DISCARDED

TORONTO & ONTARIO

CAROLYN B. HEL

Contents

DISCOVER
Toronto & Ontario

Buzzing urban centers with hip nightspots and eclectic shops. Creative chefs, international eateries, and plenty of local specialties. Historic sites and modern art museums. Romantic getaways, outdoor adventures, and activities for the kids. And all at a good value, too? That's Ontario.

Toronto is Canada's most multicultural city. Then there's Niagara Falls, Canada's most visited tourist attraction; Ottawa, the grand national capital; and theater festivals at Stratford and Niagara-on-the-Lake.

Beyond these well-known attractions, Ontario offers much more. Bordering four of the five Great Lakes as well as Hudson Bay, Ontario has more than 3,000 kilometers (2,300 miles) of shoreline. This vast forested province stretches from the southernmost point in Canada nearly to the Arctic.

With all that space, Ontario has countless options for outdoor adventures. Skate along the world's largest ice rink, hike one of Canada's longest trails, or swim in its biggest "swimming hole." Go cycling, canoeing, white-water rafting, cross-country skiing, and dogsledding. You can even scuba dive among shipwrecks on the floor of the Great Lakes.

Home to Canada's most diverse population, Ontario delivers cultural

Clockwise from top left: Killarney East Lighthouse; Toronto skyline; Waterloo Region Museum; Point Pelee National Park; Stratford's Red Rabbit bistro; Pukaskwa National Park.

adventures as well. More than half of Toronto's residents were born outside Canada, giving the city a vibrant multicultural buzz. You could breakfast on French croissants, lunch on Japanese *okonomiyaki,* and end your day with Italian, Greek, or indigenous fare.

In central Ontario, Old Order Mennonites still travel by horse and buggy and sell homemade preserves at local farmers markets. Roughly 25 percent of Canada's indigenous population lives here, so you can hike through the wilderness with a native guide or watch a performance at a First Nations-run theater. You can also follow the Underground Railroad, which sheltered people fleeing slavery during the U.S. Civil War.

Ontario has laid-back college towns and scores of wineries, maple syrup makers, and apple orchards. Take in a hockey game or take the train to a remote eco-lodge. You'll find the Thousand Islands and far more than a thousand things to do.

A thousand and counting. That's Ontario.

Clockwise from top left: historic interpreters dressed as pioneers at Upper Canada Village; the Big Nickel in Sudbury; skyscrapers in Toronto's Bloor-Yorkville district; Owen Sound's cliffs and caves.

10 TOP
EXPERIENCES

1 Toronto Art and Culture: It's more than just the world-class museums, galleries, music, and theatre. Multicultural festivals, foods, and neighborhoods make Ontario's largest city a prime destination for cultural explorers (page 23).

2 **Niagara Falls by Water, Land, or Air:** Experience Ontario's greatest waterfall—and biggest visitor attraction—by boat, along waterside cycling or hiking routes, and even by helicopter (page 107).

3 **Georgian Bay Road Trip:** Drive past the dramatic rock formations and stunning blue waters of the Bruce Peninsula to the indigenous communities on Manitoulin Island and over the pink granite hills in Killarney Provincial Park (page 24).

4 **Local Food Adventures:**
Eat your way through Toronto's restaurant scene (page 76) and follow trails devoted to cheese (page 168), butter tarts (page 226), and apple pies (page 386).

<<<

5 **Wine-Tasting:**
Get away to wine country on the Niagara peninsula (pages 139 and 129) and in Prince Edward County (page 231)... or discover emerging wine regions near Lake Huron and Georgian Bay.

>>>

6 **Northern Lakes Getaways:**
Adventure awaits from Muskoka (page 317) to the striking landscapes along Georgian Bay (page 359) and Lake Superior. (page 424).

<<<

7 **Explore Canada's Roots:** Start your history tour in Canada's first capital—the hip present-day city of Kingston (page 244). Then follow the Rideau Canal (page 255) to Ottawa, the seat of the nation's government, where you can trace the country's roots on Parliament Hill (page 273).

8 Indigenous Experiences: Learn more about indigenous culture at Manitoulin Island (page 413), Moose Factory Island (page 352), and the Curve Lake First Nations Reserve (page 222).

<<<

9 Hiking: Lace up your hiking boots! Choose day hikes in Gatineau, Algonquin, Killarney, and on Lake Superior's North Shore, or tackle the trek from Niagara to Tobermory on the Bruce Trail (page 366).

>>>

10 Scenic Waterways: Cruise along Lake Superior (page 424), the Thousand Islands (page 258), and the Rideau Canal (page 255); or dive for shipwrecks on Georgian Bay (page 369).

<<<

Planning Your Trip

Where to Go

Toronto

Canada's largest city is home to one of the most multicultural populations on the planet. The country's cultural hub, Toronto is a major center for **film** and **theater,** with a wide range of **museums,** eclectic **boutiques,** and diverse neighborhoods. The reclaimed waterfront along Lake Ontario has **performance spaces** and **art galleries,** along with a lakeside **walking and cycling trail.** This diversity has made Toronto one of North America's most exciting cities for eating, shopping, and simply exploring.

The Niagara Region

Niagara Falls is a must-see attraction, and whether it's your first visit or your 50th, feeling the spray and watching the cascading curtains crash into the river below is still a thrill. Yet Niagara is more than just the falls. Here in Ontario's **major wine-producing region,** you can sip new vintages or sample local produce, while the well-preserved town of Niagara-on-the-Lake stages the **Shaw Festival,** one of North America's premier summer theater festivals.

Lake Erie to Lake Huron

West of Toronto, sprawling suburbs give way to university towns with interesting arts scenes, wide-open farm country, and sandy beaches. Theater fans flock to the **Stratford Festival,** while in St. Jacobs, **Mennonite communities** preserve their traditional customs. You can tour Ontario's newest **wine districts,** visit Canada's southernmost point, or explore the region's dramatic history as the terminus of the **Underground Railroad.** And on **Lake Huron,** you can sit by the shore on some of the province's loveliest beaches.

Eastern Ontario

Water, water, everywhere—that's what you'll find in Eastern Ontario: along Lake Ontario (home to the **Prince Edward County** wine region and a hotbed of local food), in the **Kawarthas** region around the city of Peterborough, among the **Thousand Islands** in the St. Lawrence River, and along the **Rideau Canal** between Kingston and Ottawa. This region has plenty for the history buff, too, from **indigenous culture** to Canada's early development.

Ottawa

Canada's national capital combines history, culture, and outdoor activities. You can tour **Parliament** and numerous **grand museums,** then skate on the **Rideau Canal** (the world's largest rink), or hike through sprawling **Gatineau Park.** For foodies, Ottawa has a branch of **Le Cordon Bleu** culinary school and plenty of innovative restaurants. This bilingual city knows how to party, too, hosting the nation's biggest **Canada Day celebrations** and dozens of **festivals** year-round.

Cottage Country, Algonquin Park, and the Northeast

Getting away to "the cottage" is a long-standing Ontario summer tradition, and even without a cottage of your own, you can escape to this lake district. The highlight is **Algonquin Provincial Park,** one of the province's largest protected green spaces.

Cottage Country and Northeastern Ontario are prime **canoe trip** destinations, with an extensive network of lakes. For a more culturally focused trip, ride the **Polar Bear Express** train north to James Bay to experience the culture of one of Canada's largest aboriginal groups.

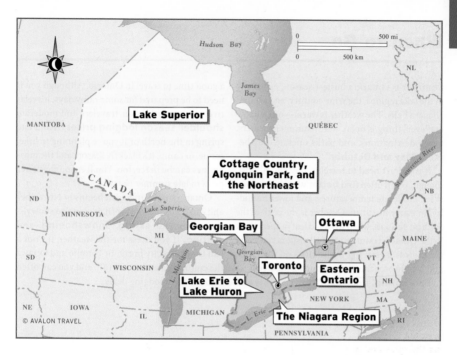

Georgian Bay

Spectacular scenery surrounds Georgian Bay, where more than 30,000 islands dot the waters. Besides **three national parks,** several beautifully remote **provincial parks,** and sections of the **Bruce Trail** (one of Canada's longest hiking routes), you'll find dramatic rock formations, Caribbean-blue water, and a network of **lighthouses** standing guard along the coast.

Ontario's earliest European pioneers built a settlement near Georgian Bay, which is now a fascinating **historical village.** On Manitoulin Island, the **Great Spirit Circle Trail** is a leader in indigenous tourism, offering numerous ways for visitors to experience First Nations culture.

Lake Superior

Craving more eco-adventure? Head north to Lake Superior. **Hiking trails** crisscross rocky cliffs, while **spectacular beaches** line Lake Superior's shores, and you can **canoe, kayak,** or **sail** to remote inlets and islands. Yet even if you're just doing a **driving tour** along the lake, the views seem to get better around every turn.

When to Go

Summer is Ontario's busiest season, especially in the lake regions, the wine country, and around Niagara Falls. The weather is warm—often hot—and everything is open. Many summer theaters, beach destinations, and parks operate only between **May and October.**

If you don't need to travel in July and August, though, you'll often find **better weather** (sunny skies, moderate temperatures, and lower humidity) in **early autumn.** October is the peak of the **foliage season,** when weekend leaf peepers flock to the Ontario countryside. Fall visitors can avoid the crowds by staying in the cities on weekends and heading for the country during the week.

Late spring, from May to early June, is also a good time to travel in Ontario. Although you'll need to be prepared for some rainy days, it's relatively quiet, with fewer travelers and moderate **shoulder-season lodging prices.** Avoid late spring in the north or if you're planning to hike, canoe, or camp; it's blackfly season, and the mosquitoes can be fierce, too. You'll encounter fewer pests in late summer or fall.

Ontario's **winter,** which begins in November and can continue into April, is cold and snowy—the season for **skiing, snowshoeing,** and **skating.** If you dress for the weather, it's not a bad time for a city break; in Toronto and Ottawa the cultural calendars are full, and you can often find excellent lodging deals.

an 1850s log cabin at the Buxton National Historic Site

Know Before You Go

Passports and Visas

United States citizens need a valid **passport, passport card,** or **Enhanced Driver's License** for travel to Canada.

All other visitors need a valid passport. Depending on your nationality, you may also need either a visitor **visa** or an **Electronic Travel Authorization** (eTA). **Visas** are not required for citizens of the United States, United Kingdom, Australia, New Zealand, Mexico, Singapore, Japan, South Korea, Israel, and most Western European countries for stays in Canada of less than six months. However, the **Electronic Travel Authorization (eTA)** is required for visa-exempt visitors who are traveling to Canada **by air.** Check with Citizenship and Immigration Canada (www.cic.gc.ca) to confirm what documents you require.

Vaccinations

No special immunizations or vaccinations are required to visit Canada, but it's always smart to ensure that your **routine immunizations** are up-to-date, particularly if you're traveling with children.

Transportation

Ontario's largest airport is **Toronto's Pearson International Airport,** with flights from across Canada, the United States, Europe, the Caribbean, Latin America, and Asia. **Ottawa** is another air gateway, with flights from major Canadian cities, along with several U.S. and some European destinations.

VIA Rail, Canada's national rail carrier, can bring you to Ontario from across the country, whether you're starting from Vancouver, Jasper, Edmonton, Saskatoon, Winnipeg, Montreal, or Halifax. From the United States, **Amtrak** has train service from New York City to Niagara Falls and Toronto. **Bus travel** is a reasonable option, too, from the northeastern United States or eastern Canada.

Toronto's comprehensive **public transportation system** makes a car unnecessary if you'll be staying in the city. Ottawa and Niagara Falls are also easy to navigate without a vehicle. Otherwise, outside the province's urban areas, you'll have more flexibility if you **drive** or **rent a car.**

The Best of Ontario

This itinerary takes you through Southern Ontario's highlights, from Toronto to Niagara Falls, the Muskoka Lakes, Algonquin Provincial Park, and Ottawa, the nation's capital. It's easiest to do if you have a car, or pick up a rental car when you leave Toronto (you won't need it in the city).

Toronto

DAY 1

Fly into **Toronto.** Visit the **CN Tower** for great views across the city and Lake Ontario. If you dare, take the **EdgeWalk,** a thrilling walk suspended outside the tower, 116 stories above the ground. Back on earth, stroll along the harbor front, then stop for lunch at **St. Lawrence Market** on your way to the galleries and shops in **The Distillery District.** Catch the ferry to the **Toronto Islands** for a late-afternoon walk or bike ride. Wrap up your day with dinner downtown or in the **Entertainment District.**

DAY 2

Spend today continuing to explore Toronto. Tour the Frank Gehry-designed **Art Gallery of Ontario** or the massive **Royal Ontario Museum.** After checking out the entertaining **Bata Shoe Museum,** have lunch in **Chinatown** or **Kensington Market,** or linger over afternoon tea at the deluxe **Shangri-La Hotel.** Wander along **Queen Street West** for shopping and gallery-hopping, have dinner at one of the eclectic restaurants, and stop for a nightcap at one of the clubs.

Niagara Falls

DAY 3

250 KILOMETERS / 155 MILES (4 HOURS ROUND-TRIP)

You're going to **Niagara Falls** for the day; either rent a car or book a day tour. Don't miss the **Hornblower Niagara Cruise,** a boat tour

Toronto has several "Chinatowns" with lots of good eating.

Niagara's Whirlpool Aero Car opened in 1916.

under the falls. Niagara Falls has plenty of other attractions, including the **White Water Walk** and the **Whirlpool Aero Car;** for the most dramatic falls views, take a **Niagara Helicopters Flightseeing Tour.** From the falls, it's a half-hour drive to **Niagara-on-the-Lake,** where you can wander the historic downtown and tour local **wineries.** Have an early dinner, then see a play at the **Shaw Festival** before returning to Toronto.

Cottage Country
DAY 4
250 KILOMETERS / 155 MILES (3.5-4 HOURS)
Today you'll make a leisurely drive northeast to Muskoka **Cottage Country,** but your first stop en route is just outside Toronto at the excellent **McMichael Canadian Art Collection.** Continuing north, visit **Muskoka Wharf** in **Gravenhurst** to cruise on a restored steamship and tour a heritage boat museum. In **Bracebridge,** browse the shops in the cute downtown and continue to **Huntsville** to have dinner and spend the night.

DAY 5
120 KILOMETERS / 75 MILES (2 HOURS)
From Huntsville, you'll enter **Algonquin Provincial Park** through the West Gate. Algonquin measures over 7,500 square kilometers (nearly 3,000 square miles), so there's plenty to explore. Go for a **hike** or rent a **canoe** at the Portage Store. Walk through the exhibits at the **Algonquin Visitors Centre;** there's usually an interesting nature program happening, as well. Try to schedule your late-summer visit for a Thursday to join in the evening **Wolf Howl.** Spend the night at one of the park lodges.

Ottawa
DAY 6
250 KILOMETERS / 155 MILES (3.5-4 HOURS)
Drive out the park's East Gate, following Highway 60 east toward **Ottawa.** Your first Ottawa-area stop will actually be across the Ottawa River in **Gatineau** at the massive **Canadian Museum of History,** where you can learn almost anything about Canada's history and culture. After checking into your Ottawa hotel, browse the shops and

Food and Wine Getaways

Ontario has plenty of gourmet getaways and scrumptious side trips for culinary tourists.

WHERE TO WIELD YOUR WHISK

Impress a special someone with some serious short-term culinary training. Hone your skills in Ottawa at **Le Cordon Bleu** (www.lcbottawa.com). On the Niagara Peninsula, both **The Good Earth Food and Wine Co.** (www.goodearthfoodandwine.com) in Beamsville and the **Wine Country Cooking School** (www.winecountrycooking.com) at the Strewn Winery in Niagara-on-the-Lake offer recreational cooking classes. In Prince Edward County, **From the Farm Cooking School** (www.fromthefarm.ca) and the **Waring House Cookery School** (www.waringhouse.com) offer courses based on the region's bounty.

RAISE A GLASS

Ontario has three major wine-producing regions: **Prince Edward County,** the **north shore of Lake Erie,** and the Niagara region, which is further subdivided into the **Niagara-on-the-Lake** and the **Twenty Valley** wine districts. Restaurants at the wineries and in the nearby towns pair local wines with creative dishes. During your wine tour, sample some **ice wine,** Ontario's signature dessert wine.

Ontario isn't all about the grape. The craft beer scene is booming across the province. It's hard to find an Ontario town without its own microbrewery. Explore Ottawa's craft breweries on a **Brew Donkey Tour** (www.brewdonkey.ca), while **Brew Tours** (www.brewtours.ca) runs beer-tasting tours in Toronto and in Muskoka's Cottage Country. Toronto's first sake brewery, the **Ontario Spring Water Sake Company** (www.ontariosake.com), has a tasting bar at its shop in the Distillery District.

TO MARKET, TO MARKET

At farmers markets, you can purchase local fruits and vegetables, cheeses, jams, honey, and baked goods directly from the producers. Some of the largest are in Toronto, at **St. Lawrence**

Sample Ottawa's famous BeaverTails snacks in the ByWard Market.

Market and at **Evergreen Brick Works;** in **St. Jacobs,** west of Toronto, which has Canada's largest year-round farmers market; and in Ottawa at the **ByWard Market.** Others include the year-round **Barrie Farmers Market** and the **Thunder Bay Country Market** up north. **Farmers Markets Ontario** (www.farmersmarketsontario.com) lists markets around the province.

FOOD TOURS

In Toronto, **The Culinary Adventure Co.** (www.culinaryadventureco.com) runs delicious neighborhood tours. Book an excursion with **Tasty Tours** (www.tastytourstoronto.com) to sample from bakeries, chocolate shops, and other sweet spots. In Ottawa, **C'est Bon Epicurean Adventures** (www.cestboncooking.ca) leads food tours of the ByWard Market, Chinatown, and Little Italy. Eat your way through Kingston with **Kingston Food Tours** (www.kingstonfoodtours.ca).

galleries in the **ByWard Market** neighborhood. Stay for dinner and catch some music at one of the clubs.

DAY 7
Get to the **Parliament Buildings** first thing in the morning to take a tour. If you're visiting in July or August, watch the **Changing the Guard,** complete with red-coated, fur-hat-wearing guards. For a dose of culture, go to either the **National Gallery of Canada** or the **Canadian War Museum,** then take an afternoon stroll or cycle along the **Rideau Canal.** Have dinner in Little Italy or Wellington West. Wrap up your Ontario week with a concert or play at the **National Arts Centre** or the **Great Canadian Theatre Company.**

Toronto Art and Culture

TOP EXPERIENCE

A long weekend in Toronto will give you time to enjoy the city's museums, galleries, and theaters. Base yourself at the arty **Drake** or **Gladstone Hotels,** or choose a lodging in the Entertainment District, like the **Hotel Le Germain, Soho Metropolitan,** or **Thompson Toronto.** Plan a day trip to see a show in either Stratford or Niagara-on-the-Lake.

Day 1
Start your museum meandering at the **Art Gallery of Ontario,** which has an extensive collection of Canadian and international art in a striking building designed by Frank Gehry. Next door, you can't help but notice the **Sharp Centre for Design**— it's the checkered box floating in the sky supported by yellow, blue, and purple "pencils."

Head east to **The Distillery District** to browse more galleries, including the **Artscape Building,** which houses more than 60 artist studios. After lunch in one of the district's cafés, go downtown to see what's happening at the always-bustling **Harbourfront Centre.** Check out the **Power Plant Gallery,** and watch the artists at work in **The Craft Studio.**

Stratford's Courthouse Square

Roy Thompson Hall

Have dinner in the **Entertainment District,** then catch a concert at **Roy Thompson Hall,** a performance of the **National Ballet of Canada,** or a play at one of the city's many theaters.

Day 2

A tour of the **Elgin and Winter Garden Theatre Centre** takes you through Toronto stage history in Canada's only "double-decker" theater. Then get a dose of world culture and natural history at the **Royal Ontario Museum.** Nearby is the eclectic **Bata Shoe Museum,** which houses more than 10,000 shoes—from doll-like slippers worn by Chinese women with bound feet to singer Elton John's sky-high platforms.

Make an excursion to the **Junction Triangle** to see what's on at the **Museum of Contemporary Art,** then take a break at one of the neighborhood's craft breweries. Your next stop is **Queen Street West,** where you can wander into whichever galleries and boutiques catch your eye and where you have lots of options for a meal. After dinner, see what's screening at the **TIFF Bell Lightbox.**

Day 3

From Toronto, it's an easy day trip to either the **Shaw Festival** in Niagara-on-the-Lake or the **Stratford Festival** in Stratford. Take a behind-the-scenes tour of the theater before lunch, then see an afternoon matinee. You'll be back in Toronto in time for a nightcap to top off your weekend of art and culture.

Georgian Bay Road Trip

TOP EXPERIENCE

The best time for this tour, which takes in the striking natural scenery around Georgian Bay, is late summer or early fall. The autumn is especially lovely, as the leaves put on their vibrant color show. Just wrap up the trip before Canadian Thanksgiving, the second weekend in October, when the ferry to Manitoulin Island stops running and many of the region's attractions close for the season.

Day 1

300 KILOMETERS / 190 MILES (4-4.5 HOURS)

From Toronto, drive northwest to the **Bruce Peninsula.** Check into a hotel in **Tobermory** or set up camp in **Bruce Peninsula National Park,** then stop into the **National Park Visitors Centre** to learn more about the region. Climb the **Lookout Tower** to take in the views, then hike to **The Grotto** and beautiful **Indian Head Cove,** with its turquoise waters and intricate rock formations. Back in town, have dinner in a café on **Little Tub Harbour.**

Day 2

Pack a picnic and take the boat to **Flowerpot Island** to explore **Fathom Five National Marine Park,** one of only three national marine conservation areas in Canada. It's a short hike from the ferry dock to the distinctive "flowerpot" rock formations. When you return to the mainland, take a **lighthouse tour,** then hike along the **Bruce Trail,** go **kayaking,** or book a **snorkeling tour** among the shipwrecks just offshore. Walk along broad **Singing Sands Beach** and watch the sun set over Lake Huron.

Day 3

FERRY (2 HOURS)

Take the morning ferry to **Manitoulin Island.** Enjoy a leisurely lunch at **Garden's Gate Restaurant,** then spend the afternoon at **Providence Bay Beach** or splash under **Bridal Veil Falls.** Spend the night on the Aundeck Omni Kaning First Nations Reserve at **Endaa-aang "Our Place,"** where you can rent a comfortable cottage or sleep in a tepee.

summertime hikers at Indian Head Cove in Bruce Peninsula National Park

Day 4

Today you're exploring Manitoulin's indigenous heritage with the **Great Spirit Circle Trail.** Arrange a workshop on traditional First Nations dance, drumming, or crafts. You can also take their **Mother Earth Nature Hike,** where a native guide will help you identify local plants and understand how they're used in traditional medicine and cooking, as you climb the **Cup and Saucer Trail.** In the evening, see a production by the indigenous **Debajehmujig Theatre Group.**

Day 5

225 KILOMETERS / 140 MILES (3-3.5 HOURS)
Get an early start today to drive to **Killarney Provincial Park,** a vast and dramatic provincial park with rugged white dolomite ridges, pink granite cliffs, pine forests, and crystal-clear lakes. You'll want to reach Killarney in time for a swim at **George Lake** and an afternoon of **hiking** or **canoeing.** You can camp in the park or stay in one of the lodges in town. Enjoy a fish-and-chips dinner at **Herbert Fisheries** while you take in the sunset over the harbor.

Day 6

200 KILOMETERS / 125 MILES (3 HOURS)
In the morning, take another hike or paddle before driving south toward **Parry Sound,** stopping for a picnic or a stretch-your-legs hike at **Grundy Lake Provincial Park** along the way. In Parry Sound, arrange a **flight-seeing tour,** the most thrilling way to take in Georgian Bay's 30,000 Islands region; if you're with a special someone, schedule a romantic sunset flight—complete with champagne. If you'd rather stay close to the ground, explore the islands with a sightseeing cruise on the *Island Queen.* In the evening, see a play, concert, or lecture at the **Charles W. Stockey Centre for the Performing Arts.**

Day 7

150 KILOMETERS / 95 MILES (2 HOURS)
Your first stop today is **Killbear Provincial Park,** about 45 minutes' drive from Parry Sound. While it's less known than Ontario's larger "destination" parks, its dramatic granite cliffs and quiet sandy beaches are well worth exploring. Later in the day, drive south to **Honey Harbour** or **Port Severn,** where you'll spend the night.

Killarney Provincial Park

Day 8

55 KILOMETERS / 35 MILES (1 HOUR)

Of the thousands of islands that dot Georgian Bay, 63 are protected in the **Georgian Bay Islands National Park.** Your destination today is **Beausoleil Island** for a full day of hiking, mountain biking, swimming, picnicking, and exploring. Back on the mainland, drive south to **Midland** for dinner and check in to a hotel, where you'll stay for the next two nights.

Day 9

Travel back in time to the 1600s at **Sainte-Marie Among the Hurons,** a historical village that reimagines the first European settlement in Ontario, where French Jesuits lived and worked with the indigenous Wendat (Huron) people. In the afternoon, go canoeing at **Wye Marsh Wildlife Centre,** or go for a hike or swim at **Awenda Provincial Park.**

Day 10

200 KILOMETERS / 125 MILES (3 HOURS)

As you begin your drive south, stop for a stroll along **Wasaga Beach,** the world's longest freshwater beach. Another worthwhile detour is the small town of **Creemore,** where art galleries, cafés, and shops line the main street. After you've had your fill of browsing, have a bite to eat before making your way back to Toronto.

With five national parks, two national marine conservation areas, and more than 300 provincially protected green spaces, Ontario has plenty of destinations for outdoor activities. Trying to figure out which adventures are for you? Start here.

GRAB YOUR HIKING BOOTS

Whether close to the cities or deep in the wilderness, Ontario has hiking trails that suit all levels of experience. One of Canada's longest hiking routes, the Bruce Trail, extends 845 kilometers (525 miles) from the Niagara region to the tip of the Bruce Peninsula. Algonquin Provincial Park has forested trails for everyone from kids to seasoned backpackers; outside of Ottawa, Gatineau Park has plenty of day-hiking options. In Killarney Provincial Park and Lake Superior Provincial Park, your rewards for climbing the Crack and the Top of the Giant trails are spectacular mountain or lake views.

PICK UP A PADDLE

For canoe-tripping or kayaking, Algonquin is a prime Ontario destination, while farther north, you can paddle for days in the wilderness surrounding Temagami or along the rocky shores and islands of Lake Superior. Just getting started with your paddle? Head for the inland lakes at provincial parks like Grundy Lake or Arrowhead, or paddle along Georgian Bay at Killarney or Killbear. You can also find gentle paddling along the Grand River from Elora to St. Jacobs to Brantford.

TAKE OFF ON TWO WHEELS

Crisscrossed with cycling paths, the Niagara region is one of Ontario's best destinations for bicycling. For longer trips, there's Ontario's epic Great Lakes Waterfront Trail, which follows the shores of Lake Huron, Lake Erie, Lake Ontario, and the St. Lawrence River for roughly 2,100 kilometers (1,300 miles) from Grand Bend all the way to the Quebec border. Unique two-wheeled Ontario tours include Windsor Eats Wine Trail Rides, where you cycle and wine-taste in the Lake Erie North Shore wine district, and Grand Experiences' "The Path Less Travelled," where you explore the Mennonite countryside by bike, visiting local homes and shops around St. Jacobs.

GO FOR A SWIM

Surrounded by four of the five Great Lakes, with over 200,000 inland lakes of all sizes, Ontario has plenty of places to swim. Popular beaches include Sandbanks on Lake Ontario in Prince Edward County, the Pinery and Sauble Beach on Lake Huron, and Wasaga Beach—the world's longest freshwater beach—on Georgian Bay. There's Providence Bay Beach on Manitoulin Island, Pancake Bay on Lake Superior, and the striking aqua waters of Elora Quarry. Even Toronto has urban beaches on its Lake Ontario shore and on the Toronto Islands.

IT'S NOT TOO COLD FOR SNORKELING AND SCUBA DIVING

You may not think of Ontario, with its chilly northern waters, as a destination for snorkeling or scuba diving. But with the Great Lakes and the St. Lawrence River claiming many ships over the decades, the region offers interesting shipwreck sites that you can explore from the deep. Prime diving destinations include the waters of the Bruce Peninsula, where close-to-shore wrecks are accessible to snorkelers, too; the Thousand Islands; and Lake Superior.

LET IT SNOW

While Ontario's hilly regions pale in comparison to Western Canada's mountains, the province has several destinations for downhill skiing and snowboarding; the largest is Blue Mountain Resort near Collingwood. One don't-miss winter experience is ice-skating on the Rideau Canal in Ottawa, which in the colder months freezes to become the world's largest outdoor skating rink. You can cross-country ski or snowshoe pretty much anywhere there's snow; several parks have extensive winter trail systems, including Arrowhead, Wasaga Beach, the Pinery, and Gatineau Park. To try your hand at dogsledding, head for Algonquin.

With adventures like these across Ontario, there's no reason to stay inside.

Romance at Niagara Falls

Oh, the lovers come a thousand miles,
They leave their home and mothers,
Yet when they reach Niagara Falls
They only see each other.

Dating back to the 1840s, this song suggests that, even in the 19th century, Niagara Falls was already a popular destination for honeymooners. And why not? What's more romantic than canoodling with your beloved in view of the rushing falls?

Romantic Sleeps

Book a room with a view of the falls, perhaps at the **Sheraton on the Falls** or the **Marriott Niagara Falls Fallsview Hotel and Spa.** Alternatively, choose a smaller upscale property, like the **Sterling Inn & Spa,** that will pamper the two of you.

For more luxurious accommodations, consider staying in Niagara-on-the-Lake at the elaborately appointed **Prince of Wales Hotel** or the deluxe modern **124 on Queen.** You could spend time at the falls during the day and retreat to this more peaceful village in the evenings.

Adventures for Two

When you've had your fill of strolling hand-in-hand in front of the cascading falls, you might want to escape from Niagara Falls's hustle and bustle. Rent bicycles—perhaps a bicycle built for two—and **cycle** the riverside path along the Niagara River Parkway, or book a private half-day wine and cycling tour to the nearby **Twenty Valley.**

Plan time for wine touring in Niagara-on-the-Lake; visit the luxurious tasting room at **Stratus Vineyards** or reserve a Taste of Gold experience at **Peller Estates Winery** to sample their top wines. The **Peller Estates Winery Restaurant** is one of the area's best lunch stops, or have your midday meal among the vines at **Ravine Vineyard Bistro** or on the patio at **Treadwell Farm-to-Table Cuisine.** Stop to lick each other's gelato at **Il Gelato di Carlotta** in Niagara-on-the-Lake.

The Hornblower Niagara Cruises take you right under the spray.

Head back to the falls for an aerial tour with **Niagara Helicopters Flightseeing,** an experience that's even more dramatic at sunset. Or take a sunset trip to the base of the falls on the **Hornblower Niagara Cruises.** For dinner, choose somewhere upscale and romantic like **Casa Mia Ristorante.**

Wrap up your day by watching the **Fireworks over the Falls,** then head back to your hotel to spark your own fire.

Northern Exposure

To see northern Ontario, combine a road trip with train travel. In fact, as you travel toward **James Bay,** you have to leave your car behind—no roads run this far north. Begin in Toronto, stop for **canoeing and hiking** in the Temagami lake lands, and continue north to Cochrane to catch the **Polar Bear Express train** to the Cree communities of Moosonee and Moose Factory Island. This trip is best in **July** or **August,** when the weather is warm, and the Polar Bear Express runs Sunday to Friday.

Day 1
455 KILOMETERS / 285 MILES (5.5-6 HOURS)
Get an early start from Toronto on your drive north to **Temagami;** allow at least an extra hour to stop to eat in Bracebridge, Huntsville, or North Bay. You'll arrive at **Smoothwater Wilderness Lodge** in time for a late-afternoon paddle on the property's lake and a leisurely family-style dinner; the lodge is the best place to eat in the area, and a bonus is the travel tips you'll get from the other guests.

Day 2
Spend the day outdoors around Temagami. Ask the Smoothwater staff to organize a canoe, kayak, or hiking trip in **Lady Evelyn Smoothwater Provincial Park.** Return to the lodge for dinner and spend the evening relaxing in the Gathering Hall.

Day 3
275 KILOMETERS / 170 MILES (3.75-4.5 HOURS)
You'll have time for a brief early-morning hike or paddle in Temagami before driving north to **Cochrane.** Arrive in time to visit the **Polar Bear Habitat** before checking into your hotel.

Day 4
Today you're going where no roads go—north toward James Bay on Ontario Northland's **Polar Bear Express** train. You'll arrive in **Moosonee** by midafternoon; walk to the docks to catch the water taxi to **Moose Factory Island.** Spend the night at the **Cree Village Ecolodge,** run by the Cree First Nation, and have dinner (with traditional indigenous ingredients) in the lodge's lovely dining room.

Day 5
You'll spend most of the day on Moose Factory Island. Visit the **Cree Cultural Interpretive Centre** to learn more about Cree culture, language, traditional medicine, and food. Walk over to the **Moose Cree Complex;** part shopping mall, part community center, it's the hub of the First Nations reserve, so you can glimpse what local life is like on this remote island. After lunch, take a **boat tour to James Bay.**

The Polar Bear Express heads south in the late afternoon and will take you as far as **Cochrane,** where you'll need to spend the night.

Day 6
720 KILOMETERS / 450 MILES (9-10 HOURS)
In the morning, begin your long drive back to Toronto. If you have time, add a stopover in Huntsville and a visit to **Algonquin Provincial Park.**

historic headstones at Uncle Tom's Cabin Historic Site

Several Oscar-winning films—*Lincoln, Django Unchained,* and *12 Years a Slave*—focused on the period surrounding the U.S. Civil War, when thousands of enslaved African Americans fled north toward Canada. These refugees traveled along the Underground Railroad, a network of safe houses that provided them with shelter. But what happened to these former slaves once they reached Canada's promised land?

Many crossed into Canada into what are now the Southwestern Ontario communities of Windsor, Amherstburg, Chatham, Dresden, and Buxton. At sites throughout this region, you can explore the **African Canadian Heritage Route,** tracing the history of the former slaves and their new life in Canada. Before you set out, look at the online resources provided by the **Ontario Heritage Trust** (www.heritagetrust.on.ca).

DRESDEN

In Dresden, **Uncle Tom's Cabin Historic Site** (www.uncletomscabin.org) tells the story of former slave and abolitionist Reverend Josiah Henson, whose memoirs may have been part of the inspira-tion for Harriet Beecher Stowe's historic antislavery novel, *Uncle Tom's Cabin.*

BUXTON

Farther west, the Buxton Settlement became the largest black settlement in Canada, with one of North America's first integrated schools. Many descendants of these early settlers still live in the region, and you can learn more about their heritage at the **Buxton National Historic Site and Museum** (www.buxtonmuseum.com).

WINDSOR

Built and operated by descendants of formerly enslaved people who traveled here on the Underground Railroad, the **John Freeman Walls Historic Site and Underground Railroad Museum** (www.undergroundrailroadmuseum. com), outside Windsor, brings the fugitive slave experience to life. As you walk into the nearby woods, you hear hound dogs attempting to track you down (fortunately, it's just a recording). You also learn more about the family who settled here and tour the 1846 log cabin, where they raised nine children.

Toronto

Look for ★ to find recommended sights, activities, dining, and lodging.

Highlights

★ **CN Tower:** Toronto's tallest building has two observation levels and a revolving restaurant, all with great views across the city and the lake. Daredevils can even take the "EdgeWalk," a thrilling walk suspended *outside* (yes, outside!) the tower, 116 stories above the ground (page 37).

★ **Harbourfront Centre:** There's always something happening in this waterfront arts complex. Watch artists at work in their studios, browse gallery exhibits, take in a play or a lecture, go ice-skating, or stroll the walkways along the lake (page 39).

★ **The Toronto Islands:** Only a 10-minute ferry ride from downtown, these small islands in Lake Ontario are the city's backyard, where you can lounge at the beach, ride a bike, or have a picnic. The awesome views of the city skyline are a bonus (page 43).

★ **The Distillery Historic District:** Where whiskey was once king, the Victorian-era brick buildings that housed the world's largest distillery have been converted into a cool arts district full of galleries, artist studios, shops, cafés, and theaters (page 49).

★ **Royal Ontario Museum:** Inside this massive museum of natural history and world cultures, you'll find everything from Egyptian mummies to British neoclassical dining rooms, Buddha statues to medieval armor—and scads of kid-pleasing dinosaur skeletons (page 50).

★ **Bata Shoe Museum:** This quirky—and fun—gallery of footwear traces the history and culture of a wide swath of humanity by showcasing what people wore on their feet (page 51).

★ **Art Gallery of Ontario:** In a striking Frank Gehry-designed building, Toronto's art museum is one of the largest in North America,

with significant collections of Canadian, Inuit, African, and Oceanic art. The architecture alone merits the price of admission (page 55).

★ **Queen Street West:** Lined with art galleries, funky shops, eclectic eateries, and happening bars, the west end of Queen Street is one of the city's "in" arts districts (page 57).

★ **The McMichael Canadian Art Collection:** It's worth the trip to these forested grounds north of the city for this excellent all-Canadian art museum, with significant works by Canada's Group of Seven, noteworthy early-20th-century landscape painters (page 62).

Canadians may typically be modest about their country's attractions, but Toronto has plenty to boast about. With more than 5.9 million people living in the metropolitan area, it's the country's largest city and Ontario's provincial capital. As Canada's cultural hub, it's home to one of the most multicultural populations on the planet.

About half of metropolitan Toronto's residents were born outside Canada, hailing from China, India, Italy, the Caribbean, the Philippines, the Middle East, Portugal, and more—name a country and Toronto probably has residents who used to call it home. This diversity has made Toronto one of North America's most exciting cities for eating, shopping, and exploring. You can wander through Little India, Koreatown, Greektown, and several Chinatowns.

Toronto is often called "Hollywood North" for the number of movies made here; every September, the Toronto International Film Festival draws stars to one of North America's major film fests. Toronto is also a center for English-language theater, with dozens of theaters and repertory companies. A significant event on the city's calendar is the annual Pride Week, one of the world's largest LGBTQ pride celebrations.

Set on Lake Ontario, Toronto is reclaiming its waterfront, which now houses performance spaces and art galleries, along with a lakeside walking and cycling trail. Skyscrapers stand side by side with Victorian-era buildings downtown, while farther afield museums and eclectic shops satisfy culture- and couture-seekers alike. Whether you want to wrap up your day with a contemporary dinner from one of the city's hottest chefs or unwind over a drink in a neighborhood club, you'll find it all in Toronto.

PLANNING YOUR TIME

Toronto is a year-round destination. Summer is the most popular time to visit, particularly if you're traveling with kids. Everything is open, and you'll find plenty of festivals and special events. Just prepare for hot, humid weather.

Previous: Nathan Phillips Square; Take your skyline photos from the Toronto Islands. **Above:** the CN Tower.

Toronto

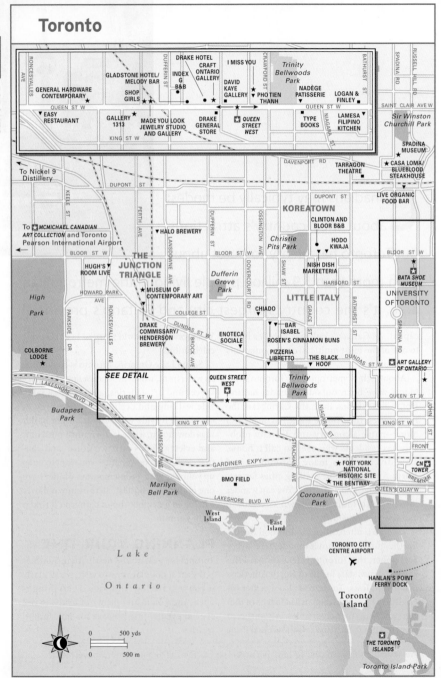

RONCESVALLES AVE

GENERAL HARDWARE CONTEMPORARY ★

GLADSTONE HOTEL/ MELODY BAR
SHOP GIRLS ★

DUFFERIN ST

INDEX G B&B

DRAKE HOTEL
CRAFT ONTARIO GALLERY

I MISS YOU

DAVID KAYE GALLERY ▼

CRAWFORD ST

★ PHO TIEN THANH

Trinity Bellwoods Park

NADÈGE PATISSERIE

BATHURST ST

LOGAN & FINLEY ★

SPADINA RD

RUSSELL HILL RD

SAINT CLAIR AVE W

QUEEN ST W

★ EASY RESTAURANT

GALLERY 1313 ★

MADE YOU LOOK JEWELRY STUDIO AND GALLERY

DRAKE GENERAL STORE

QUEEN STREET WEST

KING ST W

NIAGARA ST

TYPE BOOKS

LAMESA FILIPINO KITCHEN

Sir Winston Churchill Park

SPADINA MUSEUM

★ CASA LOMA/ BLUEBLOOD STEAKHOUSE

To Nickel 9 Distillery

DUPONT ST

KEELE ST

PERTH AVE

DAVENPORT RD

TARRAGON THEATRE

LIVE ORGANIC FOOD BAR

DUPONT ST

KOREATOWN

CLINTON AND BLOOR B&B

To ★ MCMICHAEL CANADIAN ART COLLECTION and Toronto Pearson International Airport

▼ HALO BREWERY

DUFFERIN ST

OSSINGTON AVE

Christie Pits Park

HODO KWAJA

BLOOR ST W

BATA SHOE MUSEUM ★

SPADINA RD

BLOOR ST W

LANSDOWNE AVE

BLOOR ST W

DOVERCOURT RD

SHAW ST

NISH DISH MARKETERIA

HARBORD ST

UNIVERSITY OF TORONTO

High Park

HUGH'S ROOM LIVE

THE JUNCTION TRIANGLE

★ MUSEUM OF CONTEMPORARY ART

HOWARD PARK AVE

Dufferin Grove Park

COLLEGE ST

LITTLE ITALY

GRACE ST

BATHURST ST

PARKSIDE DR

RONCESVALLES AVE

DRAKE COMMISSARY/ HENDERSON BREWERY

DUNDAS ST W

BROCK AVE

CHIADO ▼

ENOTECA SOCIALE ▼

★ BAR ISABEL
ROSEN'S CINNAMON BUNS

SPADINA AVE

ART GALLERY OF ONTARIO ★

COLBORNE LODGE ★

PIZZERIA LIBRETTO ▼

THE BLACK HOOF ▼

DUNDAS ST W

★

LAKESHORE BLVD W

SEE DETAIL

QUEEN ST W

QUEEN STREET WEST

Trinity Bellwoods Park

QUEEN ST W

JOHN ST

Budapest Park

JAMESON AVE

KING ST W

NIAGARA ST

KING ST W

FRONT ST

GARDINER EXPY

STRACHAN AVE

★ FORT YORK NATIONAL HISTORIC SITE
★ THE BENTWAY

CN TOWER ✚

BREMNER

Marilyn Bell Park

BMO FIELD ★

LAKESHORE BLVD W

Coronation Park

QUEEN'S QUAY W

West Island

East Island

L a k e

O n t a r i o

TORONTO CITY CENTRE AIRPORT ✈

HANLAN'S POINT FERRY DOCK ■

Toronto Island

Toronto

0   500 yds

0   500 m

✚ THE TORONTO ISLANDS

Toronto Island Park

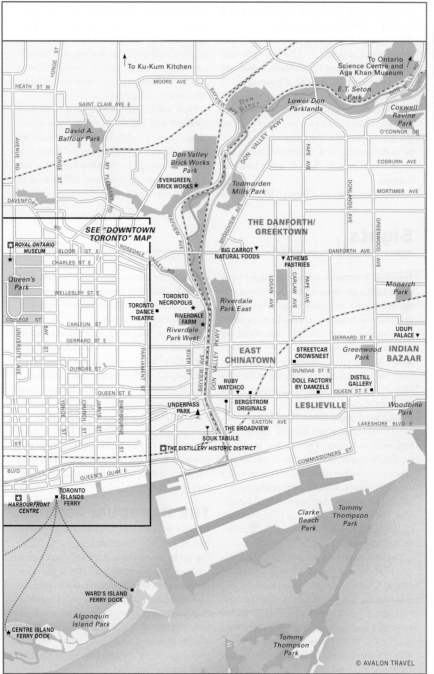

Torontonians are quick to point out that the "lake effect" that dumps piles of snow on their upstate New York neighbors has a different result in their city. Toronto's position on Lake Ontario's northern shore moderates the winter weather, and the city averages 115 centimeters (45 inches) of snow per year—less than Buffalo can get on a single day. Sure, it's cold and often snowy in winter, but Toronto has great museums, the cultural season will be in full swing, and accommodations are often less expensive than at other times of the year.

The best seasons for a Toronto trip, though, are spring and fall. The weather should be temperate, especially in autumn, and the cultural calendar will be full. If you'll be in town in September during the Toronto International Film Festival, a major event on the city's cultural agenda, book accommodations well in advance.

How much time do you need to explore Toronto? You could visit for a weekend and catch the city's highlights or stick around for weeks and still have plenty to do. Toronto is also close enough to **Niagara Falls** that you can take a day trip there and still be back in town for supper.

Sights

Toronto's downtown core is just inland from the Lake Ontario waterfront. Downtown and the Harbourfront contain the city's oldest neighborhoods and its newest developments, where narrow streets laid out in the city's early days are a short walk from water-view skyscrapers. The city's landmark CN Tower is here, and you can catch a ferry to the Toronto Islands, a waterfront green space a quick cruise from downtown.

Like most major cities, Toronto has noteworthy museums of art, science, and natural and cultural history. The city has some less typical museums, too: galleries of textiles and ceramics, a hockey museum, even a museum devoted to shoes. You can tour the city halls—old and new—and visit the provincial legislature, the fort where the city was first settled, a high-tech aquarium, and the only "double-decker" theater in Canada.

Beyond the museums and sights, Toronto's lure is its diverse neighborhoods, including several Chinatowns, an Indian district, and communities that have Greek, Korean, and Portuguese roots. There's bohemian, multicultural Kensington Market, with its cheap eateries and offbeat shops, and Cabbagetown, with well-manicured Victorian homes. For art and shopping, head for the Distillery District, Queen Street West, or Leslieville on the city's east side. And then there's the Harbourfront, with its galleries, gardens, and green spaces to enjoy on a sunny city day.

If you're planning to visit several of Toronto's major attractions, consider purchasing a **CityPass** (www.citypass.com, adults $88, ages 4-12 $59), which covers admission to the CN Tower, Royal Ontario Museum, Casa Loma, Ontario Science Centre, and Toronto Zoo. In addition to discounted admission, the pass lets you bypass the ticket lines at most attractions. Buy a CityPass online or at any of the included attractions; it's good for nine consecutive days beginning with the first day that you use it.

THE HARBOURFRONT

In mild weather, the Lake Ontario shore is one of Toronto's loveliest areas, with walking paths along the waterfront, parks, and lots of things to see and do. While the lakeshore is only a short walk from downtown, the Gardiner Expressway, the elevated highway that bisects the city, cuts off the Harbourfront from the rest of the city. Several streets, including Bay, York, and Lower Simcoe Streets, pass underneath the expressway, so you can walk from downtown.

Three Days in Toronto

DAY 1

Start with a visit to the observation decks at the **CN Tower** to get a scenic overview of the city. Walk down to the lakeshore to take in the island views. See what's showing at the **Power Plant Gallery** and browse the art studios and galleries at **Harbourfront Centre.** Then catch the streetcar east to **St. Lawrence Market** and to the **Distillery District** to check out the shops and have something to eat.

After lunch, head for one or more of the city's major museums: the **Art Gallery of Ontario** for contemporary art in a striking Frank Gehry-designed building; the **Royal Ontario Museum** if you're into world cultures and natural history; or the **Bata Shoe Museum** for, well, shoes—but shoes like you've never seen before. Have dinner in the Entertainment District, then see a comedy show at **Second City,** a concert at **Roy Thompson Hall,** or a play at any of the downtown theaters.

DAY 2

Visit the city's "castle on the hill," the lavish **Casa Loma.** Then take a **food tour** or poke around the **Kensington Market** and **Chinatown** districts, where you have lots of options for a casual lunch.

Spend the afternoon browsing the galleries and shops along **Queen Street West.** Stay in the West End for dinner, perhaps Italian at **Enoteca Sociale** or **Pizzeria Libretto** or contemporary Spanish fare at lively **Bar Isabel.** Later in the evening, see what's happening at the **Drake** or **Gladstone Hotels.**

DAY 3

Take a half-day trip north to see **The McMichael Canadian Art Collection,** a museum of Canadian art with an exceptionally strong collection of works by the Group of Seven, noted landscape painters who worked in Ontario in the early 1900s. On your way back into town, stop in the Junction Triangle for the **Museum of Contemporary Art** and have lunch or a snack at the **Drake Commissary** nearby.

Back in the city, catch the ferry to the **Toronto Islands,** where you can bike, walk, or simply enjoy the city views. In the evening, try the inventive indigenous cuisine at **Ku-Kum Kitchen,** pair sake and izakaya-style small plates at **Omai Restaurant,** or savor a multicourse feast at **Ruby Watchco.** Wrap up your Toronto stay with cocktails and a view at **The Rooftop,** atop the Broadview Hotel, or in the historic **Library Bar** at the Fairmont Royal York Hotel.

★ CN Tower

If you've seen photos of the Toronto skyline, you've seen the iconic **CN Tower** (301 Front St. W., at John St., 416/868-6937, www.cntower.ca, subway: Union, 9am-10:30pm daily, adults $38, seniors $34, ages 4-12 $28). At 457 meters (1,500 feet) high, the tower, which opened in 1976 to provide telecommunications capabilities for the city, held the record for the world's tallest building for many years. Even if loftier skyscrapers have taken away its title, this is still one tall building.

Once you've boarded the glass elevators and rocketed 113 stories to the LookOut level (the elevator ride takes only 58 seconds), the views stretch out over the city and Lake Ontario. The next thrill is a walk across the see-through **Glass Floor;** it's 346 meters (1,136 feet) straight down.

If you want to get even higher, go up to the **SkyPod,** the next observation level, at 447 meters (1,465 feet), 34 stories above the LookOut. Sky Pod access is an additional $15.

For extreme thrill seekers, there's the **EdgeWalk** (www.edgewalkcntower.ca, mid-Apr.-mid-Nov., $225, including admission to other tower attractions), where you walk outside (yes, outside!) around the roof of the

Toronto Budget Tips

On a budget? Don't worry: Toronto has plenty of free and low-cost attractions. Here's how to stretch your dollars while exploring Toronto.

- There's no charge to wander the **St. Lawrence Market, the Distillery District, Kensington Market,** or any of the city's multicultural neighborhoods—although you may want to budget for snacks along the way.

- Walk along the Harbourfront or browse the galleries and shops along **Queen Street West,** all for free.

- Tours of the **Ontario Legislative Assembly** are free, and there's no charge to explore the grounds at the **Evergreen Brick Works.**

- A trip to the **Toronto Islands** will cost a small ferry fare, but once you're there, you can stroll, picnic, and lounge on the sand without spending a penny.

- Many of Toronto's museums offer free or discounted admission at certain times. The **Royal Ontario Museum** has reduced admission on Friday after 5:30pm. The **Art Gallery of Ontario** is free on Wednesday 6pm-9pm. The **Bata Shoe Museum** offers "pay what you can" admission on Thursday 5pm-8pm. Admission to the **Gardiner Museum** is half price on Friday 4pm-9pm.

- Take one of the city's free walking tours. Locals lead free guided walks of their neighborhoods or other favorite places around town on the **Toronto Greeter** tours. The **Heritage Toronto Walks,** highlighting a neighborhood's architectural, cultural, or natural history, are free as well, as are the Royal Ontario Museum's **ROM Walks.**

tower restaurant, 116 stories (356 meters, 1,168 feet) above the ground. You're harnessed to a safety rail, but the daring can lean out over the edge. When you're suspended outside the building, it's probably not the time to tell you that lighting strikes the tower an average of 75 times per year, but don't worry: The EdgeWalk closes during high winds and electrical storms.

The tower's flagship dining room is the revolving **360 Restaurant at the CN Tower** (416/362-5411, www.cntower.ca/360, 11am-3pm and 3:30pm-10:15pm daily May-Oct., 11am-2pm and 4:30pm-10:15pm daily Nov.-Apr., lunch prix fixe $58-72, dinner prix fixe $65-79), which makes a complete revolution every 72 minutes, giving you great views over the city. Though meal prices are high, they include access to the LookOut level and Glass Floor, and you can bypass the ticket line. At the base of the tower is casual **Le Café** (8:30am-7pm daily).

With two million people visiting the tower

every year, ticket lines can be long, and visitors must pass through airport-style security checkpoints. Arrive before 11am or after 3pm, and buy your tickets online in advance, to minimize your wait time. Purchasing a CityPass, which includes CN Tower admission, also lets you skip the box office lineups. At certain times throughout the year, you can purchase a timed ticket online (adults $45, seniors $41, ages 4-12 $35), which costs a little more but gives you access to the LookOut level at a specific time.

Ripley's Aquarium of Canada

Housing more than 16,000 marine animals in 5.7 million liters (1.5 million gallons) of water, Toronto's modern aquarium, **Ripley's Aquarium of Canada** (288 Bremner Blvd., 647/351-3474, www.ripleyaquariums.com, subway: Union, 9am-11pm daily) has North America's biggest collection of sharks, along with all manner of other aquatic creatures.

The aquarium's galleries each highlight a

different aquatic habitat or type of marinelife. The Canadian Waters gallery showcases eels, lobsters, gigantic octopi, and other creatures who inhabit the Great Lakes and the country's coastal regions. The colorful Planet Jellies exhibit surrounds you with graceful jellyfish, while in the Dangerous Lagoon, which you pass through on a moving walkway, sharks, stingrays, and other fearsome-looking fish swim all around. "Please touch" exhibits let the kids get their hands wet, and interactive shows are offered in different galleries throughout the day.

Purchase timed entry tickets online for visits between 9am and 7pm for a slightly reduced fee: adults $31, seniors and ages 6-13 $21, ages 3-5 $9. Regular walk-up tickets are adults $35, seniors and ages 6-13 $24.25, ages 3-5 $12. Adjacent to the CN Tower, the aquarium is generally open nightly till 11pm but occasionally closes earlier to host private events; check the website or phone before making an evening visit.

Rogers Centre

Toronto's professional baseball team, the Blue Jays, plays in the **Rogers Centre** (1 Blue Jays Way, 416/341-1000, www.rogerscentre.com, subway: Union), a massive arena that also hosts megaconcerts, performances, and other events by luminaries ranging from U2 to the Dalai Lama. Opened in 1989 adjacent to the CN Tower, the building's claim to fame is its roof; it's the world's first fully retractable roof, which can open or close in 20 minutes. The **Blue Jays Stadium Tours** (416/341-2770, adults $17, seniors and ages 12-17 $13, ages 3-11 $10) offer sports fans a one-hour guided tour of the facility.

Buy tickets for Rogers Centre events online or at the **box office** (Gate 9, Bremner Blvd., 10am-7pm Mon.-Fri., 10am-5pm Sat.-Sun.).

★ Harbourfront Centre

Harbourfront Centre (235 Queens Quay W., 416/973-4000, www.harbourfrontcentre.com, hours vary) is activity central for arts and literary events and for enjoying the outdoors. Inside this four-hectare (10-acre) lakeside complex of buildings are numerous art galleries, artist studios, theaters, and shops, and outdoors, a walkway wends along the waterfront. Stop at the center's information desks, or check the comprehensive website, to see what's happening.

Inside **Bill Boyle Artport** are several small art galleries, and you can watch artists at work in **The Craft & Design Studios** (10am-8pm

You can see more than 16,000 aquatic creatures at Ripley's Aquarium of Canada.

Downtown Toronto

© AVALON TRAVEL

KENSINGTON
MARKET

PLANET
TRAVELER ●

OXFORD ST
NASSAU ST

GOOD EGG ■
JUMBO
EMPANADAS ▼
POW WOW CAFE ▼

AUGUSTA AVE

MOTHER'S ■
DUMPLINGS

HURON ST
BALDWIN ST
CECIL ST
BEVERLEY ST

OMAI ■
RESTAURANT

MCCAUL ST

COLLEGE ST

SPADINA AVE

HARBORD ST

SPADINA AVE

BATHURST ST

BORDEN ST
BRUNSWICK AVE
MAJOR ST
SUSSEX AVE

Central
Technical
High School

HARBORD ST

ALBANY AVE
HOWARD AVE
WELLS ST

BRUNSWICK AVE

BLOOR ST W

LOWTHER
SUITES ■

LOWTHER AVE

BERNARD AVE

HURON ST

SAINT GEORGE ST

BLOOR-
YORKVILLE

DAVENPORT RD

BATA SHOE ✦
MUSEUM

TORONTO

NONA MACDONALD ■
VISITORS CENTRE

UNIVERSITY
OF TORONTO ●
ART CENTRE

HOSKIN AVE

U
N
I
V
E
R
S
I
T
Y

O
F

MASSEY COLLEGE
RESIDENCES ●

ROYAL
CONSERVATORY
OF MUSIC

PRINCE ARTHUR AVE

ROYAL ONTARIO ✚
MUSEUM

WHOLE FOODS ■
MARKET

HAZELTON
HOTEL ●

AVENUE RD

YORKVILLE
VILLAGE

YORKVILLE AVE

HAZELTON AVE

QUEEN'S PARK CRESCENT W

Queen's
Park

ONTARIO ✦
LEGISLATIVE
ASSEMBLY

UNIVERSITY AVE

GERRARD ST

COLLEGE ST

GROSVENOR ST

ST JOSEPH ST

WELLESLEY ST W

QUEEN'S PARK CRESCENT E

GARDINER ★
MUSEUM

CHARLES ST W

SAINT MARY ST

BAY ST

PUSATERI'S ●

SCOLLARD ST

DAVENPORT RD

Ramsden
Park

CHELSEA ■
HOTEL ●

SALAD KING ▼

BANH MI ■
BOYS

GERRARD ST W

YONGE ST

BAY ST

WELLESLEY ST E

PLANTA ▼
OKONOMI ★
HOUSE

HOLT ▼
RENFREW

YONGE ST

GRANBY ST
MCGILL ST

LES AMIS B&B ■

BUDDIES IN ■
BAD TIMES
THEATRE

WOOD ST

MAITLAND ST

DUNDONALD ST

CHURCH ST

CAA THEATRE ■

ISABELLA ST

SABAI SABAI ■

CHARLES ST E

HUDSON'S ■
BAY

ARTHUR CONAN ★
DOYLE ROOM

BLOOR ST E

PARK RD

CLUNY DR

CRESCENT RD

CARLTON ST
JARVIS ST

CHURCH-
WELLESLEY
VILLAGE

EARL ST

MT PLEASANT RD

ROSEDALE VALLEY RD

SOUTH DR

GERRARD ST E

Allan Gardens
ALLAN GARDENS ★
CONSERVATORY

HOMEWOOD AVE

SHERBOURNE ST

BLEECKER ST

WELLESLEY ST E

SHERBOURNE ST

HOWARD ST

ELM AVE

DALE AVE

David A.
Balfour
Park

GLEN RD

CABBAGETOWN

WELLESLEY ST E

PARLIAMENT ST

Mon.-Sat., 10am-6pm Sun.). **The Centre Shop** (416/973-4993, noon-5pm daily) sells cool, arty stuff, from jewelry to craft supplies to housewares.

Look for the smokestack to find the **Power Plant Gallery** (231 Queens Quay W., 416/973-4949, www.thepowerplant.org, 10am-5pm Tues.-Sun., 10am-8pm Thurs., free), a contemporary art gallery in a former 1920s power station. The eclectic exhibits change regularly, so there's always something new to see.

To get to Harbourfront Centre, take the subway to Union Station, then walk (about 10 minutes) or catch the no. 509 Exhibition or no. 510 Spadina streetcar west to Harbourfront Centre.

Toronto Music Garden

What do a cellist and a garden designer have in common? In Toronto, they have a garden: **Toronto Music Garden** (479 Queens Quay W., www.harbourfrontcentre.com, dawn-dusk daily year-round, free). Renowned cellist Yo-Yo Ma collaborated with garden designer Julie Moir Messervy to create this waterfront green space inspired by J. S. Bach's "First Suite for Unaccompanied Cello." In Messervy's design, each movement within the piece corresponds to a different section of the garden.

Perhaps the best way to appreciate the music garden is to come for the music. **Summer Music in the Garden** (416/973-4000, www.harbourfrontcentre.com, 7pm Thurs., 4pm Sun. late June-mid-Sept.) is a series of free one-hour classical and world-music concerts.

From Union Station to the garden, take the no. 509 Exhibition or no. 510 Spadina streetcar west to Spadina Avenue.

Fort York National Historic Site

As you stand next to the restored 19th-century barracks, surrounded by condo and office towers, with the hum of city traffic buzzing in the background, it's hard to imagine that this urban pocket was once the first significant settlement in the Toronto area. In 1793, the lieutenant governor of Upper Canada, John Graves Simcoe, and his troops began building a garrison at Fort York, now the **Fort York National Historic Site** (250 Fort York Blvd., 416/392-6907, www.fortyork.ca, 10am-5pm daily mid-May-early Sept., 10am-4pm Mon.-Fri., 10am-5pm Sat.-Sun. early Sept.-mid-May., adults $14, seniors $10, ages 13-18

the Power Plant Gallery at Harbourfront Centre

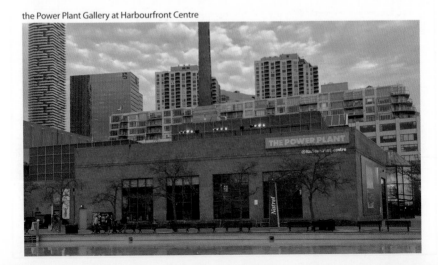

$8, ages 6-12 $6), which would become the territory's new capital. Upper Canada's original capital had been in Niagara—dangerously close, Simcoe thought, to the U.S. border.

Moving the capital north didn't keep it safe, though. During the War of 1812, American troops attacked and burned Fort York. The British quickly began to rebuild, and many of the buildings now standing—including two blockhouses, several barracks, and two powder magazines—date to this period of reconstruction, between 1813 and 1815. It's the largest collection of original War of 1812 buildings in Canada. A modern exhibit center outside the fort explains the historical context and the involvement of the indigenous people who lived on this land.

From Union Station or the Harbourfront, take the no. 509 Exhibition streetcar west to Fort York Boulevard, and follow the signs to the fort. You can also take the subway to Bathurst station (Bloor-Danforth line), then catch the no. 511 Bathurst streetcar southbound; it stops on the fort's eastern side.

The Bentway

Underneath the Gardiner Expressway, near the Fort York Visitor Centre between Strachan Avenue and Bathurst Street, **The Bentway** (416/304-0222, www.thebentway.ca) is a 1.75-kilometer-long (1.1 mile) urban gathering place. It's not a park exactly, but more like a city plaza and walking path. The Bentway hosts arts and music events. In winter, there's a short outdoor skating trail. It's eventually slated to extend east to Spadina Avenue.

★ THE TORONTO ISLANDS

A short ferry ride across the harbor from downtown, the **Toronto Islands** (415/397-2628, www.toronto.ca) are the city's backyard, where both residents and visitors go to lounge at the beach, cruise around by bike or kayak, or have a picnic. The awesome views of the skyline, from the ferries and from the islands themselves, are a bonus; take those picture-postcard city snapshots here.

The "Toronto Islands" consist of several small islands connected by bridges. Ferries dock at Centre Island, Ward's Island to the east, and Hanlan's Point to the west.

Restrooms and drinking water are available on the islands, and there are several places to eat, including the **Island Café** (20 Withrow St., 416/203-6460, www.islandcafeto.com, 8am-9pm Mon.-Thurs., 8am-10pm Fri., 9am-10pm Sat., 9am-9pm Sun. late May-mid.-Oct.,

New towers dwarf the historic buildings at Fort York.

$10-16), on Ward's Island, and the more tour-isty **Shopsy's Island Deli Bar and Grill** (416/203-0405, www.shopsys.ca, 11am-8pm daily mid-June-early Sept., $10-16), next to the Centre Island docks.

Centre Island

Centre Island is the entertainment hub, with an amusement park, gardens, bicycle and boat rentals, and beaches. If you have young kids, head for the **Franklin Children's Garden,** with play structures, a tree house, and a the-ater with summer storytelling events. There's a beach by the pier on Centre Island, but if you walk or cycle either direction from there, you'll find prettier, less populated sand.

Rent bikes at **Toronto Islands Bike Rentals** (416/203-0009, www. torontoislandbicyclerental.com, 11am-5pm May-Sept., $8 per hour, tandems $15 per hour, cash only) near the Centre Island pier, across the island from the ferry dock. You can also rent fun "quadricycles," four-wheeled pedal bikes seating two ($17 per hour) or four ($30 per hour) people. It takes about an hour to cycle a loop of the islands. You can take bi-cycles over from the mainland, except on the Centre Island ferry on busy summer weekends.

In summer, the **Boat House** (416/397-5166, 11am-6pm Mon.-Fri., 11am-7pm Sat.-Sun. June-early Sept., 11am-6pm Sat.-Sun. early-late Sept.) rents **canoes, kayaks,** and **pedal boats.** From the Centre Island docks, follow the main path past the amusement park, cross the bridge near the fountains, and then bear left (east) toward the Boat House.

A big draw for the kids is **Centreville Theme Park** (604/203-0405, www. centreisland.ca, 10:30am-8pm daily July-early Sept., call or check the website for hours May-June and mid-late Sept.), with a 1907 carousel, a Ferris wheel, bumper boats, a roller coaster, and other old-time carnival attractions. If you arrive on the Centre Island ferry, it's hard to sneak past the amusements without the kids noticing; the park is a short walk from the ferry dock.

Admission to the amusement park is free, but you'll pay to ride the rides. A sheet of 25 ride tickets costs $26, or you can buy an all-day pass. Individual passes are based on height; one-day passes for adults and kids over four feet tall are $42, under four feet tall $32. Family all-day passes are $125. Passes are dis-counted if you buy them online.

Ward's Island

Ward's Island looks like an urban cottage col-ony, with the islands' only community of per-manent residents, a beach, and a playground. Wander past the lakeside homes and imagine living here yourself. The mostly sandy **Ward's Island Beach** can be less crowded than some of the others.

Toronto Island SUP (416/899-1668, www. torontoislandsup.com, 9am-9pm Sat.-Sun. May-Sept., 1st hour $30, $10 per additional hour) rents stand-up paddleboards on week-ends from Ward's Island Beach. On weekdays, it rents paddleboards from the Algonquin Bridge (13 Algonquin Bridge Rd., 10:30am-8pm Mon.-Fri. May-Sept.) on the island's la-goon; from the Ward's Island ferry dock, turn right and walk for about five minutes to the bridge. Toronto Island SUP also offers guided SUP tours and SUP yoga classes; check its website for schedules and prices.

Hanlan's Point

If you see airplanes coming in over the harbor, so low that you think they're going to land on your ferry, it's because they're headed to the Toronto Island Airport, near Hanlan's Point, which also has parks and beaches, including **Gibraltar Beach,** west of the pier. Nearby, the stone **Gibraltar Point Lighthouse,** built in 1808-1809, is the oldest surviving light-house on the Great Lakes and the second old-est in Canada. There's a **clothing-optional beach** at Hanlan's Point.

Getting There and Around

Catch the **ferry** (9 Queens Quay W., at Bay St., 416/392-8193, www.toronto.ca, round-trip adults $7.70, seniors and ages 15-19 $5.05, ages

2-14 $3.75) to the islands from the Jack Layton Ferry Terminal near the Westin Harbour Castle Hotel. Buy your tickets online in advance or in person at the ferry terminal.

From downtown, ferries run to Centre Island, Hanlan's Point, and Ward's Island. You can disembark at one and return from another. The schedules for the three ferries are different, however, so be sure to check. While schedules vary seasonally and by time of day, Centre Island boats (mid-Apr.-mid-Oct.) run most frequently, with summer departures every 15-30 minutes. Boats to Hanlan's Point (mid-Apr.-mid-Oct.) and Ward's Island (year-round) typically operate every 30-60 minutes in summer. Only the Ward's Island ferry runs year-round.

Cars are not allowed on the islands, so you'll need to get around on foot or by bicycle. Cycling is a good way to tour these flat islands, which are crisscrossed with pathways.

DOWNTOWN AND THE FINANCIAL DISTRICT
Hockey Hall of Fame
Are you a hockey fan? Then make the pilgrimage to the **Hockey Hall of Fame** (Brookfield Pl., 30 Yonge St., 416/360-7735, www.hhof.com, subway: Union, King, 9:30am-6pm Mon.-Sat., 10am-6pm Sun. late June-early Sept., 10am-5pm Mon.-Fri., 9:30am-6pm Sat., 10:30am-5pm Sun. early Sept.-late June, adults $19, seniors $15, ages 4-13 $13), a museum devoted to the sport and its star players, on the lower level of the Brookfield Place office tower. Exhibits include the legendary Stanley Cup. Two theaters show archival footage of hockey game highlights and the "be a player" zone lets you wield your own stick.

Design Exchange
The former Toronto Stock Exchange, a 1937 art deco building with a limestone and pink granite facade, now houses the **Design Exchange** (234 Bay St., 416/363-6121, www.dx.org, 9am-5pm Wed.-Fri., noon-4:30pm Sat.-Sun.), a gallery space devoted to

Canadian design. Admission prices vary by exhibition. Ask the staff if you can take a peek at the well-preserved former trading floor on the second level.

Elgin and Winter Garden Theatre Centre
The only "double-decker" theater in Canada, and one of less than a dozen ever built worldwide, the **Elgin and Winter Garden Theatres** (189 Yonge St., 416/314-2901, subway: Queen) are two full-size theaters—stacked one on top of the other. Constructed as a vaudeville house, the Elgin opened in December 1913 on the main level; the Winter Garden upstairs opened two months later. While the Elgin is traditional in style, with detailed gold plasterwork and red upholstered seats, the Winter Garden was designed to resemble a garden. Its walls are painted with floral murals, and real leaves hang from the ceiling, like a garden arbor.

As the vaudeville era ended, the lower-level theater became a movie house in the 1930s and 1940s, but by the 1970s, it had become a porn palace. The Winter Garden, shuttered in 1928, was all but abandoned. In 1981, the Ontario Heritage Foundation purchased the building and launched a multiyear restoration project.

While the Elgin had been renovated repeatedly over the years (the lobby had been painted 27 times), the Winter Garden was essentially preserved from the 1920s, hidden under decades of grime. The restoration team couldn't use water or other liquids to clean the wall murals, which had been created with water-soluble paint. Instead, they used more than 385 kilograms (850 pounds) of raw bread dough, rolling it over the murals to lift off the dirt. The team also harvested more than 5,000 beech branches to replace the crumbling leafy ceiling.

Since the restored theaters reopened in 1989, they've been used primarily for touring productions—dramas, musicals, ballets, and operas—as well as various special events. For an event calendar and tickets, contact Ticketmaster (855/622-2787, www.ticketmaster.ca) or phone the theater directly.

The **Ontario Heritage Trust** (www.heritagetrust.on.ca) runs fascinating 90-minute **tours** (5pm Thurs., 11am Sat. year-round, adults $12, seniors and students $10, cash only) of the theater complex that take you through both theaters and tell you more about the building's history and restoration. Arrive at the theater 15 minutes before the scheduled tour time.

Old City Hall

Toronto architect Edward James Lennox (1854-1933), who later designed the even more ornate Casa Loma, crafted the intricately carved Romanesque Revival stone building now known as Toronto's **Old City Hall** (60 Queen St. W., www.toronto.ca, subway: Queen, 8:30am-4:30pm Mon.-Fri.). When it opened in 1899, it was the largest municipal building in North America.

On the building's exterior, Lennox included stone caricatures that represented politicians of his era. At the main entrance on Queen Street, marked by three stone archways, look closely at the top of the columns on the west side of the center arch and you might spot a face with a handlebar mustache—that's Lennox himself.

Old City Hall was actually the Toronto's third city hall building. The first, which burned down in 1849, was on the current site of the St. Lawrence Market. The St. Lawrence Market building was the second city hall from 1845 to 1899.

Surrounding skyscrapers now dwarf the landmark 103-meter (300-foot) clock tower adorning the structure that housed city offices and council chambers until the mid-1960s. Today, Old City Hall is used as a court building. Visitors can walk around inside (after you clear the security check), taking in the finely detailed mosaic floors and marble walls, but no interior photos are allowed. The city plans to relocate the courts and open a new Museum of Toronto inside; in the interim, the building may close to visitors, so check the city website before visiting.

Toronto City Hall

Two curved towers flanking a spaceship-style pod? Finnish architect Viljo Revell designed the distinctive complex of buildings that is the **Toronto City Hall** (100 Queen St. W., www.toronto.ca, subway: Queen, Osgoode), which opened in 1965. (Sadly, the architect died 10 months before the building's opening ceremony.)

When you enter City Hall from the plaza, you can't miss the massive white column in the center of the rotunda; it's the support structure for the **City Council Chambers** that sit above it. If you'd like to attend a council meeting, check the city website (www.toronto.ca) to see when the council is in session.

To the right of the main entrance (on the east wall) is the **"nail mural,"** a wall sculpture called *Metropolis* that artist David Partridge (1919-2006) crafted from 100,000 nails. Other artwork is on view around the building's 1st and 2nd floors; feel free to browse.

To the left of the entrance is a **scale model of the city.** The buildings in the model that are colored pink are those designated as historically or architecturally significant.

There are no public tours of City Hall, but ask at the lobby reception desk for a free **self-guided tour booklet,** which points out many of the building's noteworthy features. The tour booklet is also available online on the city website.

Free concerts and festivals frequently take place on **Nathan Phillips Square,** the plaza in front of City Hall, which is named for the former Toronto mayor who was in office from 1955 to 1962. The plaza's reflecting pool, a pleasant spot for a rest or picnic in summer, becomes a **skating rink** in winter. The arches that span the pool are the **Freedom Arches,** dedicated in 1991 "to the millions who struggled, including Canadians, to gain and defend freedom and to the tens of millions who suffered and died for the lack of it."

Campbell House Museum

Built in 1822 when the Toronto area was still a frontier outpost, the Georgian-style **Campbell House Museum** (160 Queen St. W., at University Ave., 416/597-0227, www. campbellhousemuseum.ca, subway: Osgoode, 9:30am-4:30pm Tues.-Fri., noon-4:30pm Sat.-Sun. late May-late Sept., 9:30am-4:30pm Tues.-Fri., noon-4:30pm Sat. late Sept.-late Dec. and Jan.-late May, adults $6, seniors and ages 13-18 $4, ages 5-12 $3) is the oldest remaining house from the original Town of York. On the 30- to 45-minute guided tours, you'll learn about early Toronto history and about the lives of Judge William Campbell—the sixth chief justice of Upper Canada—and his wife, Hannah, who built and resided in the house. Although few original furnishings remain, the house is outfitted with elegant period pieces that reflect the Campbells' well-to-do status.

Campbell House was originally located 1.5 kilometers (0.9 miles) to the southeast. After being threatened with destruction in 1972, it was moved to its current location, one block west of City Hall.

Mackenzie House

Illegitimate children, mental illness, political intrigue, sibling rivalry, even suicide are all part of the history of William Lyon Mackenzie (1795-1861) and his family, who moved to this Georgian row house in 1859, just two years before his death. Yes, when you take a 45-minute tour of **Mackenzie House** (82 Bond St., 416/392-6915, www.toronto. ca, subway: Dundas, noon-5pm Sat.-Sun. Jan.-Apr., noon-5pm Tues.-Sun. May-early Sept., noon-4pm Tues.-Fri., noon-5pm Sat.-Sun. early Sept.-Dec., adults $7, seniors and ages 13-18 $4, ages 5-12 $3), two blocks east of Dundas subway station, you'll learn about Mackenzie's official biography as a journalist, political reformer, and politician who became the first mayor of the city of Toronto. Yet the guides also share personal details about his life that make a visit here more than just a historic house tour.

Mackenzie published a reform-minded newspaper, the *Colonial Advocate,* and one section of the house is now a working 1850s replica of Mackenzie's Toronto print shop, with an original 19th-century printing press.

Ryerson Image Centre

Interested in contemporary photography? Then visit the cutting-edge gallery of the **Ryerson Image Centre** (33 Gould St., 416/979-5164, www.ryerson.ca/ric, subway: Dundas, 11am-6pm Tues. and Thurs.-Fri., 11am-8pm Wed., noon-5pm Sat.-Sun., free), on the Ryerson University campus. You'll recognize the modern glass-and-steel building by the larger-than-life photos of Gloria Steinem, Albert Einstein, and other notables on the exterior. Exhibits in the three exhibition spaces change several times a year; complimentary tours of the current shows are offered at 2:30pm Tuesday-Sunday.

Textile Museum of Canada

Quilts, clothing, carpets, kimonos, pillow covers, and hats—you'll find all these and more at the **Textile Museum of Canada** (55 Centre Ave., www.textilemuseum.ca, 11am-5pm Thurs.-Tues., 11am-8pm Wed., adults $15, seniors $10, over age 5 $6, families $30; 5pm-8pm Wed. admission by donation). The museum's permanent collection includes more than 12,000 objects that come from 200 regions around the world and span almost 2,000 years. They're shown in rotating exhibits, along with changing exhibitions of contemporary and historical textiles from Canada and abroad. Free **guided tours** of the galleries are offered at 2pm Sunday.

The subway station closest to the museum is St. Patrick; you can also take the no. 505 Dundas streetcar to Chestnut Street.

St. Lawrence Market

From the Town of York's earliest days, the area bounded by Front, Jarvis, King, and Church Streets was a market district. In 1845, the town built a city hall nearby on

Front Street, which housed the mayor's office, council chambers, the police station, and the jail, as well as a produce and poultry market. When the city again outgrew these quarters and constructed a new municipal building—now known as Old City Hall—on Queen Street in 1899, the market began to take over the former city offices, evolving into the **St. Lawrence Market** (Front St. E., between Market St. and Jarvis St., 416/392-7219, www.stlawrencemarket.com).

The St. Lawrence Market complex now has three main buildings: South Market, which is the main destination for food, North Market, and St. Lawrence Hall. The market is four blocks east of Union Station. You can also take the no. 504 King streetcar to Jarvis Street.

SOUTH MARKET

The **South Market** (93 Front St. E., 8am-6pm Tues.-Thurs., 8am-7pm Fri., 5am-5pm Sat.) is packed with market stalls selling cheeses, meats, and produce as well as prepared foods. Not all of it is locally produced, but some is, so look hard if you're into local goodies.

On the South Market's 2nd floor, the city-run **Market Gallery** (www.toronto.ca, 10am-4pm Tues.-Thurs., 10am-6pm Fri., 9am-4pm Sat., adults $8, seniors and ages 13-18 $7, ages 5-12 $5) mounts changing exhibitions that reflect the city's art, culture, or history. The gallery space housed the Toronto City Council Chamber in the late 1800s.

For a detailed history of the market district, book a 90-minute **St. Lawrence Market History Walking Tour** (647/393-8687, bruce.bell2@sympatico.ca, www.brucebelltours.ca, 10am Tues.-Sat., adults $30) with guide Bruce Bell. Reservations are required; book by phone or email.

The **Market Kitchen** (416/860-0727, www.themarketkitchen.ca), on the mezzanine level of the South Market, offers cooking classes (2-3 hours, $50-90 pp) on topics ranging from baking scones to cooking with beer to preparing Spanish tapas. Book in advance on the website.

Note that the South Market is closed Sunday-Monday.

NORTH MARKET

Across Front Street from the South Market building, the North Market has been a place for area farmers to sell their wares since 1803. It is still a year-round Saturday **farmers market** (5am-3pm Sat.) and Sunday **antiques market** (dawn-5pm Sun.), though at the time of this writing, a new North

St. Lawrence Market

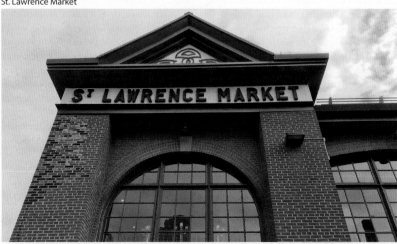

Market building was being constructed, and these weekend markets had relocated temporarily to 125 The Esplanade, south of the South Market building.

ST. LAWRENCE HALL

The stately cupola-topped building at the corner of King and Jarvis Streets is **St. Lawrence Hall** (157 King St. E., www.stlawrencemarket. com). Built in 1850, the hall was once one of the city's social hubs, hosting concerts, lectures, and balls. The hall also played a role in the abolitionist movement, when the North American Convention of Coloured Freemen, an abolitionist group, met here in 1851 to discuss the issue of former slaves fleeing the United States. After debating whether to encourage these refugees to start new lives in Canada, the Caribbean, or Africa, the 53 delegates concluded that Canada was the best destination.

St. Lawrence Hall is now primarily a city office building, but visitors can go up to the **East Room,** on the 3rd floor, to see the small exhibit about the notables who lectured, performed, or visited here, from Canadian politician and journalist William Lyon Mackenzie to abolitionist leader Frederick Douglass to circus impresario P. T. Barnum.

★ The Distillery Historic District

Toronto was once home to the world's largest distillery, the Gooderham and Worts Distillery, founded in 1832. Though the stills have long been stilled, the five-hectare (13-acre) site east of downtown has been redeveloped into **The Distillery Historic District** (55 Mill St., 416/364-1177, www. thedistillerydistrict.com), where the Victorian-era brick industrial buildings now house galleries, shops, cafés, and theaters, as well as high-end condominiums.

The Distillery Historic District is bounded by Parliament, Mill, and Cherry Streets. From downtown, take the no. 514 Cherry streetcar to the Distillery Loop, or ride the no. 504 King streetcar to Parliament Street, then walk two blocks south. You can also follow a **walking path** along the Esplanade between the St. Lawrence Market and the Distillery District, bordering David Crombie Park.

GALLERIES AND ARTIST STUDIOS

The **Artscape Building** (15 Case Goods Lane, www.torontoartscape.on.ca, noon-5pm Wed.-Sun.) houses more than 60 artist

The Distillery Historic District

studios, many of which are open for browsing, and you may be able to watch the artists at work.

The **Corkin Gallery** (7 Tank House Lane, 416/979-1980, www.corkingallery.com, 10am-6pm Tues.-Sat., noon-5pm Sun.) has one of the coolest art spaces in the Distillery District, displaying contemporary works amid the brick columns, steel girders, and soaring ceilings of the building's original structure.

At the **Deaf Culture Centre** (34 Distillery Lane, 416/203-0343, www.deafculturecentre. ca, 11am-6pm Tues.-Sat., noon-5pm Sun., free), browse a small museum about the deaf community and about technological innovations and communications tools for the deaf. The center also offers resources for deaf individuals and their families.

BREWERIES AND DISTILLERIES

Toronto's first sake brewery, **Ontario Spring Water Sake Company** (51 Gristmill Lane, 416/365-7253, www.ontariosake.com, noon-6pm Sun.-Thurs., noon-7pm Fri., 11am-7pm Sat.) has a retail store and tasting bar in the Distillery District. One-hour weekend brewery tours (1pm and 3:30pm Sat.-Sun., $15 pp) take you through the facility, where you learn about the sake-making process and taste several varieties. Reservations are recommended for tours; phone to book.

Mill Street Brewery (21 Tank House Lane, 416/681-0338, www.millstreetbrewpub. ca, store 11am-9pm Mon.-Thurs., 11am-10pm Fri.-Sat., 11am-8pm Sun., brewpub 11am-10pm Sun.-Mon., 11am-11pm Tues.-Wed., 11am-midnight Thurs., 11am-2am Fri.-Sat.) produces more than a dozen varieties of beer in this Distillery District microbrewery. Tours of the brewery (4pm Mon.-Tues.; 4pm, 5pm, 6pm, and 7pm Wed.-Fri.; hourly 1pm-7pm Sat.-Sun., $10) include tastings; check in 15 minutes before the tour time.

Spirit Of York Distillery Co. (12 Trinity St., 416/777-0001, www.spiritofyork.com, noon-8pm Mon.-Wed., noon-9pm Thurs., noon-10pm Fri.-Sat., noon-9pm Sun.) produces vodka and gin that you can sample at the glam circular bar in the tasting room, where big windows look into the distilling area.

Underpass Park

Underneath a tangle of streets east of the Distillery District, **Underpass Park** (29 Lower River St., free) transformed a neglected space beneath the Eastern Avenue, Richmond Street, and Adelaide Street overpasses into a street art gallery. Toronto-based artist Paul Raff designed a public art piece, *Mirage*, with 57 reflective stainless steel octagons that sparkle from the "ceiling" beneath the overpasses, while other artists have decorated the overpass columns with colorful murals and paintings.

BLOOR-YORKVILLE AND THE ANNEX

Bloor Street bisects the city from west to east, and its central section, between Yonge Street and Avenue Road, is the **Bloor-Yorkville** (www.bloor-yorkville.com) neighborhood. An upscale shopping and dining destination, Bloor-Yorkville houses several of the city's top cultural attractions, including the Royal Ontario Museum and the Bata Shoe Museum.

West along Bloor Street between Avenue Road and Bathurst Street, **The Annex** (www. bloorannex.ca) is more residential and more bohemian. Many of its cafés and shops cater to students and staff at the nearby University of Toronto.

★ Royal Ontario Museum

A visit to the venerable **Royal Ontario Museum** (ROM; 100 Queen's Park, 416/586-8000, www.rom.on.ca, subway: Museum, St. George, 10am-5:30pm Sat.-Thurs., 10am-8:30pm Fri., adults $20, seniors $17, ages 15-19 and students $15.50, ages 4-14 $14, discounted admission after 5:30pm Fri.) is like a stroll through the history of the world. In this massive museum of natural history and world cultures, you'll find everything from Egyptian mummies to British neoclassical dining rooms, Buddha statues from China and India, armor from medieval Europe, and, of course, lots of kid-pleasing dinosaur skeletons.

Approach the museum building on the Queen's Park side and you'll see an imposing stone face with arched windows that dates back to the early 1900s. But when you come around to Bloor Street, it looks like an altogether different structure. Architect Daniel Libeskind designed this contemporary addition, the **Michael Lee-Chin Crystal,** a series of five interlocking glass and steel prisms that appear to hang off the building's Bloor Street facade.

Take a free 45-minute **tour** (daily, times vary) to get your bearings—either an introduction to the museum's highlights or a more in-depth look at a particular aspect of the collection. The ROM also offers lectures, children's programs, and other special events; check the website for schedules. Avoid lines at the ticket counter by buying your tickets online in advance. Some special exhibitions have higher admission prices.

Gardiner Museum

Exhibiting ceramics from ancient times to the present, the **Gardiner Museum** (111 Queen's Park, 416/586-8080, www.gardinermuseum. on.ca, subway: Museum, 10am-6pm Mon.-Thurs., 10am-9pm Fri., 10am-5pm Sat.-Sun., adults $15, seniors $11, students $9, under age 18 free, half price 4pm-9pm Fri.) shows pieces like a Zapotec funerary urn (created AD 500-700), porcelain from Japan and China, and English delftware from the 17th and 18th centuries. To learn more about the museum's exhibits and collections, take a free **guided tour** (2pm daily).

If ogling these fine ceramics pieces inspires you to get your own hands dirty, try a two-hour drop-in **clay class** (6pm Wed. and Fri., 1pm Sun., adults $15, seniors and students $12, under age 12 $5). Sign up online, beginning at 10am on the day of the class.

★ Bata Shoe Museum

If you think that a museum devoted to shoes would appeal only to foot fetishists or footwear-fixated fashionistas, think again. The well-designed **Bata Shoe Museum** (327 Bloor St. W., 416/979-7799, www. batashoemuseum.ca, subway: St. George, 10am-5pm Mon.-Wed. and Fri.-Sat., 10am-8pm Thurs., noon-5pm Sun., adults $14, seniors $12, students $8, ages 5-17 $5, families $24-35) traces the history and culture of a

Royal Ontario Museum

wide swath of humanity by showcasing what people wore on their feet.

Inside the asymmetrical building, designed by architect Raymond Moriyama to resemble a shoebox with its lid askew, the museum's collections include more than 10,000 shoes—from doll-like slippers worn by Chinese women with bound feet (there's even an over-shoe version for wearing while working in the fields) to singer Elton John's sky-high platform shoes. They have Queen Victoria's silk stocking and a pair of socks that Napoleon wore at Elba. Exhibit captions reveal fascinating snippets about the people who wore them.

From 5pm to 8pm Thursday, admission is pay-what-you-can (suggested donation $5).

University of Toronto

With more than 75,000 students and over 15,000 faculty and staff, the **University of Toronto** (www.utoronto.ca, subway: St. George, Museum) is Canada's largest university. The main St. George campus is roughly bounded by Bloor, Bay, and College Streets and Spadina Avenue.

As you're wandering the leafy grounds, see what's on at the **University of Toronto Art Centre** (15 King's College Circle, 416/978-1838, http://artmuseum.utoronto.ca,

noon-5pm Tues.-Sat., Sept.-June, free), which shows wide-ranging exhibits in a Romanesque Revival building. It's off Hoskin Avenue, between St. George Street and Queen's Park Crescent.

Prospective students and visitors can take a two-hour **general campus tour** (www.future.utoronto.ca, 11am and 2pm Mon.-Fri., 11am Sat., free) to learn more about the university. Tours depart from the **Nona Macdonald Visitors Centre** (25 King's College Circle, 416/978-5000).

Ontario Legislative Assembly

Although Toronto is Canada's largest city, it's not the national capital; Ottawa has that distinction. But it is the capital of the province of Ontario, which, like all Canadian provinces, has its own provincial government. Ontario's seat of government is the august **Ontario Legislative Assembly** (111 Wellesley St. W., 416/325-7500, tour information 416/325-0061, www.ontla.on.ca, subway: Queen's Park, tours 9am-5pm Mon.-Fri., 9am-4:30pm Sat.-Sun. mid-May-June, 9am-5:30pm Mon.-Fri., 9am-4:30pm Sat.-Sun. July-early Sept., 9am-5pm Mon.-Fri. early Sept.-mid-May, free) in Queen's Park.

On the free 30-minute **tours** of the

Elton John's platform shoes on display at the Bata Shoe Museum the Arthur Conan Doyle Room at the Toronto Reference Library

St., 416/395-5577, www.torontopubliclibrary. ca, subway: Bloor-Yonge, 9am-8:30pm Mon.-Fri., 9am-5pm Sat., 1:30pm-5pm Sun., free), modeled after the study at 221B Baker Street (the mythical sleuth's residence), is full of books by and about the author of the Sherlock Holmes mysteries. Also on display is a variety of Holmes memorabilia, from his trademark pipe to comic books based on Holmes's (fictional) life, as well as Doyle's letters and papers. The collection doesn't circulate, but visitors are welcome to browse, and the helpful staff can tell you about the materials.

Casa Loma

You don't have to travel to Europe to tour a castle; Toronto has **Casa Loma** (1 Austin Terrace, at Spadina Rd., 416/923-1171, www. casaloma.org, 9:30am-5pm daily, adults $30, seniors and ages 14-17 $24, ages 4-13 $20, parking $10). This opulent "House on the Hill" overlooking the city took three years (1911-1914) to build and contains enough grand salons, towers, and elaborate gardens to satisfy most castle buffs. While kids may not care about the architecture or plush furnishings, they might enjoy climbing the twisty spiral staircase to the turret, finding secret passageways, or following the creepy underground tunnels to the horse stables (where mahogany paneling lines the deluxe stalls). You might also check out **Escape from Casa Loma** (647-243-7658, www.escapecasaloma. com, see website for schedule, $46 pp), a series of escape room games that take place inside the castle after-hours.

The castle ticket price includes a self-guided audio tour with details about the house, its owners, and its furnishings, as well as admission to a documentary film about Canadian financier Sir Henry Pellatt, who built the castle. Casa Loma is now home to the luxe **BlueBlood Steakhouse** (www. bluebloodsteakhouse.com, 5pm-midnight Sun.-Wed., 5pm-1am Thurs.-Sat.), which opens after the castle closes to daytime visitors.

From downtown, the most direct route to

building, which opened in 1893, you'll get a brief history of the building and the structure of Ontario's government. Guides share interesting tidbits about members of the provincial parliament (though they're more historical than scandalous). Tour schedules vary depending on what's happening in the building, so it's a good idea to phone ahead. Several other tours are available as well; check the website for details.

Visitors are welcome to observe the provincial parliament in action, which, during the legislative session, is typically 10:30am-6pm Monday and 9am-6pm Tuesday-Thursday. Pick up a free access pass from the Special Constable at the legislature's south basement entrance. Staff at the information desk in the main lobby can also answer questions about tours and parliament sessions.

Arthur Conan Doyle Room

Are you a fan of Sherlock Holmes? On the 5th floor of the Toronto Reference Library, the **Arthur Conan Doyle Room** (789 Yonge the castle is to take the subway to Dupont station (Spadina-University line). Exit the subway, walk north two blocks on Spadina Road, and climb the Baldwin Steps (a 110-step staircase) to the castle.

Spadina Museum

Across the road from Casa Loma, the large but decidedly more modest historic house that now houses the **Spadina Museum** (285 Spadina Rd., 416/392-6910, www.toronto. ca, noon-5pm Sat.-Sun. Jan.-Mar., noon-5pm Tues.-Sun. Apr.-early Sept., noon-4pm Tues.-Fri., noon-5pm Sat.-Sun. early Sept.-Dec., adults $9, seniors and ages 13-18 $6.50, ages 6-12 $5.50) is more typical of an upper-class family home from the early 20th century. Built in 1886, the house belonged to the well-to-do Austin family, and nearly all the furnishings, from the ornate art deco wallpaper to the billiards table, are original to the home.

Like Casa Loma, the Spadina Museum is at the top of the Baldwin Steps, a short walk (but a steep climb) from Dupont station.

KENSINGTON MARKET, CHINATOWN, AND VICINITY

Head west of downtown for art, food, and shopping, where the city's diverse neighborhoods are particularly fun to explore when you're hungry.

Kensington Market

Kensington Market isn't a market building. Rather, it's a market neighborhood, filled with vendors' stalls and international eateries that span the globe. There's a Chilean empanada place near a Mexican taco joint, an Indian spice vendor opposite a Latino meat market, and a plethora of fruit sellers, bakeries, nut vendors, cheese shops, and inexpensive clothing outlets. On a mild evening, sidewalk cafés are packed, and people spill out of restaurants and bars onto the streets. Most of the action takes place along Augusta Avenue, Baldwin Street, and Nassau Street, west of Spadina Avenue between Dundas and College Streets.

Generations of immigrants have settled in the Kensington Market area, which gives it its multicultural vibe. In the second half of the 19th century, working-class immigrants from England and Ireland made the neighborhood their home. Then, between 1905 and 1930, Jews fleeing persecution in Europe settled here, many opening small shops that resemble those still lining the narrow streets today. After World War II, Caribbean, Chinese, South Asian, and Latin American newcomers joined the European settlers in the market district.

To get to Kensington Market, take the no. 506 Carlton streetcar to Major Street or Augusta Avenue, or take the no. 510 Spadina streetcar and get off anywhere between Dundas and College.

"Original" Chinatown

Toronto's first Chinatown, settled in the early 1900s, was originally located along Elizabeth Street, near Dundas Street, behind the current Toronto City Hall. When the city began appropriating land in the neighborhood during the late 1940s and early 1950s, with a plan to build a new city hall and public square, many Chinatown businesses closed, but others moved west into the district now known as Toronto's original Chinatown. Chinese groceries, herbalists, and restaurants line Spadina Avenue and Dundas Street, extending north to College Street and south toward Queen Street. The neighborhood has grown increasingly diverse, with Vietnamese and other Southeast Asian businesses joining the Chinese vendors, and hip eateries and cafés adding to the mix. It's a fun place to browse and, of course, eat.

To get to Chinatown, take the no. 505 Dundas or no. 506 Carlton streetcar to Spadina Avenue. You could also take the no. 510 Spadina streetcar and get off anywhere between Dundas and College.

★ Art Gallery of Ontario

Born Frank Owen Goldberg in Toronto in 1929, the internationally acclaimed architect now known as Frank Gehry grew up not far from the **Art Gallery of Ontario** (AGO, 317 Dundas St. W., 416/979-6648 or 877/225-4246, www.ago.net, subway: St. Patrick, 10:30am-5pm Tues. and Thurs., 10:30am-9pm Wed. and Fri., 10:30am-5:30pm Sat.-Sun., adults $19.50, seniors $16, students and ages 6-17 $11, families $49; free admission 6pm-9pm Wed.). The Art Gallery is one of North America's largest museums, with more than 80,000 works, so perhaps it's fitting that Gehry designed the facility's dramatic building, which opened in 2008. While Gehry has constructed buildings all over the world—from the Guggenheim Museum Bilbao in Spain and the Experience Music Project in Seattle to the Walt Disney Concert Hall in Los Angeles—the AGO was his first project in Canada.

Among the highlights of the museum's collection, beyond the building itself, are its Canadian collections, which include significant works by the Group of Seven (early-20th-century landscape artists) and by contemporary Inuit artists. The AGO has the largest collection of African and Oceanic art in a Canadian art museum, the largest public collection of work by the British sculptor Henry Moore (1898-1986), and a major European Old Masters collection that's particularly strong in Italian and Dutch painting from the 1600s and French impressionist works from the 1800s.

The best way to get an overview of the museum's extensive collection is to take the 60-minute **AGO Highlights Tour** (11am, noon, 1pm, and 3pm Tues., Thurs., and Sat.-Sun., 11am, noon, 1pm, 3pm, and 7pm Wed. and Fri., free).

When you need a break, you can get coffee and pastries in the 2nd-floor Galleria Italia espresso bar. For sandwiches, salads, and light meals, there's **caféAGO.** The museum's main dining room is **AGO Bistro** (noon-2:30pm and 5:30pm-10pm Tues.-Fri., 11am-2:30pm and 5:30pm-10pm Sat., 11am-3pm Sun., lunch $14-24, dinner $22-33), which serves contemporary fare.

The museum is three blocks west of the St. Patrick subway station. The no. 505 Dundas streetcar stops at McCaul and Beverly Streets are both in front of the AGO.

Ontario College of Art & Design

If you can imagine a black-and-white-checkered box floating in the sky, supported only by yellow, blue, and purple pencils, then you can begin to envision one of Toronto's most distinctive buildings, the Sharp Centre for Design at the **Ontario College of Art & Design** (OCAD, 100 McCaul St., 416/977-6000, www.ocad.ca, subway: St. Patrick).

The floating box, or tabletop, section of the building is 9 meters (29.5 feet) tall, 31 meters (102 feet) wide, and 84 meters (275 feet) long and houses studios and classrooms. Twelve colorful hollow steel legs, each measuring 30 meters (100 feet)—or roughly the equivalent of a 10-story building—support the "tabletop." British architect Will Alsop, in partnership with the Toronto-based Robbie/Young + Wright Architects, designed this unusual structure, which opened in 2004.

The building is most remarkable from the exterior. There are no public tours of the interior, but you can go inside to view exhibitions at **Anniversary Gallery,** a small experimental gallery space on the second level.

OCAD has other galleries in the neighborhood that are open to the public. Its flagship **Onsite Gallery** (199 Richmond St. W., noon-8pm Wed., noon-7pm Thurs.-Fri., noon-5pm Sat.-Sun., free) mounts exhibits in contemporary art, design, and digital media. To see what OCAD students and recent graduates are up to, stop into **Ignite Gallery** (165 Augusta Ave., 1pm-6pm Wed.-Sun., free).

401 Richmond

South of Queen Street at Spadina Avenue

Family-Friendly Toronto

Ripley's Aquarium of Canada has plenty for kids to see and do.

Toronto has plenty of activities to engage children of all ages.

- Ride to the top of the **CN Tower** and let your little daredevils jump on the Glass Floor, 113 stories above the ground.

- Check out the sharks, jellyfish, and more than 16,000 other aquatic creatures at **Ripley's Aquarium of Canada.**

- The dinosaurs and mummies at the **Royal Ontario Museum** have lots of kid appeal, as do the hands-on exhibits at the **Ontario Science Centre** and the animals at **Riverdale Farm.** Young hockey fans won't want to miss the **Hockey Hall of Fame.**

- If it's a nice day, take the ferry to the **Toronto Islands,** especially if your youngsters love amusement parks. You can also rent bikes and go exploring.

- Older kids might enjoy a family version of an **Urban Quest** walking tour, where you follow a series of clues through the city, or an escape game, like **Escape from Casa Loma.**

- When it's time to eat, wander the **St. Lawrence Market** and let everyone pick out their favorite bites. In Chinatown, have dim sum or watch the dumpling makers at work at **Mother's Dumplings.**

- Several attractions in suburban Toronto are popular with the kids, too, including **Canada's Wonderland** (Canada's Wonderland Rd., Vaughan, 905/832-8131, www.canadaswonderland. com), an amusement park that's home to Canada's tallest and fastest roller coaster; **LEGOLAND Discovery Centre** (1 Bass Pro Mills Dr., Vaughan, 855/356-2150, www. legolanddiscoverycentre.ca/toronto), for kids ages 3-10 who love colorful LEGO blocks; and the **Toronto Zoo** (2000 Meadowvale Rd., Toronto, 416/392-5929, www.torontozoo.com), which has more than 5,000 animals.

- Toronto's most family-friendly place to stay is the **Chelsea Hotel,** a mega-size property (it's Canada's largest lodging) with an indoor pool with a 40-meter (130-foot) waterslide, a "Kid Centre" for games, arts, and crafts, and a roster of family activities.

is **401 Richmond** (401 Richmond St. W., 416/595-5900, www.401richmond.net), a rehabbed brick heritage building that's home to artists, galleries, art shops, and other cultural businesses. Poke around and see what's happening, or check out **Open Studio** (416/504-8238, www.openstudio.on.ca, noon-5pm Tues.-Sat.), an artist-run printmaking center, and **Swipe Design|Books+Objects** (416/363-1332, www.swipe.com, 11am-7pm Mon.-Fri., 11am-6pm Sat.), which sells design books and lots of cool design stuff. **Spacing Store** (416/644-1017, www.spacingstore.ca, 11am-7pm Mon.-Fri., 11am-6pm Sat.) carries fun, arty Toronto souvenirs, from subway station coasters to books, T-shirts, and socks.

Graffiti Alley

You'll find murals and street art throughout Toronto, but one of the most famous graffiti destinations is in the Entertainment District. Canadian comedian and political commenter Rick Mercer popularized **Graffiti Alley** when he began filming his "rants"—observations on whatever is currently annoying him—as he walked down the vividly tagged alleyway. Officially known as Rush Lane, the alley is located between Queen Street West, Spadina Avenue, Richmond Street West, and Portland Street.

THE WEST END

Toronto's farther-west-of-downtown neighborhoods include some of the city's hippest districts, filled with galleries, restaurants, and funky boutiques.

TOP EXPERIENCE

★ Queen Street West

As you head west from downtown through the Entertainment District along Queen Street, the shops and eateries change from chains and mainstream brands to smaller, independent businesses. Farther west, this funky neighborhood gets a mouthful of a moniker: West Queen West. Though it still has a grunge feel

in parts, this "in" arts district is packed with eclectic shops and galleries, arty hotels, and hip bars.

Run by the Ontario Crafts Council, the small **Craft Ontario Gallery** (1106 Queen St. W., 416/925-4222, www.craftontario.com, 11am-6pm Mon., 10am-6pm Tues.-Wed., 10am-7pm Thurs.-Sat., 11am-5pm Sun.) shows works by Ontario craftspeople. At the **David Kaye Gallery** (1092 Queen St. W., at Dovercourt Rd., 416/532-9075, www.davidkayegallery.com, 11am-6pm Wed.-Fri., 11am-5pm Sat.-Sun.), you'll find paintings, objects, and jewelry by a mix of up-and-coming and more established artists.

Housed in a former police station, **Gallery 1313** (1313 Queen St. W., 416/536-6778, www.g1313.org, 1pm-6pm Wed.-Sun.) is an artist-run space that shows contemporary Canadian art. **General Hardware Contemporary** (1520 Queen St. W., 416/821-3060, www.generalhardware.ca, noon-6pm Wed.-Sat.), in a former hardware store west of Lansdowne Avenue, exhibits contemporary art by Canadian and international artists.

High Park

On the far west side of the city, Toronto's largest public park, **High Park** (1873 Bloor St. W., 416/397-2628, www.toronto.ca, subway: High Park, dawn-dusk daily, free) has Grenadier Pond, hiking trails, playgrounds, gardens, and even a small **zoo** (Deer Pen Rd., 7am-dusk daily, free) with cows, sheep, bison, llamas, peacocks, and deer.

To see what's where in the park, you can catch the "trackless train" (10:30am-dusk Sat.-Sun. Apr. and Sept.-Oct., 10:30am-dusk daily May-Aug, adults $4.50, seniors and kids $3.50), which makes a 30-minute tour of the park grounds.

Another park attraction is the 1837 **Colborne Lodge** (11 Colborne Lodge Dr., 416/392-6916, www.toronto.ca, noon-5pm Tues.-Sun. May-Aug., noon-5pm Sat.-Sun. Sept., noon-4pm Tues.-Sun. Oct.-Dec., noon-4pm Fri.-Sun. Jan.-Apr., adults $7, seniors and ages 13-18 $4, ages 4-12 $3), the former home of John and Jemima Howard, who founded High Park.

To reach most park sights, take the Bloor subway, which runs along the park's northern border, to High Park station. If you're going to Colborne Lodge, on the south side of the park, it's easier to take the no. 501 Humber/Long Branch streetcar to Colborne Lodge Drive; from there, it's a short walk up the road.

The Junction Triangle

While the west Toronto neighborhood known as the Junction Triangle may be far from the city center, it's emerging as an arts hub, due in part to the opening of the Museum of Contemporary Art. New restaurants and craft breweries are adding to the mix in this triangle of land between Lansdowne Avenue, Dundas Street West, and Dupont Street.

MUSEUM OF CONTEMPORARY ART

Relocated in 2018 to a revamped former aluminum foundry in the Junction Triangle, the **Museum of Contemporary Art** (MOCA, 158 Sterling Rd., 416/395-0067, www.museumofcontemporaryart.ca, noon-8pm Mon. and Wed.-Fri., 10am-6pm Sat.-Sun., adults $10, students $5) shows cutting-edge creations by Canadian and international artists, working in many different media. Admission to the ground-floor gallery is free; you pay admission for the main exhibit spaces on the 2nd and 3rd floors. More than 20 local artists will work in studio spaces on the building's upper levels.

The fastest way to get to the museum from downtown is to ride the UP Express, the train that connects Union Station to Pearson Airport, to Bloor station; from there, it's about a 10-minute walk to MOCA. You can also take the subway (Bloor-Danforth line) to Lansdowne station, a 15-minute walk to the museum. The no. 504 King streetcar can take you to Dundas Street West at Bloor Street, also about 15 minutes on foot to the museum; the streetcar is convenient if you're already in one of the West End neighborhoods, but it's a slow ride from the city center.

For refreshments before or after your museum visit, stop into nearby **Drake Commissary** (128 Sterling Rd., 416/432-2922, www.drakecommissary.ca, 8:30am-10pm Sun.-Wed., 8:30am-midnight Thurs., 8:30am-1am Fri.-Sat., lunch $6-19, dinner $6-27), an art-filled bakery, bar, and eatery that the Drake Hotel team runs in a rehabbed brick industrial space. Besides scones, muffins, and other pastries, you can share hummus or duck pâté, nibble open-faced sandwiches from prawn and avocado to pickled herring with beets, or grab a slice of pizza. The evening menu adds larger plates like smoked brisket or kale lasagna. To drink, sip fresh juices, cold-brew coffee, local craft beers, and imaginative cocktails.

BREWERIES AND DISTILLERIES

Near Drake Commissary and MOCA, **Henderson Brewery Company** (128A Sterling Rd., 416/863-8822, www.hendersonbrewing.com, 11am-11pm daily) offers samples and pours pints in its brewery tasting room. Their flagship, Henderson's Best amber ale, is a classic English-style bitter, and they regularly craft seasonal brews like Target Practice, a Belgian blond brewed with tart cherries.

The beer masters at tiny **Halo Brewery** (247 Wallace Ave., 416/606-7778, www.halobrewery.com, 3pm-9pm Tues.-Fri., 11am-9pm Sat.-Sun.) are always experimenting, creating a small range of distinctive brews, all with vividly colored geometric labels. In the brewery tasting room, you might find Shapeshifter, a sour, grapefruit-y IPA; Tokyo Rose, a saison infused with rose hips; or Magic Missile, a dry-hopped pale ale.

If you venture farther northwest, you can sample a unique spirit made from a distinctively Ontario ingredient. Rather than distilling its vodka from grain or potatoes, **Nickel 9 Distillery** (90 Cawthra Ave., Unit 100, 647/341-5959, www.nickel9distillery.com, 3pm-9pm Thurs.-Fri., 11am-9pm Sat., 11am-5pm Sun.) crafts its Northern Temple Vodka

Nickel 9 Distillery

from apples. Try it at this microdistillery's sample bar.

THE EAST END

Exploring Toronto's east side is less about seeing "sights" and more about exploring different neighborhoods and communities.

The area surrounding Church and Wellesley Streets may officially be **Church-Wellesley Village** (www.churchwellesleyvillage.ca), but as the longtime hub of Toronto's large gay and lesbian community, its unofficial name is the Gay Village.

East of Parliament Street, between Gerrard and Wellesley Streets, lies **Cabbagetown.** According to legend, the immigrants who settled here in the 1800s could afford to eat only the cabbage they grew themselves—giving rise to the Cabbagetown name. Nowadays, you might still have to eat cabbage to afford the pricey, meticulously preserved Victorian homes in this now well-to-do corner of town. This urban district has several outdoor attractions

(all accessible via the no. 506 Carleton streetcar): **Allan Gardens Conservatory** (19 Horticultural Ave., 416/392-1111, www.toronto.ca, 10am-5pm daily, free), greenhouses with more than 1,500 square meters (16,000 square feet) of plants; **Riverdale Farm** (201 Winchester St., 416/392-6794, www.toronto.ca, 9am-5pm daily, free), a kid-friendly farm and gardens; and the 1850 **Toronto Necropolis** (200 Winchester St., 416/923-7911, 8am-8pm mid-Mar.-Sept., 8am-dusk daily Oct.-mid-Mar.), a leafy, park-like cemetery where a number of notable Torontonians are interred, including William Lyon Mackenzie (Toronto's first mayor), politician Jack Layton (who led the country's New Democratic Party [NDP] from 2003 until his death in 2011), and Anderson Ruffin Abbot (1837-1913), the first Canadian-born Black surgeon.

Stretching east along Danforth Avenue between Chester and Pape Avenues is the Danforth, the neighborhood also known as **Greektown** (www.greektowntoronto.com) because it was historically the center of Toronto's Greek community. You'll still find souvlaki shops, traditional cafés, and baklava-filled bakeries, but the Danforth has become popular with young families who shop in the organic market and frequent the local yoga studio.

Around Broadview Avenue and Gerrard Street is one of Toronto's smaller Chinatowns. This **East Chinatown** actually has a significant Vietnamese population, which means lots of pho and banh mi shops. The no. 506 Carlton streetcar will take you to this community.

Farther east along Gerrard are the sari shops and curry-scented dining rooms of Little India, in the neighborhood called the **Indian Bazaar** (www.gerrardindiabazaar.com). Take the no. 506 Carlton streetcar and get off when you begin to see Indian shops.

Ride the no. 501 Queen Street streetcar east from downtown, and you'll reach the gentrifying neighborhoods of **Queen East** and **Leslieville,** which are drawing the artistically inclined to their galleries, cafés, and increasingly hip restaurants and shops. Continuing east is the residential neighborhood known as **The Beaches.** It borders Lake Ontario, with lakefront walkways and, yes, beaches, making it a pleasant spot for a day's excursion.

GREATER TORONTO
Evergreen Brick Works

For more than 100 years, the Don Valley Brick Works made many of the bricks that built Toronto, including notable buildings like Old City Hall and Massey Hall. When the brick works ceased operations in 1986, this complex of buildings northeast of downtown fell into disrepair. Graffiti artists began using its huge brick walls as their canvases, and performance artists held underground raves in the abandoned factory.

In 1991, the site took on a new identity with the launch of **Evergreen Brick Works** (550 Bayview Ave., 416/596-7670, www.evergreen. ca), whose mission was to restore the 16 buildings and create a new environmental design and education center. Since then, Evergreen Brick Works has started a variety of "green" programs to bring nature back into the city. If you're interested in green design, local food,

cycling, or a host of environmental issues, pay a visit here.

To get your bearings in this sprawling complex, stop into the **Young Welcome Centre** (9am-5pm Mon.-Fri., 8am-5pm Sat., 10am-5pm Sun.) and see what's on for the day. Workshops, exhibits, and other special events take place throughout the year; a calendar is posted on the website. **Hiking trails** wend through the property, too.

The best time to visit is on the weekend, when a large **farmers market** (8am-1pm Sat. late May-Oct., 10am-3pm Sun. late June-Oct., 9am-1pm Sat. Nov.-late May) sets up shop, with vendors selling local produce, cheeses, honey, maple syrup, baked goods, and a variety of prepared foods. In mild weather, it's in the outdoor pavilion; in winter, it moves into the Welcome Centre. You can also sit down for a meal at **Café Belong** (416/901-8234, www. cafebelong.ca, 11:30am-3pm Mon.-Tues., 11:30am-9pm Wed.-Fri., 10am-10pm Sat., 10am-3pm Sun., lunch $16-32, dinner $22-44), which emphasizes local foods.

To get here, take the subway (Bloor-Danforth line) to Broadview station, where you can catch a free shuttle to the Brick Works. The shuttle stop is next to the park on Erindale Avenue, on the east side of

Ontario Science Centre

Broadview Avenue, just north of the station. The shuttles run every 30-45 minutes.

Ontario Science Centre

"Please touch" exhibits are common at many science museums, but at the well-designed **Ontario Science Centre** (770 Don Mills Rd., at Eglinton Ave. E., www.ontariosciencecentre.ca, 10am-4pm Mon.-Fri., 10am-8pm Sat., 10am-5pm Sun., adults $22, seniors, students, and ages 13-17 $16, ages 3-12 $13, IMAX film $6 extra, parking $10), exhibits go beyond button-pushing and computer-based games to promote real explorations of the material. Besides the expected displays about space, the human body, and the earth, you can investigate prejudice, stereotyping, and racism in the thought-provoking exhibit called *A Question of Truth*. While a play area will entertain the little ones, even jaded teens can find cool stuff here, particularly in the Innovation Centre, where activities range from creating and testing paper airplane designs to constructing a pair of shoes.

This sprawling museum is built into a hillside in the Don Valley, northeast of the city center. From downtown, take the subway (Yonge-University line) to Eglinton Station.

Then take the no. 34 Eglinton East bus to Don Mills Road. The museum is a short walk south on Don Mills Road.

Alternatively, ride the Bloor-Danforth line to Pape Station, in the Danforth (Greektown) neighborhood, where you transfer to the no. 25 Don Mills bus north. Get off at St. Dennis Drive, in front of the Science Centre.

Aga Khan Museum

In a dramatic contemporary building facing a reflecting pool, the **Aga Khan Museum** (77 Wynford Dr., 416/646-4677 or 844/859-3671, www.agakhanmuseum.org, 10am-6pm Tues. and Thurs.-Sun., 10am-8pm Wed., adults $20, seniors $15, students and ages 14-17, ages 6-13 $10, parking $10, free admission 4pm-8pm Wed.) exhibits art and artifacts from across the Muslim world, spanning from centuries past up to today.

Take a **guided tour** (11am Tues.-Sun., see website for additional tour times) to learn more about the museum's collections or an **architecture tour** (12:45pm Tues.-Sun.) to get the story on its unique design; the fee for either tour is $10 for adults, $5 for seniors and students, in addition to regular museum admission. The museum hosts lectures, concerts, and other events. On weekends, pop-up

The Aga Khan Museum exhibits art from across the Muslim world.

musical performances take place throughout the day; check the website for details. The museum's **Diwan** restaurant (416/646-4670, 11:30am-2:30pm Tues.-Sun.) serves dishes from across the Middle East, while a small café offers tea and baklava.

To reach the museum by public transit from downtown, take the subway (Yonge-University line) to Eglinton Station and change to bus no. 34C, Eglinton East. The bus, about a 25-minute trip, will take you to Wynford Drive at Garamond Court, near the museum. Another transit option is to take the Bloor-Danforth subway to Broadview Station. Change to bus no. 100/100A Flemingdon Park; it's a 25-minute ride to Wynford Drive at Wynford Heights Crescent, which is a short walk from the museum.

★ The McMichael Canadian Art Collection

You wouldn't expect to find a major museum of Canadian art way out in the woods. Yet this 6,000-piece collection of works by Group of Seven, First Nations, Inuit, and contemporary artists sits on 40 hectares (100 acres) of forested land in the village of Kleinburg, north of the city.

What is now **The McMichael Canadian Art Collection** (10365 Islington Ave., Kleinburg, 905/893-1121 or 888/213-1121, www.mcmichael.com, 10am-5pm daily May-early Sept., 10am-5pm Tues.-Sun. early Sept.-Apr., adults $18, seniors and ages 5 and over $15, family $36, parking $7) got its start when Robert and Signe McMichael began collecting Canadian art in their rural home. In the 1960s, they donated their collection and residence to the province of Ontario to become a public museum.

You can easily spend several hours exploring the McMichael, which has significant holdings of works by the Group of Seven among its all-Canadian galleries; six of these artists are buried on the property in the Artist Cemetery, which you can visit. There's also a sculpture garden and a network of walking trails.

The McMichael is 45 kilometers (28 miles) north of downtown Toronto, a 40-60-minute drive. If you are traveling from Toronto to the Muskoka region, Georgian Bay, or other points north of the city, you can detour to the McMichael along the way.

Using public transit, reaching the McMichael is doable but complicated; routings involve connecting from Toronto's subway and buses to the **York Region's public transit system** (www.yorkregiontransit.com), where bus no. 13 runs along Islington Avenue to the gallery.

Entertainment and Events

Toronto is not only Canada's largest city, it's the country's cultural capital, home to many of Canada's premier cultural institutions: the Toronto Symphony Orchestra, the National Ballet of Canada, the Canadian Opera Company, and the Canadian Stage Company. But the city has a more contemporary side, too. Toronto hosts an annual fringe festival in July and an international writers' fest in October. Among the liveliest summer events are a popular carnival celebrating Caribbean culture and annual Pride Week, one of the world's largest LGBTQ pride celebrations.

The acclaimed Second City comedy company has a Toronto branch, and the city has a range of professional and local theater groups. Don't forget the nightclubs, jazz bars, and sports pubs broadcasting all hockey, all the time.

If you're looking for theaters, concert halls, and clubs, you'll find some near Dundas Square; others cluster in the Entertainment

District, on and around King Street west of the downtown core.

To find out what's going on, the best sources are the online arts and entertainment publications, *Now* (www.nowtoronto.com) and *blogTO* (www.blogto.com). The **City of Toronto** (www.toronto.ca) and **Tourism Toronto** (www.seetorontonow.com) both post online event calendars.

NIGHTLIFE

The neighborhood known as the Entertainment District, around King Street West from St. Andrew station west to Bathurst Street, has lots of clubs and bars, as does West Queen West (Queen Street from Ossington to Gladstone). For hotel bars and lounges, you'll find plenty of options in the Entertainment District and around downtown.

Though the hub of the LGBTQ community was once the Church and Wellesley neighborhood, known as the **Gay Village** (www.churchwellesleyvillage.ca), queer culture now extends around the city, including the west-side district dubbed **Queer West** (along Ossington Ave. and Queen St. W., www.queerwest.org).

Bars and clubs go in and out of fashion, so check locally to see what's going on.

Rock, Jazz, and Blues

Jazz club **The Rex** (194 Queen St. W., 416/598-2475, www.therex.ca, subway: Osgoode) hosts 1,000 gigs a year. Two bands play nightly Monday-Thursday, there are three shows on Friday, and at least four groups take the stage on Saturday and Sunday, beginning most weekends at noon. A range of live music acts performs at **Hugh's Room Live** (2261 Dundas St. W., 416/533-5483, www.hughsroomlive.com, subway: Dundas West), a reinvention of the late, lamented Hugh's Room club, a long-standing folk and blues destination.

Bands from Willie Nelson to the Talking Heads to the Tragically Hip have all taken the stage at the **Horseshoe Tavern** (370 Queen St. W., 416/598-4753, www.horseshoetavern.

com) since the club first opened in 1947. These days, it's going for an indie vibe, booking up-and-coming new music acts. Take the no. 501 Queen streetcar to Spadina Avenue, or the no. 510 Spadina streetcar to Queen Street. All kinds of events happen at **The Underground at the Drake Hotel** (1150 Queen St. W., 416/531-5042 or 866/372-5386, www.thedrakehotel.ca), from DJ dance parties and indie band concerts to film screenings and comedy shows. Get there on the no. 501 Queen streetcar. The events at the Gladstone Hotel's **Melody Bar** (1214 Queen St. W., 416/531-4635, www.gladstonehotel.com) are as eclectic as the hotel itself, including TV trivia, karaoke nights, and indie music shows.

Big-name rock and pop concerts perform at the city's two sports and entertainment arenas: **Scotiabank Arena** (40 Bay St., 416/815-5400, www.aircanadacentre.com, box office 10am-6pm Mon.-Sat.), which is slated to be renamed Scotiabank Arena, and **Rogers Centre** (1 Blue Jays Way, 416/341-1000, www.rogerscentre.com, box office 10am-7pm Mon.-Fri., 10am-5pm Sat.-Sun.). For online or phone sales for events at either venue, contact **Ticketmaster** (855/985-5000, www.ticketmaster.ca).

Bars, Pubs, and Lounges

The classic dark-wood-paneled **Library Bar** (100 Front St. W., 416/368-2511, www.fairmont.com, 11:30am-1am Mon.-Fri., 5pm-1am Sat.-Sun.) at the venerable Fairmont Royal York Hotel feels ever so sophisticated, particularly when you're savoring one of its famous martinis. Afternoon tea is served here on weekends, with seatings at noon, 12:30pm, and 2:30pm Saturday and Sunday. A chic spot for a drink is the Thompson Toronto Hotel's **Lobby Bar** (550 Wellington St. W., 416/601-3554, www.thompsonhotels.com, 5pm-2am daily), where the bar glows with white light and the wall mural is a whimsical interpretation of the Toronto skyline. In the Entertainment District, meet for a pre- or post-theater libation at **Victor Restaurant and Lounge** (30 Mercer St., 416/883-3431,

Around the World in a Toronto Day

In this city there are Bulgarian mechanics, there are Eritrean accountants, Colombian café owners, Latvian book publishers, Welsh roofers, Afghani dancers, Iranian mathematicians, Tamil cooks in Thai restaurants, Calabrese boys with Jamaican accents, Fushen deejays, Filipina-Saudi beauticians, Russian doctors changing tires; there are Romanian bill collectors, Cape Croker fishmongers, Japanese grocery clerks, French gas meter readers, German bakers, Haitian and Bengali taxi drivers with Irish dispatchers.

Toronto writer Dionne Brand in her novel *What We Long For*

Although Brand included this description of Toronto in a work of fiction, there's nothing fictional about the city's multicultural makeup. About half of metropolitan Toronto's residents were born outside of Canada, hailing from nearly every part of the globe. And throughout the city, you'll find diverse enclaves where you can explore the food and culture of Toronto's various communities.

Perhaps the most visible of these neighborhoods are Toronto's Chinatowns—and Toronto has several of these predominantly Chinese districts, not surprisingly, since the Chinese are among Toronto's largest visible-minority groups. Downtown, the **"original" Chinatown**, extending outward from the intersection of Spadina Avenue and Dundas Street, is a traditional immigrant neighborhood, where you'll find Chinese groceries, herbalists, and plenty of modest—and tasty—restaurants. The smaller **East Chinatown** is located around Broadview Avenue and Gerrard Street; it has a significant Vietnamese population as well.

Toronto has several large Chinese communities in the suburbs of Scarborough east of downtown, Mississauga to the west, and Richmond Hill and Markham to the north. The northern suburbs, in particular, are wealthier communities than the central-city Chinatowns, with higher-end restaurants and shops, many concentrated in malls, catering to this more upscale demographic. The **Pacific Mall** (4300 Steeles Ave. E., Markham, www.pacificmalltoronto.com) is one of the largest Asian malls in North America.

Toronto also has a significant South Asian community. Many South Asian immigrants once made their homes in Toronto's **Little India** neighborhood, also known as the Indian Bazaar, in the city's East End along Gerrard Street East. While Indian residents—and restaurants—have moved throughout Toronto and its suburbs, you'll still find a concentration of eateries, jewelers, and clothing shops here that cater to the Indian community.

Many Greek immigrants settled along Danforth Avenue, particularly between Chester and Pape Streets, in the district called the Danforth, or **Greektown.** The neighborhood has gentrified and lost some of its Greek character as younger families and trendier shops have moved in, but Toronto's Greek community, one of the largest outside Greece, still shops in the markets and traditional bakeries, lingers over coffee and pastry in the cafés, and dines on classic dishes like dolmades (grape leaves) and souvlaki.

Although Toronto's Korean community isn't as concentrated in one neighborhood as some other ethnic groups, the city does have a **Koreatown,** on Bloor Street West, around Christie Street. Markets, restaurants, and karaoke bars cater both to Koreans and others who enjoy the lively district's vibe.

In the early 20th century, many European immigrants settled on Toronto's west side. **Little Italy,** primarily along College Street, west of Bathurst, and **Little Portugal,** on Dundas Street, near Ossington, today seem to have a lot of overlap, with Italian restaurants on the "Portuguese" streets and Portuguese bakeries on the "Italian" ones. And many contemporary eateries have moved in alongside the more traditional businesses. No matter; there's still good eating in these districts.

The streets on and around Roncesvalles Avenue, in the city's West End, were settled by Polish immigrants, giving the community the nickname **Little Poland.** This neighborhood still has Polish businesses, primarily bakeries, delis, restaurants, and travel agencies, although the district no longer has a predominantly Polish population. In a recent census, Polish was the second most widely spoken language in the neighborhood. The first? Chinese.

www.victorrestaurant.com, 5pm-11pm daily), a stylish lounge in the lobby of Hotel Le Germain.

Comedy

The Toronto branch of the Chicago-based sketch comedy club **Second City** (51 Mercer St., 416/343-0011 or 800/263-4485, www.secondcity.com, shows generally 8pm Mon.-Thurs., 7:30pm and 10pm Fri.-Sat., 7:30pm Sun., $20-30) has cabaret-style shows every night.

Games

Whether you're into low-tech table tennis or high-tech virtual reality, **The Rec Room** (255 Bremner Blvd., 416/815-0086, www.therecroom.com, 11am-midnight Sun.-Wed., 11am-1am Thurs., 11am-2am Fri.-Sat.) is a gamer's paradise. In a historic former railway roundhouse near the CN Tower, you can enter "The Void," an immersive virtual world, or show off your skills at more than 80 arcade games. Take a break with an Ontario beer or Canadian whisky and a wood-fired pizza (there's a long list of pub eats, too). Regular entertainment, from trivia nights to video dance parties, keeps things hopping. Kids are welcome until 11pm; after that, you must be 19 or older.

Travel back in time to Victorian-era Toronto as you try to solve a series of mysteries. "The Secret of Station House No. 4" (1 hour, $40-46), an escape game set in the 1870s George Brown House, is just one of the history-themed escape games that **Secret City Adventures** (647/243-7658, www.secretcityadventures.com) offers in historic locations around the city. You can test your skills in several games at Casa Loma (1 hour, $40-46) and with an adventure at Black Creek Pioneer Village (90 minutes, $30-$42). See the Secret City website for game schedules and specific locations.

THE ARTS
Theater

Toronto is one of the world's hubs of English-language theater, with dozens of theater venues in the metropolitan area. A number of professional repertory companies are based here, many of which focus on Canadian plays. The city's large theaters also host major musicals and other touring productions.

The **Canadian Stage Company** (416/368-3110, www.canadianstage.com), one of Canada's largest not-for-profit theater companies, produces contemporary Canadian and international plays. Their main stage is the

The Rec Room is a gamer's paradise.

Bluma Appel Theatre (St. Lawrence Centre for the Arts, 27 Front St. E., 416/366-7723 or 800/708-6754, www.stlc.com, subway: Union). They also perform at the smaller **Berkeley Street Theatre** (26 Berkeley St.); from downtown, take the no. 504 King streetcar east to Ontario Street. In the summer, the company goes outdoors for the **Canadian Stage in High Park** (High Park Amphitheatre, 1873 Bloor St. W., late June-early Sept.), a pay-what-you-can outdoor production; bring a picnic.

The **Factory Theatre** (125 Bathurst St., 416/504-9971, www.factorytheatre.ca) produces a full season of all-Canadian plays, with many world premieres. Founded in 1970, the Factory was the first company to present only Canadian works. The no. 511 Bathurst streetcar stops at Adelaide Street, near the theater. You can also take either the no. 501 Queen or no. 504 King streetcars to Bathurst Street. Another long-standing local company, **Tarragon Theatre** (30 Bridgman Ave., at Howland, 416/531-1827, www.tarragontheatre. com, subway: Dupont) has been producing a mix of new plays, Canadian works, and classic and contemporary international theater since 1970. Since 1969, **Theatre Passe Muraille** (16 Ryerson Ave., 416/504-7529, www. passemuraille.ca) has produced edgy contemporary works. The small Queen West theater space is two blocks from the no. 501 Queen streetcar's Bathurst Street stop. The professional **Soulpepper Theatre Company** (www.soulpepper.ca) stages the classics, including Tolstoy, Tennessee Williams, David Mamet, and more contemporary works, at the **Young Centre for the Performing Arts** (50 Tank House Lane, 416/866-8666, www. youngcentre.ca) in the Distillery District.

Buddies in Bad Times Theatre (12 Alexander St., 416/975-8555, www. buddiesinbadtimes.com, subway: Wellesley) is a not-for-profit professional company that has been producing queer theater since 1979. Its plays focus primarily on gay, lesbian, bisexual, and transgendered identity issues. You never know quite what you'll find on the **World Stage at Harbourfront Centre** (235 Queens Quay W., 416/973-4000, www. harbourfrontcentre.com), but expect creative contemporary Canadian and international performances. On the east side, **Streetcar Crowsnest** (345 Carlaw Ave. at Dundas St. E., 647/341-7390 ext. 1010, www.crowstheatre. com) is a two-theater complex at the base of a condo tower; it's home to **Crow's Theatre**, which produces new Canadian plays. Bus no. 72 between Union and Pape Stations stops at the theater, or you can take the no. 506 Carlton streetcar to Gerrard Avenue at Carlaw and walk south.

Canada's oldest continuously operating legitimate theater (built in 1907), the beaux arts **Royal Alexandra Theatre** (260 King St. W., between Simcoe St. and Duncan St., 416/872-1212 or 800/461-3333, www.mirvish.com, subway: St. Andrew) hosts a variety of plays and musicals. The 2,000-seat **Princess of Wales Theatre** (300 King St. W., at John St., 416/872-1212 or 800/461-3333, www.mirvish. com, subway: St. Andrew), which opened in the Entertainment District in 1993, is one of Toronto's newer stages. Large-scale musicals, including *Miss Saigon, The Lion King,* and *The Sound of Music,* are a mainstay of the theater. Opened in 1920 as a vaudeville house, the **Ed Mirvish Theatre** (244 Victoria St., 416/872-1212 or 800/461-3333, www.mirvish.com, subway: Dundas) was once Canada's largest movie theater; it originally had 3,373 seats. These days it stages major musicals such as *Billy Elliot,* as well as other theater and dance productions.

The **Elgin and Winter Garden Theatre Centre** (189 Yonge St., 416/314-2901, subway: Queen), the only "double-decker" theater in Canada, houses two full-size theaters. Drama, musicals, ballet, and opera, as well as various special events, go on stage here. For an event calendar and tickets, contact **Ticketmaster** (855/622-2787, www.ticketmaster.ca) or phone the theater directly.

Only the facade of the **CAA Theatre** (651 Yonge St., 416/872-1212 or 800/461-3333, www.mirvish.com, subway: Bloor-Yonge) was saved when the building, which began life in 1911 as a private residence, was rebuilt in 2005. It's now a venue for live theater and concerts.

Live Music

The **Toronto Symphony Orchestra** (416/598-3375, www.tso.ca), one of Canada's major orchestras, performs at **Roy Thompson Hall** (60 Simcoe St., 416/872-4255, www.roythomson.com, subway: St. Andrew), the 2,600-seat concert hall with a distinctive curved facade designed by noted Canadian contemporary architect Arthur Erickson (1924-2009). Purchase symphony tickets at the Roy Thompson box office, by phone, or online. Opened in 1982 in the Entertainment District, the theater hosts other concerts as well as the TSO events.

Built in 1894, venerable **Massey Hall** (178 Victoria St., at Shuter St., 416/872-4255, www.masseyhall.com, subway: Dundas, Queen) was once Toronto's most important venue for classical concerts, opera, jazz, and other events, hosting appearances by Enrico Caruso, George Gershwin, Glenn Gould, Oscar Peterson, Bob Dylan, Gordon Lightfoot, and the Dalai Lama. The theatre is slated to close in 2018 for a multiyear revitalization project, so check the website for updates.

Canada's largest opera troupe is the Toronto-based **Canadian Opera Company** (416/363-8231 or 800/250-4653, www.coc.ca). They perform at the **Four Seasons Centre for the Performing Arts** (145 Queen St. W., subway: Osgoode). Buy tickets by phone or in person from the Four Seasons Centre box office, or online at the opera website. From the Bolshoi Ballet to the Soweto Gospel Choir, the 3,191-seat **Sony Centre for the Performing Arts** (1 Front St. E., 855/872-7669, www.sonycentre.ca, subway: Union) presents international dance, music, and theatrical productions. Tickets are available online through Ticketmaster (www.ticketmaster.ca) or at the theater box office.

The **St. Lawrence Centre for the Arts** (27 Front St. E., 416/366-7723 or 800/708-6754, www.stlc.com, subway: Union) has

four music organizations in residence. **Music Toronto** (www.music-toronto.com) presents traditional and modern chamber music, while **Opera in Concert** (www.operainconcert.com) produces operas that are rarely seen in Canada. The professional **Toronto Operetta Theatre** (www.torontooperetta.com) presents operetta, light opera, and musical theater featuring Canadian performers. The **Hannaford Street Silver Band** (www.hssb.ca), a professional brass band, performs several concerts throughout the year. Visiting musicians and other performers also take to the stage at the St. Lawrence Centre. Contact the St. Lawrence box office for tickets, or order online. At the **Royal Conservatory of Music** (273 Bloor St. W., 416/408-0208, www.rcmusic.ca, subway: St. George) in the Bloor-Yorkville neighborhood, notable Canadian and international musical acts, including those working in classical, chamber, early, and world music, perform at the 1,135-seat **Koerner Hall.**

Dance

The **National Ballet of Canada** (416/345-9595 or 866/345-9595, https://national.ballet.ca), one of the world's top dance companies, works its artistic magic at the **Four Seasons Centre for the Performing Arts** (145 Queen St. W., subway: Osgoode). Tickets are available online from the ballet company website, or from the Four Seasons Centre box office in person or by phone.

One of Canada's leading contemporary dance companies, **Toronto Dance Theatre** (416/967-1365, www.tdt.org), established in 1968, performs several Toronto shows a year, either at Harbourfront Centre or at its own Winchester Street Theatre (80 Winchester St.) in Cabbagetown, a short walk from the Parliament Street stop on the no. 506 Carlton streetcar. On the upper level of the Queen's Quay Terminal at Harbourfront Centre, **Fleck Dance Theatre** (207 Queens Quay W., 416/973-4000, www.harbourfrontcentre.com) plays host to a variety of local, national, and international dance performers.

Cinema

If you're interested in film, don't miss visiting the **TIFF Bell Lightbox** (350 King St. W., 416/599-8433 or 888/599-8433, www.tiff.net). The distinctive contemporary glass building is not only headquarters for the annual Toronto International Film Festival, it's also home to the **TIFF Cinematheque,** which screens a wide range of movies throughout the year, and a **gallery** that shows film-related exhibits.

The lazy days of summer mean outdoor movies, right? The **Free Flicks** series (Harbourfront Centre, 235 Queens Quay W., 416/973-4000, www.harbourfrontcentre.com, July-Aug., check the website for schedule, free) screens films on summer Wednesday nights.

Literary Events

The **International Festival of Authors** (235 Queens Quay W., 416/973-4760 or 416/973-4000, www.ifoa.org) hosts weekly readings and other literary events from September to June at Harbourfront Centre. **Pages Unbound** (www.pages-unbound. com) runs a series of periodic literary evenings at the **Gladstone Hotel** (1214 Queen St. W., 416/531-4635, www.gladstonehotel. com) and at other venues around the city; see their website for details.

FESTIVALS AND EVENTS
Spring

Photography buffs should schedule a Toronto visit during the **Scotiabank CONTACT Photography Festival** (416/539-9595, www.scotiabankcontactphoto.com, May), which showcases works by more than 1,000 local, national, and international artists at more than 200 venues around town. During the last weekend in May, more than 150 museums, historic buildings, art spaces, condos, and religious institutions—including many that aren't usually open to the public—welcome visitors during **Doors Open Toronto** (www.toronto.ca/doorsopen, May, free). The **Toronto Jewish Film Festival** (416/324-9121, www.tjff.com, May) typically screens

90-100 movies from many different countries, some by Jewish filmmakers, others with themes of Jewish interest.

Summer

Luminato (416/368-3100, www. luminatofestival.com, June) is a two-week arts fest, featuring theater, dance, music, literature, food, visual arts, film, and even magic. Many events are free, although others require a ticket; the website has a schedule and ticket information. Though it may not be as well known as the similarly named SXSW (South by Southwest festival in Austin), Toronto's **North by Northeast Music Festival** (NXNE, 416/863-6963, www.nxne.com, June) presents Canadian and international new and indie music, as well as avant-garde film and digital media. One of the world's largest LGBTQ pride celebrations, **Toronto Pride Month** (416/927-7433, www.pridetoronto. com, June) features marches, parades, and entertainment as well as a street fair and family activities. The annual Pride Parade is a highlight.

Jazz aficionados converge for the annual **Toronto Jazz Fest** (416/928-2033, www. torontojazz.com, June-July), featuring more than 350 performances at locations around the city. The Beaches neighborhood gets into the jazz act, too, with the long-running, free **Beaches Jazz Fest** (416/698-2152, www. beachesjazz.com, July). You never quite know what you'll see at the **Toronto Fringe Festival** (416/966-1062, www.fringetoronto. com, July), an eclectic lineup of more than 150 plays and theatrical performances. The **Toronto Caribbean Carnival** (416/391-5608, www.carnival.to, July-Aug.) is a month-long celebration of all things Caribbean, with music, dance, street parties, food, and a whopper of a parade.

Toronto's Greek community welcomes visitors to Danforth Avenue during the annual **Taste of the Danforth** (416/469-5634, www.tasteofthedanforth.com, Aug.), a weekend of food, music, kids' activities, and more. For many Torontonians, it's not summer till you've been to the **Canadian National Exhibition** (416/393-6300, www.theex.com, Aug.-Sept.), a waterfront fair with carnival rides, a dog show, farm animals, a garden show, and all sorts of concerts and special events.

Fall

The city's premier cultural event is the **Toronto International Film Festival** (www.tiff.net, Sept.), which screens more than 300 movies from around the world and draws celebrities from across the globe. Advance ticket sales generally begin in July, although the detailed festival lineup isn't announced until about two weeks before opening night. Contact the **TIFF Bell Lightbox** (350 King St. W., 416/599-8433 or 888/599-8433) to find out when tickets go on sale. Stay up all night for Toronto's annual **Nuit Blanche** (www.nbto.com, Oct.), a sundown-to-sunrise celebration of the contemporary arts. A major literary festival, the **Toronto International Festival of Authors** (www.ifoa.org, Oct.) is 11 days

of readings, discussions, and interviews with authors from across Canada and abroad. Most events take place at **Harbourfront Centre** (235 Queens Quay W., information 416/973-4760, tickets 416/973-4000, www.harbourfrontcentre.com).

Winter

Get your holiday shopping done, or pick up a unique souvenir, at the **One of a Kind Show and Sale** (416/960-3680, www.oneofakindshow.com, Nov.-Dec.), an annual arts and crafts market. During the **Cavalcade of Lights** (www.toronto.com), the city lights its official Christmas tree in Nathan Phillips Square, outside City Hall. The tree-lighting ceremony, complete with concerts and outdoor ice-skating, takes place the last weekend of November; the square remains illuminated through December. The smaller winter sibling of the Toronto Fringe Festival, the **Next Stage Theatre Festival** (www.fringetoronto.com, Jan.) presents a lineup of new plays.

Shopping

Toronto is a Canadian art center with a good mix of galleries, craft shops, and arts-oriented shops. The city has a growing cohort of homegrown fashion designers, so it's worth browsing the boutiques. You'll also find many of the same chain stores that populate malls across North America.

SHOPPING DISTRICTS

The largest mall in the downtown area, **Eaton Centre** (220 Yonge St., 416/598-8560, www.torontoeatoncentre.com, subway: Dundas or Queen, 10am-9:30pm Mon.-Fri., 9:30am-9:30pm Sat., 10am-7pm Sun.) has more than 230 stores, extending along Yonge Street from Queen to Dundas Streets. Most are Canadian or international chains, including Abercrombie & Fitch, H&M, Lululemon Athletica, and Roots.

In the **Bloor-Yorkville** neighborhood (subway: Bloor-Yonge, Bay, St. George), Bloor Street is lined with a mix of midrange and upscale chain stores, from Banana Republic to Brooks Brothers; on some side streets, you'll find independent boutiques. **Yorkville Village** (55 Avenue Rd., 416/968-8600, www.yorkvillevillage.com) houses a collection of high-end shops, including Jacadi, Judith & Charles, and Cop.Copine.

Galleries, clothing shops, and design studios populate the restored industrial buildings in the **Distillery District** (www.thedistillerydistrict.com), east of downtown. If you continue east into funky **Leslieville,** along Queen Street East, you'll find more independent designers and vintage furniture shops. On **Queen Street West,** there's a mix of chains and independent shops, with the more creative independents winning out as you continue west to **West Queen West** (from Bathurst Street to Gladstone Avenue). Off Queen Street, **Ossington Avenue** is a mini hub for cool shops and restaurants.

DEPARTMENT STORES

Founded in 1670 as a fur-trading company, the **Hudson's Bay Company**—Canada's oldest corporation—has grown to become the country's largest retailer. Its flagship chain of department stores, with locations across Canada, is known as The Bay. Among the many Toronto branches, there's one downtown near **City Hall** (176 Yonge St., 416/861-9111, www.thebay.com, subway: Queen, 10am-9:30pm Mon.-Fri., 9:30am-9:30pm Sat., 10am-7pm Sun.) and another in the **Bloor-Yorkville** neighborhood (44 Bloor St. E., 416/972-3333, subway: Bloor-Yonge, 10am-7pm Mon.-Wed. and Sat., 10am-9pm Thurs.-Fri., 11am-6pm Sun.).

Upscale fashion emporium **Holt-Renfrew** (50 Bloor St. W., 416/922-2333, www.holtrenfrew.com, subway: Bloor-Yonge, 10am-8pm Mon.-Wed. and Sat., 10am-9pm Thurs.-Fri., 11am-7pm Sun.) boasts top international designers and personal service, with prices to match.

BOOKS AND MAGAZINES

A classic independent bookstore that's a lovely spot to browse downtown, **Ben McNally Books** (366 Bay St., 416/361-0032, www.benmcnallybooks.com, 9am-6pm Mon.-Fri., 11am-5pm Sat.) also hosts readings and other literary events. The no. 501 Queen streetcar stops at Bay Street, a block from the shop.

Independently owned **Type Books** (883 Queen St. W., 416/366-8973, www.typebooks.ca, 10am-6pm Mon.-Wed., 10am-7pm Thurs.-Sat., 11am-6pm Sun.) not only has a good selection of all types of books, it also sponsors readings and literary events. Take the no. 501 Queen streetcar to Strachan Avenue.

If you want a book by a local chef, find it at **Good Egg** (267 Augusta Ave., 416/593-4663, www.goodegg.ca, 10am-6pm Mon.-Sat.,

shoppers in Bloor-Yorkville

11am-6pm Sun.), a Kensington Market bookshop that carries cookbooks, food books, and foodie magazines, along with kitchen gadgets and food gifts from Toronto and elsewhere.

CLOTHING, SHOES, AND ACCESSORIES
Queen Street West

Need a flannel shirt or stylish blazer? See what's on the racks at **Logan & Finley** (670 Queen St. W., 416/769-9732, www.loganandfinley.com, 11am-7pm Mon.-Fri., 10am-6pm Sat., noon-6pm Sun.), which stocks casual Canadian-made clothing and accessories for men and women. Work by more than 100 local jewelry designers is on view at **Made You Look Jewelry Studio and Gallery** (1338 Queen St. W., 416/463-2136, www.madeyoulook.ca, 10am-8pm Mon.-Fri., 10am-6pm Sat., noon-5pm Sun.). They'll also custom-design special pieces.

Part boutique and part art gallery, **Shopgirls** (1342 Queen St. W., 416/534-7467, www.shopgirls.ca, 11am-7pm Mon.-Fri.,

shops on Queen Street West

Designer Christina Bergstrom creates the vibrantly colored women's clothes she sells in her Leslieville shop, **Bergstrom Originals** (781 Queen St. E., 416/595-7320, www.bergstromoriginals.com, 11am-7pm Mon.-Wed. and Sat., 11am-8pm Thurs.-Fri., noon-6pm Sun.). Bergstrom complements her own pieces with shoes and accessories by other designers from near and far. To get here from downtown, take the no. 501 Queen streetcar eastbound to Saulter Street. Playful contemporary and vintage-inspired dresses are ready to rock and roll at **Doll Factory by Damzels** (1122 Queen St. E., 416/598-0509, www.damzels.com, 11am-6pm Tues.-Sat., noon-5pm Sun.). Designers Kelly Freeman and Rory Lindo sell their own line, *Damzels in This Dress,* along with other clothing, gifts, and accessories. Take the no. 501 Queen streetcar to Caroline Avenue.

GIFTS AND NOVELTIES
Design geeks could lose themselves for hours at cool **Bergo Designs** (28 Tank House Lane, 416/861-1821, www.bergo.ca, 10am-7pm Mon.-Thurs., 10am-8pm Fri.-Sat., 11am-6pm Sun.) in the Distillery District. Alvar Aalto, Philippe Starck, and other international designers are represented, but you'll find quirky jewelry, toys, and gifts for your artsy friends, created by up-and-coming craftspeople.

Pawing through the assortment of stuff in the **Drake General Store** (1151 Queen St. W., 416/346-0742, www.drakegeneralstore. ca, 10am-7pm Mon.-Wed., 10am-8pm Thurs.-Sat., 10am-6pm Sun.) is like visiting a cool friend who has a collection of weird and wonderful things. Need a stick-on mustache? Check. A classic CBC radio bag? Check. Croissant-shaped earrings, Canadian Mountie cocktail napkins, or same-sex cake toppers? Check, check, and check. In addition to the Queen West location, they have shops in the Hudson's Bay stores downtown (176 Yonge St., lower level, 416/861-6009, 9:30am-9:30pm Mon.-Sat., 9am-7pm Sun.) and in

10am-6:30pm Sat., noon-5pm Sun.) is a collective that sells clothing, jewelry, and artwork by Canadian designers. Just north of Queen Street, **I Miss You** (63 Ossington Ave., 416/916-7021, noon-6pm daily) stocks good-quality vintage designer labels and other clothing and accessories, including lots of 1960s cocktail dresses.

Distillery District
For beautifully crafted jewelry, handbags, and other accessories, peruse the wares—many by Toronto-based artisans—at **Corktown Designs** (5 Trinity St., 416/861-3020, www. corktowndesigns.com, 10am-7pm Mon.-Thurs., 10am-8pm Fri.-Sat., 11am-7pm Sun.).

Leslieville
More than 200 Canadian designers created the distinctive clothing, jewelry, ceramics, glass, and other works at the **Distill Gallery** (1360A Queen St. E, 416/304-0033, www. distillgallery.com, hours vary seasonally), for both browsing and buying.

Bloor-Yorkville (100 Bloor St. E., 416/538-2222, ext. 457, 10am-7pm Mon.-Wed. and Sat., 10am-9pm Thurs.-Fri., 11am-6pm Sun.).

OUTDOOR GEAR

For clothing, boots, or camping supplies, visit **Mountain Equipment Co-Op** (MEC, 400 King St. W., 416/340-2667, www.mec.ca, 10am-9pm Mon.-Fri., 9am-7pm Sat., 10am-6pm Sun.), the Toronto branch of Canada's largest outdoor retailer. The store rents out tents, sleeping bags, canoes, kayaks, cross-country skis, and snowshoes. You must become a co-op member to make a purchase; anyone can join by paying a lifetime membership fee of just $5.

Sports and Recreation

Whenever the sun shines, residents flock to the lakefront, the Toronto Islands, or the city's many parks, where there are numerous paths for walking and cycling. When winter comes, ice-skating keeps Toronto folks busy (unless they head north to the downhill ski and snowboard resorts). And year-round, Toronto is Canada's hub for professional sports, especially hockey, baseball, and basketball.

PARKS AND BEACHES

The city's best beaches are on the **Toronto Islands** (ferry: Jack Layton Ferry Terminal, 9 Queens Quay West at Bay St., 416/392-8193, www.toronto.ca, round-trip adults $7.70, seniors and ages 15-19 $5.05, ages 2-14 $3.75).

The south shore has several narrow but sandy stretches on Lake Ontario. There's also Ward's Island Beach, Gibraltar Beach, even a clothing-optional beach at Hanlan's Point. For a more urban beach experience, head for the pink umbrellas at **Sugar Beach** (25 Dockside Dr., at Queen's Quay E., www.waterfrontoronto.ca, dawn-dusk daily, free). Part of Toronto's ongoing waterfront redevelopment, this stretch of sand at the foot of Lower Jarvis Street faces Lake Ontario in the shadow of the Redpath Sugar Factory. You can't swim here, but it's a popular spot to sit in the sun. **HTO Park** (339 Queens Quay W.), a similar urban beach, is downtown west of Harbourfront Centre.

summertime at Toronto's Sugar Beach

The city's most beautiful parkland is **High Park** (1873 Bloor St. W., 416/397-2628, www.toronto.ca, subway: High Park, dawn-dusk daily, free). The park is in the city's west end, south of Bloor Street, with a large pond, playgrounds, hiking trails, and even a small zoo.

Note that the Lake Ontario waters are not always clean enough for safe swimming, so check the water quality before you dive in. Phone the city's **Beach Water Quality Hotline** (416/392-7161) or see the Beach Water Quality page on the city website (www.toronto.ca). City staff also post signs at the beach if bacteria levels are too high for healthy swimming.

HIKING

The **Toronto Islands** (ferry: Jack Layton Ferry Terminal, 9 Queens Quay W. at Bay St., 416/392-8193, www.toronto.ca, round-trip adults $7.70, seniors and ages 15-19 $5.05, ages 2-14 $3.75) and **High Park** (1873 Bloor St. W., 416/397-2628, www.toronto.ca, subway: High Park, dawn-dusk daily, free) are popular hiking destinations. You can also hike the trails that wend around the property at the **Evergreen Brick Works** (550 Bayview Ave., 416/596-7670, www.evergreen.ca).

BICYCLING

Toronto has hundreds of kilometers of bike lanes on city streets. However, if you're not an experienced urban cyclist, you may want to stick to one of the off-road cycling trails. The 56-kilometer (35-mile) **Martin Goodman Trail** runs along the Toronto lakeshore. It's part of the 2,100-kilometer (1,300-mile) **Great Lakes Waterfront Trail,** which follows the shores of Lake Huron, Lake Erie, and Lake Ontario from Grand Bend to the Quebec border. The **Toronto Islands** (ferry: Jack Layton Ferry Terminal, 9 Queens Quay W. at Bay St., 416/392-8193, www.toronto.ca, round-trip adults $7.70, seniors and ages 15-19 $5.05, ages 2-14 $3.75) are another popular cycling spot. You can rent bikes ($8 per hour, tandems $15 per hour) and four-wheeled pedal bikes ("quadricycles") that

seat two ($17 per hour) or four ($30 per hour) near Centre Island pier.

To figure out the best cycling routes around Toronto, try the useful **Ride the City** (www.ridethecity.com/toronto) mapping tool, which plots the safest route between two points. You can get more information about cycling in Toronto, as well as a bike-route map, at the **City of Toronto website** (www.toronto.ca).

Bike Share Toronto (www.bikesharetoronto.com), a public bike-sharing system, lets you pick up a bike from rental stations around the city, ride it to your destination, and return it to the nearest station when you arrive. The basic rental fee is $7 for 24 hours (or $15 for 72 hours); if you keep your rides short (up to 30 minutes per trip), that's all you pay. Since the service is designed for short hops, there are additional fees for each half-hour beyond the initial 30 minutes. Bikes are located throughout the downtown area (look for rental stations near subway stops), around the University of Toronto, and in many other neighborhoods; there's a location map on the Bike Share website.

KAYAKING AND CANOEING

At **Harbourfront Canoe and Kayak Centre** (283A Queens Quay W. at Rees St., 416/203-2277 or 800/960-8886, www.paddletoronto.com), you can rent canoes ($50/two hours, $90 per day), kayaks (single $40/two hours, $70 per day, double $50/two hours, $90 per day), and stand-up paddleboards ($40/two hours, $70 per day). You can also rent canoes, kayaks, and pedal boats on the **Toronto Islands** (ferry: Jack Layton Ferry Terminal, 9 Queens Quay W. at Bay St., 416/392-8193, www.toronto.ca, round-trip adults $7.70, seniors and ages 15-19 $5.05, ages 2-14 $3.75) during the summer. The rental shop is in the Boat House on Centre Island.

ICE-SKATING

Popular places to ice-skate are on the pond in front of City Hall, which becomes the seasonal **Nathan Phillips Square Rink** (100 Queen St.

Canada's First Urban National Park

Rouge National Urban Park will be Canada's first urban national park.

Imagine a "national park." Don't you think of an expansive wilderness, far from city skyscrapers, traffic jams, and noise? But on the eastern borders of metropolitan Toronto, Canada's newest nationally protected outdoor space will be the country's first urban national park: **Rouge National Urban Park** (416/264-2020, www.pc.gc.ca, year-round, free).

A 79-square-kilometer (30-square-mile) parcel of land stretching from Lake Ontario in the south to the community of Markham in the north, more than 20 times larger than New York's Central Park, Rouge Park has been a recreational playground for the Toronto region for many years. However, as development increasingly encroached on the parkland, many Torontonians began lobbying to provide greater protection for this natural area. In 2011, Rouge Park was approved to become part of Canada's national park system.

While Parks Canada is still finalizing the administrative details for Rouge to obtain its full national park status, the park is open to the public. Hiking trails crisscross Rouge Park's forested areas, and park staff lead periodic guided walks. You can look out over the Little Rouge Creek Valley from the **Glen Eagles Vista Trail** (7 Twyn Rivers Dr., Toronto)—a great place to take in the fall colors—or go for a swim in Lake Ontario from sandy **Rouge Beach** (195 Rouge Hills Dr., Toronto). Campers can pitch a tent or park their RV in the 125-site **Glen Rouge Campground** (7450 Kingston Rd., Toronto, 855/811-0111, www.trca.ca, May-Oct., $28-33 tent sites, $41-44 electrical sites), the only camping spot within Toronto city limits. Glen Rouge also has five **oTENTiks** ($120/night), platform tents that can sleep up to five people.

Several sections of the park are accessible by public transit from downtown Toronto. To reach Glen Eagles, bus no. 86A Scarborough from the Kennedy subway station will drop you near the park. To Rouge Beach, you can take bus no. 54A Lawrence East from Eglinton station to the intersection of Lawrence Avenue East and Starspray Boulevard; alternatively, catch the GO Train to Rouge Hill, which is 1.3 kilometers (0.8 miles) from the beach entrance. A national park that you can reach by public transit? How cool and urban is that!

W., 416/304-1400, www.toronto.ca, 10am-10pm daily, skate rentals adults $10, ages 12 and under $5), and at Harbourfront Centre's lakeside **NatrelRink** (Queen's Quay W., 416/973-4000, www.harbourfrontcentre.com, 10am-10pm Sun.-Thurs., 10am-11pm Fri.-Sat., skate rentals adults $12.50, ages 12 and under $6.25). You can also skate on **The Bentway Skate Trail** (416/304-0222, www.thebentway.ca, 11am-9pm Sun.-Thurs., 11am-11pm Fri.-Sat., skate rentals $10), under the Gardiner Expressway at the Fort York Visitor Centre (250 Fort York Blvd.). Skating season is weather-dependent but typically begins in late November or early December and continues until March.

SPECTATOR SPORTS

As in most Canadian cities, hockey is Toronto's major sport, and the team to root for is the National Hockey League's **Toronto Maple Leafs** (www.nhl.com/mapleleafs). They take to the ice at the **Scotiabank Arena** (40 Bay St., 416/815-5400, www.aircanadacentre.com). The same facility is the home court for the **Toronto Raptors** (www.nba.com/raptors), in the National Basketball Association.

The **Toronto Blue Jays** (416/341-1234 or 888/654-6529, www.mlb.com/bluejays), in Major League Baseball's American League, play their home games at **Rogers Centre** (1 Blue Jays Way, 416/341-1000, www.rogerscentre.com) from spring through fall. Buy tickets online at **Ticketmaster** (www.ticketmaster.ca) or in person at the Rogers Centre **Box Office** (Gate 9, Bremner Blvd., 10am-7pm Mon.-Fri., 10am-5pm Sat.-Sun.).

The city's Canadian Football League team, the **Toronto Argonauts** (416/341-2746, www.argonauts.ca), and the professional men's soccer team, **Toronto FC** (416/360-4625, www.torontofc.ca), play at **BMO Field** (170 Princes' Blvd., http://bmofield.com) on the Exhibition Place grounds, west of downtown. Tickets are available through **Ticketmaster** (www.ticketmaster.ca). To get to BMO field, take the no. 509 Harbourfront streetcar west from Union Station to Exhibition, or catch the no. 511 Bathurst streetcar south from Bathurst station (Bloor-Danforth line) to Exhibition. You can also take the GO train from Union Station to Exhibition.

Explore Toronto's waterfront in a kayak or a traditional voyageur canoe.

Food

Toronto has some of Canada's top restaurants, a roster of celebrity chefs, and innovative dining rooms serving wildly creative cuisine. In this multicultural city, you can also find everything from Vietnamese noodle shops to roti stands, Filipino cocktail lounges to French bistros, even eateries showcasing traditional ingredients of the country's indigenous communities.

TOP EXPERIENCE

FOOD AND DRINK TOURS

The Culinary Adventure Co. (877/317-4870, www.culinaryadventureco.com) runs a number of different Toronto food tours, including St. Lawrence Market (adults $69, ages 6-14 $59), Chinatown and Kensington Market (adults $79, ages 5-14 $69), and Riverside and Leslieville (adults $79, ages 6-14 $59). Their website lists tour details and times.

Indulge your sweet tooth as you explore Kensington Market, Trinity-Bellwoods, or other districts with **Tasty Tours** (www.tastytourstoronto.com, adults $49-59, ages 7-12 $35-45), which offers guided 2-2.5-hour neighborhood walks with snacking stops at bakeries, chocolate shops, and other sugary destinations. Check their website for tour schedules and locations.

Would you rather sip your way around the city? **Brew Tours** (416/562-2435, www.brewtours.ca) takes you to several craft breweries on its neighborhood beer tours, including the "Jitney Junction" ($109 pp) and the "Westend Wallop" ($109 pp).

DOWNTOWN AND THE FINANCIAL DISTRICT

If you're hungry downtown, go underground. Cafés and snack shops line the PATH network that runs underneath the city-center streets. **St. Lawrence Market** (93 Front St. E., 416/392-7219, www.stlawrencemarket.com, 8am-6pm Tues.-Thurs., 8am-7pm Fri., 5am-5pm Sat.) is a fun place to browse, whether you're looking for produce, cheeses, or a more substantial lunch. The **Nathan Phillips Square Farmers Market** (100 Queen St. W., 8am-2:30pm Wed. July-mid-Oct.) takes over the plaza in front of City Hall on Wednesdays in summer and fall.

More than a dozen Toronto chefs have assembled at **Assembly Chef's Hall** (111 Richmond St. W., 647/557-5993, subway: Osgoode, www.assemblychefshall.com, 7am-10pm Mon.-Fri., 10am-10pm Sat., check the website for Sun. hours), offering quick-service cuisine ranging from barbecue to ramen to cake.

Contemporary

With sturdy pine tables and walls decorated with old photos, **The Gabardine** (372 Bay St., at Richmond, 647/352-3211, www.thegabardine.com, subway: Queen, 8am-10pm Mon.-Fri., breakfast $8-12, lunch & dinner $15-30) looks like it has always been in the Financial District; surprisingly, it opened in 2011. In the morning, stop in for pastries, oatmeal, or a breakfast sandwich; later, it's upscale pub fare, such as sandwiches like buttermilk fried chicken or Italian sausage, or larger plates: chicken potpie, seared flat-iron steak, or cod tacos. Because it caters to the office crowd, the Gabardine is closed weekends.

Toronto's oldest restaurant, **The Senator** (249 Victoria St., 416/364-7517, www.thesenator.com, subway: Dundas, 7:30am-2:30pm Mon., 7:30am-9pm Tues.-Fri., 8am-2:30pm and 4:30pm-9pm Sat., 8am-2:30pm Sun., lunch $16-24, dinner $18-30) certainly looks the part, with burgundy vinyl booths, a checkerboard floor, and a 1920s-style lunch counter. While the evening menu concedes to modern tastes, with house-smoked salmon and burgers made of naturally raised beef, it's daytime classics like fresh-squeezed orange juice, eggs Benedict, roast turkey with stuffing, and homemade meat loaf that have been bringing in the customers for decades.

Asian

The **Banh Mi Boys** (399 Yonge St., 416/977-0303, www.banhmiboys.com, subway: College, Dundas, 11am-10pm Mon.-Fri., 11am-9pm Sat., noon-7pm Sun., $5-10) have made Vietnamese baguette sandwiches cool, serving modern versions laden with grilled pork, lemongrass tofu, even duck confit. Graffiti-inspired wall art, along with fusion tacos like kalbi beef and sides like kimchi fries, amp up the hipster quotient at this fast-food joint with style. There's a second location with the same hours on the west side (392 Queen St. W., 416/363-0588). **Salad King** (340 Yonge St., 2nd Fl., 416/593-0333, www.saladking.com, subway: Dundas, 11am-10pm Mon.-Thurs., 11am-11pm Fri., noon-11pm Sat., noon-9pm Sun., $7-12) doesn't specialize in salads. It's a cheap and cheerful Thai eatery that's convenient for a quick bite downtown. It serves curries, noodles, and several choices for vegetarians. If you do want a salad, try the green papaya version.

Toronto was all abuzz when New York chef David Chang opened a branch of his uber-cool, modern Japanese **Momofuku** (190 University Ave., 647/253-8000, www.momofuku.com, subway: St. Andrew, Osgoode) in the Shangri-La Hotel, starting with the casually hip **Noodle Bar** (ground floor, 11:30am-3pm and 5pm-10:30pm Sun.-Mon., 11:30am-3pm and 5pm-11pm Tues.-Sat., $10-20), which serves ramen, pork buns, and other Asian small plates. As this book went to press, they were revamping their other eateries at this location; check online for updates.

Bakeries and Cafés

If you've never sampled the Canadian bacon known as peameal, or even if you have, a good place to try it is at the St. Lawrence Market's **Carousel Bakery** (416/363-4247, www.stlawrencemarket.com), which sells the "world-famous peameal bacon on a bun" for a tasty, meaty lunch. Not a meat eater? The market's **Cruda Cafe** (647/346-6502, www.crudacafe.com, 9am-6pm Tues.-Thurs., 8am-7pm Fri., 6am-5pm Sat.), on the lower level, sells fresh juices, smoothies, raw wraps, and other vegetarian fare.

A handy spot for a snack or light meal in the Distillery District is **Brick Street Bakery** (27 Trinity St., 416/214-4949, www.brickstreetbakery.ca, 8:30am-6pm Sun.-Mon., 8:30am-7pm Tues.-Thurs., 8:30am-8pm Fri.-Sat., $5-10). Croissants, brioche, and scones pair with morning coffee; later in the day, sandwiches include lamb *kofta* (a lamb burger with fennel slaw), a chicken and bacon club, or a vegetarian combo of portobello mushrooms, red peppers, and basil purée. Revive your flagging energy with a cookie or mini tart.

Stop into **SOMA Chocolatemaker** (32 Tank House Lane, 416/815-7662, www.somachocolate.com, 10am-8pm Mon.-Sat., 11am-6pm Sun.) in the Distillery District to sniff the chocolatey goodness and watch the chocolate makers at work. It's not easy to choose between the beautifully crafted bonbons and pastries, freshly made gelatos and sorbets, and hot chocolate drinks, including the Mayan chocolate spiced with ginger, orange peel, and chili. As their tagline says, it's "a place to eat, drink, and worship chocolate." Amen.

Tiny **Roselle Desserts** (362 King St. E., 416/368-8188, www.roselleto.com, 11am-6pm Wed.-Thurs., noon-6pm and 8pm-11pm Fri., 11am-6pm and 8pm-11pm Sat., 11am-5pm Sun.) crafts picture-perfect French-style pastries, from macarons to their signature banana éclairs. They make a mean dark chocolate sea salt cookie, too. They're north of the Distillery District, and on the no. 504 King streetcar line.

THE ENTERTAINMENT DISTRICT

Centered on King Street West from University Avenue to Bathurst Street, this downtown neighborhood is home to many of the city's theaters, concert venues, and hip restaurants.

Contemporary

The Oliver and Bonacini Restaurants group runs two eateries in the TIFF Bell Lightbox Theatre. Café-style **O&B Canteen** (330 King St. W., 416/288-4710, www.obcanteen.comom, 11am-10pm Mon., 11am-11pm Tues.-Fri., 10am-11pm Sat., 10am-10pm Sun., $8-26), in a window-lined see-and-be-seen street-level room, is perfect for a quick bite before a show, with audience favorites like pizzas, sandwiches, pastas, roast chicken, and grilled salmon. Their grab-and-go counter (8am-5pm Mon.-Fri., 10am-5pm Sat.-Sun.) offers pastries and light meals to take out.

The more expensive seats—and more innovative menus—are upstairs in **Luma Restaurant** (416/288-4715, www. lumarestaurant.com, 11:45am-10pm Mon.-Tues., 11:45am-11pm Fri., 4pm-11pm Sat., lunch $16-27, dinner $21-34), where you can lunch on kale salad with pickled grapes, clam carbonara, or housemade duck sausage. In the evening, start with a cocktail like the Bottomless Havana (gin, pineapple, chamomile, and cinnamon) or the High Park (rye, sweet vermouth, and black walnut bitters), before digging into Oscar-worthy entrées like steelhead trout with squash and prairie grains or roasted pork chop with pretzel spaetzle.

Bistro-style **Marben** (488 Wellington St. W., 416/979-1990, www.marbenrestaurant. com, 5pm-10pm Tues.-Fri., 10:30am-3pm and 5pm-10pm Sat.-Sun., brunch $15-21, dinner $21-34) is popular for brunch, with dishes like baked eggs over squash and potato hash or a classic British-style fry-up. When the sun goes down, sup on Ontario-raised pheasant or tri-tip steak with heirloom carrots and beets. Get here on the no. 510 Spadina streetcar to Wellington, or the no. 504 King to Spadina or Portland.

French

Ask Torontonians to recommend a classic French bistro and the name you'll keep hearing is **Le Select Bistro** (432 Wellington St. W., 416/596-6405, www.leselect.com, 11:30am-9:30pm Mon., 11:30am-10pm Tues.-Thurs., 11:30am-10:30pm Fri., 11am-10:30pm Sat., 10:30am-9:30pm Sun., lunch $14-30, dinner $16-35), an old favorite for steak frites, *choucroute garnie* (pork with sauerkraut), cassoulet, and other traditional bistro dishes. Always busy for brunch, they also offer a post-theater menu. Take the no. 504 King streetcar to Spadina or Portland, or the no. 510 Spadina to Wellington.

ITALIAN

Lounge at the long communal tables at ever-so-stylish ★ **Buca** (604 King St. W., 416/865-1600, www.buca.ca, 5pm-10pm Sun.-Wed., 5pm-11pm Thurs.-Sat., $18-36), and start your evening with Italian shared plates like house-cured *salumi* or crispy pig's ears. The unusual pastas might include handmade duck egg *bigoli* with duck-offal ragù or pork-blood spaghetti, and the pizzas might be topped with braised pork with capers and mascarpone or potatoes and artichokes. The cave-like wine room has an intimate atmosphere. Take the no. 504 King streetcar to Portland Street. The same team runs nearby **Bar Buca** (75 Portland St., 416/599-2822, 7:30am-2am Mon.-Fri., 8am-2am Sat.-Sun.), which opens with espresso and pastries, and carries on with wine and Italian small plates till the wee hours.

Asian

From his start as a Hong Kong kitchen apprentice to his rise as a Food Network star, chef Susur Lee has been wowing (and occasionally exasperating) the food world. **Luckee** (328 Wellington St. W., 416/935-0400, www.luckeerestaurant.com, noon-2pm and 5:30pm-11pm Tues.-Fri., 11am-2:30pm and 5:30pm-11pm Sat.-Sun., dim sum $8-24, dinner $13-33), a cool red-hued restaurant and bar at the Soho Metropolitan Hotel, takes the chef back to his Chinese roots, with uniquely Susur twists on Cantonese,

Shanghai, and Sichuan dishes. Try the delicate lobster and asparagus dumplings or the black pepper beef.

Bakeries and Cafés

SOMA Chocolatemaker (443 King St. W., at Spadina, 416/599-7662, www.somachocolate.com, 9am-8pm Mon.-Thurs., 9am-9pm Fri., noon-9pm Sat., noon-6pm Sun.), an artisanal chocolate and gelato café with its original location in the Distillery District, lures those with a sweet tooth with hot chocolate, truffles, pastries, and ice cream.

BLOOR-YORKVILLE AND NORTH

Gourmet grocer **Pusateri's** (57 Yorkville Ave., at Bay St., 416/925-0583, www.pusateris.com, subway: Bay, 7:30am-8pm Mon.-Wed. and Sat., 7:30am-9pm Thurs.-Fri., 7:30am-7pm Sun.) is like a miniature Whole Foods Market, selling produce, cheeses, breads, and prepared foods. Prices are high, but so is the quality. Speaking of **Whole Foods Market** (87 Avenue Rd., 416/944-0500, www.wholefoodsmarket.com, subway: St. George, Bay, 9am-10pm Mon.-Fri., 9am-9pm Sat.-Sun.), the large natural foods retailer has an outpost in Yorkville Village.

Indigenous

Drawing on his roots growing up on Manitoulin Island's Wikwemikong Unceded Reserve, chef Joseph Shawana incorporates ingredients from indigenous communities across Canada into the inventive dishes he conceives at ★ **Ku-Kum Kitchen** (581 Mt. Pleasant St., 416/519-2638, www.kukumkitchen.com, 11am-3pm and 5pm-10pm Wed.-Sat., 11am-3pm Sun., lunch $16-18, dinner $20-28). You might try rich, creamy rabbit liver mousse served with baked bannock, caribou with squash and foraged mushrooms, even seal loin paired with golden beets and appealingly bitter microgreens. The staff is happy to explain the menu and make suggestions. Reservations are a good idea in this small storefront space. The restaurant is about a 15-minute walk from Eglinton Station (Yonge-University line).

Steak

If you think old-fashioned glamour has gone out of style, you haven't been to luxe **BlueBlood Steakhouse** (1 Austin Terr., 416/353-4647, www.bluebloodsteakhouse.com, subway: Dupont, 5pm-midnight Sun.-Wed., 5pm-1am Thurs.-Sat., kitchen closes 11pm, $34-200) inside Casa Loma, Toronto's

BlueBlood Steakhouse at Casa Loma

castle. In this imposing, wood-paneled dining room decorated with portraits of the British queen and Prince (the late American singer-songwriter), it's all about the meat, sourced from across North America and served in portions ranging from large (8 ounces) to massive (44 ounces), along with other classics like Caesar salad prepared tableside and Baked Alaska set aflame for dessert. In a castle, after all, would you expect anything less?

Vegetarian

When you need a plant-based break from museum hopping or Bloor-Yorkville shopping, there's **Planta** (1221 Bay St., 647-348-7000, www.plantarestaurants.com, subway: Bay, Bloor-Yonge, 11:30am-3pm and 5pm-9pm Mon.-Tues., 11:30am-3pm and 5pm-10pm Wed.-Fri., 11:30am-2:30pm and 5pm-11pm Sat., 10:30am-3pm and 5pm-9pm Sun., $14-24), a creative, plant-filled vegetarian eatery, where you can share plates like coconut ceviche, creamy and crispy cauliflower "tots," kale Caesar salad with pickled onions, or eggplant lasagna with smoked tofu. The owners run another downtown joint, **Planta Burger** (4 Temperance St., 647/348-7000, subway: Queen, King, 11:30am-7:30pm Mon.-Sat., $8-11), for veggie burgers and dairy-free milk shakes.

Live Organic Food Bar (264 Dupont St., at Spadina, 416/515-2002, www.livefoodbar. com, subway: Dupont, 11:30am-9:30pm Mon.-Thurs., 11:30am-10pm Fri.-Sat., 11am-9pm Sun., $12-23) is a vegan café near Casa Loma. This chipper orange and green space looks like one of their colorful composed salads, like the Detox, brimming with kale, parsley, kelp noodles, seaweed, and avocado. Among the many raw choices are sweet potato "sushi" and a sunflower sesame hummus wrap. Even the drinks nod to health-consciousness, in cocktails like a vodka, lavender, and *kombucha* blend.

Asian

With its cartoon logo, red lanterns, and fast-food ambience, **Okonomi House** (23 Charles St. W., 416/925-6176, subway: Bloor-Yonge, 11am-3pm and 4:30pm-10pm Mon.-Fri., noon-3pm and 4:30pm-10pm Sat., $7-13) looks like a Japanese Denny's. But no matter—you're here for the *okonomiyaki,* a savory pancake that resembles a cross between an omelet and a crepe. Fried with cabbage, onions, and your choice of beef, pork, bacon, vegetables, squid, or shrimp, it's a quick, filling meal. It's worth the extra $0.50 to add salty bonito (fish flakes) and seaweed to punch up the flavor.

At **Sabai Sabai Kitchen and Bar** (81 Bloor St. E., 647/748-4225, www.sabaisabaito. ca, subway: Bloor-Yonge, 11am-10pm Mon.-Thurs., 11am-11pm Fri.-Sat., 4pm-10pm Sun., $12-16), the motto is "peace, love & sticky rice." And even if the bold-flavored northern Thai dishes, designed to share, won't solve the world's problems, they're still tasty. Try the *khao soi* (noodles with chicken or beef swimming in a rich coconut-milk curry broth), grilled beef salad with fresh herbs, and garlicky stir-fried morning glory greens. Vegans have lots of options here.

KENSINGTON MARKET AND CHINTATOWN

Inexpensive eateries abound around Kensington Market and in Toronto's original Chinatown, alongside a growing number of hip dining spots.

Indigenous

Son of an Anishinaabe mother and a Jewish father, chef-owner Shawn Adler at Kensington Market's **Pow Wow Café** (213 Augusta Ave., 416/551-7717, 11am-8pm daily, $12-16) is known for his tacos: fry bread piled with beef or vegetarian chili, cheddar cheese, tomatoes, cilantro, and other vegetables. He does fusion varieties as well, topped with pork souvlaki or jerk chicken. At brunch, he cooks up corn pancakes with maple syrup and a hearty platter of scrambled eggs, venison sausage, duck bacon, and fry bread. This compact and casual storefront has a few tables inside and a few more on the sidewalk patio.

Latin American

The only thing "jumbo" about this tiny Kensington Market shop may be the appetites of the patrons who flock here for the signature stuffed pastry. **Jumbo Empanadas** (245 Augusta Ave., at Nassau, 416/977-0056, www.jumboempanadas.ca, 9am-8pm Mon.-Sat., 11am-8pm Sun., $5-9) serves tasty Chilean empanadas filled (more traditionally) with beef or chicken with olives and hard-boiled egg, or (more Toronto) with vegetables, including a spinach-mushroom-pepper mélange. Take the no. 510 Spadina streetcar to Nassau Street, or the no. 506 Carlton streetcar to Major or Augusta.

Asian

One block of Baldwin Street, between McCaul and Beverley Streets, near the Art Gallery of Ontario, is lined with small local eateries. It's easy to walk right past petite ★ **Omai Restaurant** (3 Baldwin St., 647/341-7766, www.omairestaurant.ca, subway: St. Patrick, noon-3pm and 5:30pm-10:30pm Mon.-Thurs., noon-3pm and 5:30pm-midnight Fri., 5:30pm-midnight Sat., lunch $12-23, small plates $4-16), but don't. It's a sake bar with a thoughtful selection of rice wines by the glass to pair with *temaki* (hand rolls) and izakaya-style small plates. Try the tamago roll amped up with truffle oil or the refreshing *sunomono* with crunchy puffed buckwheat.

In Chinatown, watch the deft dumpling makers at work at **Mother's Dumplings** (421 Spadina Ave., 416/217-2008, www.mothersdumplings.com, 11:30am-10pm Sun.-Thurs., 11:30am-10:30pm Fri.-Sat., $8-12), which specializes in *jiaozi,* steamed or boiled dumplings native to northeastern China. Order a steamer or three—filled with shrimp, egg, and chive; cabbage, mushroom, and tofu; or pork with pickled cabbage—to pair with excellent northern-style side dishes, like tofu strip salad (bean curd dressed with peppers and fragrant cilantro) or garlicky smashed cucumbers. Take the no. 510 Spadina streetcar to College or Nassau Streets, or the no. 506 Carlton streetcar to Spadina Avenue.

A dingy basement room with about as much ambience as, well, a dingy basement room, **Chinese Traditional Buns** (536 Dundas St. W., 416/299-9011, www.chinesetraditionalbuns.ca, 11:30am-10pm Mon.-Thurs., 11:30am-10:30pm Fri.-Sun., $6-15) nonetheless cooks up simple, scrumptious specialties of China's western regions. Try the Xi'an cured pork sandwich (like a Chinese pork slider), or any of the hand-pulled noodles, including the ground meat-topped *dan dan mien.* It's in Chinatown, just west of Spadina Avenue; take the no. 505 Dundas streetcar to Spadina, or the no. 510 Spadina streetcar to Dundas.

Sheltered from the busy food court in the Village by the Grange building, the surprisingly serene **Manpuku** (105 McCaul St., 416/979-6763, www.manpuku.ca, subway: St. Patrick, 11:30am-8pm Mon.-Wed., 11:30am-11pm Thurs.-Fri., noon-11pm Sat., $5-7) is a good choice for an inexpensive Japanese meal near the Art Gallery of Ontario, which is across the street. Choose from simple udon noodle soups, rice plates, and curries.

THE WEST END

Some of Toronto's most interesting eateries are along West Queen West, Ossington Avenue, and Dundas Street West—a hotbed of casually contemporary bistros, tapas joints, and fun and funky dining rooms.

Although no longer exclusively old-world Italian, Toronto's **Little Italy** (www.littleitalyintoronto.ca) district, along College Street west of Bathurst, is lively with sidewalk cafés and trattorias. Look for traditional Portuguese breads and the sweet custard tarts known as *pasteis de nata* in bakeries and cafés along Dundas Street West in **Little Portugal** (www.littleportugal.ca). **Koreatown** (www.koreatownbia.com) centers on Bloor Street West, between Bathurst and Christie Streets, where, in addition to restaurants serving traditional pork bone soup, spicy fried chicken, or grill-it-yourself barbecued meats, you'll find authentic Korean pastries.

Contemporary

"Party like you're in Barcelona" could be the motto of lively **Bar Isabel** (797 College St., 416/532-2222, www.barisabel.com, 6pm-midnight Sun.-Tues., 6pm-2am Fri.-Sat., $9-69), where the inventive tapas, accompanied by equally imaginative cocktails, have earned plenty of kudos. You might sip an Isabel Fashioned (made with bourbon and Spanish brandy) while you graze on mussels escabeche, Serrano ham, and shishito peppers, or go big with whole sea bream ceviche or an entire grilled octopus. The signature dessert is a Basque cake topped with sherry cream. Ride the no. 506 Carlton streetcar to Shaw.

With horse tartare, beef tongue and beets, and sweetbreads *alla puttanesca*, the menu at **The Black Hoof** (928 Dundas St. W., at Bellwoods Ave., www.theblackhoof. com, 6pm-midnight Thurs.-Sun., small plates $13-25, cash only) reads like a challenge—at least if you don't normally nibble the nasty bits. But if you're eager to embrace nose-to-tail eating, join the hordes at this mod meatery for tapas and a cocktail or glass of wine. No reservations are accepted. The no. 505 Dundas streetcar will get you here. Next door, the same owners run Haitian-inspired **Rhum Corner** (926 Dundas St. W., 647/346-9356, www.rhumcorner.com, 6pm-1am Sun.-Wed., 6pm-2am Thurs.-Sat., kitchen closes at 11pm) for Caribbean snacks and drinks.

Indigenous

In a tiny Koreatown storefront restaurant, its exterior painted to resemble a birch forest, **Nish Dish Marketeria** (690 Bloor St. W., 416/855-4085, www.nishdish.com, subway: Christie, 10am-7pm Tues.-Fri., 9am-6pm Sat.-Sun., $7-11) starts the day with boar or bison breakfast sandwiches and coffee roasted by a local First Nation; order yours as an *anishnakano* (aka an americano). For lunch, try the salmon-corn cakes, an elk burger, or the "Three Sisters Stew," a generous dill-topped bowl of green beans, squash, and corn.

Italian

Every neighborhood needs a sociable wine bar and Italian eatery like ★ **Enoteca Sociale** (1288 Dundas St. W., 416/534-1200, www. sociale.ca, 5pm-11pm daily, $12-46), where you can bring the family, a pal or two, or a special someone to sample from the large selection of wines and Roman-style plates. There are several pastas, like tagliatelle with turkey ragù or gnocchi with smoked ricotta, trout crudo, and heartier plates like whole grilled sea bream. Book ahead—the restaurant is small and frequently busy—and get here on the no. 505 Dundas streetcar to Dovercourt, west of Ossington.

Always-packed **Pizzeria Libretto** (221 Ossington Ave., at Dundas, 416/532-8000, www.pizzerialibretto.com, 11:30am-11pm daily, pizzas $13-19) tames the hungry hordes with Neapolitan-style pizza, paired with interesting salads like arugula with pears, walnuts, and piave cheese, or antipasto platters laden with cured meats and regionally made cheeses. Take the no. 505 Dundas streetcar to Ossington Avenue. They've added locations downtown (155 University Ave., 416/551-0433, subway: St. Andrew, 11:30am-11pm daily), in the Entertainment District (545 King St. W., at Portland St., 647/352-1200, 11:30am-11pm daily), and in the Danforth (550 Danforth Ave., 416/466-0400, subway: Chester, Pape, 11:30am-10pm Sun.-Thurs., 11:30am-11pm Fri.-Sat.).

Portuguese

When you tire of grunge waitstaff, warehouse-bare rooms, and hipper-than-thou pig's ear-filled menus, retreat to old-world **Chiado** (864 College St., 416/538-1910, www. chiadorestaurant.com, noon-2:30pm and 5pm-10pm Mon.-Fri., 5pm-10pm Sat.-Sun., lunch $19-35, dinner $35-55), where dignified waiters wear crisp white aprons and candlelit tables are dressed in starched white cloths. The menu is "progressive Portuguese"; the salt cod is grilled, then roasted with olive oil and garlic, and traditional *piri piri* sauce glazes the pan-seared monkfish. If the prices seem rich,

Rosen's Cinnamon Buns

come for a selection of tapas ($7-19). Take the no. 506 Carlton streetcar west to Ossington Avenue.

Asian

West Queen West isn't only about hip cafés and dining spots. If you're craving a comforting bowl of soup, head for **Pho Tien Thanh** (57 Ossington Ave., 416/588-6997, 11am-10pm daily, $8-15), which specializes in the traditional Vietnamese noodle soup called pho. Take the no. 501 Queen streetcar to Ossington, then walk two blocks north.

Lamesa Filipino Kitchen (669 Queen St. W., 647/346-2377, www.lamesafilipinokitchen.com, 5pm-10pm Tues.-Fri., 11am-3pm and 5pm-10pm Sat., 11am-3pm and 5pm-9pm Sun., $12-26) aims to make this Asian cuisine more accessible, creating modern interpretations of Filipino classics in versions designed for sharing. The friendly crew running this fun restaurant, west of Bathurst Street, is quick to tell you about dishes like *lechon kawali* (crispy pork belly with pickled papaya) or chicken adobo with chimichurri, and to pour your Filipino Shandy (beer and *calamansi* juice) or Lolo Cool J (bourbon, ginger, pineapple syrup, and lemon).

Bakeries and Cafés

Take the no. 501 Queen streetcar to Strachan Avenue to find **Nadège Patisserie** (780 Queen St. W., 416/368-2009, www.nadege-patisserie.com, 8am-8pm Mon.-Wed., 8am-9pm Thurs.-Sat., 8am-7pm Sun.), which crafts luscious pastries, macarons, and chocolates. If you need some goodies downtown, they have a branch on the PATH underground walkway at Richmond Adelaide Centre, between York and Sheppard Streets (416/350-2014, 7:30am-6:30pm Mon.-Fri.).

During a weekend with her extended family, Toronto-based food writer Amy Rosen realized that the one food that brought joy to everyone from toddlers to seniors were her homemade cinnamon buns. So she opened a take-out-only storefront bakery, **Rosen's Cinnamon Buns** (825 College St., at Ossington Ave., 416/534-2856, www.amyrosen.com, 8am-4pm Wed.-Sun.), to sell her freshly baked, not-too-sweet treats.

It's not easy to get into the **Easy Restaurant** (1645 Queen St. W., 416/537-4893, 9am-4pm daily, $10-19), at least on weekends, when this funky diner has long been an all-day-breakfast favorite. The only problem with ordering the signature *huevos divorciados* (poached eggs with black beans, tortillas, salsa, guacamole, and ancho chili jam) is that you'll be hungry again in about three days. Take the no. 501 Queen or the no. 504 King streetcar to Roncesvalles Avenue.

The specialty at Korean bakery **Hodo Kwaja** (656 Bloor St. W., 416/538-1208, subway: Christie, www.hodokwaja.ca, 9am-10pm Mon.-Sat.) is walnut cake, a walnut-shaped pastry filled with red-bean paste or a slightly sweet potato mixture. Also delicious are the brown sugar pancakes with peanuts; check the website for current baking times, so you can eat these excellent snacks while they're hot.

THE EAST END

What to eat in Toronto's East End? Head to the Danforth, also known as Greektown, for Greek food, Little India (the Indian Bazaar) for food from South Asia, and Leslieville for fine contemporary fare in laid-back neighborhood settings. **Big Carrot Natural Foods** (348 Danforth Ave., 416/466-2129, www.thebigcarrot.ca, subway: Chester, 9am-9pm Mon.-Fri., 9am-8pm Sat., 10am-6pm Sun.) is a well-stocked natural foods market in the Danforth.

Contemporary

At ★ **Ruby Watchco** (730 Queen St. E., 416/465-0100, www.rubywatchco.ca, dinner Tues.-Sat., $56 prix fixe), imaginative chef and co-owner Lynn Crawford, of Food Network Canada's *Pitchin' In*, and her team serve a four-course prix fixe menu that changes every night. Examples of Crawford's wow-worthy locally sourced spreads include cod salad with frisée and cucumber radish; fried chicken with hot honey mustard, charred broccoli with lemon butter, and heirloom carrots; and dark chocolate mousse with bourbon cherries and caramel. Peruse the weekly dishes on the bistro's website; book online or by phone. From downtown, take the no. 501 Queen streetcar east to Broadview.

Greek

The menu is simple at **Athens Pastries** (509 Danforth Ave. at Logan Ave., 416/463-5144, www.athenspastries.com, subway: Chester, Pape, 9am-11pm Sun.-Thurs., 9am-midnight Fri.-Sat., $4-6), a Greek café in the Danforth neighborhood. It includes spinach-, cheese-, or meat-filled pies wrapped in a flaky phyllo dough, as well as a few sweets, including *loukoumades* (honey doughnuts) that pair beautifully with a strong cup of coffee.

Indian

A long-established restaurant in the Little India neighborhood, **Udupi Palace** (1460 Gerrard St. E., 416/405-8189, www.udupipalace.ca, noon-10pm Sun.-Thurs., noon-11pm Fri.-Sat., $6-12) specializes in south Indian vegetarian and vegan dishes, including a lengthy list of *dosas*, crisp pancakes that come stuffed with combinations of potatoes, onions, vegetables, or *paneer* (a cheese). Don't expect much ambience in the cavernous space; it's all about the food. Take the no. 506 Carlton streetcar to Ashdale Avenue.

Middle Eastern

If you're wandering east of the Distillery District, in the neighborhood dubbed the Canary, stop for a quick bite at bright and airy **Souk Tabule** (494 Front St. E., 416/583-5914, www.souktabule.com, 11am-9pm Sun. and Tues.-Thurs., 11am-9:30pm Fri.-Sat., $7-15), which serves modern Middle Eastern fare. Mezze like *foule* (warm fava bean dip), fried cauliflower, and *labni* (yogurt cheese) come with fresh-baked *saj*, a flatbread. A selection of salads, sandwiches, and larger plates, like grilled chicken kebabs or falafel with *mujaddara* (rice and lentils), round out the menu. Try a fresh mint tea or chai latte with a sesame cookie or other sweet.

Accommodations

Like most metropolitan areas, Toronto offers a range of lodgings from international luxury hotels to arty boutique properties to homey B&Bs. Accommodations are concentrated downtown, in the Entertainment District, and in the Bloor-Yorkville neighborhood, but anything within walking distance of the subway or streetcar can be convenient. AirBnB is also an option in Toronto.

If you're on a tight budget, and you're visiting in summer, check out the residence halls on the University of Toronto campus, which offer basic but good-value rooms. Otherwise, for accommodations under $100, you're generally looking at hostels. Outside the Christmas-New Year's holiday period, rates are typically lowest in winter.

Beware that most Toronto hotels, particularly those downtown, charge for parking, which can add more than $50 per day to your tab. While free Wi-Fi is widespread, a few larger hotels still charge for Internet access.

DOWNTOWN AND THE FINANCIAL DISTRICT
Under $100

There's always something going on at the **HI-Toronto Hostel** (76 Church St., subway: King, 416/971-4440 or 877/848-8737, www.hostellingtoronto.com, $33-67 dorm, $140-210 d), whether it's a pub crawl, karaoke night, or a summer barbecue. The hostel has more than 140 beds across nine floors in 6-, 8-, 10-, and 14-bed dorms (male only, female only, and mixed); quad rooms with bunk beds; and private doubles with en suite baths. A basement café serves breakfast and dinner, and there is a common kitchen. Wi-Fi is free. The no. 504 King streetcar stops a block away at Church Street.

$100-150

One block east of busy Yonge Street, **Les Amis B&B** (31 Granby St., 416/591-0635, www. bbtoronto.com, subway: College, $95-105 s, $125-145 d, parking $13.75), in a narrow 1870s town house, is on a quiet residential street. The five cozy guest rooms have wide-board floors, down duvets, and simple furnishings. On the 2nd floor, one room has a private bath, while the other two share a bath; the two 3rd-floor rooms share an adjacent bath. Owners Paul-Antoine and Michelle Buer serve meat-free breakfasts. Paul-Antoine is a photographer, and photos of his travels adorn the walls.

$150-300

Built in the early 20th century, the 56-room **Hotel Victoria** (56 Yonge St., 416/363-1666 or 800/363-8228, www.hotelvictoria-toronto.com, subway: King, $169-439 d) is a petite but pretty boutique inn downtown. The style starts in the art deco lobby with a black granite fireplace and marble columns and continues upstairs, where rooms have black furniture, white duvets, and gold accents, along with coffeemakers and free Wi-Fi. The standard rooms are cozy; for more space (plus a mini fridge), opt for a deluxe king or deluxe queen.

Don't expect luxury at the 18-story **Bond Hotel** (65 Dundas St. E., subway: Dundas, 416/362-6061, www.bondplace.ca, subway: Dundas, $165-450 d, Wi-Fi $8.95, parking $25), but do expect simple comfort and style. Of the 285 guest rooms, with white duvets and flat-screen TVs, the least expensive standard rooms are quite small, but some of the larger "deluxe" rooms have two separate sleeping areas—not separate rooms, but somewhat private. The building has a fitness room, and parking is available in a nearby garage. The no. 505 Dundas streetcar stops at Bond Street, right out front.

If you don't need a lot of space and you want a central downtown location, consider the **Strathcona Hotel** (60 York St., 416/363-3321, www.thestrathconahotel.com, subway:

Union, $179-479 d, Wi-Fi $10). The rooms in this 12-story building, decorated with white duvets and gray accents, cover the basics—decent beds, coffeemakers, TVs—with no extraneous frills. The street-facing rooms are noisier but bright; the interior rooms are quieter and darker.

Canada's largest hotel and Toronto's most family friendly, the 1,590-room **Chelsea Hotel** (33 Gerrard St. W., 416/595-1975 or 800/243-5732, www.chelseatoronto.comom, subway: College, $245-399 d, $385-549 suite), feels like a small city. There's always something for kids to do, including an indoor pool with a big waterslide, games and crafts in the "Kid Centre," and a teen lounge with video games, foosball, and movies. Relax in the top-floor adults-only pool and fitness room. Rooms range from 25-square-meter (275-square-foot) standards with a king, queen, or two doubles to slightly larger kitchenette units to two-bedroom "Family Fun" suites with bunk beds and a play area. Wi-Fi is free; parking is $35 (self-parking) and $45 (valet) daily.

With its colored neon lighting and sleek martini lounge, the lobby at the **Pantages Hotel Toronto Centre** (200 Victoria St., 416/362-1777 or 855/852-1777, www.pantageshotel.com, subway: Queen, $219-479 d) has a space-age air. Upstairs, you'll feel like a contented Buddha in the 89 serene suites, which have hardwood floors, kings or queens topped with white duvets, kitchenettes, and washer-dryers. For more active relaxation, head for the well-equipped 24-hour fitness room. The hotel is one block south of Dundas Square, one block west of Yonge Street.

The **Cambridge Suites Hotel** (15 Richmond St. E., 416/368-1990 or 800/463-1990, www.cambridgesuitestoronto.com, $257-417 d, parking $27) may not be as stylish as trendier boutique properties, but you get a lot of space for your money. The 229 modern units are all two-room suites with separate living and sleeping areas (with a flat-screen TV in each room), as well as kitchenettes with fridges, microwaves, coffeemakers,

Fairmont Royal York

dishes, and cutlery. The top floor of the 22-story building has a small workout room, hot tub, and sauna. Rates include Wi-Fi.

As skinny as a guru, the 27-story tower of the **Executive Hotel Cosmopolitan Toronto** (8 Colborne St., 416/350-2000 or 800/958-3488, www.cosmotoronto.com, $199-429) has a Zen feel. Each floor has only five sleek, modern guest rooms, with wood floors and kitchenettes; they even come with yoga mats. The larger Deluxe Suites, with washer-dryers, are configured either as a studio with sleeping and sitting areas or as a one-bedroom unit with a separate living room. Head for the fitness room or book a treatment in the spa. **Tip:** For the best views, ask for a room on the 20th floor or above. A mandatory 6 percent "hotel amenity fee" covers Wi-Fi and local phone calls.

Over $300

Built in 1929, the ★ **Fairmont Royal York** (100 Front St. W., 416/368-2511 or 866/540-4489, www.fairmont.com, subway: Union,

$305-739 d, parking $59) was once the tallest building in the British Empire. Both the staff and the more than 1,300 rooms are gracious and welcoming, whether you're the Queen of England (yes, she's stayed here) or a regular Joe. Have a drink in the dark-paneled Library Bar or dinner in the contemporary **Epic** restaurant (419/860-6949, www.epicrestaurant. ca, 7am-10am, noon-2pm, and 5:30pm-10pm Mon.-Fri., 7am-2pm and 5:30pm-10pm Sat.-Sun., lunch $16-36, dinner $36-49), where the solicitous servers will ensure you're well cared for whether you're dining with a client, a special someone, or your great-aunt Tillie. A skylight illuminates the indoor pool; the updated fitness room is open 24/7. Sign up for Fairmont's frequent-stay program to get free Wi-Fi during your stay.

They don't build hotels like this anymore. Retaining the elegance of a bygone era, the majestic ambience of **The Omni King Edward** (37 King St. E., 416/863-9700, www. omnihotels.com, subway: King, $319-375 d, parking $48) begins in the lobby, with its ornate columns and plasterwork, soaring ceiling, and marble floors. Most of the 301 rooms aren't quite as grand, but they're comfortable, traditionally furnished retreats from the bustle of the surrounding Financial District. Register for the Omni loyalty program before your stay to get complimentary Wi-Fi.

One King West (1 King St. W., 416/548-8100 or 866/470-5464, www.onekingwest. com, subway: King, $259-509 d), a deluxe, centrally located condominium-hotel, caters to business travelers and couples with sleekly modern apartments for short or extended stays. The building combines the elegance of a former 1880s bank headquarters with a new tower that soars above the original structure. The suites are larger than typical hotel rooms and have kitchens with dishwashers and laundry facilities. Parking (valet only) is $49 per day; fortunately, you can leave the car at home, since you can walk to the underground PATH network and the subway.

Opposite City Hall, the **Sheraton Centre Hotel** (123 Queen St. W., 416/361-1000, www.

sheratontoronto.com, subway: Osgoode, $399-579 d) has 1,377 guest rooms in two towers; the taller rises 43 stories above downtown. The rooms feel business casual, with white duvets, large desks, and leather armchairs. The higher-priced club rooms on floors 36-42 have the best city views and provide access to the top-floor lounge, with complimentary breakfast, evening hors d'oeuvres, and Internet access (which normally costs $15 per day). Alternatively, join the Starwood frequent stay program for free Wi-Fi. There's an indoor-outdoor pool and a spacious health club. Parking is valet only ($50 per day).

Larger-than-life photos of sports stars adorn the guest room walls of the deluxe, intimate ★ **Hotel Le Germain Maple Leaf Square** (75 Bremner Blvd., 416/649-7575 or 888/940-7575, www.germainmapleleafsquare. com, subway: Union, $439-779 d). With down duvets, espresso machines, and 40-inch flat-screen TVs, the 167 contemporary rooms have the expected luxuries. Many of the glass-walled showers open to the bedrooms; pull the shades if you're feeling modest. The athletic artwork may inspire a visit to the well-equipped fitness room, and the expanded continental breakfast has cheeses, charcuterie, and pastries. Rates include Wi-Fi; parking (valet only) is $49 per night.

The Ivy at Verity (111d Queen St. E., 416/368-6006, www.theivyatverity.ca, $409-429 d) is a discreetly upscale boutique lodging inside a members-only private club for high-powered professional women. Accommodations are open to anyone, but the indoor pool, exercise room, and spa are for women only. The four deluxe guest rooms are decorated with eclectic light fixtures, balconies overlooking the pocket courtyard, and marble baths with rain showers and heated floors. Continental breakfast is served, and guests have access to the members' lounge for drinks or light meals. **George Restaurant** (647/496-8275, www.georgeonqueen.ca, noon-2:30pm Mon., noon-2:30pm and 5:30pm-9:30pm Tues.-Fri., 5:30pm-9:30pm Sat., lunch $19-27, dinner $26-37) shares the building, which once housed a chocolate factory, and provides room service for Ivy guests.

There's a lot to love at the luxurious, Asian-style **Shangri-La Hotel Toronto** (188 University Ave., 647/788-8888 or 866/344-5050, www.shangri-la.com, subway: St. Andrew, Osgoode, $480-700), including always at-your-service staff, a window-lined fitness facility, a hammam spa, and an indoor pool with private cabanas and subtle lighting. And that's before you even walk into the 202 generously proportioned rooms and suites, outfitted with both terrycloth robes and kimonos, iPads to use during your stay, 46-inch flat-screen TVs, and capacious spa-like baths. Not pampered enough? Take afternoon tea (with sweets and finger sandwiches) in the lobby; the tea menu lists 75 varieties.

More than 450 original artworks decorate the deluxe, subtly Canadian-themed **Ritz-Carlton Toronto** (181 Wellington St. W., 416/585-2500 or 800/542-8680, www.ritzcarlton.com, subway: St. Andrew, $518-799 d). The 263 guest rooms are on floors 6-20; choose a south-facing high-floor room for views of the lake, or splurge on a spacious corner suite with bamboo floors and a separate living area. You can see the CN Tower from the indoor saltwater pool, and the large fitness center has the expected equipment. Book a massage, facial, or yoga class at the **Spa** (www.spamyblendtoronto.com). The restaurant **ToCa** (for "Toronto, Canada"; 6:30am-10:30am, 11:30am-2:30pm, and 5pm-10pm Mon.-Fri., 7am-10:30am, 11:30am-2:30pm, and 5pm-10pm Sat., 7am-10:30am, 11:30am-2pm, 2:30pm-4:30pm, and 6pm-10pm Sun.; lunch $20-38, dinner $28-48) serves Italian dishes with ingredients from Ontario and across the country.

THE ENTERTAINMENT DISTRICT
$150-300

Style without frills could be the slogan of **The Beverley Hotel** (335 Queen St. W., 416/493-2786, www.thebeverleyhotel.ca, $159-309 d), an 18-room European-style lodging.

Decorated with black-and-white photos, the guest rooms—on floors 2-4 above the hotel's restaurant—are small, simple sleeping spaces with white linens, flat-screen TVs, iPod docks, modern baths, and free Wi-Fi. The most spacious, the XL, have large, street-facing windows; most other units have interior, frosted-glass windows, but if you're just here to snooze, maybe you won't care. Get here on the no. 501 Queen streetcar to John Street.

Hotel Ocho (195 Spadina Ave., 416/593-0885, www.hotelocho.com, $189-330 d) is a trendy 12-room inn in a rehabbed 1902 industrial building. In the spare but comfy rooms, the Ocho has kept many original features—exposed brick, stocky wood beams, factory-size windows—while adding flat-screen TVs, modern baths with rain showers, and contemporary art. Even if you don't stay here, stop into the espresso bar (with free Wi-Fi) or have cocktails and snacks in the lounge. The Ocho is two blocks north of Queen Street West; take the no. 501 Queen streetcar to Spadina or the no. 510 Spadina streetcar to Queen.

Over $300

With 92 rooms and suites, the **Soho Metropolitan** (318 Wellington St. W., at Blue Jays Way, 416/599-8800 or 866/764-6638, www.metropolitan.com/soho, $310-600 d) feels quiet and intimate, occupying the first four floors of a condominium tower. In the bright and airy guest rooms, floor-to-ceiling windows, large walk-in closets, and marble baths with heated floors are standard. Set aside time for a workout in the health club or indoor lap pool. The hotel's **Luckee Restaurant and Bar** tempts with modern Chinese cuisine from celeb chef Susur Lee, and **Wahlburgers** sports bar is all about the burgers. Take the no. 504 King streetcar to Peter Street, then walk two blocks south.

Celebrity spotters might want to hang out at the luxury 96-room **BISHA Hotel** (80 Blue Jays Way, 416/551-2800 or 844/275-1726, www.bishahoteltoronto.com, $299-669 d), on the first eight floors of a 44-story hotel-condo tower. Even if you don't spot stars in the black velveteen-walled lobby or in the dark lobby bar, you'll feel like a celeb in your chic black-and-white room where the pop art pops with color. At **KŌST** (437/800-5938, www.kosttoronto.com, 7am-10:30pm Sun.-Tues., 7am-11:30pm Wed.-Sat., breakfast $12-17, lunch $14-21, dinner $14-45), the rooftop restaurant with an infinity pool on the terrace (and views of the Lake Ontario shoreline and the CN Tower), you can watch the sunset with cocktails and Baja-style small plates, while mornings bring sunny city vistas with avocado toast or fruit-topped coconut pancakes. On the 2nd floor, **Akira Back** (437/800-5967, www.akirabacktoronto.com, 5pm-11pm daily, $17-49), named for its Seoul-born, Aspen-raised star chef, serves inventive Japanese-Korean fare.

Like its sister property at Maple Leaf Square, 11-story **Hotel Le Germain** (30 Mercer St., 416/345-9500 or 866/345-9501, www.germaintoronto.com, $310-710 d), on a quiet side street one block from King, is run by a hip and helpful crew offering au courant accommodations with down duvets and large baths, many with glass showers facing the bedroom. Have a complimentary cappuccino in front of the fireplace in the lobby lounge, or head for the rooftop terrace, which has a

putting green. Stylish **Victor Restaurant** (416/883-3431, www.victorrestaurant.com, 6:30am-11am and 5pm-10:30pm Mon.-Sat., 6:30am-11am Sun., $18-42) serves sharing plates and other contemporary dishes that work before theater or after an evening out. Wi-Fi is free; parking (valet only) is $50 per night.

From the expansive lobby bar with its cartoon-style mural of the Toronto skyline, to the 102 guest rooms with sleek dark wood, white linens, and whimsical orange chairs, to the rooftop infinity pool overlooking the city, **Thompson Toronto** (550 Wellington St. W., at Bathurst St., 416/640-7778 or 888/550-8368, www.thompsonhotels.com, $386-699 d) is one stylish spot. You won't go hungry here, either: **Thompson Diner** (416/601-3533, 6am-3am daily, $12-18) is an upscale almost 24-hour diner and bar, and window-lined **Colette Grand Café** (647/348-7000, www.colettetoronto.com, 11:30am-2:30pm Mon., 11:30am-2:30pm and 5pm-10pm Tues.-Wed., 11:30am-2:30pm and 5pm-11pm Thurs.-Fri., 10am-2:30pm and 5pm-11pm Sat., 10am-2:30pm Sun., lunch $19-36, dinner $28-44) is a chic Mediterranean dining destination. The no. 504 King streetcar stops one block away at Bathurst Street.

coconut pancakes at KŌST in the BISHA Hotel

BLOOR-YORKVILLE AND THE ANNEX
Under $100

From Wi-Fi-equipped "phone booths" to electrical outlets in the lockers, the little touches make **Planet Traveler** (357 College St., 647/352-8747, www.theplanettraveler.com, $42-49 dorm, $101-115 d), a privately-run hostel near Kensington Market, stand out. There's a colorful lounge, communal kitchen, coin-op laundry, and rooftop deck with views across downtown. The small dorms have six beds, a bath, and big windows. Basic private rooms share a bath with four other rooms, and there's an additional common washroom down the hall. Rates include continental breakfast and Wi-Fi. Take the no. 506 Carlton streetcar to Augusta Avenue, or the no. 510 Spadina streetcar to College Street.

$150-300

In the residential Annex neighborhood, **Lowther Suites** (88 Lowther Ave., 416/925-4600, www.lowthersuites.com, subway: St. George, Spadina, $130-395 d) has five spacious one- or two-bedroom apartments with full kitchens and washer-dryers in a renovated brick mansion. Rates include Internet access and parking. The property caters to independent travelers—there's no common area, food service, or other hotel-style services (although a caretaker is on call). It's well suited to longer-term stays.

Over $300

Among Toronto's many luxurious lodgings, one of the most deluxe is the intimate **Hazelton Hotel** (118 Yorkville Ave., 416/963-6300 or 866/473-6301, www.thehazeltonhotel.com, $705-929 d, parking $49). The 77 sizable, sound-insulated rooms have amenities like 47-inch flat-screen TVs, roomy rain showers, heated bath floors, and plush mattresses. There is a spa, health club, and indoor lap pool. The attentive concierge service will arrange whatever you need. The hotel even has a private screening room in case you're hosting a film premiere or a playoff party. If you're not traveling by chauffeured limousine, Bay is the most convenient subway station.

THE WEST END
$100-150

How about a stay in an art gallery? The main floor of **Index G B&B** (50 Gladstone Ave., 416/535-6957, www.indexgbb.com, $95-100 s, $105-125 d) is a contemporary gallery space. Upstairs are four spare but arty guest rooms with original artwork on the walls. In the morning, help yourself to a simple continental breakfast (cereal, fruit, yogurt, coffee, tea) in the gallery. Wi-Fi is free. The no. 501 Queen streetcar stops at Gladstone Avenue, one block away, and the building is a short stroll from the West Queen West action.

$150-300

Personable proprietor Albert Tan welcomes guests to the **Clinton and Bloor B&B** (390 Clinton St., 416/538-0417, www.clintonandbloor.com, subway: Christie, $189-209 d, $289 suite) in his comfortable townhome on a residential Koreatown street. The high-ceilinged top-floor suite runs the length of the house, with ample closet space. The rear-facing room on the 2nd floor has a sleigh bed and a mini fridge; the sunny front room is a bit smaller. All have private baths. Breakfasts include deliciously nutty granola from Albert's secret recipe.

As much a place to lounge, drink, and eat as to sleep, the arty ★ **Drake Hotel** (1150 Queen St. W., 416/531-5042 or 866/372-5386, www.thedrakehotel.ca, $239-429 d) is a cultural hub on West Queen West. Guest rooms range from the cozy Crash Pad (just big enough to crash) to the progressively larger Dens, Salons, and Suite, with hardwood floors, exposed brick walls, TVs, and original artwork. If you're staying with a special someone, you can order champagne, flowers, or something from the cheeky Pleasure Menu, from plumes of feathers to all manner of sex toys.

The funky ★ **Gladstone Hotel** (1214 Queen St. W., 416/531-4635, www.gladstonehotel.com, $259-475) is a evolved from a rooming house to a strip club to its present incarnation as a smart boutique hotel. The furnishings in the 58 rooms trace these eras, too, mixing mid-century pieces with vinyl record players and contemporary art. French press coffeemakers, Wi-Fi, air-conditioning, and nightly turndown service add to the comfort. The lobby-level Café + Bar takes you from morning coffee to evening drinks, and **The Civic** (5pm-10pm Mon.-Thurs., 5pm-11pm Fri., 10am-3pm and 5pm-11pm Sat., 10am-3pm and 5pm-10pm Sun., dinner $20-56), with red leather banquettes and brick walls, updates upscale comfort food, from mushroom toast to steaks to a juicy, flavorful roast chicken. The property's showplace is **The Rooftop**, a buzzing lounge with a panoramic city view.

PEARSON INTERNATIONAL AIRPORT
$150-200

If you have an early departure or late arrival at the airport, hole up for the night at the cool, good-value **ALT Hotel Toronto Airport** (6080 Viscount Rd., Mississauga, 905/362-4337 or 855/855-6080, http://toronto.althotels.ca, $179-199 d). The 153 compact rooms in this modern 14-story tower are technology friendly, with free Wi-Fi, lots of outlets for plugging in your devices, bedside reading lamps, flat-screen TVs, and iPod alarm clocks. In the lobby, you can shoot some pool or have a drink at the bar. When it's time to catch your flight, pick up a "grab-and-go" meal (fruit, pastries, salads, or sandwiches), then take the free Terminal Link train right to the gates.

The Drake Hotel is a hub of activity on West Queen West.

combination art gallery and hotel in a restored 1889 building. The 37 rooms are all unique, designed by different artists. In the Teen Queen, the walls are plastered with photos of teen idols, while the Offset resembles a sleek urban loft. Most aren't large, but they are way cool, with flat-screen TVs, iPod docks, and Wi-Fi, and the hotel hosts all sorts of fun music, art, and literary events.

THE EAST END
Over $200

Built in 1891, ★ **The Broadview** (106 Broadview Ave., 416/362-8439, www.thebroadviewhotel.ca, $233-499 d) has

Information and Services

VISITOR INFORMATION

Tourism Toronto (416/203-2500 or 800/499-2514, www.seetorontonow.com), the city's convention and visitors association, has loads of information on its website to help you plan a Toronto visit, including a calendar of local events. At Union Station, the provincial **Ontario Travel Information Centre** (65 Front St. W., 416/314-5899, www.ontariotravel.net) provides information about travel around Toronto and elsewhere in the province.

MEDIA AND COMMUNICATIONS

Canada's two national newspapers, the *Globe and Mail* (www.theglobeandmail.com) and the *National Post* (www.nationalpost.com), are headquartered in Toronto, and the city has two other daily newspapers, the *Toronto Star* (www.thestar.com) and the *Toronto Sun* (www.torontosun.com). *Toronto Life Magazine* (www.torontolife.com), published monthly in print and available online, covers the arts, restaurants, and things to do, as does *Now* (www.nowtoronto.com), *Where Toronto* (www.where.ca), *blogTO* (www.blogto.com), and *Post City News* (www.postcity.com).

Transportation

GETTING THERE

As Canada's largest city, Toronto has flights from many parts of the world, as well as train and bus connections from around Ontario, from major Canadian cities, and from many U.S. points.

Air
PEARSON INTERNATIONAL AIRPORT

Toronto's **Pearson International Airport** (YYZ, 6301 Silver Dart Dr., Mississauga, 416/247-7678 or 866/207-1690, www.torontopearson.com) is Canada's largest, with flights from across Canada, the United States, Europe, and Asia. The airport is 24 kilometers (15 miles) northwest of downtown in the suburb of Mississauga. Most major Canadian and U.S. carriers and many international airlines fly into Toronto.

Pearson Airport has two terminals, Terminal 1 and Terminal 3. Check with your airline or the airport website to confirm which terminal you need. The free **Terminal Link**

Train runs between the two terminals and to Viscount Station, where some rental car shuttles pick up customers and where the ALT Hotel Toronto Airport is located.

The fastest way to travel between Pearson Airport and downtown is to ride the **Union-Pearson Express** (www.upexpress.com, 5:30am-1am daily, one-way adults and ages 13-19 $12.35, seniors $6.20, ages 12 and under free, families $25.70), a rail link between Union Station and Pearson Airport, with stations at Terminal 1, the Weston and Bloor GO stations, and at Toronto's Union Station. Travel time is about 25 minutes.

Regular public transit services can also take you between downtown and the airport; it's slower but cheaper than the Union-Pearson Express. From the airport, catch the **no. 192 Airport Rocket bus** ($3.25) to the subway. It runs to Kipling station, on the Bloor-Danforth line, which goes from west to east across the city. Get a transfer on the bus, so you don't have to pay another fare to board the subway. The first no. 192 bus leaves the airport at about 5:30am Monday-Saturday and at 7:30am Sunday; the last departure from the airport is at 2am. Service runs every 10 to 20 minutes.

You need exact change to pay your fare on the bus. You can also purchase a single-fare ticket from a **TTC ticket machine** inside Terminal 1, on the Ground Transportation level, just inside from where the TTC buses stop. The machines accept cash or credit cards. Once you're on the subway, you'll need to transfer again from the Bloor-Danforth line if you're headed to the Union Station area, the Harbourfront, or other points downtown. Get off at St. George Station, and change to the Yonge-University-Spadina line heading southbound.

Between 2am and 5am, when the no. 192 Airport Rocket isn't running, you can take the **no. 300A Bloor-Danforth bus** ($3.25), which operates from the airport into the city along Bloor Street and Danforth Avenue, essentially following the route of the Bloor-Danforth subway line. Buses run about every 30 minutes.

A taxi from Pearson Airport to downtown Toronto is a flat rate of $45-70, according to your destination, and generally takes 45-60 minutes, depending on traffic conditions. Ride-sharing services Uber and Lyft can also pick you up at Pearson Airport.

TORONTO CITY AIRPORT
Toronto has a second, smaller airport on the Toronto Islands, **Billy Bishop Toronto City Airport** (YTZ, www.billybishopairport.com). **Porter Airlines** (416/619-8622 or 888/619-8622, www.flyporter.com) is the main carrier serving this airport. Porter flies from Toronto to the Ontario cities of Ottawa, Windsor, Sudbury, Sault Ste. Marie, Timmins, and Thunder Bay. It also flies to Montreal, Quebec City, Halifax, Fredericton, Moncton, and St. John in Canada and to Boston, Chicago, Newark, and Washington Dulles in the United States. **Air Canada** (514/393-3333 or 888/247-2262, www.aircanada.com) flies from Toronto City Airport to Montreal.

For an airport on an island, Toronto City Airport is surprisingly easy to get to, in part because it's so close to downtown. You can walk through an underground **pedestrian tunnel** between the airport and the mainland, or hop on the **free ferry** (5:30am-midnight daily, every 15 minutes) between the airport and the foot of Bathurst Street. One of the world's shortest ferry routes, the crossing takes only a few minutes. Once you're on the mainland, you can take Porter Airlines' free **shuttle bus** downtown, which departs approximately every 15 minutes. The downtown shuttle stop is on the west side of the Fairmont Royal York Hotel (York St. at Front St. W.), opposite Union Station. Alternatively, you can catch the no. 509 streetcar to Union Station or the no. 511 streetcar to the Bathurst subway station.

BUFFALO-NIAGARA INTERNATIONAL AIRPORT
If you're traveling to Toronto from the United States, you may find lower fares to **Buffalo-Niagara International Airport** (BUF, 4200 Genesee St., Buffalo, NY, 716/630-6000 or 877/359-2642, www.buffaloairport.com). Flying into Buffalo can also be convenient if you're planning to visit the Niagara region as part of your trip, since you can stop in Niagara between Toronto and Buffalo.

The cheapest way to travel between Toronto and the Buffalo airport is by bus. **Megabus** (705/748-6411 or 866/488-4452, www.megabus.com, 3-3.5 hours, $15-25) operates several buses a day in each direction. **Greyhound** (www.greyhound.ca, 3.75-4.75 hours, $14-25) also runs several times a day between Toronto and Buffalo airport, with a 30-minute layover in downtown Buffalo. Several other shuttle and limo services operate between Toronto and Buffalo airport; check the Buffalo airport website for a complete list.

Train
Toronto's rail depot is **Union Station** (65 Front St. W., www.toronto.ca/union_station) downtown. VIA Rail, Amtrak, and GO

Transit trains all run to Union Station, which is also a stop on the Toronto subway (Yonge-University-Spadina line).

VIA RAIL

Toronto is a hub for **VIA Rail** (888/842-7245, www.viarail.ca) trains that travel across Canada. Trains from the east travel to Toronto from Ottawa, Kingston, and Montreal; you can connect in Montreal for Quebec City, Moncton, and Halifax. Trains traveling west go to Winnipeg, Saskatoon, Edmonton, Jasper, and Vancouver. Shorter routes within Ontario operate between Windsor, London, and Toronto; between Sarnia, London, and Toronto; and between Niagara Falls and Toronto.

From Montreal to Toronto (5-5.25 hours, one-way economy adults $51-250, ages 2-11 $25-125), VIA Rail runs six trains a day in each direction Monday-Friday and five on Saturday and Sunday. From Ottawa to Toronto (4.25-4.75 hours, one-way economy adults $50-243, ages 2-11 $25-122), ten trains run in each direction Monday-Friday, seven on Saturday, and eight on Sunday. Most Montreal and Ottawa trains stop at Kingston en route to Toronto. There are several daily trains between Windsor and Toronto (4-4.5 hours, one-way economy adult $50-178, ages 2-11 $25-89) and one a day between Sarnia and Toronto (4.75 hours, one-way economy adults $44-158, ages 2-11 $23-79). Both the Windsor and Sarnia trains travel via London. VIA Rail runs one train daily in each direction between Toronto and Niagara Falls (2 hours, one-way adults $25-77, ages 2-11 $13-39).

VIA's flagship route, **The Canadian,** crosses Canada from Vancouver to Toronto via Jasper, Edmonton, Saskatoon, and Winnipeg. If you do the trip nonstop, it takes 3.5 days. There are departures three times a week in each direction May through mid-October and twice a week the rest of the year. Fares vary by class of service; choose from options that include a seat, a bunk, or a private cabin. Within Ontario, you can catch the Canadian to Toronto from Sudbury, although the train stops in that community in the middle of the night.

AMTRAK

The Amtrak **Maple Leaf** (800/872-7245, www.amtrak.com, 12.5 hours, adults $121-153, ages 2-12 $61-92) travels from New York City's Penn Station to Toronto's Union Station (65 Front St. W.). The train runs once a day, with major stops at Poughkeepsie, Albany, Syracuse, Rochester, Buffalo, Niagara Falls (New York), Niagara Falls (Ontario), St. Catharines, and Oakville en route to Toronto.

If you're coming from Detroit, you can cross the border to Windsor and catch the VIA Rail train from there. From Chicago and U.S. points farther west, there's no direct rail service to Toronto. You can either take the Amtrak **Wolverine** train from Chicago to Detroit (6.5 hours), where you can cross the border and transfer to VIA Rail; or take Amtrak's **Lake Shore Limited** from Chicago to Buffalo (10.5 hours). From Buffalo, change to the **Maple Leaf** or catch a bus on to Toronto. On any of these routings, be prepared for long layovers.

GO TRAINS

GO Transit (416/869-3200 or 888/438-6646, www.gotransit.com) operates a network of trains and buses that travel between the suburbs and surrounding communities and Toronto's city center. It's primarily a commuter option, so most schedules are optimized for business days, with lots of service into Toronto in the mornings and out of the city in the evenings, and less frequent service midday and on the weekend. GO Trains link Toronto with Oakville, Burlington, Hamilton, Milton, Brampton, Georgetown, Barrie, Richmond Hill, Markham, Lincolnville, and Oshawa. GO also provides seasonal service to Niagara Falls, running weekends and holidays from late May through mid-October.

Bus

The **Toronto Coach Terminal** (610 Bay St., 416/393-7911) is the city's main long-distance bus depot, located one block north of the corner of Dundas and Bay. The closest subway station is Dundas, two blocks east. You can also take the no. 505 Dundas streetcar to Bay Street.

GREYHOUND

Greyhound (800/661-8747, www.greyhound.ca) reaches Toronto from many Canadian and U.S. cities, although many routes involve a change of buses along the way. Greyhound runs frequent buses between Toronto and Ottawa (5.25-6 hours, one-way adults $38-89, ages 2-11 $31-68); from Montreal (8.25-9.5 hours), passengers change in Ottawa; from Quebec City (Sainte-Foy), transfers are in both Montreal and Ottawa. From the west, Greyhound reaches Toronto from Calgary (52 hours) and Winnipeg (32 hours), stopping in Thunder Bay, Sault Ste. Marie, and Sudbury en route. From Vancouver, passengers change buses in Calgary; from Edmonton, transfer in Calgary or Winnipeg.

From the United States, Greyhound runs buses to Toronto from New York City (10.5-13.15 hours, one-way adults $47-107, ages 2-11 $38-86), with stops in Syracuse and Buffalo. To Toronto from Boston (14.5-18.25 hours), transfer in Buffalo or Syracuse; from Philadelphia (14-17.75 hours), changes buses in New York City. Greyhound has several daily buses to Toronto from Detroit (5.75-7.75 hours), with stops in Windsor and London, and three a day from Chicago (12-13 hours).

ONTARIO NORTHLAND

Ontario Northland (800/461-8558, www.ontarionorthland.ca) runs buses between Toronto and Northeastern Ontario, including the Muskoka Lakes, Parry Sound, Sudbury, Temagami, and Cochrane.

MEGABUS

Megabus (705/748-6411 or 866/488-4452, www.megabus.com) has some of the best fares to Toronto from Niagara Falls (1.75-2.5 hours, one-way $16-24), Kingston (2.75-3 hours, one-way $22-66), Montreal (6 hours, one-way $22-59), New York City (11.5-12.25 hours, one-way $35-99), Syracuse (6.5 hours, one-way $10-75), Washington DC (14.5 hours, one-way $35-109), Baltimore (13.5 hours, one-way $35-109), and Philadelphia (11.75 hours, one-way $30-99). On some routes, one-way sale fares may drop as low as $1, so check the website for deals, particularly if you have flexible travel dates.

GO BUSES

In addition to a commuter train network, **GO Transit** (416/869-3200 or 888/438-6646, www.gotransit.com) runs buses between surrounding communities and downtown Toronto. GO Transit buses arrive and depart from the **Union Station GO Bus Terminal** (141 Bay St., at Front St. W.), not from the Toronto Coach Terminal. Among the main GO Toronto services are bus routes from Niagara Falls, St. Catharines, Hamilton, Kitchener, Waterloo, Cambridge, Guelph, Orangeville, Barrie, and Peterborough.

Car

Toronto is 450 kilometers (280 miles) from Ottawa, 558 kilometers (349 miles) from Montreal, 2,115 kilometers (1,322 miles) from Winnipeg, 1,926 kilometers (1,204 miles) from Halifax, and a long-haul 4,550 kilometers (2,844 miles) from Vancouver.

Several major highways run in and around the Toronto area. The **Gardiner Expressway** follows the lakeshore into downtown. West of the city, it connects with Queen Elizabeth Way (known as the QEW), which despite its noble-sounding name is a traffic-clogged multilane highway that continues around Lake Ontario to Hamilton and the Niagara region. East of downtown, the Gardiner meets the Don Valley Parkway, a main route from the eastern and northeastern suburbs. **Highway 401** crosses the region north of Toronto proper. It's the main east-west route across Southern Ontario, extending east to Quebec and west to Windsor. **Highway 407** (www.407etr.com), an electronic toll highway, parallels Highway 401 farther north. Tolls are charged automatically by distance and time of travel; the end-to-end charge is $33-50. Even if you've driven from out of the province, or from the United States, your license plate information will be recorded and you'll receive a bill. Note, though, that most rental car companies do not allow you to drive their cars on the 407.

FROM THE UNITED STATES

From the United States, Toronto is 160 kilometers (100 miles) from Buffalo, New York; 808 kilometers (505 miles) from New York City; 906 kilometers (566 miles) from Boston; 378 kilometers (236 miles) from Detroit; and 854 kilometers (534 miles) from Chicago. The nearest highway border crossings from the United States are at the Peace, Rainbow, Whirlpool, and Queenston-Lewiston Bridges near Niagara Falls; the Blue Water Bridge on Highway 402 and I-69/94 at Sarnia/Port Huron on the Michigan border; the Ambassador Bridge or the Detroit-Windsor Tunnel between Detroit and Windsor; or via the Thousand Islands Bridge east of Gananoque.

GETTING AROUND

Toronto is built on the shores of Lake Ontario. Beginning at the lake and heading north, downtown Toronto includes the Harbourfront, the Financial District, and a mix of residential and commercial neighborhoods. Downtown extends north to Bloor Street, a main east-west street that borders the University of Toronto campus. North of Bloor is Midtown, where you'll find many of Toronto's residential neighborhoods alternating with commercial developments.

Yonge Street, Toronto's main north-south artery, bisects the city, beginning at the lakeshore and continuing north well beyond the city limits. "East" addresses are east of Yonge; "west" addresses are west of Yonge. Pay careful attention to the "east" and "west" designators: 1200 Queen Street East would be in Leslieville in the city's far east end, while 1200 Queen Street West is eight kilometers (five miles) away on the city's west side.

Toronto has a comprehensive public transit system, including a subway, streetcars, and buses, so it's easy to get around the city without a car. The **Toronto Transit Commission** (TTC, 416/393-4636, www.ttc.ca) runs the transit network within the city. Use the online Trip Planner (www.ttc.ca) to figure out the best way to get from one point to another. The TTC website also has detailed maps of the streetcar and bus routes.

TRANSIT FARES AND PASSES

The fare structure is the same for TTC subways, streetcars, and buses. To pay cash for a single ride (adults $3.25, seniors and ages 13-19 $2.10, ages 12 and under free) in the subway stations, pay your fare (using cash, credit, or debit cards) at the ticket collector's booth. On buses or streetcars, pay your fare when you board; you will need exact change.

Toronto is phasing out the city's paper transit **tickets** and coin-like **tokens**, replacing them **Presto cards** (www.prestocard.ca), electronic shared value cards. With a Presto card, which is normally sold for $20, including a $6 deposit, transit fares are slightly discounted (adults $3, seniors and ages 13-19 $2.05), and you don't have to hunt for exact change before boarding a vehicle. Using a Presto card also gives you a discount on the Union-Pearson Express. You can purchase a Presto card online (and have it mailed to you), or buy it at the Gateway newsstands in most Toronto subway stations. Once you have a card, reload it online or at the subway stations' self-service Presto machines.

Subway

The Toronto subway has four lines: two main lines that are most useful to visitors and two shorter "spur" lines that extend service into the suburbs. The two main lines are the **Bloor-Danforth line,** which runs east-west across the city, following Bloor Street and Danforth Avenue, and the

Toronto's extensive streetcar network can take you across the city.

Yonge-University-Spadina line, which runs on a roughly U-shaped route. From its southernmost point at Union Station, a section of the Yonge-University-Spadina route runs north along Yonge Street to Finch station in North Toronto. The other section follows University Avenue in the downtown area, and then continues northwest to Vaughan Metropolitan Centre, in the Toronto suburbs. You can transfer free of charge between the two lines at Spadina, St. George, and Bloor-Yonge station.

The subway operates 6am-1:30am Monday-Saturday and 8am-1:30am Sunday. Trains generally run every few minutes, slightly less often late at night and on Sunday.

Streetcar

The TTC operates a network of streetcars that run along major streets downtown and beyond. Most streetcars run 24 hours a day. Among the more useful routes for visitors are:

- **No. 501 Queen:** The system's longest route travels along Queen Street from the West End through downtown to Leslieville and the Beaches.

- **No. 504 King:** Operates from Dundas West station along Roncesvalles Avenue in the West End, along King Street through downtown, continuing east past the Distillery District, then turning north along Broadview Avenue, and connecting to the Bloor-Danforth subway at Broadview station.

- **No. 505 Dundas:** Travels east-west along Dundas Street.

- **No. 506 Carlton:** From High Park in the West End, runs along College Street, Carlton Street, and Gerrard Street, and connects to Main Street station on the Bloor-Danforth subway line.

- **No. 509 Harbourfront:** Travels between Union Station and Exhibition Place, passing Harbourfront Centre and Fort York en route.

- **No. 510 Spadina:** Runs between Spadina station (on both the Bloor-Danforth and Yonge-University-Spadina subway lines) and Union Station, via Spadina Avenue and Queen's Quay along the harbor.

Between 1:30am and 5am, the **Blue Night Network,** an overnight bus service, operates along some streetcar routes. Stops are marked with a blue band, and service runs at least every 30 minutes. Blue Night service runs along the Queen, King, Carlton, and Spadina streetcar routes as the no. 301 Queen, no. 304 King, no. 306 Carlton, and no. 310 Spadina.

Bus

In downtown Toronto, you can reach most places by subway or streetcar. As you venture farther from the city center, buses become more convenient. To figure out if buses travel to your destination, enter your starting and ending point into the **TTC's online Trip Planner** (www.ttc.ca). The TTC website also maps all the bus routes in the city. Buses typically run 6am-1am Monday-Saturday and

8am-1am Sunday. Between 9pm and 5am, anyone traveling alone on Toronto city buses can ask to be let off between stops, so you don't have to walk as far to your destination.

From 1:30am to 5am, the overnight **Blue Night Network** runs buses along the Bloor-Danforth and Yonge subway routes. The no. 300 Bloor-Danforth bus operates along Bloor Street and Danforth Avenue between Pearson Airport to Victoria Park Avenue, while the no. 320 Yonge bus follows Yonge Street from Union Station north to Steeles Avenue. Blue Night buses also run along many regular bus routes. Stops are marked with a blue band, and service runs at least every 30 minutes. The **TTC website** (www.ttc.ca) has maps and schedules of all Blue Night buses.

The PATH Network

Underneath downtown Toronto, the **PATH** (www.torontopath.com) is a 30-kilometer (19-mile) network of interconnected underground walkways. You can walk from building to building, protected from the weather. You'll often find more stores and services underground along the PATH walkways than you will at street level; in fact, the PATH is the largest underground shopping complex in the world. The PATH extends from Union Station north to City Hall, Eaton Centre, and the Toronto Coach Terminal, bounded roughly by Yonge Street to the east and University Avenue to the west, with a couple of spurs continuing west into the Entertainment District. Multicolored directional signs mark the walkways.

Following the PATH can be confusing for newcomers, because you don't have the landmarks you see at street level. Many signs direct you to particular buildings, rather than streets, and you may not know whether you want to go, for example, toward the Canadian Pacific Tower or First Canadian Place. Use the online PATH map to help you get oriented.

Taxi and Ride-Sharing Services

Except for the flat-rate fares from Pearson Airport, Toronto taxis are metered, so make sure the driver uses the meter. Rates start with an initial $4.25 charge, with an additional charge of $1.75 for every kilometer traveled. Short trips around the downtown area can cost $10-15. You can hail taxis on the street, although it's often easier to find them in front of hotels, train or bus stations, shopping centers, and attractions such as museums. Call **416/TAXICAB** (416/829-4222, www.416-taxicab.com) from anywhere in Toronto and you'll be connected to local taxi services. Both **Uber** and **Lyft** operate in Toronto.

Car

Unless you plan to explore the suburbs or take day trips out of town, it's easier to get around Toronto without a car. Traffic can be heavy, with rush hours extending at least 7am-9am and 4pm-6pm Monday-Friday. Many downtown streets are one-way, and turns, both left and right, are often restricted from major arteries. While right turns are allowed at red lights in Ontario, they're often prohibited in downtown Toronto; look for signs at the intersection.

Drivers must yield to streetcars. When a streetcar stops, the cars behind it must stop at least two meters (six feet) behind and wait for passengers to board or unload.

PARKING

There's metered on-street parking throughout Toronto, but the rate varies by location ($1.50-4 per hour), so be sure to check the meter or ticket dispenser. Some streets have single-space meters that take coins only. Others have ticket dispensers that take either coins or credit cards and give you a ticket to put on your car's dashboard. The city also operates 160 parking lots containing about 20,000 spaces. The **Toronto Parking Authority** (www.greenp.com) has a useful parking lot finder that shows the location and rates at all municipal parking lots. When booking a hotel reservation, ask about the cost and availability of parking if you're planning to bring a car. Daily parking charges can add significantly to your costs.

CAR RENTALS

All the major North American car rental companies have outlets at Toronto's **Pearson Airport** (YYZ, 6301 Silver Dart Dr., Mississauga, 416/247-7678 or 866/207-1690, www.torontopearson.com), and most have offices downtown as well:

- **Alamo** (877/222-9075, www.alamo.ca)

- **Avis** (800/879-2847, www.avis.ca)

- **Budget** (800/268-8900, www.budget.ca)

- **Dollar** (800/848-8268, www.dollarcanada. ca)

- **Enterprise** (800/261-7331, www.enterprise rentacar.ca)

- **Hertz** (800/654-3131, www.hertz.ca)

- **National** (877/222-9058, www.nationalcar. ca)

- **Thrifty** (800/847-4389, www.thrifty.com)

A number of smaller car rental agencies have offices near Pearson Airport, and it's worth checking to see if their rates are lower than the major companies. They provide shuttles to their locations from the terminals or from the airport's Viscount Station, which you can reach on the free **Terminal Link Train** from either Terminal 1 or Terminal 3.

- **Advantage Car Rentals** (905/w38-3432882, www.advantagecarrentals.com)

- **Discount Car Rentals** (416/249-5554, www.discountcar.com)

- **Payless Car Rental** (416/416-863-8444, www.paylesscar.com)

- **Zoom Rent-A-Car** (416/222-4473, www. zoomrentals.com)

Note that most rental-car companies do not allow you to drive on Highway 407; if you do, they'll charge you a premium over the basic toll charges.

Tours
WALKING TOURS

One of the best ways to get to know a city is to meet local residents. **Toronto Greeters** (aka TAP into TO!, 416/338-2786, www.toronto. ca/tapto, year-round, free) offers free two- to three-hour tours of a Toronto neighborhood led by a local "greeter," an enthusiastic resident and volunteer tour guide. Choose which neighborhood to visit and note whether you have a specific interest (such as architecture or food), or let the greeter select a favorite area. Request a greeter at least a week in advance; sign up or get more information on the program website.

Heritage Toronto Walks (416/338-0684, www.heritagetoronto.org, May-Oct.) are free walking tours that highlight a neighborhood's history, whether architectural, cultural, archaeological, or natural. Check their online schedule for walk times and locations.

Urban Adventures (800/691-9320, www. urbanadventures.com) offers several different walking tours, including "Beer Makes History Better" (4 hours, $48), which combines a walking tour through the St. Lawrence Market and Distillery District with stops at several pubs for a brew; a tour of Kensington Market and Chinatown (2 hours, $37); and When Pigs Fry (3 hours, $76), where you'll learn why Toronto is nicknamed "Hogtown" and taste bacon, sausage, and other pork snacks along the way.

The Urban Adventures guides also run free walking tours as **The Tour Guys** (647/230-7891, www.tourguys.ca), including several different 90-minute guided walks downtown. Although there's no charge for these tours, you're encouraged to tip your guide. One popular excursion is their "Graffiti Tour," a walk through the street art hubs of Graffiti Alley and the side streets off Queen Street West. Check their website for a current schedule.

On an **Urban Quest** (www.urbanquest. com, year-round, $10), you solve a series of clues that lead you from place to place around town. Typically lasting around 1.5 hours, the quests end at a mystery restaurant where you can have lunch or dinner (not included in the quest fee). You can do a quest with any number of people, but most are designed for two to four.

The Royal Ontario Museum runs **ROM Walks** (416/586-8097, www.rom.on.cas, usually 2pm Sun. and 6pm Wed. May-Oct., free), guided walks that highlight the history and architecture of particular neighborhoods. Check the website for the weekly schedule.

BOAT TOURS

Take a two-hour sail around Toronto Harbour on a traditional 50-meter (165-foot) three-masted schooner with the **Toronto Tall Ship Boat Cruises** (416/203-2322 or 800/267-3866, www.tallshipcruisestoronto.com, May-Sept., adults $31, seniors $27.50, ages 5-15 $17, ages 0-4 $3).

Want to see Toronto from a traditional voyageur canoe? **Canoe Toronto** (283 Queens Quay W., 416/993-4224, www.canoetoronto.com, May-Sept.) runs a 2.5-hour Toronto Islands paddle ($49) with a stop on Centre Island. Canoes can accommodate 6-20 paddlers each.

The Niagara Region

Look for ★ to find recommended
sights, activities, dining, and lodging.

Highlights

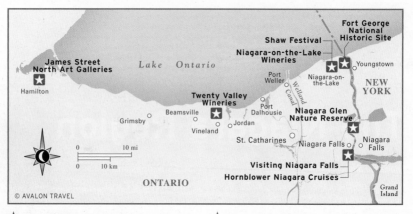

© AVALON TRAVEL

★ **Visiting Niagara Falls:** No matter how many times you've seen these thundering water-falls—the Horseshoe Falls on the Ontario side of the Niagara River and the American Falls on the New York banks—they're still spectacular (page 107).

★ **Hornblower Niagara Cruises:** Since the 1840s, ferryboats have taken visitors to the base of the falls, so put on your rain poncho and climb aboard. A cruise with these modern ships is still the best way to hear the crashing waters and feel the spray (page 108).

★ **Niagara Glen Nature Reserve:** The window-lined Nature Centre at this park north of the falls has great views of the Niagara River Gorge. Take a guided hike through the reserve or hit the trails on your own (page 112).

★ **Shaw Festival:** From April through October, the town of Niagara-on-the-Lake hosts one of North America's major theater festivals, devoted to the works of Irish playwright George Bernard Shaw, along with more contemporary plays (page 127).

★ **Niagara-on-the-Lake Wineries:** With more than two dozen wineries clustered in this small region, you can easily stop at many producers—and sample many varieties—in a short visit (page 129).

★ **Fort George National Historic Site:** An important battleground during the War of 1812, this restored fort overlooking the Niagara River is now a national historic site. Learn about the Niagara region's early history and watch staff demonstrate traditional weaponry, cook on an open hearth, and perform fife and drum music (page 133).

★ **Twenty Valley Wineries:** This growing viticultural district, encompassing the towns of Beamsville, Vineland, and Jordan, produces ice wine, Ontario's distinctive dessert wine, as well as other varietals (page 139).

★ **James Street North Art Galleries:** En route to or from the Niagara region, stop off in the edgy, arty city of Hamilton to browse its local art scene (page 146).

Niagara Falls, an easy drive south of Toronto or across the border from New York State, is one of the most-visited destinations in Canada. Families, honeymooners, tour groups, and everyone in between make their way to this iconic attraction. Whether it's your first falls visit or your 50th, feeling the spray on your face, watching the cascading curtains tumble and crash into the river below, or glimpsing a rainbow arching over the torrents is still a thrill.

Yet Niagara is more than just the falls. Beyond the town of Niagara Falls, with its quirky mix of stunning natural beauty and honky-tonk tourist lures, the Niagara region offers plenty of attractions. The Niagara Peninsula is Ontario's major wine-producing region, and a prime destination for a wine country getaway. Wine-tasting lures visitors to Niagara-on-the-Lake, home to more than two dozen wineries, and to the Twenty Valley, a popular wine-touring day trip from Niagara Falls. Niagara-on-the-Lake is also home to one of North America's premier theater festivals—the Shaw Festival, which produces works by noted Irish playwright George Bernard Shaw along with more contemporary playwrights.

Built in the 1820s, the Welland Canal provides a shipping route between the Great Lakes, from St. Catharines south to Port Colborne. Freighters, barges, and pleasure craft continue to navigate the canal's eight locks, and you can watch megaships up close as they lock through.

Outdoors lovers can explore an extensive network of cycling paths that crisscrosses the Niagara Peninsula, or set out on the Bruce Trail, an 800-kilometer (500-mile) hiking route that extends to the tip of the Bruce Peninsula. History lovers will find numerous historic sites that date to the War of 1812. A worthy detour on your way to or from Niagara is Hamilton, an edgy, up-and-coming city known for its art scene and inventive restaurants.

PLANNING YOUR TIME

You can easily visit Niagara Falls on a day trip from Toronto or upstate New York, but there's

---

Previous: rainbow over Niagara Falls; Horseshoe Falls. **Above:** Ten Thousand Buddhas Sarira Stupa.

The Niagara Region

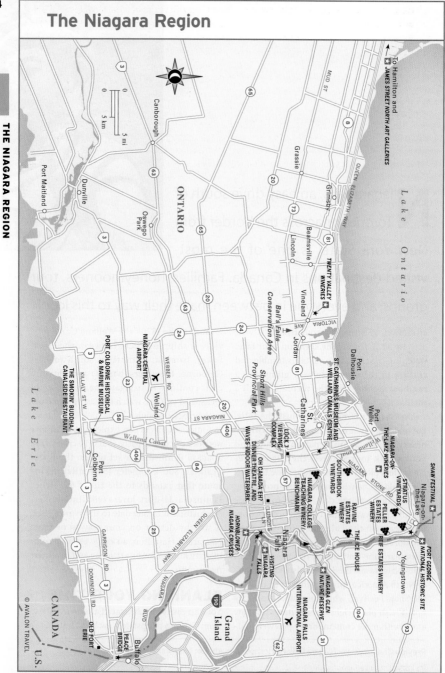

To Hamilton and
JAMES STREET NORTH ART GALLERIES

ONTARIO

Lake Ontario

Lake Erie

CANADA
U.S.

© AVALON TRAVEL

plenty to do on the Niagara Peninsula to occupy a long weekend. Plan a day at Niagara Falls, another day in Niagara-on-the-Lake, and at least part of a third touring the Twenty Valley Wine Country.

Summer is Niagara's peak season. From late June through early September, everything is open, and most attractions keep long hours, from 9am until at least 7pm-8pm. The Shaw Festival kicks off with preview productions in April, then ramps up its schedule June through September, continuing through October.

Weekends are busiest in both Niagara Falls and Niagara-on-the-Lake, especially in summer and early fall, so you'll find more accommodations options (and often lower prices) if you can visit midweek. Many Niagara Falls attractions open for the season in April or May and close in late October or early November. Visiting the falls during the spring or fall "shoulder" periods outside the June-August peak can mean fewer crowds. September and October are harvest season for the region's vineyards, making it a popular wine-touring time. The falls themselves are, obviously, there year-round, and you can save significantly on accommodations by visiting midwinter, when far fewer tourists are around. Just prepare for snow and cold temperatures.

Whenever you visit, check attractions' opening hours before you set out, because many Niagara-area sights change their hours with the seasons.

Niagara Falls

The city of Niagara Falls is home to about 88,000 people and hosts more than 12 million visitors every year—all because of the spectacular torrents of water that cascade down the Niagara River. Long popular as a honeymoon destination, Niagara Falls has plenty of appeal for everyone from kids to seniors.

The Niagara River connects two of the Great Lakes—Lake Ontario and Lake Erie—and also separates Canada from the United States. That means that there are actually two cities named Niagara Falls—one in Ontario, the other across the river in New York State—and two main waterfalls: Horseshoe Falls on the Canadian side and American Falls on the New York side. The Ontario side of the river is more developed, with numerous attractions in addition to the falls, mixing history, green space, and, unfortunately, plenty of tacky tourist traps.

The area along the Niagara River closest to Horseshoe Falls is known as **Table Rock,** where a large visitors center houses several attractions. The **Fallsview** area, with its skyscraping hotels, is atop the Niagara Escarpment, a steep climb up the hill above Table Rock.

To the north of Table Rock along the river is **Queen Victoria Park** and the departure point for **Hornblower Niagara Cruises,** a deservedly popular boat ride that takes you under the falls. Up the slope north of the Hornblower docks is **Clifton Hill,** with numerous places to stay, as well as the flashing neon of arcades, wax museums, and other kitschy attractions.

North along the river is the **Whirlpool** area, where the river makes a 90-degree turn. A number of parks and natural attractions are clustered between the Whirlpool and **Queenston,** a historic district 12 kilometers (7.5 miles) north of the falls. The **WEGO bus** runs along the Niagara Parkway to all the major attractions and has other routes to take you around the city of Niagara Falls.

Away from the river, Queen Street is the main business route through "downtown" Niagara Falls, although there's actually more development along Ferry Street and Lundy's Lane, which run east-west from the river across the city to the Queen Elizabeth Way

Niagara Falls

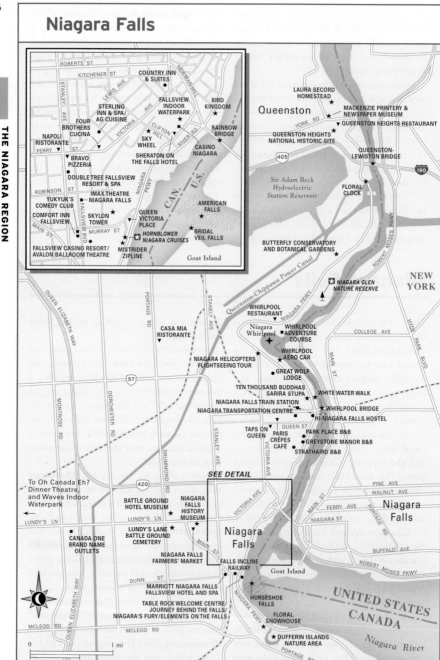

ROBERTS ST
KITCHENER ST
LEWIS AVE
STANLEY AVE
NEWMAN HILL
COUNTRY INN & SUITES
FALLSVIEW INDOOR WATERPARK
BIRD KINGDOM
STERLING INN & SPA/ AG CUISINE
FOUR BROTHERS CUCINA
VICTORIA AVE
CLIFTON HILL
RIVER RD
RAINBOW BRIDGE
NAPOLI RISTORANTE
FERRY
SKY WHEEL
CASINO NIAGARA
BRAVO PIZZERIA
SHERATON ON THE FALLS HOTEL
ROBINSON ST
DOUBLE TREE FALLSVIEW RESORT & SPA
NIAGARA PKWY
CAN.
U.S.
AMERICAN FALLS
YUKYUK'S COMEDY CLUB
IMAX THEATRE NIAGARA FALLS
FALLSVIEW BLVD
SKYLON TOWER
QUEEN VICTORIA PLACE
COMFORT INN FALLSVIEW
MAIN ST
MURRAY ST
HORNBLOWER NIAGARA CRUISES
BRIDAL VEIL FALLS
FALLSVIEW CASINO RESORT/ AVALON BALLROOM THEATRE
MISTRIDER ZIPLINE
Goat Island

LAURA SECORD HOMESTEAD
MACKENZIE PRINTERY & NEWSPAPER MUSEUM
Queenston
YORK RD
QUEENSTON HEIGHTS RESTAURANT
QUEENSTON HEIGHTS NATIONAL HISTORIC SITE
405
QUEENSTON-LEWISTON BRIDGE
190
Sir Adam Beck Hydroelectric Station Reservoir
FLORAL CLOCK
NEW YORK
BUTTERFLY CONSERVATORY AND BOTANICAL GARDENS
NIAGARA GLEN NATURE RESERVE
Queenston-Chippawa Power Canal
WHIRLPOOL RESTAURANT
QUEEN ELIZABETH WAY
PORTAGE RD
STANLEY AVE
CASA MIA RISTORANTE
Niagara Whirlpool
WHIRLPOOL ADVENTURE COURSE
NIAGARA PKWY
COLLEGE AVE
HYDE PARK BLVD
WHIRLPOOL AERO CAR
57
NIAGARA HELICOPTERS FLIGHTSEEING TOUR
GREAT WOLF LODGE
TEN THOUSAND BUDDHAS SARIRA STUPA
WHITE WATER WALK
MAIN ST
DORCHESTER RD
NIAGARA FALLS TRAIN STATION
NIAGARA TRANSPORTATION CENTRE
WHIRLPOOL BRIDGE
HI-NIAGARA FALLS HOSTEL
TAPS ON QUEEN
QUEEN ST
PARK PLACE B&B
MONTROSE RD
DRUMMOND RD
PARIS CRÊPES CAFÉ
VICTORIA AVE
GREYSTONE MANOR B&B
STRATHAIRD B&B
SEE DETAIL
420
PINE AVE
WALNUT AVE
To Oh Canada Eh? Dinner Theatre, and Waves Indoor Waterpark
BATTLE GROUND HOTEL MUSEUM
NIAGARA FALLS HISTORY MUSEUM
FERRY AVE
MAIN ST
Niagara Falls
LUNDY'S LN
LUNDY'S LN
NIAGARA ST
PORTAGE RD
CANADA ONE BRAND NAME OUTLETS
LUNDY'S LANE BATTLE GROUND CEMETERY
MAIN ST
Niagara Falls
BUFFALO AVE
DUNN ST
NIAGARA FALLS FARMERS' MARKET
FALLS INCLINE RAILWAY
Goat Island
ROBERT MOSES PKWY
MARRIOTT NIAGARA FALLS FALLSVIEW HOTEL AND SPA
UNITED STATES
TABLE ROCK WELCOME CENTRE/ JOURNEY BEHIND THE FALLS/ NIAGARA'S FURY/ELEMENTS ON THE FALLS
HORSESHOE FALLS
FLORAL SHOWHOUSE
CANADA
Niagara River
MCLEOD RD
MCLEOD RD
DUFFERIN ISLANDS NATURE AREA
PORTAGE RD
To Old Fort Erie

0   1 mi
0   1 km

© AVALON TRAVEL

Two Days in Niagara

DAY 1

Start your Niagara Falls visit with a walk past **Horseshoe Falls**, close enough that you can feel the spray. **Journey Behind the Falls** gives you another up-close perspective of the rushing water; on some summer Sundays, you can even do yoga beside the falls. Another highlight is a **Hornblower Niagara Cruise** that takes you past the American Falls and into the Horseshoe Falls basin. Keep your camera handy.

Head to downtown Niagara for lunch, perhaps a savory crepe at **Paris Crêpes Café**. Then catch the WEGO bus north along the river to ride the historic **Whirlpool Aero Car** above the Niagara gorge, take a hike at the **Niagara Glen Nature Reserve**, or walk through the **Niagara Parks Botanical Gardens** and visit the **Butterfly Conservatory**.

Stop off at the small but modern **Niagara Falls History Museum** to learn more about the region's past, including the daredevils who've tried to cross the falls, and then go for a sunset spin on the **Sky Wheel** or simply walk past the falls again. Keep the romance going with the imaginative **AG Cuisine** or the classic Italian **Casa Mia Ristorante**.

DAY 2

In the morning, check out of your hotel and make your way to **Niagara-on-the-Lake**, detouring into Queenston to see the **Laura Secord Homestead** and other historical attractions, then tour the **Fort George National Historic Site**. Have an early lunch at a winery restaurant, perhaps **Peller Estates Winery Restaurant** or **Ravine Vineyard Bistro**, before setting off on a wine-tasting tour. Pause for a slice of pie at the **Pie Plate Bakery and Café** or a butter tart at **The Fruit Shack**.

If you're not too tired, rent a bike and pedal along the **Niagara River Recreation Trail** to enjoy the riverside views. Then settle into your hotel or B&B and freshen up before dinner at **Backhouse**, **Treadwell Farm-to-Table Cuisine**, or **Zees**.

Finish your busy day with a play at the **Shaw Festival**. If you need a treat before bed, it's an easy stroll from the theatre to **Il Gelato di Carlotta**.

(QEW), the highway that connects Toronto with the Niagara region.

★ VISITING NIAGARA FALLS

Niagara's falls aren't the world's tallest or widest falls, but they certainly rank among the most spectacular. The Niagara Falls began forming during the last ice age, more than 12,000 years ago, and they have actually moved 11 kilometers (7 miles) during that period. They originally began north of their present location, near the Niagara Glen.

The best free vantage point for viewing the falls is near the **Table Rock Welcome Centre** (6650 Niagara Pkwy., www.niagaraparks.com), adjacent to the Horseshoe Falls. Be prepared for spray to mist around you, even as you walk or stand nearby.

The larger **Horseshoe Falls,** often called the Canadian Falls (on the Ontario side of the Niagara River), are 670 meters (2,200 feet) wide and curve in a semicircular "horseshoe" from bank to bank. While the Horseshoe Falls measure only 57 meters (188 feet) from top to bottom, more than 168,000 cubic meters (44 million gallons) of water crash over the falls every minute during daylight hours.

On the New York shore, the **American Falls** have a gentler curve. In fact, unless you see them from above, they look like a straight curtain of water stretching 260 meters (850 feet) wide and 21 to 34 meters (70-110 feet) tall, depending on where you measure.

A third narrow waterfall, known as **Bridal Veil Falls,** almost looks like part of the

American Falls, since it's just beside it, separated from the American Falls by Luna Island. The Bridal Veil Falls measure 17 meters (56 feet) across.

★ Hornblower Niagara Cruises

Boat tours to the base of the falls have been running since the 1840s, when the *Maid of the Mist* ferry began operating as a sightseeing boat. Over the years, the *Maid* transported such notable passengers as Princess Diana and her sons, U.S. presidents Theodore Roosevelt and Jimmy Carter, Soviet president Mikhail Gorbachev, and actor Marilyn Monroe. **Hornblower Niagara Cruises** (5920 Niagara Pkwy., 905/642-4272 or 855/264-2427, www.niagaracruises.com, daily Apr.-Nov., check the website for seasonal schedules, adults $26, ages 5-12 $16) operates the tour routes from the Canadian side of the falls; they're still the best way to hear the thundering waters and feel the spray.

Departing every 15 minutes from 8am to dusk, the Hornblower catamarans, which accommodate up to 700 passengers, cruise past the American Falls and into the Horseshoe Falls basin. The ride lasts about 20 minutes, and yes, despite the free rain ponchos, you will get wet, but you'll want to get as close as you can to the falls views. Hornblower also offers 40-minute Falls Illumination tours and Fireworks tours (adults $40, ages 5-12 $36), on select dates, departing at 8:30pm (early Sept.-Oct.) or 9:30pm (May-early Sept.), with a bar and music on board; they post schedules on their website and at their ticket office.

The *Maid of the Mist* still runs from the American side of the falls, leaving from Prospect Point in the **Niagara Reservation State Park** (716/284-8897, www.maidofthemist.com, adults US$19.25, ages 6-12 $11.20).

Journey Behind the Falls

The **Journey Behind the Falls** (Table Rock Welcome Centre, 6650 Niagara Pkwy., www.niagaraparks.com, daily year-round, check the website for seasonal schedules, adults $20, ages 6-12 $13 mid-Apr.-Dec., adults $13.15, ages 6-12 $11.55 Jan.-mid-Apr.) lets you see the waterfalls from a different perspective. You start your journey in an elevator that descends 45 meters (150 feet) through the rock beside the Horseshoe Falls. Then you walk through underground tunnels to two observation decks, where the falls crash beside you. The spray on the observation platforms can be drenching, so protect your camera gear, your guidebook, and anything else that you don't want waterlogged. Allow about 30 minutes to explore, longer if you're with kids who relish the falls' chilly shower.

Save this attraction for a warm day if you can; the spray can feel frigid. From January through mid-April, the lower observation deck, which gives you the best falls view, is closed (it's too icy), so admission prices are reduced.

Want to work on your downward dog beside the rush of the waterfall? On several summer Sunday mornings, Niagara Parks offers **Namaste Niagara** (www.niagaraparks.com, $50 pp), a 45-minute yoga session on the lower deck at Journey Behind the Falls, followed by breakfast at their Queenston Heights restaurant. Check their website or social media channels for dates and details.

Niagara's Fury

A two-part multimedia show, *Niagara's Fury* (Table Rock Welcome Centre, 6650 Niagara Pkwy., www.niagaraparks.com, daily year-round, check the website for seasonal schedules, adults $15, ages 6-12 $9.75) tries to explain how the falls were created, starting with a short cartoon. Then you move into a circular theater where lightning flashes, the earth shakes, and water pours from the ceiling as you "experience" the birth of the falls.

Older kids may think *Niagara's Fury* is cool, but the crashing thunder and shaking floor may frighten younger ones. Although the entire show lasts less than 20 minutes, give it a miss if you're short on time; the real falls are far more dramatic.

The American Side of the Falls

spring flowers at the American Falls

There are two cities named Niagara Falls—one on the Ontario side of the Niagara River and another on the opposite bank in New York State. On the New York side, the falls area is part of the **Niagara Reservation State Park** (716/278-1796, www.niagarafallsstatepark.com). You'll find the best views of the falls at **Prospect Point,** right next to the American Falls. The overall views of the American Falls are more majestic from the Canadian shore, but you're closer to the spray on the U.S. side. The historic *Maid of the Mist* tour boats (716/284-8897, www.maidofthemist.com, mid-May-early Nov., call or check the website for seasonal schedules, adults US$19.25, ages 6-12 US$11.20), which take you right under the falls, now operate only from Prospect Point.

If you want to feel the spray full in your face, head for **Goat Island,** where you can descend alongside Bridal Veil Falls on the **Cave of the Winds** (716/278-1730, www.niagarafallsstatepark. com, mid-May-late Oct., call or check the website for seasonal schedules, adults US$17, ages 6-12 US$14), which follows a wooden walkway to a platform just six meters (20 feet) from the falls. You'll receive a rain poncho, but you should still expect to get wet. You can learn more about the falls and their history at the multimedia **World Changed Here Pavilion** (year-round, call or check the website for seasonal hours, adults $7, ages 6-12 $5), which remains open when the Cave of the Winds tours are closed for the winter.

If you plan to visit several attractions on the American side, consider purchasing the **Niagara Falls USA Discovery Pass** (adults $46, ages 6-12 $35), valid June through late October, which covers discounted admission to the *Maid of the Mist,* Cave of the Winds, Aquarium of Niagara, and the Niagara Adventure Theater.

The **Rainbow Bridge** connects Niagara Falls, Ontario, with Niagara Falls, New York. You can cross the bridge by car, on foot, or by bike, but remember: Even if you're just strolling across for the afternoon, this is an international border and you need to *bring your passport.*

For more information, contact **Niagara USA Official Visitor Center** (10 Rainbow Blvd., Niagara Falls, NY, 716/285-8600 or 877/325-5787, www.niagarafallsusa.com, 8:30am-7pm daily June-mid-Sept., 8:30am-5pm daily mid-Sept.-May). *Moon Niagara Falls* (www.moon.com), by Joel A. Dombrowski, has lots more details about exploring the American side of the Falls.

MistRider Zipline

For a thrilling ride into the Niagara gorge, take a zip on the **MistRider Zipline to the Falls** (5920 Niagara Pkwy., 800/263-7073, www.wildplay.com/niagara-falls, mid-Apr.-late Nov., call or check the website for seasonal schedules, ages 7 and up $60 pp). You'll whiz past the American Falls, traveling 670 meters (2,200 feet) to land on the observation deck at the base of Horseshoe Falls. The launch site is on the riverbank 1.3 kilometers (.8 miles) north of Horseshoe Falls, near the Hornblower Cruises ticket office; it's on the WEGO bus route.

White Water Walk

As you go north of Horseshoe Falls, the Niagara River bucks and churns through a section known as the Whirlpool Rapids. Rated as Class VI white water—defined as "extremely difficult to successfully maneuver . . . usually considered unrunnable"—the rushing rapids slicing through the deep gorge are impressive, even from the shore, where the **White Water Walk** (4330 Niagara Pkwy., www.niagaraparks.com, daily mid-Apr.-Oct., check the website for seasonal schedules, adults $13, ages 6-12 $8.45) gives you an up-close look.

After taking an elevator 70 meters (230 feet) into the gorge and walking through a tunnel to the riverbank, you follow a 300-meter (0.25-mile) boardwalk along the Niagara River rapids. Stairs lead to two observation areas at the river's edge. A small exhibit area near the elevators profiles some of the daredevils who attempted various stunts on the Niagara River or over the falls—just don't try these tricks yourself. Not only is stunting extremely dangerous (only a few of the adventurers survived), it's now illegal, and trespassers can face hefty fines.

The White Water Walk is four kilometers (2.5 miles) north of Horseshoe Falls, on the WEGO bus route. You follow the walk at your own pace, but most people find that 30-45 minutes is enough time.

Whirlpool Aero Car

Over thousands of years, the Niagara River slowly eroded a path through the Niagara Escarpment, creating a deep canyon called the Great Gorge. North of the falls, as the river wends through the gorge, it makes a sharp right-angle turn, which forces the water into a counterclockwise spin. This unusual churning water formation, the Niagara River Whirlpool, is difficult to see from shore (without a long, steep hike), but it's easily visible from above, aboard the **Whirlpool Aero Car** (3850 Niagara Pkwy., www.niagaraparks.com, daily mid-Apr.-early Nov., check the website for seasonal schedules, adults $15, ages 6-12 $9.75).

The unusual-looking Aero Car, designed by Spanish engineer Leonardo Torres Quevedo, has been transporting passengers over the Whirlpool since 1916. You stand in the red cable car, which is attached to the overhead cables by a sunshine-yellow contraption that looks like half of a giant bicycle wheel. As you ride across the gorge and back, the views extend up and down the river.

The Aero Car is 4.5 kilometers (3 miles) north of Horseshoe Falls, on the WEGO bus route. Although the ride itself takes just 10 minutes round-trip, the Aero Car accommodates only 35 people and tickets are issued for specific times, so be prepared to wait.

Skylon Tower and Sky Wheel

For an aerial view of the falls, take the "yellow bug" elevators—they do resemble yellow beetles—that scoot up the outside of the **Skylon Tower** (5200 Robinson St., 905/356-2651 or 888/975-9566, www.skylon.com, 8am-midnight daily summer, 9am-10pm daily winter, adults $15.02, ages 3-12 $9.22) to the observation deck 236 meters (775 feet) in the sky. You can also buy a combination ticket that includes a show in the 3-D/4-D theater (adults $20.82, ages 3-12 $12.70). Tickets are discounted if you purchase them online in advance.

Yet another vantage point for viewing the falls is the 8- to 12-minute whirl on the

Sky Wheel (4950 Clifton Hill, 905/358-4793, www.skywheel.ca, year-round, call or check the website for seasonal hours, adults $12, ages 3-12 $7), a 53-meter (175-foot) Ferris wheel on which you ride in enclosed gondolas. The vistas of the American Falls are great; you see the Horseshoe Falls at a greater distance. The **Clifton Hill Fun Pass** (www.cliftonhill.com, adults $29.95, ages 3-12 $19.95), available online, includes admission to the Sky Wheel along with several other commercial attractions (Zombie Attack, anyone?).

SIGHTS
Museums

Lundy's Lane, which runs east-west across the city of Niagara Falls, was the site of a major battle between American and British troops in the War of 1812. Both sides suffered some of the heaviest casualties of the war during the Battle of Lundy's Lane on July 25, 1814. Neither side won the battle, but American troops withdrew south to Fort Erie, setting the scene for the Battle of Fort Erie later that summer.

Along Ferry Street and Lundy's Lane (Ferry changes its name west of Main St.), several sights help you learn more about Niagara's 19th-century history. In an 1874 stone building with a modern glass-walled addition, the **Niagara Falls History Museum** (5810 Ferry St., 905/358-5082, www.niagarafallshistorymuseum.ca, 10am-5pm Tues.-Sun., 10am-9pm Thurs., adults $5, ages 6-19 $4, free admission 5pm-9pm Thurs.) houses more than 25,000 artifacts relating to the region's past, with exhibits about the history of the falls, including the daredevils who've tried to cross them, and about the War of 1812. Additional exhibitions in the temporary gallery change several times a year. Kids can try on soldiers' uniforms or walk a tightrope over the "falls."

A short walk farther west, the **Lundy's Lane Battle Ground Cemetery** (6110 Lundy's Lane, www.niagarafalls historymuseum.ca), also known as the Drummond Hill Cemetery, is on the site where the Lundy's Lane battle was fought. The cemetery has a mix of historic and more recent graves, including a monument honoring Laura Secord, a Canadian heroine during the War of 1812 who is buried here. Pick up a guide to the cemetery at the Niagara Falls History Museum or online on the museum's website.

On the 30-minute guided tours of

the Sky Wheel

the **Battle Ground Hotel Museum** (6151 Lundy's Lane, 905/358-5082, www. niagarafallshistorymuseum.ca, 11am-5pm Fri.-Sun. late May-Aug., donation), a restored wood-frame tavern, you'll learn about life in Niagara Falls from the 1830s to the 1850s, when the falls were already a tourist attraction and travelers gathered in taverns such as this one. The museum also houses some artifacts from the War of 1812.

Ten Thousand Buddhas Sarira Stupa

One of Niagara's most incongruous sights might be the peaceful **Ten Thousand Buddhas Sarira Stupa** (4303 River Rd., 905/371-2678), also called the Cham Shan Buddhist Temple. Built in the 1990s, it looks as if it were transported directly from Asia. The seven-story pagoda houses Buddhist arts and artifacts (11am-4pm Sat., 10am-3pm Sun. June-mid-Oct.), while a smaller Buddhist temple (10am-5pm daily) is in an adjacent building. A walk around the property may help you recover your Zen state after Niagara's tourist frenzy.

★ Niagara Glen Nature Reserve

Some of the best views of the Niagara River and gorge are from the window-lined—and free—Nature Centre at the **Niagara Glen Nature Reserve** (3050 Niagara Pkwy., 905/354-6678, www.niagaraparks.com, daily year-round, free). Inside the **Nature Centre** (10am-5pm daily mid-Apr.-early Nov., free), a small exhibit area includes a Touch Table to explore rocks, fossils, and animal skulls found in the gorge, as well as displays about the area's flora and fauna.

The glen has about four kilometers (2.5 miles) of hiking trails that descend into the Niagara gorge. The **River Path** is a particularly scenic route that follows the Niagara River all the way to the Whirlpool. This trail has lots of steep climbs and descents, so Niagara Parks staff recommend allowing at least three hours round-trip. Pick up a trail map at the Nature Centre or get one online at www.niagaraparks.com.

Park naturalists lead one-hour guided hikes (11am and 2pm daily May-Aug., $7), where you learn more about the area's history, geology, plants, and wildlife as you explore the walking paths. Because some of the terrain is quite steep, these guided walks are best suited for adults and older children.

Niagara Glen is eight kilometers (five miles) north of Horseshoe Falls, on the WEGO bus route.

Butterfly Conservatory and Botanical Gardens

More than 2,000 butterflies flit around the **Butterfly Conservatory** (2405 Niagara Pkwy., 905/356-8119, www.niagaraparks.com, daily year-round, call or check the website for seasonal hours, adults $15, ages 6-12 $9.75), alighting on the tropical flowers and on visitors' arms and heads. Start your visit with a short video about butterflies and their habits, from which you learn, among other things, that butterflies smell with their antennae and taste with their feet. The family-friendly conservatory is a good choice for a chilly day, since inside it's warm year-round.

The Butterfly Conservatory is on the grounds of the **Niagara Parks Botanical Gardens** (2565 Niagara Pkwy., 905/356-8554, www.niagaraparks.com, dawn-dusk daily year-round, free, parking $5), a 40-hectare (100-acre) expanse of manicured grounds, ornamental flowers, and herb gardens, crisscrossed with walking paths. Among the flowering highlights are rhododendrons and irises, which typically peak in June, and roses that bloom from mid-June into September; check the website for a detailed bloom schedule.

The gardens and Butterfly Conservatory are nine kilometers (six miles) north of Horseshoe Falls, on the WEGO bus route, opposite the Niagara Glen Nature Reserve.

Floral Clock

As you're traveling along the Niagara Parkway between the falls and Queenston, stop to check the time at this 12-meter-wide (40-foot-wide) working **Floral Clock** (14004 Niagara Pkwy., www.niagaraparks.com, dawn-dusk daily, free), inlaid with more than 15,000 plants. Ontario Hydro, the regional power company, created this floral attraction in 1950. Its hour hand measures 4.5 meters (14.5 feet); the minute hand is 5.3 meters (17.5 feet). Niagara Parks staff change the clock's botanical design twice a year.

The Floral Clock is 11.5 kilometers (7 miles) north of Horseshoe Falls, on the WEGO bus route.

Bird Kingdom

Housed in a former corset factory, the world's largest free-flying indoor aviary, **Bird Kingdom** (5651 River Rd., 905/356-8888 or 866/994-0090, www.birdkingdom.ca, 9:30am-5pm daily, last admission 4:15pm, adults $18, ages 4-15 $14, parking $3 per hour), is fun for children, especially on a bad-weather day. In the small aviary, more than 40 species of tiny birds flit about, while in the main glass-walled sanctuary, nearly 400 birds representing approximately 80 species, including brilliant orange-red scarlet ibis, African royal starlings, and multicolored macaws, fly around you as you wander the paths. Ask at the admission desk or check online for the daily schedule of animal encounters and activities, from bat feeding to snake handling. Tickets are discounted if you buy them online in advance.

The Bird Kingdom is 2.5 kilometers (1.5 miles) north of the Horseshoe Falls, just north of the Rainbow Bridge.

ENTERTAINMENT AND SHOPPING
Nightlife

Jay Leno, Aretha Franklin, Olivia Newton-John, Sean Penn, and Ringo Starr have all performed at the 1,500-seat **Avalon Ballroom Theatre** (6380 Fallsview Blvd., 888/325-5788, www.fallsviewcasinoresort.com), in the Fallsview Casino Resort, which has a regular lineup of concerts, Broadway-style musicals, comedians, and other shows. Children under

age 19 are not permitted in the theater. Buy tickets through the theater box office or from **Ticketmaster** (www.ticketmaster.ca).

As long as you don't mind a few corny jokes about Mounties and beavers, the dinner theater *Oh Canada Eh?* (8585 Lundy's Lane, 905/374-1995 or 800/467-2071, www.ohcanadaeh.com, 6:15pm daily July-Aug., 6:15pm Sat.-Thurs. mid-Apr.-June and Sept.-mid-Oct., adults $55-75, ages 13-18 $45-75, ages 3-12 $40-75) is an evening of rollicking good fun. While you tuck into a hearty multicourse meal featuring dishes from across Canada, enthusiastic performers take you on a cross-country journey of Canadian music, from Newfoundland sea shanties to songs by Joni Mitchell, Neil Young, k.d. lang, and Leonard Cohen. Kids under age 12 enter free with the purchase of certain adult tickets; check the website or phone for details. Show-only tickets without dinner are also available (adults $35, ages 13-18 $30, ages 3-12 $25).

There are more laughs at **YukYuk's Comedy Club** (Sheraton Four Points Hotel, 6455 Fallsview Blvd., 800/899-9136, www.yukyuks.com, $12-17), which typically presents five stand-up comedy shows every week (Thurs.-Sat.).

Among the many places where Niagara Falls can separate you from your money are its two casinos: **Casino Niagara** (5705 Falls Ave., 905/374-3598 or 888/325-5788, www.casinoniagara.com) and the **Fallsview Casino** (6380 Fallsview Blvd., 888/325-5788, www.fallsviewcasinoresort.com), Canada's largest gaming facility. Both casinos are open 24 hours daily; guests must be at least 19 years old to enter.

Cinema

The **IMAX Theatre Niagara Falls** (6170 Fallsview Blvd., 905/358-3611 or 866/405-4629, www.imaxniagara.com, shows on the hour year-round, call or check the website for seasonal schedules, adults $15, ages 4-12 $11) screens "you are there" films about the falls and the daredevils who've tried to plummet over the rushing water. Also on-site is the **Daredevil Exhibit** (adults $9.30, kids $7.50), which tells the stories of the falls-plunging thrill seekers. Combination tickets for the IMAX movie and exhibit (adults $24, kids $18) are available, as are packages that include the movie, the exhibit, and admission to the nearby Skylon Tower (adults $39, kids $28). Buy your tickets online for discounted admission.

Festivals and Events
The **Fireworks over the Falls** (www. niagaraparks.com) illuminate the night sky at 10pm Monday through Friday, from mid-May through early September; check the website for fireworks dates at other times of year. In July and August, there are free concerts featuring local bands at 8pm in Queen Victoria Park before the fireworks begin.

During the **Winter Festival of Lights** (www.wfol.com, Nov.-Jan., free), the falls are illuminated nightly, and fireworks over the falls continue weekly on Fridays. Additional light displays are at the Dufferin Islands Nature Area and at several other locations around the city.

Shopping
What would a mega tourist attraction be without an outlet mall? Just off the QEW, west of the falls, the 30-plus stores at the **Canada One Brand Name Outlets** (7500 Lundy's Lane, 905/356-8989, www.canadaoneoutlets. com, 10am-9pm Mon.-Sat., 10am-6pm Sun.) carry a variety of North American brands such as Guess, Coach, Reebok, Roots, and Nike.

SPORTS AND RECREATION
Parks
At the peaceful **Floral Showhouse** (7145 Niagara Pkwy., 905/354-1721, www. niagaraparks.com, 9:30am-5pm daily, adults $5, ages 6-12 $3.75), floral displays change with the seasons, including geraniums in June, begonias in early autumn, and poinsettias, cyclamen, and azaleas in December. In summer, you can stroll through the gardens surrounding the showhouse, which is 500 meters (0.3 miles) south of Horseshoe Falls, on the WEGO bus route.

Dufferin Islands Nature Area (6345 Dufferin Isle Rd., at Niagara Pkwy., www. niagaraparks.com, dawn-dusk daily, free) is crisscrossed with walking trails that explore the region's natural side. You can follow the paths and bridges that connect several small islands. From November to January, lighting displays illuminate the islands as part of the annual **Winter Festival of Lights** (www. wfol.com). The nature area is 750 meters (0.5 miles) south of the falls, between the Floral Showhouse and the Rapidsview Parking Lot.

Hiking
Ontario's premier hiking route, the 800-kilometer (500-mile) **Bruce Trail**, which runs all the way to the northern tip of the Bruce Peninsula, begins in Queenston. Throughout the year, the **Niagara Bruce Trail Club** (www.niagarabrucetrail.org) offers frequent hikes of varying lengths and levels of difficulty; nonmembers are welcome. After you participate in more than one or two hikes, the club will ask you to become a member ($50/year).

The **Greater Niagara Circle Route** (www.niagararegion.ca or www. niagaracyclingtourism.com) includes more than 140 kilometers (87 miles) of paved walking or cycling trails. It loops around the Niagara Peninsula, following the Niagara River south from Niagara-on-the-Lake to Niagara Falls and then to Fort Erie, turning west to Port Colborne, north along the Welland Canal to St. Catharines, and east to return to Niagara-on-the-Lake.

Biking
The Niagara region has a bike-sharing program, **Zoom BikeShare** (905/468-3401, www.zoombikeshare.com, $5/hour), that enables you to pick up a bike at one location in Niagara Falls or Niagara-on-the-Lake and return it at any of the other designated locations.

The program launched in 2018 with about a dozen rental spots; check their website for specifics. To rent a bike, download the Zoom BikeShare mobile app, Movatic.

Whirlpool Adventure Course

WildPlay's **Whirlpool Adventure Course** (3500 Niagara Pkwy., 800/263-7073, www.wildplay.com/niagara-falls, May-mid-Oct., call or check the website for seasonal hours) offers three different options for climbing, swinging, and zipping through a network of ropes and aerial adventures above the Niagara gorge. Start with the Classic Course ($40), and if that's not enough of a thrill, add the challenging Extreme Course ($30 extra). Youngsters can test their skills on the lower Kids Course (ages 5-12 $20).

The Whirlpool Adventure Course is 8.2 kilometers (5.1 miles) north of Horseshoe Falls, on the WEGO bus route.

Water Parks

Sixteen waterslides, a huge wave pool, and a water play area keep families splashing at the **Fallsview Indoor Waterpark** (5685 Falls Ave., 905/374-4444 or 888/234-8413, www.fallsviewwaterpark.com, call or check the website for seasonal hours, day pass $45-50). The park offers accommodations packages with several nearby hotels, including the Sheraton on the Falls, Crowne Plaza Niagara Falls-Fallsview Hotel, Skyline Hotel & Waterpark, and Clifton Victoria Inn at the Falls.

The **Waves Indoor Waterpark** (8444 Lundy's Lane, 905/356-8444 or 866/707-0030, www.americananiagara.com, call or check the website for seasonal hours, $35 pp), located at the Americana Resort on the west end of Lundy's Lane, also has a wave pool, waterslides, a kiddie play structure, and whirlpools.

FOOD

If you're at home in chain restaurants, you'll be happy eating in Niagara Falls. The chains are cheek by jowl on the streets surrounding the falls, particularly along Clifton Hill. For independent eateries, Queen Street, the still-reviving downtown district, is worth checking out, as is the area on Ferry Street near Stanley Avenue. It's also a short drive to Niagara-on-the-Lake, where you'll find more dining options.

The small **Niagara Falls Farmers Market** (5943 Sylvia Pl., 905/356-7521, www.niagarafalls.ca/farmersmarket, 6am-noon Sat.) operates year-round near the intersection of Main and Ferry Streets.

Niagara Parks Restaurants

The Niagara Parks agency runs convenient restaurants and snack bars at several of the visitors centers around Niagara Falls. Meals range from basic sandwiches to high-end fare, but all emphasize Ontario ingredients; hours vary seasonally.

The flagship dining room, **Elements on the Falls** (6650 Niagara Pkwy., 905/354-3631, www.niagaraparks.com, year-round, $20-42), has great views of the Horseshoe Falls and a contemporary menu that ranges from salads and sandwiches to pastas and steaks. Other Parks restaurants include **Queen Victoria Place Restaurant** (6345 Niagara Pkwy., 905/356-2217, late Apr.-late Oct., $16-34), the **Whirlpool Restaurant** (3351 Niagara Pkwy., 905/356-7221, late Apr.-late Oct., $13-18), and the **Queenston Heights Restaurant** (14184 Niagara Pkwy., Queenston, 905/262-4274, May-mid-Oct., lunch $9-24).

Fallsview

Hidden on the lower level of the Sterling Inn, stylish ★ **AG Cuisine** (Sterling Inn, 5195 Magdalen Ave., 289/292-0005, www.agcuisine.com, 5:30pm-9:30pm Tues.-Sun., $28-37) earns kudos for its creative cuisine. With retro white banquettes, red drapes, and twinkling chandeliers, the dining room channels the Rat Pack, while the food is ever so au courant. Not only does executive chef Cory Linkson favor regional ingredients in his artfully plated dishes, but the restaurant even runs its own farm, supplying fresh ingredients for squash velouté, locally raised beef tenderloin with an almond-brie crust, or a risotto of farm vegetables. The well-constructed wine list emphasizes Niagara producers.

Want to eat above it all? In the Skylon Tower's **Revolving Dining Room** (www. skylon.com, 11:30am-3pm and 4:30pm-10pm daily, lunch $29-54, dinner $41-59), which makes a complete rotation every hour, even a hamburger will set you back $29, but tower admission is free when you ride up for a meal. For families, the **Summit Suite Buffet Dining Room** (11:30am-3pm and 5pm-10pm Mon.-Sat., 10:30am-3pm and 5pm-10pm Sun., lunch adults $30, children $13, dinner adults $40, children $16), which also includes tower admission, is a better value.

Ferry Street

The Ferry Street area has several popular Italian restaurants.

For good food, moderate prices, and a family-friendly feel, all within walking distance from Clifton Hill, **Bravo Pizzeria** (5438 Ferry St., 905/354-3354, www.bravopizzeriagrill. com, 11:30am-midnight daily, $14-36) specializes in pizzas cooked in the wood-fired oven, from Greek-style with feta, olives, and spinach to the *arrabbiata,* loaded with spicy sausage, calabrese salami, and peppers. Soups, salads, panini, and pastas round out the menu. The beer selection features brews from 70 countries; parking is free.

Italian classics done well have kept the traditional family-run **Napoli Ristorante** (5485 Ferry St., 905/356-3345, www. napoliristorante.ca, 4pm-close daily, $15-42) in business since 1962. Start with the arancini (rice balls stuffed with mozzarella and peas), or a salad of lettuce, escarole, and Tuscan kale. Then share a pizza; tuck into a pasta, such as the *orecchiette abruzzese* (shaped like "little ears" and tossed with rapini and homemade sausage); or fuel up with the veal chop or the chicken stuffed with butternut squash. Wines include both Niagara and Italian labels. Parking is free.

Another old favorite, family-operated **Four Brothers Cucina** (5283 Ferry St., 905/358-6951, www.fourbrotherscucina. com, 11:30am-11pm daily, lunch $8-14, dinner $17-34) can get you in and out fast with their express lunch menu of salads, Italian sandwiches, and pastas; try the "mini dining adventure," a greatest-hits sampler plate of lasagna, ravioli, and fettucine with a meatball. There's no reason to rush, though: settle into your red leather chair to savor

AG Cuisine earns kudos for its imaginative dishes.

the bruschetta topped with fresh tomatoes and basil, homemade gnocchi, or chicken parmigiana.

Queen Street and North

France's loss became Niagara's gain after chef-owner Thierry Clement left his homeland and opened **Paris Crêpes Café** (4613 Queen St., 289/296-4218, www.pariscrepescafe.com, 11am-2pm and 5pm-8pm Mon.-Fri., 10am-2pm and 5:30pm-8pm Sat., 10am-2pm and 5pm-8pm Sun., $11-36), a French bistro and *crêperie* in downtown Niagara Falls. The classic crepes are the must-haves, particularly savory buckwheat versions like the Sud Ouest (stuffed with duck confit, onion jam, Swiss cheese, and a sunny-side-up egg); sweet varieties include dark chocolate, chestnut, and salted caramel.

The full-bodied Red Cream Ale, lighter Charleston Lager, and creamy Vanilla Wheat are among the brews on tap at **Taps on Queen** (4680 Queen St., 289/477-1010, www.tapsbeer.ca, noon-11pm daily, $10-17), a local microbrewery and pub with a sidewalk patio. To go with your beer, choose pizza, burgers, or comfort fare like vegetable curry or fish-and-chips.

Gracious old-world ★ **Casa Mia Ristorante** (3518 Portage Rd., 905/356-5410, www.casamiaristorante.com, 5pm-midnight Mon. and Sat., 11:30am-2:30pm and 5pm-midnight Tues.-Fri., $21-55) feels light-years away from the whirl of the falls. The traditional Italian offerings include cannelloni fiorentina (stuffed with ground veal and spinach) or rack of lamb with a Dijon-rosemary crust. Choose among 30 wines by the glass and hundreds more by the bottle. In the less formal bar, you might share a salumi plate, grilled calamari, pizza, or veal parmigiana. Located about a 15-minute drive north of Horseshoe Falls, the restaurant offers free transportation to and from area hotels.

ACCOMMODATIONS

Niagara Falls has thousands of rooms, in everything from bare-bones motels to homey B&Bs to glitzy hotel towers. In general, the closer you are to the falls, the higher the price, and any room with even a partial falls view will cost more than a viewless lodging.

Accommodations cluster in several main areas. The Fallsview area, on the Niagara Escarpment above Horseshoe Falls, has predominantly high-end hotel towers and some of the best falls views. A mix of basic chain hotels and more upscale properties lines the streets of Clifton Hill. North of the falls, along River Road and the surrounding residential streets, are numerous bed-and-breakfasts. Along Ferry Street and Lundy's Lane west of the falls, you'll find a mix of old-fashioned roadside motels and more modern chains. Some of the cheapest rooms are on the west end of Lundy's Lane (which, despite its picturesque name, is a busy multilane boulevard), near the entrance to the QEW; just budget for parking near the falls or plan to take the bus, because it's too far to walk.

Rates are generally highest in July-August and during holiday weekends. Fall weekends, when the leaves are in full color, are also busy. Room rates can fluctuate wildly, even within the same month, so check different travel dates if your plans are flexible.

Under $150

Near the bus and train stations downtown, **HI-Niagara Falls Hostel** (4549 Cataract Ave., 905/357-0770 or 888/749-0058, www.hostellingniagara.com, $35-39 dorm, $90 d) provides cheap beds, space to hang out, and activities ranging from barbecues to pub crawls. Sleeping options include cramped four-, six-, and eight-bed dorms and tiny double-bed private rooms, all with shared baths. Linens and towels are included, as is a light continental breakfast. You can prep your own meals in the communal kitchen or play pool in the basement lounge. Wi-Fi is free.

Staying at **Strathaird Bed & Breakfast** (4372 Simcoe St., 905/358-3421, www.strathairdinn.com, Apr.-Oct., $85-125 d) is like visiting a favorite aunt and uncle. Owners Tom and Val Jackson offer a warm Scottish welcome to their modest but comfortable home, encouraging you to have a cup of tea or relax on the porch. The three guest rooms upstairs cover the basics: queen beds, en suite baths, air-conditioning, and Wi-Fi, and you'll fuel up with a full Scottish breakfast of eggs, bacon, beans, tomatoes, and fruit. Rates include parking, or if you phone ahead, they'll pick you up at the train or bus station. The WEGO bus stops one block away.

$150-250

A full hot breakfast is served in the formal dining room at **Greystone Manor B&B** (4939 River Rd., 905/357-7373 or 877/237-4746, www.greystone-manor.ca, $130-248 d), but the atmosphere in this restored 1908 home is anything but stiff. The double-size living room has plenty of space for lounging, yoga, or dancing (owner Barbara Grumme, who's a wealth of local information, teaches ballroom dance, and you can arrange a lesson). Upstairs, the four queen-bed air-conditioned guest rooms (three en suite, one with a private bath across the hall) are simple but cozy. Wi-Fi, phone calls within North America, and parking are free.

Owners Carolyn and Gary Burke have lived in their 1886 heritage home—with its own turret—for more than 30 years, and they share their local knowledge with their guests at the **Park Place B&B** (4851 River Rd., 905/358-0279, www.parkplaceniagara.ca, $185 d). Each of the two upstairs guest rooms has a king bed, a fireplace, and a large bath with a whirlpool tub; a third suite is in the carriage house. You can choose breakfast delivered to your room or served by candlelight in the Victorian-style dining room. The WEGO bus stops one block away.

Among Clifton Hill's many family-friendly midrange chains, a good choice is the **Country Inn & Suites** (5525 Victoria Ave., 905/374-6040 or 800/830-5222, www.countryinns.com, $124-348 d, parking $10 per day). Though there's nothing especially country-like about this seven-story hotel, it has what families need, including standard rooms with two queen beds (and larger one-bedroom suites), an indoor pool, a fitness room, complimentary buffet breakfast, and Internet access. Rates drop significantly outside the July-August high season.

Across the street from the Fallsview Casino, the **Comfort Inn-Fallsview** (6645 Fallsview Blvd., 905/358-9353 or 800/463-1938, www.comfortinnfallsview.ca, $149-299 d) gives you a Fallsview location for moderate rates. The rooms are standard chain-hotel style, but the kids will appreciate the indoor and outdoor pools. If you need more space, ask about the slightly larger family rooms, with two queen beds and a sleep sofa, or the two-bedroom family suites. Wi-Fi is free.

A more upscale option in the Fallsview neighborhood is the 19-story **DoubleTree Fallsview Resort & Spa** (6039 Fallsview Blvd., 905/358-3817 or 800/730-8609, www.niagarafallsdoubletree.com, $134-255 d, parking $16) with a ski-lodge-style lobby decorated with lots of wood and stone. One of the hotel's nicest features is the indoor pool on the lower level, where there's also a fitness room and guest laundry. Most of the 224 simple but comfortable guest rooms have two queen beds; all have small refrigerators, coffeemakers, and Wi-Fi. For more space, book a one-bedroom suite with a separate sitting area and sofa bed. Rooms on the 16th floor or above have views of the American Falls.

Over $250

Occupying a 1928 former dairy, the boutique ★ **Sterling Inn & Spa** (5195 Magdalen St., 289/292-0000 or 877/783-7772, www.sterlingniagara.com, $250-390 d) has a three-story milk bottle above its entrance. Inside, the 41 contemporary guest rooms are spare but spacious, with couples-courting features like king beds, fireplaces, and large steam showers or whirlpool baths for two. Overall, the feel is upscale, if not deluxe, but pampering touches include a breakfast tray delivered to your room and an on-site spa offering couples massages. Wi-Fi and parking are included.

The prime rooms at the contemporary **Sheraton on the Falls Hotel** (5875 Falls Ave., 905/374-4445 or 888/229-9961, www.sheratononthefalls.com, $189-609 d, parking $29-49 per day), a 669-room mirrored tower opposite the American Falls, are those overlooking the waterfalls, of course. You'll pay a significant premium for falls-view rooms, but the upcharge is smaller midweek and outside summer high season. Facilities include indoor and outdoor pools, a fitness center, and a spa overlooking the falls; Casino Niagara is nearby. A daily resort fee ($15.95) covers Wi-Fi, phone calls within Canada and to the United States, and two WEGO bus tickets.

Another top choice for falls-view rooms is the 23-story **Marriott Niagara Falls Fallsview Hotel and Spa** (6740 Fallsview Blvd., 905/357-7300 or 888/501-8916, www.niagarafallsmarriott.com, $191-599 d, parking $35 per day). Of the 432 guest rooms, the higher-floor units have the best perspective of the falls; the suites, including a two-level loft unit with floor-to-ceiling windows, have some of the most dramatic vantage points. Even the indoor pool overlooks Horseshoe Falls. Wi-Fi is $10 per day.

Your kids may not care about seeing the falls once they're at **Great Wolf Lodge** (950 Victoria Ave., 905/354-4888 or 800/605-9653, www.greatwolf.com, $260-579 d), a resort that features a wave pool and several waterslides. Amenities include several eateries and snack bars, a spa for adults, a spa for preteens, and a nightly story hour for little ones. The standard family suite has two queens or one queen plus a sleep sofa, or you can choose a fun themed suite. Rooms have microwaves and mini fridges. Room rates include waterpark access, which is limited to hotel guests. The lodge is seven kilometers (4.5 miles) north of the Horseshoe Falls.

A 30-story tower, the **Fallsview Casino Resort** (6380 Fallsview Blvd., 888/325-5788, www.fallsviewcasinoresort.com, $269-349 d) feels like a small city. The lobby, with its art deco-style ceiling, checkerboard floor, and Doric columns, channels the French belle epoque, while the 374 guest rooms are sparer, perhaps to avoid competing with the views of the falls from most rooms. There's an indoor pool, a spa, a collection of shops and boutiques, 16 restaurants and fast-food outlets, and the casino itself, Canada's largest gaming facility. The 1,500-seat theater hosts concerts, comedy shows, and other big-name entertainment.

INFORMATION AND SERVICES
Visitor Information

A good source for guidance about things to do and places to stay in Niagara Falls is **Niagara Falls Tourism** (905/356-6061 or 800/563-2557, www.niagarafallstourism.com), the city's visitor and convention bureau.

The **Niagara Parks Commission** (877/642-7275, www.niagaraparks.com) operates several seasonal information offices that can help you once you're in town. Their objective is to encourage you to visit Niagara Parks attractions (and sell tickets), but they provide information as well. They open at 9am daily June-August:

- **Table Rock Welcome Centre** (6650 Niagara Pkwy., near Horseshoe Falls)
- **Grand View Marketplace Welcome Centre** (outside the Hornblower Niagara Cruises ticket booths)
- **Clifton Hill Welcome Centre** (Clifton Hill at Falls Ave.)
- **Murray Street Welcome Centre** (near Queen Victoria Pl.)
- **Rapidsview Welcome Centre** (south of the falls at the Rapidsview parking lot).

Discounts and Passes

Niagara Parks sells passes—all available online, at the Niagara Parks Welcome Centres, or at any of the included attractions—that offer discounts for various attractions.

The **Niagara Falls Adventure Pass Classic** (www.niagaraparks.com, Apr.-Nov., adults $65, ages 6-12 $43) includes admission to the Hornblower Niagara Cruises, Journey Behind the Falls, *Niagara's Fury,* and the White Water Walk, along with two days' transportation on the WEGO buses. For the same price, you can choose the **Niagara Falls Adventure Pass Nature,** which covers admission to Hornblower Niagara Cruises, Whirlpool Aero Car, Floral Showhouse, and Butterfly Conservatory, as well as two days of WEGO rides.

Want to do it all? The **Niagara Falls Adventure Pass Plus** (www.niagaraparks. com, Apr.-Nov., adults $110, ages 6-12 $79) covers the Hornblower Niagara Cruises, Journey Behind the Falls, *Niagara's Fury,* White Water Walk, Whirlpool Aero Car, Floral Showhouse, Butterfly Conservatory, Old Fort Erie, Laura Secord Homestead, McFarland House, and Mackenzie Printery, along with two days' transportation on the WEGO buses, rides on the incline railway, and a shuttle to Niagara-on-the-Lake.

GETTING THERE

The main commercial airports serving the Niagara region are in Toronto and Buffalo. Niagara Falls has train service from Toronto and Buffalo, with connections to other Canadian and U.S. cities, and you can get there by bus from a variety of destinations as well. By car, it's about two hours' drive from Toronto and less than an hour from Buffalo, traffic and border crossings permitting.

If you're traveling between Niagara and Buffalo or other U.S. points, remember that you must cross an international border. Allow extra time for border formalities, and make sure you have your passport.

Air
TORONTO

Toronto's **Pearson International Airport** (YYZ, 6301 Silver Dart Dr., Mississauga, 416/247-7678 or 866/207-1690, www. torontopearson.com) has flights from across Canada, the United States, and overseas. All the chain car rental agencies, and several local rental companies, have offices at Pearson Airport.

The most direct way to travel from Pearson to Niagara Falls is to take the **Niagara Air Bus** (905/374-8111 or 800/206-7222, www. niagaraairbus.com, 2 hours, one-way $95), a door-to-door airport shuttle. Book online at least three days in advance for a 5 percent discount. **Greyhound** (800/661-8747, www. greyhound.ca, 1.75 hours, one-way adults $15-28) service between Pearson and the **Niagara Transportation Centre** (4555 Erie Ave., Niagara Falls) is much less expensive than the Air Bus, as long as your travel schedule aligns with the daily trip. If you're stopping off in Toronto anyway, there are many more bus and train options to Niagara Falls from downtown Toronto.

BUFFALO

Flying from the United States, you may find cheaper flights into **Buffalo-Niagara International Airport** (BUF, 4200 Genesee St., Buffalo, NY, 716/630-6000, www. buffaloairport.com). All the major North American car rental agencies operate at the Buffalo airport.

The cheapest way to reach Niagara Falls from Buffalo airport is by bus, particularly if you can nab a discount deal on **Megabus** (866/488-4452, www.megabus.com, 1.25-1.5 hours, one-way $1-11). **Greyhound** (800/661-8747, www.greyhound.ca, 1.25-2.5 hours, one-way $11-21) also runs regular buses on this route. Both carriers travel to the **Niagara Transportation Centre** (4555 Erie Ave., Niagara Falls).

Several taxi, shuttle, and limo services offer more frequent, but more expensive, service between Buffalo airport and Niagara Falls. The most economical carrier will depend on the number of people in your party. Check the airport website (www.buffaloairport.com) for additional transportation information.

- **Buffalo Airport Express** (716/472-8580 or 800/604-1570, www.buffaloairportexpress.

Bridges to Niagara

To travel between the United States and Canada in the Niagara region, you have to cross the Niagara River on one of four bridges. All are toll bridges; you pay the toll when you're *entering* Canada. The bridges can get clogged with traffic, so before you choose your route, check the border lineups online or by phone through the **Niagara Falls Bridge Commission** (800/715-6722, www.niagarafallsbridges.com). You can also get border crossing updates from the **U.S. Customs and Border Protection** (http://bwt.cbp.gov) and the **Canadian Border Services Agency** (www.cbsa-asfc.gc.ca).

The **Peace Bridge** (www.peacebridge.com, 24 hours daily, CAD$4.75 or US$3.75) is the southernmost crossing, linking I-190 from the Buffalo area with the QEW in Fort Erie.

The **Rainbow Bridge** (www.niagarafallsbridges.com, 24 hours daily, CAD$4.75 or US$3.75) directly connects Niagara Falls, Ontario, with Niagara Falls, New York. The main highway routes to this bridge are the QEW on the Canadian side and I-190 on the U.S. side.

You must have a NEXUS card to cross the **Whirlpool Bridge** (www.niagarafallsbridges.com, 7am-11pm daily, CAD$4.75 or US$3.75), north of the Rainbow Bridge. NEXUS is a prescreened traveler program designed to expedite border crossings for frequent travelers between the United States and Canada. To get more information about NEXUS, contact the **U.S. Customs and Border Protection** (www.cbp.gov) or the **Canadian Border Services Agency** (www.cbsa-asfc.gc.ca).

North of the falls, the **Queenston-Lewiston Bridge** (www.niagarafallsbridges.com, 24 hours daily, CAD$4.75 or US$3.75) connects Queenston, Ontario, and Lewiston, New York. This is the closest bridge to Niagara-on-the-Lake.

com): Scheduled shuttle service to or from major Niagara Falls hotels.

- **Buffalo Airport Shuttle** (716/685-2550 or 877/750-2550, www.buffaloairportshuttle.com): Scheduled shuttle service to or from major Niagara Falls hotels.

- **Buffalo Airport Taxi** (716/633-8294 or 800/551-9369, www.buffaloairporttaxi.com, 8am-8pm daily, one-way $65 pp): Scheduled shuttle service to or from major Niagara Falls hotels.

- **Niagara Air Bus** (905/374-8111 or 800/206-7222, www.niagaraairbus.com, one-way $100 pp, 5 percent discount for 3-day advance online booking): Door-to-door service to or from any Niagara Falls address.

Train

VIA Rail, GO Trains, and Amtrak all provide service to the **Niagara Falls Train Station** (4267 Bridge St.), which is north of the falls, one block from the Queen Street downtown district. **VIA Rail** (888/842-7245, www.viarail.ca, 2 hours, one-way adults $25-77, ages 2-11 $13-39) runs one train daily in each direction between Toronto's Union Station (65 Front St. W.) and Niagara Falls.

From June through early September and on May and October holiday weekends, **GO Transit** (416/869-3200 or 888/438-6646, www.gotransit.com, Fri.-Sun., two hours, round-trip adults $37.50) runs weekend and holiday train service from Toronto's Union Station. These seasonal GO trains run as the **bike train**, with coaches specifically designed to carry bicycles. The rest of the year, you can take the GO train between Toronto and Burlington, then change to a bus between Burlington and Niagara Falls (2.75 hours, one-way adults $19.30, seniors and ages 6-12 $9.65).

Amtrak's Maple Leaf (800/872-7245, www.amtrak.com) line travels from New York City's Penn Station to Toronto's Union Station, stopping in Niagara Falls. The train runs once daily, with major stops at

Niagara on Two Wheels

The Niagara region is one of Ontario's most bicycle-friendly areas, crisscrossed with bike routes and cycling paths. To get yourself and your bike to Niagara, take the **Bike Train** (www.biketrain. ca), operated by **GO Transit** (416/869-3200 or 888/438-6646, www.gotransit.com). From late June through early September, and on May and October holiday weekends, bike trains running between Toronto's Union Station and Niagara Falls on Friday, Saturday, Sunday, and holidays have coaches specifically designed to carry bicycles.

The Niagara Region website (www.niagararegion.ca, click on "Maps and Trails") has an online regional cycling route planner that allows you to specify your starting point, the approximate distance you want to ride, the level of difficulty, and types of sights you might like to see along the way. They also have a bike map app that you can download to a mobile device. For more information about bicycling in the Niagara region, check the website for the **Niagara Cycling Tourism Centre** (www.niagaracyclingtourism.com) or the **Regional Niagara Bicycling Committee** (www.rnbc.info), which both have regional cycling maps and resources.

While many accommodations will provide places for you to store your bike, **Cycle and Stay Niagara** (www.cycleandstayniagara.com) is a network of B&Bs located on or near a bike route that are particularly cyclist-friendly. If your Niagara cycling adventures whet your appetite for seeing more of Ontario by bike, explore **Ontario By Bike** (www.ontariobybike.ca), which can help you plan cycling trips across the province.

THE GREATER NIAGARA CIRCLE ROUTE

The Greater Niagara Circle Route (www.niagararegion.ca) includes more than 140 kilometers (87 miles) of mostly paved cycling trails, which lets you cycle to many of the area's highlights. The trail loops around the Niagara Peninsula, following the Niagara River south from Niagara-on-the-Lake to Niagara Falls and on to Fort Erie. It then turns inland between Fort Erie and Port Colborne, running along the Welland Canal from Port Colborne to St. Catharines before returning to Niagara-on-the-Lake.

The circle route is actually made up of a number of shorter trails, so if you don't want to cycle the whole loop, you can choose one or more of the following routes:

- The **Niagara River Recreational Trail** (www.niagaraparks.com) follows the Niagara River 56 kilometers (35 miles) from Fort George in Niagara-on-the-Lake past Niagara Falls

---

Poughkeepsie, Albany, Syracuse, Rochester, Buffalo, and Niagara Falls (New York) before crossing into Canada. The New York City-Niagara trip (one-way adults $88-121, ages 2-12 $44-77) takes 9.5 hours.

Bus

Long-distance buses, including those from Toronto and New York City, arrive at and depart from the **Niagara Transportation Centre** (4555 Erie Ave., 905/357-2133), across the street from the Niagara Falls Train Station. **Megabus** (866/488-4452, www. megabus.com) has frequent service between Toronto's Central Bus Station (610 Bay St.) and Niagara Falls. The trip takes about two hours, and fares can be as low as $1 each way (yes, really), although more typical one-way fares are $14-21. Megabus also travels between Niagara Falls and Hamilton (1.5 hours, one-way $10).

From the United States, **Greyhound** (www.greyhound.ca, 10-11 hours, one-way adults US$49-78) has several daily buses from New York City to Niagara Falls.

Car

Niagara Falls is 130 kilometers (80 miles) southeast of Toronto. From downtown Toronto, you can take the Gardiner Expressway west to the QEW. Follow the to Fort Erie. The section of the trail between Niagara-on-the-Lake and the falls is one of the region's most popular.

- Crossing the southern end of the Niagara Peninsula, parallel to the Lake Erie shore, the paved **Friendship Trail** (www.forterie.ca) runs 16 kilometers (10 miles) from Seaway Park in Port Colborne to Fort Erie, where it joins the Niagara River Recreational Trail.

- The **Welland Canals Trail** (www.welland.ca) is a 42-kilometer (27-mile) north-south cycling path that connects St. Catharines and Port Colborne, along the Welland Canal.

GREAT LAKES WATERFRONT TRAIL

The Great Lakes Waterfront Trail (www.waterfronttrail.org) follows the shores of Lake Huron, Lake Erie, Lake Ontario, and the St. Lawrence River from Grand Bend, through the Niagara region, all the way to the Quebec border. Extending for roughly 2,100 kilometers (1,300 miles), the trail, which also has a section in Northern Ontario connecting Sudbury to Sault Ste. Marie, includes a mix of dedicated off-road cycling paths and on-road routes, typically on less trafficked residential streets, although some sections do run along the shoulder of major roads.

On the Niagara Peninsula, the waterfront trail connects the towns of Port Colborne, Fort Erie, Niagara Falls, Niagara-on-the-Lake, St. Catharines, Lincoln, and Grimsby, continuing on to Hamilton and north to Toronto.

NEW YORK TO NIAGARA

If you want to ride your bike from New York State to the Niagara region, you can. Cyclists are allowed to cross the Peace Bridge between the Buffalo area and Fort Erie. You don't have to pay the toll, but you do need the same documents (including your passport) as you do if you're coming by other means of transportation. You can pick up the Niagara River Recreation Trail or the Friendship Trail on the Ontario side of the bridge. NOTE: Due to construction work, the Peace Bridge is closed to cyclists until at least spring 2019.

Cyclists can also cross the Rainbow Bridge ($1). If you're in Niagara Falls—either Ontario or New York—and you want to cross over to the other Niagara Falls, the Rainbow Bridge is the most direct route. Again, passports are required. Cyclists and pedestrians are not allowed on the Queenston-Lewiston Bridge.

QEW south as it skirts the Lake Ontario shore, then passes Hamilton and St. Catharines. Exit onto Highway 420 east, which will take you into Niagara Falls.

Coming from the United States, Niagara Falls is 40 kilometers (25 miles) from Buffalo, New York. Interstate 190 from Buffalo goes north to the four bridges over the Niagara River, which separates New York from Ontario.

Tours from Toronto

Many tour companies offer one-day excursions from Toronto to Niagara Falls. Prices and services vary widely, from bare-bones backpacker trips to deluxe limousine tours. In general, you'll save money exploring on your own, but the convenience of a tour may be worth the extra money.

- **Niagara Day Tour** (905/465-0890, www. niagaradaytour.com, daily Apr.-Oct., Tues., Thurs., Sat.-Sun. Nov.-Mar., adults $79, ages 4-12 $44) runs good-value smaller-group Niagara Falls excursions that include an hour to explore Niagara-on-the-Lake, a wine tasting at Reif Estates Winery (including a sample of their ice wine), and stops at the Floral Clock and the power stations on the Niagara River, before arriving in Niagara Falls, where you'll have 2.5-3 hours to explore. They pick you up in downtown Toronto at the Strathcona Hotel (60 York St., opposite Union Station) or the DoubleTree by Hilton (108 Chestnut St., near Yonge/Dundas Square) at 8am or 8:30am; you'll be back in Toronto around 6pm. You can also book the tour with the Hornblower Niagara Cruise included (adults $99, ages 4-12 $59).

- Departing from downtown Toronto hotels between 7:30am and 8am and returning to Toronto between 4:30pm and 5pm, **Queen Tour** (905/597-6160, www.tourstoniagarafalls.com, adults $89, ages 3-11 $79) includes time to explore Niagara Falls and Niagara-on-the-Lake; quick stops at the Whirlpool Rapids and a winery; and round-trip transportation from Toronto.

- **King Tours** (www.kingtours.ca, adults $100) offers a similar day trip, departing slightly later, with hotel pickups between 8am and 9am. You'll stop in Niagara-on-the-Lake and pass by the Floral Clock, Queenston Heights, and the Whirlpool Aero Car en route to Niagara Falls. The tour includes a winery stop plus 2-3 hours of free time at the falls. You'll be back in Toronto by 7pm. They offer a package with a Hornblower Niagara cruise (adults $120), too.

- **GrayLine Tours** (www.grayline.ca, adults $169, seniors $153, ages 5-11 $108) runs daily 9.5-hour trips from Toronto that include a buffet lunch, a Hornblower Niagara boat tour, and stops at the Whirlpool Rapids, the Floral Clock, and a winery. Their "Freedom Tour" (adults $136, seniors $119, ages 5-11 $87) includes the same stops without meals. Both include return transportation from many Toronto hotels, departing around 10am.

GETTING AROUND

You can easily walk along the river near the falls, between Table Rock and the Hornblower Niagara cruise docks, and up to Clifton Hill, where many hotels are located. You can also walk between Horseshoe Falls and the Fallsview hotel district, although it's a fairly steep climb up the hill. Cycling is another good option; you can pedal the 56-kilometer (35-mile) Niagara River Recreation Trail between Niagara-on-the-Lake and Fort Erie.

Bus

Operated by the City of Niagara Falls and the Niagara Parks Commission, the **WEGO bus** (www.wegoniagarafalls.com, check the website for seasonal hours, 24-hour/48-hour pass adults $8/12.50, ages 6-12 $5/9) is a convenient year-round shuttle bus. Its several useful routes converge at the Table Rock Welcome Centre and transport you around Niagara Falls. The **Niagara Falls Adventure Pass** (www.niagaraparks.com) includes two free days of WEGO bus rides.

The WEGO Green Line travels along the Niagara Parkway, stopping at all the major Niagara Parks attractions, as well as the bus and train station downtown. If you've driven to the falls area, you can park your car in any of the Niagara Parks day lots ($30/day) and catch the WEGO bus to the falls and other points of interest.

The Blue Line loops through the Fallsview and Clifton Hill districts, while the Red Line runs through Clifton Hill and continues out along Ferry Street and Lundy's Lane—handy if you'd like to visit the Niagara Falls History Museum or if you're staying at a Lundy's Lane hotel.

Daunted by the steep hill between the Fallsview district and the falls themselves? The **Falls Incline Railway** (www.niagaraparks.com, ages 6 and over one-way $2.75, all-day pass $7) transports passengers up and down the 30-meter (100-foot) embankment between the Table Rock Welcome Centre and Fallsview Boulevard, near the Fallsview Casino and the Skylon Tower. The ride is quick—about one minute—but you overlook Horseshoe Falls along the way.

Car

Parking near the falls is quite limited. If

you can leave the car at home or at least at your hotel, you'll save yourself some parking hassles. There is free, seasonal parking at **Queenston Heights Park** (14184 Niagara Pkwy.) and at the **Whirlpool Aero Car** (3850 Niagara Pkwy.), which are both north of the falls, on the WEGO bus route. You can purchase an annual parking pass for **Niagara Glen** (3050 Niagara Pkwy.) or the **Butterfly Conservatory** (2565 Niagara Pkwy.), also on the WEGO route, for $15.

Parking passes valid at other Niagara Parks lots, including **Rapidsview Parking Lot** (7651 Niagara Pkwy.), **Queen Victoria Place** (6349 Niagara Pkwy.), and the **Falls Lot** (6635 Niagara Pkwy.) directly behind Horseshoe Falls, are $30/day; a pass good for a full year is $55. The Niagara Parks website (www.niagaraparks.com) has more details about parking locations.

When driving around the falls, watch out for pedestrians. Many become captivated by the waterfalls and thus completely oblivious to traffic.

Tours

It lasts only 12 minutes, but a **Niagara Helicopters Flightseeing Tour** (3731 Victoria Ave., 905/357-5672, www.niagara helicopters.com, 9am-sunset daily, adults $144, couples $280, kids $89) is an exciting way to see the falls from a different perspective. Aboard a six-passenger Bell 407 helicopter, your flight path takes you along the Niagara River, over the Whirlpool, past the American Falls, and around Horseshoe Falls; their semicircular horseshoe shape is most apparent from the air. You don headphones to listen to narration about the sights along the way.

VICINITY OF NIAGARA FALLS
Queenston

Thirteen kilometers (8 miles) north of Niagara Falls and 11 kilometers (6.8 miles) south of downtown Niagara-on-the-Lake, the quiet village of Queenston houses several historic sites.

QUEENSTON HEIGHTS NATIONAL HISTORIC SITE

British and Canadian troops clashed with the American invaders in the Battle of Queenston Heights, one of the early skirmishes of the War of 1812 fought on Niagara soil. Through the British won the battle, the British commander, Major General Isaac Brock, was killed.

A helicopter tour is an exciting way to see the falls.

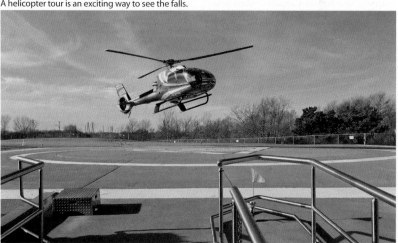

The battle site is now the **Queenston Heights Park** (www.niagaraparks.com), with gardens and picnic tables, as well as **Brock's Monument,** a national historic site honoring the fallen British military leader. Parks Canada runs **interpretive programs** (905/468-4257, www.pc.gc.ca, 10am-5pm daily May-Aug., 11am-4pm Mon.-Fri. and 10am-5pm Sat.-Sun. Sept.-mid-Oct., adults $4.50, ages 6-16 $3.50) at the monument, or you can follow a self-guided tour.

MACKENZIE PRINTERY AND NEWSPAPER MUSEUM

In 1824, political reformer and journalist William Lyon Mackenzie (1795-1861) began publishing a newspaper, the *Colonial Advocate,* in this Queenston house. This ivy-covered stone building, which dates to the late 1700s, is now the **Mackenzie Printery and Newspaper Museum** (1 Queenston St., 905/262-5676, www.niagaraparks.com or www.mackenzieprintery.org, 10am-5pm daily mid-May-early Sept., 11am-5pm Sat.-Sun. early-Sept.-Oct., adults $6.25, ages 6-12 $4.05). Exhibits are devoted to Mackenzie's life and work, the early history of the Niagara-York (now Toronto) region, and the development of printing technology from the 18th century to the present. The museum also houses Canada's oldest printing press, a wooden device built in Britain in 1760, which was used to print Ontario's first newspaper, the *Upper Canada Gazette,* in 1793.

Guided tours run 30-45 minutes and include plenty of hands-on activities. You can set your name in movable type—and learn how hard it was to be a printer's apprentice. The printery is 13.3 kilometers (8.3 miles) north of Horseshoe Falls.

LAURA SECORD HOMESTEAD

During the War of 1812, Laura Ingersoll Secord and her husband, James, were ordered to billet several American soldiers in their Queenston home. One night, they overheard the American officers planning an attack on

Laura Secord, "Canada's Paul Revere," is buried in Lundy's Lane Battle Ground Cemetery.

British forces at nearby Beaverdams. Since James had been wounded several months earlier during the Battle of Queenston Heights, Laura decided that she would go warn the British commander, based near Thorold, of the impending American assault. Her 32-kilometer (20-mile) journey on foot through the dense woods took 18 hours. As a result of Secord's information, the British set up an ambush and defeated the Americans in the Battle of Beaverdams on June 24, 1813.

Secord is often called "Canada's Paul Revere," after the man who made a similar journey during the American Revolution to warn that British troops were on the move from Boston. The home where she and her husband lived, the **Laura Secord Homestead** (29 Queenston St., 905/262-4851, www.niagaraparks.com, 10am-5pm daily mid-May-early Sept., 11am-5pm Sat.-Sun. early Sept.-Oct., adults $9.70, ages 6-12 $6.30) is now a museum, where guides in period dress lead 30-minute tours, providing information about Secord's life and times.

Also on the property is the gothic-style **Queenston Chapel,** a Methodist church built in the 1860s and subsequently moved to the Secord Homestead site.

The homestead is 13.3 kilometers (8.3 miles) north of Horseshoe Falls, a short walk from the Mackenzie Printery.

Old Fort Erie

In 1764, at the Niagara Peninsula's southeastern point, a short hop across the river to the New York shore, the British built their first fort in Ontario. The fort became a base for an alliance of British, Loyalist, and Iroquois soldiers during the American Revolution (1775-1783), but it took its place in history during the War of 1812 when it became Canada's bloodiest battlefield. During the six-week Siege of Fort Erie in 1814, more than 3,000 troops were killed or wounded. Later that year, as American troops were withdrawing to Buffalo, they destroyed what remained of the fort.

It wasn't until the 1930s that **Old Fort Erie** (350 Lakeshore Rd., Fort Erie, 905/871-0540, www.niagaraparks.com, 10am-5pm daily mid-May-early Sept., 10am-4pm Mon.-Fri. and 10am-5pm Sat.-Sun. early-Sept.-Oct., adults $12.50, ages 6-12 $8.15) was restored and opened to the public. You can tour the fort, wandering into the soldiers' barracks, officers' quarters, kitchens, and other buildings, where costumed staff tell you about the history of the fort and the region.

Old Fort Erie is 19 kilometers (12 miles) south of Niagara Falls. It's a pretty drive along the Niagara Parkway, although it's a bit faster to take the QEW. Parking at the fort is free.

Niagara-on-the-Lake

Although it's just 20 kilometers (12.5 miles) up the road from Niagara Falls, the small town of Niagara-on-the-Lake (NOTL) feels like it's on a different planet. While the city of Niagara Falls teeters between brash, honky-tonk, and naturally spectacular, NOTL is more reserved, with a cute main street, historical attractions that date primarily from the War of 1812, a peaceful lakeshore, and dozens of B&Bs. The town's main attractions are theater and wine. It's home to the highly regarded Shaw Festival, as well as more than two dozen wineries.

Niagara-on-the-Lake's historic downtown centers on Queen Street, bounded by Lake Ontario and the Niagara River. The village of Virgil, along Niagara Stone Road (Highway 55), is the commercial hub, while the more rural village of St. Davids to the south is where you'll find several of the wineries.

★ SHAW FESTIVAL

"You see things; and you say 'Why?'
But I dream things that never
were; and I say 'Why not?'"

Perhaps Shaw Festival founder Brian Doherty had these words from George Bernard Shaw's 1921 play *Back to Methuselah* in mind when he conceived the idea of a summer festival devoted to Shaw's work. Whatever his inspiration, Doherty, a lawyer, playwright, and Shaw fan, launched the **Shaw Festival** (10 Queen's Parade, 905/468-2172 or 800/511-7429, www.shawfest.com, Apr.-Oct.) in the summer of 1962, when he produced eight performances of Shaw's *Don Juan in Hell* and *Candida*.

Author George Bernard Shaw (1856-1950) had no connection to Niagara-on-the-Lake. Born in Dublin, Ireland, in 1856, he wrote 63 plays, five novels, numerous essays, and more than 250,000 letters during his 94-year life, most of which he lived in England. The festival's original mandate was to perform plays by Shaw and his contemporaries, who include Chekhov and Tennessee Williams. More recently, directors have expanded this mission to include plays about the period when Shaw lived, as well as works by contemporary playwrights who are controversial or political

Niagara-on-the-Lake

Lake Ontario

SOUTHBROOK VINEYARDS

NEOB LAVENDER BOUTIQUE

To Niagara College Teaching Winery

NIAGARA STONE RD

TOWNLINE RD

EAST AND WEST LINE

LINE 1 RD

LINE 2 RD

LAKESHORE RD

STREWN WINERY

CONCESSION RD 7

CONCESSION RD 6

LINE 5 RD

LINE 6 RD

LINE 7 RD

LINE 8 RD

PIE PLATE BAKERY & CAFE

THE FRUIT SHACK

NIAGARA KAYAK RENTALS

VIRGIL

CONCESSION RD 4

FARMERS MARKET AT THE VILLAGE

LAKESHORE RD

EAST AND WEST LINE

LINE 3 RD

FOUR MILE CREEK RD

To Ravine Estates Winery

CONCESSION RD 3

CONCESSION RD 2

ESKOOT NIAGARA

BACKHOUSE

WILLOW CAKES & PASTRIES

GLOBETROTTERS BED & BREAKFAST

OAST HOUSE BREWERS

STRATUS VINEYARDS

ZOOM LEISURE BIKES

Niagara-on-the-Lake

SEE DETAIL

SHAW FESTIVAL

Fort Niagara State Park

LINE 4 RD

NIAGARA STONE RD

PELLER ESTATES WINERY

BROCKAMOUR MANOR

QUEEN'S PARADE

JOHN ST

NIAGARA ST

CONCESSION RD 1

REIF ESTATES WINERY

GRAND VICTORIAN BED & BREAKFAST

MCFARLAND HOUSE

FORT GEORGE NATIONAL HISTORIC SITE

PUMPHOUSE ART CENTRE

NIAGARA

Youngstown

THE ICE HOUSE

NIAGARA PKWY

RIVER RD

ZOOM LEISURE BIKES

CANADA
U.S.

Niagara River

Joseph Davis State Park

Lewiston

RIVER RD

ROBERT MOSES PKWY

CREEK RD 1

PLETCHER RD

SWAN RD

NEW YORK

190

0   1 km
0   1 mi

© AVALON TRAVEL

Detail (inset)

REGENT ST

PRIDEAUX ST

124 ON QUEEN

ROYAL GEORGE THEATRE

IL GELATO DI CARLOTTA

COPPER DREAMS BED & BREAKFAST

TREADWELL FARM-TO-TABLE CUISINE

NIAGARA-ON-THE-LAKE CHAMBER OF COMMERCE VISITOR CENTRE

NIAGARA HISTORICAL SOCIETY MUSEUM

CASTLEREAGH ST

DAVY ST

KING ST

JOHNSON ST

QUEEN ST

PRINCE OF WALES HOTEL

NIAGARA APOTHECARY MUSEUM

FRONT ST

Niagara R.

REGENT ST

ZEES

SHAW FESTIVAL

FESTIVAL THEATRE/ STUDIO THEATRE

Simcoe Park

WELLINGTON ST

QUEEN'S PARADE

GATE ST

BYRON ST

RICARDO ST

DELATER ST

QUEEN'S LANDING/ TIARA

in the same way that Shaw was during his lifetime.

The Shaw Festival operates as a repertory theater, with plays running simultaneously on three stages. The festival company typically includes 65-70 actors per season, many of whom return year after year—as do many patrons.

Tickets

The festival typically announces the lineup for its upcoming season at the end of the previous summer. You can order tickets (adults $35-117) online, by phone, or in person at any of the festival theaters.

You can save money on tickets by attending discounted preview performances before a play's official opening, as well as Sunday-evening shows. Discounted tickets are available at certain performances for students ($25), patrons under age 30 ($30-40), and seniors (from $48). Families can purchase a youth ticket (under age 18) for $29 with each regular adult ticket.

Theaters

The Shaw Festival stages its productions at three theaters in Niagara-on-the-Lake. Its flagship venue is the 856-seat **Festival Theatre** (10 Queen's Parade), which opened in 1973 on the east end of downtown. The building also houses the 200-seat **Jackie Maxwell Studio Theatre.** Parking in the Festival Theatre lot costs $15 during performances.

The festival's other stage is the 304-seat **Royal George Theatre** (85 Queen St.), a former vaudeville house on NOTL's main street. The closest parking is on the surrounding streets.

Tours

For a fascinating behind-the-scenes experience, take the hour-long **backstage tour** (11am Sat. and 10am Sun. Apr.-May; 11am Tues.-Wed. and Sat., 10am Sun. June-Oct., $10) of the Festival Theatre. You'll learn about the festival's history; visit the rehearsal hall (staff estimate that actors rehearse one hour for each minute they spend on stage); tour the dressing rooms; walk through the wardrobe shop, which occupies a staff of 40 (nearly three-quarters of the costumes used on stage are new every year); and find out more about set design and construction. Tours are only $5 if you also purchase a ticket to a performance.

Lectures and Workshops

The festival offers a variety of talks, readings, and special events throughout the season. Look for the following events, and get more information about these and other activities at www.shawfest.com:

- **Pre-show Chat:** Before many evening performances at the Festival Theatre, a company member hosts a free introduction to the play at 7:30pm (6:30pm on Sundays) mid-May to early September.

- **Continue the Conversation:** After select matinees, join a free moderated discussion about the afternoon's production.

- **Tuesday Q & A:** Following most Tuesday-evening performances, you can stay for a free question-and-answer session with company members.

TOP EXPERIENCE

★ WINERIES

Niagara-on-the Lake has more than two dozen wineries along Highway 55 (Niagara Stone Rd.); on York Road in St. Davids, toward Queenston; along the Niagara River Parkway and the concessions (rural roads) parallel to the parkway; and on Lakeshore Road skirting Lake Ontario.

Most NOTL wineries are open year-round and charge a small fee ($2-5) for tastings; if you purchase wine, you may get credit for your tasting fee. Larger wineries offer regularly scheduled tours, but smaller facilities may offer tours only by appointment or not at all. The **Wineries of Niagara-on-the-Lake** (www.wineriesofniagaraonthelake.com) has more details about the region's winemakers and a downloadable touring map.

Winery Tours

If you want to leave the driving to someone else (a good idea if you're drinking), or combine cycling and wine touring, consider these winery day tours:

- **Crush on Niagara Wine Tours** (905/562-3373 or 866/408-9463, www.crushtours.com, $99-139)

- **Grape Escape Wine Tours** (905/468-9959 or 866/935-4445, www.tourniagarawineries.com, $64-144)

- **Niagara Getaway Wine Tours** (905/933-4384, www.niagaragetaways.com, $69-139)

- **Niagara Wine Tours International** (905/468-1300 or 800/680-7006, www.niagaraworldwinetours.com, $65-139).

The Niagara College Teaching Winery

The Niagara College Teaching Winery is Canada's only licensed teaching winery, where students study winemaking, viticulture, and marketing and staff a working winery on 15 hectares (38 acres) of vineyards. Stop into the college-run **Wine Visitor and Education Centre** (135 Taylor Rd., 905/641-2252, www.niagaracollegewine.ca, 10am-6pm daily May-Oct., 11am-5pm Sun.-Fri., 10am-5pm Sat. Nov.-Apr.) for information about area wineries and tastings of the college's wines, including the reserve wines known as the Dean's List. As this book went to press, the college was constructing a **Teaching Distillery** next door; check the college website (www.niagaracollege.ca) for updates.

Ravine Estates Winery

The tasting room at family-owned **Ravine Estates Winery** (1366 York Rd., St. Davids, 905/262-8463, www.ravinevineyard.com, 11am-6pm Sun.-Thurs., 11am-8pm Fri.-Sat.) is in a historic clapboard home built in the early 1800s. They make merlot, cabernet franc, chardonnay, and sauvignon blanc, among others, and offer several types of tours. Stop here if you're hungry; they run a market-inspired **bistro** and a summertime pizza patio.

Wine makes the "Dean's List" at the Niagara College Teaching Winery.

Southbrook Vineyards

You can't miss the striking azure wall—200 meters (650 feet) long and 3 meters (10 feet) high—that slices across the fields at **Southbrook Vineyards** (581 Niagara Stone Rd., 905/641-2548 or 888/581-1581, www.southbrook.com, 10am-6pm daily mid-May-mid-Oct., 11am-5pm daily mid-Oct.-mid-May), marking the entrance to Canada's first certified biodynamic winery. Inside, you can sample wines in the sleek glass-walled tasting pavilion; they're known for chardonnays and cabernet-merlot blends. Tours of the vineyards and winery are offered on weekends; call or check the website for a schedule. The farm-to-table **Vineyard Bistro** (noon-5pm Fri.-Sun. late May-mid-Oct., $8-16) serves pizzas outside on the patio.

Stratus Vineyards

With a marble bar, library-style shelves lined with wines, and views across the fields, the tasting room at **Stratus Vineyards** (2059

Niagara Food and Wine Events

With so many wineries and local food producers around the Niagara Peninsula, it's no surprise that several festivals and events showcase the area's wine and food. The Niagara region's wineries kick off the summer tasting season at the **Niagara Homegrown Wine Festival** (www. niagarawinefestival.com, June) with two weekends of food and wine events.

Every Wednesday in summer, more than 20 local food trucks, craft brewers, and winemakers join forces for **The Supper Market** (Market at the Village, 111 Garrison Village Dr., Niagara-on-the-Lake, www.marketatthevillage.ca, 4:30pm-9pm Wed. mid-May-mid-Sept.), a festive alfresco food fair that feels like a community party. There's live music, too.

Wouldn't running be more fun if you could stop for chocolate along the way? That's the philosophy behind **The Chocolate Race** (www.thechocolaterace.com, May), a 2.5K, 5K, and 10K walk and run with a chocolate-dipping stop en route and more chocolate treats at the finish line.

In the fall, the **Niagara Grape and Wine Festival** (www.niagarawinefestival.com, Sept.) celebrates the harvest with tastings, concerts, and other special events. It's worth braving the winter weather for the **Niagara Ice Wine Festival** (www.niagarawinefestival.com, Jan.), when tastings, winery tours, a gala party, and other festivities highlight the region's distinctive dessert wines. You can also sample ice wines and more at the **Twenty Valley Winter WineFest** (www.20valley.ca, Jan.).

Niagara Stone Rd., 905/468-1806, www. stratuswines.com, 11am-5pm daily) feels like a luxurious lounge, rather than a muddy-boots winery. Tasting flights of four wines ($10) are served in crystal stemware, and special events, including cheese tastings, concerts, and upscale picnics, take place throughout the season. Their signature wines are blends, labeled simply Stratus White and Status Red. It's also the first winery in the world to receive Leadership in Energy and Environmental Design (LEED) certification, a green-building stamp of approval.

Peller Estates Winery

Best known for chardonnay, riesling, and ice wine, the winery in a grand château at **Peller Estates Winery** (290 John St. E., 905/468-4678 or 888/673-5537, www.peller. com, 10am-9pm Mon.-Thurs., 9am-10pm Fri.-Sun. June-Sept., 10am-7pm Sun.-Thurs., 10am-9pm Fri.-Sat. Oct.-May) produces several lines of wines, from the affordable Family Series to the mid-priced Private Reserve and the high-end Signature Series. They offer multiple options for tastings and tours, and their restaurant is one of the area's most deluxe.

Reif Estates Winery

Opened in 1982, the German-style **Reif Estates Winery** (15608 Niagara Pkwy., 905/468-7738, www.reifwinery.com, tastings 10am-6pm daily Apr.-Oct., 10am-5pm daily Nov.-Mar., tours 11:30am, 1:30pm, and 3:30pm daily Apr.-Oct., Sat.-Sun. Nov.-Mar., $5) specializes in gewürztraminer and riesling, but they also make chardonnay, pinot noir, cabernet merlot, cabernet franc, and other wines. In addition to the standard tastings, you can book a variety of special options, including a blind tasting of either a red or white flight ($20). In good weather, graze on grilled pizzas or sample wine gelato in their **Wine Sensory Garden.**

The Ice House

On a hot summer afternoon, the sign for "ice wine slushies" may lure you down the lane to **The Ice House** (14774 Niagara Pkwy., 905/262-6852, www.theicehouse.ca, 10:30am-7pm daily June-Oct., 11am-5:30pm daily Nov.-May.), a small producer of, yes, ice wine. They make several ice wine varieties: white vidal, riesling, and a more unusual cabernet sauvignon. Sample them in their tasting room as you learn more about how ice wine is made.

If only every slushie shop could make their chilled treats with ice wine!

BREWERIES

In a bright red barn, the beer masters at **Oast House Brewers** (2017 Niagara Stone Rd., 289/868-9627, www.oasthousebrewers.com, 10am-5pm Sun.-Thurs., 10am till late Fri., 10am-7pm Sat., tours 11:30am and 3:30pm Sat.-Sun., $10) specialize in farmhouse ales, including saison, biere de mars, and other brews that age in the bottle. They concoct lots of seasonal beers, though their signature Barnraiser pale ale is always available. You can have a taster or a pint on the patio out back; on Friday nights year-round, the brewery hosts live music. The 45-minute weekend brewery tours wrap up with samples.

The **Niagara College Teaching Brewery** (135 Taylor Rd., 905/641-2252, ext. 4099, www.ncteachingbrewery.ca) is Canada's first teaching brewery—a two-year program where students learn all aspects of the beer business. Sample the students' brews in the campus retail shop (10am-6pm daily May-Oct., 11am-5pm Sun.-Fri., 10am-5pm Sat. Nov.-Apr.).

SIGHTS

Stop into the **Niagara Historical Society Museum** (43 Castlereagh St., 905/468-3912, www.niagarahistorical.museum, 10am-5pm daily May-Oct., 1pm-5pm daily Nov.-Apr., adults $5, seniors $3, students $2, kids $1) to learn more about the history of the Niagara region. Housed in the first building in Ontario built specifically as a museum (the original structure dates to 1907), the exhibits here trace Niagara's history from the early aboriginal communities to the founding of Upper Canada through the War of 1812 and into the present day.

A pharmacy that operated on the town's main street for more than 140 years, the **Niagara Apothecary Museum** (5 Queen St., 905/468-3845, www.niagaraapothecary. ca, noon-6pm daily mid-May-June and Sept.-mid-Oct., noon-6pm Mon.-Fri. and

Oast House Brewers specialize in farmhouse ales.

11am-6pm Sat.-Sun. July-Aug., donation) is still filled with many of its original medicine jars and bottles.

One of Niagara-on-the-Lake's oldest buildings, **McFarland House** (15927 Niagara Pkwy., www.niagaraparks.com, noon-5pm daily mid-May-early Sept., noon-5pm Sat.-Sun. early Sept.-Oct., adults $6.25, ages 6-12 $4.05) is also one of the town's few structures to have survived the War of 1812. Scottish immigrant John McFarland settled here when the British crown granted him 246 hectares (608 acres) of land to reward his services as a boatbuilder to King George III. McFarland and his descendants lived in this 1800 Georgian-style house for more than 140 years. As you tour the restored home, you can learn more about life in the area from 1800 to 1830. Afternoon tea is served in the garden in summer.

The small gallery in the **Niagara Pumphouse Art Centre** (247 Ricardo St., 905/468-5455, www.niagarapumphouse.ca, 11am-4pm Tues.-Sun. Apr.-Dec., free) shows work by local artists. It's worth a look at the building itself, a Victorian structure overlooking the Niagara River that supplied the town's water from 1891 to 1983.

★ Fort George National Historic Site

Between 1796 and 1799, British troops built a fort to protect the Niagara River—an important supply route to the Great Lakes—as well as the growing town of Newark (now Niagara-on-the-Lake). When the Americans attacked the Niagara region during the War of 1812, U.S. troops bombed Fort George and forced the British to withdraw in May 1813. The Americans occupied Fort George until December 1813, when the British forced them to retreat to Fort Niagara, on what is now the New York side of the river. British troops once again took control of Fort George and held it through the duration of the war. By the 1820s, however, the British had built a new stronghold nearby at Fort Mississauga (on the grounds of what is now the Niagara-on-the-Lake Golf Club), and Fort George was abandoned.

Today, at the **Fort George National Historic Site** (51 Queens Parade, 905/468-6614, www.pc.gc.ca or www.friendsoffortgeorge.ca,

10am-5pm daily May-Oct., 10am-5pm Sat.-Sun. Apr. and Nov., noon-4pm Sat.-Sun. Dec.-Mar., adults $11.70, seniors $10.05, parking $6), visitors can tour the restored fort's buildings and grounds, including two blockhouses that served as soldiers' quarters, the 1796 powder magazine (the only structure to survive the War of 1812), the officers' quarters, and the kitchen, where costumed guides often cook snacks for visitors on the open hearth. Guides staff many of the buildings and can tell you about the history of the period. Fife and drum corps periodically perform, and staff demonstrate how to operate muskets like those used during the War of 1812.

Parks Canada guides lead three-hour **electronic scooter tours** (9am Fri.-Sun. June-Aug., Sat. Sept., $39 pp) that start by buzzing around the town's historic sites before you tour the fort itself. For more details or to book, contact the fort or eSkoot Niagara (289/271-0663, www.eskoot.com).

ENTERTAINMENT AND EVENTS

The **Shaw Festival** (10 Queen's Parade, 905/468-2172 or 800/511-7429, www.shawfest. com) is obviously the main entertainment in town. Even outside the regular April-to-October season, the festival hosts films,

staff dressed as 19th-century soldiers at Fort George

holiday performances, and other special events. They post a detailed event calendar on their website.

Music Niagara (905/468-5566 or 800/511-7429, www.musicniagara.org, mid-July-mid-Aug., $25-50) is a long-running summer festival of classical, jazz, blues, and choral music concerts at wineries, churches, parks, and other venues around town.

SHOPPING

Queen Street is downtown's main shopping street, lined with boutiques, galleries, and restaurants, most designed for visitors. Outside downtown, midway between the QEW and the historic district, Niagara Stone Road (Hwy. 55) is the region's commercial hub.

For Shaw books and other memorabilia, visit **Bernard's** (10 Queen's Parade, 905/468-2172 or 800/511-7429, 9am-8pm daily May-Oct., 9am-6pm daily Nov., 9am-5pm Mon.-Sat. Dec., 9am-6pm Mon.-Sat. Jan.-Apr.), the gift shop in the Festival Theatre lobby.

Husband-and-wife team Robert and Melissa Achal founded the **NEOB Lavender Boutique** (758 Niagara Stone Rd., 905/682-0171, www.neoblavender.com, 10am-6pm daily), and they readily share their passion for their 8,000 lavender plants and other flowers and herbs. They've stocked their shop with oils, lotions, and other body products, as well as lavender cookies and even lavender-scented coffee. Tours of the fields and greenhouse ($5) are offered on the hour from 11am to 3pm May-October.

Banana Republic, Forever 21, J. Crew, Lululemon Athletica, and Kate Spade are among the discounted brand names sold at the large **Outlet Collection at Niagara** (300 Taylor Rd., 905/687-6777, www.outletcollectionatniagara.com, 10am-9pm Mon.-Sat., 10am-6pm Sun.), just off the QEW.

SPORTS AND RECREATION

Both walkers and cyclists enjoy the 56-kilometer (35-mile) **Niagara River Recreation Trail,** which begins in Niagara-on-the-Lake and follows the Niagara River south to Niagara Falls and on to Fort Erie. You can rent bicycles from **Zoom Leisure Bikes** (431 Mississauga St., 905/468-2366 or 866/811-6993, www.zoomleisure.com, 8:30am-7pm daily Apr.-Oct., half-day $20, full-day $30). They also manage **Zoom BikeShare** (905/468-3401, www.zoombikeshare.com, $5/hour), a bike-sharing program that enables you to pick up and return a bike at locations throughout Niagara Falls and Niagara-on-the-Lake. They offer several cycling tours, too, including a 3.5-hour winery tour ($69) that visits several local wineries, a craft beer and wine tour ($79), and a picnic wine tour ($90).

Tour company **Niagara Wine Tours International** (443 Butler St., 905/468-1300, www.niagaraworldwinetours.com, 9:30am-8pm daily, $12/hour, half day $20, full day $30) rents bikes as well.

eSkoot Niagara (477 Mississauga St., 289/271-0663, www.eskoot.com, daily May-Oct., three hours $39-59 pp, full day $69-79 pp) rents electric scooters that you can use to explore the area. You must know how to ride a bike and be at least 18 years old (or 16 if an adult family member accompanies you).

Contact **Niagara Kayak Rentals** (1511 Niagara Stone Rd., 905/328-1048, www.niagarakayak.com) to get out on the water. They offer several kayaking options, including a two-hour paddle along Lake Ontario (single $50, double $85) or a two-hour paddle in the Niagara River from Queenston Heights to NOTL (single $80, double $140).

Visiting in winter? You can go ice-skating on the grounds of Fort George National Historic Site at the **Vintage Parks Canada Ice Rink** (51 Queens Parade, 905/468-6614, www.pc.gc.ca, 1pm-4pm and 5pm-8pm Mon.-Thurs., 2pm-5pm and 6pm-9pm Fri., 10am-1pm, 2pm-5pm, and 6pm-9pm Sat., 10am-1pm and 2pm-4pm Sun. Dec.-Mar. weather permitting). Skate rentals are available at the concession stand on evenings and weekends (5pm-9pm Mon.-Fri., 10am-9pm Sat., and 10am-4pm Sun.).

FOOD

Queen Street downtown is lined with places to eat, although you'll often find better value in other parts of town. Several wineries have excellent restaurants, too.

Contemporary

Benchmark (135 Taylor Rd., 905/641-2252, ext. 4619, www.ncbenchmark.ca, 11:30am-2pm Tues.-Thurs., 11:30am-2pm and 5pm-9pm Fri.-Sat., $17-28), the student-run restaurant at Niagara College, is teaching its pupils about local, seasonal cuisine. Your locally grown greens might come with an Ontario cider vinaigrette, and the duck, glazed with college-made honey, may have been raised nearby. The wine list draws from the college's own labels and other Niagara producers. Reservations are required. For a lighter bite, stop into **Bench to Go** (8:30am-2pm Mon.-Fri. June-Aug., 8am-3:30pm Mon.-Fri. Sept.-May, $4-8), which sells good-value salads, sandwiches, and a daily hot dish, plus pastries and coffee.

Ignore the setting in the nondescript strip mall. At **Backhouse** (242 Mary St., 289/272-1242, www.backhouse.xyz, 5pm-9pm Wed.-Thurs, 5pm-10pm Fri., 11:30am-2:30pm and 5pm-10pm Sat., 11:30am-2:30pm and 5pm-9pm Sun., $16-32), the creative "cool climate" cuisine shines, in dishes like wood-fired cauliflower with Ontario peanuts, locally raised duck with celeriac mousse, and trout in an oyster mushroom-pinot noir jus. You can select tasting menus at both lunch ($49) and dinner ($69-99), with optional wine pairings.

Even if it weren't conveniently sited opposite the Festival Theatre, it would be worth dining at **Zees** (Shaw Club Hotel, 92 Picton St., 905/468-5715, www.niagarasfinest.com/restaurants/zees, 11:30am-2:30pm and 5pm-8:30pm Sun.-Thurs., 11:30am-2:30pm and 5pm-9pm Fri.-Sat. May-Nov, 11:30am-2:30pm and 5pm-8:30pm Sun., 5pm-8:30pm Mon.-Thurs., 5pm-9pm Fri., 11:30am-2:30pm and 5pm-9pm Sat. Dec.-Apr., lunch $15-24, dinner $18-36) for its comfortable ambience and solicitous service. The just-imaginative-enough plates might range from a salad of roasted and pickled beets with local goat cheese to a turkey sandwich with cranberry aioli at midday, or salmon croquettes with fire-roasted peppers, root beer-braised short ribs, or seafood pappardelle in the evening.

Overlooking Lake Ontario, the pretty **Tiara** (Queen's Landing Hotel, 155 Byron St., 905/468-2195 or 888/669-5566, www.vintage-hotels.com, 11am-2pm and 5pm-9pm Mon.-Sat., 11:30am-2pm and 5pm-9pm Sun., brunch prix fixe $34, lunch $16-21, dinner $34-49) sparkles for its views. The midday menu includes salads, sharing plates like a goat cheese fondue, and interesting sandwiches, like the "antipasto panini," filled with prosciutto, smoked mozzarella, and charred vegetables. Dinner is more formal, with entrées like braised rabbit with mushrooms and polenta or house-made linguini with seafood and vermouth cream. Tiara is also popular for a refined Sunday brunch.

An early promoter of local food in the Niagara region, classy **Treadwell Farm-to-Table Cuisine** (114 Queen St., 905/934-9797, www.treadwellcuisine.com, 11:30am-2:15pm and 5pm-10pm daily spring-summer, call for off-season hours, lunch $21-26, dinner $35-40) continues to feature regional products in dishes like a salad of seared wild mushrooms topped with a crispy poached egg or Ontario rainbow trout with potato rösti and kale. The wine list highlights Ontario labels, they serve several Ontario ciders, and the beers are mostly Ontario craft brews. Reserve in advance for this dining destination.

Winery Restaurants

Bison carpaccio with a cured egg yolk. Black truffle linguini with ice wine-poached lobster. These are just some of the imaginative, locally focused dishes you might find at **Peller Estates Winery Restaurant** (290 John St. E., 905/468-6519 or 888/673-5537, ext. 2, www.peller.com, noon-3pm and 5:30pm-8:30pm Sun.-Thurs., noon-3pm and 5pm-9pm

Fri.-Sat., lunch $25-45, dinner prix fixe $95), a splurge-worthy dining room in the winery's grand château. At lunch, you can order a la carte or choose a tasting menu (4 courses $65, 5 courses $75, with optional wine pairings). At dinner, the chef serves a lavish five-course fixed menu.

Set amid the vines at the Ravine Vineyard Estate Winery, casual-chic **Ravine Vineyard Bistro** (1366 York Rd., St. Davids, 905/262-8463, www.ravinevineyard.com, noon-8:30pm Mon.-Fri., 11am-8:30pm Sat.-Sun., $15-36) serves modern bistro fare with Niagara ingredients. Look for dishes like a salad of raw, pickled, and poached Niagara pears with spinach and smoked almonds, a burger topped with house-smoked bacon and aged cheddar, or slow-roasted Ontario pork with cider-stewed vegetables.

Bakeries and Cafés

Amid the scones and croissants that lure morning lingerers, and the gorgeous-looking cakes and tarts (including mini ones, just right for a picnic), **Willow Cakes and Pastries** (242 Mary St., 905/468-2745, www.willowcakes.ca, 7am-7pm daily July-Aug., 8am-6pm daily Sept.-June), a petite café just outside downtown, bakes quiche, pork pies, and other savory dishes for a light lunch.

Sandwiches, tacos, and creative pizzas are all fine choices at the country-style **Pie Plate Bakery and Café** (1516 Niagara Stone Rd., Virgil, 905/468-9743, www.thepieplate.com, 11am-7pm Tues.-Thurs., 11am-9pm Fri.-Sat., 11am-7pm Sun.; call or check the website for off-season hours, $6-18), but remember, you're here for the pie: strawberry in June-July, blueberry June-September, peach July-September, and pumpkin in the fall. Whole pies will feed the family; you can eat the individual mini pies right now.

Italian-style ice cream parlor ★ **Il Gelato di Carlotta** (59 Queen St., 905/468-8999, www.gelatodicarlotta.com, 11am-10pm Mon., 11am-11:30pm Tues.-Sun. mid-Apr.-mid-Oct; call or check the website for off-season hours) lures crowds with its frozen treats.

The signature flavor is Crema di Carlotta, a citrus cream, though the rich dark chocolate is pretty irresistible. There is a Niagara Falls branch in the Fallsview Casino (6380 Fallsview Blvd., 905/356-8999, 10am-10pm Sun.-Thurs., 10am-midnight Fri.-Sat.).

Groceries and Markets

Produce, prepared foods, and baked goods are available at the **Farmers Market at the Village** (111 Garrison Village Dr., www.farmersmarketatthevillage.ca, 8am-1pm Sat. late May-mid-Oct.), off Niagara Stone Road (Hwy. 55). **The Fruit Shack** (1267 Niagara Stone Rd., 905/468-9821, www.thefruitshack.com, 9am-6pm daily mid-June-mid-Oct., 9am-6pm Thurs., 9am-5pm Fri.-Sat. mid-Oct.-June) sells local produce, meats, and homemade baked goods. The butter tarts are particularly delicious.

ACCOMMODATIONS

The **Niagara-on-the-Lake Chamber of Commerce** (www.niagaraonthelake.com) can book rooms for you at more than 200 area lodgings. Search for lodging availability and prices on their website. For bed-and-breakfast listings and bookings, contact the **Niagara-on-the-Lake Bed-and-Breakfast Association** (905/468-0123, www.niagarabedandbreakfasts.com). For summer weekend stays, particularly at the smaller B&Bs, book well in advance.

$100-200

Owners Donna and Fernando Vieira are avid travelers, so it's no surprise that they've filled **Globetrotters Bed & Breakfast** (642 Simcoe St., 905/468-4021 or 866/835-4446, www.globetrottersbb.ca, $140-160), a guesthouse on a suburban cul-de-sac, with original art and mementos from their journeys. Draped with colorful sheer curtains, the Sultan's Tent suite looks seductive, although its attached twin-bed room could accommodate a family or friends. The compact Crystal Palace room, on the main floor, has bright blue walls and a hand-painted headboard.

Rates include a full breakfast, Wi-Fi, and parking.

$200-300

A short walk from Queen Street and the theaters, the **Copper Dreams Bed & Breakfast** (28 Johnson St., 905/468-7097, www.copperdreams.ca, $210-230 d) was built in the 1870s to house military officers and their families. You won't feel confined to your quarters in the three updated guest rooms, each with a queen bed, fireplace, and modern bath. The largest, the Newark Room, has a soaker tub for two. A multicourse breakfast, Wi-Fi, and parking are included in the rates.

Built in the 1860s as a summer "cottage," the stately ★ **Grand Victorian Bed & Breakfast** (15618 Niagara Pkwy., 905/468-0997, www.grandvictorian.ca, $210-270 d) has a large wraparound porch and regal architectural details—12-foot ceilings, original woodwork, stained glass windows, and numerous fireplaces. The six guest rooms have four-poster or canopy beds, antique wardrobes, and other period details; one has a private sundeck. Rates include Wi-Fi. You can arrange a tour and tasting at Reif Estates Winery next door or play tennis on the courts out back—if you can rouse yourself from that fantastic porch.

The owners of ★ **Brockamour Manor** (433 King St., 905/468-5527, www.brockamour.com, $229-289 d) serve elaborate breakfasts that will start your day right, as you trade travel tips and theater reviews with fellow guests. Wander into the billiards room to work off your meal with a round of pool or lounge over the newspaper. The six guest rooms are spacious, with classic furnishings and modern touches like gas fireplaces, DVD players, and Wi-Fi.

Over $300

Comprising several buildings in the historic district, **124 on Queen** (124 Queen St., 905/468-4552 or 855/988-4552, www.124queen.com, $300-580 d) is a plush place to lay your head. The least expensive rooms have a king or queen bed with a flatscreen TV, Keurig coffeemaker, and mini fridge; up the price scale, added amenities include fireplaces and kitchenettes. The one- and two-bedroom villas ($440-890) have full kitchens and laundry facilities. You can work out in the small fitness room 24-7, and the spa offers massages and facials. Room rates include Wi-Fi, unlimited local phone calls, parking, and a local shuttle service.

Queen's Landing (155 Byron St., 905/468-2195 or 888/669-5566, www.vintage-hotels.com, $280-560 d), a majestic Georgian-style brick inn that looks like it's been on the lakeshore for generations, was actually built in 1990. While the furnishings are classic, it doesn't have the creakiness of an old-fashioned hotel. Some of the 140 rooms have fireplaces or jetted tubs; the best have views over Lake Ontario. There's also an indoor pool. The hotel hosts lots of business events, but you won't be out of place on a weekend escape.

Built in 1864, the refined ★ **Prince of Wales Hotel** (6 Picton St., 905/468-3246 or 888/669-5566, www.vintage-hotels.com, $300-560 d) wows with its elaborately decorated public spaces, from the lobby's ornate inlaid wood floor to the classic drawing room, where afternoon tea is served daily. There is an indoor pool and the Secret Garden spa. The decor varies in the 110 traditionally appointed guest rooms; some have antique four-poster beds, Tiffany lamps, or fireplaces, but all have modern amenities, from rain showers to heated towel racks. The location couldn't be better, right in the town center.

INFORMATION AND SERVICES

The **Niagara-on-the-Lake Chamber of Commerce** (26 Queen St., 905/468-1950, www.niagaraonthelake.com, 10am-6pm daily May-Oct., 10am-5pm daily Nov.-Apr.) runs a visitors center downtown on the lower level of the courthouse. They can also help you find a place to stay.

Cooking Classes

On the grounds of Strewn Winery, the **Wine Country Cooking School** (1339 Lakeshore Rd., 905/468-1229, www.winecountrycooking.com, mid-Jan.-Nov.) offers recreational cooking classes on Saturdays. Most classes, in which you cook and eat a seasonal meal with wine pairings, are taught 10am-3pm, but evening classes (4pm-9pm) are available. Call or check their website for a detailed schedule.

GETTING THERE

Niagara-on-the-Lake is on the northeast tip of the Niagara Peninsula, bordering Lake Ontario and the Niagara River. It's 135 kilometers (85 miles) southeast of Toronto and 20 kilometers (12.5 miles) north of Niagara Falls.

Air

Toronto's **Pearson International Airport** (YYZ, 6301 Silver Dart Dr., Mississauga, 416/247-7678 or 866/207-1690, www.torontopearson.com) and **Buffalo-Niagara International Airport** (BUF, 4200 Genesee St., Buffalo, NY, 716/630-6000, www.buffaloairport.com) are the commercial airports closest to Niagara-on-the-Lake. The **Niagara Air Bus** (905/374-8111 or 800/206-7222, www.niagaraairbus.com), a door-to-door airport shuttle, can take you from either Pearson (one-way $109) or Buffalo (one-way $96) to Niagara-on-the-Lake; book online at least three days in advance for a 5 percent discount.

Train

Niagara-on-the-Lake does not have direct train service, but on summer weekends, **GO Transit** (416/869-3200 or 888/438-6646, www.gotransit.com) runs trains from Toronto to St. Catharines, where you can pick up a connecting shuttle bus to NOTL.

Car

From Toronto to Niagara-on-the-Lake, take the QEW south, passing Hamilton and St. Catharines. At exit 38B, follow the Niagara-on-the-Lake signs to Highway 55, which is also Niagara Stone Road. Go northeast on Highway 55 for 12 kilometers (7 miles) until it ends at Queen Street. Turn right toward the downtown business district and the Shaw Festival Theatre.

From Buffalo and points south in the United States, take I-190 north to the Queenston-Lewiston Bridge. Once you've crossed to the Ontario side, the most scenic route is to follow the Niagara River Parkway into Niagara-on-the-Lake.

Shaw Festival Bus from Toronto

The easiest way to make a day trip from Toronto for a Shaw Festival show is to ride the **Shaw Express** (905/468-2172 or 800/511-7429, www.shawfest.com, Wed., Thurs., Sat., Sun. Apr.-Oct., round-trip $25 pp), a direct bus from downtown Toronto to Niagara-on-the-Lake. In Toronto, buses depart at 10am from the Fairmont Royal York Hotel (York St. at Front St. W.), opposite Toronto's Union Station; return buses leave the Festival Theatre at 5pm (4pm Sundays). On some Saturdays in July and August, there's an 11pm departure from NOTL, which enables you to see an evening performance. You must have a ticket to a Shaw Festival play to ride the bus. Book your bus ticket online or by phoning the festival box office.

Shuttle from Niagara Falls

From May to late October, you can take a **Niagara Parks shuttle** (www.niagaraparks.com, one-way adults $7, ages 6-12 $5) between the Floral Clock in Niagara Falls and Fort George in Niagara-on-the-Lake. It makes several stops in Queenston en route. The shuttle operates once an hour in each direction and connects with the Niagara Falls WEGO buses.

GETTING AROUND

You can easily walk around the downtown heritage district, between the theaters, the shops, and the lake, and many accommodations are also within walking distance. Few of the wineries are within an easy walk of downtown, though, so you'll need to have a car or bicycle—or book a wine tour—to get out to the tasting rooms. **Niagara-on-the-Lake Transit** (905/468-3266, www.notl.org, $3) provides limited bus service around downtown and between downtown, Niagara College, and the Outlet Collection at Niagara.

Niagara-on-the-Lake has plenty of pleasant cycling routes, including the Niagara River Recreation Trail south toward Niagara Falls. You can reach many of the wineries along country roads by bicycle—at least if you don't drink too much en route.

Parking around town is somewhat limited, particularly on Queen Street and around the theaters. The town website (www.notl.org) has an online parking map that shows parking lots, meter rates and durations, and free parking locations.

Walking Tours

The **Niagara Historical Society** offers one-hour walking tours of Niagara-on-the-Lake (11am Sat.-Sun. June-Aug., $10, including admission to the Niagara Historical Society Museum). **Old Town Tours** (289/292-3532 or 888/492-3532, www.oldtowntours.ca, 10:30am and 2:30pm daily May-Sept., adults $20, ages 7-12 $10) runs two-hour walking tours through the town's historic district as well.

The Twenty Valley

The Twenty Valley lies in the north-central section of the Niagara Peninsula, west of Niagara Falls and Niagara-on-the-Lake. This wine region is centered on the towns of Beamsville, Vineland, and Jordan, yet it is close enough to Toronto, Niagara Falls, and Niagara-on-the-Lake for a day of wine touring or a getaway weekend.

TOP EXPERIENCE

★ TWENTY VALLEY WINERIES

At last count, the Twenty Valley had roughly 40 wineries, and new ones crop up regularly. The peak season for wine touring is during the fall harvest, generally mid-September through early October; July and August are popular, too, with the vineyards full and lush and the weather hot. Most wineries remain open year-round, though many reduce their hours from November to April. Most charge a small fee ($2-5) for tastings, which you can usually credit toward wine purchases.

Winery Tours

For tours that stop at several Twenty Valley wineries, or for cycling tours through wine country, contact the following tour operators:

- **Crush on Niagara Wine Tours** (905/562-3373 or 866/408-9463, www.crushtours.com, $89-139)

- **Grape Escape Wine Tours** (905/468-9959 or 866/935-4445, www.tourniagarawineries.com, $64-144)

- **Niagara Wine Tours International** (905/468-1300 or 800/680-7006, www.niagaraworldwinetours.com, $65-139).

Beamsville

Owner Nicolette Novak grew up on the property that's now home to **The Good Earth Food and Wine Co.** (4556 Lincoln Ave., 905/563-6333, www.goodearthfoodandwine.com, winery 11am-5pm daily summer, 11am-4pm daily winter, restaurant 11am-4pm Mon.-Fri., 11am-5pm Sat.-Sun.), where she and her staff make riesling, rosé, cabernet franc, and pinot noir, among others, which Novak describes as "good for food." Sample these for yourself in the tasting room, or sit down for lunch in the bistro. Their recreational **cooking school** offers two- or three-hour

The Twenty Valley

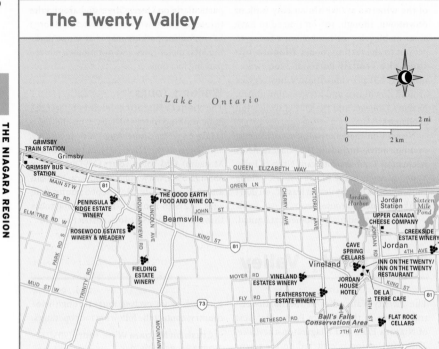

cooking classes focusing on local ingredients; check the website or phone for schedule and prices.

The striking wood-and-stone building that houses the family-owned **Fielding Estate Winery** (4020 Locust Lane, 905/563-0668 or 888/778-7758, www.fieldingwines.com, 11am-6pm daily June-Sept., 11am-5:30pm daily Oct.-May, tours noon and 2pm daily, $10 pp) overlooks the fields and vineyards, a particularly lovely setting for wine tasting. The winery is known for aromatic whites, especially riesling and pinot gris. In addition to regular winery tours, you can book a private tasting ($10); reserve ahead.

On the 32-hectare (80-acre) property at **Peninsula Ridge Estate Winery** (5600 King St. W., 905/563-0900, www.peninsularidge. com, 10am-6pm daily June-Oct., 10am-5pm daily Nov.-May), the winemakers produce

cabernet sauvignon, merlot, syrah, chardonnay, sauvignon blanc, and pinot noir. Stop by for tastings; tours are available by appointment.

The beehives behind **Rosewood Estates Winery and Meadery** (4352 Mountainview Rd., 905/563-4383 or 866/633-3248, www. rosewoodwine.com, tastings daily 11am-6pm Mon.-Sat., 11am-5pm Sun. June-Oct., 11am-5pm Thurs.-Mon. Oct.-May) provide raw materials for Niagara's first mead (honey wine), as well as several varieties of honey. They make wine, too, including pinot noir and riesling. You can drop in for tastings, but tours ($20) must be booked online in advance.

Vineland

Vineland Estates (3620 Moyer Rd., 905/562-7088 or 888/846-3526, www.vineland.com,

10am-6pm daily May-Oct., 11am-5:30pm Sun.-Thurs., 10am-6pm Fri.-Sat. Nov.-Apr., tours noon daily May-Oct., noon Sat.-Sun. Nov.-Apr., $15) released their first vintage back in 1983, which makes them an old-timer in these parts. The signature wines are cabernet franc and riesling, and Vineland makes a distinctive drink called Vice, a blend of their Vidal ice wine and vodka. A small market above the spacious tasting room sells cheeses and offers cheese tastings. The winery restaurant serves lunch and dinner, and the property has two guesthouses.

Not only are the grapes used at the **Featherstone Estate Winery** (3678 Victoria Ave., 905/562-1949, www.featherstonewinery. ca, 11am-5:30pm daily June-Aug., 11am-5:30pm Fri.-Sun. Apr.-May and Sept.-Dec.) grown without pesticides, the winery relies on sheep grazing in the vineyards as a natural way to prune the vines. The fleecy animals give their name to the Black Sheep Riesling; the winery also produces merlot, pinot noir, and cabernet franc, among others. On summer weekends, you can sit on the veranda for pizza and a glass of wine (noon-4pm Sat.-Sun. mid-May-early Sept.).

Jordan

Think wine tasting can be staid, even snooty? Visit laid-back **Flat Rock Cellars** (2727 7th Ave., 905/562-8994, www. flatrockcellars.com, 10am-6pm Sun.-Fri., 10am-7pm Sat. May-Oct., 10am-5pm Sun.-Fri., 10am-6pm Sat. Nov.-Apr.), where you can tour ($10, by reservation only) the vineyards and cellars, learn about their "gravity flow" production process, and sample their wines, which include riesling, chardonnay, and pinot noir.

The winery building at **Cave Spring Cellars** (3836 Main St., www. cavespringcellars.com, 905/562-3581 or 888/806-9910; 10am-6pm daily June-Sept., 10am-5pm Sun.-Thurs., 10am-6pm Fri.-Sat. Oct.-May), in Jordan Village, was built in 1871 and houses Ontario's oldest functioning wine cellar. The current winery, founded in 1986, specializes in riesling, including ice wines, and also makes well-regarded pinot noir, chardonnay, and cabernet franc. Drop into the tasting bar or choose among several tour and private tasting options (from $20 pp, advance reservations required).

Talk with the "Creek Geeks" at the relaxed tasting bar at **Creekside Estate Winery** (2170 4th Ave., 905/562-0035 or 877/262-9463, www.creeksidewine.com, 10am-6pm daily May-Nov., 10am-5pm daily Dec.-Apr., tours 2pm Sat.-Sun. June-Oct.), where you can sample their sauvignon blanc, cabernet shiraz, or other varieties. A unique experience is the **"Up the Creek" tour** (May-Sept., $7), a "dirty boots" adventure where you help out in the vineyard and then do a guided tasting as reward for your labor. **The Deck @ Creekside** (11:30am-9pm Fri., 11:30am-3:30pm Sat.-Mon. mid-May-mid-Oct., $12-21) sates weekend visitors with salads, burgers, and meats from the smoker. There's live music Friday evenings.

BALL'S FALLS CONSERVATION AREA

Beyond the Twenty Valley's wineries are several conservation areas where you can go hiking, and the rolling hills make for pleasant cycling. Billing itself as "Niagara's Other Falls," **Ball's Falls Conservation Area** (3292 6th Ave., Jordan, 905/562-5235, www. ballsfalls.ca, grounds 8am-8pm daily May-Oct., 9am-4pm daily Nov.-Apr., adults $7, seniors and students $5) has 10 kilometers (six miles) of hiking trails, including routes that lead to two waterfalls: the 27-meter-tall (90-foot) Lower Falls, and the 11-meter-tall (35-foot) Upper Falls. The falls run strongest in the spring, and the grounds are a pretty picnic spot.

In a modern, environmentally sensitive building, the **Ball's Falls Centre for Conservation** (9am-4pm daily) has exhibits about the plants and animals that live in the region. Also on-site is a collection of **heritage buildings** (10am-3pm daily Apr.-Oct.), including a flour mill, a church, a blacksmith shop, and the home that belonged to the Ball family, who settled here in 1807. Guides take you around the buildings and demonstrate milling, weaving, and other 19th-century skills.

FOOD
Beamsville

A salad of seasonal vegetables. A cheese or charcuterie platter to share. A grilled cheese sandwich with caramelized onions. That's the simple, fresh fare on offer at the **Good Earth Food and Wine Company** (4556 Lincoln Ave., 905/563-6333, www. goodearthfoodandwine.com, 11am-4pm Mon.-Fri., 11am-5pm Sat.-Sun., $15-25; call or check the website for off-season hours), where you can lunch on the patio overlooking the vineyards (or inside the dining room). They kick off the weekend with "TGIF Casual Fridays" (5pm-7:30pm Fri., $15-25), once-a week dinners.

Housed in an 1885 Queen Anne revival manor house, **The Restaurant at Peninsula Ridge** (5600 King St. W., 905/563-0900, ext. 35, www.peninsularidge.com, noon-2:30pm and 5pm-9pm Wed.-Sat., 11:30am-2:30pm Sun., lunch $15-26, dinner $25-40) bills its style as "casual fine dining." That means that at lunch, your choices will range from a grilled portobello mushroom sandwich to steelhead trout with fingerling potato lyonnaise, while you might sup on prosciutto-wrapped chicken, short ribs with sweet potato purée, or grilled venison with a northern bean cassoulet.

Vineland

In a former farmhouse overlooking the vineyards, **Vineland Estates Winery Restaurant** (3620 Moyer Rd., 905/562-7088 or 888/846-3526, www.vineland.com, noon-3pm and 5pm-9pm daily May-Dec., noon-3pm and 5pm-9pm Wed.-Sat., noon-3pm Sun. Jan.-Apr., lunch $14-26, dinner $16-36) serves upscale wine-country fare. At midday, you might choose citrus-cured rainbow trout with wheat berries or gnocchi

with pulled chicken and squash. For dinner? Perhaps tagliatelle with kale pesto and rabbit, or pickerel paired with beef cheek pastrami. Multicourse tasting menus are available at lunch ($39) and dinner ($85), with optional wine pairings.

Jordan

Need some cheese for your wine-country picnic? Visit **Upper Canada Cheese Company** (4159 Jordan Rd., 905/562-9730, www. uppercanadacheesecompany.com, 10am-5pm daily), which produces several cheeses, including the camembert-style Comfort Cream and the semisoft Niagara Gold, from the milk of local Guernsey cows.

De La Terre Café (3839 Main St., 905/562-4567, www.delaterre.ca, 8am-5pm Mon.-Sat., 10am-5pm Sun., $7-13), in a little house in Jordan Village, makes top-notch baked goods (mmm, cinnamon buns, spelt scones, and pecan squares) and sandwiches, like sweet potato hummus with kale-almond pesto or back bacon with Swiss cheese and greens. Soups and salads round out the short menu; to drink, they serve coffee, beer, wine, and cider. The same owners run a take-out-only **bakery** in Vineland (3451 King St., 905/562-1513, 8am-4pm daily).

After a hard day of wine touring, maybe you just want to kick back with a burger and a beer. The **Jordan House Tavern** (3751 Main St., 905/562-9591, www.jordanhouse. ca, 11am-11pm Sun.-Thurs., 11am-1am Fri.-Sat., $12-15) is your joint. Served in a homey room with a stone fireplace and timbers from the original 1840s saloon that stood on this site, the unfussy, well-executed menu includes hearty burgers, straightforward sandwiches, salads, and bar snacks. There's live music most Friday and Saturday nights.

The formal, white-tablecloth **Inn on the Twenty Restaurant** (3836 Main St., 905/562-7313, www.innonthetwenty.com, 11:30am-3pm and 5pm-9pm daily, call or check the website for off-season hours, lunch $12-30, dinner $22-42), with a wall of windows looking across the countryside, is a special-occasion spot. An early adopter of the Niagara regional food movement, the kitchen creates contemporary cuisine that draws on local products. In the evening, starters might include greens with ice wine-poached pears or a beet tart with honeyed goat cheese, while the entrée could be rack of Ontario lamb served with salt-roasted Jerusalem artichokes. The wine list includes labels from Cave Springs Cellars (under the same ownership) and other Ontario producers.

ACCOMMODATIONS
Vineland
At the entrance to **Vineland Estates Winery** (3620 Moyer Rd., 905/562-7088 or 888/846-3526, www.vineland.com) are two self-contained lodgings. The cozy one-bedroom B&B Cottage ($200 d) is designed for a couples escape. The staff provide a complimentary bottle of wine and provisions for a make-your-own breakfast, but you might not see another soul during your stay. The larger Estate Guesthouse ($350) looks like a suburban home. Accommodating a family or group of friends, it has three bedrooms, a living room, and kitchen facilities; breakfast provisions and a bottle of wine are included, too.

Jordan
Owned by the proprietors of Cave Spring Cellars and the more upscale Inn on the Twenty, the **Jordan House Hotel** (3751 Main St., 905/562-5336 or 800/701-8074, www.jordanhouse.ca, $159-229 d) is an excellent choice for moderately priced wine-country accommodations. It's an upscale two-story motel attached to a historic tavern, with contemporary chocolate-brown and royal-blue linens, flat-screen TVs, coffeemakers, and simple but functional baths. Expect no frills, done well.

Looking for a romantic wine-country escape? The ★ **Inn on the Twenty** (3845 Main St., 905/562-5336 or 800/701-8074, www.innonthetwenty.com, $279-409 d) has the region's most deluxe accommodations,

staffed by an attentive team. The 27 spacious rooms, all more than 500 square feet, are all different, furnished with a mix of antiques and contemporary pieces; some have a separate sitting area and sleeping alcove, some have private terraces, while others are two-level lofts, with a living room and upstairs bedroom. Most have fireplaces and whirlpool tubs. The spa, in an adjacent 1840s building, offers massage, facials, reflexology, and other services. **Jordan Village** (www.jordanvillage.com) has a small collection of boutiques and galleries nearby.

INFORMATION AND SERVICES
For information about the Twenty Valley region, contact the **Twenty Valley Tourism Association** (905/562-3636, www.20valley.ca). The **Wine Council of Ontario** (905/562-8070, ext. 221, www.winecountryontario.ca) can provide more details about the area wineries.

GETTING THERE AND AROUND
To explore the Twenty Valley, you'll either need to have a car or arrange for a tour. Cycling is another option, although it's hilly terrain.

Train or Bus
For rail service to the Twenty Valley, the closest **VIA Rail** (888/842-7245, www.viarail.ca) stations are in Grimsby (99 Ontario St.) or St. Catharines (5 Great Western St.), where the Toronto-Niagara Falls trains stop. **Megabus** (866/488-4452, www.megabus.com) runs frequent buses from Toronto to Grimsby (Main St. at Christie St., 1 hour, $1-11) and St. Catharines (70 Carlisle St., 1.25-1.5 hours, $1-17).

Car
Highway 81 is the main east-west route across the Twenty Valley, running between Grimsby and St. Catharines. From Toronto, take the QEW south toward the Niagara Peninsula. It's

95 kilometers (59 miles) to Beamsville (exit 64, Ontario St.), 100 kilometers (62 miles) to Vineland (exit 57, Victoria Ave.), and 102 kilometers (64 miles) to Jordan (exit 55, Jordan Rd./Hwy. 26).

From Niagara Falls, the simplest route is to take the QEW north. To Jordan it's 34 kilometers (21 miles), to Vineland 36 kilometers (22 miles), and to Beamsville 41 kilometers (25 miles).

St. Catharines and the Welland Canal

The Great Lakes are part of an extensive shipping route that extends from Lake Superior to the Atlantic Ocean. But until the 1800s, a significant natural obstruction—Niagara Falls—blocked the passage between Lake Ontario and Lake Erie. William Hamilton Merritt (1793-1862), a St. Catharines entrepreneur, proposed the idea of a canal across the Niagara Peninsula, connecting the two lakes. He began raising money, and in 1824, construction began on the first Welland Canal.

Building the canal involved finding a way for ships to "climb the mountain," otherwise known as the Niagara Escarpment; Lake Erie is roughly 100 meters (326 feet) higher in elevation than Lake Ontario. The solution was a series of locks that lift ships traveling south through the canal and let them descend the same distance when they journey from Lake Erie to Lake Ontario. After the first Welland Canal opened in 1829, it was rebuilt three times, refining the route and improving the lock technology. The current canal, the fourth, opened in 1932.

At 43.5 kilometers (27 miles), the Welland Canal is about half the length of the Panama Canal. On the Lake Ontario side, the canal starts in St. Catharines, the peninsula's largest city. It heads south through Thorold and Welland before reaching the town of Port Colborne, where it meets Lake Erie on the Niagara Peninsula's south shore. Ships transit the canal between April and December. It takes roughly 9-10 hours for a boat to make the journey between the two lakes.

SIGHTS

You can bicycle the entire length of the Welland Canal if you follow the **Welland Canals Trail** (www.welland.ca), a 42-kilometer (27-mile) cycling path that runs from St. Catharines to Port Colborne.

St. Catharines Museum and Welland Canals Centre

The exhibits in the well-designed **St. Catharines Museum and Welland Canals Centre** (1932 Welland Canals Pkwy., St. Catharines, 905/984-8880 or 800/305-5134, www.stcatharines.ca, 9am-5pm daily, donation $4), located at Lock 3 on the canal, illustrate the history of the Welland Canal and the St. Catharines area. One section of the museum houses the **Ontario Lacrosse Hall of Fame,** devoted to Canada's official summer sport (the official winter sport is hockey).

A highlight is behind the museum, where you can climb to the **viewing platform** to watch the massive ships pass through the locks. The museum posts a schedule showing when the next ships expect to arrive, and also sends out these details on its Twitter feed (www.twitter.com/StCMuseum).

Port Colborne Historical and Marine Museum

The **Port Colborne Historical and Marine Museum** (280 King St., Port Colborne, 905/834-7604, www.portcolborne.ca, noon-5pm daily May-Dec., free) is a complex of several historic buildings, including an 1835 log schoolhouse (one of the region's oldest), an 1880s blacksmith shop, and a Victorian-era home that now houses **Arabella's Tea Room** (2pm-4pm June-Sept.), which serves home-made biscuits and jam to visitors. Also on the property is the 1901 **Neff Steam Buggy,** thought to be the oldest surviving Ontario-made automobile.

FOOD

Searching for enlightenment, or at least dinner, from the far corners of the globe, **The Smokin' Buddha** (265 King St., Port Colborne, 905/834-6000, www.thesmokinbuddha.com, 4:30pm-9pm Tues., 11:30am-10pm Wed.-Sat., $12-15) cooks up small plates, curries, and noodles that take inspiration from Asia, Latin America, India, and the Middle East. Try the Japanese-style *sobo* pockets, sweet tofu stuffed with smoked salmon, sprouts, rice, and wasabi mayo, or go global with Korean beef noodles, Thai curries, or chicken enchiladas. The location in the town's old train station, with exposed brick walls and wooden benches, puts you in the mood for your journey.

Stop in for a beer or a bite at the friendly **Canalside Restaurant** (232 West St., Port Colborne, 905/834-6090, www.canalside.ca, lunch and dinner from 11:30am daily, lunch $10-17, dinner $10-25) facing the Welland Canal. Canalside carries a long list of brews

from Canada and abroad, including its own Lock 8 Lager, and the crowd-pleasing pub menu runs from burgers and sandwiches to pastas, seafood, and steaks.

INFORMATION AND SERVICES

The **St. Catharines Tourism Information Centre** (1932 Welland Canals Pkwy., St. Catharines, 800/305-5134, www.tourismstcatharines.ca), inside the St. Catharines Museum and Welland Canals Centre, has information about the canal and the surrounding region. For information about Port Colborne and the Niagara Peninsula's south shore, contact the **Port Colborne Visitor Information Centre** (76 Main St. W., Port Colborne, 905/834-5722 or 888/767-8386, www.portcolborne.ca, 9am-6pm daily).

GETTING THERE AND AROUND

Unless you're planning to bicycle around the Welland Canal region, you really need a car, as public transit is limited. **VIA Rail** (888/842-7245, www.viarail.ca) trains run to St. Catharines (5 Great Western St.), where you could rent a car to continue your explorations or head off on your bike.

Hamilton

Midway between Toronto and Niagara Falls, Hamilton has an arty, edgy side. Canada's ninth-largest city was once defined by its steel plants, but today artists are opening galleries and studios in its brick storefronts, funky shops are luring both locals and visitors, and young families are moving in as a more affordable urban alternative to nearby Toronto. With a growing number of hip cafés and cool eateries, it's even been nicknamed "Brooklyn of the North." Make a stopover en route to Niagara Falls or a day trip from Toronto to check out what's new.

SIGHTS AND ACTIVITIES
Art Gallery of Hamilton

Surprise: Ontario's third-largest public art gallery is in Hamilton. The **Art Gallery of Hamilton** (123 King St. W., 905/527-6610, www.artgalleryofhamilton.com, 11am-6pm Wed. and Fri., 11am-8pm Thurs., noon-5pm Sat.-Sun.) has a wide-ranging collection, emphasizing 19th-century European and Canadian historical works, African sculpture, and contemporary art from Canada and abroad. Every Wednesday, Saturday, and Sunday at 1pm, you can take a free tour of some aspect of the gallery's collection.

The Level Two Gallery upstairs is always free, but there's a charge to visit the Level One Gallery (adults $10, seniors and students $8, ages 6-17 $4, families $25). On the first Friday of every month, admission to the entire museum is free 4pm-8pm.

★ James Street North Art Galleries

The **James Street North Gallery District** (www.jamesstreetnorth.ca) downtown is the center of Hamilton's arts community. Most galleries are open Wednesday to Saturday afternoons.

As you wander the street, some galleries to look for include: **The Assembly** (4 Cannon St. E., at James St. N., 289/799-3794, www.assemblygallery.ca, noon-5pm Fri.-Sat.), **Hamilton Artists Inc.** (155 James St. N., 905/529-3355, www.theinc.ca, noon-5pm Wed.-Thurs. and Sat., noon-6pm Fri.), **Centre3 for Print and Media Arts** (173 James St. N., 905/524-5084, www.centre3.com, 10am-6pm Mon.-Fri., 11am-5pm Sat.), and **You Me Gallery** (330 James St. N., 905/523-7754, www.youmegallery.com, noon-5pm Wed.-Sun.).

The liveliest time to explore James Street North is during the monthly **ArtCrawl,** the second Friday of every month, when galleries up and down the street stay open late. The biggest crawl of them all is September's **SuperCrawl** (www.supercrawl.ca), which adds music, dance, and theater events for a weekend-long arts festival.

Dundurn National Historic Site

Beyond modern art, Hamilton has history to explore. Dundurn Castle, at **Dundurn National Historic Site** (610 York Blvd., 905/546-2872, www.hamilton.ca, noon-4pm Tues.-Sun., adults $11.50, seniors and ages 13-17 $9.50, ages 6-12 $6, families $30), has a connection to the contemporary British royals. Camilla, Duchess of Cornwall, who is the second wife of Charles, Prince of Wales, is the great-great-great-granddaughter of Sir Allan Napier MacNab (1798-1862) and his wife, Mary, who built and lived in this stately mansion with their daughters, Sophia and Minnie. A lawyer, entrepreneur, and politician, MacNab served as premier of the United Province of Canada, the pre-Confederation union of what would become the provinces of Ontario and Quebec.

Completed in 1835, the home has more than 40 rooms restored to the Victorian era, from grand public spaces to modest servants' quarters (the family had eight live-in servants). Visits are by one-hour guided tour only. To learn more about life in the castle, read *The Diary of Sophia MacNab,* which the older MacNab daughter wrote when she was 13, the year her mother died. It's available in the gift shop.

Royal Botanical Gardens

Located northwest of downtown at the Hamilton-Burlington line, the **Royal Botanical Gardens** (680 Plains Rd. W., Burlington, 905/527-1158, www.rbg.ca, 10am-8pm daily late Apr.-Oct., 10am-5pm daily Nov.-late Apr., adults $16, seniors and students $13, ages 4-12 $9, families $37) has more than 1,100 hectares (2,700 acres) of flowers, plants, and trees, and more than 30 kilometers (19 miles) of walking trails. There are roses and magnolias, cherry trees and tulips, and one of the most extensive collections of lilacs in the world. The gardens are open year-round; some exhibits are indoors.

Waterfalls

Hamilton is sometimes called the "City of Waterfalls" for the more than 100 streams that cascade down slopes around the region. In the Dundas area west of downtown, the 22-meter (72-foot) **Webster's Falls** (Fallsview Rd., off Short Rd.) and the narrower but taller (41-meter, 135-foot) **Tew's Falls** (Harvest Rd.) have a short walking trail between them. The **Hamilton Conservation Authority** (www.

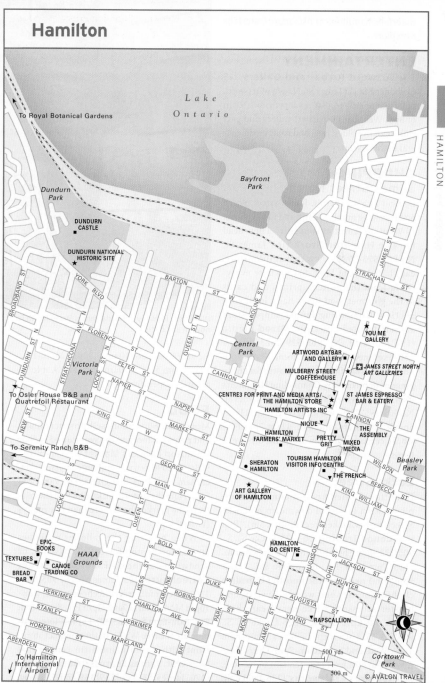

Hamilton

Lake Ontario

To Royal Botanical Gardens

Dundurn Park

Bayfront Park

DUNDURN CASTLE

DUNDURN NATIONAL HISTORIC SITE

BROADBAND ST

YORK BLVD

BARTON ST

STRACHAN ST E

JAMES ST N

DUNDURN ST

STRATHCONA AVE N

FLORENCE ST

QUEEN ST N

CAROLINE ST N

Central Park

YOU ME GALLERY

ARTWORD ARTBAR AND GALLERY

JAMES STREET NORTH ART GALLERIES

Victoria Park

PETER ST

NAPIER ST

CANNON ST W

MULBERRY STREET COFFEEHOUSE

CENTRE3 FOR PRINT AND MEDIA ARTS/ THE HAMILTON STORE

ST JAMES ESPRESSO BAR & EATERY

NEW ST

LOCKE ST N

KING ST

NAPIER ST

HAMILTON ARTISTS INC

NIQUE

CANNON ST E

To Osler House B&B and Quatrefoil Restaurant

THE ASSEMBLY

MARKET ST

BAY ST N

HAMILTON FARMERS' MARKET

PRETTY GRIT

MIXED MEDIA

Beasley Park

To Serenity Ranch B&B

GEORGE ST

SHERATON HAMILTON

TOURISM HAMILTON VISITOR INFO CENTRE

WILSON ST

REBECCA ST

LOCKE ST S

MAIN ST W

THE FRENCH

KING WILLIAM ST

QUEEN ST S

ART GALLERY OF HAMILTON

BOLD ST

EPIC BOOKS

HAAA Grounds

HAMILTON GO CENTRE

HUGHSON ST N

JOHN ST N

JACKSON ST

TEXTURES

CANOE TRADING CO

HESS ST

CAROLINE ST

DUKE ST

HUNTER ST E

BREAD BAR

HERKIMER ST

CHARLTON AVE

ROBINSON ST

PARK ST

MCNAB ST

AUGUSTA ST

STANLEY ST

HERKIMER ST W

JAMES ST

YOUNG ST

RAPSCALLION

HOMEWOOD ST

MARKLAND ST

BAY ST

ABERDEEN AVE

Corktown Park

To Hamilton International Airport

0   500 yds

0   500 m

© AVALON TRAVEL

waterfalls.hamilton.ca) lists more waterfalls to explore.

ENTERTAINMENT

The **Artword Artbar and Gallery** (15 Colbourne St., at James St. N., www.artword. net, from 6pm Wed.-Sat., events from 7:30pm or 8pm Wed.-Sat.) is part art gallery and part club, with live blues, jazz, and roots music several nights a week.

SHOPPING
James Street North

Beyond its art galleries, James Street North has a growing number of fun and funky shops.

Want a Hamilton souvenir? Then head for **The Hamilton Store** (165 James St. N., 905/973-2932, www.thehamiltonstore. ca, 11:30am-5pm Wed.-Sat.), where everything from the posters, prints, and cards to the gourmet food items has a local connection. Combining an art supply store and art-focused gift shop, **Mixed Media** (154 James St. N., 905/529-2323, http:// v2.mixedmediahamilton.com, 11am-5pm Tues.-Sat.) is another spot to browse for crafty presents or mementos. Channeling Hamilton's industrial-art vibe, **Pretty Grit** (128 James St. N., 905/393-7809, www.prettygrit.ca, 11am-6pm Tues.-Thurs. and Sat., 11am-7pm Fri.) stocks ceramics, housewares, and other gift items.

Locke Street

Hamilton's other up-and-coming shopping district is west of downtown on Locke Street (www.lockestreetshops.com). Pop into **Canoe Trading Co** (233 Locke St. S., 905/523-0606, https://canoetradingco.com, 11am-7pm Mon.-Fri., 10am-6pm Sat., 11am-5pm Sun.) to peruse the (mostly) Canadian clothing for men and women, jewelry, and hipster accessories like beard care kits. Check out **Epic Books** (226 Locke St. S., 905/525-6538, www.epicbooks.ca, 10am-6pm Tues.-Wed. and Sat., 10am-8pm Thurs.-Fri., noon-5pm Sun.), an independent bookstore, and **Textures Craftworks** (236 Locke St.

Hamilton's formerly industrial James Street North is now an arts district.

S., 905/523-0636, 10am-5:30pm Mon.-Fri., 10am-5pm Sat., 9:30am-3pm Sun.), a local artists' cooperative.

FOOD

More than 60 vendors sell produce, meat, and prepared foods at the year-round indoor **Hamilton Farmers Market** (35 York Blvd., 905/546-2096, www.hamiltonfarmersmarket. ca, 8am-6pm Tues. and Thurs.-Fri., 7am-5pm Sat.). Note the historic Birks Clock in the center of the market that's more than five meters (17 feet) high.

When browsing the galleries on James Street North, stop for coffee, pastries, or sandwiches at the cool **Mulberry Street Coffeehouse** (193 James St. N., 905/963-1365, www.mulberrycoffeehouse.com, 7am-10pm Mon.-Thurs., 7am-11pm Fri., 8am-11pm Sat., 8am-6pm Sun., $3-13). Laptop-toters appreciate the free Wi-Fi. In the compact storefront with a gold-painted tin ceiling that houses **St. James Espresso Bar & Eatery** (170 James St. N., 289/389-6565, www.

saint-james.ca, 8am-5pm Mon.-Sat., 9am-4pm Sun., $7-16), you can refresh with coffee drinks, pancakes, or avocado toast.

Lively **Nique** (30 Vine St., 905/529-8000, www.niquerestaurant.ca, 11:30am-3pm and 5pm-midnight Mon.-Thurs., 11:30am-3pm and 5pm-2am Fri., 5pm-2am Sat., 11am-3pm and 5pm-midnight Sun., lunch $14-22, dinner $18-36), just off James Street, is a fun spot for drinks, snacks, or a full meal. Start with a cocktail or craft beer and a plate of the signature sushi nachos, then graze on a salad of roasted veggies with smoked yogurt or dig into world-wandering plates like shrimp curry, farfalle with crispy kale, or steak. Love chocolate? The massive square of chocolate cake with espresso icing conveniently arrives in its own take-out container.

The downtown block housing **The French** (37 King William St., 905/528-3737, www.thefrench.ca, noon-3pm and 5pm-10pm Mon.-Thurs., noon-3pm and 5pm-10:30pm Fri., 10am-3pm and 5pm-10:30pm Sat., 10am-3pm and 5pm-9pm Sun., lunch $13-26, dinner $19-39, brunch $8-24) has become a "restaurant row," with several intriguing dining options. This French-inspired bistro in a restored stone and brick building is smart enough for a business lunch but casual enough for a relaxed evening out. The menu updates bistro classics, from a niçoise salad to a root vegetable tagine to duck confit. Between lunch and dinner (3pm-5pm), the French stays open for snacks and drinks.

The guiding principle at **Bread Bar** (258 Locke St. S., 905/522-2999, www.breadbar.ca, 8am-10pm daily, $9-30), a neighborhood bakery by day and mellow pizzeria by night, is that "good ingredients matter." Those good ingredients turn up in salads, sandwiches, and mighty fine pizzas, whether topped with brie, roasted garlic, and arugula; apple, smoked cheddar, and bacon; or other flavorful combinations. Wheel in your stroller, bring in your date, or roll in with your pals, and you'll feel equally at home.

In a snug downtown storefront, eclectic **Rapscallion** (61 Young St., 905/522-0088, www.rapscallionrestaurant.com, 5pm-11pm daily, $5-15) gets imaginative with its meat, concocting a changing assortment of sharing plates like Tongue and Cheek (confit tongue with braised veal cheek) or the Rudolph (venison tartare with pickled tomatoes). But don't fret, plant lovers: the kitchen gets equally creative with vegan "charcuterie," puff pizza with butternut squash purée, and other

Webster's Falls, Hamilton

veggie-friendly fare on its periodic Meatless Mondays.

Serving inventive contemporary fare, **Quatrefoil Restaurant** (16 Sydenham St., Dundas, 905/628-7800, www.quatrefoilrestaurant.com, noon-3pm and 5pm-10pm Tues.-Sat., lunch $17-26, dinner $35-44), west of downtown, put Hamilton on the fine-dining map. At lunch, try the rainbow trout with beluga lentils, or the updated eggs Benedict. In the evening, Cornish hen might be paired with potato gnocchi and a leek purée, while the locally raised beef might be served with rutabaga gratin and mustard jelly. It's straightforward, stylish, and scrumptious.

ACCOMMODATIONS

If you want to stay right downtown, **Sheraton Hamilton** (116 King St. W., 905/529-5515 or 888/627-8161, www.sheratonhamilton.com, $155-299 d) has all the standard business-class amenities. Otherwise, Hamilton has a couple of lovely B&Bs outside the city center.

Grand ★ **Osler House B&B** (30 South St. W., Dundas, 289/238-9278, www.oslerhouse.com, $165-195 d) feels like a place you might have inherited if your relations were minor royalty. Owners Gary Fincham and Sara Burnet-Smith bought, designed, and furnished this 1848 Georgian-style home, which has high ceilings, a grand staircase, spacious rooms, oriental rugs, antiques, and capacious baths with heated floors in the three guest rooms upstairs. Enjoy the gracious parlor or the more casual billiards room; breakfast may include beautifully carved fresh fruit, apricot scones with homemade jam, and a carefully rolled omelet.

On a rural road between Hamilton and Brantford, owner Shane Burry has transformed a suburban home into **Serenity Ranch B&B** (2171 Wilson St. W., Ancaster, 905/920-2447 or 800/659-3714, www.serenityranchbb.com, $99-199 d). Each of the five traditionally furnished guest rooms, with pillow-top mattresses and remote-controlled lights, has a fridge with complimentary

The French is one of several restaurants along King William Street.

beverages, a microwave with free popcorn, and a flat-screen TV with a DVD player. Rates include a full breakfast. There's a complimentary guest laundry and a lovely porch overlooking the fields.

INFORMATION AND SERVICES

The **Tourism Hamilton Visitor Information Centre** (28 James St. N., 905/546-2666 or 800/263-8590, www.tourismhamilton.com, 9am-4pm Mon.-Fri.) can provide information about things to see and events around the region.

GETTING THERE AND AROUND

An alternative to Toronto's busy Pearson Airport, **Hamilton International Airport** (YHM, 9300 Airport Rd., 905/679-1999, www.flyhamilton.ca) is 14 kilometers (nine miles) south of downtown. **WestJet** (888/937-8538, www.westjet.com) is the airport's main carrier, with nonstop flights to Calgary year-round, November through April flights to Edmonton, Halifax, Winnipeg, Orlando, and Las Vegas, and summer service to Vancouver. **Air Canada** (888/247-2262, www.aircanada.com) has a daily flight in each direction between Hamilton and Montreal year-round, and discount carrier **Flair Airlines** (204/888-4357, www.flairairlines.com) flies to Edmonton, Winnipeg, and Abbotsford, BC.

Buses and trains arrive at and depart from the **Hamilton GO Centre** (36 Hunter St. E., 416/869-3200, www.gotransit.com), an art deco-style building downtown with frequent service to Toronto's Union Station (1-1.25 hours, one-way adults $12.45, seniors and kids $6.25). **Megabus** (866/488-4452, www.megabus.com) can take you to Niagara Falls (1.5-1.75 hours, one-way $10).

Hamilton is midway between Toronto and Niagara Falls. It's 65 kilometers (40 miles) southwest of Toronto, a straight shot down the Queen Elizabeth Way (QEW). To Niagara Falls, continue south on the QEW for another 70 kilometers (44 miles).

You can explore downtown Hamilton without a car. It's a short walk from the train-bus station to the Art Gallery and Farmers Market; the James Street North Gallery District is also within walking distance. To visit other attractions, get around on the city's bus system, the **Hamilton Street Railway** (905/527-4441, www.hamilton.ca, one-way $3).

a plush guest room at Hamilton's Osler House B&B

Lake Erie to Lake Huron

Bounded by two Great Lakes, the tri-angle of Ontario stretching west from Toronto includes arty university towns, great theater, traditional Mennonite communities, African Canadian historical sights, craft breweries, wineries,

and plenty of lakeside beaches and parks. Most are close enough to Toronto for a weekend getaway.

About 90 minutes' drive west of Toronto are the twin cities of Kitchener-Waterloo, where high tech has reshaped this formerly industrial region and launched a fledgling arts scene. As Kitchener-Waterloo embraces technology, St. Jacobs and the surrounding farm country are home to Mennonite communities that hold fast to their traditional ways, while the nearby villages of Elora and Fergus are among Ontario's most beautiful small towns.

Theatergoers make regular pilgrimages to Stratford for its namesake theater festival, which presents works by Shakespeare and more contemporary playwrights. Like its British namesake (yes, it's on the River Avon), the town also has plenty of high-end restaurants and browse-worthy shops. While considerably smaller than its UK counterpart, the

city of London is Canada's 10th-largest metropolitan area. Its large student population has given rise to culture, shops, and pubs.

Many towns in Southwestern Ontario were the last stop on the Underground Railroad, the network of safe houses that sheltered slaves escaping plantations in the U.S. South. In Windsor, Amherstburg, Buxton, and Chatham, sights from that era dramatically illustrate this history. Along Lake Erie's shores you can tour a growing wine district, visit the southernmost point on the Canadian mainland, or hop the ferry to laid-back Pelee Island. To the west, the Lake Huron shore is lined with beachfront vacation towns and plenty of places to sit by the shore and watch the sun set.

PLANNING YOUR TIME

Kitchener-Waterloo and Stratford are easy day trips from Toronto. For a weekend getaway, tour the historic sites and wineries of

Previous: a Mennonite family's buggy; Canada's southernmost mainland point in Point Pelee National Park. **Above:** Kitchener-Waterloo is a high-tech hub.

Look for ★ to find recommended sights, activities, dining, and lodging.

Highlights

★ **St. Jacobs:** This small town outside Kitchener-Waterloo is a base for learning more about the region's traditional Mennonite community. You can see farmers driving horse-drawn buggies, and purchase homemade jams, quilts, and other handcrafted items from Mennonite families (page 163).

★ **Stratford Festival:** Running annually from April through October, North America's largest classical repertory theater has been producing plays by William Shakespeare and more contemporary playwrights since 1953 (page 170).

★ **Buxton National Historic Site and Museum:** This museum and its adjacent historic buildings recount the fascinating story of the Buxton Settlement, which became the largest 19th-century African Canadian community in Canada (page 188).

★ **Point Pelee National Park:** On a spit of land jutting into Lake Erie, the southernmost tip of Canada's mainland is a major stopover point for migrating birds, particularly in spring (page 190).

★ **Pelee Island:** A peaceful getaway for a day, a weekend, or more, this rocky island in Lake Erie is the southernmost point in Canada. Bring your bike (or rent one on the island); it's a good spot for cycling (page 193).

★ **John Freeman Walls Historic Site and Underground Railroad Museum:** Built and operated by the descendants of

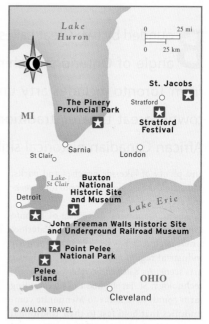
© AVALON TRAVEL

escaped slaves, this open-air museum illustrates the arduous journey north on the Underground Railroad to freedom in Canada (page 201).

★ **The Pinery Provincial Park:** The 10-kilometer (six-mile) powdery sand beach at this popular park is one of the loveliest on Lake Huron (page 205).

Lake Erie to Lake Huron

0

0

20 mi

50 km

MICHIGAN

Saginaw Bay

Ann Arbor

Flint

Detroit

Windsor

PELEE ISLAND

Amherstburg

Kingsville

Leamington

Lakeshore

Tilbury

POINT PELEE NATIONAL PARK

JOHN FREEMAN WALLS HISTORIC SITE AND UNDERGROUND RAILROAD MUSEUM

CHATHAM-KENT BLACK HISTORICAL SOCIETY

Chatham-Kent

Blenheim

Ridgetown

Rodney

BUXTON NATIONAL HISTORIC SITE AND MUSEUM

UNCLE TOM'S CABIN HISTORIC SITE

Dresden

Lake St. Clair

St. Clair

Port Huron

Sarnia

Petrolia

Plympton-Wyoming

Watford

Strathroy

Glencoe

St. Thomas

London

Ingersoll

Aylmer

Tillsonburg

Port Stanley

Malahide

Delhi

Port Dover

Norfolk

Nanticoke

Forest

Lambton Shores

THE PINERY PROVINCIAL PARK

Grand Bend

South Huron

Bayfield

Goderich

Kincardine

Southampton

Exeter

Lucan

St. Marys

Mitchell

Clinton

Bluewater

Blyth

Wingham

Listowel

Mt Forest

Clinton

STRATFORD FESTIVAL

Stratford

New Hamburg

Woodstock

ST. JACOBS

Waterloo/ Kitchener

Cambridge

Paris

Brantford

Haldimand

Dunwille

Port Colborne

Caledonia

St. Catharines

Stoney Creek

Burlington

Oakville

Milton

Markham

Mississauga

Toronto

Vaughan

Acton

Guelph

Rockwood

Fergus

Elora

Orangeville

Eloro

Hamilton

Lake Ontario

Lake Huron

Lake St. Clair

Lake Erie

CANADA

UNITED STATES

OHIO

PENNSYLVANIA

NY

Erie

Dunkirk

© AVALON TRAVEL

Southwestern Ontario, or hang out in one of the Lake Huron beach towns.

For a more complete tour, plan to spend a week to 10 days. Start by exploring the museums in Kitchener-Waterloo and the Mennonite communities around **St. Jacobs.** Allow a day to browse the shops and swim in the quarry in the pretty village of **Elora,** and another day or two to visit Stratford and see at least one play at the **Stratford Festival.** From Stratford, drive to Lake Huron and spend a couple of days relaxing in **Bayfield** or at **The Pinery Provincial Park.** Stop off in **London** as you make your way southwest to visit the African Canadian heritage sights around Chatham, wine-tour near Amherstburg and Kingsville, and sightsee in Windsor. If you have time, head over to **Pelee Island** to cycle, walk, or just unwind.

Kitchener-Waterloo and Vicinity

Billing itself as "Canada's technology triangle," the formerly industrial communities of Kitchener-Waterloo (aka "K-W") and nearby Cambridge have reinvented themselves with high tech. BlackBerry helped put Waterloo on the innovation map after launching its smartphone here back in 1999. More than 400 tech firms, including Google, Open Text, and Christie, have since established K-W offices, and graduates of University of Waterloo's well-regarded computer science, mathematics, and engineering programs regularly start up technology ventures in the region.

This high-tech development is triggering a renaissance in other areas, notably the arts. The region has several excellent small museums and galleries, clustered in downtown Kitchener or uptown Waterloo (the city's central area), and an increasingly robust calendar of arts events. There's a feeling of excitement here that makes it worth exploring.

Well before the high-tech boom, many early settlers arrived from Germany, and a wildly popular event remains the annual Oktoberfest, the largest such festival outside of Germany. The most visible day-to-day legacy of this Germanic heritage is in the countryside around K-W, particularly around the village of St. Jacobs, where many residents are traditional Old Order Mennonites, whose simple buggy-driving, technology-shunning lifestyle contrasts sharply with the online-obsessed world of their more urban neighbors. See it while you still can.

SIGHTS
Kitchener-Waterloo Art Gallery

Compact yet cool, the **Kitchener-Waterloo Art Gallery** (101 Queen St. N., Kitchener, 519/579-5860, www.kwag.ca, 9:30am-5pm Mon.-Wed., 9:30am-9pm Thurs., 9:30am-5pm Fri., 10am-5pm Sat., 1pm-5pm Sun., free) shows contemporary Canadian and international artworks from the 4,000-piece permanent collection and in changing exhibits. Located in the Centre in the Square theater building, the gallery stays open late before performances.

THEMUSEUM

Part children's museum and part "museum of ideas," **THEMUSEUM** (10 King St. W., Kitchener, 519/749-9387, www.themuseum. ca, 10am-9pm Wed., 10am-4pm Thurs.-Sun., over age 14 $12, ages 3-13 $9, everyone $5 Wed.) has plenty of things for kids to do, but as you climb to the higher floors in the open, multitiered space, exhibits become more sophisticated, like the recent *Science of Sexuality* or *Digital Dynamics,* which highlighted games, new media art, and other interactive works.

There's nothing "children's museum" about the on-site eatery, **B@THEMUSEUM**

Kitchener-Waterloo

(519/742-2337, www.bhere.ca, 11am-11pm Tues.-Thurs., 11am-1am Fri., 11am-midnight Sat., 11am-9pm Sun., $12-21), which has a rustic wood, beer-hall vibe and pairs its internationally influenced menu of dumplings, tacos, and pastas with craft brews and fun cocktails.

Waterloo Region Museum

Starting with its striking, multicolored glass exterior, the **Waterloo Region Museum** (10 Huron Rd., Kitchener, 519/748-1914, www.waterlooregionmuseum.com, 9:30am-5pm daily May-early Sept., 9:30am-5pm Mon.-Sat.,

11am-5pm Sun. early Sept.-Apr., adults $11, seniors and students $8, ages 5-12 $5, families $25) isn't your ordinary historical museum. Multimedia exhibits trace the region's roots from its aboriginal inhabitants to today's high-tech businesses. Behind the museum, travel back to 1914 in the **Doon Heritage Village** (9:30am-5pm daily May-early Sept., 9:30am-4pm Mon.-Sat., 11am-4pm Sun. early Sept.-mid-Oct., 9:30am-5pm Mon.-Fri. mid-Oct.-Dec.), where costumed staff re-create early-20th-century life.

The museum and heritage village are nine

kilometers (six miles) southeast of downtown Kitchener, about a 15-minute drive.

Woodside National Historic Site

The **Woodside National Historic Site** (528 Wellington St. N., Kitchener, 519/571-5684 or 888/773-8888, www.pc.gc.ca, 10am-4pm daily mid-May-Sept., 10am-4pm Thurs.-Sun. Oct.-mid-Dec., adults $3.90, seniors $3.40) is the boyhood home of William Lyon Mackenzie King (1874-1950), Canada's longest-serving prime minister. Set in wooded, park-like grounds, the house has been restored to its appearance in 1891, when Mackenzie King was a teenager, and includes some furnishings that belonged to the King family. Interpreters in period costume tell you about the home and its history.

Schneider Haus

The oldest home in Kitchener, the 1816 **Schneider Haus** (466 Queen St. S., Kitchener, 519/742-7752, www.schneiderhaus.ca, 10am-5pm Wed.-Sat., 1pm-5pm Sun. mid-Feb.-June and early Sept.-mid-Dec., 10am-5pm Mon.-Sat., 1pm-5pm Sun. July-early Sept., adults $6, seniors and students $5, ages 5-12 $4, families $15) belonged to a Pennsylvania German Mennonite farm family. Although the house today is just a few blocks from the city's urban center, it once sat on a 181-hectare (448-acre) farm, and within the restored home it's still the 1800s. Costumed staff cook, put up pickles, spin, or do chores appropriate to the season, and interpret 19th-century farm life and Mennonite customs.

Canadian Clay and Glass Gallery

Changing its exhibits several times a year, the **Canadian Clay and Glass Gallery** (25 Caroline St. N., Waterloo, 519/746-1882, www.theclayandglass.ca, 11am-6pm Mon.-Fri., 10am-5pm Sat., 1pm-5pm Sun., free) features contemporary clay and glass works, often in conjunction with multimedia, painting, and other genres, by artisans from Canada and

THEMUSEUM is a museum of ideas.

farther afield. Do your gift shopping in the museum's first-rate boutique, which sells distinctive jewelry, stained glass pieces, ceramics, and glass sculptures by more than 140 Canadian craftspeople.

Fashion History Museum

Flannel shirts? Denim jackets? Whatever preconceptions you might have about Canadian fashion, the **Fashion History Museum** (74 Queen St. E., Cambridge, 519/654-0009, www.fashionhistorymuseum.com, noon-5pm Wed.-Sun. mid-Mar.-mid-Dec., ages 13 and up $5) may turn them on their heads. In a 1929 brick former post office, this small museum mounts inventive changing exhibits about everything from everyday clothing to shoes to couture in Canada from the 1700s to the present.

ENTERTAINMENT AND EVENTS

The weeklong Kitchener-Waterloo **Oktoberfest** (519/570-4267, www.

oktoberfest.ca, Oct.), which claims to be the largest Bavarian festival outside Munich, celebrates the region's German heritage with beer, music, beer, food, and more beer. For craft beer, look for **Craftoberfest** (www.kwcraftoberfest.com, Oct.), an autumn weekend in downtown Kitchener celebrating local microbrews.

Part of a network of Ontario regional theaters, the **Hamilton Family Theatre Cambridge** (46 Grand Ave. S., Cambridge, 519/621-8000, www.draytonentertainment.com) stages crowd-pleasing plays on its sleek, modern stages.

FOOD

In the **Kitchener Market** (300 King St. E., Kitchener, 519/741-2287, www.kitchenermarket.ca, 8am-3pm Tues.-Fri., 7am-2pm Sat.), vendors sell Croatian, Caribbean, and other international food to go. On Saturday, the lower level houses a large **farmers market** (7am-2pm Sat.).

Need a coffee break? Coffee roaster and cool hangout **Settlement Coffee** (www.settlementco.ca) has locations near Google's headquarters in Kitchener (1 Victoria St. S., 226/971-0739, 7am-9:30pm Mon.-Thurs., 7am-9pm Fri., 8am-9pm Sat., 8am-8pm Sun.) and in Uptown Waterloo (23 King St. N., 519/954-6622, 7:30am-9:30pm Mon.-Thurs., 7:30am-9pm Fri., 8am-9pm Sat., 8am-8pm Sun.).

It's easy to pass right by **Sabletine** (203 King St. S., Waterloo, 519/568-7373, www.sabletine.com, 8am-5:30pm Tues., 8am-6pm Wed.-Fri., 9am-5pm Sat., 10:30am-4pm Sun., $8-10), but don't. This petite café bakes chocolate croissants, lemon tarts, and other fine French pastries, along with daily soups, sandwiches, and interesting salads, like a hearty wheat-berry Waldorf with apples, cranberries, and nuts.

Two Goblets (22 Ontario St. N., Kitchener, 519/749-1829, www.twogoblets.com, 11:30am-2pm and 5pm-9pm Tues.-Fri., 4pm-9pm Sat., lunch $18, dinner $21-23) specializes in schnitzel, with more than a dozen variations, as well as goulash, cabbage rolls, and other hearty dishes that show off K-W's central European roots. You can fill your own goblets with wine from Germany, Canada, and farther afield. At lunchtime, the restaurant offers an all-you-can-eat buffet.

The inventive menu changes every day at ★ **The Berlin** (45 King St. W., Kitchener, 519/208-8555, www.theberlinkw.ca, 5pm-10pm Tues.-Sat., 11am-2pm and 5pm-9pm Sun., $27-38), a lively bistro with high ceilings and rustic wood floors. You might find grilled baby squid with purple daikon, flaky lingcod paired with beans, leek oil, and grapes, or juniper-sauced wood-fired venison among the distinctive dishes that use plenty of local ingredients. Bring your appetite and an open mind.

Known for its flavorful lamb spaghetti (Ontario-raised lamb, marinated tomatoes, wilted spinach, and several types of mushrooms served over pasta) and for its daily-changing curry creation, **The Red House** (30 William St. W., Waterloo, 226/647-4687, www.redhouseuptown.ca, 11:30am-9pm Tues.-Thurs., 11:30am-10pm Fri., 10:30am-3pm and 4pm-10pm Sat., lunch $16-21, dinner $21-34) is a contemporary fine-dining restaurant in a comfortably relaxed setting. And yes, it's located in a cozy red house.

With exposed brick walls, a lengthy booze list, and lots of grazing options, always-busy **Bauer Kitchen** (187 King St. S., Unit 2, Waterloo, 519/772-0790, www.thebauerkitchen.ca, 11am-11pm Mon.-Tues. and Fri., 11am-midnight Wed.-Thurs., 9am-1am Sat., 9am-11pm Sun., lunch $11-25, dinner $15-38) is the kind of place where you can meet up for drinks or bring the gang for a laid-back meal. Snack on fried calamari with pickled peppers and hoisin-glazed duck wings, or dig into burgers, pizzas, pasta, or steaks.

Langdon Hall Country House Hostel's **Dining Room** (1 Langdon Dr., Cambridge, 519/740-2100, www.langdonhall.ca, 7am-10:30am, noon-2pm, and 5:30pm-9pm Mon.-Fri., 7:30am-10:30am, noon-2pm, and 5:30pm-9pm Sat., 7:30am-10:30am,

Side Trip: Brantford and the Six Nations

South of Kitchener-Waterloo and west of Hamilton, the city of Brantford claims the invention of an indispensable modern technology: the telephone. Home to the Six Nations of the Grand River Territory, comprising the Onondaga, Cayuga, Seneca, Mohawk, Oneida, and Tuscarora, the region is also worth a detour for its First Nations heritage sites. Contact the **Brantford Visitor and Tourism Centre** (399 Wayne Gretzky Pkwy., 519/751-9900 or 800/265-6299, www.discoverbrantford.com) for more information about the area.

THE INVENTION OF THE TELEPHONE

Alexander Graham Bell (1847-1922) lived with his family in the 1858 farmhouse that is now the **Bell Homestead National Historic Site** (94 Tutela Heights Rd., 519/756-6220, www.bellhomestead.ca, 9:30am-4:30pm Tues.-Sun., adults $7, seniors and students $6, ages 7-12 $4.75). The family purchased the property in 1870 after emigrating from Scotland. Sitting by the river behind the house in what he called his "dreaming place," Bell reportedly had the inspiration that led him to develop his most famous invention. Guides in period costume tell you about the Bell family's life, Bell's research, and the history of the telephone.

As you travel rural roads in this part of Ontario, be on the lookout for **barn quilts** (www.barnquilttrails.ca), replicas of colorful fabric quilts painted on the sides of area barns. There's one on the Bell Homestead property.

EXPLORING THE SIX NATIONS

The **Six Nations Tourism** office (2498 Chiefswood Rd., Ohsweken, 519/758-5444 or 866/393-3001, www.sixnationstourism.ca, 9am-4:30pm Mon.-Fri., 10am-3pm Sat.-Sun. May-Sept., 9am-4:30pm Mon.-Fri. Oct.-Apr.) has a small exhibit area; staff also answer questions about local First Nations attractions and culture.

Writer and poet E. Pauline Johnson (1861-1913) was born to a Mohawk father and English mother in the 1853 manor house that's now **Chiefswood National Historic Site** (1037 Hwy. 54, Ohsweken, 519/752-5005, www.sixnationstourism.ca, 10am-3pm Tues.-Sun. late May-early Sept., adults $2). She became one of the earliest First Nations authors to earn wide recognition in Canada. On the 30-minute guided tours ($5), you can learn more about her life, work, and family that spanned two cultures.

Her Majesty's Royal Chapel of the Mohawks (301 Mohawk St., Brantford, 519/756-0240, www.mohawkchapel.ca, 10am-3pm Tues.-Sun. mid-May-early Sept., $5) was the first Protestant house of worship in Upper Canada and remains Ontario's oldest surviving church. Built by the British in 1785, it was given to First Nations who supported the British during the American

noon-2:30pm, and 5:30pm-9pm Sun., prix-fixe brunch $72, lunch $26-34, dinner $40-58) is a special-occasion destination with gracious staff. Using local ingredients, the chefs might concoct arctic char paired with vanilla-scented parsnips and cardamom cream or thyme-roasted beef with truffle pudding. Dessert might feature a *mille feuille* with caramel mousse. Dress up and book in advance. You can also dine in the more casual but still luxe **Wilks' Bar** (noon-9:30pm daily, $17-39), where menu choices include fish-and-chips or cider-glazed ham hock with a ramp purée.

ACCOMMODATIONS

Prices rise and availability plummets during university graduations and other special events, but otherwise, you shouldn't have trouble finding a room in or around Kitchener-Waterloo.

Eleanor Roosevelt, Elton John, and Lady Gaga have all stayed at **The Walper Hotel** (20 Queen St. S., Kitchener, 519/745-4321 or 800/265-8749, www.walper.com, $179-279 d), built in 1893 in Kitchener's downtown. Now completely revamped into a cool boutique

Alexander Graham Bell's former home in Brantford

Revolutionary War. One of two Royal Chapels in North America, this simple wood-frame structure is the only such chapel located on First Nations land. Thayendanegea, the Mohawk chief, soldier, and statesman more commonly known as Joseph Brant, for whom the present-day city is named, is buried in a tomb beside the chapel.

The **Woodland Cultural Centre** (184 Mohawk St., Brantford, 519/759-2650, www. woodlandculturalcentre.ca, 9am-4pm Mon.-Fri., 10am-5pm Sat.-Sun. late May-mid-Oct., 9am-4pm Mon.-Fri., 10am-5pm Sat. mid-Oct.-late May, adults $7, seniors $5, ages 5-18 $5) houses a museum exhibiting archeological, historical, and cultural artifacts from the Six Nations communities, as well as periodic First Nations art shows.

Hungry? On the Six Nations reserve, the **Burger Barn** (3000 4th Line, Ohsweken, 519/445-0088, www.burgerbarn.ca, 8am-9pm daily, $6-20) should be your destination, if you like big meaty patties with imaginative toppings. The Smokey Mountain is piled high with Canadian bacon, cheddar, and barbecue sauce, the Luau with monterey jack, grilled pineapple, ham, and hot peppers, and there's even a Mac & Cheeseburger, topped with, yes, macaroni and cheese. You can order breakfast, sandwiches, poutine, or steak, but it's called the *Burger Barn* for a reason.

hotel, the 92 guest rooms have been upgraded with mid-century furnishings, flat-screen TVs, stylish robes, and on-trend equipment for brewing your own pour-over coffee. Hang out over cocktails in **The Lokal** (5pm-9pm Mon.-Fri.), the second-floor lounge, or pop next door for a bite at **TWH Social** (1 King St. W., Kitchener, 519/745-8478, www.twhsocial. com, 11am-11pm Mon.-Thurs., 11am-midnight Fri., 10am-midnight Sat., 10am-9pm Sun.), the hotel's lower-level bistro. Room rates include Wi-Fi; budget $25/day for valet parking or $14/day for self-parking in a nearby garage.

Near Uptown Waterloo, the nine-story, business-friendly **Delta Hotels by Marriott Waterloo** (110 Erb St., Waterloo, 519/514-0404 or 844/254-5047, www.marriott.com, $144-269 d, parking $12) has 194 contemporary rooms, most with a king-size bed, as well as fridge, coffee/tea station, and safe; Wi-Fi is included. Get your workout done in the good-sized fitness center, which has several treadmills, elliptical trainers, and stationary bikes, or in the indoor pool, where a skylight gives the space an outdoor feel.

Fancy classical appointments like elaborately carved bedsteads, lamps shaped like peacocks, and ornate gas fireplaces? Then drive 23 kilometers (14 miles) west of Waterloo to **Puddicombe House** (145 Peel St., New Hamburg, 519/662-2111 or 855/699-2111, www.puddicombehouse.com, $149-209 d), built in 1868 in the village of New Hamburg. The six guest rooms are furnished with antiques and period pieces, as well as flat-screen TVs and air-conditioning. While you may have to crawl around to find the electrical outlets, there's complimentary Wi-Fi throughout the inn. Guests can take breakfast (included in the rates) in one of the three dining rooms, which also serve lunch and dinner.

Play tennis or croquet on the lawn or lounge by the pool at posh ★ **Langdon Hall Country House Hotel and Spa** (1 Langdon Dr., Cambridge, 519/740-2100, www.langdonhall.ca, $325-725 d). Enjoy afternoon tea in the conservatory or stroll the gardens or the 12 kilometers (7.5 miles) of wooded trails before heading for the whirlpool, sauna, and steam room or booking a treatment in the spa. The grand 1902 brick manor was the summer house of New York-born Eugene Langdon Wilks, great-grandson of American mogul John Jacob Astor. Twelve of the 60 elegant guest rooms are in the main house, while the rest are in two separate wings, with overstuffed chairs, fireplaces, and luxurious baths with soaker tubs. The buffet breakfast is lavish.

INFORMATION AND SERVICES

Waterloo Regional Tourism Marketing Corporation (519/585-7517 or 877/585-7517, www.explorewaterlooregion.com) provides information about sights, activities, events, and accommodations in Kitchener, Waterloo, Cambridge, St. Jacobs, and the surrounding towns.

GETTING THERE
Air

The **Region of Waterloo International Airport** (YFK, 4881 Fountain St., Breslau, 519/648-2256 or 866/648-2256, www.waterlooairport.ca) is located east of K-W. **WestJet** (888/937-8538, www.westjet.com) has a direct daily flight from Calgary with connections to Vancouver, Edmonton, and other western Canadian cities.

Alternatively, fly into Toronto's **Pearson International Airport** (YYZ, 6301 Silver Dart Dr., Mississauga, 416/247-7678 or 866/207-1690, www.torontopearson.com), which has many more flight options, and either rent a car or catch the bus to K-W. **Greyhound** (800/661-8747, www.greyhound.ca) runs buses between Toronto Pearson and Kitchener (15 Charles St. W., 1-2 hours, one-way adults $10-38) several times daily. Airways Transit's **Toronto Airporter Bus Service** (519/886-2121, www.airwaystransit.com, 1.5-2 hours, one-way $101 for 1 person, $128 for 2, $144 for 3) provides shared-ride door-to-door service between Pearson and Kitchener-Waterloo.

Train

Both **VIA Rail** (888/842-7245, www.viarail.ca, 1.75 hours, one-way adults $25-66, ages 2-11 $13-33) and **GO Transit** (416/869-3200 or 888/438-6646, www.gotransit.com, 2-2.5 hours, one-way adults and students $17.70, seniors and ages 6-12 $8.85) run trains between Toronto's Union Station and **Kitchener Station** (126 Weber St. W., 888/842-7245).

Bus

Greyhound (800/661-8747, www.greyhound.ca) operates numerous daily buses from Toronto to Kitchener (1.75-2 hours, one-way adults $10-38), as well as several buses a day from Toronto to the University of Waterloo (1.5-2.5 hours, one-way adults $10-38). **Megabus** (866/488-4452, www.megabus.com) runs buses from Kitchener to Hamilton (1.5 hours, one-way adults $10).

Car

Downtown Kitchener is 105 kilometers (65 miles) southwest of central Toronto, about 90 minutes (except at rush hours); take Highway 401 west to exit 278, where you'll pick up Highway 8 west. Exit onto King Street east if you're heading to central Kitchener. Uptown Waterloo is five kilometers (three miles) northwest of downtown Kitchener. From Highway 8, you can either take King Street East and continue through Kitchener and into Waterloo, or take Highway 85 north to Erb Street East and go west.

GETTING AROUND

Kitchener-Waterloo is launching a light-rail system that should work with the region's existing bus network to allow you to explore K-W car-free. **Grand River Transit** (GRT, 519/585-7555, www.grt.ca) runs a comprehensive network of light rail and buses around the region. The light rail, known as ION, has stations throughout downtown Kitchener and Uptown Waterloo, extending to the Conestoga Mall, where you can make connections for St. Jacobs. Out-of-town buses arrive at the **Kitchener Bus Terminal** (15 Charles St. W.), a short walk from the **Victoria Park ION station** and a hub for GRT buses. From there,

both light rail and buses connect downtown Kitchener with Uptown Waterloo. Kitchener with Uptown Waterloo. Use the **EasyGO trip planner** (www.grt.ca) to plot your route.

It's much easier to explore farther afield with a car. Most major car rental agencies have offices in Kitchener-Waterloo. However you're getting around, pay particular attention to the directional and city designations in street addresses: 10 King Street East in Kitchener is not near 10 King Street North in Waterloo.

★ ST. JACOBS

This small town north of Waterloo is a base for learning more about the region's Mennonite community, who settled here in the 1800s. Many Mennonites continue to observe traditional customs, traveling in horse-drawn buggies, wearing unadorned clothing, and farming, canning, and quilting as they have for generations.

St. Jacobs's attractions are in two separate areas. The Market District, where you'll find the year-round farmers market, as well as a collection of outlet stores, is three kilometers (1.9 miles) south of St. Jacobs Village, which houses the Visitors Centre and several smaller attractions. While both the market and village are worth a visit, they're undeniably

Ontario apples at the St. Jacobs Farmers Market

touristy, so make time to explore the surrounding countryside for a clearer glimpse of Mennonite life.

The Market District

Canada's largest year-round farmers market, **St. Jacobs Farmers Market** (878 Weber St. N., 519/747-1830, www.stjacobs.com, 7am-3:30pm Thurs. and Sat. year-round, 8am-3pm Tues. mid-June-early Sept., free) is like a department store of farm markets, where you can buy everything from tomatoes to T-shirts to toenail clippers. The aisles are often as packed as a carnival midway on a hot summer's night.

Many shopkeepers, particularly those selling fruits and vegetables, homemade jams and pickles, or locally produced maple syrup, are Mennonites—the men in traditional black jackets and straw hats, the women in long dresses and bonnets, with their buggies parked behind their stalls. Look for their seasonal produce, homemade baked goods, and quilts and other crafts.

One of the market's most popular snack stalls is the **Fritter Company,** which turns apple slices into crispy, batter-fried apple fritters. Prepare for long lines if you want a fritter fix.

St. Jacobs Village

Stop into the St. Jacobs Visitor Information Centre, not just for information about the region (which they have plenty of), but to see **The Mennonite Story** (1406 King St. N., 519/664-3518, www.stjacobs.com/mennonite-story, 11am-5pm Mon.-Sat., 1:30pm-5pm Sun. Apr.-Dec., 11am-4:30pm Mon.-Sat., 2pm-4:30pm Sun. Jan.-Mar., donation $5) on the lower level. This informative exhibit includes a video about the Old Order Mennonites in the St. Jacobs region, a history of the Mennonites' European roots, including a replica of a cave where their Swiss ancestors hid from their persecutors, a reproduction of a Mennonite meetinghouse, and another video that explains about life in modern Mennonite communities from Brazil to Mexico to Zimbabwe.

If you think a model railroad is just for kids or train geeks, you haven't visited the **St. Jacobs & Aberfoyle Model Railway** (1440-3 King St. N., 519/664-3737, www.stjacobsmodelrailway.com, 10am-5pm Sat., noon-5pm Thurs. and Sun. early July-Aug., 10am-5pm Sat., noon-5pm Sun. May-early July and Sept.-mid-Dec., adults $8, seniors $7, children $5), a fascinating miniature world depicting Southern Ontario life in the 1950s. Yes, there are tiny trains, but this elaborate diorama, hand-built by a group of local residents over the past 40-plus years, comes complete with the local movie house, a Mennonite meetinghouse, and even a farmer in his outhouse.

At **Hamel Brooms** (1411 King St. N., 10:30am-5pm Mon.-Sat., noon-5pm Sun.), you can watch the staff make straw brooms as they've done since the early 1900s. The **Country Mill** (1441 King St. N., 10am-6pm Mon.-Sat., noon-5:30pm Sun.) is primarily a collection of shops, but the building also houses the modest **Maple Syrup Museum of Ontario** (519/664-3626, free).

When you need liquid refreshment, order a taste or a pint at **Block Three Brewing Company** (1430 King St. N., Unit 2, 519/664-1001, www.blockthreebrewing.com, 11am-6pm Sun.-Wed., 11am-9pm Thurs.-Sat.), a local microbrewery.

Mennonite Cultural Tours

Outfitter **Grand Experiences** (888/258-0441, www.grand-experiences.com) offers a unique pedal-powered way to explore Mennonite culture in and around St. Jacobs. On the "Path Less Traveled" tour, you'll cycle gently rolling rural roads to visit a Mennonite-run harness shop, where you can talk with the owner about driving a horse-drawn buggy. Have lunch on a nearby farm with the gregarious family matriarch, who runs a quilting business and keeps a sizeable vegetable garden. You'll also visit a Mennonite general store and the West Montrose Covered Bridge. A half-day canoe excursion along a quiet section of the Grand

The Old Order Mennonites

Most of the roughly 4,000 Mennonites who live in and around St. Jacobs are known as "Old Order Mennonites." The Old Order community is what many people envision when they think of Mennonites: men and women wear traditional clothing, the men in dark suits and black or straw hats, the women in simple long dresses and bonnets. They reject contemporary conveniences, like cars and computers. In this patriarchal society, women may work before they are married, but once they tie the knot, their responsibilities are at home. Large families, with an average of seven children, are common. Women don't wear makeup or jewelry and typically sew the long, plain dresses that they and their daughters wear.

Old Order Mennonites settled in Ontario in the 1800s and can trace their roots to Switzerland in the 1500s. While many of the Old Order now have electricity and telephones in their homes, they shun other technologies, from automobiles and clothes dryers to radios and TVs. Most speak a German dialect, although all learn English at school. The Old Order communities run their own schools, which children typically attend through grade 8 or age 14.

The Old Order Mennonites are private people, but you can learn more about their communities and customs if you're respectful of their beliefs and traditions. Drive along the back roads outside St. Jacobs and you'll likely see horse-drawn buggies trotting alongside your car, or black-hatted men pedaling along on their bicycles. On Sunday, you may see lines of buggies heading to the meetinghouse.

Many Mennonite families sell produce, eggs, homemade jams, and quilts from their farms in the countryside around St. Jacobs. They'll post a sign at the end of their driveway if they're open for business. You're welcome to chat while you're browsing their wares or making a purchase, but remember that they're running a business, not opening their homes to gawking travelers. Also, Mennonites frown on picture taking (they believe it can lead to the sin of pride), so don't snap photos of people, and ask permission before photographing their buggies or the products they're selling.

You can stop into the Mennonite-run **Wallenstein General Store** (7278 Hwy. 86, at Hwy. 10, 519/669-2231), about 12 kilometers (7.5 miles) northwest of St. Jacobs, which sells the traditional hats, religious books, fabrics, and farm supplies used in the Old Order community. Their homemade morning glory muffins ($1) are tasty, too.

Northeast of St. Jacobs, the **Lost Acres Variety Store** (12 Covered Bridge Dr., West Montrose, 519/669-5689) is also Mennonite-run (note the extra-large packages of Jell-O for sale). It's adjacent to Ontario's only remaining covered bridge, the **West Montrose Covered Bridge,** built in 1881; it's known as the "Kissing Bridge" because it offered couples traveling by horse and buggy a secluded spot to smooch.

To find other Mennonite-owned businesses, simply drive the country lanes—if the sign says "No Sunday Sales," it's likely run by a Mennonite family. In addition to produce vendors and quilters, look for furniture makers and other artisans.

At the **St. Jacobs Visitor Information Centre** (1406 King St. N., 519/664-1133 or 800/265-3353, www.stjacobs.com), pick up the helpful free booklet *The Plain and Simple Facts: Inside the Old Order Mennonite Community of the St. Jacobs Area,* which explains more about the community's beliefs and traditions, courtship and marriage customs, schools, and child-rearing practices. They also sell other books about Mennonite culture and traditions.

River and accommodations in St. Jacobs are also included.

You can book this trip as a two-day, one-night tour ($389/person) or as a two-day, two-night package ($489/person) that includes a behind-the-scenes visit to the St. Jacobs Farmers Market. Another option is a one-day cycling-only version of the tour ($100/person) that doesn't include lodging or canoeing.

Entertainment and Events

Near the farmers market, the year-round

St. Jacobs Country Playhouse (40 Benjamin Rd. E., 519/747-7788, www.draytonentertainment.com) stages musicals and other lighter fare. At the more intimate St. Jacobs Schoolhouse Theatre (11 Albert St., 519/638-5555, www.draytonentertainment.com), in an 1867 stone school in St. Jacobs Village, you can watch professional theater productions with cabaret-style seating.

The annual Quilt and Fibre Art Festival (800/265-3353, www.stjacobs.com), typically held over several days in late May, showcases quilt work by regional artisans. Quilts are displayed in St. Jacobs, Kitchener-Waterloo, and surrounding towns. As part of the festival, quilts are auctioned off at the New Hamburg Mennonite Relief Sale (www.nhmrs.com), one of Canada's largest quilt auctions.

Food and Accommodations

You won't go hungry at the St. Jacobs Farmers Market (878 Weber St. N., 519/747-1830, www.stjacobs.com, 7am-3:30pm Thurs. and Sat. year-round, 8am-3pm Tues. mid-June-early Sept.), with plenty of stalls selling snacks and more substantial meals.

Pick up a Dutch apple square, butter tart, or other sweet from the Stone Crock Bakery (1402 King St. N., 519/664-3612, www.stonecrock.ca, 6:30am-6pm Mon.-Sat., 11am-5:30pm Sun.). Next door, the family-style Stone Crock Restaurant (1396 King St. N., 519/664-2286, www.stonecrock.ca, 7am-3pm Mon.-Tues., 7am-8pm Wed.-Sat., 11am-8pm Sun.) sets up a buffet at lunch (Mon.-Sat., $19) and dinner (Fri.-Sun., $25); among the à la carte options are solid dishes like roast turkey, cabbage rolls, and pot roast.

Jacob's Grill (1398 King St. N., 519/664-2575, www.jacobsgrill.ca, 11:30am-9pm Mon.-Wed., 11:30am-10pm Thurs.-Sat., 11:30am-5pm Sun., $12-25) tries to bridge the gap between traditional and contemporary with a menu that includes macaroni and cheese, steak, barbecue ribs, and Thai noodles. The Stone Crock and Jacob's are under the same ownership.

In St. Jacobs Village, owner Claire Bowman keeps three neat second-floor guest rooms at Baumann House Bed & Breakfast (25 Spring St., 519/664-1515, www.bbcanada.com/3205.html, $95 d), and she can tell you everything about touring the region. One room has twig furniture, another has a spool bed topped with a red velvet coverlet, and a third, with twin beds, is done all in lavender; rooms share one bath upstairs and a half bath on the main level. Breakfast specialties include herb and cheese omelets and pancakes with local maple syrup.

St. Jacobs also has several chain motels close to the farmers market, including the family- and business-friendly Homewood Suites (45 Benjamin Rd., 519/514-0088, http://homewoodsuites3.hilton.com, $149-239 d), which has modern one- and two-bedroom apartment-style units with full kitchens as well as an indoor pool. Rates include a buffet breakfast daily and an evening social hour (Mon.-Thurs.).

Information and Services

The knowledgeable staff at the St. Jacobs Visitor Information Centre (1406 King St. N., 519/664-1133 or 800/265-3353, www.stjacobs.com, 11am-5pm Mon.-Sat., 1:30pm-5pm Sun. Apr.-Dec., 11am-4:30pm Mon.-Sat., 2pm-4:30pm Sun. Jan.-Mar.) can offer directions, point out things to do, and answer questions about the area's Mennonite community. There's a seasonal Visitor Information Centre (15 Farmers Market Rd., 519/883-3953, 9am-5pm Mon.-Fri., 8am-4pm Sat., 11am-5pm Sun. May-Oct.) opposite the farmers market.

Getting There and Around

St. Jacobs is eight kilometers (five miles) north of Waterloo via Highway 85. King Street, the village's main street, runs between the village and the market district.

A fun way to get around St. Jacobs is aboard the heritage Waterloo Central Railway (www.waterloocentralrailway.com, adults $20, ages 2-10 $15). Stops include Waterloo

(90 Northfield Dr. W.), St. Jacobs Market (330 Farmers Market Rd.), and St. Jacobs Village (50 Isabella St.). The train operates three trips a day on Tuesday (mid-June-Aug.), Thursday (mid-May-mid-Oct.), and Saturday (mid-Apr.-late Oct.).

Grand River Transit (519/585-7555, www. grt.ca) bus no. 21 runs every 20-30 minutes between the Conestoga Mall (550 King St. N., Waterloo) and St. Jacobs, and also connects the Market District and St. Jacobs Village. Buses run about every 30 minutes; there's no service after 7pm Monday-Friday, after 4pm Saturday, or on Sunday. From downtown Kitchener, the GRT light rail system can take you to the mall.

ELORA AND FERGUS

Frequently named to lists of Ontario's prettiest small towns, the communities of Elora and Fergus make enjoyable stopovers as you're traveling around the province. Scottish pioneers settled the Elora-Fergus region in the mid-1800s, building well-crafted homes from the abundant limestone quarried nearby. Many of these imposing stone structures still stand, housing galleries, shops, and inns.

Sights and Activities

Limestone was once dug from the depths of the **Elora Quarry** (319 Wellington County Rd. 18, 519/846-5234, www.grandriver.ca, 11am-8pm Mon.-Fri., 10am-8pm Sat.-Sun. June-early Sept., adults $10, seniors $7.50, ages 6-14 $5). Surrounded by stone cliffs, the quarry's deep, strikingly blue water now makes it the town's summertime swimming hole.

The Grand River rushes through **Elora Gorge** (7400 Wellington County Rd. 21, Elora, 519/846-9742, www.grandriver.ca, May-mid-Oct., adults $7, seniors $5.50, ages 6-14 $3), creating a natural tubing park (9am-7pm daily late June-early Sept., 9am-7pm Sat.-Sun. May-late June and early-late Sept., $5) in the 22-meter-deep (72-foot-deep) chasm; you can rent a tubing gear package with an inner tube, helmet, and life jacket ($30). Three kilometers (1.9 miles) of hiking trails wend along

the river, where experienced canoeists and kayakers also come to run the white water. Bring a picnic and spend the afternoon.

In a majestic building that belies its origins as a poorhouse, the **Wellington County Museum** (536 Wellington County Rd. 18, Fergus, 519/846-0916, ext. 5221, www. wellington.ca/museum, 9:30am-4:30pm Mon.-Fri., 1pm-5pm Sat.-Sun., donation) has well-designed exhibits about the area's past. The building was constructed in 1877 as a refuge for the region's impoverished and homeless population.

Entertainment and Shopping

See what's firing in the hot shop at **Blown Away Glass Studio** (6506 Wellington Rd., Elora, 519/846-8268, www. blownawayglassstudio.com, 10am-6pm Tues.-Fri., 10am-5pm Sat., 11am-4pm Sun.), which sells original glass art. Looking for something crafty to do with your partner? How about "One Hot Date"? It's an introductory two-hour glassblowing workshop for couples.

Painter Kreso Cavlovic likes to keep the door open at his **Gallery Vernissage Art Studio** (78 Metcalfe St., Elora, 519/729-5063) so visitors can stop in to watch him work and have a chat. His gallery is one of many along Elora's downtown streets.

A modern movie house inside the 1860s former Commercial Hotel, the **Gorge Cinema** (43 Mill St. W., Elora, 519/846-0191, www.gorgecinema.ca) is Canada's longest continuously running repertory cinema.

Food and Accommodations

Friendly **Café Creperie** (40 Mill St. W., Elora, 519/846-1618, www.cafecreperie.ca, 11am-2pm Wed., 11am-2pm and 5pm-11pm Thurs.-Fri., 11am-4pm Sat.-Sun., $9-15) serves coffee, salads, and both savory and sweet crepes. **Elora Brewing Company** (107 Geddes St., Elora, 519/805-2829, www. elorabrewingcompany.ca, 11am-11pm Mon.-Thurs., 11am-1am Fri.-Sat., 11am-9pm Sun., $10-32) offers beer and updated pub fare in its historic stone building. When the weather's

The Oxford County Cheese Trail

Love cheese? Plan a detour through one of rural Ontario's cheese-making regions. Oxford County, located between Kitchener-Waterloo, Stratford, and London, has been "cheese country" since Canada's first cheese factories opened here in the 1860s. At its peak, the region had 98 cheese makers. Today, the **Oxford County Cheese Trail** (www.oxfordcountycheesetrail.ca) highlights cheeses past and present with a network of cheese producers, restaurants, and attractions.

Several cheese makers sell their wares or offer tours, including **Mountainoak Cheese** (3165 Huron Rd., New Hamburg, 519/662-4967, www.mountainoakcheese.ca, 9am-5pm daily). Owners Adam and Hannie van Bergeijk were cheese makers in their native Holland, and they now specialize in gouda that they produce and age on their farm. You can drop into their farm store, but appointments are required for a one-hour tour of their facilities ($7 pp), which includes tasty samples.

Operating since 1874, **Bright Cheese & Butter** (816503 County Rd. 22, Bright, 519/454-4810, www.brightcheeseandbutter.com, 9am-5pm Mon.-Fri., 9am-4pm Sat.) is primarily a production facility, but you can purchase cheddars, asiago, and fresh cheese curds in their retail shop.

To learn more about how cheese is made, look through the window at **Gunn's Hill Artisan Cheese** (445172 Gunns Hill Rd., Woodstock, 519/424-4024, www.gunnshillcheese.ca, 9am-5pm Mon.-Sat.); they're typically producing cheese weekdays between 9:30am and noon. This family-owned business emphasizes firm, Swiss-style cheeses. If you like fresh curds, visit Fridays at 1pm.

What's a chocolate shop doing on a cheese trail? **Chocolatea** (38 King St. E., Ingersoll, 519/495-6020, www.chocolatea.ca, 10am-6pm Tues.-Fri., 10am-3pm Sat.) crafts small-batch chocolates using cream from local dairies, locally produced honey, maple syrup, fruit, and even beer.

The **Ingersoll Cheese & Agricultural Museum** (290 Harris St., Ingersoll, 519/485-5510, www.ingersoll.ca, 10am-5pm daily June-Aug., 10am-5pm Mon.-Fri. Sept.-May, donation) traces the history of the local dairy industry. A featured exhibit tells the story of the 3,300-kilogram (7,300-pound) "Mammoth Cheese," crafted by local producers and shipped to England in 1866 as a publicity stunt. This event inspired poet James McIntyre to pen "Ode on the Mammoth Cheese," which begins, "We have seen the Queen of cheese, Laying quietly at your ease, Gently fanned by evening breeze, Thy fair form no flies dare seize."

fine, sit at the garage door-style windows and watch the whole town stroll by.

Welcoming owners Kathleen Stanley and Roger Dufau operate ★ **Drew House B&B** (120 Mill St., Elora, 519-846-2226, www.drewhouse.com, $135 d) in a historic stone farmhouse and former barn set around a lovely garden. In the coach house, six guest rooms are decorated in a French country style. The owners have filled an alcove with books to read and provide coffee, tea, and cold drinks. In the main house are two multiple-bedroom suites for 5-8 people ($270-420). The ample hot breakfast, served family-style, is a highlight. There's Wi-Fi in the main house but not in the coach house rooms.

In a stately stone manor, the **Breadalbane Inn & Spa** (487 St. Andrew St. W., Fergus, 888/842-2825, www.breadalbaneinn.com, $130-195), pronounced "bruh-DAHL-bun," has seven traditional rooms, with four additional suites in the carriage house. It also has two restaurants: Italian **Scozia** (519/843-4770, 11:30am-11pm Mon.-Sat., 11:30am-10pm Sun., $13-29) serves pastas, pizzas, steak, and, in a nod to the town's Scottish heritage, haggis-stuffed ravioli. The relaxed **Fergusson Room Pub** (519/843-4770, 11am-11pm Sun.-Thurs., 11am-1am Fri.-Sat., $12-20) takes the Scottish theme further, with bangers and mash and shepherd's pie alongside other pub fare; there's plenty of beer on tap, too.

Slated to open in 2018, the **Elora Mill**

Ingersoll Cheese & Agricultural Museum

Contemporary bistro **SixThirtyNine** (639 Peel St., Woodstock, 519/536-9602, www. sixthirtynine.com, 11am-2pm and 5pm-10pm Wed.-Fri., 5pm-10pm Sat., 5pm-8:30pm Sun., $30-38) is an excellent cheese-friendly choice. Start with arancini filled with Gunn's Hill Five Brothers cheese before moving on to roast chicken with aged cheddar gnocchi. Book a seat at the counter to watch the kitchen action.

Want more cheese? **Tourism Oxford** (www.tourismoxford.ca) can provide more details about the trail and the surrounding region, including an online map.

Hotel & Spa (77 Mill St. W., Elora, www. eloramill.ca) is a 30-room boutique inn in a 19th-century riverside mill; check the website for updates and rates.

Practicalities

Check the website for **Elora-Fergus Tourism** (www.elorafergus.ca) for more information about the region. Elora is 115 kilometers (70 miles) northwest of Toronto and 30 kilometers (19 miles) north of Waterloo. Fergus is five kilometers (three miles) northeast of Elora. Public transit around the region is nonexistent, so plan to come by car.

Stratford

The main attraction in this town of 30,000 is the Stratford Festival, North America's largest classical repertory theater. Originally known as the Stratford Shakespeare Festival, it presents not only works by the Bard on the stage; the festival also includes productions by other classical and more contemporary playwrights.

Even if theater isn't your thing, Stratford makes a good getaway, just two hours from Toronto. Due to the presence of the Stratford Chefs School, the town has a large number of high-end restaurants, and you can entertain yourself with music, shopping, and special events throughout the year. If you're not coming for theater, visit Sunday-Tuesday, when fewer productions are staged, or outside the festival season, when accommodations are easier to find; prices and crowds both peak from July through September.

★ STRATFORD FESTIVAL

Stratford-born journalist Tom Patterson hatched the idea for a hometown festival devoted to William Shakespeare's works. He then convinced British actor and director Tyrone Guthrie to become its first artistic director. The inaugural production—*Richard III*, with Alec Guinness playing the lead—took to the stage in July 1953 in a giant canvas tent.

Today, the **Stratford Festival** (519/273-1600 or 800/567-1600, www.stratfordfestival.ca) has produced thousands of plays, many by Shakespeare, but many also by other classical and more contemporary playwrights. The festival opens with preview performances in late April or early May and continues through October. July-September are the busiest months, with multiple plays running in repertory. Beyond the plays, the festival offers theater tours, lectures, and special events.

Tickets

Ticket sales (519/273-1600 or 800/567-1600,

www.stratfordfestival.ca) for the upcoming season typically start in January. If you're hoping to visit during a July or August weekend or any holiday period, buy tickets and book your accommodations as early as you can. Many regular patrons who return year after year reserve their lodgings for the following season before they even leave town.

Ticket prices range from $35 to more than $120, depending on the type of play, dates, and seat location. Seniors, students, and families can purchase discounted tickets, and you can sometimes buy last-minute "rush" tickets for 20-50 percent off; they're sold two hours before the performance by phone or at the box office, but not online. On some Sunday, Tuesday, and Thursday evenings, two-for-one tickets are available. See the festival website for details and other discount offers.

Theaters

Stratford Festival plays are normally performed at four venues. The largest, the 1,826-seat **Festival Theatre** (55 Queen St.), built in 1957, is east of the town center in Upper Queen's Park. Two performance spaces are right downtown: the 1,090-seat **Avon Theatre** (99 Downie St.) and the 260-seat **Studio Theatre** (34 George St. E.), behind the Avon. In 2018, the **Tom Patterson Theatre** (111 Lakeside Dr.) closed pending a major reconstruction; check the festival website for updates.

Tours and Talks

For a behind-the-scenes look at the Stratford Festival, take the one-hour **Festival Theatre Tour** (55 Queen St., www.stratfordfestival.ca, 9am and 9:15am Wed.-Sun. June-early Nov., adults $10, seniors $8, students $6). You'll also learn more about the current season and past productions.

On the one-hour **Costume and Props Warehouse Tour** (350 Douro St., www.

Stratford

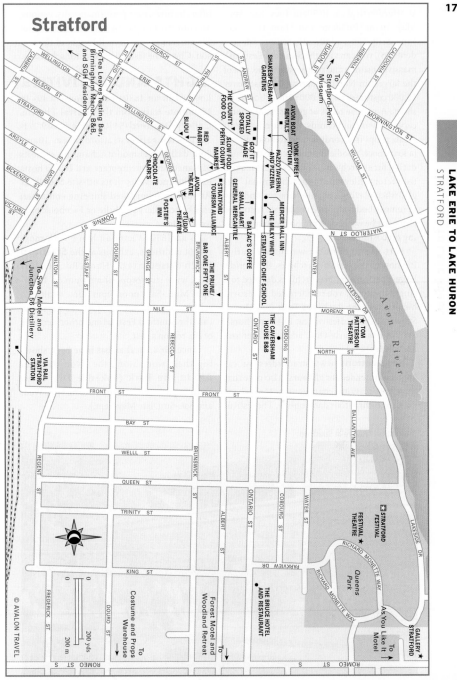

To
Stratford-Perth
Museum

SHAKESPEAREAN
GARDENS

AVON BOAT
RENTALS

YORK STREET
KITCHEN

TOTALLY
SPOKED

GOT IT
MADE

THE COUNTY
FOOD CO.

PAZZO TAVERNA
AND PIZZERIA

MERCER HALL INN

BIJOU

RED
RABBIT

PERTH COUNTY
FOOD MARKET

THE MILKY WHEY

SMALL MART
GENERAL MERCANTILE

STRATFORD CHEF SCHOOL

CHOCOLATE
BARR'S

AVON
THEATRE

STRATFORD
TOURISM ALLIANCE

BALZAC'S COFFEE

FOSTER'S
INN

STUDIO
THEATRE

THE PRUNE/
BAR ONE FIFTY ONE

To Tea Leaves Tasting Bar,
Birmingham Manor B&B,
and SGH Residence

To Tea Leaves Tasting Bar,
Birmingham Manor B&B,
and SGH Residence

To Swan Motel and
Junction 56 Distillery

VIA RAIL
STRATFORD
STATION

THE CAVERSHAM
HOUSE B&B

TOM
PATTERSON
THEATRE

Avon River

STRATFORD
FESTIVAL
THEATRE

Queens
Park

THE BRUCE HOTEL
AND RESTAURANT

To
Costume and Props
Warehouse

To
Forest Motel and
Woodland Retreat

As You Like It
Motel

To

GALLERY
STRATFORD

© AVALON TRAVEL

0   200 yds

0   200 m

CHURCH ST

ERIE ST

WELLINGTON ST

ST ANDREW ST

ST PATRICK ST

WELLINGTON ST

NELSON ST

CAMBRIA ST

STRATFORD ST

ARGYLE ST

MCKENZIE ST

VICTORIA

ST DAVID ST

GEORGE ST

DOWNIE ST

MILTON ST

FALSTAFF ST

DOURO ST

GRANGE ST

NILE ST

REBECCA ST

BRUNSWICK ST

ALBERT ST

ONTARIO ST

WATER ST

COBOURG ST

MORENZ DR

NORTH ST

FRONT ST

FRONT ST

BAY ST

WELLL ST

QUEEN ST

TRINITY ST

KING ST

BRUNSWICK ST

ALBERT ST

ONTARIO ST

COBOURG ST

WATER ST

REGENT ST

FREDERICK ST

DOURO ST

ROMEO ST

ROMEO ST

MORNINGTON ST

HIBERNIA ST

CALEDONIA ST

WILLIAM ST

WATERLOO ST N

LAKESIDE DR

BALLANTYNE AVE

RICHARD MONETTE WAY

PARKVIEW DR

RICHARD MONETTE WAY

LAKESIDE DR

HURON ST

stratfordfestival.ca, 10:30am Tues.-Sat. Apr.-May, 10am, 10:30am, and 11am Tues.-Sat. June-early Nov., adults $10, seniors $8, students $6), you can visit the Stratford Festival's massive costume and props warehouse, one of the largest in North America; it houses over 55,000 costumes and 10,000 pairs of boots and shoes. Amid the racks of gowns, pantaloons, capes, crowns, and swords, you learn how staff create props from ordinary household objects (a foam pool "noodle" might become the foundation for an archway), how designers make a thin actor achieve the proper abdominal "jiggle" when playing a portly character, and how to remove body odor from elaborate costumes that can't be washed. Wrap up the tour by trying on costumes.

Part of the costume-warehouse building houses the festival's archives, the world's largest performing-arts archives devoted to a single theater. If you're interested in festival history, take the **Archives Tour** (350 Douro St., www.stratfordfestival.ca, 10:45am Thurs.-Fri. mid-June-early Oct., adults $8, seniors and students $6).

Reservations (www.stratfordfestival.ca) are recommended for all tours. Also note that there are occasional changes to the tour schedules, so confirm tour dates online. The festival offers lectures, post-performance discussions, and other informal ways to learn more about the current productions throughout the season. Check the festival website for schedules.

SIGHTS AND ACTIVITIES

Located in an 1880s pump house a 10- to 15-minute walk from the Festival Theatre, **Gallery Stratford** (54 Romeo St. S., 519/271-5271, www.gallerystratford.on.ca, 10am-5pm daily, free) mounts changing exhibits of Canadian contemporary art. It also hosts exhibits and events in its off-site **Steelbox Art Lab**, a repurposed shipping container; check the gallery's website or Facebook page for details.

In an 1880s Victorian home with more recent additions, exhibits at the **Stratford Perth Museum** (4275 Huron Rd., 519/393-5311, www.stratfordperthmuseum.ca, 10am-4pm Mon.-Sat., noon-4pm Sun., adults $7, seniors and students $6, ages 6-12 $5) showcase the Stratford Festival and other elements of the region's past.

Since 1968, local artists have been showing their work along the Avon River at **Art in the Park** (Lakeside Dr., www.artintheparkstratford.com, 10am-5pm Wed. and Sat.-Sun. late May-Sept.).

the Festival Theatre in Stratford

ENTERTAINMENT AND SHOPPING

Though Stratford is known for its classical theater productions, **SpringWorks** (www. SpringWorksFestival.ca, Oct.), the town's "Indie Theatre and Arts Festival," showcases more avant-garde music, dance, and theater performances. During the month-long **Stratford Summer Music** (www. stratfordsummermusic.ca, mid-July-mid-Aug.), more than 100 concerts, from jazz to Mozart to organ recitals, take place.

Ontario Street is downtown Stratford's main shopping street, with boutiques, galleries, pubs, and cafés. **Small Mart General Mercantile** (119 Ontario St., 519/508-6300, www.small-mart.ca, 10am-6pm Mon.-Sat., 11am-5pm Sun.) sells a quirky mix of clothing with classic Canadian logos, T-shirts, retro candies, watches, and miscellaneous cool stuff. Tiny **Got It Made** (27 Ontario St., 10am-5pm Tues.-Sat., noon-4pm Sun.) carries jewelry, cards, and crafts by local artisans.

The Milky Whey (118 Ontario St., 519/814-9439, www.themilkywhey.ca, 10am-6pm Tues.-Fri., 9:30am-6pm Sat., 11am-4pm Sun. June-early Sept., 10am-5pm Tues.-Fri., 9:30am-5:30pm Sat., 11am-3pm Sun. Mar.-May and early Sept.-Dec., 11am-3pm Tues.-Wed., 10am-5pm Thurs.-Sat., 11am-3pm Sun. Jan.-Feb.) is the place for cheese, with lots of regionally produced varieties.

Given their last name, Derek and Jacqueline Barr may have been destined to open a chocolate shop: theirs, which sells rich handmade truffles, as well as caramels and other candies, is called **Chocolate Barr's** (55 George St. W., 519/272-2828, www.chocolatebarrs.com, 9am-6pm Mon.-Sat., 10am-5pm Sun.), of course.

SPORTS AND RECREATION

The 113-kilometer (70-mile) **Avon Trail** (www.avontrail.ca) runs from St. Marys northeast to Conestogo, passing through the Stratford area. The Avon Trail Association organizes regular volunteer-led day hikes.

Visitors are welcome; check the website for a schedule.

Stratford is compact enough for exploring by bike. Rent your wheels from **Totally Spoked** (29 Ontario St., 519/273-2001, www.totallyspoked.ca, 9am-5:30pm Mon.-Wed. and Fri., 9am-8pm Thurs., 9am-5pm Sat., noon-4pm Sun. spring-summer, 10am-5:30pm Tues.-Wed. and Fri., 10am-7pm Thurs., 10am-5pm Sat., noon-4pm Sun. fall-winter; half day $20-35, full day $35-55). **Avon Boat Rentals** (30 York St., 519/271-7739, www.avonboatrentals.ca, 9am-dusk daily May-Oct.) rents canoes, kayaks, and bicycles alongside the Avon River. You can also take a 30-minute **river cruise** aboard the *Juliet III* pontoon boat.

Many of the flowers in the **Shakespearean Gardens** (Huron St., at York St.), a pretty spot to stroll near the Avon River and the Perth County Court House, are mentioned in Shakespeare's plays.

FOOD

With the professional Stratford Chefs School in town, as well as an audience of hungry, well-heeled theatergoers, Stratford is a great spot for a gourmet splurge. Reservations are strongly recommended during the summer, and they're essential if you're trying to have dinner before the theater. If you're watching your budget, Stratford still offers good eating, with bakeries, cafés, and locally focused bistros.

While Stratford restaurants are open daily from May or June through August or September, many reduce their hours, or close altogether, outside the summer high season. A notable exception is the Stratford Chefs School dinners (Oct.-early Mar.).

Food Tours

Buy a pass to the **Stratford Chocolate Trail** ($30) and you can sample six chocolate offerings—truffles, teas, cookies, ice cream, even chocolate martinis—at any of 20 locations around town. If beer and pork are more your style, check out the **Stratford Bacon &**

Stratford Chefs School

One reason that Stratford has such a dynamic restaurant scene is the presence of the **Stratford Chefs School** (136 Ontario St., 519/271-1414, www.stratfordchef.com) is a professional culinary institute that trains 30-40 aspiring chefs every year. These students aren't just holed up in the lecture hall; they cook for the public, too. You can sample what these young chefs are learning during the school's annual **Dinner Series** (Tues.-Sat. late-Oct.-early Mar., $55-85 pp), held in the school's modern downtown facility.

Every year, the school brings in international guest chefs who work with the students and oversee diners' meals. You may not have the chance to visit Rome or Mendoza, Argentina, to eat in the restaurants that chefs Cristina Bowerman (Glass Hostaria) or Matias Aldasoro (Casa del Visitante) run, but you can dine on their dishes in Stratford. Other dinners feature chefs from across Canada.

If you'd like to get into the kitchen yourself, consider the **Open Kitchen program** (Mar.-Sept., $40-75 pp), with 1- to 3-hour hands-on cooking classes and culinary workshops designed for home cooks, taught in the school's professional training kitchens. You might learn to prepare pasta or vegetarian fare, try out pressure cookers or other kitchen gadgets, or work on techniques for preserving food or making pastry.

The school's website lists the schedule of dinners, guest chef appearances, courses, and other events. And who knows? The student prepping your salad today may be the Ferran Adrià or Thomas Keller of the future.

Ale Trail ($30), which includes hoppy drinks and porcine snacks at several local purveyors. Purchase passes for either trail at the **Stratford Tourism Alliance** (47 Downie St., 519/271-5140 or 800/561-7926, www.visitstratford.ca) in person or online.

Karen Hartwick, who owns the **Tea Leaves Tasting Bar** (433 Erie St., 519/273-1201 or 800/733-0376, www.stratfordtealeaves.com, 11am-5pm Wed.-Sat. and by appointment), is a certified tea sommelier who can teach you all about blacks, greens, herbals, and more. She carries more varieties in her petite shop, including her own unique blends, and offers complimentary tastings.

Need something with a little more kick? Visit **Junction 56 Distillery** (45 Cambria St., 519/301-2911, www.junction56.ca, 10:30am-4:30pm Tues.-Wed., 10:30am-6pm Thurs.-Fri., 10:30am-5pm Sat., tours 11am Sat., tastings $1/each, tours $15 pp) to try its gin, vodka, and "moonshine" whiskey; the latter is an unaged spirit brewed from corn.

Contemporary

At lunch, ★ **Red Rabbit** (64 Wellington St., 519/305-6464, www.redrabbitresto.com,

11:30am-2:30pm and 5pm-9pm daily, call or check the website for off-season hours; lunch and a la carte dinner $12-19, prix fixe dinner $49-54) is known for its chicken and waffles and its umami-packed mushroom burger. Staff will tell you that, among the sandwiches, the spicy hot chicken has a cult following, too. Early evenings in this stylish bistro, with exposed brick walls and a long bar, bring an inventive two- or three-course pretheater menu (Tues.-Sat.), perhaps sesame-dressed asparagus or Asian-style shrimp cakes to start, then braised pork shoulder with roasted veggies and tahini, or lingcod in a green chili-charred tomato broth. After 7:30pm and on Sunday and Monday evenings, they relax again with sharing plates, salads, and burgers. Plenty of local craft beers are always on offer.

Bijou (105 Erie St., www.bijourestaurant.com, 5pm-10pm Tues.-Sat. late Mar.-Nov.), a petite French-inspired bistro, pairs casual—refurbished wood floors, a chalkboard menu—with white tablecloths and a kitchen committed to sourcing locally. Pretheater dinner is prix fixe (5pm-8pm, two-courses $46-48), where you might select a starter like creamy pumpkin-squash soup, followed by a trio of trout (seared, smoked, and caviar) or dry-aged rib eye with cauliflower cheese purée. After 8pm, the à la carte menu ($12-18) offers small plates like duck tenders with Swiss chard or chicken spaghetti with smoked bacon, and "food flights," like a beet salad board with greens, goat cream, and candied nuts.

One of Stratford's original fine-dining restaurants, **The Prune** (151 Albert St., 519/271-5052, www.theprune.com, dinner 4:30pm-10pm Tues.-Sat. mid-May-mid-Oct.) is still a favorite dining destination for theatergoers. Pairing classical French techniques with local ingredients, the kitchen creates dishes like pan-seared trout with rapini and broad beans, lamb sirloin with a chanterelle and sweet corn ragout, or risotto with roasted carrots and carrot tops. Prix fixe meals are $59, $75, and $85 for two, three, or four courses. For a still interesting but more informal meal or after-theater snack, tuck into their **Bar One Fifty One** (4:30pm-10pm Tues.-Wed., 4:30pm-midnight Thurs.-Sat., $10-18) for smoked gouda arancini, salmon rillettes with pickled onions, or braised beef pie.

The classy Bruce Hotel has an equally refined restaurant, lit by contemporary chandeliers. **The Restaurant at the Bruce** (89 Parkview Dr., 519/508-7100, www.thebruce.ca, breakfast 7:30am-10:30am daily, lunch 11:30am-1:30pm daily, dinner 5pm-9pm Tues.-Sat., breakfast $17-19, lunch $15-25, dinner $28-39 or prix fixe $80-95) serves locally focused contemporary cuisine, including bison tartare with grilled spelt and fermented currants, duck breast and crispy pork paired with baby kale and preserved apricot, and venison with celeriac purée. The wine list is strong on Ontario labels.

Italian

Pazzo Taverna and Pizzeria (70 Ontario St., 519/273-6666 or 877/440-9666, www.pazzo.ca, pizzeria 11:30am-9pm Sun.-Thurs., 11:30am-midnight Fri.-Sat., lunch $14-16, dinner $15-25, taverna 5pm-10pm Wed.-Sun., dinner $21-30) is two restaurants in one. On the lower level is a casual pizzeria, with salads, pastas, panini, and excellent pizzas. On the main floor is a more upscale restaurant, with sleek white chairs and oversize windows, where the updated Italian classics might include herb-stuffed pork tenderloin with Jerusalem artichoke purée, risotto with roasted mushrooms and thyme, or chicken scaloppine.

Stratford's Pazzo Taverna and Pizzeria is two restaurants in one.

Bakeries and Cafés

Named for French playwright Honoré de Balzac, **Balzac's Coffee** (149 Ontario St., 519/273-7909, www.balzacs.com, 6:30am-7pm Mon.-Fri., 7am-7pm Sat.-Sun.) would be right at home in Paris, with its high ceilings, embossed wallpaper, and excellent coffees. Nibble pastries or sandwiches or linger over a cup of joe. More fair-trade coffee options are available at **Revel** (37 Market Pl., 519/305-1600, www.revelstratford.ca, 8am-5pm Mon.-Fri., 8am-6pm Sat., 9am-3pm Sun.); in warm weather, they have a tap for nitro coffee.

Don't expect a bland assortment of lettuce and shredded carrots on the salad bar at **The County Food Co.** (38 Erie St., 519/275-2665, www.countyfoodco.com, 10am-5pm Mon., 10am-7pm Tues.-Sat. summer, 10am-4pm Mon.-Fri. winter, $6-13), a café and takeout shop that emphasizes local ingredients; you might find fresh kale with dried cranberries, mustard-dressed chickpeas, or beets with caramelized onions and pecans. They make sandwiches, too, including the signature stuffed pork schnitzel. Try the oversize oatmeal cookies.

Cheerful and unpretentious **York St. Kitchen** (51 York St., 519/273-7041, www.yorkstreetkitchen.com, 11am-3pm daily, $8-13) has been serving interesting yet inexpensive eats since the mid-1990s. It's known for hearty sandwiches, like the Mennonite (summer sausage, cheddar, and corn relish) and the "Lee-Shawich" (black forest ham, melted Brie, and apple butter). "Monster" cookies and other sweets have fans, too.

Groceries and Markets

Stratford has two farmers markets: the **Stratford Farmers Market** (Stratford Rotary Complex, 353 McCarthy Rd., 519/271-5130, www.stratfordfairgrounds.com, 7am-noon Sat. year-round) and the **Slow Food Perth County Market** (Market Square, behind Stratford City Hall, 10am-2pm Sun. May-mid-Oct.; Falstaff Family Centre, 35 Waterloo St. N., 10am-2pm Sun. mid-Oct.-Apr.).

ACCOMMODATIONS

For a fairly small community, Stratford has a large number of lodgings, including motels, inns, and many B&Bs. What you won't find are inexpensive accommodations, at least during the summer theater season. If you're on a tight budget, come from Toronto for the day, or consider driving in from London.

On the **Stratford Tourism Alliance** website (www.visitstratford.ca), you can search for available lodgings by date, location, and various features. The Stratford Festival also runs an accommodations booking service (800/567-1600, www.stratfordaccommodations.com). For more B&B options, try the **Stratford and Area Bed & Breakfast Association** (www.bbstratford.ca).

Under $100

One of Stratford's only budget accommodations is the **SGH Residence** (130 Youngs St., 519/271-5084, www.sgh.stratford.on.ca/residence, $72 s, $88 d), a residence hall with basic shared-bath rooms on the grounds of the Stratford Hospital. Rates include breakfast and parking.

$100-150

In this price range, you'll find well-maintained motels—not fancy, but comfortable. The trade-off is that you're not within walking distance of downtown.

The star of the show at the old-fashioned, family-run **Swan Motel** (960 Downie St., 519/271-6376, www.swanmotel.ca, May-late Oct., $118-142 d), two kilometers (1.2 miles) south of the town center, is the pretty manicured grounds, with gardens, picnic tables, and an outdoor pool. You get a warm welcome from longtime owners Peter and Colleen Pola before checking into one of 24 simple rooms with mini fridges, coffeemakers, and free Wi-Fi. Though there's no restaurant, you can stop into the lobby for complimentary morning muffins, coffee, and tea.

At the 18-room **As You Like It Motel** (379 Romeo St. N., 519/271-2951, www.asyoulikeit.on.ca, late Apr.-early Nov., $115-160 d), 3.5

kilometers (2.2 miles) northeast of the town center, the updated linens and carpets, mixed with the old-time furniture, give the spaces a cool, almost mid-century-modern vibe. Rooms have mini fridges and free Wi-Fi. You can have a light continental breakfast in the dining area behind the front desk, and there's a pool out back.

$150-250

Owners Elena Pastura and Dom Tassielli at the **Birmingham Manor B&B** (240 Birmingham St., 519/273-6545 or 888/391-9996, www.birminghammanor.com, $155-195) are drama fans who can update you on the local art and theater scene. They've outfitted the living room of their 1904 Victorian home with masks and other theater memorabilia, while upstairs are four traditional guest rooms with canopy or sleigh beds and antique furnishings. Three have modern en suite bathrooms, the fourth has a huge private bath (with a claw-foot tub) down the hall. Multicourse breakfasts start with fresh fruit, move on to baked eggs or another hot dish, and wrap up with sweets like quinoa chocolate cake.

Though it's less than a 10-minute drive from town, the **Forest Motel and Woodland Retreat** (2941 Forest Rd., 519/271-4573, www.forestmotel.on.ca, $149-245 d) feels like just that: a retreat into the woods. A short stroll from peaceful Lake McCarthy, the 19 motel rooms with sturdy pine furniture are simple but snug, with fridges, microwaves, coffeemakers, and free Wi-Fi. Outside, you can lounge on the waterside patios or take a canoe for a leisurely paddle. Rates include continental breakfast.

Buttermilk pancakes and a spinach-feta strata are among the breakfast specialties at **The Caversham House B&B** (155 Cobourg St., 519/271-7882 or 866/998-7882, www.thecavershamhouse.com, $165-225 d), a friendly lodging in a 1906 Edwardian house where you can read in the book-lined living room and enjoy homemade cookies in the evening. The three guest rooms aren't large, but they're well designed, with original oak floors, air-conditioning, and free Wi-Fi; the Henley Suite's private balcony overlooks the garden.

Stratford has several small inns on the upper floors of downtown historic buildings, including **Foster's Inn** (111 Downie St., 519/271-1119 or 888/728-5555, www.fostersinn.com, $179-225 d), with nine unfussy, loft-style guest rooms on the second and third stories. Hang out downstairs in

a Victorian-style room at Birmingham Manor B&B

the friendly bar or have meals in the brightly painted restaurant; the three-cheese omelet will fuel you for the day. They don't have parking, but a free lot is two blocks away. Wi-Fi is included.

Also above a downtown restaurant and beer hall, the 14 rooms at the **Mercer Hall Inn** (108 Ontario St., 519/271-1888 or 888/816-4011, www.mercer.beer, $137-265 d) are all decorated differently. They're not deluxe, but they're modern, with Keurig coffeemakers and mini fridges; some have whirlpool tubs, some have fireplaces, and room 209 has a river view. Rates include Wi-Fi.

Over $250

Stratford didn't have a true luxury lodging until **The Bruce Hotel** (89 Parkview Dr., 519/508-7100 or 855/708-7100, www.thebruce.ca, $295-650 d) opened near the Festival Theatre. At this high-end 25-room property, guest rooms are large, with Frette linens and deep tubs. Detail-obsessed owner Jennifer Birmingham personally laid more than 660,000 mosaic tiles in the hotel's baths, while on the lobby wall is a hand-painted map of the world as it looked in 1564—the year Shakespeare was born. Other amenities include a small indoor pool, a fitness room, a library, a game room, and a suitably deluxe restaurant.

INFORMATION AND SERVICES

The **Stratford Tourism Alliance** (47 Downie St., 519/271-5140 or 800/561-7926, www.visitstratford.ca, 9am-5pm Mon.-Fri., 10am-4pm Sat. May, 9am-6pm Mon.-Fri., 10am-6pm Sat.-Sun. June-Aug., 9am-5pm Mon.-Fri., 10am-6pm Sat., 10am-2pm Sun. Sept., 9am-5pm Mon.-Fri., 10am-4pm Sat. Oct.-Apr.) runs a helpful visitors center stocked with information about the region. Their website lists scads of things to see and do.

GETTING THERE

Stratford is 150 kilometers (93 miles) southwest of Toronto, 45 kilometers (28 miles) southwest of Kitchener, and 60 kilometers (37 miles) northeast of London.

Air

The closest airports to Stratford are **Waterloo International Airport** (YKF, 4881 Fountain St. N., Breslau, 519/648-2256, www.waterlooairport.ca) or **London International Airport** (YXU, 1750 Crumlin Rd., London, 519/452-4015, www.londonairport.on.ca), but Toronto's **Pearson International Airport** (YYZ, 6301 Silver Dart Dr., Mississauga, 416/247-7678 or 866/207-1690, www.torontopearson.com) has flights from many more destinations. **Stratford Airporter Shuttle** (519/273-0057 or 888/549-8602, www.stratfordairporter.com, 2.5 hours, one-way $89 pp, $129 for 2 people) provides transportation from Pearson to Stratford. They also run private shuttles to the Waterloo and London airports.

Train

You can catch the train to **VIA Rail's Stratford Station** (101 Shakespeare St., 888/842-7245, www.viarail.ca) from Toronto (2.25 hours, one-way adults $33-85, ages 2-11 $16-43), although the Stratford Direct Bus is less expensive and better aligned with the festival performance schedule. VIA Rail also operates between Stratford and London (1-1.25 hours, one-way adults $23-45, ages 2-11 $12-23).

Bus

The Stratford Festival runs the convenient **Stratford Direct Bus** (800/567-1600, www.stratfordfestival.ca, round-trip $29), which lets theatergoers come from Toronto without a car. From mid-April to late May and from mid-October through early November, buses depart Toronto's Intercontinental Hotel (225 Front St. W. at Simcoe St.) at 10am daily, which brings you to Stratford in time for an afternoon matinee. The return buses depart Stratford at 5pm. From late May through mid-October, there are two buses a day in each direction, leaving Toronto at 10am and

Side Trip: St. Marys

Twenty kilometers (12 miles) southwest of Stratford and 45 kilometers (28 miles) northeast of London, the small community of St. Marys is known as "Stonetown" for the limestone dug from the area's quarries and the classical stone buildings that line the downtown streets.

The Quarry (425 Water St., 519/284-3090, www.townofstmarys.com, 1pm-8pm daily late June-Aug., adults $4.75, seniors $4.50, ages 3-18 $3.50, families $13.25), built into a former stone quarry, is Canada's largest outdoor swimming pool. Swimmers can use the changing rooms in the adjacent Lind Sportsplex.

Also in town is the **Canadian Baseball Hall of Fame** (386 Church St. S., 519/284-1838, www.baseballhalloffame.ca, adults $7.50, seniors $6, ages 6-16 $3.75, families $15), crammed with memorabilia. In 2018, the museum closed for renovations; check ahead before visiting.

For a bite to eat, swing into **Little Red's Pub and Eatery** (159 Queen St. E., 226/661-2233, www.littlereds.ca, 11am-2pm and 5pm-9pm Tues.-Sat., $11-20) for pub classics like fish-and-chips or burgers (including an option made with Ontario-raised bison) and other chef's whims using local ingredients, from a daily salad feature to lake fish to smoked pork chops.

3pm, and returning from Stratford at 5pm and 11pm. Book at least one day in advance; you must have a ticket to a festival performance or event.

Car

From Toronto, it's about a two-hour drive to Stratford. Take Highway 401 west to exit 278 onto Highway 8 west toward Kitchener. Then follow Highway 7/8 west from Kitchener to Stratford. As you enter Stratford, Highway 7/8 becomes Ontario Street, the town's main east-west street.

GETTING AROUND

If you're staying downtown, you can easily walk to restaurants and shops. The Stratford Festival's theaters are scattered around the town center; two are right downtown, and the largest, the Festival Theatre, is 1.5 kilometers (0.9 miles) east of downtown. To walk to the Festival Theatre, follow the riverfront path or go east on Ontario Street, then north on Queen Street.

Downtown street parking is metered, and while it's inexpensive, it's limited to three hours, so pull into a lot if you're parking for a meal and a show. If the free parking on the streets surrounding the Festival Theatre is full, try the large Queen Street lot near the theater ($15). Street parking is free on Sunday.

City of Stratford Transit (519/271-0250, www.stratfordcanada.ca, one-way adults $2.75, seniors and students $2.50) operates limited bus service around town. Buses run about every 30 minutes (hourly on Sunday), but the last buses leave at 9:30pm Monday-Friday, 7:30pm Saturday, and 5pm Sunday, so they're not convenient for post-theater transportation. If you need a taxi, phone **City Cab** (519/272-2222) or **Radio Cab** (519/271-4242).

London

Canada's 10th-largest city makes a convenient stopover between Toronto and Lake Huron or if you're exploring Southwestern Ontario. It's home to one of Canada's major universities—the University of Western Ontario—which gives the town a youthful feel, along with lots of craft breweries and several worthwhile museums.

SIGHTS

In the city center, six-hectare (15-acre) **Victoria Park** (bounded by Dufferin Ave., Central Ave., Clarence St., and Wellington St.) is a great place for a picnic. You'll often find festivals, concerts, and other special events here. At the park's southwest corner is grand **St. Peter's Cathedral** (196 Dufferin Ave., 519/432-3475, www.cathedral.rcec.london. on.ca), built in the 1880s to resemble a 13th-century French Gothic cathedral. Visitors are welcome to take a peek inside or to attend mass.

Museum London (421 Ridout St. N., 519/661-0333, www.museumlondon.ca, noon-5pm Tues.-Sun., noon-9pm Thurs., donation) exhibits a mix of historical art, contemporary art, and historical artifacts. Canadian architect Raymond Moriyama, who designed Toronto's Bata Shoe Museum and the Ontario Science Centre, as well as the Canadian War Museum in Ottawa, designed London's distinctive silvery museum, which was planning an expansion as this book went to press; check its website for updates. The museum's **Rhino Lounge** (519/850-5111, 11am-4:30pm Tues.-Wed. and Fri.-Sun., 11am-8:30pm Thurs., www.rhinolounge.ca) is a cool spot for coffee, pastries, or vegetarian light bites; lunch (Tues.-Fri., $14-21) and Sunday brunch ($25) is served in the stylish **River Room** (519/850-2287, www.northmoore.ca/theriverroom), overlooking the river.

Wander through London's oldest surviving residence, the 1834 **Eldon House** (481 Ridout St. N., 519/661-0333, www.eldonhouse.ca, noon-5pm Tues.-Sun. May-Sept., noon-5pm Wed.-Sun. Oct.-Dec., noon-5pm Thurs.-Sun. Jan.-Apr., donation), and you can imagine yourself a guest of the well-to-do Harris family, who lived in this white clapboard home for four generations. Among its idiosyncratic furnishings are an umbrella stand made from an elephant's foot, gold-embossed faux-leather wallpaper that the family brought back from Japan in 1897, and a melodeon (a miniature organ).

London played an important role in medical history, when local doctor Frederick Banting (1891-1941) conceived the idea of extracting insulin from a pancreas as a treatment for diabetes. Thanks to Banting's research, insulin was first used successfully in a human trial in 1922, and Banting received the Nobel Prize in Medicine the following year. Banting's former home is now the **Banting House National Historic Site** (442 Adelaide St. N., 519/673-1752, www. diabetes.ca, noon-4pm Tues.-Sat., adults $5, seniors and students $4, families $12), where guides recount the history of his life and his discovery in 45-minute tours.

BREWERIES

Founded in London in 1847, the Labatt Brewing Company still makes beer here. To learn more about the brewing process, take a two-hour **Labatt Brewery Tour** (150 Simcoe St., 519/850-8687 or 800/268-2337, londontour@labatt.com, www.labatt.com, Mon.-Fri., $12) that wraps up with a beer tasting. You must book in advance (8am and 4pm Mon.-Fri.) by phone or email.

London also has a growing craft beer scene. Start your self-guided tasting tour at **London Brewing** (521 Burbrook Pl., 226/667-6363, www.londonbrewing.ca, noon-9pm Wed.-Fri., 11am-9pm Sat., noon-5pm Sun.), a co-operatively-run brewery and pub in an east

London

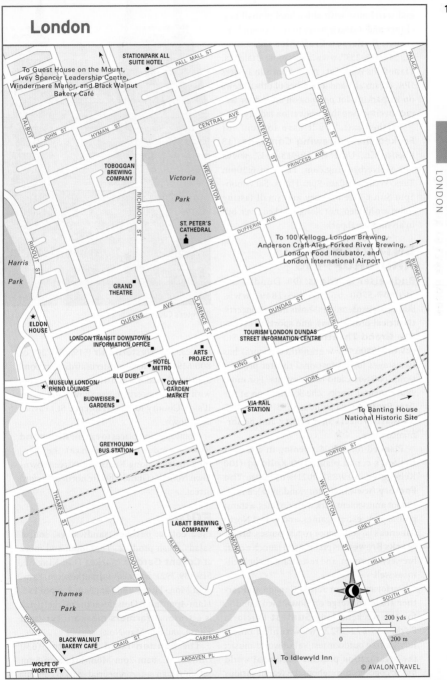

STATIONPARK ALL
SUITE HOTEL

PALL MALL ST

PALACE
ST

To Guest House on the Mount,
Ivey Spencer Leadership Centre,
Windermere Manor, and Black Walnut
Bakery Café

COLBORNE
ST

CENTRAL AVE

WATERLOO
ST

TALBOT
ST

JOHN ST

HYMAN ST

PRINCESS AVE

TOBOGGAN
BREWING
COMPANY

Victoria

Park

RICHMOND
ST

WELLINGTON
ST

ST. PETER'S
CATHEDRAL

DUFFERIN AVE

To 100 Kellogg, London Brewing,
Anderson Craft Ales, Forked River Brewing,
London Food Incubator, and
London International Airport

Harris

Park

RIDOUT
ST

BURWELL
ST

GRAND
THEATRE

AVE

QUEENS

CLARENCE ST

DUNDAS ST

ELDON
HOUSE

WATERLOO
ST

LONDON TRANSIT DOWNTOWN
INFORMATION OFFICE

TOURISM LONDON DUNDAS
STREET INFORMATION CENTRE

ARTS
PROJECT

HOTEL
METRO

KING ST

YORK ST

BLU DUBY

MUSEUM LONDON/
RHINO LOUNGE

COVENT
GARDEN
MARKET

BUDWEISER
GARDENS

VIA RAIL
STATION

To Banting House
National Historic Site

GREYHOUND
BUS STATION

HORTON ST

WELLINGTON

THAMES
ST

GREY ST

LABATT BREWING
COMPANY

RIDOUT
ST S

TALBOT
ST

RICHMOND
ST

HILL ST

Thames

Park

SOUTH ST

0   200 yds

WORTLEY RD

BLACK WALNUT
BAKERY CAFÉ

CRAIG ST

CARFRAE ST

0   200 m

WOLFE OF
WORTLEY

ARDAVEN PL

To Idlewyld Inn

© AVALON TRAVEL

end warehouse with old-school pinball machines and a dozen beers to try. Around the corner, **Anderson Craft Ales** (1030 Elias St., 548/888-2537, www.andersoncraftales.ca, 11am-9pm Wed.-Sat., noon-5pm Sun.) offers IPA, cream ale, and a number of other brews on its parking-lot patio or on an indoor terrace overlooking the production facility.

Farther east, you'll have to hunt for **Forked River Brewing Company** (45 Pacific Ct., Unit 4, 519/913-2337, www.forkedriverbrewing.com, 11:30am-6:30pm Tues.-Wed., 11:30am-9pm Thurs.-Sat., noon-5pm Sun.). The brewery and small tasting room are hidden, not along a forked river, but in an industrial park.

ENTERTAINMENT AND SHOPPING

Budweiser Gardens (99 Dundas St., 519/667-5700 or 866/455-2849, www.budweisergardens.com) hosts major concerts, theatrical productions, and sporting events. The **Grand Theatre** (471 Richmond St., 519/672-8800, www.grandtheatre.com) has two stages for professional theater productions, concerts, and other events. For more experimental works, check what's on at the **Arts Project** (203 Dundas St., 519/642-2767, www.artsproject.ca), a gallery and performance space.

Planned for a 2018 opening in a former Kellogg's cereal plant, **100 Kellogg** (100 Kellogg Ln., 519/852-0021)will house **The Factory** (www.thefactorylondon.ca), a huge indoor amusement park with zip lines, a trampoline park, escape games, and one of North America's largest indoor ropes courses. **Silver Stacks Brewery** is planning to launch a craft brewery, taproom, and restaurant in the facility as well.

Performers from across Canada and farther afield converge on downtown London for the weekend-long **Sunfest** (Victoria Park, 519/672-1522, www.sunfest.on.ca, July), a free outdoor festival of world music; the organization presents additional world music concerts throughout the year at various

St. Peter's Cathedral

venues. The **Western Fair** (519/438-7203 or 800/619-4629, www.westernfairdistrict.com, Sept.) is London's old-time country expo, with rides, concerts, horse shows, and more. It's on County Road 2 (Florence St.) east of downtown.

Boutiques and places to eat line **Richmond Row** (www.downtownlondon.ca), the shopping district along Richmond Street downtown from the Grand Theatre north to Oxford Street.

FOOD

Find coffee, pastries, sandwiches, soups, salads, fresh produce, Thai food, and more at **Covent Garden Market** (130 King St., 519/439-3921, www.coventmarket.com, 8am-6pm Mon.-Thurs. and Sat., 8am-7:30pm Fri., 11am-4pm Sun.). Outside on the market plaza is a seasonal **farmers market** (8am-2pm Thurs. and Sat. May-Nov.).

The **London Food Incubator** (630 Dundas St., 8am-7pm Mon.-Fri., 8am-5pm Sat.-Sun.), an entrepreneurial market concept in the city's east end, houses a small grocery, the **Fire Roasted Coffee Company** (519/438-5225, www.fireroastedcoffee.com, 8am-7pm Mon.-Fri., 9am-5pm Sat.-Sun.), and several prepared foods businesses where you can pick up lunch or a snack.

For scrumptious muffins, cookies, quiche, and other baked goods, head to the ★ **Black Walnut Bakery Café** (134 Wortley Rd., 519/439-2253, www.blackwalnutbakerycafe. com, 7am-6pm Mon.-Sat., 8:30am-5pm Sun.) in the Wortley Village neighborhood south of downtown. If you're in a savory mood, try the flaky spinach pie; they also serve sandwiches and soups midday. And if you're lucky, there'll be slices of fresh fruit pie. A second, more central branch is on Richmond Row (724 Richmond St., 519/850-2253, 7:30am-6pm Mon.-Fri., 8am-6pm Sat., 8:30am-5pm Sun.).

A cavernous tasting room, sports bar, and eatery, **Toboggan Brewing Company** (585 Richmond St., 519/433-2337, www. tobogganbrewing.com, noon-11pm Sun.-Thurs., noon-midnight Fri.-Sat., $11-23) crafts beers like Lunatic Fridge IPA and Mr. Insurance Man Blonde, along with seasonal brews. Take a seat at the long bar to watch the game on the big screen, or dig into pub grub like pizza, full-meal salads, or tacos (try

the panko-crusted Ontario perch variety). The biergarten terrace is a spirited summer hangout.

London's bistro with buzz is the adventurous **Wolfe of Wortley** (147 Wortley Rd., 519/854-6004, www.wolfeofwortley.com, from 5pm Tues.-Sun., small plates $7-30), which brothers Gregg and Justin Wolfe opened in Wortley Village. The signature cocktails, like the "Wake Up You're on Fire" (bourbon, coffee liqueur, Cointreau, and chili bitters) or the "Sour Power" (bourbon, Aperol, amaro, and lemon), pair well with small plates: oysters, charcuterie, and veggies like brussels sprouts with grapes and blue cheese or house-made "pickles and ferments." Among the inventive proteins are pork loin with a 63° egg and kale, and rainbow trout with carrots and coconut.

ACCOMMODATIONS

London has a slew of basic chain motels south of downtown on Wellington Road. Otherwise, accommodations cluster downtown or near the University of Western Ontario campus north of the center.

Under $100

A cross between a dormitory and a hotel, the no-frills **Guest House on the Mount**

Toboggan Brewing Company

(Ignatia Hall, 2nd Fl., 1486 Richmond St., 519/641-8100, www.guesthouseonthemount.ca, $49-89 s, $59-119 d) attracts guests of all ages. The spacious hotel-style rooms are simply furnished, with a bed and a TV; you can choose shared bath, half bath (with a toilet and sink), or a private bath. Facilities include a lounge, laundry, shared kitchen, and free Wi-Fi. The guesthouse is north of the university campus, on the grounds of the Windermere on the Mount retirement home; follow the signs to Ignatia Hall.

$100-200

Though it caters to conferences and business travelers, the **Ivey Spencer Leadership Centre** (551 Windermere Rd., 519/679-4546, www.iveyspencerleadershipcentre.com, $129-154 d) is an excellent option for vacationers, too. On 30 forested acres on the University of Western Ontario campus, the sprawling complex is built around a 1930s brick manor, expanded to encompass 125 guest rooms with comfy beds, one-cup coffeemakers, fridges, and big work desks with lots of outlets and Wi-Fi. Work out in the spacious fitness center, tuck into the big buffet spread for breakfast, and wash your grubby gear in the complimentary guest laundry. You can borrow a bike to explore the campus, too.

Windermere Manor (200 Collip Circle, 519/858-1391 or 800/997-4477, www.windermeremanor.com, $140-160 d), also on the UWO campus, looks the part of a university lodging, with an ivy-covered stucco exterior and dark woodwork lining the hallways. The rooms are comfortable if somewhat dated, with floral drapes and oak furnishings, though flat-screen TVs, fridges, one-cup coffeemakers, and Wi-Fi are standard. Included in the rates is breakfast at **Restaurant Ninetyone** (519/858-5866, www.restaurantninetyone.ca), overlooking the wooded grounds.

In a lane facing Covent Garden Market, **Hotel Metro** (32 Covent Market Pl., 519/518-9000 or 866/626-3876, www.hotelmetro.ca, $139-225 d) is set in a former shoe factory warehouse. The best of the 20 contemporary loft-style rooms, with iPod docks, modern baths with rain showers, and Wi-Fi, are on the 4th (top) floor, where they have exposed brick walls and oversize windows. This boutique lodging doesn't have its own parking lot, so park next door in the Covent Market garage ($13 per day) or hunt for parking on nearby streets. The hotel's restaurant, **Blu Duby** (519/433-1414, www.bluduby.com, 11am-11pm Mon.-Thurs., 11am-midnight Fri.-Sat., 4pm-9pm Sun., lunch $13-17, dinner $21-40), hums with a friends-hanging-out vibe. It cooks up nibbles like lamb "lollipops" and Korean-style dumplings and larger plates such as beef short ribs and chickpea cakes with harissa-tomato sauce.

One block from Richmond Row, the **StationPark All Suite Hotel** (242 Pall Mall St., 519/642-4444 or 800/561-4574, www.stationparkinn.ca, $169-228 d, parking $24/day) is popular with business travelers and families who appreciate the suites with a bedroom and separate living area. The "superior" suites on floors 9-14 are a little brighter and have newer furnishings, but all rooms are equipped with mini fridges, microwaves, and coffeemakers. Continental breakfast and Internet access are included.

Over $200

Built in 1878 as a private home, the **Idlewyld Inn** (36 Grand Ave., 519/432-5554, www.idlewyldinn.com, $155-339 d) is a rambling mansion with bay windows, stained glass, gingerbread trim, and a turret. The original owner, Charles Smith Hyman, served as London's mayor, a federal cabinet minister, and captain of Canada's national cricket team, and you can imagine this Victorian notable receiving guests in the formal dining room (which now serves breakfast, lunch, and dinner). While retaining some of the period features, the 21 guest rooms have updated decor and amenities that include flat-screen TVs and Wi-Fi. Rates include breakfast and parking.

INFORMATION AND SERVICES

Tourism London (519/661-5000 or 800/265-2602, www.londontourism.ca) runs two helpful visitors centers that provide information about the London area: the **Dundas Street Information Centre** (267 Dundas St. at Wellington St., 8:30am-4:30pm Mon.-Fri., 10am-5pm Sat.-Sun. late May-mid-Oct., 8:30am-4:30pm Mon.-Fri. mid-Oct.-late May) downtown, and the **London Tourist Information Centre** (696 Wellington Rd. S., 8:30am-12:30pm and 1:30pm-4:30pm Mon.-Fri., 10am-5pm Sat.-Sun.) between Highway 401 and the city center. They deliver lots of local information online, too.

GETTING THERE
Air

London International Airport (YXU, 1750 Crumlin Rd., 519/452-4015, www.londonairport.on.ca) is 10 kilometers (six miles) northeast of downtown. **Air Canada** (888/247-2262, www.aircanada.com) flies to Toronto and Ottawa; **WestJet** (888/937-8538, www.westjet.com) has direct flights to Toronto, Winnipeg, Calgary, Vancouver, and Orlando.

A taxi between the airport and downtown London costs $30-35. **Avis** (www.avis.com), **Enterprise** (www.enterpriserentacar.ca), **Hertz** (www.hertz.ca), and **National** (www.nationalcar.ca) have car rental offices at the London airport. **London Transit** (www.ltconline.ca) buses can take you between the airport and downtown (Mon.-Fri.); take bus no. 36 from the airport to Fanshawe College, then change to bus no. 4 or no. 20 heading downtown.

You'll find many more flight options via **Toronto's Pearson Airport** (YYZ, 6301 Silver Dart Dr., Mississauga, 416/247-7678 or 866/207-1690, www.torontopearson.com). **Robert Q Airbus** (105 Wharncliffe Rd. S., 519/673-6804 or 800/265-4948, www.robertq.com, 2.25 hours, one-way adults $65.50,

seniors and students $62.25, kids under 12 $32.75) runs shuttles between Pearson Airport and London. It's much cheaper to take the **Greyhound** bus between Pearson and London's **Greyhound Bus Station** (101 York St., 519/434-3250 or 800/661-8747, www.greyhound.ca, 2-2.5 hours, one-way adults $23-49), as long as your schedule matches up with one of the several daily buses.

Train

London is easy to reach by train. The Toronto-Windsor and Toronto-Sarnia trains all stop at London's downtown **VIA Rail station** (205 York St., 888/842-7245, www.viarail.ca). Most trains between Toronto and London (one-way adults $37-128, ages 2-11 $20-65) make the trip in 2.25-2.5 hours, but check the schedule: a couple chug along for 3.5 hours. Windsor to London (one-way adults $38-104, ages 2-11 $20-52) takes 1.75 hours.

Bus

Greyhound operates numerous daily buses from Toronto to the London **Greyhound Bus Station** (101 York St., 519/434-3250 or 800/661-8747, www.greyhound.ca, 2.15-3 hours, one-way adults $21-53) downtown.

Car

London is 195 kilometers (120 miles) southwest of Toronto, a 2- to 2.5-hour drive. Either take the QEW to Highway 403 to Highway 401 or pick up Highway 401 directly. From Highway 401, take exit 187 and follow Wellington Road north toward downtown.

GETTING AROUND

Downtown London is compact enough to explore on foot, and the extensive bus system, run by **London Transit** (519/451-1347, www.ltconline.ca, adults $2.75), can take you farther afield. Phone or stop into the **Downtown Information Office** (150 Dundas St., 7:30am-7pm Mon.-Fri., 8:30am-6pm Sat.) if you need transit help.

LONDON

LAKE ERIE TO LAKE HURON

Southwestern Ontario

In the 1800s, at least 30,000 enslaved African Americans fled from the United States to freedom in Canada. Following the Underground Railroad, a network of safe houses and churches that sheltered the refugees, the majority of those enslaved people crossed into Canada into what is now Southwestern Ontario. Many remained in the region, with significant settlements in Windsor, Sandwich, Amherstburg, Chatham, Dresden, and Buxton, and many of their descendants live here today. A number of sites throughout Southwestern Ontario enable you to explore this African Canadian Heritage Route, tracing the history of the former slaves and their new life in Canada.

Windsor, now this region's largest city, continues to be a magnet for newcomers, attracting immigrants from many nations. An industrial city, it has several worthwhile museums, and its restaurants offer a multiethnic cornucopia. Southwestern Ontario is also a growing winemaking region, where you can go wine-tasting and exploring, particularly around the towns of Amherstburg, Harrow, and Kingsville.

For more information about this part of the province, check out the website for **Ontario's Southwest** (519/290-8687, www.ontariossouthwest.com), the region's tourism organization.

CHATHAM AND VICINITY

Many formerly enslaved people settled in Chatham and the nearby communities of Dresden and Buxton, where several sites explore the history of these African Canadian settlements.

Uncle Tom's Cabin Historic Site

The **Uncle Tom's Cabin Historic Site** (29251 Uncle Tom's Rd., Dresden, 519/683-2978, www.uncletomscabin.org, 10am-4pm

Tues.-Sat., noon-4pm Sun. mid-May-June and Sept.-Oct., 10am-4pm Mon.-Sat., noon-4pm Sun. July-Aug., adults $7, seniors and ages 13-17 $6, ages 6-12 $4.50, families $20) tells the story of former slave and abolitionist Reverend Josiah Henson (1796-1883), who was born on a plantation in Maryland, then sold to a slave owner in Kentucky before following the Underground Railroad to Canada. Settling near Dresden in 1842, he helped establish the Dawn Settlement, a community that became a refuge for formerly enslaved people. In 1852, American writer Harriet Beecher Stowe published her historic anti-slavery novel *Uncle Tom's Cabin,* which some historians say was based in part on Henson's memoirs.

Start your visit by watching a video introducing Josiah Henson, the history of slavery in the United States and Canada, and the settlements that former slaves set up in Southwestern Ontario. Then visit the gallery, where exhibits explore these topics in more detail. You can tour several restored buildings, including Henson House, the reverend's last residence, as well as a local church built in the 1880s. Inside the church, look for the booklet *Sounds of Freedom,* which explains that many songs that slaves sung contained coded messages. "The Gospel Train's a-Comin'," for example, would alert other enslaved people that a group was planning an escape. You can also visit the small cemetery where Henson is buried.

The Uncle Tom's Cabin Historic Site is located west of Dresden, 30 kilometers (19 miles) north of Chatham, near the intersection of Highways 21 and 15.

Chatham-Kent Black Historical Society

In the 1850s, as more blacks established themselves in the Chatham area, the town became a center for African Canadian intellectual life,

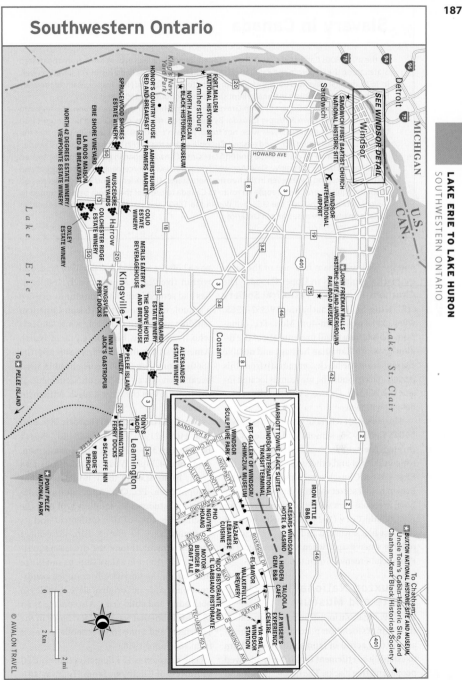

Southwestern Ontario

MICHIGAN

Detroit

U.S. ——— CAN.

Sandwich

Windsor

SEE WINDSOR DETAIL

HOWARD AVE

WINDSOR INTERNATIONAL AIRPORT

SANDWICH FIRST BAPTIST CHURCH NATIONAL HISTORIC SITE

FORT MALDEN NATIONAL HISTORIC SITE

Amherstburg

NORTH AMERICAN BLACK HISTORICAL MUSEUM

HONOR'S COUNTRY HOUSE BED AND BREAKFAST

King's Navy Yard Park

PIKE RD

AMHERSTBURG FARMERS MARKET

SPRUCEWOOD SHORES ESTATE WINERY

ERIE SHORE VINEYARD

LA ROOS MAISON BED & BREAKFAST

NORTH 42 DEGREES ESTATE WINERY/ VIEWPOINTE ESTATE WINERY

MUSCEDERE VINEYARDS

Harrow

COLCHESTER RIDGE ESTATE WINERY

OXLEY ESTATE WINERY

COLIO ESTATE WINERY

Lake Erie

To ★ PELEE ISLAND

Kingsville

KINGSVILLE FERRY DOCKS

INN 31/ JACK'S GASTROPUB

MERLIS EATERY & THE GROVE HOTEL AND BREW HOUSE

MASTRONARDI ESTATE WINERY

PELEE ISLAND WINERY

ALEKSANDER ESTATE WINERY

Cottam

Lake St. Clair

JOHN FREEMAN WALLS HISTORIC SITE AND UNDERGROUND RAILROAD MUSEUM

Leamington

LEAMINGTON FERRY DOCKS

TONY'S TACOS

SEACLIFFE INN

BIRDIE'S PERCH

FT PELEE DR

★ POINT PELEE NATIONAL PARK

IRON KETTLE B&B

Lake Erie

To Chatham, ★ BUXTON NATIONAL HISTORIC SITE AND MUSEUM, Uncle Tom's Cabin Historic Site, and Chatham-Kent Black Historical Society

0   2 mi

0   2 km

© AVALON TRAVEL

MARRIOTT TOWNE PLACE SUITES

WINDSOR INTERNATIONAL TRANSIT TERMINAL

WINDSOR SCULPTURE PARK

SANDWICH ST

HURON CHURCH RD

UNIVERSITY AVE

WYANDOTTE

COLLEGE AVE

CRAWFORD AVE

ART GALLERY OF WINDSOR/ CHIMCZUK MUSEUM

PHO NGUYEN HOANG

MAZAAR LEBANESE CUISINE

MOTOR BURGER AND CRAFT ALE

OUELLETTE AVE

PARENT AVE

GILES

NICO RISTORANTE AND 'IL GABBIANO RISTORANTE

CAESARS WINDSOR HOTEL & CASINO

EL-MAYOR

A HIDDEN GEM B&B

RIVERSIDE DR

WALKERVILLE BREWERY

TALOOLA CAFE

J.P. WISER'S EXPERIENCE CENTRE

VIA RAIL WINDSOR STATION

WALKER RD

SEMINOLE AVE

TECUMSEH RD E

Slavery in Canada

By the mid-1800s Canada was a safe haven for enslaved people escaping north from the United States along the Underground Railroad, but unfortunately Canada had a history of slavery as well. In 1629, the first slave was transported from Africa to the colony of New France. Many of the early British and French settlers in Canada kept slaves throughout the 1600s and 1700s.

In 1793, Lieutenant Governor John Graves Simcoe prohibited the importation of slaves into the region then known as Upper Canada. By this decree, no new slaves could be brought into the province, but existing slaves were not freed. It wasn't until 40 years later, in 1833, that the British Slavery Abolition Act freed enslaved people across the British Empire, including Canada.

The migration of slaves from the United States into Canada began in earnest after the United States passed the 1850 Fugitive Slave Act, which required law enforcement officers to apprehend and return escaping slaves, even in the free northern states. The Underground Railroad developed to shelter fugitive enslaved people en route to Canada to prevent them from being returned to slavery in the South. Until the U.S. Civil War in the 1860s, thousands fled north to freedom in Canada, many of them settling in Ontario.

and by 1861, Chatham had one of the largest black populations in Upper Canada. The **Chatham-Kent Black Historical Society** (177 King St. E., Chatham, 519/352-3565, www.ckbhs.org, 11am-4pm Mon.-Fri., donation) maintains a small museum about the region's African Canadian heritage and notable citizens from the black community from this period and beyond. The museum is located inside the W.I.S.H. Centre, a community center near downtown.

Museum staff will take visitors on **guided tours** (adults $6, seniors and students $5) through the neighborhood, pointing out historic buildings and other sites, including the First Baptist Church where abolitionist John Brown held a secret meeting in 1858, and the BME Freedom Park with its sculpture of Mary Ann Shadd Cary (1823-1893), who became the first black woman in North America to publish a newspaper when she launched The Provincial Freeman in Ontario in 1853.

★ Buxton National Historic Site and Museum

In 1849, an abolitionist organization called the Elgin Association purchased 3,650 hectares (9,000 acres) of land south of Chatham to establish a settlement for formerly enslaved people and free blacks. The new settlers would pay $2.50 per acre to buy a parcel of land, and within five years, approximately 150 families had settled here. The community opened a school, which educated African Canadian children and began attracting white students who lived nearby, becoming one of North America's first integrated schools. By the 1860s, more than 2,000 people lived in what became known as the Buxton Settlement; at the time, it was the largest black settlement in Canada.

The **Buxton National Historic Site and Museum** (21975 A. D. Shadd Rd., North Buxton, 519/352-4799, www.buxtonmuseum.com, 1pm-4:30pm Wed.-Sun. May-June and Sept., 10am-4:30pm daily July-Aug., 1pm-4:30pm Mon.-Fri. Oct.-Apr., adults $6, seniors and students $5, families $20) tells the fascinating story of this settlement and its community. A 20-minute film introduces the settlement; among the museum's artifacts is a berth from a slave ship, its small size illustrating the horrifically cramped conditions on board, and original slave shackles in both adult and child sizes. Also on-site is an 1852 log cabin that was the oldest home in the settlement and a one-room schoolhouse used from 1861 until 1968.

The museum is 15 kilometers (nine miles) southwest of Chatham. From Highway 401, take exit 81 onto County Road 27/Bloomfield Road south, and turn right (west) onto 8 Line/County Road 14 and left (south) onto A. D. Shadd Road.

Food and Accommodations

Ask locals where to have dinner and they'll direct you to the **Chatham Breakfast House & Grille** (525 Grand Ave. E., 519/355-1279, www.chathambreakfasthouse.ca, 7am-8pm Tues.-Thurs., 7am-2pm and 5pm-9pm Fri., 8am-2pm and 5pm-9pm Sat., 8am-2pm Sun., lunch $10-17, dinner $18-38). Despite the name, this homey, long-popular eatery, with red and black booths, is a Portuguese-style *churrascaria* specializing in intensely juicy *piri piri* chicken, steaks, and ribs. They do serve breakfast, with the usual eggs and French toast suspects; at lunchtime, look for sandwiches like pork cutlets with sautéed onions and a variety of panini, plus that delicious chicken.

The surprisingly cool ★ **Retro Suites Hotel** (2 King St. W., 519/351-5885 or 866/617-3876, www.retrosuites.com, $159-249 d) is located in a restored block of Victorian-era buildings. The 45 rooms are wildly different, from the Easy Rider, with an antique motorcycle hanging from the ceiling, and Game Time, a sports lover's dream, to the Log Cabin, a Canadian north woods fantasy of pine walls, a log bedframe, and a light fixture with antlers. The hotel's dining room, the **Chilled Cork Restaurant and Lounge** (7am-9pm Mon.-Fri., 8am-9pm Sat., 8am-2pm Sun., lunch $10-19, dinner $17-43), specializes in pastas and steaks.

Practicalities

Chatham is off Highway 401, 290 kilometers (180 miles) southwest of Toronto and 110 kilometers (68 miles) from London. From Highway 401, take exit 90 and go north on Highway 40/Communication Road toward Wallaceburg; then turn left onto Park Avenue East, toward the center of town. From Windsor, 80 kilometers (50 miles) to the southwest, take Highway 401's exit 81, Bloomfield Road; follow Bloomfield Road north, then turn right (east) onto Park Avenue West. **Chatham-Kent Tourism** (25 Creek Rd., Chatham, 519/360-1998 or 800/561-6125, www.visitck.ca) can provide information about the region.

Pupils studied in this one-room schoolhouse until 1968.

KINGSVILLE AND LEAMINGTON

Along the Lake Erie shore, the towns of Kingsville and Leamington are popular with bird-watchers—Point Pelee National Park is a highlight. The surrounding land is farm country, where you can visit a growing number of wineries. Ferries to Pelee Island leave from Kingsville and Leamington.

★ Point Pelee National Park

The southernmost point on Canada's mainland, the waterfront **Point Pelee National Park** (1118 Point Pelee Dr., Leamington, 519/322-2365 or 888/773-8888, www.pc.gc.ca, www.friendsofpointpelee.com, adults $7.80, seniors $6.80), jutting into Lake Erie, is an important stopover point for migrating birds; more than 390 species have been identified in the vicinity, with the greatest variety during the annual spring migration, typically the first three weeks of May. The **Festival of Birds** (www.festivalofbirds.ca, May) celebrates this annual migration with guided birding hikes, birding presentations, and other special events. Monarch butterflies also migrate through the Point Pelee region; visit from late August through early October for the best butterfly viewings.

At the park **Visitors Centre** (10am-5pm daily mid-late Apr., 6am-5pm daily early-late May, 10am-5pm Mon.-Fri., 10am-7pm Sat.-Sun. late May-early Sept, 10am-5pm Mon.-Fri., 10am-6pm Sat.-Sun. early Sept.-Oct.), you can walk through exhibits about the region's flora and fauna; periodic "creature feature" presentations include live animals. Several short hiking trails start nearby.

Most visitors head directly to the scenic "Tip of Canada," the narrow spit of land at the park's southern end, where waves roll in from both sides of the lake. The road between the Visitors Centre and the tip is closed to private vehicles from spring through fall. The park service runs the free **Shuttle to the Tip** (10am-4pm daily mid-late Apr., 6am-5pm daily early-mid-May, 10am-5pm Mon.-Fri., 10am-7pm Sat.-Sun. late May-early Sept., 7am-4pm Mon.-Fri., 7am-6pm Sat.-Sun. early-Sept.-early Oct., 10am-4pm daily early-late Oct.), which takes visitors close to the park's endpoint. From the shuttle drop-off point, there's a one-kilometer (0.6-mile) loop trail to the tip and back. As an alternative to the shuttle, you can walk the 2.5-kilometer (1.5-mile) road between the Visitors Centre and the tip. Swimming is prohibited near the tip because currents can be quite strong. To

paddling through the marsh at Point Pelee National Park

swim, head for the sandy beaches along the park's western shore.

Follow the **Marsh Boardwalk Trail,** a one-kilometer (0.6-mile) loop through the cattails, to experience the marshy habitat of the park's eastern side, or climb the lookout tower overlooking the marsh. To explore the marsh from the water, you can rent canoes ($20 for 1 hour, $10 for each additional hour) at the nearby **Marsh Store** (519/322-1654, May-mid-Oct.), which also sells snacks. The park offers one-hour guided **Freighter Canoe Tours** (July-early Sept., $7.30 pp, families $20) of the marsh in their "Cattail Cruiser" 10-person canoes. **Farm Dog Cycles** (519/551-1613, www.farmdogcycles.com, 10am-5pm Sat.-Sun. late May-early Sept., $10 per hour, half day $20, full day $30) rents bicycles from a stand near the boardwalk.

Designated a Dark Sky Preserve, the park stays open till midnight several times a year for stargazing during its **Dark Sky Nights.** Get the schedule from the Visitors Centre or the park website. The park is open year-round, although some services, including the Shuttle to the Tip, are seasonal. Park admission rates are reduced slightly from November through March.

CAMPING

Point Pelee National Park doesn't have a campground, but the park does have 24 year-round **oTENTiks** ($120/night), furnished platform tents that each sleep up to six. Bring your own bedding and food; water taps, toilets, and showers are a short walk away. Make oTEN-Tik reservations at 877/737-3783 or https://reservation.pc.gc.ca.

Wineries

Canada's southernmost winery, **Pelee Island Winery** (455 Seacliff Dr./County Rd. 20, Kingsville, 519/733-6551 or 800/597-3533, www.peleeisland.com, 9am-6pm Mon.-Sat., 11am-5pm Sun., tours noon, 2pm, and 4pm daily, adults $5, seniors $4) grows its grapes on Pelee Island but makes most of its wines—pinot grigio, riesling, cabernet

merlot, cabernet franc, ice wine, and more—at this Kingsville location. Tours include a video about the winemaking process, a walk through the winery, and a tasting.

Most other Kingsville-area wineries are small, family-owned properties, including **Mastronardi Estate Winery** (1193 Concession 3 E., Kingsville, 519/733-9463 or 800/320-5040, www.mastronardiwines.com, 11am-5pm daily May-Dec., 11am-5pm Fri.-Sun. Jan.-Apr., tours by appointment) and **Aleksander Estate Winery** (1542 County Rd. 34, Ruthven, 519/326-2024, www.aleksanderestate.com, 11am-6pm Mon.-Fri., 11am-5pm Sat.-Sun., tours by appointment).

Food

Its walls decorated with local art, funky **Merlis Eatery & Beveragehouse** (4 Main St., Kingsville, 519/733-0110, 11am-8pm Mon.-Thurs., 11am-9pm Fri.-Sat., $8-18) dishes out coffee, homemade soups, sandwiches, and vegetarian options, plus local wine, craft beer, and occasional live music.

Lively **Jack's Gastropub** (31 Division St. S., Kingsville, 519/733-6900, www.jacksdining.com, 11:30am-9pm daily, $10-18), in an early 1900s brick building, serves pub snacks, sandwiches, potpies, and Lake Erie perch. It stocks a decent selection of Ontario beers, too. Upstairs are the three guest rooms of **Inn 31** (http://inn31.com, $139-149 d), furnished with antique-style pieces, mixed with modern accessories, and puffy duvets on the queen beds.

Look up inside the multilevel **Grove Brew House** (12 Main St. E., Kingsville, 519/712-8812, www.mygrovebrewhouse.com, 11:30am-11pm Sun.-Thurs., 11:30am-midnight Fri.-Sat., $11-24), a craft brewery and restaurant adjacent to the Grove Hotel. Beer tanks sit on a catwalk over the bar, and black-and-white street-style art hangs from the walls. In addition to the brews, which include Paradise Lager and Westcott Cream Ale, the menu offers interesting sandwiches and pizzas. Try the perch sliders with crisp coleslaw and onion chips.

On your way to Point Pelee National Park, stop at the "Bustaurant," a big red double-decker bus that houses **Birdie's Perch** (625 Point Pelee Dr., Leamington, 519/551-7043, www.birdiesperch.ca, 11am-11pm daily May-mid-Oct., $4-15), a restaurant and take-out shop offering fish-and-chips, tacos, sandwiches, and ice cream.

Walk into **Tony's Tacos** (52 Erie St. S., Leamington, 519/326-0110, 10am-8:30pm Tues.-Sun.) and you'll think you've wandered into a convivial cantina in small-town Mexico. The walls are bright orange, the merengue music blares, and the traditional tacos are heaped with meat. Ask for the house-made green hot sauce. On weekends, hunker down over a steaming bowl of *posole* (soup made with corn or hominy) or *menudo* (tripe stew).

Accommodations

When the Instagram hashtags are posted in the breakfast room, you know you're not staying in your grandmother's B&B. The personable young owners of the ★ **Iron Kettle B&B** (7005 County Rd. 46, Comber, 519/687-2377, www.ironkettlebb.com, $145 d)—he's a chef, she's a teacher—run this 19th-century brick manor with a broad grassy lawn as a stylish six-room inn. Original details abound, from the pine floors to the exposed brick walls; fast Wi-Fi and modern private baths are among the contemporary amenities. Breakfast is a highlight, starting with fresh fruit and warm-from-the-oven scones, croissants, and other pastries, along with a hot dish, maybe quiche with sweet potatoes and ham. The inn is 22 kilometers (14 miles) north of Leamington and 40 kilometers (25 miles) southwest of Chatham.

The funkiest place to stay in town is **The Grove Hotel** (12 Main St. E., Kingsville, 519/712-9087, www.mygrovehotel.com, $159-239 d), restored from its origins as a former 1850s temperance hotel to a fun boutique inn with an on-site craft brewery. It's full of quirky touches—the reception desk is made of old suitcases—and the 18 guest rooms are all different; the Brewmaster's Suite has an entrance directly into the brewpub. Rates include Wi-Fi, continental breakfast in the lobby, a 24-hour self-serve coffee bar, and a beer flight in the pub.

At the **Hellemsfield Inn** (2 Mill St. W., at Division St. S., Kingsville, 519/733-5250, www.bbcanada.com, $100-110 d), owners Carol and Scott Sitler created self-contained guest quarters in their 1872 Greek Revival-style home. The two bedrooms, one upstairs

Iron Kettle B&B

and one on the main level, aren't large, so the space is well suited to sociable types or couples traveling together who'd enjoy hanging out by the wood-and-stone fireplace in the cheery common living area. The owners serve a full breakfast on Saturday and Sunday, and a lighter continental spread during the week.

You can practically roll out of bed and onto the Pelee Island ferry (at least when it's leaving from the Leamington docks) when you stay at the **Seacliffe Inn** (388 Erie St. S., Leamington, 519/324-9266, www.seacliffeinn. com, $139-299 d). The 23 nautical-themed motel-style rooms with sturdy wooden furnishings are comfortable enough, and you can grab a beer or a bite in the downstairs lounge.

Information and Services

Leamington was once known as the "Tomato Capital of Canada" for the extensive tomato crop that grows nearby and for the large Heinz plant that once dominated the town. Reflecting this tomato heritage, Ontario's most unusual tourism office may be the **Leamington Tourist Information Booth** (Talbot St. W. at Mill St. W., www.leamington. ca), which is shaped like a giant tomato. Pick up local information and pose for tomato photos. **Tourism Windsor, Essex, and Pelee Island** (333 Riverside Dr. W., Suite 103, Windsor, 519/255-6530 or 800/265-3633, www.visitwindsoressex.com) also provides information about Kingsville and Leamington.

Getting There and Around

You'll want a car to explore the Kingsville-Leamington area. From Toronto (350 kilometers, 215 miles) or London (170 kilometers, 107 miles), take Highway 401 to Highway 77 south to Leamington. Kingsville is 15 kilometers (nine miles) west of Leamington. County Road 20, which is Seacliff Drive in Leamington and Main Street in Kingsville, connects the two towns. From Windsor, follow Walker Road south to Highway 3 east. Exit at Division Road/County Road 29 for Kingsville (40 kilometers, or 25 miles) or at

Erie Street for Leamington (50 kilometers, 30 miles).

Ferries to Pelee Island (www. ontarioferries.com) leave from Leamington (Erie St. S., 519/326-2154, Apr.-July) and Kingsville (Lakeview Ave. at Park St., 519/733-4474, Aug.-Dec.). To travel between Kingsville-Leamington and northern Ohio, you can take the Pelee Island ferry to or from Sandusky.

★ PELEE ISLAND

Canada's southernmost point is this laid-back little island in Lake Erie, where most visitors come simply to escape the mainland's hustle and bustle. In fact, the island's name, which locals pronounce "PEE-lee," comes from the French *pelée*, meaning "bare." Pelee is ringed with beaches—it's a peaceful spot for cycling and bird-watching, and there's even a winery—but otherwise, you won't find many sights. As one island innkeeper said, "There's nothing to do here, but it takes at least three days to do it."

Pelee's summer population is about 1,500, but only 300 hardy souls live on the island year-round. Many accommodations and eateries open in April or May and close in October or November. Even during the high season, business hours can be erratic; if few visitors are around, or if the owner has something else to do, places can close unexpectedly, so call ahead.

Travel on and off the island is also weather-dependent. While Pelee has some of Canada's warmest weather, winds can whip up along Lake Erie, causing the ferry from the mainland to delay or even cancel service. Ferries run April through mid-December.

Cycling is an easy way to get around the island; from the west ferry dock, it's 10 kilometers (six miles) north to the lighthouse (one-way), 1.2 kilometers (0.75 miles) south to the Pelee Island winery, and four kilometers (2.5 miles) south to Fish Point. Bring your own bike on the ferry or rent one from **Comfortech Bike Rental** (1023 West Shore

Rd., 519/724-2828, www.peleebikerental.com, daily May-Oct.) near the West Dock.

Sights

Jam-packed with artifacts, photos, and fossils, the **Pelee Island Heritage Centre** (1073 West Shore Rd., 519/724-2291, www.peleeislandmuseum.ca, 10am-5pm daily May-Oct., adults $3, seniors $2.50, students $2), a small museum opposite the ferry docks, is a good place to start your island explorations. Exhibits detail the island's geology, ecology, and human history, and you can learn about shipwrecks that plagued the surrounding waters.

South of the ferry docks, at the intersection of West Shore Road, **Pelee Island Winery** (20 East West Rd., 519/724-2469 or 800/597-3533, www.peleeisland.com, 11am-4pm Sun.-Thurs., 11am-7pm Fri.-Sat. mid-May-mid-June, 11am-8pm daily mid-June-early Sept., 11am-4pm daily early Sept.-mid-Oct.), one of the country's oldest winemaking operations, was established in 1866 as Vin Villa Winery. At the Island Pavilion visitors center, find out more about the winemaking process and walk among the 223 hectares (550 acres) of grapes. Ninety-minute tours (noon and 2pm daily mid-May-mid-June and early Sept.-mid-Oct., noon, 2pm, 4pm, and 6pm mid-June-early Sept., adults $5, seniors $4) include a wine tasting. The winery's **Deli Hut** serves burgers, pizza, and snacks.

On West Shore Road north of the dock, be on the lookout for **Stoneman,** a massive stone *inukshuk* sculpture, designed by local resident Peter Letkeman. The kids at the Pelee Island Public School gave Stoneman his name.

On the island's northeast tip, follow the short trail in **Lighthouse Point Provincial Nature Reserve** (www.ontarioparks.com) to the 1834 limestone lighthouse. There's a small pebbly beach, but no restrooms or other facilities.

At the **Stone Road Alvar Conservation Area** (www.erca.org, dawn-dusk daily year-round, free) in the island's southeast, you can wander the rocky shore to see one of

Pelee Island's distinctive natural features: alvars. Areas of limestone covered with a thin layer of topsoil, alvars allow unique vegetation to grow. Butterfly spotters have seen five rare species here: the giant swallowtail, tawny emperor, Acadian hairstreak, hackberry butterfly, and sachem skipper. From the West Dock, take West Shore Road to East West Road, and then turn south on Stone Road.

A popular bird-watching spot is the **Fish Point Provincial Nature Reserve** (519/825-4659, www.ontarioparks.com), a stopover point for migrating birds. There's a beach, but no facilities. Follow West Shore Road south until it becomes McCormick Road, then continue south to Fish Point. Other island beaches include **Sunset Beach** (West Shore Rd., north of the ferry docks) and **East Park Beach** (East Shore Rd., just north of East West Rd.).

Entertainment and Events

Birders and their friends flock to Pelee Island for the annual **Spring Song Weekend** (www.peleeislandmuseum.ca, May), which typically includes a bird-watching race and an evening banquet with a presentation by a guest author. Canadian authors from Margaret Atwood to Alice Munro to Lawrence Hill have participated.

A major local event is the annual **Pelee Island Pheasant Hunt** (www.pelee.org, Oct.-Nov.), started in the 1900s as a way to control the island's burgeoning pheasant population. More recently, it has become a sporting event, with pheasants raised for the hunt on the Pelee Island Pheasant Farm. The hunt draws hundreds of visitors during the last two weeks of October and the first week of November; if hunting isn't your thing, visit another time.

Food

The island has restaurants, but not many. You can buy picnic supplies and groceries at the **Co-op Grocery Store** (347 North Shore Rd., 519/724-2910) on the island's north end. If there's something specific you want, though, bring it from the mainland.

Tiny **Conorlee's Bakery and Delicatessen** (5 North Shore Rd., 519/724-2321, 8:30am-4pm Sun.-Wed., 8:30am-8pm Thurs.-Sat. summer, call for off-season hours), in a little yellow cottage, serves pastries and coffee in the mornings, deli sandwiches and pizza later in the day.

Crammed with buoys, sailing flags, and other nautical gewgaws, the funky dining room at **The Anchor and Wheel** (11:30am-8:30pm daily summer, call for off-season hours, $15-35) looks like it washed ashore from a Jimmy Buffet song. Start with a tropical drink in the Tiki Bar, but the real action is on the dinner plates, laden with bountiful portions of fish, prime rib, or pasta.

Your basic island bar, **Scudder Beach Bar and Grill** (325 North Shore Rd., 519/724-2902, lunch and dinner daily May-Sept., $8-13) serves wings, wraps, fried fish, and other pub fare. Bands liven things up most summer weekends.

Accommodations and Camping

Pelee Island has a few modest inns and B&Bs; on busy July and August weekends, arrange a place to stay before you hop on the ferry. For links to cottage rentals, check the Pelee Island website (www.pelee.org).

New owners took over the former Wandering Pheasant Inn and renamed it for their friendly pooch: **The Wandering Dog Inn** (1060 East West Rd., 519/724-2270, https://thewanderingdoginn.com, May-Nov., $105-185 d). The original Victorian inn building houses seven simple guest rooms with shared baths. In an adjacent cottage-style block, the five rooms are larger and furnished with Victoriana (and en suite baths). You can walk to the water in less than five minutes. The inn is adults only, except in the family suite ($225), which can sleep up to six.

In owner Jeri Marentette's modern home on the island's north shore, **Lucky Stone Beach House B&B** (295 North Shore Rd.,

519/724-9932, www.luckystonebeachhouse.com, May-Sept., $150-175 d) has three comfortable guest rooms. The Blue Room, on the lower level, has a private bath; upstairs, the Yellow and Green Rooms share bath facilities. Rates include breakfast and Wi-Fi.

The **East Park Campground** (1362 East Shore Rd., 519/724-2200, www.pelee.org, May-early Nov., $25) has 25 sites for tents and trailers, a short walk from East Beach. There are no electrical hookups, but there are washrooms with showers, as well as a small store.

Information and Services

The **Municipality of Pelee Island** (519/724-2931 or 866/889-5203, www.pelee.org) is the best source of local island information. If you'd like a guide to organize your Pelee Island visit, contact **Explore Pelee: Pelee Island Tours** (519/325-8687, www.explorepelee.com). Owner Anne Marie Fortner and her team can tell you anything you need to know about the island and offer several bike tours ($40-60 pp), as well as van-based tours ($30 pp) that explore Pelee's geology, agriculture, or history.

Getting There

Pelee Island is located in Lake Erie, south of Kingsville and Leamington and north of Sandusky, Ohio. Between April and mid-December, the **Pelee Island Transportation Company** (519/724-2115 or 800/661-2220, www.ontarioferries.com, one-way adults $7.50, seniors $6.25, ages 6-12 $3.25, bicycles $3.75, cars $16.50) runs 90-minute ferries to the island. Note that from the Ontario mainland, ferries leave from different points depending on the season. April through July, ferries depart from the **Leamington Docks** (Erie St. S., Leamington, 519/326-2154), while August to December, boats leave from the **Kingsville Docks** (Lakeview Ave. at Park St., Kingsville, 519/733-4474). The fare is the same from either point. Because of weather conditions, the ferry will occasionally be rerouted to the alternate dock, so it's always smart to confirm your departure and arrival points.

In summer (late June-early Sept.), ferries run 3-4 times daily in each direction. Check the website or phone for the exact schedule, for off-season hours (when departures are much less frequent), and for any unexpected schedule changes.

Travelers from the United States can catch the ferry from the **Sandusky Docks** (Jackson St. at Shoreline Dr., Sandusky, OH, late Apr.-Sept., 1.75 hours, one-way adults $13.75, seniors $11.25, ages 6-12 $6.75, bicycles $6.50, cars $30). Call or check the website for seasonal schedules.

If you're traveling between Sandusky and Pelee, remember your passport! You're crossing an international border and must clear customs and immigration. If you're taking a car on the ferry, advance reservations (519/326-2154 or 800/661-2220) are required, whether from the Ontario mainland or from the United States.

From mid-December to March, the only way on and off the island is by air. **Pelee Island Transportation Company** (519/724-2115 or 800/661-2220) flies regularly between Windsor and **Pelee Island Airport** (Centre Dyke Rd., 519/724-2265). **Griffing Flying Service** (419/734-5400, www.flygriffing.com) flies to Pelee from Erie-Ottawa International Airport near Sandusky.

Getting Around

Pelee Island is about 13 kilometers (eight miles) from north to south and about six kilometers (3.8 miles) across. The island has no public transportation, but there are taxis, or you can bring a car or bike from the mainland on the ferry.

AMHERSTBURG, HARROW, AND VICINITY

One of the oldest settlements in Southwestern Ontario, Amherstburg, on the Detroit River south of Windsor, was occupied by American forces during the War of 1812. The British burned the town's original Fort Amherstburg when U.S. troops forced them to retreat in 1813. After the war, the British regained control of the town and built Fort Malden, which is now a national historic site.

Amherstburg is also a gateway to the wine region known as **Essex Pelee Island Coast (EPIC) Wine Country** (www.epicwineries.com) along Lake Erie's North Shore, with wineries in the countryside around the adjacent community of Harrow.

Sights

In the first half of the 19th century, the British built fortifications in a strategic setting on the Detroit River to protect the Amherstburg area from American attacks. What remains of Fort Malden, now the **Fort Malden National Historic Site** (100 Laird Ave., Amherstburg, 519/736-5416, www.pc.gc.ca, 10am-5pm daily July-early Sept., 10am-5pm Wed.-Sat. mid-May-June and early Sept.-Oct., adults $3.90, seniors $3.40), dates to the 1830s. You can tour the soldiers' barracks, cookhouse, and other fort buildings; staff demonstrate musket drills, open-hearth cooking, and other elements of 19th-century military life.

Like other Southwestern Ontario communities, Amherstburg was a destination for formerly enslaved people who escaped to Canada via the Underground Railroad. The exhibits at the **North American Black Historical Museum** (277 King St., Amherstburg, 519/736-5433 or 800/713-6336, www.blackhistoricalmuseum.org, noon-5pm Tues.-Fri., 1pm-5pm Sat.-Sun., adults $7.50, seniors and kids $6.50) illustrate this history, along with other elements of the black experience in North America. Walk through a log cabin that belonged to a former slave family in the 1880s or explore one of the oldest surviving African Methodist Episcopal churches in Canada.

On the site of a former navy yard that dates to 1796, **King's Navy Yard Park** (242 Dalhousie St., Amherstburg, www.amherstburg.ca) contains lovely manicured gardens and a riverside walking path.

Wineries

The Mitchell family planted their first grapes

in 1991 and now grow nine varieties, including chardonnay, pinot noir, merlot, and cabernet sauvignon. You can drop in for tastings at their Tuscan-style **Sprucewood Shores Estate Winery** (7258 County Rd. 50 W., Harrow, 519/738-9253 or 866/938-9253, www.sprucewoodshores.com, 11am-5pm daily, tastings $2 pp) overlooking the lake, but call ahead to arrange a tour (Mon.-Fri., $6 pp).

Vidal, riesling, and baco noir are among the interesting wines at friendly **Erie Shore Vineyard** (410 County Rd. 50 W., Harrow, 519/738-9858, www.erieshore.ca, 1pm-6pm Mon.-Fri., 10am-6pm Sat., noon-5pm Sun.). Ask about their ice wine and the unusual "cabernet ice."

Bernard and Nancy Gorski have run CREW, **Colchester Ridge Estate Winery** (108 County Rd. 50 E., Harrow, 519/738-9800, www.colchesterridge.com, 11am-6pm daily late May-Sept., 11am-5pm Sun. and Wed.-Thurs., 11am-6pm Fri.-Sat. Oct.-late May), since 2006. They make an off-dry riesling and a big, flavorful cabernet, among others.

The **Viewpointe Estate Winery** (151 County Rd. 50 E., Harrow, 519/738-0690 or 866/372-8439, www.viewpointewinery.com, 11am-6pm daily) produces especially nice whites, including riesling and an unusual (but very good) auxerrois. The winery offers tours ($10 pp, reservations required) as well as cooking classes. A peaceful setting for a summer meal is the patio overlooking the vineyards at the on-site ★ **restaurant** (noon-5pm Thurs.-Mon., $14-17), which, in addition to salads, a charcuterie plate, and excellent pizzas, is known for its fried perch. The restaurant moves indoors when the weather turns. Once a month, it's open for Friday dinner, with live music; see the website for the schedule.

Family-owned **North 42 Degrees Estate Winery** (130 County Rd. 50 E., Colchester, 519/984-2684, www.north42degrees.com, 11am-6pm daily, call or check the website for off-season hours) bottled its first wines, including sauvignon blanc, riesling, gewürztraminer, pinot noir, and cabernet franc, in 2013.

Also on the property is **Serenity Lavender** (www.serenitylavender.com, 11am-5pm daily), where you can wander among the aromatic plants; the shop sells lavender products for bath, bed, and kitchen. Opened in 2017, **Bistro 42** (check the website or phone for hours, $9-33) is located above the tasting room, with walls of windows and four terraces overlooking the vineyards.

Ann Wilson left a law career in Detroit to launch **Oxley Estate Winery** (533 County Rd. 50, Harrow, 519/738-3264, www.oxleyestatewinery.com, 11am-5pm Sun.-Thurs., 11am-6pm Fri.-Sat.) with her husband, Murray, on a 38-acre property near the lake. They began making wines, including riesling, auxerrois, and chardonnay, in 2011. After your wine-tasting, have lunch in the lovely **Wine Garden** (check the website or phone for hours, Feb.-Dec., $12-19).

Opened in 1980, **Colio Estate Winery** (1 Colio Dr., just off Walker Rd., Harrow, 519/738-2241 or 800/265-1322, www.coliowinery.com, 10am-5pm Mon.-Sat., 11am-5pm Sun.) makes a number of different wines, from the easy-drinking Girls' Night Out line to more premium varieties like the Bricklayer cabernet merlot, in its large (for this region, anyway) winery. Tours (2pm daily May-Dec.) visit the production facilities, crushing room, barrel room, and shop.

The Muscedere family began planting grapes in 2003, and you can sample the fruits of their labor, particularly their full-bodied cabernet sauvignon and other reds, at **Muscedere Vineyards** (7457 County Rd. 18, Harrow, 519/738-1145, www.muscederevineyards.com, 11am-5pm daily, tastings $5). The tasting room is on the lower level of the family's brick home; at midday in warm weather, they serve **pizza** (Fri.-Sun. mid-May-June and Sept.-mid-Oct., daily July-Aug.) from a wood-fired oven on the garden patio.

WINE TOURS

One of the best ways to explore the Lake Erie North Shore wineries and the gently rolling surrounding countryside is by bicycle. On the guided **Windsor Eats Wine Trail Rides** (519/982-5212, www.winetrailride.ca, May-Sept., $95 pp, $130 tour plus bike rental), you cycle to several wineries, taste wines at each stop, and have a communal multicourse meal at a winery, park, or local farm. These well-run tours, usually offered once a month and averaging 20-25 kilometers (12-16 miles) of cycling, draw groups of 30-50 people, and they're sociable experiences, whether you come alone or with companions. Ticket sales end two days before each event, so book online in advance.

Events

Since the 1800s, **The Harrow Fair** (McAfee St., off County Rd. 20, Harrow, 519/738-3262, www.harrowfair.com, late Aug. or early Sept.) has been showcasing the region's produce and livestock and showing visitors an old-fashioned good time. Besides plenty of eating, activities include horse shows, sheep shearing, and musical entertainment.

Food

The **Amherstburg Farmers Market** (7860 County Rd. 20, Amherstburg, 519/730-1253, www.amherstburgfarmersmarket.com, 8:30am-1:30pm Sat. mid-May-mid-Oct.) takes place at the Malden Community and Cultural Center.

Along Dalhousie Street in town, you'll find several casual dining spots, including **Dalhousie Bistro** (219 Dalhousie St., Amherstburg, 519/736-0880, www.thedalhousiebistro.com, generally 10am-3pm Sun.-Thurs., 10am-9pm Fri.-Sat., $8-29) in a Victorian house opposite King's Navy Yard Park, serving salads, sandwiches, wine-friendly platters of cheeses and charcuterie, and other light meals. If you like waffles, try the delicious made-from-scratch version here.

Accommodations

Amherstburg and the rural wine country nearby have a handful of B&Bs. For more accommodation options, consider staying in Kingsville or Windsor, which are within a short drive of the Amherstburg area.

The upscale **La Roos Maison Bed & Breakfast** (309 Martin Lane, Harrow, 519/890-1657, www.laroosmaison.com, $129-199 d) has five guest rooms in a sprawling modern home directly on the lakeshore. The ceilings in the common living room soar two stories high, and three rooms have balconies facing the water, including the huge Lakefront

the tasting room at family-run Muscedere Vineyards

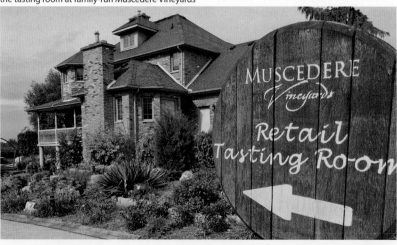

3, with vibrant rust-hued walls, black-and-white furnishings, and a gas fireplace. The two smallest rooms share a bath. Rates include Internet access and a full breakfast.

Robert and Debbie Honor have been running ★ **Honor's Country House Bed-and-Breakfast** (4441 Concession 4 S., Amherstburg, 519/736-7737, www.honorscountryhousebb.com, $100-125 d) in their 1920 farmhouse for more than 25 years. With deep roots here, they can tell you all about the community. The B&B's common areas, including a comfy living room and a dining room with guest fridge and microwave, are done in craftsman style. Upstairs, the two simply furnished guest rooms have private baths. After a hearty breakfast, you might want to just sit on the front porch and watch the world go by.

Information and Services

Amherstburg's **Tourism Office** (268 Dalhousie St., Amherstburg, 519/730-1309, www.amherstburg.ca) provides information about things to do in the vicinity. You can also get information from **Tourism Windsor, Essex, and Pelee Island** (333 Riverside Dr. W., Suite 103, Windsor, 519/255-6530 or 800/265-3633, www.visitwindsoressex.com), the regional tourism association. The **Essex Pelee Island Coast (EPIC) Wine Country** website (www.epicwineries.com) lists wineries in the region.

Getting There and Around

Downtown Amherstburg is 35 kilometers (22 miles) west of Kingsville and 25 kilometers (15 miles) south of Windsor; County Road 20 connects these three communities. Most of the wineries are on or near County Road 50, along the Lake Erie shore.

WINDSOR

If you're interested in history, in distilleries and breweries, or in sampling international foods, make a stop in Windsor, an ethnically diverse industrial city on the Canadian side of the Detroit River facing the Detroit skyline.

The region was one of Ontario's earliest settlements; it was the oldest French colony west of Montreal. In later years, Canada's distillery industry got its start here, and the region's history entwined with that of the United States, first over the issue of slavery and then during the Prohibition era.

More recently, the city has become a magnet for immigrants from around the world, with nearly one-quarter of its 215,000 people born outside Canada. Windsor's Little Italy district is along Erie Street, south of the city center, and Wyandotte Street, which runs east-west across downtown, offers a snapshot of Windsor's other ethnic communities, particularly its Lebanese and Asian populations.

Breweries and Distilleries

Hiram Walker, J. P. Wiser, and Henry Corby were among Canada's spirits industry pioneers, launching distilleries in the Windsor region in the 1850s. Many Hiram Walker employees and their families took up residence in "Walker's Town," the planned community that Walker built east of downtown Windsor, which is now the gentrifying Walkerville neighborhood of stately brick homes and hip cafés.

On January 17, 1920, the U.S. Congress ratified the 18th Amendment to the U.S. Constitution, which banned the manufacture, sale, and transport of alcoholic beverages, ushering in the era of Prohibition. Many Canadian provinces enforced a similar alcohol ban. In Ontario, the Liquor Control Act prohibited public drinking, but it didn't outlaw either the manufacture or export of liquor. Distilleries in the Windsor region capitalized on this loophole; more than 75 percent of the alcohol consumed in the United States during the 1920s and early 1930s traveled across the Detroit River.

North America's largest distillery by capacity, Hiram Walker & Sons still operates on the Walkerville riverfront, where you can learn about its flagship brands at the **J. P. Wiser's Experience Centre** (2072 Riverside Dr. E., 519/561-5684, www.jpwiserstour.ca, tours

1pm and 3pm Fri., $15 pp). Ninety-minute tours take you through the story and production process of Canadian whisky, and you'll sample four varieties. Don't forget your ID; you must be 19 or older to take the tour.

At **Walkerville Brewery** (525 Argyle Rd., 519/254-6067, www.walkervillebrewery.com, 11am-6pm Sun.-Wed., 11am-7pm Thurs. and Sat., 11am-9pm Fri.), the tasting bar and taproom occupy a high-ceilinged former whiskey warehouse. Among its microbrews are the easy-drinking Honest Lager and a flavorful India pale ale, along with seasonal beers. Take a 45-minute **guided tour** (12:30pm, 3:30pm, and 5pm Sat., $7 pp) for details about the brewery's history and beer-making process.

The region's growing community of craft brewers and distillers have joined together to create the **Barrels Bottles & Brews Trail** (www.barrelsbottlesbrews.ca), a self-guided tasting route. Check the website for more places to sip and sample.

On a **Windsor Eats Bikes & Beers Cycling Tour** (519/982-5212, www.windsoreats.com, May-Oct., $70 pp, $100 tour plus bike rental), you cycle to several breweries for tours and tastings, with samples of food along the way. Tours usually run once a month and average 20 kilometers (12 miles) of cycling. Check the website for schedules.

Another Windsor Eats excursion, the four-hour **Drinks of Walkerville Walking Tour** (www.windsoreats.com, 11am Sat. and Sun., $85 pp), offered year-round, takes you through this neighborhood's distilling and brewing history. You'll sample whiskeys at the J. P. Wiser Brand Centre, taste beer at Walkerville Brewery, and learn about the district and its boozy past.

Museums and Galleries

A cool contemporary building overlooking the river houses two museums. The **Art Gallery of Windsor** (401 Riverside Dr. W., 519/977-0013, www.agw.ca, 11am-5pm Wed.-Sun., adults $10, students and ages 6-17 $5) showcases Canadian art, particularly works by artists from Southwestern Ontario. At 2pm on Saturday and Sunday, the museum offers free gallery tours.

Chimczuk Museum (401 Riverside Dr. W., 519/253-1812, www.citywindsor.ca, 10am-5pm Tues.-Sat., 11am-5pm Sun., adults $5, seniors, students, and ages 3+ $4), with exhibits about area history, including the local First Nations and Métis communities, is located on the first floor of the art gallery building. The museum is named for Joseph Chimczuk (1897-1990), who immigrated to Windsor from what is now Ukraine; after a career at the Ford Motor Company, he willed his estate to the City of Windsor. You can buy a discounted ticket to visit both museums (adults $12, students and ages 6-17 $7).

More than 30 outdoor sculptures line the Windsor waterfront in the **Windsor Sculpture Park** (along the Detroit River, between Huron Church Rd. and Church St., www.citywindsor.ca, free). Free one-hour **Art Cart Tours** (11am-5pm Sat.-Sun. May-June and Sept.-mid-Oct., 4pm-7:30pm Wed.-Fri. and 11am-5pm Sat.-Sun. July-Aug.) cruise through the sculpture park in an electric golf cart. Contact the Chimczuk Museum for tour details (519/253-1812, www.citywindsor.ca).

Sandwich

Southwest of downtown, the Sandwich neighborhood is the oldest permanent European settlement in Ontario, inhabited by French pioneers in the 1700s; the City of Windsor publishes a Sandwich Walking Tour (www.citywindsor.ca) describing the community's historic structures. Sandwich was also important in the region's African Canadian history as a destination for formerly enslaved people who came to Canada along the Underground Railroad. The **Sandwich First Baptist Church National Historic Site** (3652 Peter St., 519/252-4917, www.sandwichbaptistchurch.ca) is Canada's oldest active black church, beginning as a log structure in the 1820s. The current church building, which is still used for services, opened in 1851; call ahead if you'd like a building tour. Historians have found evidence of tunnels leading into the church cellar that were likely used by fugitive slaves.

★ John Freeman Walls Historic Site and Underground Railroad Museum

Ring! Ring! When you arrive at the **John Freeman Walls Historic Site and Underground Railroad Museum** (859 Puce Rd., Lakeshore, 519/727-6555, www.undergroundrailroadmuseum.org, 10:30am-3pm Tues.-Sat. May-Sept.), ring the Freedom Bell to call the "conductor," who will guide you around this open-air museum, built and operated by descendants of John Freeman Walls and his wife, Jane King Walls, fugitive slaves who traveled here from North Carolina on the Underground Railroad. As you walk into the nearby woods, following the path of former slaves, you hear the hound dogs attempting to track you down (fortunately, it's just a recording). You also tour the Walls's 1846 log cabin, where they raised nine children, and which became a safe house for formerly enslaved people; watch a video about the family's history; and visit the family cemetery.

The museum is 35 kilometers (22 miles) east of Windsor. Take Highway 401 to exit 28, Highway 25/Puce Road, and go north to the site. Hours can be irregular, so call before visiting.

Food

Windsor has a large Lebanese population and several excellent Middle Eastern restaurants. Bring your family or friends to the brightly lit **El-Mayor** (936 Wyandotte St. E., 519/258-7645, www.elmayorrestaurant.com, 9am-1am Sun.-Thurs., 9am-3am Fri., 9am-4am Sat., $7-26), the better to share the overflowing platters of falafel, kebabs, *shawarma,* and salads. Another excellent Lebanese eatery is the more upscale **Mazaar Lebanese Cuisine** (372 Ouellette Ave., 519/967-9696, www.mazaar.ca, 11am-9pm Mon., 11am-10pm Tues.-Thurs., 11am-11pm Fri., noon-11pm Sat., noon-9pm Sun., $9-28), which has live music Friday and Saturday.

If you're craving a bowl of hot beef noodle soup, or other inexpensive Vietnamese classics, the friendly but bare-bones **Pho Nguyen Hoang** (510 Wyandotte St. W., 519/977-0852, 9am-9pm Thurs.-Tues., $4-12) can oblige.

Cozy **Taloola Café** (396 Devonshire Rd., 519/254-6652, www.taloolacafe.com, 8am-10pm Tues.-Fri., 9am-10pm Sat., 10am-4pm Sun., $6-17) has exposed brick walls and wood

where the Underground Railroad had its end: Southwestern Ontario

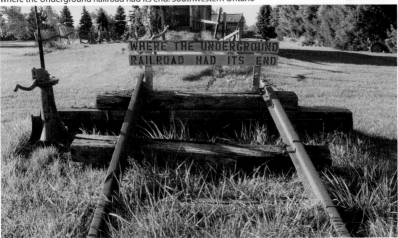

floors and a menu of vegetarian-friendly salads, sandwiches, and rice bowls as well as all-day breakfast, coffees, and teas. Try the Blue Green Salad of kale, blue cheese, cranberries, and walnuts. Local musicians often perform on Friday and Saturday nights.

Motor Burger and Craft Ale (888 Erie Street E., 519/252-8004, www.thisismotor. com, 11:30am-9pm Mon.-Thurs., 11:30am-10pm Fri., noon-10pm Sat., noon-8pm Sun., $13-22) is a nanobrewery and gastropub, brewing one-of-a-kind beers like Deja Blue (a Saskatoon berry hefeweizen), Sexy Saison, and Fast Eddy's, a German-style golden ale. Sit at one of the long bars and dig into their signature Deux Chevaux burger, mounded high with smoked bacon, gruyere, caramelized onions, and spinach. Also on the lengthy burger list are a shrimp burger with mango-avocado salsa; a veggie patty made from assorted seeds and beans; and a beef burger slathered with porchetta and peanut butter.

In Windsor's "Little Italy," locally popular choices include **Nico Ristorante** (851 Erie St. E., 519/255-7548, www.nicoristorante. com, 11:30am-2pm and 5pm-11pm Tues.-Fri., 5pm-11pm Sat., lunch $15-25, dinner $19-35) and **Il Gabbiano Ristorante** (875 Erie St. E., 519/256-9757, www.ilgabbiano.com,

4:30pm-9pm Sun. and Tues., 11:30am-2pm and 4:30pm-9pm Wed.-Thurs., 11:30am-2pm and 4:30pm-10pm Fri., 4:30pm-10pm Sat., $13-38).

Accommodations

Windsor has a cluster of high-rise chain hotels near the riverfront and a few B&Bs around town.

A Hidden Gem B&B (406 Moy Ave., 519/988-9260 or 844/878-7436, www. windsorhiddengembb.com, $115 d) is an excellent value, with two enormous suites in a brick Victorian home in residential Walkerville. The 2nd-floor Green Suite includes a sitting area with a comfy sofa, while the 3rd-floor Loft Suite, decorated in pastel blues, has a window seat and café table under the eaves, as well as a whirlpool tub. Hosts Sue and Troy, who serve a full hot breakfast, provide guests with a book of suggested things to do and places to eat, and they're happy to chat about the community and local activities.

Downtown, though not riverside, **Marriott TownePlace Suites** (250 Dougall Ave., 519/977-9707 or 888/236-2427, www.marriott. com, $158-229 d, parking $15) has 128 family-friendly studio and one-bedroom suites with kitchenettes and separate sleeping/sitting

Motor Burger and Craft Ale

spaces that were updated in 2017. Rates include breakfast and Wi-Fi.

The city's top lodging is the glitzy **Caesars Windsor Hotel and Casino** (377 Riverside Dr. E., 519/258-7878 or 800/991-7777, www.caesarswindsor.com, $159-299 d), with 758 rooms in two riverfront towers (to stay in the Forum Tower, you must be at least 19 years old; all ages are welcome in the Augustus Tower). Riverside rooms on the upper floors have views of the Detroit skyline. In addition to the gaming rooms, the hotel has a spa, an indoor pool, a fitness facility, and several restaurants.

Information and Services
The website of **Tourism Windsor, Essex, and Pelee Island** (333 Riverside Dr. W., Suite 103, 519/255-6530 or 800/265-3633, www.visitwindsoressex.com, 8:30am-4:30pm Mon.-Fri.) is an excellent resource for travel planning, with listings for hotels, attractions, and upcoming events in Windsor and surroundings.

Getting There
AIR
Windsor International Airport (YQG, 3200 County Rd. 42, 519/969-2430, www.yqg.ca) is 12 kilometers (7.5 miles) southeast of downtown. **Porter Airlines** (www.flyporter.com) flies to Toronto's City Airport, **Air Canada** (www.aircanada.com) goes to Toronto Pearson Airport, and **WestJet** (888/937-8538, www.westjet.com) flies nonstop to Calgary. **Transit Windsor**'s (www.citywindsor.ca) no. 8 Walkerville bus runs between the airport and Riverside Drive downtown every 30-60 minutes (less often on weekends). A taxi from the airport to most downtown points should be $20-25.

Across the U.S. border, about 40 kilometers (25 miles) from Windsor off I-94, **Detroit Metro Airport** (DTW, 734/247-7678, www.metroairport.com) has more options for flights to U.S. cities and overseas. **Robert Q Airbus** (519/673-6804 or 800/265-4948, www.robertq.com, 1.25 hours, one-way adults $51,

seniors and students $48, under age 12 $26) runs a shuttle between Detroit Airport and the Windsor Holiday Inn (1855 Huron Church Rd.). **Courtesy Transportation** (519/977-9700, www.courtesytransportation.com) and **Classic Shuttle** (519/796-4634, www.classicshuttle.ca) also provide transportation between DTW and downtown Windsor.

TRAIN
From the **VIA Rail Windsor Station** (298 Walker Rd., at Riverside Dr., 888/842-7245, www.viarail.ca), trains run to London (1.75 hours, one-way adults $38-104, ages 2-11 $20-52) and Toronto (4-4.5 hours, one-way adults $50-178, ages 2-11 $25-89).

U.S. rail carrier **Amtrak** (800/872-7245, www.amtrak.com) runs trains from Chicago to Detroit, where you can cross the border into Windsor. Unfortunately, the convenient Windsor Tunnel Bus doesn't stop at the Detroit train station (11 W. Baltimore Ave.). The simplest option is to take a cab from the Amtrak station to one of the tunnel bus stops downtown. Alternatively, catch the **QLINE** streetcar (313/528-3044, https://qlinedetroit.com, US$1.50) at the Baltimore Street station to Congress Street (20 minutes); from there, it's a short walk to the tunnel bus stop either at the corner of Griswold and Congress Streets or at the Detroit Tunnel Plaza.

BUS
Windsor's bus station is the **Windsor International Transit Terminal** (300 Chatham St. W., 519/254-7575, www.citywindsor.ca) downtown. **Greyhound** (800/661-8747, www.greyhound.ca) runs a nighttime bus between Toronto and Windsor (4.25-5.5 hours, adults one-way $29-73). The same bus stops in London (2.25 hours, adults one-way $22-53).

Between downtown Detroit and downtown Windsor, you can catch Transit Windsor's **Tunnel Bus** (www.citywindsor.ca, 519/944-4111, 5:30am-12:30pm Mon.-Sat., 8am-midnight Sun., one-way $5). In Windsor, the bus arrives at and departs from the Windsor International Transit Terminal; you can also get off at Caesars Windsor Hotel and Casino (377 Riverside Dr. E., 519/258-7878 or 800/991-7777, www.caesarswindsor.com). In Detroit, you can catch the bus at Cobo Center (1 Washington Blvd.), the Rosa Parks Transit Center (E. Park Pl. at State St.), or at the Detroit Tunnel Platform (Randolph St. at Renaissance Dr. N.), near the Mariner's Church opposite the Renaissance Center. Assuming no traffic or border delays, the trip takes only 20-25 minutes.

CAR

Windsor has two 24-hour international border crossings: the **Detroit-Windsor Tunnel** (www.dwtunnel.com) and the **Ambassador Bridge** (www.ambassadorbridge.com). Tolls in the tunnel vary slightly depending on which direction you're traveling: from Detroit to Windsor (US$5) or from Windsor to Detroit (US$4.50). Bridge tolls (US$5) are the same in either direction.

Check current border lineups online at **U.S. Customs and Border Protection** (http://bwt.cbp.gov) and the **Canadian**

Border Services Agency (www.cbsa-asfc. gc.ca). Always allow extra time if you're catching a plane, or if you have a time-critical appointment, on the opposite side. Remember that passports are required for travel between the United States and Canada.

To Windsor from Toronto, 365 kilometers (225 miles) to the northeast, it's a direct drive down Highway 401. Allow 4-4.5 hours. From London, it's 185 kilometers (115 miles).

Getting Around

Ouellette Avenue is the main north-south street in downtown Windsor and the dividing line between "east" and "west" addresses. Riverside Drive and Wyandotte Street cross the city from east to west. **Transit Windsor** (www.citywindsor.ca, one-way $3) runs buses throughout downtown.

You'll want a car for exploring Southwestern Ontario's wineries or African Canadian heritage sites. Car rental companies with Windsor offices include **Avis** (www.avis. com), **Budget** (www.budget.ca), **Discount** (www.discountcar.com), **Enterprise** (www. enterpriserentacar.ca), and **National** (www. nationalcar.ca).

Along Lake Huron

Lake Huron is famous for its sunsets. As the sun illuminates the darkening sky with streaks of gold, people come to the beach to watch, pausing as if to say good night to the day. And even though you know the sun will rise and set again tomorrow, there's something about watching it hover over the lake that makes you want to stop and watch it one more time.

During the day, the blue lake and its beaches are equally compelling, since Huron is lined with lovely stretches of sand. In the lakeside towns, you'll find lighthouses and small museums, galleries and theaters, and a growing number of breweries and wineries, but it's the beach—and the sunset—that will

draw you again and again to the second largest of the Great Lakes.

From Toronto, there's no direct highway to Lake Huron, so you'll need to slow down as you meander through rural towns along the way. But that's okay—the leisurely drive gives you time to tune into the laid-back vibe of the lakeshore. Once you reach Lake Huron, Highway 21, known as the Bluewater Highway, connects lakeside towns from Sarnia north to Southampton.

GRAND BEND

Grand Bend has a long, sandy beach on Lake Huron and the honky-tonk feel of a summer tourist town. There are ice cream stands and T-shirt shops, cheek-by-jowl rental cottages, and packs of young folks cruising the beach and the bars looking for a good time. Plenty of families return to the beach year after year. Visit outside of frenetic July and August, though, and Grand Bend quiets down into a pleasant spot for a weekend by the shore. Just outside of town is a provincial park with a spectacular dune-backed expanse of sand.

★ The Pinery Provincial Park

One of the most beautiful beaches along Lake Huron is just south of Grand Bend. At **The Pinery Provincial Park** (9526 Lakeshore Rd./Hwy. 21, 519/243-2220, www.ontarioparks.com or www.pinerypark.on.ca, year-round, $17 per vehicle), the 10-kilometer (six-mile) powdery sand beach, backed by the undulating dunes topped with waving grasses, feels like it goes on forever. While the beach is wildly popular in summer, the day-use area is divided into nine sections, so you can explore till you find a spot to lay your towel.

The **Visitors Centre** (519/243-8574, 10am-5pm daily July-Aug., 10am-5pm Sat.-Sun. Sept.-June), near the campgrounds on the park's west side, runs various nature programs in summer. Near the Visitors Centre you can rent bicycles ($10-15 per hour, $25-50 per day), or canoes and kayaks ($12-15 per hour, $25-45 per day) to paddle along the Old Ausable River Channel.

Ten short hiking trails, from one to three kilometers (0.6-2 miles), wend through the park. With the exceptions of the challenging **Nipissing Trail,** which climbs to a lookout atop the park's largest dune ridge, and the longer **Wilderness Trail,** most trails are easy enough to explore with kids. Pick up trail guides at the Visitors Centre. The 14-kilometer (8.7-mile) **Savannah Multiuse Trail** loops through the park, more or less paralleling the road, making it a more pleasant (and safer) option for pedestrians and cyclists.

In winter, you can cross-country ski or snowshoe along 40 kilometers (25 miles) of trails. You can rent skis and snowshoes (9:30am-3pm Sat.-Sun., adults $12 per hour, ages 6-17 $10 per hour) at the Visitors Centre.

The park entrance is eight kilometers (five miles) south of Grand Bend on Highway 21. Once you arrive, park your car and explore on foot or by bicycle. The park road is a 12-kilometer (7.5-mile) one-way loop, so to revisit a spot you just passed, it's a long way around again.

Entertainment and Events

Several plays run in repertory every summer at **Huron Country Playhouse** (70689 B Line, off Hwy. 81, 519/238-6000 or 855/372-9866, www.draytonentertainment.com, mid-May-early Sept.). If you thought that old-time drive-in movies were long gone, think again: Grand Bend's **Starlite Drive-in Theatre** (36,752 Crediton Rd., 519/238-8344, www.starlitedriveintheatre.com) still screens films nightly in July and August and on weekends in the spring and fall.

Food and Accommodations

Restaurants, shops, and motels line Ontario Street (Hwy. 21) and Main Street. The **Lambton Shores Farmers Market** (1 Main St., www.grandbendfarmersmarket.ca, 8am-1pm Wed. late May-early Oct.) sets up in the parking lot of the Colonial Hotel.

The aroma of fresh baked goods may lure you into **Grandpa Jimmy's Scottish Bakery** (36 Ontario St. N., 519/238-5055 or 877/225-5907, www.grandpajimmys.com, 9am-5pm Tues.-Sat., 10am-5pm Sun., call for off-season hours). Don't resist; the scones have just the right amount of sweetness (try a berry one in season). For a beach picnic, pick up traditional sausage rolls, meat pies, breads, or pastries. Like any good grandfather's house, this one has toys for the kids (and magazines for the grown-ups).

For pastries and coffee, or sandwiches and salads to go, pull off the highway into **Highway Girl Fine Food** (15 Ontario St. S., 613/539-1741, 7am-6pm Tues.-Fri., 8am-5pm Sat., 8am-4pm Sun.), which also carries teas, jewelry, and other locally made products.

Side Trip: Local Food and Wine

In the countryside and small towns around **Grand Bend,** visit wineries and cider-makers, herb farms and orchards, for a taste of the region's local flavors.

The first winery to set up shop in "Huron Shores," one of Ontario's newest winemaking areas, is homey **Alton Farms Estate Winery** (5547 Aberarder Line, Plympton-Wyoming, 519/899-2479, www.altonfarmsestatewinery.com, noon-6pm Sat.-Sun.). Owners Anne and Marc Alton began planting grapes on their small farm in 2006, experimenting with different varieties, and now produce small batches of 8-12 wines every year. Sample their Aberarder Red (a cabernet blend), chardonnay, and other wines in the tasting room on the lower level of their home. On summer weekends, they serve pizza and wine on their patio.

Dark Horse Estate Winery (70665 B Line, Grand Bend, 519/238-5000, www. darkhorseestatewinery.com, 10am-6pm Mon.-Thurs., 10am-9pm Fri.-Sat., 11am-5pm Sun. June-Aug., 10am-6pm Tues.-Thurs., 10am-9pm Fri.-Sat., 11am-5pm Sun. Sept., 11am-6pm Thurs.-Sat., 11am-5pm Sun. Oct.-May, tours 11am and 2pm Sun.-Fri. June-Oct., call or check the website for off-season hours, $15 pp) is located in a swanky, 2,900-square-meter (31,000-square-foot) stone and glass building outside Grand Bend. Sample individual tastes or flights that include Unapologetically Bold baco and One Horse Town chardonnay.

Much of Ontario is apple country, and plenty of different varieties grow at family-run **Twin Pines Orchards & Cider House** (8169 Kennedy Line, Thedford, www.twinpinesorchards. com, 9am-5pm Sat. and 1pm-5pm Sun. Jan.-Aug., 9am-5pm Mon.-Sat. and 11am-5pm Sun. Sept.-Oct., 9am-5pm Mon.-Sat. and 1pm-5pm Sun. Nov.-Dec.). Sample British-style hard ciders and shop for homemade preserves, honey, and other goodies.

Breathe deeply at **Forest Glen Herb Farm** (8333 Glendale Dr., Lambton Shores, 519/899-4372, www.forestglenherbfarm.com, 10am-5pm daily) as you wander the fields full of herbs and flowers. Owner and horticulturalist Cynthia Cook teaches a variety of classes, from cooking with herbs to making jam. If you want to stay a while longer, book one of the two rooms in the **Forest Glen Bed and Breakfast** ($125-140 d), a 19th-century Edwardian home on the farm.

In a former school building that gives this long-standing dining spot its name, family-oriented **Schoolhouse Restaurant** (19 81 Crescent St., 519/238-5515, www.grandbendschoolhouse.ca, Apr.-Dec., breakfast $4-14, lunch/dinner $10-30) serves hearty breakfasts; burgers, sandwiches, and big salads like roasted beets with greens, apple, walnuts, dried cranberries, and feta cheese; and meat loaf, chicken potpie, and more "Olde School Favorites." Teacher won't mind if you order dessert, particularly when chocolate brownie sundaes or classic carrot cake are on the bill of fare.

Old-fashioned family dining has kept the tables full since the 1950s at friendly **Aunt Gussie's Country Dining** (135 Ontario St. S., 519/238-6786, www.auntgussies.ca, 8am-8pm Tues.-Sat., 8am-3pm Sun, breakfast $5-12, lunch/dinner $10-25), south of the town center. Stop in for breakfast before heading to the beach; later, fuel up on classics like burgers, open-face turkey sandwiches with mashed potatoes and gravy, potpie, and smoked pork chops.

The **Bluewater Motel** (121 Ontario St. S./Hwy. 21, 519/238-2014, www.thebluewatermotel.com, Mar.-Jan., from $99 d) is a well-maintained, family-run, and family-friendly property with an outdoor pool. The 22 standard motel units cover the basics: decent beds, fridges, TVs, and included Wi-Fi. Out back are five cottages that sleep 2-6. It's a one-kilometer (0.6-mile) walk along Lake Road to the town's South Beach and about the same distance along Highway 21 to

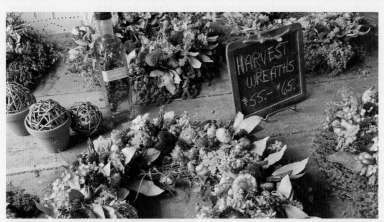

dried herbs and flowers at Forest Glen Herb Farm

Another nearby bed-and-breakfast option is **Through Windows Past B&B** (64 King St. W. Forest, 519/786-5070, www.throughwindowspast.ca, $100-125 d), which well-traveled hosts Joy and Glen Starkey run in their 1893 Victorian home, furnished with antiques and family heirlooms. The aptly named Turret Suite has a bathroom as large as some studio apartments. For more information about things to taste and other experiences in this Lake Huron region, contact **Tourism Sarnia-Lambton** (519/336-3232 or 800/265-0316, www.ontbluecoast.com) or **Ontario's Southwest** (519/290-8687, www.ontariossouthwest.com).

the town center. Farther south, **Whispering Pines Motel** (10456 Lakeshore Rd./Hwy. 21, 519/238-2383, www.whisperingpinesmotel. org, $114-169 d) has similar rooms and facilities.

CAMPING

The Pinery Provincial Park (9526 Lakeshore Rd./Hwy. 21, 519/243-2220, www. ontarioparks.com or www.pinerypark. on.ca, tent sites $42-45, electrical sites $47-52) has the second-largest campground in the Ontario Provincial Park system (only Algonquin is larger), with 1,000 campsites in three camping areas; 404 of the sites have electrical hookups. The Dunes and Burley Campgrounds (May-Sept.) have sites near the beach; the Riverside Campground

(year-round) is inland near the river. All areas have flush toilets and showers.

The **Riverside Campground** has 12 **yurts** ($98), with electricity, electric heat, and a gas grill outside. The yurts sleep up to six, in two sets of bunk beds (one double and one single bunk). This area also has a rustic camping **cabin** ($141) accommodating five and a four-person deluxe yurt ($141) that has a kitchenette with a microwave, mini fridge, and coffeemaker. Bring sleeping bags, cooking gear, and food.

Book in advance for this popular park, especially to camp in summer or on any holiday weekend. Contact the **Ontario Parks Reservation Service** (888/668-7275, www. ontarioparks.com, reservation fee online $11, by phone $13).

Practicalities

For visitor information, contact the **Grand Bend and Area Chamber of Commerce and Tourism** (1 81 Crescent St., 519/238-2001 or 888/338-2001, www.grandbendtourism.com, 10am-6pm Mon.-Sat., 10am-5pm Sun. June-Aug., noon-4pm Mon.-Fri. Sept.-May).

Grand Bend is 220 kilometers (137 miles) west of Toronto, about a 3.5-hour drive. Follow Highway 401 west to Kitchener, then take Highway 8 west to Stratford. From there, continue west to Mitchell, then follow Highway 23 south to Highway 83, which meets Highway 21 just north of Grand Bend. Alternatively, pick up Highway 7 south from Stratford, then take Highway 20 toward Fullarton, where you'll connect with Highway 83.

BAYFIELD AND VICINITY

If Grand Bend is a teenager in a bikini scarfing down hot wings or soft ice cream, Bayfield is her proper hat-wearing great aunt—more about heritage buildings, luxurious inns, and art galleries than catching rays in the sand. In the mid-1800s, Bayfield became a well-to-do port, shipping grain from area farms. Although the coming of the railroad, which didn't extend to Bayfield, ended the town's shipping industry, many stately lodgings and homes date to this prosperous era. What's new in Bayfield are the number of young entrepreneurs opening cafés, delis, and other businesses in this once staid town.

North of Bayfield, **Goderich** isn't primarily a tourist community, though its unusual octagonal downtown "square" and its pleasant boardwalk along Lake Huron are worth a stop. Inland, the town of **Blyth** has a well-regarded summer theater and an emerging craft beer and wine-producing scene.

Sights and Recreation
BAYFIELD

Bayfield's town square, **Clan Gregor Square,** is now a park surrounded by historic structures, while shops, galleries, lodgings, and restaurants line sedate Main Street,
just off the square. **Pioneer Park** overlooks Lake Huron, with steps that descend to the lovely town beach.

The **Bayfield Historical Society** (20 Main St., 519/441-3224, www.bayfieldhistorical.ca, 10pm-5pm Wed.-Sun. June-early Sept., by appointment early Sept.-May) runs a small museum and archives with photos, letters, and other documents about the town's history. The society leads historical walking tours (1pm and 3pm Sat. July-Aug., $5) around town.

For more active pursuits, visit **Outside Projects** (6 Main St., 519/565-4034, www.outsideprojects.net, 10am-5pm daily), an outdoor gear store that rents bikes (half day $22, full day $40), stand-up paddleboards ($40/hour, half day $60), and, in winter, snowshoes. It also organizes guided hikes, bike excursions, and snowshoe tours.

Cruise Lake Huron from Bayfield Harbor on the **Drift lobster boat** (519/525-0522, www.driftbayfield.com, 2pm or 7:30pm summer, weather permitting, $130 pp), a 36-foot former Nova Scotia lobster trawler built in 1973 that owner Peter Keightley (who runs Bayfield's Drift restaurant) restored and converted into a 12-passenger touring vessel. Cruises run with a minimum of four people; they can match you with other parties if your group is smaller.

GODERICH

Designed in the 1800s, **The Square** at the center of Goderich is actually an octagon where eight roads converge: North, South, East, West, Colborne, Hamilton, Kingston, and Montreal Streets. City offices are in the middle, while places to eat and shop line the surrounding streets.

A scenic 1.5-kilometer (.9-mile) boardwalk along Lake Huron connects Goderich's three free public beaches: **Main Beach** at the north end, **St. Christopher's Beach** in the middle, and **Rotary Cove Beach** to the south. The industrial buildings that you see from Main Beach belong to Compass Minerals' salt mine and processing plant. The mine, 550 meters

(1,800 feet) below Lake Huron, is the world's largest underground salt mine.

Goderich is the western terminus of the 127-kilometer (79-mile) **Goderich to Guelph Rail Trail** (www.g2grailtrail.com), a walking and cycling route along a former railway line. As this book went to press, the trail wasn't fully complete, but you can explore its Goderich end, starting from the Menesetung Bridge off North Harbour Road.

Wineries and Breweries

Among the beers that **Cowbell Brewing Company** (40035 Blyth Rd., Blyth, 519/523-4724, www.cowbellbrewing.com, 11am-8pm) turns out in its barn-like timber-frame building, completed in 2017, are the unfiltered Kölsch-style Absent Landlord, Doc Perdue's Bobcat (a West Coast red ale), and Lorna Bray Fly Girl, a nitro oatmeal stout. The tasting bar has 30 taps where you can try the house brews, as well as beer from other local producers. Wander the catwalk above the brewing room on your own or book a guided brewery tour ($15 pp) on which you can learn about the company's history, its products, and its environmental goals; it's working to become North America's first carbon-neutral brewery.

Drop in for a tasting at family-owned **Maelstrom Winery** (78925 Sanctuary Line, Seaforth, 519/233-9463, www.maelstromwinery.ca, 11am-6pm daily), which produces frontenac blanc, chardonnay, marechal foch, and other cold-climate wines from its eight-acre vineyard, set in the countryside east of Bayfield and south of Blyth. They make still, sparkling, and ice cider, too. To book a tour with one of the owners, reserve online in advance.

Entertainment and Events

The annual **Bayfield Writers' Festival** brings authors to town for a weekend of readings and other events. Get tickets from the **Village Bookshop** (24 Main St. N., Bayfield, 519/565-5600), which hosts readings and literary events throughout the year.

Food

For coffee, pastries, and a window into the local community, stop at **Shopbike Coffee Roasters** (11 Main St. N., Bayfield, 519/565-5625, www.shopbikecoffee.com, 8am-4:30pm Mon.-Fri., 8am-5pm Sat., 8am-4pm Sun.) or **Charles St. Market Café** (19 Main St. N., Unit B, Bayfield, 519/565-4783, www.charlesstreetmarket.com, 9am-2pm Mon.-Fri., 9am-5pm Sat.-Sun.).

the tasting bar at Cowbell Brewing Company

The relaxed **Black Dog Village Pub and Bistro** (5 Main St. N., Bayfield, 519/565-2326, www.blackdogpubbistro.ca, 11:30am-close daily summer, 11:30am-close Thurs.-Sun. fall-spring, lunch $11-20, dinner $13-33) serves salads, frittatas, and sandwiches midday, adding curries, steaks, and larger plates in the evening. There are 20 beers on tap and a large whiskey selection.

Owner Peter Keightley spent several years in Japan, which inspired him to open a funky Japanese-inspired restaurant, **Drift** (9 Main St. N., Bayfield, 519/525-0522, www.driftbayfield.com, 11am-9pm Sun. and Tues.-Thurs., 11am-10pm Fri.-Sat. summer; 5pm-9pm Thurs., 5pm-10pm Fri., noon-9pm Sat., noon-3pm Sun. fall-spring, small plates $4-12), back in his hometown. He serves izakaya-style small plates, from wakame salad to karage chicken to sushi, with fun cocktails and Ontario-made sake. On weekends, the restaurant morphs into a late-night **disco** (10pm-3am Fri.-Sun.). Keightley keeps a small **sailboat** (from $85 d) docked on Bayfield Harbor that he rents out as sleeping quarters to overnight guests; the boat sleeps two snugly and has a tiny galley kitchen. Restrooms with showers are in the marina, a short walk from the dock. Book through AirBnB (www.airbnb.ca) or phone the restaurant for information.

Cowbell Kitchen (40035 Blyth Rd., Blyth, 226/909-0066, www.cowbellbrewing.com, 11am-9pm Sun.-Thurs., 11am-11pm Fri.-Sat., $13-29), the big, bustling restaurant at Cowbell Brewing Company, pairs its beers with creative pub fare, from pizzas to burgers to inventive sandwiches, like smoked pork with coleslaw or an Ontario lamb burger with olive tapenade. The must-have dessert is beer pie, chocolate custard flavored with the brewery's Fly Girl stout, with a pretzel-graham cracker crust and a marshmallow meringue top.

Accommodations

The old-timey **Albion Hotel** (1 Main St., Bayfield, 519/565-2641, www.thealbionhotel.com, $115-155 d) has been taking guests since 1856. Of the four simply furnished, country-cottage guest rooms upstairs, the largest has a four-poster bed and a fireplace. Rates include continental breakfast. The pub is a popular local hangout; the dining room (11:30am-midnight Mon.-Sat., 11:30am-11pm Sun., $12-25) serves burgers, sandwiches, fish-and-chips, and steaks.

Ontario's longest continually operating

breakfast at The Little Inn of Bayfield

inn, **The Little Inn of Bayfield** (26 Main St. N., Bayfield, 519/565-2611 or 800/565-1832, www.littleinn.com, $205-325 d) was a stagecoach stop in the 1830s. Its 16 traditionally appointed guest rooms of varying sizes and configurations, including suites with a whirlpool tub or gas fireplace, occupy the 1st, 2nd, and 3rd floors. **The Willow Room** (8am-10:30am and 5pm-8:30pm daily, call or check the website for off-season hours, dinner $26-44), the inn's formal dining room with tall arched windows facing the street, serves breakfast, dinner, and Sunday brunch (9am-2pm). The locally sourced menu might feature pickerel with charred asparagus or cider-glazed Ontario lamb with Moroccan olives. You can also have a drink or a meal in the more relaxed **Four in Hand Taproom** (11:30am-8:30pm daily, lunch $16-24, dinner $17-36). Room rates include a full breakfast; dinner packages are available.

At **The Ashwood** (34777 Bayfield River Rd., Bayfield, 519/565-4444, www.theashwood.com, $129-195 d), new owners revamped a former roadside motel outside the town center into a hip lodging with a bourbon bar. The simple rooms, with wood floors and linens in neutrals and whites, have king or queen beds, flat-screen TVs, mini fridges, and free Wi-Fi. There's also a two-level family suite that sleeps six ($195-229).

Practicalities

Bayfield is 215 kilometers (134 miles) west of Toronto. Take Highway 401 west toward Kitchener, then continue west on Highway 8. At the town of Seaforth, pick up Highway 3 west, which meets Highway 21 (the Bluewater Hwy.) south of Bayfield. From London, 85 kilometers (53 miles) to the southwest, follow Highway 4 north to Brucefield, then take Highway 3 west to Highway 21.

Goderich is 21 kilometers (13 miles) north of Bayfield on Highway 21. The shortest route from Bayfield to Blyth (35 miles, or 22 miles) is to take Highway 21 north to Highway 13 east, then Highway 4 north.

Bayfield and Area Chamber of Commerce (www.villageofbayfield.com) provides information about the community. For Goderich information, see www.goderich.ca.

KINCARDINE, SOUTHAMPTON, AND VICINITY

Settled by Scottish settlers in the mid-1800s, Kincardine grew up from the lumber, fishing, and salt-producing industries. In 1968, a new technology changed this Lake Huron town's fortunes: Canada's first commercial nuclear power plant was built on the lakeshore north of town.

Summer life in nearby Southampton revolves around the pretty, sandy beach, just a short walk from downtown. But there's also a first-rate museum, which serves as the starting point for an island lighthouse tour.

Sights and Recreation

In addition to its sandy town beach, which runs for more than a kilometer (0.6 miles) along the lake, Kincardine's sights are linked to its marine past and its nuclear future.

An active lighthouse since 1859, the light station that now constitutes the **Point Clark Lighthouse National Historic Site** (529 Lighthouse Rd., Point Clark, 519/395-3735, www.huronkinloss.com, 10am-5pm daily late June-early Sept., adults $7.50, ages 12 and under $5) is one of six "imperial towers" that guided ships along Lake Huron and Georgian Bay. The 34-meter (110-foot) limestone tower, topped by a 12-sided lantern, is 18 kilometers (11 miles) south of Kincardine.

An octagonal lighthouse was constructed in 1881 on the harbor in the center of Kincardine. Still an operating light, it's now the **Kincardine Lighthouse and Museum** (236 Harbour St., Kincardine, 519/396-3150 or 800/268-3838, www.brucecoastlighthouses.com, 11am-5pm daily July-early Sept.).

The **Chantry Island Lighthouse** was built in 1859 on an island off the coast of Southampton. Because the island is now a Federal Migratory Bird Sanctuary, home to nesting colonies of great blue herons, double-crested cormorants, and great egrets, among others, access is restricted. To tour the lighthouse, reserve in advance with **Chantry Island Tours** (89 Saugeen St., 519/797-5862 or 866/797-5862, www.chantryisland.com, tours 1pm and 3pm Sat.-Sun. late May-June and early Sept., 1pm and 3pm Mon.-Fri., 9:30am, 1pm, and 3pm Sat.-Sun. July, 9:30am, 1pm, and 3pm daily Aug., $30 pp); the two-hour tour includes the boat ride to the island and a guided hike to the lighthouse.

One of the Lake Huron shore's most unusual attractions illustrates the role that nuclear power plays in the region. At the **Bruce Power Visitors Centre** (3394 Bruce Rd. 20, Tiverton, 519/361-7777 or 866/748-4787, www.brucepower.com, 9am-4pm daily July-Aug., 9am-4pm Mon.-Fri. Sept.-June, free), you can learn more about the nuclear industry and the workings of the local power plants, though the educational exhibits have a decidedly pro-nuclear bent. Outside are the spinning turbines of Ontario's first commercial wind farm (www.huronwind.com). The Bruce Power Visitors Centre is 20 kilometers (12.5 miles) north of Kincardine. Go north on Highway 21 to Highway 15/Main Street west toward Inverhuron; then take Highway 23 north to Concession 4 west.

Even if you've never wanted to surf, spend a few minutes with Tarah Coates, the surf-passionate owner of **SurfSup Eco Shop and Rentals** (889 Queen St., Kincardine, 519/955-0533, www.surfsupecoshop.com), and you'll find you can't wait to get out on Lake Huron, which—surprise!—is a popular surfing spot. Coates is an enthusiastic advocate for all things involving water and boards, including surfing, SUP-ing, and SUP surfing (surfing on a stand-up paddleboard). The shop rents boards (two hours $20, full day $35) and wetsuits ($5 with a board rental), offers lessons and classes including SUP yoga, and runs SUP tours; check its website or call for schedules.

You may not think about touring a museum on a sunny day in a beach town, but even if it's not raining, it's worth visiting the excellent **Bruce County Museum and Cultural Centre** (33 Victoria St. N., Southampton, 519/797-2080 or 866/318-8889, www.brucemuseum.ca, 10am-5pm Mon.-Sat., 1pm-5pm Sun. summer, 10am-5pm Tues.-Sat. fall-spring, adults $8, seniors and students $6, ages 4-12 $4). The modern, interactive exhibits focus on the region's heritage and culture, with displays about shipwrecks, marine history, and local life.

The Southampton area is home to the Saugeen First Nation, an Ojibwa people. The nation runs the open-air **Saugeen Amphitheatre and Gardens** (519/797-2781 or 800/680-0744, www.saugeenfirstnation.ca, free), which are open to the public. The amphitheater is 3.5 kilometers (two miles) north of Southampton on Highway 21.

Events

Kincardine celebrates its Scottish heritage during the annual **Kincardine Scottish Festival and Highland Games** (www.kincardinescottishfestival.ca, July), with kilt-wearing pipe bands, Highland dancing, and "heavy events," a traditional athletic competition that includes stone and hammer throws and the caber toss.

Food

In Kincardine, everyone seems to hang out at the peanuts-on-the-floor-casual **Hawg's Breath Saloon and Deli** (896 Queen St., Kincardine, 519/396-6565, 11am-10pm Mon.-Wed., 11am-11pm Thurs., 11am-midnight Fri.-Sat., $9-15), which serves beer, sandwiches, beer, burgers, and beer.

Inside this vegetable-colored storefront, painted in sunny yellows and healthy greens, **Pea Pod** (671 Goderich St., Port Elgin, 519/832-6500, www.thepeapod.ca, 9am-3pm Mon.-Sat., $9-15) serves vegan salads, sandwiches, tofu scrambles, and bowls. The Original is piled high with roasted sweet potatoes, chickpeas, shredded carrots, beets, walnuts, avocado, and hummus, while the

Rawsome dresses up cabbage, carrots, red peppers, avocado, sprouts, pineapple, and cashews with a peanut-miso sauce. To drink, choose from a long list of fresh juices and smoothies. Port Elgin is 28 kilometers (17 miles) north of Kincardine and 7.5 kilometers (4.5 miles) south of Southampton.

Outlaws may never have slept in the former Southampton Hotel, but today, this 1867 building houses **Outlaw Brew Co** (196 High St., Southampton, 519/797-1515, www. outlawbrewco.com, 11:30am-9pm Mon.-Sat., 11am-5pm Sun., $13-18), a microbrewery and tavern. Beers like The Sheriff IPA or Two Moon Junction, an unfiltered wheat beer, are complemented by chicken wings, pulled pork, and other pub grub. For an espresso or chai latte to go, stop by the coffee pickup window, around the corner from the main entrance.

Accommodations

Along Highway 21 in Kincardine are a couple of newer chain motels, including **Holiday Inn Express & Suites Kincardine** (2 Millennium Way, 877/660-8550, www.ihg. com).

Restaurants, shops, and a few places to stay cluster along High Street, Southampton's "downtown," on either side of Albert Street (Hwy. 21). At the comfortable **Chantry Breezes Bed & Breakfast** (107 High St., Southampton, 519/797-1818, www. chantrybreezes.com, rooms $159-189 d, cottages $189-239), one block from the beach, accommodations include three Victorian-style guest rooms and two small guest cottages out back. Guests gather in the large, window-lined parlor, the formal dining room, or out on the porch.

Opposite the Chantry Breezes, the more basic yellow brick Victorian **Southampton Inn & Spa** (118 High St., Southampton, 519/797-5915 or 888/214-3816, www. thesouthamptoninn.com, $145-165 d) is far from fancy, but the seven country-style rooms have mini fridges and private baths; three are suites with separate sitting areas. Room rates include Wi-Fi, parking, and a light breakfast.

Practicalities

If you're traveling along the Lake Huron coast, it's 45 kilometers (28 miles) on Highway 21 from Kincardine to Southampton. Southampton can also be a base for exploring the southern Bruce Peninsula; it's 20 kilometers (12 miles) south of Sauble Beach via Highway 13.

Both Kincardine and Southampton are about 225 kilometers (140 miles) northwest of Toronto. By car to Kincardine, you can either head toward Guelph, where you can take Highway 7 north and west to Highway 9, which goes into Kincardine, or pick up Highway 10 north to Orangeville, where you turn west. The most direct route from Toronto to Southampton is via Highway 10 to Owen Sound, where you can connect with Highway 21 south.

The **Kincardine Visitor Information Centre** (519/396-2731 or 866/546-2736, www.visitkincardine.ca) and **Southampton Tourism** (800/387-3456, www.visitsouthampton.ca) provide visitor information for the region.

Eastern Ontario

As you travel along the shores of Lake Ontario, the St. Lawrence River, the network of interconnected lakes in the Kawartha region, or the Rideau Canal, you're never far from a beach or a boat. If it's an island getaway you seek,

you have literally thousands to choose from. Eastern Ontario is home to the Thousand Islands. Another island destination, Prince Edward County, has a booming food and wine scene that draws gourmets and oenophiles from Toronto and beyond.

Kingston, the region's largest city, was the first capital of Upper Canada in 1841, and many historic structures from the 1800s remain. Whether at a 19th-century fort, the grand city hall, or any number of restored downtown buildings, history is very present in present-day Kingston. The city is a good base for day trips to the Thousand Islands, to Prince Edward County, or into the backcountry at provincial parks just north of town. Eastern Ontario offers more opportunities for adventure in the Peterborough area, whether it's going back in time at a pioneer village, exploring an aboriginal community or ancient aboriginal rock carvings, or simply vacationing in a lakeside cottage. Whether you're organizing a brief holiday or traveling across the province, the eastern districts serve up plenty of fun (and tasty) detours along the way.

PLANNING YOUR TIME

Many Eastern Ontario destinations are close enough to Toronto or Ottawa for a weekend getaway. They're also convenient stopping points between Toronto and Montreal. You can easily spend a weekend at a lakeside resort around **Peterborough,** exploring **Kingston'**s museums, or sampling the wineries, restaurants, and comfortable inns in **Prince Edward County.**

If you have a week, you could travel from Toronto along **Lake Ontario,** stopping off in the lakeside towns of Port Hope or Cobourg, spend a couple of days wine touring in Prince Edward County, explore Kingston for a day or two, and continue east through the **Thousand Islands.** In 10 days to two weeks, you could make a loop from either Toronto or Ottawa, adding stops at some of the provincial parks and the lakes in the Kawarthas.

Previous: jumping into adventure in the Kawarthas region; Boldt Castle in the Thousand Islands. **Above:** Prince Edward County's birds nest in style at quirky Birdhouse City.

Look for ★ to find recommended sights, activities, dining, and lodging.

Highlights

© AVALON TRAVEL

★ **Canadian Canoe Museum:** This well-designed museum in Peterborough traces Canadian historical and cultural developments through the country's waterways and watercraft (page 218).

★ **Petroglyphs Provincial Park:** One of the largest concentrations of petroglyphs in North America, Petroglyphs Provincial Park is a sacred First Nations site with more than 900 symbols carved into a massive marble slab (page 221).

★ **Prince Edward County Wineries:** If you enjoy good wine and local food, this booming wine region is a great place for a getaway and is an easy drive east of Toronto (page 231).

★ **Sandbanks Provincial Park:** Like the beach? This expansive and popular Prince Edward County park has some lovely ones and giant sand dunes, too (page 236).

★ **Fort Henry:** There's always something happening at these 19th-century fortifications overlooking the city of Kingston. You can tour the barracks, attend "Victorian school," and watch the Sunset Ceremonies, with military maneuvers, music, and fireworks (page 244).

★ **Kingston Penitentiary:** Tour the forbidding edifice that once housed many of Canada's most notorious criminals (page 247).

★ **Kingston Food Tours:** Pair local history with good eating (and drinking) on these deliciously entertaining urban walking tours (page 249).

★ **Thousand Islands Boat Tours:** The best way to see the Thousand Islands is by water. Choose from a variety of cruises around the islands, departing from Gananoque or from the nearby town of Rockport (page 258).

★ **Fulford Place:** George Taylor Fulford made his fortune selling "Pink Pills for Pale People," and he used the considerable proceeds to build this opulent 35-room mansion overlooking the St. Lawrence River in Brockville (page 263).

★ **Upper Canada Village:** Travel back to the 1860s at one of Ontario's largest and best-preserved historic villages. Chat with costumed interpreters as they go about their daily business as millers, bakers, or blacksmiths, and join in traditional activities, from milking the cows to riding in a horse-drawn barge (page 265).

Eastern Ontario

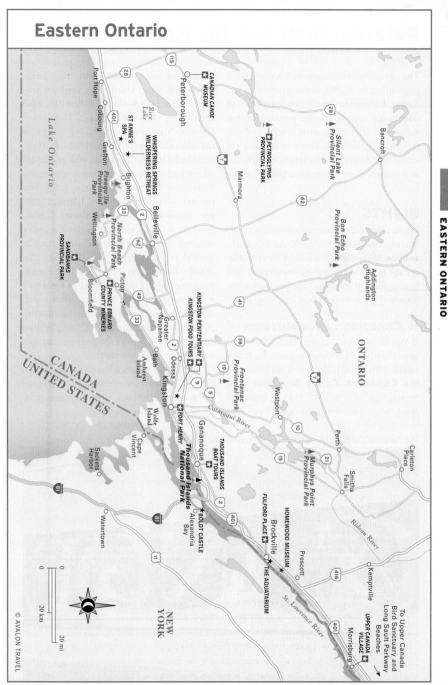

Lake Ontario

Port Hope
Cobourg
Grafton
Wellington
Brighton
Belleville
Bloomfield
Picton
Greater Napanee
Bath
Amherst Island
Odessa
Kingston
Wolfe Island
Gananoque
Cape Vincent
Sackets Harbor
Watertown
Alexandria Bay
Brockville
Prescott
Kemptville
Morrisburg

Peterborough
Marmora
Bancroft
Addington Highlands
Westport
Perth
Smiths Falls
Carleton Place

Rice Lake

CANADIAN CANOE MUSEUM
PETROGLYPHS PROVINCIAL PARK
ST ANNE'S SPA
WHISPERING SPRINGS WILDERNESS RETREAT
Presqu'ile Provincial Park
North Beach Provincial Park
SANDBANKS PROVINCIAL PARK
PRINCE EDWARD COUNTY WINERIES
KINGSTON FOOD TOURS
KINGSTON PENITENTIARY
Silent Lake Provincial Park
Bon Echo Provincial Park
Frontenac Provincial Park
FORT HENRY
Thousand Islands National Park
THOUSAND ISLANDS BOAT TOURS
BOLDT CASTLE
Murphys Point Provincial Park
HOMEWOOD MUSEUM
FULFORD PLACE
THE AQUARIUM
UPPER CANADA VILLAGE

CANADA
UNITED STATES

ONTARIO

NEW YORK

Cataraqui River
St. Lawrence River
Rideau River

To Upper Canada Bird Sanctuary and Long Sault Parkway Beaches

© AVALON TRAVEL

0
20 km
0
20 mi

115
28
401
33
2
62
49
33
28
62
41
38
19
9
5
2
10
15
21
47
401
2
401
416

81
81
11

Peterborough and the Kawarthas

The city of Peterborough, with a year-round population of 81,000, is the gateway to the Kawartha region. Two hours northeast of downtown Toronto (traffic permitting), the Kawarthas is a rural district of lakes and waterways, provincial parks, and lakeside resorts. Visit to explore the region's aboriginal and cultural heritage or for a holiday at the lake.

SIGHTS

While several Peterborough attractions, including the Canoe Museum, the Lift Lock, and the Art Gallery, are within the city, others are in the surrounding countryside and lake regions. In planning your itinerary, allow time to travel between these far-flung sites.

★ Canadian Canoe Museum

If you think that a canoe museum would appeal only to boating enthusiasts, think again. The well-designed exhibits at the **Canadian Canoe Museum** (910 Monaghan Rd., 705/748-9153 or 866/342-2663, www.canoemuseum.ca, 10am-5pm Mon.-Wed. and Fri.-Sat., 10am-8pm Thurs., noon-5pm Sun., adults $12, seniors, students, and ages 5-17 $9.50, families $30) aren't just about watercraft. They trace Canada's history and culture, exploring how the lakes and rivers that cross the country—and the boats that provided vital transportation links along those waterways—have influenced the nation's development. Yes, the exhibits illustrate how different peoples across Canada built and used canoes, from the West Coast First Nations' massive whaling canoes to the birchbark canoes of central and eastern Canada, but they also detail cultural developments, like how canoes became an integral part of Ontario's recreational culture. You can often watch artisans at work in the galleries, carving paddles, building canoes, or doing related crafts, or take a workshop where you can learn these skills yourself.

The Canoe Museum has announced plans to move to a new waterfront facility near the Peterborough Lift Lock. Check the website for updates on this new location.

The Canadian Canoe Museum traces the country's history through its boats.

Peterborough and the Kawarthas

Kinmount

Chandros Lake

504

To Silent Lake
Provincial Park

Apsley

504

**Kawartha
Highlands
Provincial
Park**

507

28

PETROGLYPHS
PROVINCIAL PARK

Kasshabog
Lake

46

49

36

Woodview

VIAMEDE
RESORT

56

Lower
Buckhorn
Lake

Upper
Stoney
Lake

Cameron
Lake

23

BEACHWOOD
RESORT

Stoney
Lake

22

44

Sturgeon
Lake

Pigeon
Lake

CURVE LAKE
FIRST NATION
CULTURAL CENTRE

6

36

Buckhorn
Lake

WHETUNG
OJIBWA
CENTRE

Warsaw Caves
Conservation Area

29

32

28

Kawartha
Lakes

7

STILLWATER
BY THE LAKE

SEE DETAIL

Peterborough

7

2

CANADIAN
CANOE MUSEUM

LANG PIONEER
VILLAGE MUSEUM

10

35

2

ISLAND SPIRITS

115

7

ZIM ART
RICE LAKE
GALLERY

Rice
Lake

2

Bailieboro

4TH LINE
THEATRE

DOO DOO'S
BAKERY

28

9

35

115

9

10

0   8 mi

0   8 km

Cobourg

401

Lake   Ontario

© AVALON TRAVEL

PETERBOROUGH
BUS STATION

PETERBOROUGH
LIFT LOCK

BLACKHONEY CAFE
LA HACIENDA

HUNTER ST

ARMOUR RD

BRIO GUSTO

CHARLOTTE

PETERBOROUGH INN
& SUITES HOTEL

SILVER BEAN CAFÉ

SHERBROOKE

PETERBOROUGH
& THE KAWARTHAS
TOURISM

TWO DISHES
COOKSHOP

Little Lake

Del Crary
Park

LIFTLOCK CRUISES

PARK ST

GEORGE ST

ART GALLERY
OF PETERBOROUGH

LANSDOWNE   ST

PETERBOROUGH
FARMERS' MARKET

CANADIAN
CANOE MUSEUM

Underwater Dining at Lock 21

Imagine paddling a voyageur canoe into the world's highest hydraulic lift lock, then enjoying drinks and dinner beneath the lock system. Welcome to **Underwater Dining at Lock 21** (705/742-2201 or 800/461-6424, www.thekawarthas.ca, $295 pp).

Departing from the Peterborough Lift Lock Visitor Centre (353 Hunter St. E.), you'll start with a guided paddle in an 11-meter (36-foot) voyageur canoe that you and 15 other guests navigate along the waterway and into the lift lock. Your boat will rise as the lock chamber begins to fill, and you'll be lifted nearly 20 meters (65 feet). After paddling out of the lock, you'll go into lockmaster's booth to learn more about the lift lock's operation. You'll paddle back into the lock for your descent, followed by cocktails and appetizers, with live music.

Descending through a series of narrow stairways and tunnels, the lockmaster will guide you into the lock's lower chamber for dinner—with 1,700 tons of water in the boat chamber above you. The evening wraps up with dessert and ghost stories; the lock is reportedly the site of several paranormal experiences.

Underwater Dining is offered several times between June and September. The events sell out almost as soon as they're announced. Sign up for the email newsletter from **Peterborough & the Kawarthas Tourism** (www.thekawarthas.ca) to be notified of upcoming dates.

Peterborough Lift Lock

Aboriginal people have traversed Ontario's network of interconnected lakes and waterways since at least 9000 BC. When European fur traders arrived in the 17th century, they also used these water routes to explore and trade. In the 1800s, settlers lobbied for an inland canal to make water travel easier and to gain access to markets across what is now Ontario.

The first lock on what became the **Trent-Severn Waterway** (www.pc.gc.ca/trent) was built in 1833 at the town of Bobcaygeon; by the 1880s, additional locks made it possible to travel smoothly through several of the Kawartha Lakes. Today, the Trent-Severn Waterway, with more than 40 locks, connects Lake Ontario with Georgian Bay, running 386 kilometers (241 miles) across central Ontario. Recreational boaters are the waterway's primary users.

The waterway's must-see is Peterborough's **Lock 21,** which opened in 1904 and is the highest hydraulic lift lock in the world; rising 19.8 meters (65 feet), it's essentially an elevator for boats. To experience going up and down in the lock, (there are great views from the top), take an informative two-hour sightseeing cruise with **Liftlock Cruises** (Little Lake Peterborough Marina, George St., 705/742-9912 or 888/535-4670, www.liftlockcruises.com, daily mid-May-mid-Oct., call or check the website for seasonal schedules, adults $28.75, seniors $26.50, ages 5-12 $15.50, ages 4 and under $3.50).

On land, you can learn about the waterway system at the **Peterborough Lift Lock Visitor Centre** (353 Hunter St. E., 705/750-4950, www.pc.gc.ca, 9am-6pm daily July-Aug., 10am-4pm daily mid-May-June and Sept.-mid-Oct.), which Parks Canada runs near Lock 21.

Art Gallery of Peterborough

There's usually something new to see at Peterborough's lakeside art museum, the **Art Gallery of Peterborough** (250 Crescent St., 705/743-9179, www.agp.on.ca, 9am-5pm Mon.-Fri., 9am-8pm Wed., 11am-5pm Sat.-Sun. July-Aug., 11am-5pm Tues.-Sun. Sept.-June, free). The gallery hosts four or five exhibitions every year, emphasizing Canadian contemporary art, and the shop stocks ceramics, jewelry, textiles, and other work by regional artists. The gallery also organizes the weekend-long **Kawartha Autumn Studio**

Tour every September, when local artists open their studios to visitors.

Lang Pioneer Village Museum

Many settlers came to the Peterborough area in the 1800s from England, Scotland, and Ireland. To learn about the lives of these pioneers, visit **Lang Pioneer Village Museum** (104 Lang Rd., off Hwy. 34, Keene, 705/295-6694 or 866/289-5264, www. langpioneervillage.ca, 10am-3pm Mon.-Fri. late May-mid-June, 10am-4pm daily late June-early Sept., adults $10, seniors and students $8, ages 5-14 $5, families $30), where more than 25 buildings date from the 1820s to the 1880s.

Newly arrived settlers would typically build a simple log cabin, like the 1820s Fife Cabin. As they became more established, they would construct larger homes, like the 1840s Fitzpatrick House or the comparatively more comfortable 1870s Milburn House. In addition to these restored homes, there's a general store, church, and schoolhouse, as well as the reconstructed shops of the village carpenter, tinsmith, printer, and blacksmith. The weaving shop houses two authentic Jacquard looms, rarely seen in North America. Costumed guides help bring the village to life.

Developed in partnership with the local Curve Lake and Hiawatha First Nations, the village's Aabnaabin Camp illustrates and interprets traditions of the region's indigenous people. See demonstrations of paddle- or snowshoe-making, learn about medicinal plants, or listen to traditional stories.

In autumn (early Sept.-Dec.) the village is open weekdays for guided fall color tours, available by reservation only. The village is 18 kilometers (11 miles) southeast of Peterborough. Take Highway 7 east for 10 kilometers (six miles), then turn south on County Road 34 (Heritage Line). From there, it's six kilometers (3.7 miles) to Lang Road and the village entrance.

★ Petroglyphs Provincial Park

Containing one of the largest concentrations of petroglyphs—rock carvings made by indigenous people—in North America, **Petroglyphs Provincial Park** (2249 Northey's Bay Rd., Woodview, 705/877-2552, www.ontarioparks.com, 10am-5pm daily mid-May-Oct., $14.50 per vehicle) is an active sacred site for First Nations people.

No one knows for sure when the Algonquian people carved the more than 900

The Art Gallery of Peterborough shows Canadian contemporary art.

symbols onto the massive crystalline marble slab here, now protected in a large glass building constructed around the rock. Experts date the carvings, which include human figures as well as snakes, turtles, and other animals, at somewhere between 600 and 1,100 years old. Park interpreters can help identify the carvings and share ideas about their traditional meanings. All park visitors must register at the **Learning Place Visitor Centre,** where you can watch a 20-minute film about the site and view exhibits about the region's aboriginal traditions, before heading for the petroglyphs.

Although the park is regularly open until 5pm, arrive by 3:30pm so you have time to drive to the site, visit the Learning Place, and see the glyphs. The province's park service manages the site in partnership with the local Curve Lake First Nation. Due to the site's spiritual importance, no photos are allowed.

The park is 55 kilometers (34 miles) northeast of Peterborough. Take Water Street/Highway 29 north, continue north on Highway 28, and turn right (east) onto Northey's Bay Road, which leads to the park entrance. There are no camping facilities or accommodations within the park.

Curve Lake First Nations Reserve

If a visit to the petroglyphs piques your curiosity about First Nations heritage and culture, your next stop should be the **Curve Lake First Nations Reserve** (www.curvelakefirstnation.ca). More than 750 Ojibwa people live on this reserve, with 1,400 more in the surrounding communities.

At the **Curve Lake First Nation Cultural Centre** (1024 Mississauga St., 705/657-2758, www.curvelakeculturalcentre.ca, 8:30am-4:30pm Mon.-Thurs., 8:30am-4pm Fri., adults $3, seniors and ages 5 and over $2), curator Anne Taylor, the cultural archivist who manages the facility, or one of her staff uses the displays of drums, baskets, and beadwork to introduce visitors to the culture and history of the Curve Lake people. The staff discuss traditional teachings, explain how particular items are used, and answer your questions. The Cultural Centre is on the main floor of the nation's government offices; look for the "Curve Lake Business Centre" sign.

The **Whetung Ojibwa Centre** (875 Mississauga St., 705/657-3661, www.whetung. com, 9am-5pm daily, free) is part souvenir

wild rice from the Curve Lake First Nation

shop, part art gallery, and part museum. It stocks everything from inexpensive doodads to high-quality works by regional aboriginal artists. Poke around the museum room on the lower level, which is crammed with buffalo bones, arrowheads and other artifacts, photographs, and traditional craftwork.

Another way to experience First Nations culture is to attend the annual **Curve Lake Pow Wow** (www.curvelakefirstnation.ca, 3rd weekend of Sept.), a festival of traditional music and dance that's open to the public.

Curve Lake Reserve is 35 kilometers (22 miles) northwest of Peterborough on a peninsula surrounded by lakes; the only direct road access is from the north. From Peterborough, take Water Street/Highway 29 north, then continue north on Buckhorn Road/Highway 23. At Curve Lake Road/Highway 22, turn left (west); the road (called Mississauga St.) will turn south onto the reserve.

Warsaw Caves Conservation Area

Do you or your kids enjoy underground exploring? At **Warsaw Caves** (289 Caves Rd., Warsaw, 705/652-3161 or 877/816-7604, www.warsawcaves.com, caves daily mid-Apr.-Nov., park and campground daily mid-May-mid-Oct., $15 per vehicle), you can climb, slither, and crawl through a series of seven narrow caverns formed in the limestone bedrock, ranging in size from 40 meters (130 feet) to 91 meters (300 feet) long. While you don't need technical climbing skills, you do need to clamber over rocks and scoot through dark narrow passageways; it's like an underground jungle gym.

There's no light in the caves, so you'll need a flashlight—a headlamp is best to keep your hands free (you can purchase one at the gatehouse). Wear sturdy shoes and clothes that can get dirty or wet, and don't enter the caves alone. Download the park's *Spelunkers' Guide* from the website, or pick up a copy at the gatehouse; it gives tips for tackling each cave.

While you might want to skip the caves themselves if you're claustrophobic, the forested conservation area also has several short hiking trails, including one that leads to the **Disappearing River,** a quirk of nature in which the Indian River disappears into the limestone, reemerging farther downstream. Beyond this underground section, the Indian River is typically a placid place to paddle. Canoe rentals ($12 per hour, 2-hour minimum, $48 per day) are available. The caves are 25 kilometers (15 miles) northeast of Peterborough via County Road 4.

Kawartha Highlands Provincial Park

Ontario's largest park south of Algonquin, the wilderness expanse of **Kawartha Highlands** (613/332-3940, www.ontarioparks.com) encompasses 37,587 hectares (92,879 acres). With a series of interconnected lakes and waterways, this is an excellent spot for canoeing. Park staff have mapped out recommended canoe routes, with stopovers at some of the park's 121 backcountry campsites.

The park doesn't rent canoes. For canoes and other gear, contact **Adventure Outfitters** (1828 8th Line, Lakefield, 705/652-7986, www.adventureoutfitters.ca, $40 per day, $70 per weekend) or **Wild Rock Outfitters** (169 Charlotte St., Peterborough, 705/745-9133, www.wildrock.net, $45 per day, $35 per additional day).

You can reach the park's east side via Highway 28 and west side from Highway 507. From Peterborough, the park's closest entrance is about 50 kilometers (30 miles) to the north.

Silent Lake Provincial Park

For an outdoor stopover en route to Algonquin Provincial Park's East Gate, visit **Silent Lake Provincial Park** (Hwy. 28, Cardiff, 613/339-2807, www.ontarioparks.com, mid-May-mid-Oct. and early Dec.-mid-March, $17 per vehicle). The park has hiking trails, beaches, three mountain bike routes, canoeing, and two campgrounds, including 10 yurts.

The day-use area has a sandy beach and a large, grassy picnic area. From here, you

From Zimbabwe to Ontario

One of the Peterborough area's most unexpected attractions is out in the farmland south of the city. At the **Zim Art Rice Lake Gallery** (855 2nd Line, Bailieboro, 705/939-6144, www.zimart. ca, 11am-6pm daily June-mid-Oct., by appointment mid-Oct.-May), Fran Fearnley showcases high-quality stone carvings by artists from Zimbabwe.

After doing volunteer work in South Africa, Fearnley was introduced to the stonework, known as Shona sculpture, from nearby Zimbabwe. She now returns to Africa every winter to scout out new artworks to exhibit and sell back in Ontario. She has established an artist-in-residence program that brings a stone sculptor to her property every summer to promote their work and teach sculpting workshops to both adults and children.

For two weeks every September, Fearnley sets up a sprawling outdoor exhibition, showing more than 200 sculptures outdoors among her trees and gardens. Outside of this September period, you can view a smaller selection of sculptures around the grounds. Admission is free, but donations, which support community programs in Zimbabwe, are welcome.

The gallery is 23 kilometers (14 miles) south of downtown Peterborough, outside the town of Bailieboro. From Highway 115, take Bensfort Road south to County Road 2. Turn right and follow County Road 2 for about eight kilometers (five miles), then turn right onto 2nd Line.

can reach the easy, 1.5-kilometer (0.9-mile) **Lakehead Loop** hiking trail, which is good for kids. Serious hikers may want to circle the lake on the 15-kilometer (nine-mile) **Lakeshore Hiking Trail** (4-6 hours, strenuous). You can rent canoes and kayaks at **Pincer Bay** canoe launch (8:30am-5pm daily July-Aug.) and at the park gatehouse in spring and fall.

Silent Lake is 75 kilometers (47 miles) northeast of Peterborough, off Highway 28. For groceries and other services, head south of the park to the town of Apsley or north to Bancroft.

ENTERTAINMENT AND EVENTS

Since 1991, the excellent **4th Line Theatre** (Winslow Farm, 779 Zion Line, Millbrook; box office 4 Tupper St., Millbrook, 705/932-4445 or 800/814-0055, www.4thlinetheatre. on.ca, July-Aug.) has performed original plays with Canadian historical themes on a farm 30 kilometers (19 miles) southwest of Peterborough. The outdoor shows start at 6pm; bring a picnic to enjoy before the performance, or order one ($14) from the box office a week in advance.

The **Peterborough Musicfest** (Del

Crary Park, www.ptbomusicfest.ca, late June-Aug.) presents free outdoor concerts at 8pm Wednesday and Saturday in summer.

FOOD

In downtown Peterborough, restaurants cluster around George Street, while funky Hunter Street, between George and Aylmer Streets, has lots of cafés and pubs. The dining rooms at most lake resorts are open to the public.

Peterborough Farmers Market (Lansdowne St. W. at George St. S., 705/742-3276, www.peterboroughfarmersmarket.com, 7am-1pm Sat.) operates outdoors in Morrow Park on the south end of downtown from May through October. It moves into the park's Morrow Building November through April.

If you like your coffee, pastries, salads, and sandwiches with a water view, park yourself on the shady riverside terrace at the **Silver Bean Café** (130 King St., 705/749-0535, www.silverbeancafe.com, 8am-8pm Mon.-Fri., 9am-8pm Sat.-Sun. May, 8am-9pm Mon.-Fri., 9am-9pm Sat.-Sun. June-Aug., 8am-6pm Mon.-Fri., 9am-6pm Sat.-Sun. Sept.-mid-Oct., $3-12) in Millennium Park. At cheery little **Blackhoney Café** (221 Hunter St. W., 705/750-0014, www.blackhoneycafe. ca, 8am-10pm Mon.-Thurs., 8am-11pm Fri.,

10am-11pm Sat., 10am-6pm Sun., $5-14), you can have eggs or a croque monsieur, but don't leave without sampling the sweets.

You know the portions will be substantial when the servers' T-shirts say, "Of course, you can take the rest home." Come hungry to the white brick house, painted with a rooster, where homey **Two Dishes Cookshop** (261 Charlotte St., 705/775-2650, 8:30am-3pm Tues.-Sat., 10am-3pm Sun., $8-20) dishes out plentiful breakfasts and lunches. Try the Korean-style gochujang pork bowl with kimchi, charred vegetables, and an egg piled over rice. Other popular dishes are the poached eggs and pulled pork served on corn cakes and the curried chicken salad with crispy chickpeas.

Craving enchiladas, *pollo con mole* (chicken with a chocolaty mole sauce), or traditional Mexican tacos? Say *hola* to **La Hacienda Mexican Restaurant** (190 Hunter St. W., 705/742-1559, www.lahaciendaptb.com, 11am-9pm Mon.-Wed., 11am-10pm Thurs.-Sat., 4pm-8pm Sun., lunch $5-15, dinner $10-29). Ask for their selection of salsas to spice up your dish.

With a menu that travels from a roast chicken club sandwich to pesto-broccoli pizza to shepherd's pie, **Brio Gusto** (182 Charlotte St., 705/745-6100, www.briogusto. com, 11:30am-9pm Sun.-Tues., 11:30am-10pm Wed.-Thurs., 11:30am-11pm Fri.-Sat., $15-29) is a little hard to classify. Yet this unfussy contemporary bistro, with garage-door windows that open to the street, always has something interesting to sample. Try the "Duck 'n Greens" salad topped with roasted beets, goat cheese, and shredded duck confit.

ACCOMMODATIONS

Peterborough has standard chain hotels on Lansdowne Street, both east and west of the city center. Outside of town, inns and cottage resorts sit on the shores of the many lakes.

Hotels and B&Bs

A cross between an upscale bed-and-breakfast and a lake resort, **Stillwater By the Lake** (641 Fireroute #1, 705/741-3886, www. stillwateronthelake.com, $199-249 d) overlooks Chemong Lake, about a 15-minute drive west of the city center. Welcoming owners Sunny and Peter Montgomery have a spacious one-bedroom suite on the lower level of their lakeview home, where you can sit by the fire on one of the deep couches or soak in the hot tub outside under the deck. In the morning, they'll deliver a multicourse breakfast. During

brunch at Two Dishes Cookshop

The Butter Tart Tour

butter tarts and more at Betty's Pies & Tarts

If Ontario had an official pastry, it would be the butter tart. Filled with a gooey mix of sugar, butter, and eggs, this miniature tartlet resembles American pecan pie without the nuts, although pecans or raisins are sometimes added to the dark, sugary custard. While the tarts come in other flavors, too, from coconut to peanut butter, purists stick with the "plain" versions, and some even debate whether nuts or raisins are proper additions. Whether the centers should be runny, firm, or somewhere in between is another point of fierce contention. Whatever their filling, the tarts are made in single-serving size, perfect for an afternoon snack.

The region around Peterborough is particularly rich in butter tart options, so much so that more than 50 bakeries, restaurants, and other tart makers have joined together to create the **Kawarthas Northumberland Butter Tart Tour** (http://buttertarttour.ca), a sweet self-guided sampling route over the hills and around the lakes.

You'll find some of the best butter tarts at **Doo Doo's Bakery** (187 County Rd. 28, Bailieboro, 705/939-1394, www.doodoos.ca) near Rice Lake south of Peterborough, at **Betty's Pies & Tarts** (7380 County Rd. 2, between Port Hope and Cobourg), and at **Blackhoney Café** (221 Hunter St. W., Peterborough, 705/750-0014, www.blackhoneycafe.ca), right in Peterborough.

But don't take our word for it. Take your own butter tart tour and find your favorite. Just make sure you have plenty of napkins handy.

the summer, they rent out two standalone cottages even closer to the lakeshore.

The **Peterborough Inn and Suites Hotel** (312 George St. N., 705/876-6665 or 866/446-4451, www.peterboroughinn.com, $155-205) has a central location downtown. The 32 rooms are fairly generic, but all have fridges and microwaves, and you get free Wi-Fi, parking, and continental breakfast.

Lake Resorts

Viamede Resort (595 Mt. Julian Viamede Rd., Woodview, 705/654-3344 or 800/461-1946, www.viamede.com, $249-319 d, cottages $349-549) is a traditional lake resort with modern amenities. There's tennis, kayaks, canoes, stand-up paddleboards, nine kilometers (5.5 miles) of hiking trails, a small beach, and even a working farm. In the fitness center, with a gym, yoga studio, sauna, and steam room, you can swim from the indoor pool to an outdoor one. The resort's three restaurants are a casual pub, the traditional dining room, and **Mount Julian,** which serves elegant meals by reservation only in an 1875 waterfront house. The best inn rooms and cottages overlook the lake. Rates include breakfast and most activities. Viamede is on Stoney Lake's north shore, 40 kilometers (25 miles) northeast of Peterborough, off Highway 28 near Petroglyphs Provincial Park.

At old-style, family-friendly **Beachwood Resort** (3043 Beachwood Dr., Lakefield, 705/657-3481 or 888/313-1118, www.beachwoodresort.com, $196-404 d, cottages and condos $327-550) on Lower Buckhorn Lake, 32 kilometers (20 miles) north of Peterborough, you can choose from 12 compact rooms with knotty pine walls in the main lodge or opt for cottages or apartment-style units around the wooded property. Seven of the 2- to 4-bedroom cottages, all with full kitchens, sit right on the lake; in July and August, cottages rent by the week only. Six units with kitchen facilities in the lakeside "Evergreen Condo" range from one to three bedrooms. Swim in the lake or the heated pool or rent a boat and go for a paddle. **Frederick's Dining** (mid-May-mid-Dec., lunch $11-15, dinner $18-30) serves lake fish, burgers, and other traditional fare.

A stay at ★ **Island Spirits** (Grasshopper Island, Rice Lake, 905/373-8448, www.islandspiritsricelake.ca, May-mid-Oct.), on a 25-acre private island in Rice Lake, is a one-of-a-kind experience. Gregarious owner "Captain" TJ Chernuck has built a rustic family-friendly eco-lodging that gets you back to nature with a huge dose of fun. She keeps free-roaming alpacas, chickens, and other animals, which she's happy to introduce to kids and other visitors. Guests can hike around the island, swim from a floating dock, play checkers on the giant outdoor board, or borrow canoes, kayaks, and stand-up paddleboards to get out on the water. Several secluded cabins, stocked with books, games, cooking equipment, and propane barbecues (there are no indoor kitchens), sleep four to seven ($249-335). All have outdoor privies and solar-heated showers hidden in the trees. A couple of additional cottages accommodate larger groups, and Chernuck can host a small number of campers (per weekend adults $125, kids $75). Staff meet you at the ferry dock (86 Rolling Banks Rd., Roseneath), where you leave your car, and will transport you across to the island. The ferry dock is 55 kilometers (34 miles) southeast of Peterborough and 30 kilometers (19 miles) north of Grafton.

Camping

Warsaw Caves Conservation Area (289 Caves Rd., Warsaw, 705/652-3161 or 877/816-7604, www.warsawcaves.com, daily mid-May-mid-Oct., $15 per vehicle, camping $45) has a wooded 52-site campground. The individual sites don't have water or electrical hookups, but there are central flush toilets and showers, and drinking water is available throughout the campground.

Kawartha Highlands Provincial Park (613/332-3940, www.ontarioparks.com, reservation fee online $11, by phone $13) has 108 backcountry campsites. You can reach the campsites only by canoe—there are no walk-in sites or car camping—and a permit is required.

Silent Lake Provincial Park (Hwy. 28, Cardiff, 613/339-2807, www.ontarioparks.com, day use $16.25 per vehicle, tent sites $36-42, electrical sites $42-47) has two campgrounds with a total of 157 campsites and 10 yurts ($98). Most of the campsites are set amid the evergreens away from the lake. Campers who don't mind carrying their gear a short distance might choose one of the walk-in sites close to the lakeshore, at the corner of the Pincer Bay Campground, but it's a longer walk from the showers. Both campgrounds have central showers, flush toilets, and laundry facilities.

INFORMATION AND SERVICES

Peterborough and the Kawarthas Tourism runs a year-round **Visitors Centre** (270 George St. N., 705/742-2201 or 800/461-6424, www.thekawarthas.ca, 9am-4:30pm Mon.-Fri., 10am-5pm Sat.-Sun.) downtown.

GETTING THERE AND AROUND

Peterborough is 140 kilometers (87 miles) northeast of Toronto. By car, the most direct route is to take Highway 401 east to Highway 115 north. **Greyhound** (800/661-8747, www.greyhound.ca) runs frequent buses between Toronto and **Peterborough Bus Station** (220 Simcoe St., 705/743-8045, 1.75-2.25 hours, adults $14-32, ages 2-11 $12-26).

You need a car to explore Peterborough and vicinity; many attractions are outside the city proper, and even in town, sights aren't within easy walking distance. Outside of town, navigating around the Kawartha region requires careful attention to your map or GPS, since there are few direct roads and many lakes to circumnavigate. Allow more time to reach your destination than the mileage might indicate.

Lake Ontario

As you head east from Toronto along Highway 401, suburban sprawl and industrial development give way to farms, orchards, and beaches. A string of towns along Lake Ontario—including Port Hope, Cobourg, Grafton, and Brighton—make easy stops en route to Prince Edward County, Kingston, or points farther east, or as getaway destinations for a quick holiday.

Northumberland Tourism (600 William St., Cobourg, 905/372-3329, ext. 6257, or 866/401-3278, www.northumberlandtourism.com) provides information about the region, including details about festivals, special events, cycling routes, and other activities.

PORT HOPE AND COBOURG

Port Hope's draw is its historic downtown, where many of the well-preserved buildings date to the late 1800s. Wander along Walton Street to browse in the boutiques, antiques shops, and bookstores, or hang out in one of the cafés. You might check what's happening at the **Capitol Theatre** (20 Queen St., 905/885-1071, www.capitoltheatre.com), a restored 1930s theater (and national historic site) that hosts plays, concerts, and films.

Like nearby Port Hope, Cobourg has a historic downtown district, plus a pretty sandy beach, a short stroll from the town center. Before you get too sandy, explore King Street and peek into stately **Victoria Hall** (55 King St. W.), built in 1860. The courtroom on the first floor is a replica of London's Old Bailey. On the top floor, the **Art Gallery of Northumberland** (905/372-0333, www.artgalleryofnorthumberland.com, 11am-4pm Tues.-Fri., noon-4pm Sat.-Sun., donation) shows contemporary works.

Food and Accommodations

The Waddell (1 Walton St., Port Hope, 905/885-2449 or 800/361-1957, www.thewaddell.ca, $169-249), a traditionally furnished inn in an 1845 brick building, fits right in with downtown's historic ambience. Rates include Wi-Fi and parking. Both guests and nonguests can dine on modern Italian fare downstairs in **Trattoria Gusto** (905/885-1198, www.trattoriagusto.ca, 11am-9pm Mon.-Thurs., 11am-9:30pm Fri., 10:30am-9:30pm Sat., 10:30am-9pm Sun., lunch $13-25, dinner $14-34).

Like pie? At **Betty's Pies & Tarts** (7380 County Rd. 2, between Port Hope and Cobourg, 905/377-7437, 8am-6pm Mon.-Fri., 9am-5pm Sat.-Sun. July-Aug., call for off-season hours), the tasty pastries come in both full-size and convenient single-serving sizes—the better to sample more varieties! The apple pies are good, but resisting the gooey butter tarts is futile.

If you're in town on a Saturday, stop into **Cobourg Farmers Market** (Market Square, 2nd St. and Albert St., 7am-1pm Sat. May-Oct., 8am-1pm Sat. Nov.-Dec., www.cobourgfarmersmarket.ca), which has been supplying residents and visitors with locally grown produce, cheeses, meats, breads, and pastries since 1839.

Practicalities

From Toronto, Port Hope is 100 kilometers (60 miles) and Cobourg is 120 kilometers (75 miles) east, off Highway 401. It's just over an hour's ride on **VIA Rail** (888/842-7245, www.viarail.com, one-way adults $24-64) to **Port Hope Station** (Hayward St.). VIA Rail trains stop at **Cobourg Station** (563 Division St.) en route between Toronto (1-1.25 hours, one-way adults $25-67) and Kingston (1-1.25 hours, one-way adults $38-100).

In Port Hope, pick up a brochure outlining self-guided walking or driving tours of the historic district at the **Municipality of Port Hope Tourism Office** (20 Queen St., 905/885-2004 or 888/767-8467, www.porthopetourism.ca). The **Town of Cobourg Business and Tourism Centre** (212 King St. W., 905/372-5481 or 888/262-6874, www.cobourgtourism.ca) can tell you more about what's happening around town.

GRAFTON

In Grafton, 130 kilometers (80 miles) east of Toronto and 10 kilometers (6 miles) east of Cobourg, the main attraction—St. Anne's Spa—is north of Highway 401; Grafton Village lies to the south. The Grafton area also has a "glamping" resort for an upscale outdoor-oriented stay.

St. Anne's Spa

Set on nearly 200 hectares (500 acres) high in the hills, ★ **St. Anne's Spa** (1009 Massey Rd., 905/349-2493 or 888/346-6772, www.spavillage.ca) feels like a secluded European health retreat, where you can settle in for a day of pampering. The sprawling property is built around the elegant stone main inn, but you may not care about the resort's heritage once you've had a shiatsu massage or mud wrap treatment. Take a yoga or meditation class, go for a swim (the outdoor pool looks across the hills to Lake Ontario), rejuvenate in the eucalyptus steam room, or indulge in a wide range of other spa treatments.

Overnight guests can choose a traditionally furnished room in the main inn or one of several cottages around the property. Some cottages are quite a distance from the main inn and spa building (the hotel does offer shuttle services), so they're best for a girlfriends' getaway or for couples who want to cocoon.

Spa services start at $75 for a half-hour massage, but you can choose from a number of packages, such as an All-Inclusive Day ($185-310 pp), which gets you $120 worth of spa services, a yoga or wellness class, lunch, afternoon tea, and use of the pools and other facilities; add round-trip transportation from Toronto on VIA Rail for $94 per person. Overnight packages, with lodging, three meals, and spa treatments, start at $459-499 per person per day. Most visitors to the spa stay put, so you don't need a car. You can arrange for spa staff to pick you up at the VIA Rail station in Cobourg.

Whispering Springs Wilderness Retreat

You don't have to venture far from Toronto, or even that far off Highway 401, for a getaway into the Ontario wilderness. And at **Whispering Springs Wilderness Retreat** (141 Mercer Ln., 905/349-1009, www.whisperingsprings.ca, mid-May-mid-Oct., $295-389 d), you don't even have to give up many of the comforts of home.

At this "glamping" (glamorous camping) resort, you bed down in a spacious log-framed safari tent with wood floors, electricity, a private bathroom, even a soaker tub. In the morning, staff deliver a breakfast basket with homemade granola, fresh fruit, yogurt, and pastries. Each tent comes with an outdoor kitchen that includes a coffeemaker, kettle, mini fridge, and barbecue so you can prepare other meals (if you don't want to head into town). The on-site lounge serves local craft beer, hard cider, and wines from nearby Prince Edward County. Also on the property is a hot tub, saltwater pool, an outdoor pavilion for yoga classes, and five kilometers (three miles) of hiking trails.

To reach Whispering Springs from Highway 401, take exit 497 and go north on County Road 25. In 3.6 kilometers (2.2 miles), turn left onto Turk/Dekeyser Road. Continue for 2.7 kilometers (1.7 miles) and turn left onto Mercer Lane.

BRIGHTON

This part of Ontario is apple-growing country, and orchards and farm stands line Highway 2, which parallels Highway 401 closer to the lake. Brighton celebrates the rosy fruit every autumn with a weekend-long **Applefest** (www.applefest.ca, Sept.).

Pick your own apples (mid-August through October) at family-friendly **Cricklewood Farm** (27 Grandview Rd., 613/475-4293, www.cricklewood.ca) or navigate your way through their **corn maze** (9:30am-4:30pm Sun.-Fri., 9:30am-6pm Sat. Aug.-early Nov.). The farm is off County Road 2, about three kilometers (1.9 miles) west of Brighton.

Presqu'ile Provincial Park

As its French name suggests, **Presqu'ile Provincial Park** (328 Presqu'ile Pkwy., 613/475-4324, www.ontarioparks.com or www.friendsofpresquile.on.ca, $14.50 per vehicle) is "almost an island." Set on a peninsula jutting into Lake Ontario, it's like two parks in one; flat, wide beaches line the section closest to the mainland, while the area extending between Presqu'ile Bay and the lake has both marshes and woods.

The park sees an abundance of migrating birds in the spring and fall; May and

September are popular with birders. Frogs, fish, and other creatures entertain kids at the **Nature Centre** (10am-4pm daily July-early Sept.); in summer, park staff organize guided hikes, kids' programs, and evening campfires. A lighthouse stands guard at the park's far end, where the **Lighthouse Interpretive Centre** (10am-5pm daily July-early Sept., 10am-4pm Sat.-Sun. late May-June and early Sept.-mid-Oct.) has exhibits about the area's natural and nautical past.

Accommodations and Camping

Presqu'ile's 394 campsites in eight **campgrounds** (328 Presqu'ile Pkwy., 613/475-4324, www.ontarioparks.com, late Apr.-mid-Oct., tent sites $42-45, electrical sites $47-52, reservation fee online $11, by phone $13) are popular with families. The most requested, particularly among RV campers, are the waterfront sites in the High Bluff campground, although they are not very shaded. In the Maples campground, you can reserve an **Exploration Tent** ($98), essentially a cabin with canvas walls, which sleeps four; bring sleeping bags, food, cookware, and whatever else you'd need for camping.

In town, a comfortable place to stay is **Brighton Inn Bed & Breakfast** (40 Young St., 613/475-9706 or 888/895-5807, www.brightoninn.com, $95 s, $115 d), with four guest rooms in an 1890s Victorian. Lemon crepes are a breakfast specialty of owners Don and Nikki Parks, and they'll keep your coffee cup filled while giving you tips about the area.

Practicalities

Brighton is 160 kilometers (100 miles) east of Toronto via Highway 401. It's about a 45-minute drive to the Prince Edward County wineries. Learn more about the region from the **Brighton-Cramahe Chamber of Commerce** (Cramahe Town Hall, 1 Toronto Rd., Colborne, 613/475-2775 or 877/475-2775, www.brightonchamber.ca).

Prince Edward County

Once a predominantly agricultural area, Prince Edward County, on Lake Ontario between Toronto and Kingston, has been reborn as a wine-producing district where three dozen wineries—plus a growing number of craft breweries—welcome visitors. County farms have always raised tomatoes, apples, and other produce (more than 70 canneries once operated here), but the region has jumped on the local-food bandwagon, too, with numerous restaurants featuring the county's bounty. The county is all about wine, beer, and good eating.

Prince Edward County's lodgings, restaurants, and galleries are concentrated in the communities of Picton, Bloomfield, and Wellington. The largest group of wineries is in the Wellington-Hillier area on the county's west side, with others scattered around the region. The county has several beautiful lakeside beaches, too.

High season is May through mid-October; the county is especially busy during July, August, and the autumn harvest. In early spring and late fall, some businesses reduce their hours (many restaurants close Tues.-Wed. off-season), and from January till March the county seems to hibernate. Some lodgings remain open for winter getaways, but if you're hoping to visit particular wineries or eateries, confirm that they're not on holiday themselves.

Lastly, don't mistake Prince Edward *County* for Prince Edward *Island,* the province in Atlantic Canada, even though, confusingly, Prince Edward County is also on an island. Even more confusingly, the county was once a peninsula connected to the mainland by a narrow strip of land, known as "the Carrying Place." In 1889, the Murray Canal was built at the Carrying Place, linking the Bay of Quinte with Lake Ontario but severing the county from the mainland.

★ WINERIES

Winemaking is a relatively new venture in Prince Edward County. The first winery opened in 2001, and many of the more than 35 producers are still small. At many properties you might meet the winemaker, and tours, if offered, tend to be informal. The county is best known for its white wines, although many wineries now produce reds as well.

The **Prince Edward County Winegrowers Association** (www.princeedwardcountywine.ca) has additional wine-touring tips on its website. It publishes a helpful wine-touring map that you can access online or pick up at county visitor information offices, hotels, and wineries. Most wineries charge a small fee for tastings, which they'll often waive if you purchase wine.

If you'd rather not drive while you're wine-tasting across Prince Edward County, contact one of the following companies that offer different tour options: **Beyond the Vine** (613/661-8463, www.beyondthevinepec.com); **The County Wine Tours** (www.thecountywinetours.com); or **Prince Edward County Wine Tours** (613/393-8988, www.pecwinetours.com).

Wellington

With a tasting bar in a cool, industrial hut-like structure, **Norman Hardie Vineyard and Winery** (1152 Greer Rd., 613/399-5297, www.normanhardie.com, 10am-6pm daily Apr.-Dec., 10am-5pm Mon.-Sat. Jan.-Mar.) specializes in pinot noir and chardonnay, and also produces pinot gris, muscadet, and cabernet franc. Tours are available, but staff suggest that you phone ahead. A wood-fired oven churns out freshly baked pizzas on the popular **Pizza Patio** (11am-6pm Fri.-Mon. May, 11am-6pm Thurs.-Mon. June-Oct.).

Two Days in Prince Edward County

Prince Edward County is your place for wine-tasting, beer sampling, beach going, and fine dining. Here's a delicious two-day itinerary.

DAY 1

Start your first morning in Wellington with coffee and pastries at **Enid Grace Café** before heading out to explore the local wineries near Wellington, **Rose Hall Run** and **Norman Hardie** (the latter cooks pizza on the patio). To add craft beer to your itinerary, stop at **Midtown Brewing Company** or **County Road Beer**, which both serve lunch in their tasting rooms.

After you've eaten and sampled your fill, head to the beach. Swim, explore the dunes, or go canoeing at **Sandbanks Provincial Park**. For a quieter experience, spread out your towel at **North Beach Provincial Park**.

Return to your lodging to shower and change for dinner at contemporary bistro **The Courage** in Wellington. If you're not ready to call it a night, have a nightcap on the lakeside terrace at the **Drake Devonshire Inn.**

DAY 2

Book a cooking class at **From the Farm Cooking School,** where you'll prepare lunch from local ingredients and enjoy it with county wines. In the afternoon, wander the sculpture garden at **Oeno Gallery** on the grounds of **Huff Estates,** where you can do more wine tasting if you'd like. Then head into Picton to poke around shops and galleries like **Arts on Main** or **The Red Barns**. Go for a walk at quirky **Birdhouse City** to see the more than 100 unusual birdhouses, then visit **Parsons Brewing Company** for a predinner beer tasting. Nearby, the **Merrill Inn** is an excellent choice for an evening meal.

Before you hit the road the next day, pick up sandwiches and pastries at Picton's **Agrarian Market**—in Prince Edward County, there's always one more delicious thing to eat or drink.

Known for chardonnay and pinot noir, **Rose Hall Run** (1243 Greer Rd., 613/399-1183 or 888/399-1183, www.rosehallrun.com, 10am-6pm daily May-Oct., 10am-5pm daily Mar.-Apr. and Nov.-Dec., 11am-5pm Mon.-Sat. Jan.-Feb.) is a casual place where you might meet owners Dan and Lynn Sullivan in the wine shop or around the tasting bar. You can pick up cheese, bread, and other picnic fare at the on-site **Greer Road Grocer.**

Want more wine stops? Other Wellington-area wineries include **Closson Chase Vineyards** (629 Closson Rd., Hillier, 613/399-1418 or 888/201-2300, www.clossonchase.com, 11am-5pm daily mid-Apr.-Dec., 11am-5pm Sat.-Sun. Feb.-mid-Apr.), **Karlo Estates** (561 Danforth Rd., 613/399-3000, www.karloestates.com, 11am-6pm Sun.-Thurs., 11am-8pm Fri.-Sat. May-Oct., 11am-5pm Sun.-Thurs., 11am-7pm Fri.-Sat. Nov.-Apr.), and **Sandbanks Estate Winery** (17598 Hwy.

33, 613/399-1839, www.sandbankswinery.com, 10:30am-6pm Sun.-Thurs., 10:30am-7pm Fri.-Sat. July-Aug, 10:30am-6pm daily May-June and Sept.-Oct., 10:30am-5pm daily Nov.-Apr., tours 10:30am, noon, and 2pm daily, free).

Bloomfield

One of the county's more established wineries is **Huff Estates** (2274 County Rd. 1, 613/393-5802, www.huffestates.com, 10am-6pm daily May-Dec., 10am-5pm daily Jan.-Apr., tours 11am daily), which makes riesling, chardonnay, pinot gris, vidal, merlot, and pinot noir. You can drop in for a guided tasting or winery tour. Adjacent to the winery, **Oeno Gallery** (613/393-2216, www.oenogallery.com, 10am-6pm daily high season, 11am-5pm Wed.-Mon. off-season) exhibits high-end contemporary art by international artists, including some with Ontario connections. Outside, wander

Prince Edward County

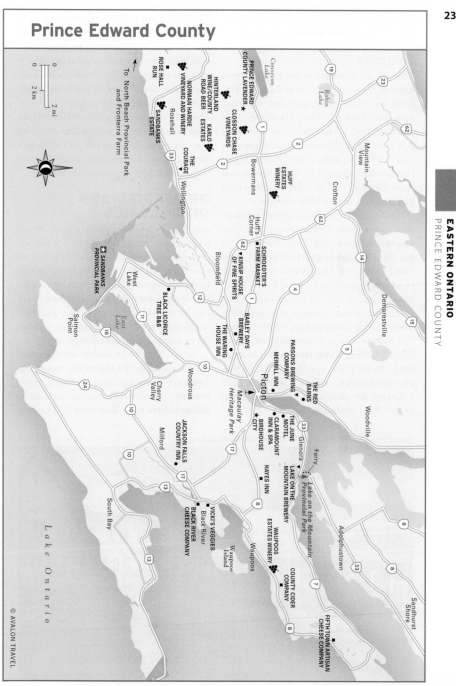

To North Beach Provincial Park
and Fronterra Farm

0 — 2 mi
0 — 2 km

ROSE HALL
RUN

SANDBANKS
ESTATE

Rosehall

NORMAN HARDIE
VINEYARD AND WINERY

HINTERLAND
WINE/COUNTY
ROAD BEER

KARLO
ESTATES

CLOSSON CHASE
VINEYARDS

PRINCE EDWARD
COUNTY LAVENDER

Consecon
Lake

Robin
Lake

THE
COURAGE

Wellington

Bowermans

HUFF
ESTATES
WINERY

Crofton

Mountain
View

Huff's
Corner

SCHROEDER'S
FARM MARKET

KINSIP HOUSE
OF FINE SPIRITS

Bloomfield

West
Lake

SANDBANKS
PROVINCIAL PARK

BLACK LICORICE
TREE B&B

East
Lake

Salmon
Point

THE WARING
HOUSE INN

BARLEY DAYS
BREWERY

Demorestville

Woodrous

Cherry
Valley

Milford

Macaulay
Heritage Park

Picton

PARSONS BREWING
COMPANY

MERRILL INN

THE RED
BARNS

Woodville

JACKSON FALLS
COUNTRY INN

CLARAMOUNT
INN & SPA

THE JUNE
MOTEL

BIRDHOUSE
CITY

Glenora

Ferry

LAKE ON THE
MOUNTAIN BREWERY

Lake on the
Mountain
Provincial Park

HAYES INN

VICKI'S VEGGIES

BLACK RIVER
CHEESE COMPANY

Black River

South Bay

WAUPOOS
ESTATES WINERY

Waupoos
Island

Waupoos

COUNTY CIDER
COMPANY

Adolphustown

Sandhurst
Shore

FIFTH TOWN ARTISAN
CHEESE COMPANY

Lake Ontario

© AVALON TRAVEL

among the more than 40 works on view in the gallery's **Sculpture Garden** (donation).

Waupoos

The county's oldest winery, **Waupoos Estates Winery** (3016 County Rd. 8, 613/476-8338, www.waupooswinery.com, 10:30am-6pm daily May-mid-Oct., 11am-4pm daily mid-Oct.-Dec, 11am-4pm Thurs.-Mon. Jan.-Apr.) opened in 2001 on manicured grounds overlooking the water east of Picton. While they produce a variety of wines, they're best known for their riesling (white) and baco (red) and make the county's first ice wine.

Tastings and several tour options are available, starting with the basic tour (11am, 1pm, and 3pm daily July-Aug., 11am, 1pm, and 3pm Sat.-Sun. Apr.-June and Sept.-Oct., $5). With views to the bay, **The Restaurant** (call or check the website for seasonal hours, lunch $15-25, dinner $20-28) serves sandwiches, salads, pastas, and a couple of larger plates midday, with contemporary locally focused fare in the evenings. Across the street, the affiliated **Clafeld Cider House and Market** (3013 County Rd. 8, 613/476-1353, www.clafeldciderhouse.com) sells sparkling hard ciders and ice ciders, along with baked goods, sandwiches, salads, and cheeses.

The County Cider Company (657 Bongards Crossroad, at County Rd. 8, 613/476-1022, www.countycider.com, 10am-6pm daily May-Oct., call for off-season hours) makes both hard (alcoholic) and nonalcoholic apple cider, as well as ice cider, a sweet dessert wine that's similar to grape-based ice wine. They fire up their pizza oven (11am-5:45pm daily July-Aug., 11am-5:45pm Tues.-Sun. late May-June and Sept.-mid-Oct.) spring to fall, serving pizzas, burgers, and salads outdoors with views across the vineyard to the lake.

BREWERIES AND DISTILLERIES

Lest you think the county is only about wine, there are breweries and a distillery, too. **Barley Days Brewery** (13730 Hwy. 33, Picton, 613/476-7468, www.barleydaysbrewery.com, 10:30am-6pm daily, call or check the website for off-season hours and for tour schedules) brews pale ale, lager, stout, and several seasonal varieties. You can take a tour that includes tastings.

Brown ale and cream ale are the main products at the small **Lake on the Mountain Brewery** (www.lakeonthemountain.com/brewery). Sample them across the road at **Miller House Café-Brasserie** (275 County

Hinterland Wine Company and its sibling, County Road Beer

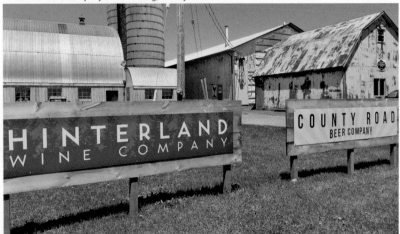

Rd. 7, Prince Edward County, 613/476-1321, www.lakeonthemountain.com, 9am-sunset daily July-Aug., 11am-sunset daily late-May-June and Sept.-Oct.), where the terrace has spectacular views above Picton Bay.

Chris and Samantha Parsons opened **Parsons Brewing Company** (876 County Rd. 49, Prince Edward County, 613/476-9977, www.parsonsbrewing.com, 11am-6pm Sun.-Thurs., 11am-7pm Fri.-Sat.), with a brewery and taproom just north of Picton. Among the roughly 15 beers you might try are Parsons Pale Ale, the unfiltered Crushable Pilsner, and Grandpa Miguel's Coffee Stout, which they brew using coffee beans that Samantha's father grows on his Guatemala farm. You can pair your drinks with tacos, tostadas, and other Mexican-inspired snacks on the sunny patio.

Opened in 2017 in a former meatpacking warehouse set back from Wellington's main street, **Midtown Brewing Company** (266 Main St., Wellington, www.midtownbrewingcompany.com, 11am-10pm Sun.-Thurs., 11am-11pm Fri.-Sat., check online for off-season hours) crafts traditional beers, from a London-style extra special bitter to a German-inspired Kölsch. Its on-site shop sells cured meats, cheeses, local produce, and prepared foods; in the brewpub, you might dig into a fried chicken sandwich or greens with trout gravlax.

First came wine, then came beer. **Hinterland Wine Company** (1258 Closson Rd., Hillier, 613/399-2903, www.hinterlandwine.com) began making sparkling wines; later, on the same property, the owners launched **County Road Beer** (613/399-5883, www.countyrdbeer.com, 11am-6pm Mon.-Sat., 11am-10pm Sun.), where they're brewing Belgian-style farmhouse ales and IPAs. Their **beer garden** (noon-5pm Mon.-Thurs., noon-7pm Fri.-Sat., 10am-4pm Sun.) uses lots of local ingredients to create dishes like a duck confit "burger," slow-roasted carrots with tahini, or smoked fish rillettes.

The tasting room at **Kinsip House of Fine Spirits** (66 Gilead Rd., Bloomfield, 613/393-1890, www.kinsip.ca, 10am-6pm daily summer, 10am-5pm Thurs.-Mon. fall-spring) is inside an ornate 1874 brick homestead, once the residence of a wealthy hops grower. You can sample vodka, gin, whiskey, and *shochu* brewed on-site.

SIGHTS

At **Macaulay Heritage Park** (35 Church St., at Union St., Picton, 613/476-3833, www.

the tasting room at Kinsip House of Fine Spirits

visitpec.ca, 9:30am-4:30pm Wed.-Sun. mid-May-Aug., 9:30am-4:30pm Sat.-Sun. Sept., adults $5, seniors and students $4, ages 5-12 $3, families $14), the 1820s **Church of St. Mary Magdalene** is now a museum of county history. Follow the timeline exhibit to learn about the area's settlement and development. Many of the county's earliest settlers were Loyalists, British supporters who left the United States in the late 1700s after the American Revolutionary War. In the room adjacent to the altar is one of the county's curiosities: a tombstone belonging to a Mr. Pierce, whose stone says he died on the nonexistent February 31, 1860. Historians have never been able to unravel the source of this error. Next door to the church is the 1830 **Macaulay House,** where costumed guides tell you about Reverend William Macaulay (1794-1874) and other settlers who lived in the county in the mid-19th century.

★ Sandbanks Provincial Park

With some of the best beaches on Lake Ontario, lakefront **Sandbanks Provincial Park** (3004 County Rd. 12, Picton, 613/393-3319, www.ontarioparks.com and www.friendsofsandbanks.org, late Apr.-mid-Oct.,

$17 per vehicle), one of the most visited destinations in the Ontario Parks system, is also known for its giant sand dunes.

The longest of the park's beaches is sandy **Sandbanks Beach,** which extends along Lake Ontario for nearly 11 kilometers (7 miles). Access to the beach is only from the south end, but you can walk along the beach literally for miles. You can also hike to the dunes along the 2.5-kilometer (1.5-mile) **Dunes Trail.** The wider three-kilometer (1.8-mile) **Outlet Beach,** on a sliver of land between Lake Ontario and East Lake, is popular with families, with more room to spread your towels; it's a good spot to swim. The famous sand dunes are at **Dunes Beach** on West Lake, where the water can be a little warmer than in Lake Ontario. The Outlet River is a good spot for **canoeing.** You can rent canoes at the Woodyard (mid-June-early Sept.), adjacent to the river.

The park's **Visitors Centre** (10am-4:30pm Thurs.-Tues., 10am-1pm Wed. mid-June-early Sept.) has exhibits about the animals and plants that live in the Sandbanks area and often has snakes, fish, or other creatures on hand. In summer, the park offers **guided dunes walks,** evening campfire programs, and other activities. At this busy park, you'll

beach day at Sandbanks Provincial Park

find fewer crowds in spring and fall, and midweek in summer.

Sandbanks is 18 kilometers (11 miles) west of Picton; take County Road 10 to County Road 11. From Bloomfield, it's 13 kilometers (eight miles) southwest on County Road 12. Coming from Bloomfield, you can bypass the park's main gate and pay your admission fee at the parking area, which may save time on crowded days.

North Beach Provincial Park

If the sands at Sandbanks feel too crowded, head for smaller **North Beach Provincial Park** (440 North Beach Rd., Consecon, 613/399-2030, www.ontarioparks.com, June-mid-Sept., $14.50 per vehicle), which juts into Lake Ontario west of Wellington. The park's three kilometers (1.8 miles) of sand occupy both sides of a narrow spit of land, with some beaches facing Lake Ontario and others fronting North Bay. A day-use park only, North Beach has restrooms and a snack bar.

Birdhouse City

The county's birds nest in style at quirky **Birdhouse City** (Macaulay Mountain Conservation Area, 224 County Rd. 8, Picton, 613/968-3434, www.quinteconservation.ca, dawn-dusk daily, free), a large field populated with more than 100 birdhouses designed as replicas of historic structures and other buildings from near and far. There's a log cabin, a church, and a B&B, even a McDonald's and the Leaning Tower of Pisa. The birdhouses are on Picton's east side; take Union Street east, which becomes County Road 8.

Lake on the Mountain Provincial Park

If you don't know the story behind **Lake on the Mountain Provincial Park** (296 County Rd. 7, Picton, 613/393-3319, www.ontarioparks.com, dawn-dusk daily, free), you might think it's just a pretty little body of water. But what makes the lake a curiosity is

that it has a constant flow of fresh water with no obvious source. Early settlers to the region assumed it must be a bottomless lake, and even modern scientists, who believe that underground springs now feed the lake, haven't been able to unravel how it formed, since the lake is 60 meters (195 feet) higher than nearby Lake Ontario.

The lake is east of Picton; follow Highway 33 to County Road 7. The parking lot overlooks Picton Bay; Lake on the Mountain is across the road.

Prince Edward County Lavender

Take a deep breath as you wander the aromatic purple fields at the 1.2-hectare (three-acre) **Prince Edward County Lavender** (732 Closson Rd., Hillier, 613/399-1855, www.peclavender.com, 10am-5pm daily Apr.-mid-Oct., 10am-5pm Wed.-Sun. mid-Oct.-Dec., $3) lavender and herb farm. In their boutique, you'll find soaps, lotions, teas, and other products, all made from the farm's plants.

ENTERTAINMENT AND EVENTS

Built in the 1920s, the **Regent Theatre** (224 Main St., Picton, 613/476-8416, www.theregenttheatre.org) shows movies and hosts concerts and other special events. The region's professional summer theater, the **Festival Players of Prince Edward County** (613/476-1991 or 866/584-1991, www.festivalplayers.ca, July-Aug.) presents shows at wineries and other county venues. **Taste Community Grown** (www.tastecommunitygrown.com, Sept.) celebrates the county's local food and wine, with tastings and special events.

SHOPPING

Shops, galleries, and cafés line the Main Streets of Picton, Bloomfield, and Wellington. Farther afield, you'll find farm stands, cheese makers, and orchards. All the wineries have shops where you can buy wine and wine-related souvenirs.

Art Galleries

Numerous artists work in the county, and you can follow the **Arts Trail** (www.artstrail. ca), a self-guided tour of galleries and studios. Wellington, Bloomfield, and Picton each have several galleries, while others are around the area. Access the Arts Trail guide online or pick up a brochure at county tourist offices, hotels, and galleries.

Arts on Main (223 Main St., Picton, 613/476-5665, www.artsonmaingallery.ca, 10am-5pm daily, call for winter hours), an artist cooperative, shows works by its members, who live and work in the county. **The Red Barns** (167 White Chapel Rd., Picton, 613/476-6808, www.theredbarns.com, 10am-5pm daily May-mid-Oct.) bills itself as "an artisan's playground," and whether you want to make art, see it made by the artists-in-residence, or browse locally created works in the gallery and shop, there's something for you on this former farm. Check its website for a schedule of workshops in stained glass, glassblowing, pottery, painting, wood carving, and blacksmithing. The property is about two kilometers (1.2 miles) north of downtown Picton, off Highway 49.

Bookshops

Books and Company (289 Main St., Picton, 613/476-3037, www.pictonbookstore.com, 9am-6pm Mon.-Sat., 10am-5pm Sun.) is a large independent bookstore that hosts readings and other literary events. It's connected to **Miss Lily's Cafe** (613/476-9289, $4-8), a light and airy spot to have a coffee, pastry, or light lunch—or curl up with a book.

Gifts

An eclectic little shop whose motto is "Celebrating Canadian design and lakeside living," **Kokito** (285 Main St., Bloomfield, 613/393-2828, www.kokito.ca, 10am-5pm daily) stocks handcrafted canoe paddles, salad tongs, soaps, leather goods, cards, and more—all Canadian-made.

Lose yourself browsing at **FRUgal & Company** (167 Main St., Picton, 613/476-5151, www.frugalandcompany.com, 10am-5pm daily), which sells old records and books, vintage clothing, dishes for your cottage, and a hodgepodge of cool retro stuff you didn't know you needed.

Gourmet Treats

You can sample handmade goat's- and sheep's-milk cheeses in the tasting room at **Fifth Town Artisan Cheese Company** (4309 County Rd. 8, Waupoos, 613/476-5755, www.fifthtown.ca, 10am-6pm daily summer, call for off-season hours). The dairy itself is a "green" building, made from more than 80 percent recycled materials.

Established in 1901, **Black River Cheese Company** (913 County Rd. 13, Milford, 613/476-2575 or 888/252-5787, www.blackrivercheese.com, 9am-7pm daily July-early Sept., 9am-5pm daily Apr.-June and early Sept.-Dec., 9am-5pm Tues.-Sun. Jan.-Mar.), 11 kilometers (eight miles) south of Picton, specializes in cheddar cheese. The aged varieties are deliciously flavorful, and the fresh curds are properly squeaky.

FOOD

As you travel around the county, you'll see farm stands on many local roads. Many county regulars make a beeline for **Schroedter's Farm Market** (1492 Hwy. 62, at Hwy. 1, Bloomfield, 613/393-2823) for one reason: freshly made doughnuts.

Near the Black River Cheese Company, **Vicki's Veggies** (81 Morrison Point Rd., off County Rd. 13, Milford, 613/476-7241, www.vickisveggies.com, May-Oct.) is a self-service stand selling organically grown vegetables. Vicki supplies many local restaurants and periodically sells her wares at Toronto's Evergreen Brickworks market. Tomatoes are a highlight in season.

Be on the lookout for **Picnic PEC** (613/242-1148, www.picnicpec.com), a pink food truck that parks at wineries around the region, dishing out interesting sandwiches like a tofu banh mi with Sriracha mayo. Check its Instagram feed (www.instagram.com/picnicpecfood) to find its current location.

Wellington

Start your day at petite **Enid Grace Café** (303 Main St., 613/399-3488, www.enidgrace.com, 7am-3pm Wed.-Mon., $6-10), where staff bake everything from scones to muffins to croissants, even bagels, in house. Pair your coffee with a slice of buttered cinnamon-raisin bread or try creamy scrambled eggs, cherry tomatoes, and fresh greens served on a toasted brioche. A small selection of soups, quiches, salads, and sandwiches rounds out the menu. Go early, before all the goodies sell out.

In a Wellington storefront with a tin ceiling, rustic wood and marble tables, and a long bar, ★ **The Courage** (298 Main St., 613/399-2233, www.thecouragebar.com, 11am-10pm Wed.-Thurs., 11am-1am Fri., 10:30am-1am Sat., 10:30am-10pm Sun., lunch/brunch $12-21, dinner $17-27) gives off the vibe of a laid-back local eatery, belying the creativity that you find in the kitchen. The "uncommon octopus" comes with sriracha potatoes, corn bisque, and pops of grapefruit gel. At midday, choose an imaginative sandwich or salad. Among the "liquid courage" at the bar is county craft beer, cider, and wine.

With sleek candlelit tables and wide board pine floors (plus friendly, knowledgeable staff), **East and Main Bistro** (270 Main St., 613/399-5420, www.eastandmain.ca, 11:30am-2:30pm and 5:30pm-9pm Wed.-Sun. Feb.-Dec., lunch $11-14, dinner $22-34) feels both stylish and totally relaxed. The menu also walks that hip-homey line; the bison sirloin might come with sautéed wild mushrooms, while the locally raised chicken might be served with chorizo-cheddar bread pudding. Sweets like a warm fruit crumble or classic crème brûlée provide a comforting conclusion. The wines are local, of course.

Bloomfield

A casual café by day, **Agrarian Bistro** (275 Main St., 613/393-0111, www.agrarianpec.ca, 11:30am-2:30pm and 5pm-8:30pm Mon.-Sat., 10am-2pm and 5pm-8:30pm Sun., dinner $14-27) morphs into a more upscale dining space at night. Local flavors take the simple fare up a notch—arugula and feta salad might include Ontario peaches, the perch for the fish cakes was caught nearby, and even grilled cheese goes upscale with caramelized onions and farm-fresh greens. On the lower level, the **Speakeasy** pub has live music most Friday-Saturday nights.

Picton

The owners of Bloomfield's Agrarian Bistro

creative plates at The Courage in Wellington

operate the **Agrarian Market** (4 Lake St., 613/476-0001, www.agrarianmarket.com, 10am-5pm Sun.-Thurs., 10am-6pm Fri., 9am-6pm Sat.), a gourmet grocery, bakery, and sandwich shop where you can pick up pastries, prepared foods, produce, cheeses, and other ingredients for a picnic at the beach or a meal at the cottage.

A cheerful spot for breakfast, coffee, or a lunch break when you're browsing Picton's galleries and shops, **The Vic Café** (222 Main St., 613/476-2233, www.theviccafe.com, 7:30am-4pm Mon.-Thurs., 7:30am-7:30pm Fri.-Sat., 9am-2pm Sun., $6-14) cooks up eggs, smoothies, and granola in the morning, with inventive rice bowls such as the Sweet Butter Albert (bacon, cheese curds, carrots, peppers, corn nuts, and pickles) later in the day.

Even if you're not staying at the ★ **Merrill Inn** (343 Main St. E., 613/476-7451 or 866/567-5969, www.merrillinn.com, 5:30pm-9pm Tues.-Sat. Feb.-Dec., $25-39), book a table in its cozy garden-level dining room for some of the county's most interesting food. Start with the signature salad—baby spinach and greens topped with local cheddar, apples, and spicy-sweet pecans—or perhaps smoked trout with a cabbage and radish slaw. Entrées might include locally raised lamb or fresh fish; the kitchen takes great care with the accompanying vegetables, too. Match your meal with a county-made wine.

Cooking Classes

With the county's emphasis on local food, perhaps it's not surprising that local cooking programs can teach you to use regional ingredients. See their websites for upcoming class schedules.

Personal chef and food writer Cynthia Peters runs **From the Farm Cooking School** (618 Burr Rd., Ameliasburgh, www.fromthefarm.ca), offering regularly scheduled hands-on **cooking classes** (9:30am-1:30pm, $125 pp) in her well-designed farmhouse kitchen, a short drive north of Bloomfield and Wellington. Guests learn about ingredients they'll be using, work in pairs to prepare

lunch, and sit down to a meal with local wines. The **Farm & Cook Thursdays** program (9am-2:30pm, $150 pp) combines a visit to an area farm to harvest what's growing, with a cooking class and lunch. In addition, Peters puts together four-hour private cooking experiences ($130 pp) for small groups as well as private all-day farm touring and cooking programs ($245 pp).

The **Waring House Cookery School** (613/476-7492 or 800/621-4956, www.waringhouse.com, $75-115 pp), at the Waring House Inn, offers a variety of cooking classes, which typically run three hours (including a meal), in a large commercial kitchen. Topics might include fall vegetables or pizzas from scratch.

ACCOMMODATIONS
Wellington

The owners of Toronto's über-cool Drake Hotel completely rebuilt a former lakeside lodging to create the **Drake Devonshire Inn** (24 Wharf St., 613/399-3338, www.drakedevonshire.ca, $369-1,700 d), where the ambience is part country cottage and part hip boutique hotel. The 14 guest rooms—some in the original circa-1897 inn and others in a new addition—range from the Stargazer Crash Pad (with a skylight but no windows) to the striking 658-square-foot Owner's Suite with a peaked ceiling and water views. Musicians perform periodically in the Pavilion, which features a full-wall cartoon-style mural, and you can hang out or play table tennis in the "Glass Box," a lounge with floor-to-ceiling glass. The window-lined **restaurant** (9am-late daily, breakfast $11-19, lunch $14-34, dinner $22-38) overlooking the lake serves creative comfort food, snacks, and booze.

Go "glamping" at **Fronterra Farm** (242 North Beach Rd./County Rd. 2, Consecon, 800/427-1257, www.fronterra.ca, mid-May-Oct., $255 d), where ten roomy log-framed tents, five in the forest and five floating on the edge of the bay, have king-size beds, sitting areas, and showers under the stars. Each tent comes with a summer kitchen where you can prep farm-fresh eggs and organic veggies from the garden. The enthusiastic young owners, who plan to open a microbrewery on the site, rent canoes and bikes and can arrange other activities around the county; book in advance and tell them what you have in mind. The farm is 15 kilometers (nine miles) west of Wellington on the road to North Beach Provincial Park.

Bloomfield

Owners Diane and Bruce Milan were organic farmers in Minnesota before decamping to the county's milder Canadian climate. They operate cozy **Hillsdale House** (332 Main St., 613/393-2952, www.bbcanada.com, $150 d), a two-room B&B in their 1890s home. Diane serves a three-course hot breakfast each morning, and Bruce is also a blacksmith; stop into his **Island Forge Gallery** (www.islandforge.ca) out back to see what he's working on.

Art and the outdoors mix at **Black Licorice Tree B&B** (1287 County Rd. 12, 613/970-3031, www.blacklicoricetree.com, $169-179 s, $189-199 d), an 1892 Victorian on a three-hectare (seven-acre) property. Sandbanks Provincial Park is a short drive down the road. Owners Mark and Melanie have outfitted the three cozy guest rooms (two in the main house, one in the adjacent carriage house) with a funky assortment of furnishings. Melanie is a ceramic artist and will happily show you her **Mena Dragonfly Studio** (www.menadragonfly.com); breakfast is served on her handmade plates.

On the grounds of Huff Estates winery, **Inn at Huff Estates** (2274 County Rd. 1, 613/393-1414 or 866/484-4667, www.huffestates.com, $209-399 d) is a modern building with 21 guest rooms done in a woodsy cottage style. All have private patios; some overlook the interior courtyard, while others look onto the vineyards. Rates include a breakfast buffet.

Picton and Vicinity

Old friends April Brown and Sarah Sklash couldn't find accommodations in the county that felt cool and relaxed enough for them and their pals, so they bought an old roadside motor lodge, revamped the 16 rooms with mid-century modern furnishings, Nespresso machines, and vibrant colors, and opened ★ **The June Motel** (12351 Loyalist Pkwy., Picton, 613/476-2424, www.thejunemotel.com, late Mar.-Nov., $129-255 d). Have a drink and snack in the Wine Lobby, hang out around the fire pit, borrow a board game, or

"glamping" tent at Fronterra Farm

join a Saturday yoga class. Need something else? Send a text to the "text message concierge," who'll make you a dinner reservation or recommend a local winery.

You don't have to be an artist to stay at **The Red Barns** (167 White Chapel Rd., 613/476-6808, www.theredbarns.com, May-Oct., $150-170 d), but artists-owners Heather Watson and Peter Josic have decorated the guest rooms in their farmhouse with original stained glass inspired by the likes of Frank Lloyd Wright and Charles Rennie Mackintosh. Families might prefer the studio-style "Summer Loft" ($250) with a kitchenette or the one-bedroom coach house ($250), with mid-century modern furnishings, a kitchen, a living room with sleep sofa, and more stained glass. Rates for the farmhouse rooms, but not the Summer Loft or the coach house, include breakfast.

The former owner of the county's oldest inn moved it across the island and spent more than 40 years painstakingly putting it back together. More recent owners of the **Hayes Inn** (2319 County Rd. 8, 613/476-9082, www.hayesinnpec.com, $185-195 d), on the road between Picton and Waupoos, finished the job, outfitting this bright and airy three-room lodging with quilts and white duvets, espresso machines, and new baths. You get a full breakfast that might include pancakes with locally made maple syrup or a vegetarian farro salad—nothing like the property's early rough-hewn tavern days.

Don't want a fussy Victorian look? The **Loyalist Lofts** (56 Mary St., 613/471-1169, www.loyalistlofts.ca, $200-250 d), in a restored 1877 brick home, rents three spacious apartments furnished in a relaxed mix of the modern and the old-fashioned. Both the first-floor Wellington Suite and the upstairs Picton Unit have two bedrooms, while the two-level Bloomfield Suite has a sleep sofa in the living room and a bedroom above. Rates include Wi-Fi and a pass to Sandbanks Provincial Park. Breakfast isn't provided, but all units have kitchens, and you're just one block from Main Street.

Food is an important part of a stay at the elegant **Merrill Inn** (343 Main St. E., 613/476-7451 or 866/567-5969, www.merrillinn.com, $245-365 d), a 13-room lodging in an 1878 brick Victorian. Not only does the inn have a fine restaurant (5:30pm-9pm Tues.-Sat.), but you get a copious breakfast buffet, as well as afternoon tea or lemonade with freshly baked cookies. The guest rooms, spread out over three floors, are all different, but all are furnished with antiques and period pieces; some

the lounge at The June Motel

have fireplaces, and the Loyalist Suite even has a working wood-burning one.

The 1860s stone farmhouse at the **Waring House Inn** (395 Sandy Hook Rd., 613/476-7492 or 800/621-4956, www.waringhouse.com, $145-340 d) comprises the inn, a garden-view restaurant, and the lively **Barley Room Pub** (with music several nights a week); the guest rooms upstairs are cozy but tiny. Rooms are more spacious in two newer lodges, furnished with classic pieces from the local Gibbard furniture company. The stone Vineyard View cottage ($299-375 d) overlooks the gardens. Rates include full breakfast. Also on the property is a **cooking school**.

Upscale **Claramount Inn & Spa** (97 Bridge St., 613/476-2709 or 800/679-7756, www.claramountinn.com, $215-269 d) is a sunny yellow Colonial Revival mansion built in 1906. The seven spacious suites in the main inn have antiques, large soaker tubs, and some fireplaces; three suites in the neighboring carriage house are decorated in a more rustic country style. You can swim in the heated saltwater pool year-round (it has a retractable roof). Rates include breakfast; in the evenings, the chef at **Clara's Restaurant** (dinner $24-37), overlooking the harbor, emphasizes local ingredients in the contemporary dishes.

Once a church parsonage, the stately limestone Victorian that houses **The Manse** (10 Chapel St., 613/476-1006, www.themanse.ca, $199-289) is now a boutique bed-and-breakfast. Decorated in rich burgundies and browns, the seven upscale guest rooms are filled with deluxe amenities, from gas fireplaces to iPod docks to plush robes. Outside, sipping drinks beside the kidney-shaped saltwater pool, surrounded by manicured gardens, you'd never know you're just off Picton's Main Street.

Innkeeper Lee Arden Lewis has drawn on her Mohawk heritage to design the homey nine-room **Jackson Falls Country Inn** (1768 County Rd. 17, Milford, 613/476-8576, www.jacksonsfalls.com, $215-245 d, suite $480-485), where the quilts, artwork, and other furnishings reflect a mix of European

and indigenous designs. Rates include breakfast and Wi-Fi. The connected building housing the **restaurant** (call or check the website for seasonal hours), which is decorated with blackboards, maps, and a wood-burning stove, was constructed in 1870 as a one-room schoolhouse. The short contemporary menu features lots of locally grown and foraged ingredients, game such as rabbit or bison, and fresh Ontario fish. The inn is 12 kilometers (7.5 miles) southeast of Picton; take County Road 8 east to County Road 17.

Camping

Sandbanks Provincial Park (3004 County Rd. 12, Picton, 613/393-3319, www.ontarioparks.com, late Apr.-mid-Oct., $17 per vehicle, tent sites $42-45, electrical sites $47-52) has 620 campsites in six campgrounds. The prime sites are at Camper's Beach, right on the lake in the Outlet River Campground. Eager campers often book these sites five months in advance. From Richardson's Campground, it's a short walk to Sandbanks Beach and a slightly longer walk to Dunes Beach. All the campgrounds have central showers and flush toilets.

The park also has two cottages for rent. The **Maple Rest Heritage House** ($312) is a four-bedroom, four-bath brick Victorian home that sleeps eight. The smaller lakeside **Jacques Cottage** ($169.50) can sleep up to six; the small master bedroom upstairs has a double bed, an adjacent open loft space has two twins, and there's a sleep sofa in the living room. Both cottages include kitchens and linens. Book either cottage—well in advance—through the Ontario Parks reservation service (519/826-5290 or 888/668-7275, www.ontarioparks.com).

INFORMATION AND SERVICES

Prince Edward County (613/476-2421 or 800/640-4717, www.thecounty.ca or http://prince-edward-county.com) can provide event listings, maps, wine-touring guides, and other information for planning a county visit. The county operates several seasonal information kiosks, including the **Bloomfield Information Kiosk** (Bloomfield Town Hall, 289 Main St., lower level, 613/393-2796) and the **Wellington Information Kiosk** (Lakeshore Farms, 467 Main St. W.).

GETTING THERE AND AROUND

Prince Edward County is 215 kilometers (135 miles) east of Toronto. Take Highway 401 east to either exit 522 (Wooler Rd. S.) or exit 525 (Hwy. 33, Trenton). You need a car to get around the county.

From Kingston, take Highway 401 west to exit 566 (Marysville) and continue south on Highway 49, or follow the slower but shore-hugging Loyalist Parkway (Hwy. 33) to Adolphustown and then catch the 10-minute **Glenora-Adolphustown Ferry** (www.mto. gov.on.ca, 6am-1:15am daily, free). The ferry leaves the Adolphustown side at 15 minutes before and 15 minutes after the hour; it departs Glenora on the hour and the half-hour. From late June through mid-October, a second ferry runs 10:15am-7:30pm, so that a boat departs from each terminal every 15 minutes.

The main road across the county is Highway 33, the Loyalist Parkway, which becomes Main Street in Wellington, Bloomfield, and Picton. If you're coming to Picton from the west, it's faster to cut across on Highway 1 east from Consecon, which rejoins Highway 33 just west of Picton.

Kingston

On June 15, 1841, Kingston became the first capital of the fledgling nation of Canada. If you're interested in history, it's worth exploring this city of 150,000, midway between Toronto and Montreal. There's a 19th-century fort, a majestic city hall, the oldest continuously running public market in Ontario, and well-regarded Queen's University, founded the same year that Kingston took on its capital-city duties.

The city was also once home to Canada's most notorious criminals, who were incarcerated in the maximum-security Kingston Penitentiary. Though the jail closed its doors in 2013, it's now open for fascinating if sobering tours.

Kingston is sometimes nicknamed "The Limestone City" for its many well-preserved stone structures (some of which are now inns or B&Bs) that date to the 1800s. Located on Lake Ontario at the southern end of the Rideau Canal, Kingston's waterfront is an important part of its heritage, too, and it makes the present-day city even more pleasant, whether you're strolling the eight-kilometer (five-mile) waterfront trail or on board a lake cruise. Yet even with all this history, there's nothing stuffy about this entertaining little city. It's compact and easy to walk around, with eclectic restaurants, casual cafés, and leafy parks.

SIGHTS

TOP EXPERIENCE

★ Fort Henry

Standing majestically on a point overlooking Kingston and the St. Lawrence River, **Fort Henry** (1 Fort Henry Dr., at County Rd. 2, 613/542-7388, www.forthenry.com, 9:30am-5pm daily mid-May-June and early Sept., 9:30am-5pm Thurs.-Tues., 9:30am-10pm Wed. July-Aug., 10am-4pm early Sept.-late Sept., adults $20, seniors $18, students ages 13-18 $16, ages 6-12 $13) was built in the 1830s to protect the town, the nearby royal dockyards, and the mouth of the adjacent Rideau Canal. Kingston was a major stop on the supply routes between Montreal, Ottawa, and points farther west, making it a strategic location for the British. British troops were stationed at the fort until 1870.

Kingston

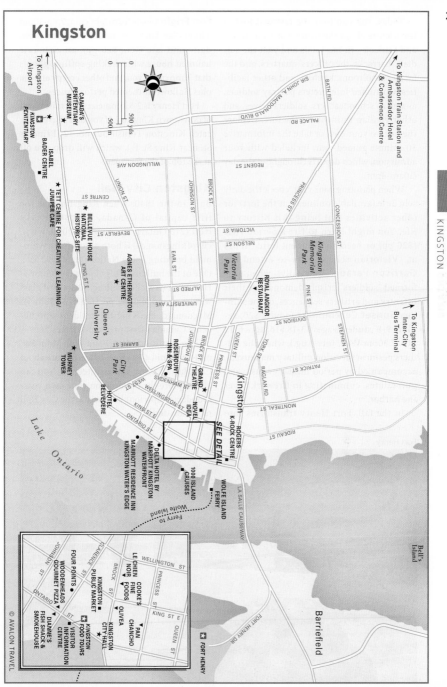

© AVALON TRAVEL

Today, you can tour the restored fort to learn more about the history of Kingston—and Canada—in the 1800s and visit the soldiers' barracks, the officers' quarters, and the fort's schoolroom, kitchen, and other facilities. Costumed interpreters portray soldiers, as well as schoolteachers, soldiers' wives, and other civilian residents of the fort. Explore the fort on your own or take the informative 50-minute guided tour, included with your admission, which departs throughout the day (10am-4pm).

When planning your visit, check the daily schedule (available online or at the fort) for other activities that bring this history to life. You might learn to fire a period rifle ($20 pp) or become a student (circa 1867) at "Victorian school." Try to attend the **Garrison Parade** (3pm daily), when uniformed "soldiers" crisply demonstrate their infantry and artillery sequences, or the summer **Sunset Ceremonies** (adults $20, seniors $18, students ages 13-18 $16, ages 6-12 $13, 7:30pm Wed. July-Aug.), when the soldiers perform precision military maneuvers, accompanied by period military music and gun salutes, culminating in fireworks over the harbor.

In the fall, Fort Henry transforms into **Fort Fright** (www.fortfright.com, 7pm-10pm Thurs.-Sat. late Sept.-mid.-Oct., 7pm-10pm daily mid-late Oct., $20 pp), an elaborate haunted house with shaking coffins, ghouls that jump out at you, and other creepy effects, plus Halloween-themed performances.

Fort Henry is 2.5 kilometers (1.5 miles) east of downtown Kingston. If you don't have a car, catch Kingston Transit Bus no. 12 (Princess St. near King St. E.), which will drop you off at the top of the fort road.

Kingston City Hall

Built in the 1840s when Kingston was the first capital of Canada, **Kingston City Hall** (216 Ontario St., 613/546-0000, www.cityofkingston.ca) is both a working government building and a National Historic Site. One of the building's highlights is Memorial Hall, with its arched ceiling, 12 stained glass windows, and massive portrait of Sir John A. Macdonald, the Kingston resident who became Canada's first prime minister.

Take a **guided tour** (10am-4pm Mon.-Sat. mid-May-mid-Oct., free) to learn more about City Hall's history and architecture. You can also explore the building on your own year-round; pick up a tour brochure at the City Hall reception desk.

Fort Henry

inside Kingston Penitentiary

Murney Tower

In the 1840s, the British built four small fortifications along the Kingston waterfront, known as the Martello Towers. The British copied these stocky round towers from a similar French structure constructed on Mortella Point on the island of Corsica (*Martello* is apparently a corruption of *Mortella*). Kingston's Martello Towers are among only 13 similar fully intact structures in the world.

One of these fortifications, the 1846 **Murney Tower** (King St. W., at Barrie St., 613/507-5181, www.kingstonhistoricalsociety. ca, 10am-5pm daily mid-May-early Sept., adults $5, seniors and students $4) is open to the public. A cannon still points out from the tower's narrow windows, and inside, a small historical museum describes the lives of the 19th-century soldiers and their families who lived in the tower.

★ Kingston Penitentiary

In 1835, the first inmates arrived at maximum-security **Kingston Penitentiary**

(560 King St. W., 613/542-7388, www. kingstonpentour.com, 8:30am-sunset Tues.-Sun. mid-May-June and early Sept.-Oct., 8:30am-sunset daily July-early-Sept., $35 pp). For more than 175 years, this forbidding limestone edifice on the waterfront housed many of Canada's most notorious criminals. The "Pen" remained an active correctional facility until 2013.

During the 90-minute tours, you will walk through the cell blocks, segregation units, workshops, and recreation yard. Former prison guards tell you what it was like to work behind the gray stone walls, sharing details about everything from prison riots to inmates' conjugal visits, although they won't name names; due to confidentiality requirements, they can't reveal specifics about any individual prisoner, even the most infamous.

If you're particularly interested in prison history, you can choose a 2.5-hour **extended tour** ($60 pp), which adds visits to the prison hospital, school, and other areas not covered in the standard tour, plus more time to talk informally with retired corrections staff.

Purchase tour tickets online in advance on the Pen tour website. You buy a ticket for a specific tour time, and you must arrive 20 minutes before your scheduled tour to complete a waiver form and other formalities. The tours are not recommended for children.

Canada's Penitentiary Museum

Opposite Kingston Penitentiary is a quirky, fascinating, and sobering museum. Housed in the former Kingston Pen's warden's residence, **Canada's Penitentiary Museum** (555 King St. W., 613/530-3122, www. penitentiarymuseum.ca, 9am-6pm Mon.-Fri., 10am-5pm Sat.-Sun. May-Oct., donation) contains a "punishment room" that displays disciplinary measures used over the years—from the strapping board to which inmates were strapped to be paddled (used as recently as 1969), to the Box, a creepy casket-like container used for solitary confinement in the 1840s. You can peek into actual jail cells, and in the "contraband room" you'll see all manner of handmade weapons and devices used for attempted escapes. Some of the volunteer guards are former corrections staff who can tell you about life on the inside. While what you learn here isn't as immersive as what you experience on the Penitentiary tour, the two activities complement each other. It's worth stopping at the museum even if you're visiting the Pen itself.

Bellevue House National Historic Site

The former home of Sir John A. Macdonald, Canada's first prime minister, **Bellevue House National Historic Site** (35 Centre St., 613/545-8666, www.pc.gc.ca, 10am-5pm daily mid-May-mid-Oct., 10am-4pm Mon.-Fri. mid-Oct.-late Oct., adults $3.90, seniors $3.40) is a sprawling 20-room white stucco mansion that Macdonald, his wife, Isabella, and their infant son rented in 1848. Macdonald hoped that the peaceful atmosphere of this Italianate country house, located about 1.5 kilometers (one mile) from central Kingston, would improve Isabella's poor health. Unfortunately, the Macdonalds' son died shortly after they moved into the house. Isabella continued to ail (she may have suffered from tuberculosis), and Macdonald found himself in financial trouble. The family left Bellevue House after only one year, relocating to a smaller and less costly home in town.

Costumed staff tell you about the Macdonald family and their home as you walk through rooms furnished with pieces from the 1840s, along with a few of the Macdonalds' possessions. On weekends in July-August, guides lead 90-minute tours (call or check the website for schedule, $7.80 pp), sharing additional details about Macdonald and his history. At other times, staff run **Alternative Facts Tours** (call or check the website for schedule and fees) about more controversial historical topics. The "Brides and Dives" tour, for example, examines Macdonald's

reputation as a womanizer and his issues with alcohol use.

At the **Visitor Centre**, adjacent to the historic house, multimedia exhibits look at the contentious issues that led up to Canada's confederation and the pros and cons of Macdonald's term as prime minister, from his personal life to indigenous history to the country's westward expansion.

Tett Centre for Creativity and Learning

In a beautifully repurposed 1820s stone building, originally constructed as a brewery, you'll find the **Tett Centre for Creativity and Learning** (370 King St. W., 343/266-0009, www.tettcentre.org, 8am-9pm Mon.-Sat., 9am-6pm Sun.). This arts hub contains a diverse assortment of small galleries, artist studios (where you might watch artists at work), and performance spaces. The center hosts arts events, as well as periodic arts workshops and classes for kids and adults. Also in the building is the waterside **Juniper Café** (www.junipercafe.ca) and the **Joe Chithalen Memorial Musical Instrument Lending Library** (www.joesmill.org), which stocks guitars, drums, violins, and many other instruments that anyone can borrow, free of charge. Individual organizations keep different hours from the general hours that the center is open to the public, so check the website for particulars and for event schedules.

Agnes Etherington Art Centre

On the Queen's University campus, the contemporary **Agnes Etherington Art Centre** (36 University Ave., 613/533-2190, www.agnes.queensu.ca, 10am-4:30pm Tues.-Fri., 1pm-5pm Sat.-Sun. May-Aug., 10am-4:30pm Tues.-Wed. and Fri., 10am-9pm Thurs., 1pm-5pm Sat.-Sun. Sept.-Apr., donation) mounts exhibits of works by artists from Canada and around the world. At 12:15pm on the third Thursday of every month, you can take a free 45-minute guided tour of the current exhibitions.

ENTERTAINMENT AND EVENTS

The **Isabel Bader Centre for Performing Arts** (390 King St. W., 613/533-2424 or 855/533-2424, www.queensu.ca/theisabel) presents theatre, film, concerts from classical to pop, and other arts events in a dramatic contemporary building on the Lake Ontario waterfront. The window-lined lobby overlooking the lake and the 500-seat concert hall, with acoustically designed wood walls and ceiling, are among the structure's most striking features; see them on a free 30-minute summertime **guided tour** of the building (July-Aug., call or check the website for schedules). Also online are details about upcoming performances and events.

First opened in 1879, the **Grand Theatre** (218 Princess St., 613/530-2050, www.kingstongrand.ca) hosts theatrical, dance, musical, and other productions by local, national, and international performers. For rock concerts, sports events, ice shows, and other big productions, head to the **Rogers K-Rock Centre** (1 The Tragically Hip Way, 613/650-5000, www.rogersk-rockcentre.com).

Every year on or around June 15, Kingston celebrates **First Capital Day** (www.cityofkingston.ca), commemorating the city's role as Canada's first capital. Clowns, contortionists, crooners, and all manner of street performers take over downtown during the weekend-long **Kingston Buskers Rendezvous** (www.downtownkingston.ca, July).

SHOPPING

Princess Street, between Ontario and Sydenham Streets, is Kingston's main downtown shopping district, with local and chain clothing shops, cafés, and other boutiques, including independent bookstore **Novel Idea** (156 Princess St., 613/546-9799, www.novelideabooks.ca, 9:30am-9pm Mon.-Fri., 9:30am-6pm Sat., 10:30am-5pm Sun.), which carries a good selection of both fiction and nonfiction.

One block south of Princess, Brock Street has a few interesting shops, including **Cooke's Fine Foods** (61 Brock St., 613/548-7721, www.cookesfinefoods.com, 10am-5:30pm Mon.-Sat.), which opened in 1865. It still has the original counters and tin ceiling, and its shelves are packed with coffees, jams, cheeses, chocolates, and other specialty foods.

FOOD

For a small city, Kingston has a large selection of good places to eat, from basic international joints to upscale contemporary dining rooms. Most are downtown around Princess, King, and Ontario Streets.

TOP EXPERIENCE

★ Food Tours

To combine a little history with a lot of eating and drinking, take an entertaining guided walk with **Kingston Food Tours** (613/704-0006, www.kingstonfoodtours.ca, year-round, see website for schedules). On the three-hour Classic Kingston downtown tour (adults $69, ages 6-12 $59), you'll learn about the city's past and its notable architecture as you sample your way through eight cafés, restaurants, and food shops; don't eat before your tour. The two-hour Beer and Bites tour (adults $69) takes you to local pubs and microbreweries to get the scoop on Kingston's craft beer scene, and of course, you'll taste the brews.

Contemporary

The exposed brick walls, tin ceiling, and rust-hued banquettes say "traditional bistro," and you'll find plenty of traditional bistro fare at **Le Chien Noir** (69 Brock St., 613/549-5635, www.lechiennoir.com, 11:30am-9pm Mon.-Thurs., 11:30am-10pm Fri.-Sat., 10am-9pm Sun., lunch $12-29, dinner $18-38). The menu takes you from omelets to burgers to Niçoise salad midday, and steak frites, duck confit, and coq au vin in the evening. You'll be equally at home here in jeans or a little black dress.

Italian

Decked out with stone walls, wooden tables, and a searingly hot pizza oven, **Woodenheads Gourmet Pizza** (192 Ontario St., 613/549-1812, www.woodenheads. ca, 11:30am-midnight daily, $10-25) is wildly popular for its eponymous pies, as well as salads and fusion variations on classic Mediterranean fare (calamari Mumbai-style, anyone?). The pizzas range from traditional tomato-and-cheese to the creative Citta (topped with brie, prosciutto, and caramelized onions) to quirky combos like the Nonna Mela, with blackened chicken, cheddar cheese, and apple butter.

At the friendly, bustling trattoria **Olivea** (39 Brock St., 613/547-5483, www.olivea.ca, 11:30am-9pm Sun.-Thurs., 11:30am-10pm Fri.-Sat., $9-25), with a wall of windows facing Market Square, the Italian-Mediterranean menu includes salads, pastas, and more substantial plates like Ligurian seafood stew or chicken under a brick. An arugula salad might pair well with one of the pastas, perhaps penne with a spicy tomato-based *arrabbiata* sauce or gnocchi with beef cheek ragù. There's live jazz Tuesday nights.

Seafood

The bright orange awnings reel in crowds to **Dianne's Fish Shack & Smokehouse** (195 Ontario St., 613/507-3474, www. dianneskingston.com, 11:30am-2pm and 4pm-9pm Mon.-Fri., 11:30am-9pm Sat.-Sun., $8-34), a bustling fish restaurant and barbecue joint with sidewalk seating. Though much of the seafood swims in from afar, the kitchen tries to use sustainable species in south-of-the-border dishes like tuna tostadas, fish tacos, or curried mussels. Smoked brisket with cocoa-coffee barbecue sauce or pulled pork carnitas please the carnivores, while local beer and a long list of tequilas keep both meat and fish fans feeling liquid.

Asian

Just out of downtown, the bare-bones but welcoming **Royal Angkor Restaurant** (523 Princess St., 613/544-9268, www.royalangkor. ca, 11am-3pm and 5pm-9pm Mon.-Fri., 4pm-9pm Sat., $10-13) is a long-standing favorite for Cambodian and Thai food. Try the hot-and-sour "Khmer Style" mix of chicken, shrimp, long beans, and tomatoes flavored with tamarind and basil; the Golden Chicken

Juniper Café

in red curry; or the Kako Khmer, chicken with green papaya, jackfruit, and eggplant.

Bakeries and Cafés

Crave a focaccia, muffin, or scone? At **Pan Chancho Bakery and Café** (44 Princess St., 613/544-7790, www.panchancho.com), the bakery (7am-6pm Mon.-Sat., 7am-5pm Sun.) sells scrumptious fresh-baked goods to go, while the sit-down café (7am-4pm daily, $10-18) whips up pastries or egg dishes in the morning, and salads, cheese plates, or creative world-rambling entrées later in the day.

At the Tett Centre for Creativity and Learning, ★ **Juniper Café** (370 King St. W., 613/344-1736, www.junipercafe.ca, 8am-6pm Mon.-Sat., 8am-5pm Sun., $8-11) has the city's only waterfront patio. Sit lakeside for morning coffee, baked goods, and breakfast sandwiches; later, the tiny kitchen turns out creative salads (like fresh greens topped with wheat berries, asparagus, feta, and pumpkin seeds) and sandwiches like roast pork with apple-Dijon compote or organic chicken with pickled onions and tomato jam; they serve Ontario wine, cider, and craft beer as well. Cookie lovers may find it hard to choose between the soft and chewy ginger or rich double chocolate varieties.

Groceries and Markets

Kingston Public Market (Springer Market Square, King St. E., between Brock St. and Clarence St., www.kingstonpublicmarket.ca, 6am-6pm Tues., Thurs., and Sat. Apr.-Nov.), behind City Hall, is the oldest market in Ontario, in operation since 1801. Selling local produce and prepared foods that change with the seasons, most of the market's action is between 8am and 3pm.

ACCOMMODATIONS

If you like staying in inns or B&Bs in stately historic buildings, you'll enjoy staying in Kingston. Downtown Kingston also has several business- and family-friendly chain hotels. The **Delta Hotel by Marriott Kingston Waterfront** (1 Johnson St., 613/549-8100 or 888/236-2427, www.marriott.com, $205-429 d) and **Marriott Residence Inn Kingston Water's Edge** (7 Earl St., 613/544-4888, www.marriottresidenceinnkingston.com, $254-504 d) are on the waterfront; **Four Points by Sheraton** (285 King St. E., 613/544-4434 or 800/325-3535, www.fourpointskingston.com, $195-254 d) is centrally located as well.

Want to know what it was really like to be a soldier in 1800s Kingston? You won't be issued a musket or army rations, but you can spend the night at **Fort Henry** (1 Fort Henry Dr., at County Rd. 2, 613/542-7388 or 800/437-2233, www.forthenry.com, $200 for up to four people, $50 for each additional person). The billets are basic—you have a cot with a mattress and not much else—and you'll need to bring a sleeping bag, pillow, and flashlight. The fort has modern washroom facilities, including hot showers, although you have to walk across the open courtyard to reach them from the guest quarters, so come prepared for the weather.

If you don't mind being a bit out of the center, consider the family-friendly **Ambassador Hotel & Conference Centre** (1550 Princess St., 613/548-3605 or 800/267-7880, www.ambassadorhotel.com, $119-259 d), a sprawling 245-room brick complex on a busy road. Varying from small queen bed units to suites, all rooms have one-cup coffeemakers and mini fridges; the nicest face conservation land behind the property. For kids, the indoor pool and 100-foot-long waterslide are highlights. Rates include Wi-Fi and parking.

Conveniently located between downtown and the Queen's campus, **Hotel Belvedere** (141 King St. E., 613/548-1565 or 800/559-0584, www.hotelbelvedere.com, $129-259 d), built in 1880 as a private home, is traditionally appointed without feeling frilly or formal. Many of the 20 antiques-filled rooms, in sizes that vary from snug to spacious, have little nooks and crannies; a set of stairs might lead into a closet, or a kitchenette might hide behind the door. Rates include Wi-Fi, parking, and a light continental breakfast (English muffin, juice, tea or coffee) served in your room or in the high-ceilinged guest parlor.

Bon Echo Provincial Park

Combining a striking outdoor setting with interesting aboriginal history, **Bon Echo Provincial Park** (16151 Hwy. 41, RR 1, Cloyne, 613/336-2228, www.ontarioparks.com or www.bonechofriends.ca, early May-mid-Oct., $14.50 per vehicle) is worth the trip, whether for a day or longer. The park is 100 kilometers (60 miles) northwest of Kingston and 130 kilometers (80 miles) northeast of Peterborough, located roughly between Toronto and Ottawa.

ABORIGINAL PICTOGRAPHS

The park's centerpiece is **Mazinaw Rock,** jutting 100 meters (325 feet) out of Mazinaw Lake and now preserved as a National Historic Site. On the front surface of the predominantly granite rock are 260 aboriginal pictographs.

Unlike the aboriginal markings at Petroglyphs Provincial Park, which were carved into the rock, the Bon Echo pictographs were drawn or painted onto the rock face. But as at Petroglyphs, the exact date of the drawings, which include turtles, canoes, and underwater creatures, is unknown. Estimates put them at somewhere between 300 and 900 years old.

You can see the Bon Echo pictographs only from the water. In summer and fall, the 26-seat **Wanderer Ferry** (round-trip adults $15, under age 12 $5) runs 45-minute tours across the lake to the pictographs. The ferry normally departs hourly (11am-4pm Mon., Wed., and Fri.-Sun. late June-early Sept., noon-3pm Fri.-Sun. early Sept.-mid-Oct.) from the docks near the park visitors center; call the park or check the **Friends of Bon Echo Provincial Park** website (www.bonechofriends.ca) to confirm the schedule. Another way to reach the pictographs is by canoe or kayak. You can't disembark at this section of the rock, but you can paddle near the drawings. Rent canoes and kayaks at the lagoon.

ON TOP OF THE ROCK

If you're atop Mazinaw Rock, you can't see the pictographs; the rock is too steep to hike or climb down. But you can hike the 1.5-kilometer (0.9-mile) **Cliff Top Trail** to a lookout on the rock's summit; in the fall, you'll have a great vista across the reds, golds, and greens of the surrounding forests. The trail is steep, but there are stairs in the steepest sections.

Like the pictographs, the Cliff Top Trail is accessible only from the water. The **Mugwump Ferry** (10:30am-3:20pm Tues., Thurs., and Fri.-Sun. late June-early Sept., 11am-2:30pm Wed. and

Guests are encouraged to mingle at ★ **Rosemount Inn & Spa** (46 Sydenham St., 613/531-8844 or 888/871-8844, www.rosemountinn.com, $175-325 d), whether it's over afternoon tea in the lounge, on the spacious front porch, or at breakfast, where a set menu is served around the community table. The nine rooms in the main inn, a stone villa built in 1850, are all different, but throughout the building you'll find leaded-glass windows, oriental rugs, and four-poster beds. Two suites in the adjacent coach house are more modern; one two-level unit has a living area and a bedroom and bath upstairs.

INFORMATION AND SERVICES

Located in the former train station, the accommodating **Tourism Kingston Visitor Information Centre** (209 Ontario St., 613/548-4415 or 888/855-4555, www.visitkingston.ca, 9:30am-6pm Sun.-Wed., 9:30am-7pm Thurs.-Sat. May-June and early Sept.-mid-Oct., 9:30am-8pm Sun.-Wed., 9:30am-9pm Thurs.-Sat. July-early Sept., 10am-4pm Sun.-Thurs., 10am-5pm Fri.-Sat. mid-Oct.-Apr.) is in Confederation Park opposite City Hall. The information center has **free Wi-Fi** and two computers with **free Internet access.**

Fri.-Sun. early Sept.-mid-Oct., round-trip $5 pp) will shuttle you from the lagoon to the start of the trail. As with the Wanderer Ferry, it's a good idea to call the park or check the **Friends of Bon Echo Provincial Park** website (www.bonechofriends.ca) to confirm the Mugwump schedule. You can also canoe across the lagoon to the trailhead.

BEACHES AND HIKING TRAILS
You can swim in Mazinaw Lake from either **Main Beach** or **North Beach.** North Beach is sandy and good for kids, although the water tends to be a little colder. Take a short hike to **The Narrows,** a point just across a narrow section of water from the rock. You can't see the pictographs from here, but at sunset, the setting sun reflects its colors on Mazinaw Rock.

The park has several other hiking trails, ranging from the easy one-kilometer (0.6-mile) **Bon Echo Creek** route to the rugged 17-kilometer (10.5-mile) **Abes Loop.**

PRACTICALITIES
Bon Echo's 532 **campsites** spread out over several areas, including 333 tent sites ($42-45), 169 electrical sites ($47-52), and 30 backcountry sites (adults $10, ages 6-17 $5). There are also six yurts ($98), 12 rustic cabins ($142) sleeping up to five, and two "Exploration Tents" ($98), which can sleep five as well; one has a view of Mazinaw Rock. Sawmill Bay is designed primarily for tent camping; there are five walk-in sites directly on Upper Mazinaw Lake, and other sites within a short walk of North Beach. Some sites in the Fairview Campground are near, but not on, the lake. Across Highway 41 from Mazinaw Lake, Hardwood Hill Campground, a wooded area high up on a hill, feels more secluded than the lakeside campgrounds, though you're farther from the lake. Also on this side of the park is a series of canoe-in backcountry campsites on Joeperry and Pearson Lakes.

If you don't want to camp, rent the **Cabin on the Hill** ($170), an 1870s log cabin that's been updated with electricity, indoor plumbing, and a kitchen. It's a short walk from North Beach and has great views of the rock. The cabin has one bedroom, plus two sleeper sofas in the living room.

The park has no food concessions. There's a small market in the village of Cloyne, about a 10-minute drive south of the park, and a larger grocery in Northbrook, farther south on Highway 41.

GETTING THERE
Air
From the small **Kingston/Norman Rogers Airport** (YGK, 1114 Len Birchall Way, 613/389-6404 www.kingstonairport.ca), eight kilometers (five miles) west of the city center, **Air Canada** (www.aircanada.com) flies to Toronto several times a day. Although the closest major international airports are **Ottawa Airport** (YOW, 1000 Airport Pkwy., Ottawa, 613/248-2000, www.ottawa-airport.ca) and **Syracuse Hancock International Airport** (SYR, 1000 Col. Eileen Collins Blvd., Syracuse, NY, 315/454-4330 www.syrairport.org), there are more flight options and direct transportation via Toronto's **Pearson Airport** (YYZ, 6301 Silver Dart Dr., Mississauga, 416/247-7678 or 866/207-1690, www.torontopearson.com).

Megabus (866/488-4452, www.megabus.com) runs several daily buses between Pearson Airport and Kingston (3.25-3.5 hours, one-way adults $50). From Ottawa Airport to Kingston, you'll either need to rent a car or go from the airport to Ottawa's train or bus station and then continue to Kingston on VIA Rail or Greyhound bus.

Train
VIA Rail's Toronto-Ottawa and Toronto-Montreal trains both stop at the **Kingston**

Train Station (1800 John Counter Blvd., 888/842-7245, www.viarail.ca). The station is 6.5 kilometers (four miles) northwest of downtown. It's a short cab ride, or you can take Kingston Transit Bus no. 18.

Bus

From the **Kingston Inter-City Bus Terminal** (1175 John Counter Blvd., 613/547-4916), **Greyhound** (800/661-8747, www.greyhound.ca) operates several daily buses to Ottawa (2.5-2.75 hours, one-way adults $21-43, ages 2-11 $20-35). **Megabus** (866/488-4452, www.megabus.com) runs buses throughout the day between Kingston and Toronto (2.75-3 hours, one-way $22-66) and from Kingston to Montreal (3-3.25 hours, one-way $10-59). From the bus terminal to downtown (five kilometers, three miles), either take a cab or catch Kingston Transit Bus no. 2 or no. 18.

Car

Kingston is 265 kilometers (165 miles) east of Toronto via Highway 401. If you're coming from the west, the easiest way to reach downtown Kingston is to take exit 615 and follow Sir John A. Macdonald Boulevard south for about six kilometers (3.7 miles). Turn left onto King Street, which will pass the Queen's University campus and continue toward downtown.

From Ottawa, 195 kilometers (123 miles) northeast of Kingston, the fastest route is to follow Highway 416 south to Highway 401 west. Exit Highway 401 at Highway 15 (exit 623) and continue south to Highway 2. Turn right (west) onto Highway 2. You'll pass Fort Henry and then cross the bridge into downtown Kingston.

GETTING AROUND

You can explore Kingston without a car, since the city's downtown is compact and easy to walk around. You can also walk from the Queen's University campus to downtown (about 1.5 kilometers, 0.9 miles). If you do have a car, consider leaving it at your hotel

when you're venturing downtown; parking can be limited.

Kingston Transit (www.cityofkingston. ca, ages 15 and over $3, day pass $8), the city's public bus system, can take you to most visitor destinations. Use the "Trip Planner" feature on the website to plot your route.

Walking Tours

Canadian history comes alive on several **self-guided audio tours** through Kingston's historic district. Created by local writer Arthur Milnes in partnership with the city of Kingston, **In Sir John A.'s Footsteps** is a one-hour walk highlighting sights important to the city during the time that Sir John A. Macdonald, Canada's first prime minister, lived and worked here. Download the free **Kingston Ontario Walking Tours app**, which contains this and a dozen other tour routes. Get more information from the City of Kingston website (www.cityofkingston.ca) or the Visitor Information Centre.

Boat Tours

To see Kingston and the nearby Thousand Islands from the water, take one of the **1000 Islands Cruises** (1 Brock St., 613/549-5544 or 800/848-0011, www.1000islandscruises.ca, Apr.-Oct., call or check the website for schedules) that depart from the pier at the foot of Brock Street, near Confederation Park. The 90-minute Discovery Cruises (adults $34, ages 4-12 $22) introduce you to local history while cruising along the waterfront from Fort Henry to the Kingston Penitentiary. The three-hour Heart of the Islands trip (adults $45, ages 4-12 $29) combines a Kingston waterfront tour with a cruise around the westernmost Thousand Islands. They also offer lunch cruises and sunset dinner tours with live music.

VICINITY OF KINGSTON
Frontenac Provincial Park

You don't have to venture far from Kingston to get into the wilderness. The 5,200 hectares (12,849 acres) of **Frontenac Provincial**

Park (6700 Salmon Lake Rd., Sydenham, 613/376-3489, www.ontarioparks.com or www.frontenacpark.ca, $14.50 per vehicle) begin less than an hour's drive north of the city. Situated on the southernmost projection of the Canadian Shield, Frontenac has a Northern Ontario landscape that doesn't require a long trek to the north. It's a popular spot for **day-hiking,** with more than 160 kilometers (100 miles) of trails ranging in length from 1.5 to 21 kilometers (0.9-13 miles).

The park's 22 lakes make for good canoeing. Although rentals aren't available in the park, you can rent a canoe from nearby outfitters such as **Frontenac Outfitters** (6674 Bedford Rd., Sydenham, 613/376-6220, www.frontenac-outfitters.com, 9am-5pm daily Apr.-Oct., $50-65 per day), south of the park entrance; they also rent kayaks ($56/day) and stand-up paddleboards ($20-26 per hour). To work on your outdoor skills, take one of the park's **wilderness skills workshops,** offered year-round, including

kayaking, snowshoeing, fishing, wilderness navigation, winter camping, and more. For some workshops, there's no fee beyond the park admission, while others have an added charge.

While Frontenac has no car camping sites, the park's 48 backcountry **campsites** (adults $12, ages 6-17 $6) are accessible on foot or by canoe. Reservations are recommended on weekends from May to October; contact the **Ontario Parks Reservations Service** (888/668-7275, www.ontarioparks.com, reservation fee online $11, by phone $13).

The park entrance is north of the village of Sydenham, 40 kilometers (25 miles) north of Kingston. From Kingston, take Sydenham Road/Frontenac County Road 9 north for about 20 kilometers (12.5 miles). Turn left onto County Road 5 into Sydenham and watch for the park sign on your right, directing you to County Road 19. From here, it's a winding 13-kilometer (eight-mile) drive to Salmon Lake Road, which enters the park.

Following the Rideau Canal

A relaxing day or weekend trip between Kingston and Ottawa is to follow the route of the Rideau Canal. The canal runs 202 kilometers (126 miles), with 47 locks and several interesting small towns along the way. Highway 15 is the main north-south route through the canal region. You can see many of the region's highlights in the triangle of three towns: Smiths Falls, Perth, and Westport. The website for the **Rideau Heritage Route Tourism Association** (www.rideauheritageroute.ca) has additional information about the Rideau region.

BOATING
Want to navigate by water? **Le Boat** (1 Jasper Ave, Smiths Falls, 800/734-5491, www.leboat.com, mid-May-mid-Oct.) offers houseboating holidays along the canal. Trips begin and end in Smiths Falls, 75 kilometers (47 miles) southwest of Ottawa and 95 kilometers (59 miles) northeast of Kingston. You can arrange holidays from three nights to two weeks, navigating as many of the 24 lock stations and 47 locks as you'd like. If you want to go from Smiths Falls to Ottawa and back by boat, you'll need at least 10 days. No boating experience is required to pilot your vessel. Staff give you instruction before you set out and provide sample itineraries and things to bring. The houseboats, accommodating between 2 and 12 people, are equipped with linens, towels, dishes, and cooking utensils. Rental rates start at about $1,400 per boat for a three-night cruise.

SMITHS FALLS

Stop in Smiths Falls (www.smithsfalls.ca) to learn more about the canal's history. Parks Canada's **Rideau Canal Visitors Centre** (34 Beckwith St. S., 613/283-5170, www.pc.gc.ca, 9am-4pm daily late May-early Sept., donation) is housed in a 19th-century mill, where exhibits detail the canal's construction (1826-1832) and its subsequent role in the region's development. Check out the Smiths Falls Locks nearby, too.

Smiths Falls' **Heritage House Museum** (11 Old Sly's Rd., 613/283-6311, www.smithsfalls.ca, 10am-5pm Sat.-Sun. May, 10am-5pm Wed., Fri., Sun., and noon-8pm Thurs. and Sat. June-Oct., 10am-4pm Thurs.-Sun. Nov.-Dec., adults $4.50, seniors $4, ages 6-18 $3.50) exhibits regional history in an 1860s Victorian home. If you have kids in tow, they'll only be interested in the house's curiosity: a two-story privy. And no, you don't want to sit on the lower level.

Smiths Falls is 75 kilometers (47 miles) southwest of Ottawa and 95 kilometers (59 miles) northeast of Kingston, along Highway 15.

PERTH

Many of the Scottish stonemasons who built the Rideau Canal settled in Perth, leaving a legacy of elegant stone homes, including **Inge-Va** (66 Craig St., 613/498-3003, www.heritagetrust.on.ca, 10am-4pm Wed.-Sun. mid-June-Aug., adults $3, ages 6-16 $1.50), an 1823 late-Georgian stone residence that is also the site of an archaeological mystery. When archaeologists excavated the site of a privy used by the Radenhurst family, who lived at Inge-Va in the mid-1800s, they were surprised to find thousands of pieces of dishes and glasses. Apparently, the family had thrown out all of their kitchenware. Historians speculate that they may have desperately hoped to stop the spread of infectious diseases that claimed 5 of their 10 children.

A unique way to explore the town is with **Perth Through the Ages** (877/283-1283, www.classictheatre.ca, Wed.-Sun. late June-Aug., adults $15, under age 13 $7.50), a theatrical walking tour through the region's history, created in conjunction with Perth's Classic Theatre Festival. While the specific tour varies annually, costumed actors lead you around town and back in time, where you might learn about the Last Duel (an infamous 1833 shootout between two feuding law students) or Perth's role in creating the record-breaking Mammoth Cheese. Call or check the website for performance details and schedules.

Murphys Point Provincial Park (2243 Elm Grove Rd./County Rd. 21, 613/267-5060, www.ontarioparks.com or www.friendsofmurphyspoint.ca, $14.50 per vehicle) tells the story of a different heritage. The Silver Queen Mine was a mica mine that operated from 1903 to 1920 in what is now the park, with the minerals shipped out along the Rideau Canal. In summer, you can tour the former mine and learn more about life as an early 20th-century miner. Murphys Point also has 20 kilometers (12.5 miles) of hiking trails and a 160-site campground (tent sites $42-45, electrical sites $47-52, rustic cabin or yurt $142, deluxe tent $98). The park is 19 kilometers (12 miles) south of Perth, via County Roads 1 and 21.

Perth and its surrounding communities form one of Ontario's major **maple syrup-producing** areas. Maple sugaring season, when syrup producers tap their trees and turn sap into syrup, takes place in March and April. Several producers welcome visitors and operate seasonal restaurants, where you can learn about the syrup-making process and (more importantly) taste the maple goodies. **Wheelers Pancake House and Sugar Camp** (1001 Highland Line, McDonalds Corners, Lanark Highlands, 613/278-2090, www.wheelersmaple.com, 9am-3pm daily) is open year-round, while favorite maple-season destinations, open in March and April, include **Temple's Sugar Bush** (1700 Ferguson's Falls Rd./County Rd. 15, Lanark, 613/253-7000, www.templessugarbush.ca) and **Fulton's**

Pancake House and Sugar Bush (399 Sugar Bush Rd., Pakenham, 613/256-3867, www.fultons.ca).

Classic album covers, from Bob Marley to the Beatles, decorate the walls of **The Hungry 7** (34 Dufferin St., 613/466-0692, 11am-9pm Mon.-Sat., $10-17), a self-described "modern diner" on Highway 7. It's run by two former Ottawa chefs who are cooking up burgers, sandwiches (try the grilled veggie), pastas, and potpies for Perth locals and hungry travelers.

Perth and District Chamber of Commerce (40 Sunset Blvd., 613/267-3200, www.perthchamber.com) can give you more information about the region. Perth is off Highway 7, a scenic alternative route connecting Toronto and Ottawa. It's also 20 kilometers (12 miles) west of Smiths Falls via Highway 43.

WESTPORT

One of the prettiest towns in the Rideau region is Westport, perched on the shores of Upper Rideau Lake, 30 kilometers (18 miles) southwest of Perth, along Highway 10. Stroll around town, or head up the ridge overlooking both the town and the lake to the 325-hectare (800-acre) **Foley Mountain Conservation Area** (off Hwy. 10, 613/273-3255, www.rvca.ca, dawn-dusk daily, $6 per vehicle). Several hiking trails wend through the woods; the lookout at Spy Rock has the best views.

A traditional family-run country inn, **The Cove Inn** (2 Bedford-on-the-Water, 613/273-3636 or 888/268-3466, www.coveinn.com, $130-180 d) has nine simple, well-kept guest rooms in the 1872 main building, which was originally a private home, and six additional rooms in the Victorian-style 1876 Fredenburgh House across the street. The **Cove's water-view dining room** (11:30am-8pm Sun.-Thurs., 11:30am-9pm Fri.-Sat., $14-30) serves pub-style dishes—burgers or hot turkey sandwiches—as well as more substantial dinner fare, with live music several nights a week.

The Thousand Islands and the St. Lawrence

The region known as the Thousand Islands extends roughly 80 kilometers (50 miles) from Kingston to Brockville, straddling both sides of the St. Lawrence River, which divides Canada and the United States. The "thousand" is more of an estimate; officially, the area has 1,864 islands. On some islands, you'll see a single home or cottage, while others support year-round communities. To be counted among the Thousand Islands, an island must be above water year-round and have at least two living trees. Two-thirds of the islands are in Canadian waters, although the overall area of the Thousand Islands is split equally between Canada and the United States.

The Thousand Islands are part of the **Frontenac Arch Biosphere Reserve** (www.frontenacarchbiosphere.ca), a United Nations designation designed to protect and promote "globally significant ecological features." The Biosphere Reserve is a 270,000-hectare (667,000-acre) region, rather than a single site, bounded roughly by the towns of Gananoque, Brockville, and Westport, and the area surrounding Frontenac Provincial Park. The Frontenac Arch's significant feature is a ridge of ancient granite that's part of the Canadian Shield, more commonly associated with the rugged landscape of the Canadian north than with Southern Ontario's flatter topography.

Long part of traditional Iroquois and Mohawk territory, the region along the St. Lawrence River's northern banks linked its fortunes to U.S.-Canadian relations. During and after the American Revolution in the late 1700s, Loyalists (American colonists who remained loyal to the British crown) fled across the border into Canada. Many of these Loyalists settled along the St. Lawrence in towns like Brockville, Prescott, and Morrisburg, which still have historic sites reflecting the Loyalist legacy.

Many attractions in the Thousand Islands are seasonal, operating from May through mid-October.

GANANOQUE AND VICINITY

The town of Gananoque—pronounced "Gan-uh-NOCK-way"—is the gateway to the Thousand Islands region. Learn more about the area's history at the small **Arthur Child Heritage Museum** (125 Water St., 613/382-2535 or 877/217-7391, www.1000islandsheritagemuseum.com, 10am-5pm daily May-early Sept., 10am-4pm early Sept.-Oct., donation) near the waterfront, where exhibits trace the region's development from its original First Nations inhabitants to the War of 1812 to the "Golden Age" of the Thousand Islands in the late 1800s, when the region became a popular tourist destination for wealthy Americans.

For views across the Thousand Islands, ride the elevator to the top of the **1000 Islands Tower** (Hill Island, www.1000islandstower.com, 9am-6pm daily May-mid-Oct., adults $12, ages 6-12 $6.75), which has three observation levels. The Tower, on Hill Island, is located between the Canadian and U.S. spans of the Thousand Islands International Bridge, 20 kilometers (12.5 miles) east of Gananoque and 40 kilometers (25 miles) west of Brockville. It's in Canadian territory, so you don't need your passport if you're coming from the Ontario side. From Highway 401, take exit 661 (Bridge to USA/Hill Island). If you're coming from the U.S. side, follow I-81 to the bridge and clear Canadian customs (remember your passport), and you'll see the tower on the right.

★ Thousand Islands Boat Tours

The best way to appreciate the Thousand Islands is from the water. **Gananoque Boat Line** (280 Main St., 613/382-2144 or 888/717-4837, www.ganboatline.com, May-mid-Oct.) operates 1-hour, 2.5-hour, and 5-hour cruises around the islands, leaving from the Gananoque waterfront. The one-hour "Beauty of the Islands" trips (10:30am, noon, 1:30pm, 3pm, 4:30pm, and 7pm daily late June-early Sept., call or check the website for spring and fall schedule, adults $25, seniors $22, ages 6-12 $14) cruise around the islands closest to shore, with commentary about their flora and fauna.

The 2.5-hour "Lost Ships of the 1000 Islands Cruise" (10:30am, 12:30pm, 1:30pm, 3:30pm, and 4:30pm daily late June-early Sept., call or check the website for spring and fall schedule, adults $38, seniors $33, ages 6-12 $15) provides recorded commentary about the history and development of the islands, giving you a more detailed picture of who has lived on various islands, past and present. You also learn about the more than 200 shipwrecks that occurred in the St. Lawrence River region, many of which still lie below the water. A cool feature: you'll see underwater images of the shipwrecks projected on overhead video screens as the cruise boat passes over their positions. These tours cruise past, but don't stop at, Boldt Castle.

BOLDT CASTLE

Visiting **Boldt Castle** (Heart Island, NY, www.boldtcastle.com, 10am-7:30pm daily late June-Aug., 10am-6:30pm mid-May-late June and late Sept., 10am-5:30pm late Sept.-mid-Oct., adults US$9.50, ages 5-12 US$6.50) is a Thousand Islands highlight. George C. Boldt, owner of New York City's Waldorf Astoria Hotel, began constructing the grandiose 120-room stone castle in 1900 in honor of his wife, Louise. For several years, a crew of more than 300 worked on the building. Unfortunately, Louise died suddenly in 1904, and George

Gananoque

ordered that all work be halted. He never returned to the property. The castle was abandoned until 1977, when the Thousand Islands Bridge Authority acquired and began restoring the property, which is now available for tours.

Gananoque Boat Line's Boldt Castle tours (5 hours, 10am and 3pm daily mid-May-late Sept., adults $49, seniors $42, ages 6-12 $18) depart the Gananoque docks; the cruise includes a two-hour stopover at Boldt Castle. You'll need to buy castle admission in addition to the boat tour ticket.

If you're short on time, Boldt Castle trips run by **Rockport Cruises** (23 Front St., Rockport, 613/659-3402 or 800/563-8687, www.rockportcruises.com, Sat.-Sun. late May-late June, daily late June-early Sept., Wed.-Sun. early-late Sept., adults $34, seniors $31, ages 5-12 $15) take 3.5 hours, including two hours to explore the castle. They depart from the town of Rockport, which is closer to the castle, 19 kilometers (12 miles) east of Gananoque. Departures from Rockport are generally at 10:30am, 12:30pm, and 2:30pm, but call or check online to confirm seasonal variations. Rockport Cruises offer a variety of shorter island cruises as well.

Heart Island, where Boldt Castle is located, is in the United States. Coming from Canada, you're crossing an **international border** and you must have a valid **passport.**

Helicopter Tours

As beautiful as the Thousand Islands are from the water, they're even more striking from the air. You can see them on a flight with **1000 Islands Helicopter Tours** (88 County Rd. 32, 613/382-3888 or 855/855-4354, www.1000islandshelicoptertours.com). Opt for a 10-minute island overview ($99 pp), add a loop over Boldt Castle on a 20-minute tour ($159 pp), or take a 30-minute flight ($229 pp) that takes in Boldt Castle as well as Singer Castle, which Frederick Gilbert Bourne, president of the Singer Sewing Machine Company, built in the early 1900s.

Sports and Recreation

A more active way to explore the Thousand Islands is by kayak. **1000 Islands Kayaking** (110 Kate St., 613/329-6265, www.1000islandskayaking.com, May-Oct., half-day single $45, tandem $75, full-day single $55, tandem $95) rents kayaks and leads guided trips (half day, 9am-noon or 1pm-4pm, adults $85, kids $65; full-day, 9am-4pm, adults $135, kids $85). They'll tailor an excursion to your interests and abilities, whether

you want to learn about the history or natural life of the islands or get a good workout. They accept walk-ins, but if you have specific interests or requests, give them a call in advance. They rent camping gear (handy if you'd like to camp in Thousand Islands National Park), offer guided multiday paddling tours, and teach kayaking lessons, including a one-day introduction to paddling.

You can cycle between Gananoque and Brockville along the pretty 37-kilometer (23-mile) section of the **Waterfront Trail** (www.waterfronttrail.org), a paved, gently rolling route that parallels the Thousand Islands Parkway. The **Tourism 1000 Islands Visitor Centre** (787 King St. E., 613/381-8427, www.1000islandstourism.com, daily May-Oct) rents bikes.

Entertainment

From May through October, the well-regarded **Thousand Islands Playhouse** (185 South St., 613/382-7020, www.1000islandsplayhouse. com), a professional company established in 1982, presents 7-10 plays in repertory in two riverfront theaters. The deck of Springer Theatre, overlooking the river, must be one of the prettiest theater lobbies anywhere.

Inside an 1860 carriage parts factory,

view of the Thousand Islands via helicopter

Gananoque Brewing Company (9 King St. E., 613/463-9131, www.ganbeer.com, noon-9pm daily May-Oct., 1pm-8pm Thurs.-Sat. Nov.-Apr.) makes a rotating assortment of beers, among them easy-drinking Rusty Putter Lager, Bellringer IPA, and Thursty Pike Pilsner, which takes its name from Thurston Pike Davis, great-grandfather of Bruce Davis, the brewery's "president and instigator." Try a tasting flight or a glass in the outdoor beer garden.

Shopping

At **Heather Haynes Gallery** (27 King St. E., 613/767-9090, www.heatherhaynes.com, 11am-5pm Mon.-Sat., 11am-4pm Sun. May-mid-Oct., 11am-5pm Wed.-Sat., 11am-4pm Sun. mid-Oct.-Apr.), local painter and multimedia artist Haynes shows her own work and that of other local artists.

Beggars Banquet Books (126 King St. E., 613/463-8998, www.beggarsbanquetbooks.com, 10am-5pm Mon.-Sat., 11am-4pm Sun.) stocks a large selection of new and used titles, including works by local authors.

Food

Wander along King Street East to find casual eateries. You're close enough to Kingston that you could head there for more dining choices.

Local favorite **Purple House Café** (165 Main St., 613/463-9296, 11:30am-9:30pm, $11-18) serves pizzas and salads outside in its lovely flower-filled garden or at the 1950s-era diner-style Formica tables inside the eponymous purple house. Homemade desserts, coffee, beer, and wine round out the menu.

Under new ownership, the former Socialist Pig Coffeehouse has morphed into funky, diner-style **Laverne's Eatery** (21 King St. E., 613/463-8800, www.laverneseatery.com, 8am-2pm Mon.-Tues., 8am-4pm Wed.-Sun.). It offers coffee and pastries, plus omelets, pancakes, salads, and sandwiches, including a smoked brisket banh mi.

Part Canadian diner and part Eastern European schnitzel parlor, the homey **Maple Leaf Restaurant/The Czech Snitzel House** (65 King St. E., 613/382-7666, www.mapleleafrestaurant.ca, 4pm-9:30pm Tues., 11am-9:30pm Wed.-Sun. May-mid-Oct., 11am-9:30pm Wed.-Sun. mid-Oct.-mid-Dec., $10-22) serves homemade borscht, spaetzle, and delicious schnitzel in either chicken or pork varieties alongside burgers, omelets, and deli sandwiches.

Modern Italian fare is on the menu at **Riva Restaurant** (45 King St. W., 613/887-2487, www.rivarestaurant.ca, 11:30am-9:30pm daily summer, 5pm-9pm Wed.-Sun. winter, lunch $9-19, dinner $12-25), a classy multi-room space where exposed brick walls and wide-board floors offset more contemporary finishes. Choose from salads, pizzas, and pastas, like the gnocchi with short-rib ragù or linguine alla carbonara (bacon-cream sauce), as well as veal marsala or steak.

Accommodations

Gananoque has several inns and B&Bs in historic buildings around the center of town. If you're looking for chain motels, like the **Quality Inn & Suites 1000 Islands** (650 King St. E., 613/382-1453, www.qualityinn1000islands.com, $95-279 d), they're jumbled together on King Street East.

In many First Nations legends, North America was called Turtle Island. Ted and Chris, owners of **Turtle Island B&B** (415 Stone St. S., 613/382-7261 or 855/382-7261, www.turtleislandbb.com, $129 d), chose this name for their relaxed lodging, where they display their collection of aboriginal arts and crafts. The three air-conditioned guest rooms in this 1922 brick Victorian are simple but cozy, with quilt-topped beds and First Nations prints on the walls. Fresh-baked scones and Belgian waffles are among the breakfast specialties.

It's easy to spot the **Sleepy Hollow Bed & Breakfast** (95 King St. W., 613/382-4377 or 866/426-7422, www.sleepyhollowbb.ca, $120-180 d), a Victorian "painted lady" decked out in yellow, purple, and green. This rambling 1905 home still has its original tin ceiling and oak wainscoting on the first floor. Upstairs, the seven guest rooms are homey and a bit old-fashioned, with period furnishings. There's a pool table for guests, and you can make yourself at home in the octagonal dining room, where owners Don and Marion Matthews serve a full hot breakfast. Wi-Fi is included in the rates.

Gananoque's only waterfront hotel is the **Gananoque Inn** (550 Stone St. S., 613/382-2165 or 888/565-3101, www.gananoqueinn. com, $169-498), which has 53 rooms across several buildings. Some of the traditional rooms in the 1896 main inn have verandas overlooking the water. The newer annex units are larger and more upscale, some with whirlpool tubs and fireplaces. The small spa offers the expected range of massages, facials, and other treatments, and the inn has two restaurants: the more formal river-view **Watermark** (from 5pm Wed.-Sun. June, daily July-Oct., dinner $25-42) and mellow **Muskie Jake's Tap and Grill** (daily year-round, call for seasonal hours, $14-28).

Information and Services

Tourism 1000 Islands (787 King St. E., 613/381-8427, www.1000islandstourism. com, daily May-Oct) runs a visitors center that provides information about Gananoque and the surrounding area. The **Thousand Islands International Tourism Council** (800/847-5263, www.visit1000islands.com) is another source of information about the islands on both the Canadian and U.S. sides of the border.

Getting There and Around

Gananoque is 30 kilometers (19 miles) east of Kingston, 290 kilometers (180 miles) northeast of Toronto, and 160 kilometers (100 miles) south of Ottawa. If you're traveling east on Highway 401, take exits 645 or 647; heading west, take exits 645 or 648. The prettiest route between Gananoque and Brockville is the 52-kilometer (32-mile) Thousand Islands Parkway, which hugs the shore parallel to Highway 401. Note that the parkway is not

the same road as Highway 2, which also parallels Highway 401.

While you don't need a car within Gananoque—it's a short walk among downtown, the waterfront, and many of the accommodations—there's no convenient bus or train service into town.

THOUSAND ISLANDS NATIONAL PARK

The first Canadian national park east of the Rockies, **Thousand Islands National Park** (613/923-5261 or 888/773-8888, www.pc.gc. ca, mid-May-mid-Oct.) was established in 1904, encompassing more than 20 islands in the St. Lawrence River. On the mainland, stop into the park's **Mallorytown Landing Visitors Centre** (1121 Thousand Islands Pkwy., Mallorytown, 613/923-5261, 10am-4pm Sat.-Sun. mid-May-mid-June and early Sept.-mid-Oct., 10am-4pm daily mid-June-early Sept., parking $6.80 per vehicle), between Gananoque and Brockville, to learn more about the region's natural and cultural history.

Two short and easy **walking trails,** from 850 meters (0.5 miles) to 1.1 kilometers (0.7 miles), start at the visitors center. For additional hiking options, head to the park's **Jones Creek area** (1270 Thousand Islands Pkwy.), east of the visitors center off the Thousand Islands Parkway. West of the visitors center, closer to Gananoque, you can hike at the **Landon Bay Centre** (302 Thousand Islands Pkwy., 613/382-2719, www. frontenacarchbiosphere.ca).

If you don't have your own boat, the best way to explore the park islands is to rent a kayak or book a paddling tour with **1000 Islands Kayaking** (110 Kate St., Gananoque, 613/329-6265, www.1000islandskayaking. com). The **Misty Isles Lodge** (25 River Rd., Lansdowne, 613/382-4232, www.mistyisles. ca) has boat rentals and offers tours as well; advance reservations are required.

The national park has 61 rustic **campsites** ($15.70) spread across several islands; 27 can be reserved through the **Parks Canada** reservation service (877/737-3783, www.reservation.pc.gc.ca, reservation fee online $11, by phone $13.50), while the remainder are first come, first served. You need a boat, canoe, or kayak to access these island campsites. You can also stay in an **oTENTik** (www.reservation.pc.gc.ca, $100), a park-managed platform tent that sleeps up to six. There are three oTENTiks on McDonald Island and two on Gordon Island (both islands have composting toilets but no running water), and five more on the mainland near the Mallorytown Landing Visitors Centre, which has restroom facilities.

If you're not traveling with camping gear, consider the park's **equipped camping service** (first night $55, subsequent nights $20). Park staff will supply you with a tent and sleeping pads for six, a camp stove, cooking gear, and dishes and utensils. You still need to bring sleeping bags or bedding, food, flashlights, and whatever other items you need. Reserve your gear at least a week in advance; call **1000 Islands Kayaking** (613/329-6265, www.1000islandskayaking.com) if you need equipment for island camping, and call the park office (613/923-5261) to reserve gear for a stay in an oTENTik on the mainland.

BROCKVILLE AND VICINITY

As you wander through the town of Brockville, on the St. Lawrence River at the east end of the Thousand Islands, you'll notice a number of grand Victorian homes, though none is grander than the mansion that local resident George Fulford built at the turn of the 20th century.

★ Fulford Place

Entrepreneur and politician George Taylor Fulford (1852-1905) made his fortune hawking "Pink Pills for Pale People." He had bought the rights to these pills, a simple iron supplement, for $53.01, and successfully marketed his wonder drug as he traveled the world in the late 1800s.

Fulford used the considerable proceeds to build **Fulford Place** (287 King St. E., 613/498-3003, www.heritagetrust.on.ca, adults $6, seniors, students, and ages 7 and over $5), an opulent 35-room Edwardian mansion overlooking the St. Lawrence River, where he lived with his wife Mary White Fulford (1856-1949) and their three children. The house was completed in 1901, but sadly, Fulford enjoyed the fruits of his labors for only a few years. In 1905, he became the first Canadian to die in an automobile accident.

The 1,900-square-meter (20,000-square-foot) home is made of marble and filled with sumptuous details—Honduran mahogany ceilings, silk wallpaper, and original stained glass windows. Many of the furnishings on view belonged to the Fulford family. Frederick Law Olmsted, who designed New York's Central Park, landscaped the Fulford Place gardens.

The schedule for Fulford Place **tours** (generally 10am-5pm daily late May-early Sept., last tour at 4pm) changes seasonally; call or check the website to confirm tour hours.

Fulford Place is east of downtown Brockville on King Street, which becomes Highway 2 on either end of town.

Homewood Museum

One of the oldest houses in Ontario, a Georgian-style stone home built in 1799-1800 is now the **Homewood Museum** (1372 Hwy. 2, Maitland, 613/498-3003, www.heritagetrust.on.ca, 10am-5pm Wed.-Sun. late May-early Sept., adults $3, under age 16 $1.50, combination ticket with Fulford Place $6). Seven generations of the Jones family lived here, and unlike many historic homes, all the furnishings inside belonged to the family, including the four-poster bed, the china and silver, and the early 19th-century surgical tools. The original owner, Solomon Jones (1756-1822), was a Loyalist and the area's first physician. Guides take you on 30-45-minute tours of the house.

Homewood Museum is east of the town of Maitland, between Brockville and Prescott. From Highway 401, take the Maitland exit and go south to Highway 2. Turn east onto Highway 2 and continue about two kilometers (1.25 miles) to the house.

Many members of the Jones family are buried in the **Blue Church Cemetery,** where numerous graves date to the late 1700s and early 1800s. The cemetery is also the final resting place of Barbara Heck, a founder of the Methodist Church. You'll find the graveyard three kilometers (1.8 miles) east of Homewood on Highway 2.

The Aquatarium

Part hands-on aquarium, part regional museum, and part adventure center, **The Aquatarium** (Tall Ships Landing, 6 Broad St., 613/342-6789, www.aquatarium.ca, 10am-5pm daily late May-early Sept., 10am-5pm Wed.-Sun. early Sept.-late May, adults $20, seniors and ages 13-17 $15, ages 4-12 $10) illustrates the Thousand Islands' maritime history and the fish, birds, and other creatures that populate its lands and waters. For the kids, there are touch tanks with crabs, starfish, and other sea life, and you can watch daily feedings in the otter tank. Multimedia exhibits let you take a virtual Thousand Islands cruise, pilot a Boston whaler, or see who wins a virtual scull race (row hard!).

Adventurers ages 8 and up can navigate a **high ropes course** rigged in a tall ship, and if you dare, free-fall—using a magnetic braking device—12 meters (40 feet) in the **AquaDrop.** The ropes course, including one AquaDrop, requires an additional $11.50 ticket; each subsequent AquaDrop is $2.

The Aquatarium is on the waterfront in downtown Brockville. From King Street (Highway 2), take Broad Street south toward the river.

Sports and Recreation

Hundreds of ships were sunk in the St. Lawrence River over the past several centuries, and many of these wrecks are now accessible to scuba divers. **Dive Brockville** (12 Water St. E., 613/345-2800, www.divebrockville.com) can organize dives and supply you with gear.

In the woods off the Thousand Islands Parkway, between Brockville and Gananoque, **Skywood Eco Adventure** (1278 Thousand Islands Pkwy., Mallorytown, 613/923-5120 or 844/470-4947, www.skywoodzip.com, 9am-5pm mid-May-Oct.) lets you play in the forest canopy, navigating an **Adventure Course** (3 hours, adults $55, ages 12-15 $48, ages 9-11 $42) that combines bridges, swings, nets, zip lines, and other aerial challenges. While the Adventure Course incorporates routes for beginner, intermediate, and more advanced adventurers, younger kids can try the **Discovery Courses** (2 hours, ages 5 and over $28), where the challenges are closer to the ground. Another experience is a two-hour guided **Zip Line Tour** (adults $62, ages 12-15 $57) over eight zip lines and bridges. Skywood has Canada's first permanent accessible zip line, the **Discovery Zip Line** (1 hour, ages 9 and over $25), which is also a good introduction for anyone new to zip lining. The Skywood website details age and weight restrictions for each activity. Reservations are recommended.

Food

Pick up a coffee and pastry at **Tait's Fresh Start Bakery** (31 King St. W., 613/865-8800, www.taitsfreshstart.com, 8am-5pm Mon.-Fri., 8am-4pm Sat.). For a light lunch, try **Boboli** (32 King St. W., 613/498-2957, 8am-5pm Mon.-Sat.), which makes homemade soup and deli sandwiches on freshly baked bread.

At **Georgian Dragon Ale House** (72 King St., 613/865-8224, 11am-11pm Mon.-Thurs., 11am-2am Fri., 9am-2am Sat., 9am-11pm Sun., $10-15), a traditional English pub, you can hang out over a beer, a burger, or a hearty Guinness pie. On weekends they serve good-value breakfast specials.

Information and Services

For more information about the Brockville area, contact the **Brockville and District Chamber of Commerce Tourism Office** (10 Market St. W., 613/342-4357 or 888/251-7676, www.brockvilletourism.com, 8am-5pm daily late May-mid-June, 8am-6pm daily mid-June-early Sept., 8:30am-4:30pm Mon.-Fri. early Sept.-late May).

Getting There and Around

Brockville is 55 kilometers (35 miles) northeast of Gananoque and 110 kilometers (68 miles) south of Ottawa via Highway 401 or Highway 2.

VIA Rail (888/842-7245, www.viarail.ca) trains run to Brockville Station (141 Perth St.) from Toronto (3-3.75 hours, one-way adults $50-167), Kingston (0.75 hours, one-way adults $23-51), and Ottawa (1.25 hours, one-way adults $25-65). The train station is about one kilometer (0.6 miles) northwest of downtown.

Megabus (866/488-4452, www.megabus.com) stops in Brockville from Kingston (one hour, one-way $1-59), Montreal (2.5 hours, one-way $10-59), and Toronto (4 hours, $10-59). The bus drops you in the parking lot of the Food Basics store (3049 Jefferson Dr.), north of Highway 401, about two kilometers (1.2 miles) from downtown. The Megabus depot is on the north side of Highway 401, and downtown is on the south; it's better to take a cab rather than trying to walk.

It's easiest to explore the region if you have a car, but Brockville's downtown area is compact and walkable. Fulford Place is 1.5 kilometers (0.9 miles) east of downtown.

PRESCOTT

Settled by the British in 1787, Prescott became a military post to defend Canada's border. Fort Wellington, now the **Fort Wellington National Historic Site** (370 Vankoughnet St., at King St., 613/925-2896, www.pc.gc.ca, 10am-5pm daily July-early Sept., 10am-5pm Thurs.-Mon. late May-June and early Sept.-mid-Oct., adults $3.90, seniors $3.40), was built during the War of 1812 to protect shipping routes along the St. Lawrence River from U.S. attack.

Nowadays, guides in period costumes demonstrate 19th-century games, crafts, open-hearth cooking, and rifle and cannon handling. The visitors center's exhibits fill in more details about the fort's role during the War of 1812, and in summer, you can take a guided tour of the fort (1:30pm Sat.-Sun. July-Aug., $7.30). Check the website for whiskey tastings and other special events.

MORRISBURG
★ Upper Canada Village

Walk back into the 1860s when you enter the gates of **Upper Canada Village** (13740 County Rd. 2, 613/543-4328 or 800/437-2233, www.uppercanadavillage.com, 9:30am-5pm daily early May-early Sept., 9:30am-5pm Wed.-Sun. early Sept.-late Sept., adults $20, seniors $18, ages 13-18 $16, ages 6-12 $13), one of Ontario's largest and best-preserved historic villages.

Not only do costumed interpreters staff all the village buildings, going about their business as 19th-century millers, shopkeepers, tavern-keepers, and bakers, they'll enthusiastically tell you about life on the cusp of the Industrial Revolution, as Upper Canada was transforming from farm country to a more mechanized society. In the woolen mill, staff operate original carding and spinning machines, powered by a water turbine that replaced the "old" technology of the spinning wheel. In the gristmill, staff grind grains that the village bakers use to bake bread, and in the sawmill, they're splitting logs with their newfangled machines. There's a cheese factory and a school, a dressmaker and a village doctor, a tinsmith, a print shop, a blacksmith, even a farm, complete with live animals.

Start in the multimedia Discovery Centre, which puts the village into its historical context. The story begins with the indigenous inhabitants (you can listen to audio clips in the Mohawk language) and continues with the Loyalists who settled here after the U.S. Revolutionary War. More exhibits explain the region's ongoing development from the Industrial Revolution into the 20th century. Kids have plenty of special activities, too. They can dress in traditional garb, learn to milk a cow, and ride along the village canal on a horse-drawn barge.

You can easily visit Upper Canada Village on a day trip from Ottawa, 80 kilometers (50 miles) to the northwest. Pick up Highway 31, which continues south all the way to Morrisburg. Turn left (east) on County Road 2; the village is 11 kilometers (6.8 miles) to the east.

From Gananoque, 110 kilometers (68 miles) to the west, follow Highway 401 to exit 758 (Upper Canada Rd.), go south, then turn left on County Road 2. From there, it's two kilometers (1.25 miles) east to the village.

Upper Canada Bird Sanctuary

Every fall, thousands of geese pass through the **Upper Canada Bird Sanctuary** (5591 County Rd. 2, Ingleside, 613/537-2024, www. stlawrenceparks.com, trails daily year-round) as they migrate south for the winter. At this 9,000-hectare (22,000-acre) preserve of woods, marsh, pastures, and waterways, you might also see great blue herons, wild turkeys, hawks, ducks, and a wide variety of common and less common birds. Even if you're not a birder, the sanctuary is a pleasant place for a walk or hike, with eight kilometers (five miles) of self-guided nature trails; in winter,

the trails are open for cross-country skiing. The visitors center (mid-May-late Oct.) has nature exhibits about the area.

The sanctuary is 14 kilometers (nine miles) east of Morrisburg, off County Road 2, near Ingleside. From Highway 401, take exits 758 or 770.

Long Sault Parkway Beaches

East of Upper Canada Village, the 11-kilometer (seven-mile) tree-lined **Long Sault Parkway** makes a scenic detour off County Road 2, crossing 11 small islands in the St. Lawrence River. At the parkway's east end, **Mille Roches Beach** (15890 Long Sault Parkway, Long Sault) is the largest public beach along the St. Lawrence River corridor, with a sandy swimming area, snack bar, picnic area, and canoe rentals. Fronting the river toward the parkway's west end, **Woodlands Beach** (15174 Long Sault Parkway, Ingleside) has swimming and picnic areas, too.

St. Lawrence Parks Commission (613/543-4328 or 800/437-2233, www.parks. on.ca) manages both beaches, which are open weekends from mid-May through mid-June, then daily until early September. Beach fees are $6 per adult (ages 13 and up) and $4.25 for seniors, up to a maximum of $17 per vehicle.

It's back to the 19th century at Upper Canada Village.

Entertainment and Events

In a theater that was once a toothbrush factory, the professional company at **Upper Canada Playhouse** (12320 County Rd. 2, 613/543-3713 or 877/550-3650, www.uppercanadaplayhouse.com, Apr.-Dec.) presents several comedies and other light plays every year.

Food and Accommodations

Sleep like a pioneer at **Upper Canada Village** (613/543-4328 or 800/437-2233, www.uppercanadavillage.com), an especially fun idea for families. Montgomery House ($195/night), a 19th-century log cabin, looks rustic, but inside, between the log walls and wide pine floors, are a living room with couches and a TV, a double Murphy bed, a full kitchen, and two baths. Upstairs under the eaves are six single beds. Linens are provided, and while officially there's no Internet service, you may be able to pick up the village's free Wi-Fi. The larger Guest House ($275/night) is a restored farmhouse with a main-floor living area, country kitchen, TV/DVD, computer with Internet access, and washer-dryer. Three bedrooms upstairs sleep eight total.

About 10 kilometers (six miles) west of Upper Canada Village in the town of Morrisburg is the lavishly decorated ★ **Russell Manor B&B** (36 1st St., 613/543-3871 or 866/401-7472, www.russellmanorbb.com, $115-150 s, $125-160 d). Starting from the upscale parlor with cream-hued rugs and overstuffed sofas, owners Michael Burton (the interior decorator) and Ron Currie (the breakfast chef) have created an elegant, romantic retreat in their 1870s manor house. Upstairs are three two-room suites with separate sitting areas, Victorian furnishings, voluminous draperies, and fine linens; a fourth room is a snug studio overlooking the garden, and a fifth is a sunny twin-bed room on the main floor.

A friendly, old-fashioned two-story motel, **McIntosh Country Inn** (12495 Hwy. 2 E., 613/543-37881 or 888/229-2850, www.mcintoshcountryinn.com, $114-209 d) has 59 basic country-style rooms in its vaguely Old English building. All have Wi-Fi, flat-screen TVs, mini fridges, and coffeemakers; some offer in-room whirlpool tubs. Like any British-style lodging, there's a pub, Mac's Tavern, where you can stop for a pint. A small outdoor pool is open in the summer.

Part curio store, part art gallery, and part old-time coffee shop, the **Basket Case Cafe** (27 Main St., 613/543-0002, 10am-6pm

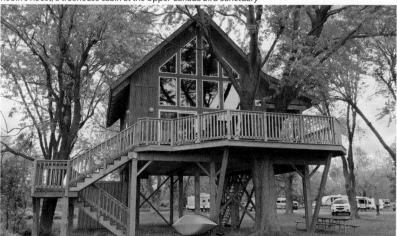

Robin's Roost, a treehouse cabin at the Upper Canada Bird Sanctuary

Tues.-Sun., call for off-season hours, $5-10), in a strip mall on County Road 2, is as crammed with stuff as your grandmother's attic. But no matter, they cook up tasty breakfasts, soups, sandwiches, and pies.

CAMPING

The **St. Lawrence Parks Commission** (613/543-4328 or 800/437-2233, www.parks. on.ca), which operates Upper Canada Village and the bird sanctuary, manages several campgrounds in the Morrisburg area. You can book campsites online beginning in February for the coming season (reservation fee $11.75).

The 300-site **Riverside-Cedar Campground** (13180 County Rd. 2, 613/543-3287, mid-May-mid-Oct., tent sites $35-37, electrical sites $41-49, cabins $95-112), along the St. Lawrence River, is closest to Upper Canada Village. Five camping cabins are available for rent.

The 69-site **Upper Canada Migratory Bird Sanctuary Campground** (5781 Country Rd. 2, Ingelside, 613/537-2024, mid-May-mid-Oct., tent sites $37-40, electrical sites $49-59, cabins $95/night Mon.-Thurs., $112/night Fri.-Sat.) is on the bird sanctuary grounds. Campsites have both water and electricity, or you can book one of the two waterfront camping cabins. The campground has showers, and there is a swimming beach along the river.

A cool lodging option in the sanctuary's campground is the treehouse-like **Robin's Roost** ($301/night), built into the trees with a deck overlooking the river. This elevated cabin can sleep six, with a queen-bed in the bedroom, a futon sofa in the living room, and a sleeping loft with a queen bed. There's a kitchenette and bathroom inside, plus an outdoor shower (or you can use the standard showers in the campground). Robin's Roost guests have use of a canoe that you can launch from the adjacent riverfront beach.

At **Mille Roches Campground** (15805 Long Sault Pkwy., Long Sault, mid-May-early Sept., tent sites $35-37, electrical sites $41-49), which occupies two small islands along the Long Sault Parkway, 63 of the 219 campsites are waterfront. This campground has restrooms, showers, and a playground.

Getting There and Around

From Ottawa, County Road 31 runs 80 kilometers (50 miles) south to Morrisburg. Following the speedier Highway 416 to Highway 401 is longer (120 kilometers, 75 miles), but it will take you about the same amount of time. Morrisburg is 140 kilometers (87 miles) northeast of Kingston along Highway 401. **VIA Rail** (www.viarail.ca) trains from Toronto or Ottawa stop in Brockville (west of Morrisburg) and in Cornwall (east of Morrisburg), but you really need a car to get around the area.

Ottawa

Look for ★ to find recommended
sights, activities, dining, and lodging.

Highlights

★ **Parliament Tours:** Any visit to Ottawa should begin on Parliament Hill, in the ornate complex of copper-roofed buildings that houses Canada's national legislature. Dozens of special events, including the nation's biggest Canada Day celebration, take place in front of Parliament (page 273).

★ **Changing the Guard:** Complete with red-coated, fur hat-wearing guards, this daily summer procession on Parliament Hill echoes its namesake ceremony at Buckingham Palace (page 275).

★ **Canadian War Museum:** The exhibitions in this striking contemporary museum west of Parliament Hill put a human face on the grim periods of war throughout Canada's history (page 280).

★ **Rideau Canal National Historic Site:** Not only is the Rideau, which stretches from Ottawa south to Kingston, the oldest continuously operating canal in North America, in winter the canal's Ottawa section transforms into the world's largest skating rink (page 281).

★ **National Gallery of Canada:** Designed by Canadian architect Moshe Safdie, the country's national art gallery has a particularly fine collection of Canadian and indigenous works. Wander out back for great city views, too (page 283).

★ **ByWard Market:** Named for both a food market and its surrounding neighborhood, this Ottawa district is foodie central, whether you're looking for a picnic lunch, a five-star meal, or a classic BeaverTails snack (page 284).

© AVALON TRAVEL

★ **Canadian Museum of History:** You can learn almost anything you want to know about Canadian history and culture in this massive—and fascinating—museum, in a distinctive curved building on the Gatineau side of the Ottawa River (page 308).

★ **Gatineau Park:** This 361-square-kilometer (89,000-acre) green space in the Quebec hills a short drive from Ottawa is the city's backyard—a haven for hiking, cycling, swimming, cross-country skiing, or snowshoeing (page 309).

Canada's national capital brims with pomp and grandeur. Parliament, the Supreme Court, the homes of Canada's prime minister and governor general—along with numerous grand museums—are here. In summer, you can even

take in the daily Changing the Guard ceremony, the iconic fur hats and red uniforms echoing the similar famous ritual at London's Buckingham Palace. History comes alive in current-day Ottawa.

Yet Ottawa isn't all about revolutions and representatives. It's an active, outdoorsy city, where residents are frequently out on foot, on skates, or on the water. The Rideau Canal, the oldest continuously operating canal in North America, transforms in winter into the world's largest skating rink. Across the river from downtown is Gatineau Park, a sprawling nature reserve crisscrossed with trails for hiking, snowshoeing, and cross-country skiing.

Ottawa also knows how to party. The city hosts the nation's biggest Canada Day celebration every July 1, and throughout the year, there's one festival after another. Even in frigid February, Ottawa's long-running winter festival, Winterlude, draws thousands of visitors from near and far.

Straddling the border with Quebec, this metropolitan area of more than one million people is one of Canada's most bilingual cities. While it may not be as francophone as Quebec City or Montreal, you'll hear plenty of French, not just in government buildings but all around the city.

If you think that Ottawa's bureaucratic culture means that its food is equally bland, think again—Ottawa is an unexpected foodie destination. The city has a branch of Le Cordon Bleu culinary school, where you can take a workshop or have a classic French meal. The capital also has plenty of innovative restaurants where you can taste the latest creations when you've had your fill of history, culture, and the outdoors.

PLANNING YOUR TIME

Ottawa is a year-round destination. As long as you're prepared for serious cold (bring heavy coats, long underwear, warm hats, boots, and

Previous: Welcome to Ottawa, Canada's national capital; boat traveling through the locks on the Rideau Canal. **Above:** Ottawa has a booming craft beer scene.

Ottawa

OTTAWA

GATINEAU

QUEBEC
ONTARIO

Ottawa River

Ottawa River Pkwy

To Diefenbunker,
Canadian Tire Centre,
and Brookstreet Hotel

SCOTT ST
RICHMOND RD
BYRON AVE
VICTORIE

FLOCK
BOUTIQUE

THYME & AGAIN

ABSINTHE CAFE &
RESTO BAR

GREAT CANADIAN
THEATRE CO

ALLIUM

SUPPLY AND
DEMAND

ART IS IN BOULANGERIE

BEYOND THE PALE
BREWING COMPANY

CANADIAN
WAR MUSEUM

CHEZ
EDGAR

LES BRASSEURS
DU TEMPS

HULL

CASINO DU
LAC-LEAMY

HOTEL HILTON
LAC-LEAMY

To GATINEAU PARK,
MacKenzie King Estate/
MacKenzie King Tearoom,
Nordik Spa-Nature and
Chelsea Pub

CHEMIN D'AYLMER

BOULEVARD DE LUCERNE

PROMENADE DE LA GATINEAU

BLVD SAINT-RAYMOND

RUE GAMELIN

BLVD DE LA CARRIÈRE

Lake
Leamy

BLVD
FOURNIER

Gatineau River

PRIME
MINISTER'S
RESIDENCE

RIDEAU
HALL

SEE "DOWNTOWN OTTAWA" MAP

NATIONAL
HOLOCAUST
MONUMENT

PARLIAMENT
HILL

OTTAWA

BOOTH ST
BRONSON AVE
GLADSTONE AVE
SOMERSET ST W
GLOUCESTER ST
WELLINGTON ST

SUSSEX DR

KING EDWARD AVE

Rideau Canal

THE
ROWAN

BANK ST

ELGIN ST

Lansdowne
Park

Commissioners
Park

NATIONAL CAPITAL
COMMISSION DRIVEWAY

CARLING AVE

TWO SIX ATE

ATELIER

Rideau River

To Ottawa International Airport

MAIN ST

RIVERSIDE DR

ALTA VISTA DR

PLEASANT PARK RD
SMYTH RD

Billings
Park

PARKDALE AVE

HOLLAND AVE

ROCHESTER ST

LAURIER HOUSE
NATL HISTORIC SITE

BENNER'S
B&B

LE CORDON BLEU

VANIER PARKWAY

VANIER PARKWAY

Richelieu
Park

HEMLOCK ROAD

RCMP MUSICAL
RIDE CENTRE

CANADA AVIATION AND
SPACE MUSEUM

PONT ALEXANDRA
CARTIER BRIDGE

PONT MacDONALD-
CARTIER BRIDGE

BLVD. MAISONNEUVE

BLVD SACRÉ-COEUR

BLVD DES ALLUMETTIÈRES

BLVD ALEXANDRE-TACHÉ

BLVD SAINT-JOSEPH

PROMENADE DE LA GATINEAU

BLVD DE LA CITÉ-DES-JEUNES

BOIE GEORGE-ETIENNE CARTIER PKWY

OTTAWA
TRAIN
STATION

TREMBLAY RD

INDUSTRIAL AVE

ST LAURENT BLVD

BELFAST RD

QUEENSWAY

COVENTRY RD

DONALD STREET

McARTHUR AVENUE

MONTREAL RD

SAINT LAURENT BLVD

AVIATION PKWY

OGILVIE RD

INNES RD

MONTREAL RD

BLAIR ROAD

CANADA SCIENCE AND
TECHNOLOGY MUSEUM

0   1 km
0   1 mi

© AVALON TRAVEL

mittens), a winter visit means fewer crowds at Parliament, the museums, and other attractions (though some reduce their hours in the winter months). In spring, the capital shakes off its winter chill as a rainbow of colorful flowers bloom, particularly during the annual Canadian Tulip Festival. And if you want the best weather, schedule your visit during the crisp, clear days of fall.

Still, it's summer when Ottawa really comes alive. Sure, the days can be hot and sticky, but the streets and museums fill with visitors, vendors set up their stalls around the ByWard Market, and one festival after another livens up the summer calendar.

If you have two or three days, you can take in many of Ottawa's highlights: tour the **Parliament** buildings; visit the **National Gallery of Canada** and the **Canadian Museum of History;** stroll, cycle, or (in winter) skate along the **Rideau Canal;** and wrap up with a wander through the **ByWard Market** district to snack on a BeaverTail (the city's iconic fried-dough treat), or have dinner at one of the many contemporary restaurants.

With four or five days, you can explore the capital in greater depth. If you're interested in government, politics, or the official life, tour **Rideau Hall** (the governor general's residence) and the **Supreme Court.** You'll have more time to explore the shops around the ByWard Market or venture farther from downtown to shop and eat in the cool Wellington West neighborhood. If you're visiting with kids, don't miss the **Canadian Museum of Nature** or an afternoon outdoors in **Gatineau Park.** Or head west of the city to the **Diefenbunker,** a quirky—and somber—museum that takes you back to Canada's Cold War era.

Sights

Ottawa's main attractions are located in the city center on either side of the Rideau Canal. Downtown Ottawa and Parliament Hill are west of the canal; the ByWard Market, National Gallery of Canada, and Royal Canadian Mint are east of the canal. Gatineau, across the Ottawa River from downtown, is where you'll find the Canadian Museum of History as well as Gatineau Park. With so many major museums, Ottawa can induce a sort of museum fatigue, so balance your sightseeing with more relaxing pursuits. A walk along the Rideau Canal or through the ByWard Market district can help revive flagging energy.

Some of Ottawa's most interesting neighborhoods aren't known for their sights, but they're worth exploring. Head for Chinatown and Little Italy, both southwest of downtown, to browse the markets or look for a meal. The funky Glebe neighborhood, which runs along Bank Street south of downtown, and Wellington West, on the city's west side, are both fun districts to ramble through for shopping and eating.

PARLIAMENT HILL

Any visit to Ottawa should begin on **Parliament Hill** (111 Wellington St., at Metcalfe St.), the legislative headquarters of Canada's national government. Even if you're not interested in the work of the federal policy wonks, the strikingly ornate complex of copper-roofed Parliament buildings above the Ottawa River is worth visiting for its architectural glamour alone.

TOP EXPERIENCE

★ Parliament Tours
The **Centre Block Guided Tour** (613/992-4793 or 866/599-4999, www.parl.ca, daily, check website for tour times, free) takes you through the main Parliament building, which opened in 1920 after a fire destroyed most of the original structure. These 20- to

Two Days in Ottawa

Do you have only two days to explore Canada's capital city? Here's how to organize your time.

DAY 1

Start with a tour of the **Parliament Buildings** and the regal **Changing the Guard** ceremony (July-Aug.), complete with fur hat-wearing sentries and plenty of military precision. Walk along the **Rideau Canal** to see boats transiting the locks. Take a peek inside the historic **Fairmont Chateau Laurier** hotel as you continue into the **ByWard Market,** where you can browse the vendors and snap your photo in front of the **Ottawa sign.** Pick up an Italian sandwich at **La Bottega Nicastro** for a picnic nearby or sit down for lunch at **Play Food and Wine.** Save room for the city's signature dessert at **BeaverTails.**

Next stop: the **National Gallery of Canada.** Make a beeline for the Canadian and indigenous galleries then check out the museum shop. On your way out, pose in front of *Maman,* the giant bronze spider sculpted by artist Louise Bourgeois. Then stop into the grand **Notre Dame Cathedral Basilica** and walk along the river to enjoy the views. If you have time, browse the boutiques along Sussex Drive.

Have an early dinner—choose between contemporary fare at **Town** or Middle Eastern cuisine at **Farouz.** Then see a play or a concert at the **National Arts Centre.**

DAY 2

Cross to Gatineau, on the Quebec side of the Ottawa River, to explore the **Canadian Museum of History.** Spend a couple of hours in the excellent Canadian history galleries, which follow the country's story from its indigenous roots to modern times. If you're not museum-ed out, return to Ottawa to tour the **Canadian War Museum,** stopping first for lunch at **Art Is In Boulangerie** and a walk through the sobering **National Holocaust Monument** opposite the museum.

Get some exercise biking along the **Ottawa River Pathway** or go rafting with **Ottawa City Adventures.** Then relax with a tasting flight at a **craft brewery** like **Beyond the Pale, Lowertown Brewery,** or **Flora Hall.**

For dinner, head to Wellington West for seafood at **Supply and Demand** or return downtown to high-end **Riviera** or deliciously vegetarian **Pure Kitchen,** which offers the bonus of a drink upstairs at cozy **Charlotte.** If it's Saturday, close out your Ottawa adventures with crazy drag-queen-led karaoke at **Shanghai Restaurant.**

60-minute tours typically begin in the foyer of the House of Commons, include an overview of Canada's parliamentary process, and, if Parliament isn't in session, visit the green **House of Commons chamber,** the color of which is modeled on the British House of Commons, and the red **Senate chamber.** Also on the tour is the gorgeous **Library of Parliament,** a circular Gothic Revival structure at the back of the Centre Block, which dates to 1876. It's one of the only parts of the original Parliament buildings that survived the devastating 1916 fire (an employee closed the library's thick iron doors, saving it from the flames). Bedecked with elaborate wood carvings and ironwork, the library houses over one million books.

The Centre Block is slated to close for a **multiyear rehabilitation project,** beginning in late 2018. During this period, no Centre Block tours will be offered. Instead, visitors will be able to tour the adjacent **West Block,** which will be the interim home of the House of Commons; the **Government Conference Centre,** where the Senate will meet during this construction period; and the **East Block,** the 1860s building that houses legislative offices.

To take any Parliament building tour, you must reserve a ticket in person on the day you want to tour. Tickets are available beginning at 9am, and they're issued for particular times. The first tours of the day are generally less crowded, so arrive early if you can. On a busy summer day, you might show up in the morning and find that the first available tour is late in the afternoon, so be prepared to adjust your schedule. Tour lengths vary depending on what's going on in the buildings; tours don't enter the Senate or House of Commons chambers when Parliament is in session. Expect airport-style security screening before you enter the building.

Between mid-May and early September, make your tour reservations at the **Capital Information Kiosk** (90 Wellington St., 9am-5pm daily), opposite Parliament Hill. Check the Parliament website (www.parl.ca) for ticketing instructions for visits during the rest of the year and for updates on the construction process.

The Peace Tower and Memorial Chamber

In the middle of Parliament's Centre Block is the landmark Peace Tower, bedecked with gargoyles and ornate stonework, its clockface visible from blocks away. Completed in 1927, the tower is dedicated to the Canadian soldiers who died in World War I. Bells in the tower chime every quarter hour, and the tower also houses a carillon, with 53 bells ranging in size from 4.5 kilograms (10 pounds) to more than 10,000 kilograms (over 22,000 pounds). From the Parliament lawn, you can listen to **free carillon concerts** (11am-noon daily July-Aug., noon-12:15pm most days Sept.-June).

Take an elevator to the Peace Tower's **observation deck** (see www.parl.ca for current hours, free) for expansive views of the surrounding area, as well as an up-close look at the carillon's bells. You can go up in the Peace Tower at the end of the Centre Block tours, or ascend the tower without taking a tour, but you still need a ticket, which follows the same ticketing procedure as the Centre Block tours. Go up first thing in the morning to avoid the crowds.

Also in the tower is the Memorial Chamber, a chapel-like space lined with stained glass windows, memorializing Canadian veterans. The chamber houses seven **Books of Remembrance** containing the names of Canadian men and women who died serving in the armed forces. Daily at 11am, during the **Turning of the Page ceremony,** a page is turned in the Books of Remembrance, so that each name is visible at least once a year. The public can view the ceremony from the chamber's entryway.

Note: The construction on Parliament Hill will close the Peace Tower and Memorial Chamber for an extended period. See the Parliament website for the current status.

Parliament Visitor Galleries

When Parliament is in session, visitors are welcome to watch the action from the Visitor Galleries in either the Senate or the House of Commons. The schedule varies, so check the Parliament website (www.parl.ca) for hours. Seating in the galleries is first come, first served; check the Parliament website (www.parl.ca) for the current ticketing procedure.

If you're Canadian, you can email or write to your Member of Parliament in advance of your visit to request a seat in the galleries. You'll then get a seat ahead of visitors who just turn up that day. Look up your MP's contact information on the Parliament website.

A popular time to visit the galleries is during the 45-minute **Question Period,** when the opposition is allowed to question the government. When Parliament is in session, Question Period in the House of Commons is usually held 2:15pm Monday-Thursday and at 11:15am Friday. The Senate Question Period takes place Tuesday-Thursday, but times vary.

You must remain quiet in the galleries—no talking is allowed—so don't bring the kids until they're old enough to sit without chatting.

★ Changing the Guard

If you're visiting Ottawa between late June and August, don't miss the **Changing the**

Downtown Ottawa

© AVALON TRAVEL

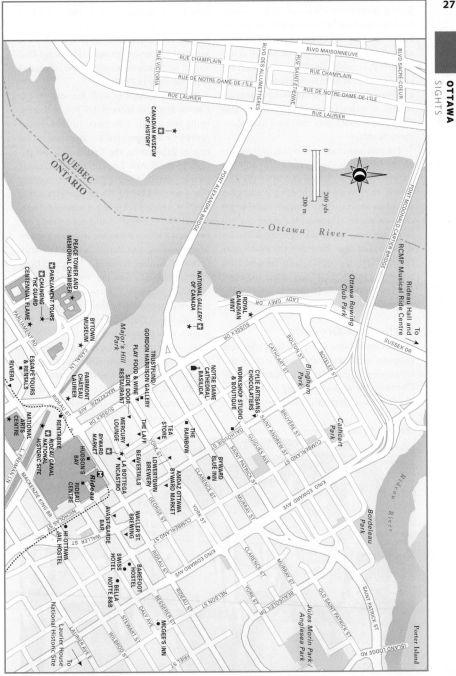

BLVD MAISONNEUVE
BLVD SACRÉ-COEUR
RUE VICTORIA
RUE CHAMPLAIN
RUE DES ALLUMETTIÈRES
RUE SAINTE-ÉTIENNE
RUE CHAMPLAIN
RUE DE NOTRE-DAME-DE-I'ÎLE
RUE DE NOTRE-DAME-DE-I'ÎLE
RUE LAURIER
RUE LAURIER

CANADIAN MUSEUM
OF HISTORY

QUEBEC
ONTARIO

PONT ALEXANDRA BRIDGE

0 200 yds
0 200 m

Ottawa River

PONT MCDONALD-CARTIER BRIDGE

To
Rideau Hall and
RCMP Musical Ride Centre

PEACE TOWER AND
MEMORIAL CHAMBER

PARLIAMENT TOURS
CHANGING
THE GUARD
CENTENNIAL FLAME

BYTOWN
MUSEUM

RIVIERA

ESCAPE TOURS
& RENTALS

PARLIAMENT HILL RD

RIDEAU CANAL

NATIONAL
ARTS
CENTRE

FAIRMONT
CHATEAU
LAURIER

Major's Hill Park

RIDEAU ST

MACKENZIE AVE

SUSSEX DR

NATIONAL GALLERY
OF CANADA

ROYAL
CANADIAN
MINT

Ottawa Rowing
Club Park

LADY GREY DR

SUSSEX DR

SUSSEX DR

BOLTON ST
BOTELER ST

Bingham
Park

CATHCART ST

Cathcart
Park

TRUSTFUND/
GORDON HARRISON GALLERY
PLAY FOOD & WINE
SIDE DOOR
RESTAURANT

NOTRE DAME
CATHEDRAL
BASILICA

WORKSHOP STUDIO
& BOUTIQUE

CYLIE ARTISANS
CHOCOLATIERS

SAINT ANDREW ST

DALHOUSIE ST

BRUYÈRE ST

CUMBERLAND ST

THE LAFF

TEA
STORE

THE
RAINBOW

LOVERTOWN
BREWERY

SAINT PATRICK ST

MERCURY
LOUNGE

BYWARD
MARKET

HUDSON'S
BAY

RIDEAU
CENTRE

Rideau

BEAVERTAILS

LA BOTTEGA
NICASTRO

ANDAZ OTTAWA
BYWARD MARKET

BYWARD
BLUE INN

GUIGUES AVE

KING EDWARD AVE

MURRAY ST

YORK ST

CLARENCE ST

GEORGE ST

WALLER ST
BREWING

AVANTGARDE
BAR

HI-OTTAWA
JAIL HOSTEL

NICHOLS ST

WALLER ST

CUMBERLAND ST

KING EDWARD AVE

YORK ST

CLARENCE ST

MURRAY ST

RIDEAU ST

NELSON ST

SWISS
HOTEL

BAREFOOT
HOSTEL

BELLA

NOTTE B&B

MCGEE'S INN

BESSERER ST

DALY AVE

STEWART ST

WILBROD ST

FRIEL ST

LAURIER AVE E

To
Laurier House
National Historic Site

MACKENZIE KING BR

L FREIMAN LN

RENTABIKE

RIDEAU CANAL
NATIONAL
HISTORIC SITE

MACKENZIE AVE

Rideau
River

Bordeleau
Park

OLD SAINT PATRICK ST

SAINT PATRICK ST

BEAUSOLEIL DR

Jules Morin Park /
Anglesea Park

Porter Island

ISLAND LODGE RD

Guard ceremony (www.parl.ca, 10am daily, free) on the lawn in front of the Parliament buildings. Dressed in ceremonial red coats and tall fur hats recalling their British counterparts at London's Buckingham Palace, the guards march in formation, accompanied by a military band. Most of the young guards are college or university students who are also Canadian armed forces reservists (cool summer job, eh?).

The ceremony takes place rain or shine. Be on the lawn by 9:45am—earlier if you want a front-row view. Before and after the ceremony, the guards march along Wellington and Elgin Streets, where it's often easier to get close-up photos. Consider watching the full ceremony one day and taking more photos on the street the next. Note that the **multiyear rehabilitation project** on Parliament Hill, beginning in late 2018, may affect the ceremonies; check the Parliament website for the current status.

Parliament Grounds

Visitors are welcome to explore the Parliament grounds, which are dotted with statues and monuments, including the **Centennial Flame** on the walkway leading to the Centre Block. It was first lit on January 1, 1967,

honoring Canada's 100th birthday. Each of the twelve segments represents one of the provinces and territories (as of 1967). Do you know which current territory is missing? That would be Nunavut, which became Canada's third territory in 1999.

One monument to look for, east of the Centre Block, is *Women Are Persons!*, honoring five female reformers. In 1916, Emily Murphy was appointed a magistrate in the city of Edmonton, the first female magistrate in the British Empire. However, many people protested her appointment, arguing that under the British North America Act of 1867—Canada's founding document—only a qualified "person" could hold public office, and a woman was not legally a person. Murphy, along with Henrietta Muir Edwards, Louise McKinney, Nellie McClung, and Irene Parlby, eventually took the "Persons Case" to Canada's Supreme Court—and lost. They persisted, appealing to the Privy Council in Britain, which finally ruled in 1929 that, yes, women were persons, too.

To guide your explorations, download or pick up *Discover the Hill: Outdoor Self-Guiding Booklet* in the **Capital Information Kiosk** (90 Wellington St., 844/878-8333, www.canada.ca, 10am-5pm daily). As with

Changing the Guard ceremony on Parliament Hill

OTTAWA
SIGHTS

A Crash Course in Canadian Government

Your visit to Ottawa will mean more if you know something about the workings of the Canadian government. The federal government has three branches: executive, legislative, and judicial. Canada's **prime minister** is the country's chief executive, and **Parliament,** the national legislature, makes Canada's federal laws.

Parliament is made up of two bodies: the House of Commons, whose 308 members are elected, and the Senate, in which—unlike the U.S. Senate—the 105 legislators are appointed. Each House of Commons member, known as a Member of Parliament or MP, represents a geographically based "riding," or district. They're elected to five-year terms. Senators can come from anywhere in the country. They can remain on the job until they reach age 75.

When a bill is introduced in Parliament, majorities in both the House of Commons and the Senate must approve it. The governor general, who is the British monarch's representative in Canada, then gives final approval—known as "royal assent"—to a bill before it becomes law.

Want to know more? The Parliament website (www.parl.ca) is an excellent resource for information about the Canadian legislative system. And if you visit Parliament Hill in Ottawa, plan to tour the House of Commons and Senate chambers and, if you can, arrange to watch a legislative session in action.

---

the rest of Parliament Hill, construction may limit access to the Parliament grounds.

DOWNTOWN

Ottawa's downtown extends west and south of Parliament Hill. Besides the many office and government buildings, several museums and attractions are downtown, as well as numerous hotels. The southern section of downtown, below Lisgar Street, is known as Centretown.

Bank of Canada Museum

How do you make a museum of banking and economics fun? When you arrive at the small **Bank of Canada Museum** (30 Bank St., 613/782-8914 or 800/303-1282, www.bankofcanadamuseum.ca, 10am-5pm Tues.-Sun., free), you create an avatar and scan an electronic bracelet to activate the entertaining high-tech activities. Design your own banknote, steer a rocket through an inflationary minefield, or learn how banknotes are produced with features that make them hard to counterfeit.

Supreme Court of Canada

With its headquarters a short walk west of Parliament Hill, the **Supreme Court of**

Canada (301 Wellington St., 613/995-5361 or 888/551-1185, www.scc-csc.gc.ca, 9am-5pm daily May-Aug., 9am-5pm Mon.-Fri. Sept.-Apr., free) is the country's highest court. Every year, the court hears 80-100 cases that it considers to have "national importance," on appeal from the federal and provincial courts. Nine judges sit on Canada's Supreme Court. By law, three justices must come from Quebec, and by convention, the remainder of the court includes three justices from Ontario, two from western Canada, and one from the Atlantic provinces.

Designed by Montreal architect Ernest Cormier (who later worked with the team designing the United Nations Headquarters in New York), the current court building was completed in 1941. From May through August, free 30-minute **tours** of the building are offered, with English-language tours starting on the hour. Reservations aren't required. Between September and April, tours run Monday through Friday only, and you must book in advance by completing the online reservation form on the court's website. Tours include an overview of Canada's judicial system, interesting historical tidbits about the court and the justices, and a walk through several rooms, including the court chambers.

The Supreme Court hears cases during three sessions each year, in winter (generally mid-Jan.-Mar.), spring (Apr.-June), and fall (mid-Oct.-Dec.). No sessions are held July-September. If you want to see the Supreme Court in action, you can; **court hearings** are open to the public on a first-come, first-served basis. Sessions normally begin at 9:30am Monday-Friday, and a second daily session is sometimes held starting at 2pm. Check the **court website** (www.scc-csc.gc.ca) for a schedule.

★ Canadian War Museum

A museum of military history could easily be dreary or downright depressing. Yet the engaging contemporary **Canadian War Museum** (1 Vimy Pl., 819/776-7000 or 800/555-5621, www.warmuseum.ca, 9am-6pm Mon.-Wed. and Fri.-Sun., 9am-8pm Thurs. late June-early Sept., 9:30am-5pm Mon.-Wed. and Fri.-Sun., 9:30am-8pm Thurs. early Sept.-Mar., 9am-5pm Mon.-Wed. and Fri.-Sun., 9am-8pm Thurs. Apr.-late June, adults $17, seniors $15, students $13, ages 3-12 $11, families $43; free admission 5pm-8pm Thurs., parking $5 per hour or $12.50 per day), located on LeBreton Flats west of Parliament Hill, is neither. The exhibitions put a human face on periods of war, illustrating not just the conflicts but also the societal issues of the times.

The four main galleries that make up the museum's permanent collection are organized chronologically. The first covers warfare on Canadian soil from the earliest days through 1885, including aboriginal conflicts, European conquests, and the War of 1812. The second (1885-1931) illustrates Canada's involvement in the South African War and World War I, while the third (1931-1945) addresses World War II. The fourth gallery begins in 1945 and continues to the present day. And because a war museum couldn't exist without tanks and airplanes, the LeBreton Gallery houses a large collection of military vehicles and artillery.

The building itself, which opened in 2005,

the Canadian War Museum

has some interesting design features. Its plant-covered "green roof" is one of the largest in North America. Notice the windows on the north peak, where Morse code spells out "Lest We Forget." The lead architect, Vancouver-born Raymond Moriyama, also designed Toronto's Bata Shoe Museum.

The War Museum is two kilometers (1.2 miles) west of the Parliament buildings. Take the Confederation Line to Pimisi Station, or catch OC Transpo bus no. 44, toward Gatineau, which travels west on Albert Street and stops in front of the museum.

National Holocaust Monument

Outside the War Museum, walk through the sobering **National Holocaust Monument** (Wellington St. at Booth St., free), which commemorates victims of the Holocaust and honors Canadian survivors. Designed by Poland-born, New York-based architect Daniel Libeskind, this angular concrete structure—with six triangular sections representing the six points of the identifying

Canadian Museum of Nature

Animalium, which houses a creepy collection of live tarantulas, hissing cockroaches, giant snails, and scorpions; a 19.8-meter (66-foot) blue whale skeleton; and the Arctic Gallery, where you can touch ice, explore the role of hunting in indigenous northern cultures, learn about scientific research in the far north, or listen to students from Nunavut and the Northwest Territories talking about their communities. The Discovery Zone has more hands-on things to do.

The museum isn't just for children, particularly during the monthly **Nature Nocturne** (adults $25), an age-19-and-over evening of music, food, and special events. The glass box that tops the entranceway is known as the **Queen's Lantern,** with great views over downtown from the top floor. Opened in 2010, it replaced the museum's original tower, which had to be dismantled back in 1916 when it began sinking into the ground.

star that the Nazis forced Jews to wear—features haunting images of Holocaust sites by Canadian photographer Edward Burtynsky.

Canadian Museum of Nature

As you walk into this castle-like Tudor Gothic structure, built in the early 1900s as Canada's first national museum building, notice the **mosaic of a bull moose** on the floor of the entrance hall. Its prominent private parts apparently created a stir among proper Ottawans in the museum's early days.

Anatomically correct moose mosaics aside, the **Canadian Museum of Nature** (240 McLeod St., 613/566-4700 or 800/263-4433, www.nature.ca, 9am-6pm Sat.-Wed., 9am-8pm Thurs.-Fri. June-early Sept., 9am-5pm Tues.-Wed. and Fri.-Sun., 9am-8pm Thurs. early Sept.-May, adults $14, seniors and ages 13-17 $12, ages 3-12 $10, free admission 5pm-8pm Thurs.), a natural history museum that focuses primarily on Canadian species, is great fun for kids. Besides the ever-popular dinosaur skeletons, highlights include the

THE RIDEAU CANAL

The Rideau Canal is more than a Canadian National Historic Site and a UNESCO World Heritage Site. In many ways, this rambling waterway and adjacent green spaces where both residents and visitors can stroll, boat, or skate is also the heart of Ottawa. Bordering the canal, just east of Parliament Hill, are two sights worth seeing if you're interested in Ottawa's heritage: the Bytown Museum and the Fairmont Château Laurier hotel.

TOP EXPERIENCE

★ Rideau Canal National Historic Site

Running 202 kilometers (126 miles) from Kingston to Ottawa, the Rideau Canal (www.pc.gc.ca) is North America's oldest continuously operating canal. After the War of 1812 between the United States and Britain, Canadians were concerned that the St. Lawrence River—a vital shipping channel between Montreal and the Great Lakes—would be vulnerable to another U.S. attack, since the Americans controlled the river's southern banks. In 1826, led by Lieutenant Colonel John By, work began on the canal that would eventually connect the Ottawa region to Lake Ontario through a series of lakes, rivers, and canals linked by 24 lock stations that allow boats to navigate its changing water levels. More than 1,000 people died constructing the canal, many of whom contracted malaria working along the swampy canal route. After six years of construction, the canal opened in 1832.

The Ottawa section of the canal runs from the Ottawa River southward, separating downtown from the ByWard Market. Between mid-May and mid-October, you can watch boats transit through the **Ottawa Locks;** the lock station closest to downtown is just north of Wellington Street, between Parliament Hill and the Fairmont Château Laurier.

Bytown Museum

To learn more about the history of Ottawa and the construction of the Rideau Canal, visit the **Bytown Museum** (1 Canal Lane, 613/234-4570, www.bytownmuseum.com, 10am-5pm Fri.-Wed., 10am-8pm Thurs. mid-May-mid-June and early Sept.-mid-Oct., 10am-7pm Fri.-Wed., 10am-8pm Thurs. mid-June-early Sept., 11am-4pm Thurs.-Mon. mid-Oct.-mid-May, adults $6.50, seniors and students $4.50, ages 5-12 $3.50, families $15, free admission 5pm-8pm Thurs.) located in Ottawa's oldest stone building, next to the Ottawa Locks. It's built on the site where the construction of the Rideau Canal began back in 1826.

Start your visit with a 20-minute video about the canal's history and check out the working model of the locks. Upstairs, exhibits trace Ottawa's development from its early days as rough-and-tumble Bytown (it was renamed Ottawa in 1855, for the Odawa, an Anishinaabe people indigenous to the area) to its naming as Canada's capital (in 1857) and beyond. The admission price includes a self-guided audio tour.

If you're visiting with children, look for the "scratch and sniff" cards illustrating local history (guess what the one about horses smells

The Rideau Canal is North America's oldest continuously operating canal.

like?). Kids can dress up in period costumes and play Victorian-era games.

Fairmont Château Laurier

Looming above the Rideau Canal, the **Fairmont Château Laurier** (1 Rideau St., 613/241-1414 or 866/540-4410, www.fairmont.com/laurier-ottawa), built in 1912, is a grand hotel that's almost as recognizable a part of the Ottawa skyline as the nearby Parliament buildings. Even if you don't stay here, stroll through the upscale lobby with its original marble floor and dark woodwork, or splurge on traditional afternoon tea in **Zoe's Lounge** (613/241-1414, 2pm-5pm Mon.-Fri., noon-5pm Sat.-Sun., reservations required, adults $42-48, children $24-26).

BYWARD MARKET DISTRICT

Home to one of Canada's oldest and largest public markets, the ByWard Market District encompasses the main market building, outdoor vendors, and the surrounding

Architect Moshe Safdie designed the National Gallery of Canada.

spider, a bronze sculpture known as *Maman,* by French American artist Louise Bourgeois (1911-2010), guards the museum entrance, standing over nine meters (30 feet) high.

Inside, the museum houses the country's largest visual arts collection. Start in the comprehensive **Canadian and indigenous art galleries,** which are organized chronologically and include a significant number of works by the Group of Seven, early-20th-century Canadian landscape artists; look for paintings by Lawren Harris (1885-1970), A. Y. Jackson (1882-1974), and Tom Thomson (1877-1917), among others. More contemporary works include paintings by First Nations artist Norval Morrisseau (1932-2007) and modern Inuit sculptures. Also visit serene **Rideau Chapel,** a 19th-century chapel from Ottawa's Convent of Our Lady of the Sacred Heart that was saved from demolition in 1972 and reconstructed in its entirety within the museum.

The always-surprising **contemporary art** exhibits are another highlight. There are also comprehensive **photography** and **European** art galleries. In addition to the permanent collections, the museum typically mounts a major exhibition every summer, as well as 12 to 14 smaller exhibits throughout the year.

One strategy for tackling such a large museum is to visit for a short time (perhaps on Thursday evening when admission is free) to get your bearings, and then return for a longer visit. Or pause for one of the 10-minute "Docent's Choice" talks, a brief overview of a specific artwork; get the schedule online or at the entrance desk. To guide your explorations, rent an **audio guide** ($5); one specialized audio program adds historical perspective to works in the Canadian art galleries, while another focuses on how fashion would have been perceived in various works.

The museum hosts concerts, films, and other special events throughout the year as well. Check its website or phone for schedules and other details. If all this culture makes you hungry, stop for tapas and a glass of wine

neighborhood, bounded roughly by Sussex Drive and St. Patrick, Cumberland, and George Streets. Whether your taste runs to museums, galleries, boutiques, or all manner of food shops and restaurants, you can easily spend hours sampling the wares in and around the ByWard Market. Stop to take your photo in front of the illuminated **Ottawa sign** on York Street, near Sussex Drive.

★ National Gallery of Canada

It's hard to say which makes a more notable landmark at the **National Gallery of Canada** (380 Sussex Dr., 613/990-1985 or 800/319-2787, www.gallery.ca, 10am-6pm Fri.-Wed., 10am-8pm Thurs. May-Sept., 10am-5pm Tues.-Wed. and Fri.-Sun., 10am-8pm Thurs. Oct.-Apr., adults $15, seniors $13, ages 12-24 $7, under age 12 free, families $30, free admission 5pm-8pm Thurs.). Is it the airy granite, glass, and steel building itself, which opened in 1988, designed by Canadian architect Moshe Safdie? Or is it the gigantic spider that sits on the museum's front plaza? The in Café 7, or head for the museum cafeteria. In the latter, the menu runs to typical sandwiches and salads, but the view across the Ottawa River—to Parliament Hill on one side and the Canadian Museum of History on the other—is one of the best in town.

Notre Dame Cathedral Basilica

Opposite the National Gallery, the twin spires of Ottawa's oldest surviving church, **Notre Dame Cathedral Basilica** (385 Sussex Dr., 613/241-7496, www.notredameottawa.com, 11:30am-6pm Mon., 9am-6pm Tues.-Sat., 8am-8:30pm Sun. May-Oct., 11:30am-6pm Mon., 10am-6pm Tues.-Fri., 2pm-6pm Sat., 8am-8:30pm Sun. Nov.-Apr., free), glint in the afternoon sun. If you think that North America has few churches to rival Europe's cathedrals, visit this grand Gothic structure, built between 1841 and 1885, with its arched columns, stained glass windows, and elaborate pipe organ. Visitors are welcome to attend church services (call or check the website for schedules), explore the architecture, or simply take sanctuary for a few moments of quiet contemplation.

Royal Canadian Mint

As the queen ages, what happens to her portrait on the country's coins? If you're interested in this and other pecuniary trivia, visit the **Royal Canadian Mint** (320 Sussex Dr., 613/993-8990 or 800/276-7714, www.mint.ca, 9am-5pm daily, Mon.-Fri. adults $6, seniors $5, ages 5-17 $3, family $15, Sat.-Sun. adults $4.50, seniors $3.75, ages 5-17 $2.25, family $11.25). Although Canada's regular-circulation coins are no longer made at this Ottawa facility (production moved to Winnipeg in 1976), the mint still manufactures investment and collection coins, military medals, and Olympic medals.

The only way to see the mint is by taking a 30-minute tour, where guides explain the production process, and you can look down on the surprisingly low-tech machines. Medals from the 2010 Winter Olympics, held

the spires of Notre Dame Cathedral Basilica

in Vancouver, are on display. Tours run frequently throughout the day; call for seasonal schedules. Make a reservation, particularly in the summer, and visit Monday to Friday to see the mint in full operation. On weekends, admission prices are lower, but the production lines are shut down, so you don't see as much.

Oh, and about the queen? Over the years, the portrait of Queen Elizabeth II that appears on Canada's coins has aged along with Her Majesty. Notice, though, that on newer coins, the monarch isn't wearing her crown. She apparently requested the crown-free likeness, so she'd appear more like a regular person.

★ ByWard Market

Lieutenant Colonel John By, who led the construction of the Rideau Canal, designed the ByWard Market and its surrounding streets back in the 1820s. He specified that George and York Streets should both be extra-wide to accommodate the horse-drawn carriages that brought goods to the market.

The centerpiece of the ByWard Market

neighborhood is the **main market building** (55 ByWard Market Square, 613/562-3325, www.byward-market.com, free), with shops selling snacks, light meals, and souvenirs; there's also a **visitor information office** and restrooms. The more interesting part of the market, though, is outside, when vendors set up stalls (generally late April or May through October) to sell produce, prepared foods, and other goodies. You'll find dozens of small shops around the market building as well.

As you wander the market area, make sure to explore the **courtyards** just east of Sussex Drive, from George Street to St. Patrick Street. They house restaurants, shops, and cafés that aren't easily visible from the main streets.

EAST OF DOWNTOWN

Several of the city's attractions are east of downtown and the ByWard Market.

Laurier House National Historic Site

Two of Canada's prime ministers lived in a mansion in the Sandy Hill neighborhood that's now the **Laurier House National Historic Site** (335 Laurier Ave. E., 613/992-8142, www.pc.gc.ca, 10am-5pm daily July-early Sept., 10am-5pm Thurs.-Mon. late May-June and early-Sept.-mid-Oct., adults $3.90, seniors $3.40).

Canada had no official prime minister's residence when Sir Wilfrid Laurier took office in 1896; a group of friends and supporters raised money to build this home, where Laurier lived from 1897 until his death in 1919. When Laurier's wife, Zoe, passed away in 1921, she bequeathed the house to William Lyon Mackenzie King, Laurier's successor as Liberal Party leader. Mackenzie King, who became prime minister that same year, moved into the house (after extensive renovations) in 1923 and lived there until he retired from politics in 1948. Guides in period costume are on hand throughout the house, which is furnished with many of Laurier's and Mackenzie King's belongings. Optional **guided tours** ($7.30) tell you more about the history of the

period. Check the website for details on occasional "live history" events where actors bring the era to life.

Laurier House is just over two kilometers (1.2 miles) east of Parliament Hill. If you don't want to walk, catch OC Transpo bus no. 19, which stops in front of the house.

Rideau Hall

Owing to Canada's history as part of the British Empire, the British monarch is still Canada's official head of state. Since the queen presumably has more to do than worry about day-to-day governance of Britain's former colonies, however, Canada's governor general acts as the queen's representative in Canada. In practice, it's the prime minister who runs the government in Canada, and the governor general's role is largely ceremonial. It's fitting, then, that the governor general's residence, **Rideau Hall** (1 Sussex Dr., 613/991-4422 or 866/842-4422, www.gg.ca, free), is a suitably ceremonial mansion, on park-like grounds northeast of the ByWard Market.

Free 45-minute **tours of Rideau Hall** (10am-4pm Sat.-Sun., by reservation 10am-4pm Mon.-Fri. May-late June, 10am-4:30pm daily late June-early Sept., noon-4pm Sat.-Sun., by reservation 10am-4pm Mon.-Fri. early Sept.-Oct., by reservation 10am-4pm daily Nov.-Apr.) explore the history of the building—built in sections from 1838 through 1940—and visit some of the grand public spaces. Imagine attending a soiree in the majestic ballroom or in the candy-striped Tent Room, where the pink fabric-draped ceiling resembles a circus tent! Tours are offered year-round, and reservations are advised. November through April, tours are by reservation only; call to book. The grounds are open daily from 8am until one hour before sunset; pick up a brochure at either entrance gate to guide your wanderings around the property. A **skating rink** (noon-5pm Sat.-Sun. early Dec.-mid-Mar.) is open for public skating on winter weekends, weather permitting.

To reach Rideau Hall from downtown or

the ByWard Market, catch **OC Transpo bus no. 9** (www.octranspo.com). On weekends, check the schedule before heading out, because service can be infrequent. En route to Rideau Hall, you might catch a glimpse of the prime minister's residence (24 Sussex Dr.), but it's not open to the public.

RCMP Musical Ride

Canada's red-coated, Stetson-wearing Mounties, officially known as the Royal Canadian Mounted Police (RCMP), are the country's national police force. But a small group of Mounties have an additional duty: performing with the **RCMP Musical Ride** (www.rcmp-grc.gc.ca/en/musical-ride). With a troop of 36 horses and riders, the Musical Ride is a cavalry drill team, executing intricate formations choreographed to music. Between May and October, the Musical Ride is frequently on tour in other parts of Canada, but they do perform periodically in Ottawa; check their website for the performance schedule.

Even when the Musical Ride is on the road, you can tour the **RCMP Musical Ride Centre** (RCMP Rockcliffe Stables, 1 Sandridge Rd., 613/741-4285, www.rcmp-grc.gc.ca/en/musical-ride, 9am-3:30pm daily May-Aug., 10am-1pm Tues. and Thurs. Sept.-Apr., free)

to meet the horses and learn more about the performing troupe. From Parliament Hill or the Rideau Centre, OC Transpo bus no. 7 will drop you near the stables.

Canada Aviation and Space Museum

If you're a fan of flying, zoom over to the hangar-like **Canada Aviation and Space Museum** (11 Aviation Pkwy., 613/993-2010, www.ingeniumcanada.org/aviation, 9am-5pm daily May-early Sept., 10am-5pm Wed.-Mon. early Sept.-Apr., adults $15, seniors and students $13, ages 3-17 $10, families $38, free admission 4pm-5pm daily) that houses Canada's largest collection of civilian and military aircraft, dating from the early 20th century to the present.

Want a bigger thrill? Strap on your goggles and take a **flight tour** (613/316-7229, 9am-5pm daily May-Oct., $65-165 pp) over Ottawa in a vintage Waco UPF-7, an open-cockpit biplane that dates to around 1939. Or book a **helicopter tour** (613/447-5662, www.heli-tremblant.com, 9am-5pm daily May-Oct., $99-199 pp) over Parliament Hill or Gatineau.

The museum is 6.5 kilometers (four miles) east of Parliament Hill. From downtown, catch OC Transpo bus no. 7 eastbound to St.

The RCMP Musical Ride tours the world from its Ottawa base.

Laurent/Eastbourne, which is a 10-minute walk to the museum.

Canada Science and Technology Museum

The **Canada Science and Technology Museum** (1867 St. Laurent Blvd., 613/991-3044, https://ingeniumcanada.org/scitech, 9am-5pm daily May-early Sept., 9am-5pm Tues.-Sun. early Sept.-Apr., adults $17, seniors and students $13, ages 3-17 $11, families $43, parking $3/hour, $8/day) entertains and educates families with fun, interactive activities. You can make your skeleton dance, experiment with sound, navigate a car on a simulated road trip, explore adaptive technology for athletes with disabilities, or learn about indigenous peoples' theories of astronomy.

The museum is 9 kilometers (5.5 miles) east of Parliament Hill. OC Transpo bus no. 86, Elmvale, will drop you on Russell Road, near Smyth Road, about a five-minute walk west of the museum.

Entertainment and Events

As the nation's capital, Ottawa's arts venues not only promote local artists but also feature Canadian performers from across the country. And with festivals year-round, there's almost always something going on. The city has a booming craft beer scene, too.

CRAFT BREWERIES

Off Bank Street south of the city center, in a historic structure with an industrial-style garage door opening to the street, **Flora Hall Brewing** (37 Flora St., 613/695-2339, www.florahallbrewing.ca, 3pm-midnight Mon.-Thurs., noon-2am Fri.-Sat., noon-midnight Sun.) crafts several types of beer, from a northeast IPA to a farmhouse saison to an English bitter, which it pours along with local guest taps. Pair your drinks with globetrotting snacks like Szechuan chicken wings or a sausage and cheese calzone.

Lowertown Brewery (73 York St., 613/722-1454, www.lowertownbrewery.ca, 11:30am-1am Sun.-Thurs., 11:30am-2am Fri.-Sat.), in the ByWard Market district, matches its hoppy pale ale, German-style lager, and red wheat beer with smoked brisket, hearty sandwiches, and other pub fare. Nearby, in the basement of a heritage building, tiny **Waller St. Brewing** (14 Waller St., 613/860-1515, www.wallerst.ca, noon-10pm Thurs.-Sat., noon-5pm Sun.) takes its inspiration from the Prohibition era, brewing beers like Speakeasy Red, Bootleg Blonde, and Moonlight Porter.

Head west of downtown for more craft beer options, including **Beyond the Pale Brewing Company** (250 City Centre Ave., 613/695-2991, www.beyondthepale.ca, 11am-9pm Tues.-Sat., 11am-6pm Sun.) in the warehouse-like City Centre complex. Check out the giant mural behind the curved bar as you sample a tasting flight of Aromatherapy IPA, Pink Fuzz grapefruit wheat, or Darkness oatmeal stout. On a sunny afternoon, sip an Ontario-brewed beer overlooking the river at the **Mill Street Brew Pub** (555 Wellington St., 613/567-2337, www.millstreetbrewery.com, 11am-11pm Mon.-Tues., 11am-midnight Wed., 11am-1am Thurs., 11am-2am Fri., 10:30am-2am Sat., 10:30am-11pm Sun), near the Canadian War Museum.

If you'd rather have a guide curate your beer tastings, book a tour with **Brew Donkey** (613/864-3659, www.brewdonkey.ca, Sat.-Sun., $72-99 pp). Their guides lead excursions to several different craft breweries around the Ottawa region every weekend. They normally post tour descriptions, times, and prices on their website six to eight weeks in advance.

NIGHTLIFE

The ByWard Market is entertainment central, full of bars, pubs, and music venues. **The**

Feeling the Chill of Canada's Cold War

Inside the Diefenbunker, it's still the 1960s.

"Attention! Warning! Take cover immediately!" As the radio announcer issues this urgent alert, the air raid siren begins to wail. Is there an incoming bomber heading straight for Ottawa? No, but at the **Diefenbunker, Canada's Cold War Museum** (3911 Carp Rd., Carp, 613/839-0007 or 800/409-1965, www.diefenbunker.ca, 11am-4pm Mon.-Fri., 10am-4:30pm Sat.-Sun. year-round, last admission 30 minutes before closing, adults $17.50, seniors $16.50, students $13, ages 6-18 $11, families $48.50), the drama and fears of the Cold War are very much alive.

Built in 1961 as a safe haven for government officials, this four-level underground bunker in the countryside outside of Ottawa was designed to survive a five-megaton bomb—more than 200 times stronger than the bomb dropped on Nagasaki during World War II. The bunker could house 500 people for up to 30 days following a nuclear attack. Fortunately, the potential nuclear catastrophe never occurred, but the bunker remained staffed and ready for use until 1994. The underground shelter, with 9,290 square meters (100,000 square feet) of living space, is now an unusual museum that vividly illustrates the Cold War era.

You can explore the Diefenbunker on your own with a complimentary iPod audio tour, but it's definitely worth taking a **guided tour** (60-90 minutes, 11am, noon, 1pm, and 2pm daily July-early Sept., 11am and 2pm daily early Sept.-June, included with admission, reservations recommended). As you enter the bunker through a 92-meter (300-foot) blast tunnel, your guide will ask each group to imagine that it's 1962 and you're joining others who've already taken refuge after a nuclear attack. You will experience a simulated decontamination procedure and medical exam before making your way through the warren of underground chambers.

The tour visits the war cabinet room, where elected officials would have plotted their strategies, as well as the prime minister's bedroom, the CBC emergency broadcast studio, and even the Bank of Canada vault designed to store 800 tons of gold. There's a recreation room with table tennis and pool tables, since you'd want to get some exercise while confined underground for 30 days. Also in the Diefenbunker are models of public fallout shelters, a cafeteria, black rotary-dial phones, huge IBM computers, and other artifacts of the era.

Tours are appropriate for children of elementary school age and older; younger children may find it unsettling. The temperature in the underground museum is a cool 17-19°C (63-66°F) year-round, so bring a sweater or light jacket. You will need a car to visit the Diefenbunker, a 30- to 40-minute drive west of downtown Ottawa. Take Highway 417 west to Carp Road and then continue north on Carp Road for 12 kilometers (7.5 miles) through the village of Carp to the Diefenbunker entrance.

Rainbow (76 Murray St., 613/241-5123, www.
therainbow.ca, hours vary) books local, national, and international blues acts, with some
R&B and jazz thrown in. DJs at **Mercury
Lounge** (56 ByWard Market Square, 613/789-
5324, www.mercurylounge.com, hours vary)
play electronic, house, jazz, funk, and anything with "soul." Ottawa's oldest tavern,
opened in 1849 as Chateau Lafayette, is now
The Laff (42 York St., 613/241-4747, www.
thelaff.ca, 11am-2am daily), with music most
nights, from Open-Mic Tuesdays to Jukebox
Fridays.

For cocktails and eclectic tacos (perhaps char siu pork belly or Baja-style
fish), find your way to the chic **Side Door
Restaurant** (18b York St., 613/562-9331,
www.sidedoorrestaurant.com, hours vary),
a lounge-style space inside a stone heritage
building. The entrance is literally the side
door, on Clarendon Court, off York Street.

Local socialists—and socialites—say "*da*"
to the eclectic mix of Soviet propaganda
posters, local art, and vast menu of Russian-
themed drinks (how about a Red Square or
a Proletarian Omelet?) at the appropriately
named **Avant-Garde Bar** (135½ Besserer
St., at Dalhousie St., 613/321-8908, www.
avantgardebar.ca, 5:30pm-2am Tues.-Sat.). If
you're hungry, share a bourgeois fish plate or a
bowl of Siberian *pelemeni* (dumplings).

Designed like an inviting living room
filled with mid-century modern furnishings,
Charlotte (340 Elgin St., 2nd floor, 613/421-
0669, www.charlotteottawa.com, 1pm-
12:30am Tues.-Wed., 1pm-1:30am Thurs.-Fri.,
6pm-1:30am Sat., 4pm-12:30am Sun.) is a cozy
lounge for drinks and a small menu of vegetarian snacks. It's upstairs above Pure Kitchen
vegetarian restaurant.

In Chinatown, **Shanghai Restaurant**
(651 Somerset St. W., 613/233-4001, https://
theshang.wordpress.com, 4:30pm-10pm
Tues.-Fri. and Sun., 4:30pm-2am Sat.) turns
into a quirky club on Saturday nights when
the owners' son, a drag queen who goes by
the name China Doll, hosts **karaoke night**
(9am-2am).

THE ARTS

The capital's major arts venue is the
National Arts Centre (NAC, 1 Elgin St.,
613/947-7000 or 866/850-2787, www.nac-
cna.ca, box office 10am-9pm Mon.-Sat., additional hours on Sun. performance days).
It's home to English- and French-language
theater, the NAC Orchestra, and a dance series. The NAC also hosts numerous festivals
and special events.

Purchase tickets for NAC events in person at the box office or from **Ticketmaster**
(www.ticketmaster.ca, 888/991-2787, service
fees apply) online or by phone. See the NAC
website for more details on buying tickets.
If you're between the ages of 13 and 29, you
can purchase last-minute **Live Rush tickets**
(www.liverush.ca) to NAC theater, music, and
dance events for only $15, plus a second ticket
for an accompanying guest of any age. Live
Rush tickets go on sale between 10am until
the performance time on the day of the show,
online or at the NAC box office. Students with
a valid student ID can purchase advance tickets at a 50 percent discount in-person at the
NAC box office.

Outside the NAC, look—or listen—
for **Oscar's Corner** (Elgin St. and Albert
St.), a larger-than-life-size bronze statue of
Canadian jazz great Oscar Peterson, created by Canadian sculptor Ruth Abernethy.
Recordings of Peterson's music play at the site,
making it seem as if the musician (1925-2007)
is still tinkling away on his piano. A popular
photo op: sit on the bench beside Peterson's
likeness.

Theater

Every year, the **National Arts Centre
English Theatre** (www.nac-cna.ca/en/
englishtheatre) typically presents five plays
in the main 800-seat theater and three plays
in the 290-seat studio theater, ranging from
classics to contemporary Canadian works. It
also produces family plays and other special
presentations.

Established in 1975, the professional **Great
Canadian Theatre Company** (GCTC, 1233

Wellington St. W., 613/236-5196, www.gctc.ca, adults $35-49, seniors and students $35) performs several contemporary plays each year, focusing on works by Canadian playwrights or with Canadian content. The first Sunday of each production's run is a pay-what-you-can performance; be at the box office at noon to buy a ticket (donation) for the 2pm show. In addition to the main-stage productions, smaller local companies present works in the black-box studio theater.

For a good yarn, **Ottawa Storytellers** (613/322-8336, www.ottawastorytellers.ca) present Speaking Out (adults $22, seniors $18, Jan.-Jun.), monthly professional storytelling performances at the National Arts Centre; see their website for performance dates. Prefer more personal stories? Check out **(un)told Ottawa** (613/322-8336, www.untoldottawa.com, see website for schedule and location, free) where tellers share tales from their lives, without notes or props.

Music

The **National Arts Centre Orchestra** (www.nac-cna.ca/en/orchestra) performs in the NAC's 2,323-seat Southam Hall. Concerts are typically held September through June.

Big-name rock, pop, country, and other musicians perform at the **Canadian Tire Centre** (1000 Palladium Dr., 613/599-0100, www.canadiantirecentre.com). The arena is a 30-minute drive (25 kilometers, 16 miles) west of downtown via Highway 417. **OC Transpo Connexion bus no. 403** (www.octranspo.com) will take you from downtown to the arena in about 45 minutes.

Dance

Canadian and international ballet and contemporary dance companies perform as part of the **NAC Dance Series** (www.nac-cna.ca/dance) at the National Arts Centre. The roster has included the National Ballet of Canada, Royal Winnipeg Ballet, Alvin Ailey American Dance Theatre, Les Ballet Jazz de Montréal, and many other well-known and lesser-known troupes.

FESTIVALS AND EVENTS

Ottawa seems to host one festival after another, particularly during the summer months. The biggest events are the Canada Day festivities, celebrating the nation's birthday on July 1, and the winter festival known as Winterlude; make your travel arrangements in advance if you'll be in town for either of these.

For a complete calendar or more information about the festivities listed here, check online at **Ottawa Festivals** (www.ottawafestivals.ca) or **Ottawa Tourism** (www.ottawatourism.ca).

Spring

More than one million tulips herald the beginning of spring during the annual **Canadian Tulip Festival** (613/567-5757 or 800/668-8547, www.tulipfestival.ca, May). The festival runs for about two weeks, with events around the city, including the ByWard Market, Lansdowne Park (Bank St., in the Glebe district), and Commissioners Park (Preston St. and Queen Elizabeth Dr.) near Dows Lake, south of downtown. Besides the opportunity to tiptoe through the tulips, the festival includes free concerts, garden parties, kids' programs, and fireworks.

Among Canada's largest literary events, the semiannual **Ottawa International Writers Festival—Spring** (613/562-1243, www.writersfestival.org, Apr.-May) offers author readings, lectures, book launches, poetry cabarets, and other literary activities at several venues around the city. Some are free; others require tickets.

Summer

Although Quebec observes all of Canada's national holidays, the province has its own *Fête Nationale* (www.tourismeoutaouais.com or www.fetenationale.quebec, June), also known as Saint-Jean-Baptiste Day, which Ottawa-Gatineau celebrates with a big outdoor concert featuring Quebecois musicians.

Held in conjunction with Canada's National Aboriginal Day, the weekend-long

Summer Solstice Indigenous Festival (613/838-5558, www.ottawasummersolstice. ca, June) showcases aboriginal artists, musicians, and dancers, with lots of kids' activities.

It's been called "Canada's biggest party"—the annual **Canada Day Celebrations** (819/997-0055 or 866/811-0055, www. ottawatourism.ca, July 1) include scads of free activities, from official ceremonies to street performers to concerts; past headliners have included the Barenaked Ladies and Serena Ryder. A highlight is the nighttime fireworks show.

Summer also brings a number of music events to town, including the **TD Ottawa Jazz Festival** (613/241-2633, www. ottawajazzfestival.com, June-July), **RBC Bluesfest** (613/247-1188 or 866/258-3748, www.ottawabluesfest.ca, July), and **Ottawa Chamberfest** (613/234-6306, www. chamberfest.com, July-Aug.).

Ottawa's Greek community welcomes visitors to join in **GreekFest** (613/225-8016, www.ottawagreekfest.com, Aug.), a 10-day party of music, dancing, and, of course, food.

Culminating in a huge Pride Parade and outdoor concert, **Ottawa Capital Pride** (613/680-3033, www.ottawacapitalpride.ca, Aug.) has been celebrating Ottawa's LGBTQ community since 1986.

Fall and Winter

Like the spring version of this book festival, the **Ottawa International Writers Festival—Fall** (613/562-1243, www. writersfestival.org, Oct.) hosts readings, book talks, lectures, and other events for the literarily inclined.

In the world's coldest national capital (a dubious honor that both Moscow and Ottawa claim), what can you do but embrace the long winter? Ottawa does just that during **Winterlude** (844/878-8333, www.winterlude. gc.ca, Feb.), a midwinter festival of outdoor fun that takes place on several February weekends. You'll find an ice sculpture competition, skating on the Rideau Canal, North America's largest outdoor snow playground, and other outdoor events. Bring your mittens!

During **Black History Month** (www. blackhistoryottawa.org, Feb.), lectures, concerts, and other special events celebrating the African Canadian experience take place around town.

Shopping

Ottawa's small cohort of local fashion designers sells its wares at boutiques around town. Visit the shops in the major museums for unique souvenirs, books, jewelry, and children's gifts.

SHOPPING DISTRICTS

Rideau Centre (50 Rideau St., 613/236-6565, www.rideaucentre.net, 9:30am-9pm Mon.-Sat., 11am-6pm Sun.) is a large mall housing Nordstrom and Simons department stores, popular North American chain stores including yoga-wear shop Lululemon, clothing retailers like the Gap and Anthropologie, and fast-food outlets like Tim Hortons and Starbucks. It's on the east side of the Rideau Canal, near the ByWard Market. Opposite Rideau Centre is a branch of the **Hudson's Bay** (73 Rideau St., 613/241-7511, www.thebay. com, 9:30am-9pm Mon.-Sat., 10am-6pm Sun.) department store.

The streets around **ByWard Market** are happy hunting grounds for shoppers looking for unique boutiques. West of the market building, **Sussex Drive** is lined with high-end clothing shops. East of the market, head to **Dalhousie Street** for more eclectic, and more affordable, fashion and housewares.

Outside the city center, the trendy **Wellington West** district is another spot to find interesting boutiques, food shops, and cafés. Start around the intersection of

Wellington and Holland and continue west along Wellington Street. From downtown, it's about a 10-minute drive or 15-minute bus ride; take OC Transpo bus no. 86 to the corner of Holland and Wellington Streets.

ART GALLERIES

Among the contemporary art galleries near the ByWard Market is **Gordon Harrison Gallery** (495 Sussex Dr., 613/746-6853, www.gordonharrisongallery.com, 10am-6pm Wed. and Sat.-Sun., 10am-8pm Thurs.-Fri.), which showcases the work of landscape painter Gordon Harrison, as well as works by other contemporary Canadian landscape artists.

During the **Wellington West 1st Thursdays Art Walk** (www.wellingtonwest.ca, 5pm-9pm Thurs., free), on the first Thursday of the month, you can visit this west-of-downtown neighborhood's art galleries. Get a list of participating galleries on the website.

locally made goods at the ByWard Market

BOOKS AND MAGAZINES

Downtown, **Perfect Books** (258A Elgin St., 613/231-6468, www.perfectbooks.ca, 10am-6pm Mon.-Wed. and Sat., 10am-9pm Thurs.-Fri., noon-5pm Sun.) is a friendly independent bookshop with a knowledgeable staff.

CLOTHING AND ACCESSORIES

Focusing on wearable clothing by Canadian female designers, with roughly half its stock made in Ottawa, funky **Workshop Studio and Boutique** (242 Dalhousie St., 613/789-5534, www.workshopboutique.ca, 10am-6pm Mon.-Wed. and Sat., 10am-8pm Thurs.-Fri., noon-5pm Sun.), near the ByWard Market, also carries accessories, purses, jewelry, and gifts.

The same owners operate **Flock Boutique** (1275 Wellington St. W., 613/695-0834, www.flockboutique.ca, 10am-6pm Mon.-Wed. and Sat., 10am-8pm Thurs.-Fri., 11am-5pm Sun.), carrying similarly eclectic Canadian-made clothing in the Wellington West neighborhood.

Another creative boutique for dresses, jewelry, and other goods for women, **Victoire** (1282-B Wellington St. W., 613/421-0089, 10am-6pm Mon.-Wed. and Sat., 10am-8pm Thurs.-Fri., 11am-5pm Sun.) describes its style as "Rock'n'Roll tea party . . . loved by rebel girls with good manners everywhere."

You gotta love the cheeky spirit of a boutique named **Trustfund** (493 Sussex Dr., 613/562-0999, www.trustfundboutique.com, 10am-6pm Mon.-Wed. and Sat., 10am-9pm Thurs.-Fri., noon-6pm Sun.). Do you need your own trust fund to afford the au courant, and not inexpensive, fashions for men and women? No, but it wouldn't hurt.

GOURMET TREATS

Watch the chocolate makers at work at **Cylie Artisans Chocolatiers** (204 Dalhousie St., 613/695-8887, www.cyliechocolat.com, 10am-6pm Wed.-Sat., 11am-5pm Sun.), crafting beautiful bonbons that look more like art than food. Purchase a gift box for a fortunate friend—or treat yourself.

Sports and Recreation

PARKS

With the park-lined Rideau Canal running through town, Ottawa feels like a green city. Downtown, you can relax in **Major's Hill Park** (Mackenzie Ave.), behind the Fairmont Château Laurier, or in **Confederation Park** (Elgin St. and Laurier Ave.), which hosts Canada Day festivities, as well as Winterlude events. The bigger **Commissioners Park** (Preston St. and Queen Elizabeth Dr.) is near Dows Lake, south of the city center. The region's largest green space is **Gatineau Park** (33 Scott Rd., Chelsea, 819/827-2020 or 800/456-3016, www.ncc-ccn.gc.ca), in the hills on the Quebec side of the Ottawa River.

SUMMER SPORTS
Cycling

The Ottawa-Gatineau region has more than 220 kilometers (137 miles) of cycling paths as part of the **Capital Pathway** network (www.ncc-ccn.gc.ca). The paths that are most accessible from the central city are the **Rideau Canal Pathway,** a flat paved trail that runs for eight kilometers (five miles) on either side of the canal; the 31-kilometer (19-mile) **Ottawa River Pathway** that takes you from Parliament Hill west to the Canadian War Museum and beyond; and the 12-kilometer (7.5-mile) paved **Rideau River Pathway,** which begins near Rideau Hall and follows the Rideau River south. Get cycling maps online at www.ncc-ccn.gc.ca or from the **Capital Information Kiosk** (90 Wellington St., 844/878-8333, www.canada.ca, 10am-5pm daily).

On **Sunday Bikedays** (www.ncc-ccn.gc.ca, late May-early Sept.), the city closes a number of roads to cars, creating additional cycling, in-line skating, running, and walking routes. In Ottawa, sections of the Sir John A. Macdonald Parkway, Colonel By Drive, and Sir George-Étienne Cartier Parkway become bikeways; in Gatineau Park, it's the Gatineau, Champlain, and Fortune Lake Parkways. Note that the Gatineau routes are hilly.

Rent bicycles from **RentABike** (2 Rideau St., at Colonel By Dr., 613/241-4140, www.rentabike.ca, 9am-5pm daily mid-Apr.-Oct. 9am-7pm daily early July-late Aug., $10-15/

A popular cycling route follows the Ottawa River.

hour, $32-50/day), at the Plaza Bridge near the Rideau Canal, or from **Escape Tours & Rentals** (65 Sparks St., 613/608-7407 or 888/667-2012, www.escapebicycletours.ca, $8/hour, $28/day). **VeloGo** (www.velogo.ca) operates Ottawa's public bike-sharing system. Its website provides instructions, rental locations, and prices.

Rafting

Prefer to do your exploring by water? You can enjoy a gentle rafting adventure without even leaving the city on a trip with **Ottawa City Adventures** (844/688-7238, www.ottawacityadventures.com, adults $75, ages 5-12 $55). This family-friendly three-hour excursion, which starts at Britannia Beach west of the city center, runs three short rapids with lots of peaceful float time in between, before ending near the Canadian War Museum. Call or check their website for seasonal schedules and transportation options.

Yoga

Join hundreds of fellow downward-doggers for **Parliament Hill Yoga** (613/230-6633, www.lululemon.com, noon-1pm Wed. May-Aug., free), a one-hour open-air yoga class on the lawn in front of the Parliament buildings. Sponsored by the local Lululemon athletic-wear store, the free noontime classes, offered on Wednesday in summer, are open to everyone, regardless of your yoga experience. However, classes may be relocated or rescheduled due to construction on Parliament Hill; call or check the Lululemon Ottawa Facebook page to confirm.

WINTER SPORTS

Even Ottawa's frigid winters don't keep locals indoors, and if you visit during the colder months, you should get outside, too. Skating on the Rideau Canal is a don't-miss experience. For cross-country skiing and snowshoeing, head for the trails in **Gatineau Park** (33 Scott Rd., Chelsea, 819/827-2020 or 800/456-3016, www.ncc-ccn.gc.ca).

The world's largest ice-skating rink, the **Rideau Canal Skateway** (613/239-5000 or 866/811-0055 information, 613/239-5234 ice conditions, www.ncc-ccn.gc.ca, generally Jan.-early Mar., free) stretches 7.8 kilometers (4.8 miles), beginning just south of Wellington and Rideau Streets and continuing beyond Dows Lake. You can rent skates at several points en route. Closest to downtown, **Capital Skates** (819/923-7039, www.capitalskates.ca, generally 10am-10pm daily, last rental 8pm, $22 for 1st 2 hours) is on the east side of the canal, between the Mackenzie King and Laurier Bridges; farther south is a second location on the west side of the canal near the intersection of the Queen Elizabeth Driveway and 5th Avenue (2pm-10pm Fri., 10am-10pm Sat.-Sun., last rental 8pm). Skate rentals are also available at **Dows Lake Pavilion** (1001 Queen Elizabeth Dr., 613/232-1001, ext. 5, www.dowslake.com, 9am-10pm daily, last rentals 1 hour before closing, adults $15 1st hour, $8 per additional hour, children $12 1st hour, $8 per additional hour). Locals recommend bringing a backpack to carry your shoes as well as water and snacks. Check the ice conditions before heading out, too, because even a brief stretch of warmer temperatures can unexpectedly close the canal to skaters.

It may seem rather sedate after cruising along on the canal, but you can also skate at the **Rideau Hall Ice Rink** (1 Sussex Dr., 613/991-4422 or 866/842-4422, www.gg.ca, noon-5pm Sat.-Sun. early Dec.-mid-Mar., free), on the grounds of the governor general's residence.

SPECTATOR SPORTS

The Senators aren't just Parliamentarians—they're also the capital's National Hockey League team. The **Ottawa Senators** (613/599-0200 or 800/444-7367, www.ottawasenators.com) play at the **Canadian Tire Centre** (1000 Palladium Dr., 613/599-0100, www.canadiantirecentre.com), 25 kilometers (16 miles) west of downtown off Highway 417, about a 30-minute drive. **OC**

Transpo (www.octranspo.com) Connexion bus no. 403 makes the 45-minute trip between downtown and the Canadian Tire Centre when there are hockey games or other events at the arena. The regular hockey season runs October to April.

The **Ottawa Redblacks** (613/599-3267 or 877/489-2849, www.ottawaredblacks.com), which played their inaugural season in the professional Canadian Football League in 2014, take to the field at **TD Place** (Lansdowne Park, 1015 Bank St.) from June through October. The city's professional soccer team, **Ottawa Fury FC** (613/599-3267 or 877/489-2849, www.ottawafuryfc.com), also play at TD Place July through October.

Food

Ottawa's reputation as a bland, beige bureaucrats' burg is changing, and no more so than in its dining scene. Imaginative contemporary fare, small plates, and international influences all make Ottawa an inspired choice for foodies.

FOOD TOURS AND CLASSES

To learn more about the culinary landscape in Ottawa's neighborhoods, book an entertaining food walk with **C'est Bon Epicurean Adventures** (613/722-8687 or 613/291-9155, www.cestboncooking.ca). Their most popular tours are the 2.5-hour ByWard Market excursions ($59) with stops at food shops, cafés, and restaurants around the market area. They offer similar tours of Chinatown, Little Italy, and Wellington West, as well as cooking courses.

Even if you're not planning to become the top chef at a gastronomic temple, you can still take a cooking class at **Le Cordon Bleu Ottawa** (453 Laurier Ave. E., 613/236-2433 or 888/289-6302, www.cordonbleu.edu, from $170 pp), the only Canadian branch of the famed French culinary school. Half-day, full-day, and multiday programs in French regional cuisine, knife skills, chocolate making, and more are offered for culinary enthusiasts; previous cooking experience is not required.

Savvy Company (613/728-8926, www.savvycompany.ca) organizes some of Ottawa's most informative and entertaining food-focused evenings. Cheese tastings are led by their in-house "cheese sommelier" and there are also wine tastings and multicourse dinners where guests mingle with local food producers. Great fun!

As you're exploring Ottawa's food shops and restaurants, look for the **Savour Ottawa** (613/699-6850, ext. 10, www.savourottawa.ca) logo. Savour Ottawa is an organization whose mandate is to promote local food and support Ottawa's development as a culinary destination. Member businesses must meet minimum standards for using local food. Their website is also a useful resource for learning about eating local in Ottawa.

DOWNTOWN

While the downtown area is filled with nondescript breakfast and lunch spots catering to local office workers or famished visitors, you can find a more interesting meal if you walk a few blocks south or west of Parliament Hill.

Contemporary

Snug storefront bistro **Clover** (155 Bank St., 613/680-8803, www.cloverottawa.ca, 11am-2pm Mon.-Tues., 11am-2pm and 5pm-9pm Wed.-Thurs., 11am-2pm and 5pm-10pm Fri., 5pm-10pm Sat., lunch $18-22, dinner $25-33), decorated with works by local artists, uses lots of local ingredients in dishes like a salad of greens and puffed grains or a braised chicken panini with Brussels sprouts slaw at midday, and steak (raised nearby) paired with soft polenta or stuffed rabbit with roasted root vegetables in the evening. Vegetarians have options as well, from sautéed chickpeas with shaved carrots to a kimchi-tofu rice bowl.

For an elegant evening out, book a table (or seat at the chef's counter) in the grand former bank that houses gourmet hot spot **Riviera** (62 Sparks St., 613/233-6262, www.dineriviera.com, 11:30am-2pm and 5pm-10pm Mon.-Thurs., 11:30am-2pm and 5pm-11pm Fri., 5pm-11pm Sat., 5pm-10pm Sun., lunch $16-28, dinner $22-46). The menu starts with tuna crudo, venison tartare, and other raw items, and then continues with appetizers like wild mushrooms on thick toast topped with a quivering egg, a changing selection of house-made pastas, and mains like bouillabaisse or duck "ham." To drink, choose from a long list of negronis and specialty cocktails.

A dark, skinny room lined with a stainless steel bar, neighborhood bistro ★ **Town** (296 Elgin St., 613/695-8696, www.townlovesyou.ca, 5pm-10pm Sun.-Thurs. and 5pm-11pm Fri.-Sat., $14-32) feels both homey and hip—a spot where you could dine solo, bring a date, or hang out with your pals. Italian-influenced sharing plates constitute most of the seasonally changing menu, where you might find rabbit risotto with carrot harissa, eggplant lasagna, or braised beef short ribs with gnocchi.

Ottawa may be a northern capital, but cheeky **Union Local 613** (315 Somerset St. W., 613/231-1010, www.union613.ca, 11:30am-2pm and 5:30pm-10pm Mon.-Fri., 10am-2pm and 5:30pm-10pm Sat., 10am-2pm Sun., late-night menu 10:30pm-2am Wed.-Sat., $24-33) proudly serves "inauthentic Southern food." The menu meanders from good ol' plates like juicy fried chicken with pepper vinegar or shrimp and grits to wilder dishes like bison tartare. Sip your way through the long list of bourbons and whiskeys or quaff a pungent house-made ginger beer. It even has a tiny on-site brewery, **Dog and Pony Brewlab** (www.dogandponybrewlab.com).

Seafood

Love oysters? **Whalesbone Oyster House** (430 Bank St., 613/231-8569, www.thewhalesbone.com, 11:30am-2pm and 5pm-10pm Mon.-Tues., 11:30am-10pm Wed.-Thurs., 11:30am-11pm Fri., 5pm-11pm Sat., 5pm-10pm Sun., lunch $12-25, dinner $26-45) has 'em, shucking several varieties from North America's East and West Coasts. Yet it's not just bivalves that has Ottawa seafoodies swimming into this laid-back Centretown joint, with its sturdy wooden tables and exposed brick walls; the menu includes a variety

duck "ham" at Riviera

of fresh fish in intriguing preparations, like mackerel with pork belly and bok choy in a shitake broth or Ontario walleye with clams and chorizo. There's another location at 231 Elgin St. (613/505-4300, 11:30am-10pm Mon., 11:30am-11pm Tues.-Wed., 11:30am-midnight Thurs.-Fri., 5pm-midnight Sat., 5pm-10pm Sun.).

If you want fresh fish without any fancy trappings (like tables and chairs), the same owners run the nearby **Whalesbone Kent** (504A Kent St., 613/231-3474, 10am-5pm Tues.-Sat.). It's primarily a fish market, but they also sell fish sandwiches and chowder to go.

Vegetarian

The straightforward but well-prepared vegetarian dishes, fresh juices, and accompanying cocktails draw plant eaters and their non-veg companions to bustling **Pure Kitchen** (340 Elgin St., 613/233-7873, www.purekitchenottawa.com, 7am-10pm Mon.-Fri., 9am-10pm Sat.-Sun., $12-20). Share some spicy cauliflower "wings" or mushroom dumplings, dig into a big salad or veggie burger, or try a hearty bowl like the Warrior, piled with falafel, quinoa, sauerkraut, kale, sweet potatoes, and grilled avocado. An "electrify" juice, blending beets, pineapple, cucumber, ginger, and turmeric, should energize you for more sightseeing.

Middle Eastern

Stylish ★ **Fairouz** (343 Somerset St. W., 613/422-7700, www.fairouz.ca, 5pm-9:30pm Sun.-Wed., 5pm-10pm Thurs.-Sat., $16-39) serves modern Middle Eastern fare in a pretty room, decorated with turquoise banquettes and marble tables in a brick Victorian. The gracious staff can help you select among plates designed to share, from crunchy, savory *muhammara* (pomegranate-cashew dip served with warm homemade pita) or *pastourma* (an excellent cured salmon) to showstopping plates like a grilled, stuffed whole trout with dill tahini. To drink, try an *arak* or the nonalcoholic Diplomat, a smooth blend of citruses and ginger beer.

Bakeries and Cafés

The **Scone Witch** (150 Elgin St., 613/232-2173, www.sconewitch.ca, 7am-7pm Mon.-Fri., 8am-4pm Sat.-Sun., scones from $2) casts its spell on lovers of the humble biscuit. Lemon poppy seed? Currant ginger? Orange cranberry? It's hard to choose a favorite flavor, so you might have to sample more than

pomegranate dip and homemade pita at Fairouz

one. At midday, try a sconewitch—a sandwich served on a freshly baked scone.

For a quick weekday bite, pop into **Bread & Sons** (195 Bank St., 613/230-5302, www.breadandsons.com, 7am-5:30pm Mon.-Fri., $4-8) for slices of vegetarian pizza, borekas (savory filled pastries), cookies, muffins, and yes, loaves of bread. Most business is takeout, though you might score a seat at the narrow wooden bar.

Whether you've got the midnight munchies, crave breakfast at 3pm, or need to refuel with a plate of meat loaf, a burger, or gooey poutine, **Elgin St. Diner** (374 Elgin St., 613/237-9700, www.elginstreetdiner.com, 24 hours daily, $6-17) is your place. It's not gourmet, but it's wholesome. If your kids can't find something they like here, send them home.

At a warehouse complex west of downtown, locals line up in the cavernous industrial space at popular bakery-café **Art Is In Boulangerie** (250 City Centre Ave., Unit 112, 613/695-1226, www.artisinbakery.com, 7am-6pm Mon.-Fri., 8am-5pm Sat., 8:30am-4pm Sun., $7-15) for pastries, inventive sandwiches, and weekend brunch. While you can pair a half-sandwich with soup or salad, consider getting your greens another time; the fresh-baked breads are swoon-worthy. Or go right to the oversized chocolate cookies, "kronuts," or other sweets. Note that the kitchen keeps slightly shorter hours than the bakery/coffee service (7am-4pm Mon.-Fri., 8:30am-4pm Sat., 9am-3pm Sun.).

BYWARD MARKET DISTRICT AND VICINITY

Despite its touristy vibe, the **ByWard Market** (55 ByWard Market Square, 613/244-4410) is still a working food market, with vendors setting up produce and other market stalls around the main market building from late April or early May through October. You'll find plenty of cafés, restaurants, and bars in this part of town, too.

Contemporary

You know a place called **Play Food and Wine** (1 York St., 613/667-9207, www.playfood.ca, noon-2pm and 5:30pm-9:30pm Mon., noon-2pm and 5:30pm-10pm Tues.-Thurs., noon-2pm and 5:30pm-11pm Fri., noon-3:30pm and 5:30pm-11pm Sat., noon-9:30pm Sun., small plates $12-19) can't be too formal. The kitchen sends out a fun assortment of small plates designed to share. Wines by the taste, glass, or bottle include options from Ontario and farther afield. Owner Stephen Beckta conceived Play as a more casual sibling to his high-end **Beckta** (150 Elgin St., 613/238-7063, www.beckta.com, 11:30am-11pm Mon.-Thurs., 11:30am-midnight Fri., 5:30pm-midnight Sat., 5:30pm-10pm Sun., lunch $24-36, dinner prix fixe $74-105) downtown; he also runs **Gezellig** (337 Richmond Rd., 613/680-9086, www.gezelligdining.com, 11:30am-2pm and 5:30pm-9:30pm Mon.-Thurs., 11:30am-2pm and 5:30pm-10pm Fri.-Sat., 10am-2pm and 5:30pm-9pm Sun., lunch prix fixe $25, dinner $28-39), a well-regarded neighborhood bistro in a former bank west of the city center.

Classic French cooking is alive and well at **Signatures** (453 Laurier Ave. E., 613/236-2499 or 888/289-6302, www.signaturesrestaurant.com, 11:30am-1:30pm and 5:30pm-9pm Tues.-Fri., 5:30pm-9pm Sat., lunch prix fixe $34, dinner $36-41), the white-tablecloth restaurant at Le Cordon Bleu, the famous culinary school's only Canadian facility, set in an 1874 Sandy Hill mansion. Yet innovation has its place, too; the rack of lamb might come with an Indian coconut eggplant roll and the seared scallops might be served with truffle risotto and XO sauce. The gracious staff tempers French formality with Canadian affability.

Bakeries and Cafés

Taking its name from the flat, oblong tail of Canada's official animal, **BeaverTails** (69 George St., 613/241-1230, www.beavertails.com) cooks up Ottawa's signature pastry: slabs of whole-wheat dough served hot from the fryer. You can slather them with all sorts of ridiculously sweet toppings, like chocolate hazelnut spread or Oreo cookies, but the simplest choices are best: cinnamon sugar, with or without a squeeze of lemon. There's another BeaverTails stand along the Rideau Canal—a popular spot to take a break while skating.

Breathe deeply when you enter the **Tea Store** (53 York St., 613/241-1291, www. teastore.ca, 9am-7pm Sun.-Thurs., 9am-8pm Fri.-Sat.), the better to take in the spicy, fruity, and earthy aromas of more than 200 varieties of tea. This peaceful tea shop and café makes a flavorful chai latte, which you can pair with pastries like tea-scented scones.

To pick up a sandwich on the run, or to gather picnic supplies, squeeze into **La Bottega Nicastro** (64 George St., 613/789-7575, www.labottega.ca, 9am-6pm Mon.-Wed. and Sat., 9am-8pm Thurs.-Fri., 10am-5pm Sun.), a jam-packed (or make that pasta-, cheese-, and *salumi*-packed) Italian deli and food shop. Choose your meat, cheese, bread, and toppings at the sandwich bar for custom-made panini ($7).

CHINATOWN, LITTLE ITALY, AND THE GLEBE

Ottawa's Chinatown (www.ottawachinatown. ca) is not strictly Chinese, particularly when it comes to eating. The neighborhood is home to a large concentration of Vietnamese eateries alongside Chinese, Korean, Japanese, and even Middle Eastern options. Somerset Street West, between Bay and Rochester Streets, is Chinatown's main street, with restaurants east and west of the colorfully painted Chinatown Gateway arch. OC Transpo bus no. 11 runs from downtown along Somerset through Chinatown.

Little Italy, along Preston Street southwest of downtown, still has traditional red-sauce restaurants, but it's the more modern, non-Italian dining rooms that make the area worth a stop. Bus no. 85 will get you to the vicinity of Little Italy. In the Glebe, centered on Bank Street south of downtown, food options include a mix of hip-grunge cafés, natural foods eateries, and contemporary restaurants. Buses no. 6 and 7 travel along Bank Street from downtown.

Contemporary

Duck Terrarium. Tombstone. The menu names alone are (almost) worth a visit to chef-owner Marc Lepine's **Atelier** (540 Rochester St., 613/321-3537, www.atelierrestaurant.ca, 5pm-8:30pm Tues.-Sat., prix fixe $125 pp, reservations essential), where dinner is an elaborate 12-course tasting menu that has flush foodies aflutter. The kitchen will make modifications for "allergies, strong dislikes, and vegetarians" but otherwise, you get whatever wildly inventive dishes are on the evening's menu. Ottawa beige and bland? Not in this atelier.

A sunny gastropub near Lansdowne Park, with blond wood tables, green walls, and a garage door opening to the street, **The Rowan** (915 Bank St., 613/780-9292, www.therowan. ca, 11:30am-2pm and 5:30pm-10pm Mon.-Fri., 10am-2pm and 5:30pm-10pm Sat., 10am-2pm and 5pm-9pm Sun., lunch $15-19, dinner $24-32) updates a classic pub menu with imaginative modern twists. At lunch, try the seared trout sandwich paired with fat potato wedges, a sweet potato and grilled veggie sandwich, or handmade pasta with bacon, parmesan, and peas. In the evening, there might be roasted cauliflower salad with chickpea hummus, pork pie, or crisp fried quail. Weekend brunch is popular, too.

It's not just the name that's clever at **Two Six Ate** (268 Preston St., 613/695-8200, www. twosixate.com, 4pm-2am Wed.-Mon., $12-22), an easygoing bistro in a Little Italy Victorian, with rough plastered walls and aged wood floors. The always-changing, designed-to-share dishes are equally engaging. You might sup on arancini made of cauliflower risotto and roasted yams, crispy fried Brussels sprouts with shawarma-style garlic sauce, or Mediterranean-flavored octopus with olive tapenade. No need to dress up; just bring your appetite for sampling. Night owls: The kitchen stays open till 2am.

Asian

The cheapest meal in town may be a banh mi (Vietnamese sandwich) from **Co Cham** (780 Somerset St. W., 613/567-6050, 10:30am-9pm daily, $3-8), where the bus fare to get here will cost more than your lunch. At this bare-bones Chinatown storefront, you can choose from several combinations of meat, pickled carrots and daikon, and fresh herbs on a bun—all for only $3 each. The menu includes other Vietnamese classics, too, from pho (noodle soup) to *bun* (rice noodles with meat, bean sprouts, and herbs). To drink, opt for tea or a fruit shake.

WELLINGTON WEST

Even though it's just a short ride west of downtown, you won't see many tourists in the Wellington West neighborhood. What you will find is lots of interesting eating, from cafés to refuel as you're browsing the boutiques, to contemporary dining rooms serving inventive food to a mostly local clientele.

Contemporary

Yes, you can sample the namesake green spirit at **Absinthe Café and Resto Bar** (1208 Wellington St. W., 613/761-1138, www.absinthecafe.ca, 11:30am-2pm and 5pm-10pm Mon.-Fri., 5:30pm-10pm Sat.-Sun., lunch $15-17, dinner $24-34); try "Death in the Afternoon" (absinthe and sparkling wine) or opt for a tasting flight of three absinthe varieties. Food options include traditional *steak frites,* but you might also find peanut-crusted cod with a fresh herb salad or ricotta and leek agnolotti with creamed kale. The candlelit dining room is decorous enough for a business meal yet relaxed enough for a night on the town.

Roast duck breast served with cornbread hash and button mushrooms is just one of the original dishes that might grace the oak tables at **Allium** (87 Holland Ave., 613/792-1313, www.alliumrestaurant.com, 5:30pm-9pm Mon., 11:30am-2pm and 5:30pm-9pm Tues.-Thurs., 11:30am-2pm and 5:30pm-10pm Fri., 5:30pm-10pm Sat., lunch $16-21, dinner $26-31), a smart-casual bistro decorated with modern art. Come for the popular Monday tapas night to sample a changing assortment of small plates ($10-32), from foie gras pâté with herbed French toast to buttermilk fried chicken with bacon aioli. The restaurant is one block north of Wellington Street.

The black seahorses on the wallpaper give chic ★ **Supply and Demand** (1335 Wellington St. W., 613/680-2949, www.

lunch at The Rowan

supplyanddemandfoods.ca, 5pm-10pm Tues.-Sat., 5pm-9:30pm Sun., $9-44) a fanciful feel, yet this über-modern kitchen plays with its food in a serious way—with top-notch results. Bring friends to this bustling brasserie, the better to sample your way through the artistically plated seafood-centric dishes. Start with something from the menu's "raw and marinated" category, perhaps buttery tuna *crudo* in a lemon-truffle oil with chips of black puffed rice.

Bakeries and Cafés

Thyme and Again Take Home Food Shop (1255 Wellington St. W., 613/722-6277, www.thymeandagain.ca, 8am-7pm Mon.-Tues., 8am-8pm Wed.-Fri., 9am-6pm Sat., 9am-5pm Sun.) is part café and part take-out shop, carrying sandwiches, prepared foods, and luscious pastries. On the second floor, the small **Exposure Gallery** (613/722-0093, ext. 225, www.exposuregallery.ca) shows work by emerging local artists.

Accommodations

Ottawa's lodging options include hostels, bed-and-breakfasts, boutique hotels, and major chain lodgings. Many hotels are located downtown, within walking distance of Parliament Hill. The ByWard Market neighborhood has several hotels and B&Bs. You'll find more B&Bs south and east of the market in residential Sandy Hill.

Perhaps because the federal government attracts businesspeople and bureaucrats for long-term stays, the capital has numerous suite hotels with kitchen facilities, many of which are comfortable for families, even if you're visiting for just a day or two. In addition to the suite hotels listed below, try **Premiere Executive Suites** (www.premieresuites.com), which rents studio, one-, and two-bedroom apartments around town for short-term stays. **AirBnB** (www.airbnb.com) lists lots of Ottawa rentals, too.

DOWNTOWN
$150-200

There are plenty of social spaces at the good-value, centrally located ★ **Alt Hotel Ottawa** (185 Slater St., 613/691-6882 or 844/258-6882, www.althotels.com, $179-209 d), from work tables to a pool table in the lobby, bar, and café, where you can have coffee or a light meal. Upstairs, the 148 simple, efficiently designed guest rooms have down duvets, convenient bedside lamps, one-cup coffeemakers, comfy reading chairs, and eclectic artwork. The small fitness room is open 24/7, and you can access the complimentary Wi-Fi throughout the property.

Built around an open atrium in a six-story 1906 building, **The Metcalfe** (123 Metcalfe St., 613/231-6555 or 844/871-6555, www.themetcalfehotel.com, $180-309 d) appeals to travelers looking for laid-back boutique style. The living room-like lobby sports a street-art mural, vintage board games, reclaimed wood beams, and library shelves, while the 106 guest rooms, some of which face into the atrium, give you modern amenities, from flat-screen TVs and coffeemakers to complimentary Wi-Fi. Guests share the fitness room and indoor pool with the Residence Inn by Marriott next door.

The spacious one- and two-bedroom suites at the **Albert at Bay Suite Hotel** (435 Albert St., 613/238-8858 or 800/267-6644, www.albertatbay.com, 1-bedroom $169-269 d, 2-bedroom $289-349 d) are a good deal for families or couples traveling together. Even the smallest of the 197 traditionally furnished units are over 74 square meters (800 square feet)—more than double the size of many hotel rooms—and all have full kitchens. There's no pool, but the fitness room overlooks the rooftop terrace. Local phone calls and Wi-Fi are included.

Over $200

Starting with a glass of sparkling wine at check-in, ★ **ARC The.Hotel** (140 Slater St., 613/238-2888 or 800/699-2516, www.arcthehotel.com, $249-399 d), a stylish 112-room boutique property, makes you feel welcome. The guest rooms, with cream-colored upholstery and dark wood furniture, have a Zen feel, with Egyptian cotton linens and Keurig coffeemakers adding a luxurious touch. The smallest rooms, dubbed "intimate queens," are indeed intimate; the king-bed units will give you more space. If a workout in the 24-hour fitness center doesn't sufficiently relax you, unwind over a cocktail in the lounge.

In a stately stone building with a green copper roof, the traditionally elegant ★ **Lord Elgin Hotel** (100 Elgin St., 613/235-3333 or 800/267-4298, www.lordelgin.ca, $189-329 d), built in 1941, is an Ottawa institution, with an excellent location near Parliament Hill. Of the 355 guest rooms with classic Biedermeier-style furnishings and free Wi-Fi, some of the nicest are the corner units overlooking the National Arts Centre. Sip cocktails in the gracious lobby lounge; on the lower level are a lap pool, hot tub, and fitness room. The hotel welcomes families and frequently offers good-value discounts.

An ample breakfast buffet, indoor lap pool and fitness facility, free Wi-Fi, and a guest laundry are among the features that make the 177-room **Residence Inn by Marriott** (161 Laurier Ave. W., 613/231-2020 or 877/478-4838, www.marriottresidenceinnottawa.com, $199-469) popular with road warriors and traveling families. The studios, with a king bed and queen sofa bed, are about the size of typical hotel rooms, but the one- and two-bedroom suites are quite large, especially the corner units; all have kitchens. The hotel hosts happy hours several nights a week where guests can mingle.

BYWARD MARKET DISTRICT AND VICINITY

In the ByWard Market district and the adjacent, primarily residential Sandy Hill neighborhood (south of Rideau St.), lodging choices range from hostels, B&Bs, and small hotels to big chain properties.

Under $100

Even if you don't usually stay in hostels, have a look at the **HI-Ottawa Jail Hostel** (75 Nicholas St., 613/235-2595 or 866/299-1478, www.hihostels.ca, $45-52 dorm, $65-68 s, $107-136 d), where some beds are in cells of the 19th-century former Carleton County Gaol (jail). The cells feel claustrophobic and noisy, with heavy grates on the doors and transom windows open to the hallways. More standard dorms and shared-bath doubles lack the cellblock ambience, but rumors of ghosts abound. Guests share the kitchen or hang out in Mugshots, the pub. Rates include Wi-Fi, breakfast, and a jail tour.

For women only, the **Barefoot Hostel** (455 Cumberland St., 613/237-0336, www.barefoothostel.com, $38-42 dorm) is Ottawa's coolest budget lodging. Inside this redbrick building near the ByWard Market, the common area with bright blue walls has space for lounging, with a flat-screen TV and computers for guest use. While there's no room to spare in the four dorms, each with four bunks, they're cheery, with wood floors and individual lockers. Guests share two modern baths. Would-be chefs, take note: the kitchen has a microwave, fridge, and toaster, but no stove. The hostel is under the same ownership as the Swiss Hotel next door.

$100-200

Occupying two sides of a brick town house on a residential street in the east end of Sandy Hill, the seven rooms at friendly, family-run **Benner's B&B** (539-541 Besserer St., 613/789-8320, www.bennersbnb.com, $95-130 d) mix traditional furnishings with contemporary pieces. All have private baths, wood floors, flat-screen TVs, and large windows; the sleek, airy Pewter Room, done in silver and white, has a private balcony, while the large King Loft has exposed brick walls and a sitting area in front of an electric fireplace. The location is

family-run Benner's B&B

a bit out of the way, but rates include parking and a full breakfast.

Co-owner Oscar Duplancic often serenades guests on the grand piano during breakfast at the aptly named **Bella Notte B&B** (108 Daly Ave., 613/565-0497 or 866/562-9569, www. bellanottebb.com, $138-188 d); Oscar and his wife, Lillian, are both professional musicians. Besides the high-ceilinged dining room with a marble fireplace, one of the nicest spaces is the cozy sitting room upstairs. The three guest rooms are simpler, with carpeted floors. The largest is the third-floor unit with sloped ceiling; another has a private balcony. The brick row house, built in 1868, was once home to Sir Alexander Campbell, one of Canada's founding fathers.

Plenty of homey touches grace three-story **McGee's Inn** (185 Daly Ave., 613/237-6089 or 800/262-4337, www.mcgeesinn.com, $118-225 d, parking $10), like the hand-carved cherry mantel in the parlor. Built in 1886, as the home of Privy Council member John McGee, this family-run inn has 14 guest rooms. Some are small, others quite large, but all have private baths and antique or period furnishings. Several have original wood fireplaces, some have whirlpool tubs for two, and a couple have private porches. Internet access and a full breakfast are included.

One of Ottawa's top midrange lodgings is the 22-room **Swiss Hotel** (89 Daly Ave., 613/237-0335 or 888/663-0000, www. swisshotel.ca, $148-228 d). From the exterior of the 1872 stone building, you'd never know that inside, the petite but stylish rooms are a riot of color balanced with crisp white duvets. Every room has an iPad, flat-screen TV, and free Wi-Fi. Owner Sabina Sauter, who has run the inn since the mid-1980s, is a tornado of enthusiasm, tending to guests' needs. Breakfast ($15) includes homemade Swiss muesli, plus freshly baked breads, cheeses, fruits, eggs, and more.

Perhaps some of the rooms in the modest, European-style **ByWard Blue Inn** (157 Clarence St., 613/241-2695 or 800/620-8810, www.bywardblueinn.com, $161-252 d) should have been named "ByWard View," since the sunny, top-floor front units—the inn's nicest—have tiny terraces with views toward Parliament Hill. The rest of the 46 rooms in this six-story building, just east of the ByWard Market, are more basic (and viewless; the cheapest are small and dark), but all have fridges, microwaves, and free Internet access. Rates include continental breakfast.

Over $200

Ottawa's landmark hotel, the castle-like ★ **Fairmont Château Laurier** (1 Rideau St., 613/241-1414 or 866/540-4410, www.fairmont. com/laurier-ottawa, $219-439 d), has a perfect location between the Rideau Canal and ByWard Market and prides itself on service. Some of the traditionally elegant rooms are smallish, but others are quite spacious, and the public spaces, like the Renaissance-style ballroom with 5.5-meter (18-foot) ceilings, are grand. The art deco pool has its original brass heat lamps. Before booking, join Fairmont's complimentary frequent-stay program; members get free Wi-Fi.

Rising 16 stories on the edge of the ByWard Market district, **Andaz Ottawa Byward Market** (325 Dalhousie St., 613/321-1234, www.andazottawa.com, $285-415 d) feels luxurious and cool without being intimidating, where staff greet you with a drink and are keen to suggest local activities. The artwork on each floor represents a different Canadian province or territory, while the 200 guest rooms are large and contemporary; ask for one above the 5th level for city views. On the top floor, the 24-hour fitness room is lined with windows, and the lounge is a great place to watch the sunset, overlooking Parliament Hill and the Ottawa River.

WEST OF THE CITY
$150-250

While **Brookstreet Hotel** (525 Legget Dr., 613/271-1800 or 888/826-2220, www.brookstreet.com, $167-250 d, parking $13), a modern 18-story tower set amid Ottawa's high-tech district west of the city, is popular with tech types on business, its resort amenities—indoor and outdoor saltwater pools, a well-equipped fitness center with drop-in yoga and other classes, bicycles, table tennis, a game room, golf, and a spa—make it a good option for active families and any visitors who don't need to be right downtown. The 276 airy, road warrior-friendly guest rooms have work

the landmark Fairmont Château Laurier

desks, Wi-Fi, bedside outlets, one-cup coffeemakers, and teakettles. Students at a local arts high school created the artworks that decorate the rooms and public spaces. With a circular bar and a fireplace, Options Lounge gives you options for cocktails and light meals, with live jazz nightly; Perspectives restaurant serves three meals a day. The hotel runs a shuttle to concerts and sports events at the Canadian Tire Centre.

Information and Services

Visitor Information

For planning a trip to Ottawa, the best source for up-to-the-minute information is **Ottawa Tourism** (150 Elgin St., Suite 1405, www.ottawatourism.ca, 613/237-5150 or 800/363-4465, 8:30am-4:30pm Mon.-Fri.). Their comprehensive website lists scores of details about the city's sights, activities, and current events. Once you arrive, pick up visitor information or get your questions answered at the **Capital Information Kiosk** (90 Wellington St., 844/878-8333, www.canada.ca, 10am-5pm daily).

Media and Communications

Ottawa's daily newspapers are the *Ottawa Citizen* (www.ottawacitizen.com) and *Ottawa Sun* (www.ottawasun.com). *Ottawa Magazine* (www.ottawamagazine.com), published monthly in print and available online, also covers the arts, restaurants, and things to do.

Transportation

GETTING THERE

Air

Ottawa International Airport (YOW, 1000 Airport Pkwy., 613/248-2125, www.yow.ca) is 15 kilometers (nine miles) south of downtown. **Air Canada** (888/247-2262, www.aircanada.ca) has nonstop flights to Ottawa from most major Canadian cities, U.S. destinations that include Boston, New York, Washington, Fort Lauderdale, and Orlando, as well as London (UK) and Frankfurt. **WestJet** (800/538-5696, www.westjet.com) flies to several Canadian and U.S. destinations, and **Porter Airways** (888/619-8622, www.flyporter.com) has flights to Toronto's City Airport, Halifax, Fredericton, St. John, and Moncton. Several U.S. carriers, including **Delta** (800/221-1212, www.delta.com) and **United** (800/864-8331, www.united.ca) serve Ottawa as well. Ottawa is also a departure point for travels to Canada's far north. **Air North** (800/661-0407, www.flyairnorth.com) connects Ottawa to Yellowknife and Whitehorse, and **Canadian North** (800/661-1505, www.canadiannorth.com) flies between Ottawa and Iqaluit.

The least expensive way to get downtown from the airport is by public transit. Catch OC Transpo **bus no. 97** (613/741-4390, www.octranspo.com, Presto/cash adults $3.45/$3.50, ages 6-12 $1.75/$1.80) outside the arrivals area; it will take you downtown in 30-35 minutes. The bus runs about every 20 minutes during the day and every 30-60 minutes at night. Paying with a Presto card, an automated fare card, is slightly cheaper than the cash fare and you can reload your card ($6) online in advance or from the automated dispenser. A taxi from the airport to the downtown area will cost $30-40; Uber also picks up passengers at the Ottawa airport.

Train

If you're traveling to Ottawa from Toronto or Montreal, the train is a fast, efficient option. **VIA Rail** (200 Tremblay Rd., 888/842-7245, www.viarail.ca) has several trains a day to both Toronto (4.25-4.75 hours, one-way adults $50-250, ages 2-11 $25-122) and Montreal (2 hours, one-way adults $38-115, ages 2-11 $20-58). The Ottawa-Toronto trains all stop in Kingston (2-2.25 hours, one-way adults $48-131, ages 2-11 $24-66), and certain trains stop in Brockville, Belleville, and Cobourg.

Ottawa's VIA Rail station is five kilometers

(three miles) southeast of the city center. From the Confederation Line's Tremblay Station, connected to the VIA Rail station, you can ride to the ByWard Market area (Rideau station) or downtown/Parliament Hill (Parliament station). A taxi from the train station to downtown will cost about $15-20, depending on traffic conditions.

Bus

Ottawa's **Central Bus Station** (265 Catherine St., 613/238-6668) is south of downtown on the edge of the Glebe neighborhood. **Greyhound** (800/661-8747, www. greyhound.ca) runs most of the bus routes in and out of Ottawa, including service to Montreal (2.5 hours, one-way adults $22-43, ages 2-11 $17-31), Toronto (5.25-6 hours, one-way adults $38-89, ages 2-11 $31-68), Kingston (2.5-2.75 hours, one-way adults $21-43, ages 2-11 $20-35), North Bay (5.5 hours, one-way adults $39-96, ages 2-11 $38-77), and Sudbury (7.75 hours, one-way adults $50-99, ages 2-11 $44-81). Greyhound also runs several buses daily between Ottawa and Montreal's Trudeau International Airport (2.25 hours, one-way adults $22-39, ages 2-11 $17-38).

Between Ottawa and either Montreal or Toronto, the train is more comfortable than the bus, but the buses travel more frequently. To go downtown from the Central Bus Station by public transit, walk two blocks east to Bank Street and catch northbound **bus no. 6** or **bus no. 7** (613/741-4390, www.octranspo. com, Presto/cash adults $3.45/$3.50, ages 6-12 $1.75/$1.80).

Car

Ottawa is located in Eastern Ontario on Highway 417. It's closer to Montreal (2-2.5 hours by car) than it is to Toronto (about a five-hour drive). From Montreal to Ottawa (200 kilometers, 125 miles), take Autoroute 40 west until it meets Highway 417 at the Ontario-Quebec provincial border.

From Toronto to Ottawa (450 kilometers, 280 miles), the most straightforward route is to follow Highway 401 east, past Kingston and Brockville, and then turn north on Highway 416, which joins Highway 417 just south of Ottawa. A more scenic route would be to pick up Highway 7 east of Toronto and follow it northeast until it meets Highway 417. You could also take Highway 401 east to Kingston, then meander north on Highway 15, through the small towns along the Rideau Canal.

From Kingston to Ottawa (200 kilometers, or 125 miles), it's about two hours by car. From the east gate of Algonquin Park to Ottawa, it's about 240 kilometers (150 miles), but the roads aren't fast, so allow 3.5 hours. Take Highway 60 east to Highway 17 east, which will join Highway 417 as you continue east into Ottawa.

GETTING AROUND

The majority of Ottawa's attractions are clustered around the downtown area, so it's easy to get around on foot. You can even walk across the bridge to the Canadian Museum of History in Gatineau (although to reach Gatineau Park and other Gatineau destinations, you'll need to have wheels of some sort). The city's comprehensive bus system is useful if you're traveling farther afield, or if you need to rest your feet.

Bus and Light-Rail

Ottawa's public transit system, **OC Transpo** (613/741-4390, www.octranspo.com), includes an extensive network of buses that travel through the city center and out to the suburbs, and as this book went to press, the city was preparing to open the **Confederation Line**, a light-rail line. Most buses operate 6am-midnight Monday-Saturday and 7am-11pm Sunday; service is frequent on weekdays, with buses running every few minutes at peak times, but less so on weekends. Bus no. 97 between the airport and downtown operates 24 hours daily.

You can either pay cash (with exact change) when you enter the bus or pay with an automated Presto card. It's slightly less expensive to use Presto, but you must purchase and load your card in advance, before you board the bus. Buy Presto cards online, and you'll receive the card in the mail; you can then activate and load it online. You can also buy Presto cards from automated dispensers in the Confederation Line stations, at Rideau Center—the **OC Transpo Sales and Information Centre** (50 Rideau St., 8:30am-9pm Mon.-Fri., 9:30am-9pm Sat., 11am-6pm Sun.) is on the 3rd floor—or inside Ottawa City Hall (110 Laurier Ave., 8:30am-5pm Mon.-Fri.).

Presto fares are $3.45 for adults, $1.70 ages 6-12; cash fares are $3.50 for adults, $1.80 ages 6-12. If you pay cash, get a transfer from the driver when you board the bus. It's your proof of payment, and it's valid for 90 minutes if you transfer to another route.

If you're going to use the buses several times in one day, buy a **DayPass** ($10.50), good for unlimited trips on the day that you purchase it. Buy the pass from the bus driver when you board (you need exact change) or from an automated dispenser in a light-rail station. The DayPass is a great deal on weekends, when the whole family (two adults and up to four kids under 12) can travel all day on a single DayPass. Use the Travel Planner on the **OC Transpo website** (www.octranspo.com) to figure out what bus or train to take and when they operate.

Downtown, many east-west buses run on Albert Street going westbound and Slater Street going east; some lines instead stop on Wellington Street, near Parliament. Going north-south, buses run on Elgin and Bank Streets. On the east side of the Rideau Canal near the ByWard Market, Rideau Street, around Rideau Centre, is a main transit point for buses heading in many directions.

Taxi

You can usually find taxis near major attractions and hotels, and at the airport, train station, and bus depot. Taxi stands are also located at several points throughout downtown. Taxis are metered. Local companies include **Blue Line Taxi** (613/238-1111, www.bluelinetaxi.com) and **Capital Taxi** (613/744-3333, www.capitaltaxi.com). Uber operates in Ottawa.

Car

Highway 417, also known as the Queensway, is the region's main east-west highway. A network of parkways winds along the rivers and the canal. If you're driving in the city center, pay attention to the many one-way streets. Wellington Street runs east-west in front of Parliament, while Elgin and Bank Streets are main north-south streets downtown. On the east side of the Rideau Canal, Sussex Drive heads north, skirting the ByWard Market neighborhood, and continuing toward Rideau Hall, the governor general's residence. Rideau Street is the main east-west road between the canal and the Rideau River.

Parking can be a challenge in downtown Ottawa. On-street parking is limited to a maximum of three hours between 7am and 7pm, so park in a lot if you'll be longer. Most lodgings charge extra—sometimes a lot extra—for parking, so ask before you book. On Saturday and Sunday, **parking is free** downtown at on-street parking meters and in city-owned parking lots. The free parking zone is bounded by Wellington Street on the north, the Rideau Canal on the east, Catherine Street on the south, and Bronson Avenue on the west. City parking lots in this area include 212 Gloucester Street and 234-250 Slater Street, both between Bank and Kent Streets. Check the city website (www.ottawa.ca) for additional parking information. Between November 15 and April 1, you cannot park overnight on city streets (between 1am and 7am) when Environment Canada forecasts a snow accumulation of seven centimeters or more. To find out if an overnight parking ban is in effect, call the city information line at 311.

Tours

A fun, family-friendly way to explore Ottawa is on an **Urban Quest** (613/853-2886, www.urbanquest.com, year-round, $10 pp), where you solve a series of clues that lead you from place to place. You can do a quest with any number of people, but most are designed for two to four. Typically lasting around 1.5 hours, quests end at a mystery restaurant where you can have lunch or dinner (not included in the quest fee).

Plunge into the Ottawa River on the **Lady Dive Amphibus Tour** (office 613/524-2221, ticket kiosk 613/223-6211, www.ladydive. com, May-mid-Oct., adults $33, seniors and students $30, ages 6-12 $23, under age 6 $12, families $89), which combines a circuit of the city's main attractions with a river cruise in an amphibious vehicle. Buy your ticket online or at their kiosk at Sparks and Elgin Streets.

With **Ottawa Walking Tours** (613/799-1774, www.ottawawalkingtours.com, over age 10 $15, under age 11 free), you get a two-hour guided historical walk around the city's main attractions. Tours depart from the Terry Fox statue opposite Parliament Hill (90 Wellington St., at Metcalfe St.). Advance reservations are required; tour schedules are posted on the website.

Gatineau

Cross the Ottawa River from downtown Ottawa, and you enter the district of Gatineau in the province of Quebec. You're still in metropolitan Ottawa, but it can feel as if you've wandered into another country. While much of Ottawa's population is bilingual, once you enter Gatineau, the first language is definitely French. Several bridges connect this Quebec region, known as the Outaouais (pronounced "oo-ta-WAY"), with the rest of metropolitan Ottawa.

Before a municipal amalgamation in 2003, Gatineau's downtown area was the city of Hull, and some people still use the older name. If an address is located in "Hull," head for downtown Gatineau.

SIGHTS

Cross the bridge to Quebec for one of the region's best museums: the Canadian Museum of History. Ottawa's largest green space, Gatineau Park, is on the Quebec side, as is a lovely Nordic-style day spa and a lively casino.

★ Canadian Museum of History

Canada's most-visited museum is the **Canadian Museum of History** (100 Laurier St., 819/776-7000 or 800/555-5621, www. historymuseum.ca, 9am-5pm Fri.-Wed., 9am-8pm Thurs. May-late June, 9am-6pm Fri.-Wed., 9am-8pm Thurs. late June-early-Sept.,

9:30am-5pm Fri.-Wed., 9:30am-8pm Thurs. early Sept.-Apr., adults $20, seniors $18, students $16, ages 3-12 $12, families $50, free admission 4pm-8pm Thurs., parking $5 per hour, $12.50 per day), a massive showcase of human history and culture displaying both comprehensive permanent collections and regularly changing temporary exhibitions.

Opened in 1989 on the banks of the Ottawa River, the building is one of Ottawa's most distinctive structures, notable for its curved, undulating walls. Alberta-born architect Douglas Cardinal, who is of Métis heritage (his other credits include the Smithsonian Institution's National Museum of the American Indian in Washington DC), was responsible for the museum's design.

The museum's showpiece is the multigallery **Canadian History Hall**, which you enter through a dramatic walkway lined with silver and white etchings illustrating people and places across the country, from iconic buildings to kids playing soccer. The exhibits themselves begin with multimedia displays about Canada's indigenous people, with stories and oral histories alongside artifacts and please-touch reproductions. The galleries continue through periods of European settlement, immigration, western expansion, and Quebec nationalism, up to the present day, with an emphasis on society and culture—the role of women settlers, the lives of Ukrainian migrants, the development of the national health care system—as much as topics of government and war.

On the museum's lower level, the **First Peoples** galleries examine indigenous issues further, emphasizing arts, stories, and traditional ways of life. Besides containing one of the world's largest collections of totem poles, the exhibits trace the history of Canada's aboriginal communities. Look for the sculpture *Spirit of Haida Gwaii* by noted First Nations artist Bill Reid (1920-1998).

Admission covers access to a "museum within the museum"—the **Canadian Children's Museum**—and to the CINE+ IMAX theater. To walk to the history museum from the Ottawa side of the river, cross the Alexandra Bridge near the National Gallery of Canada. To reach the museum by boat, board the **Au Feel de l'Eau Aqua Taxi** (819/329-2413, www.aufeeldeleau.ca, one-way adults $6, ages 12 and under $5, round-trip adults $10, children $8, cash only) at the dock near the Rideau Canal's Ottawa lock; it's on the river behind the Bytown Museum.

By bus, catch the **Société de Transport de l'Outaouais** (www.sto.ca) bus no. 31 (Cégep Gabrielle-Roy) or 67 (Station de la Cite) on Wellington Street at Metcalfe, and get off at Musée de L'Histoire (History Museum).

★ Gatineau Park

When Ottawans want to escape the city, they head for their backyard—this 361-square-kilometer (89,000-acre) green space in the Gatineau Hills—for hiking, cycling, picnicking, canoeing, or just relaxing.

Start at the **Gatineau Park Visitors Centre** (33 Scott Rd., Chelsea, 819/827-2020 or 800/456-3016, www.ncc-ccn.gc.ca, 9am-5pm daily May-Oct., 9am-4pm Mon.-Fri., 9am-5pm Sat.-Sun. Nov.-Apr.) for maps and tips from the staff to plan your explorations. The park also has a seasonal **Welcome Area** (Gamelin Blvd. at Gatineau Pkwy., Sat.-Sun. late-May-mid-Oct.) where you can stop for information.

Gatineau Park has 165 kilometers (103 miles) of **hiking trails.** The 2.5-kilometer (1.5-mile) Pink Lake Trail circles the lake of that name. Head for the Champlain Lookout for views across the Ottawa Valley, and walk the 1.3-kilometer (0.8-mile) Champlain Trail. Download a trail map from the www.ncc-ccn.

Canadian Museum of History

gc.ca website, or pick up a free copy at the Visitors Centre or in Ottawa at the **Capital Information Kiosk** (90 Wellington St., 844/878-8333, www.canada.ca, 10am-5pm daily).

You can swim in several of the park's lakes, including Meech, Philippe, and La Pêche Lakes (parking $11 per vehicle). At Philippe and La Pêche Lakes, you can rent canoes and kayaks ($20 for 1.5 hours, $25 for 2 hours, $30 for 3 hours), as well as stand-up paddle-boards ($25 for 1.5 hours, $31 for 2 hours, $37 for 3 hours).

Also in the park is the **Mackenzie King Estate** (819/827-2020, 10am-5pm Mon. and Wed.-Fri., 11am-6pm Sat.-Sun. mid-May-mid-Oct., parking $12 per vehicle), the country home of William Lyon Mackenzie King, Canada's 10th prime minister. You can tour the estate's several cottages and lush gardens (there's even an "Arc de Triomphe"), or stop for a sandwich, salad, or afternoon tea at the **Mackenzie King Tearoom** (819/827-9229, 11am-5pm Mon.-Fri., 11:30am-6pm Sat.-Sun. mid-May-mid-Oct., $10-22).

The park is open all year. Fall is one of the best times to visit Gatineau Park, when the leaves change color; come midweek to avoid the leaf-peeping crowds. In October, the park hosts its **Fall Rhapsody,** with a variety of special events. In winter, you can hike, snow-shoe, or cross-country ski; purchase a trail pass at the Visitors Centre or at any of the park's 15 departure points.

There is no public transportation to Gatineau Park. The Visitors Centre is a 20- to 30-minute drive from downtown Ottawa.

Nordik Spa-Nature

If "steam, soak, and be soothed" is your mantra, you'll be in heaven at North America's largest Nordic-style spa, **Nordik Spa-Nature** (16 Chemin Nordik, Chelsea, 819/827-1111 or 866/575-3700, www.lenordik.com, 9am-11pm Sun.-Thurs., 9am-midnight Fri.-Sat., $55 Mon.-Thurs., $65 Fri.-Sun., massages and other services extra), where the seven baths of varying

the "Arc de Triomphe" in the gardens of the Mackenzie King Estate

temperatures are outdoors amid the trees. You alternate between hot and cold treatments; there are eight saunas, an infinity pool, even a saltwater float pool. Several areas are silent—the better for relaxation—while others are set up for socializing. With a restaurant and lounge on-site, you can easily spend an entire day. Children under age 16 are not allowed.

Casino du Lac-Leamy

Gambling, as well as concerts, shows, and several restaurants, bring visitors across the bridge to Gatineau's swanky **Casino du Lac-Leamy** (1 Blvd. du Casino, 819/772-2100 or 800/665-2274, www.casino-du-lac-leamy.com, 24 hours daily).

The **Société de Transport de l'Outaouais** (STO, 819/778-8327, www.sto.ca) bus no. 200 or 400 travels from downtown Ottawa to the casino. The casino supplies free bus tickets to guests at many downtown hotels; ask the concierge at your lodging. **Au Feel de l'Eau Aqua Taxi** (819/329-2413, www.aufeeldeleau.ca) runs a shuttle boat between downtown and the casino.

FOOD AND ACCOMMODATIONS

Hearty pub food—burgers, pasta, and a don't-miss duck confit grilled cheese sandwich—will fill your belly, while the friendly vibe and beers on tap will cheer your soul at the **Chelsea Pub** (238 Old Chelsea Rd., Chelsea, 819/827-5300, www.chelseapub.ca, 11:30am-midnight Mon.-Fri., 11am-midnight Sat., 11am-11pm Sun., $12-17). Established as a tavern in 1875, it's one of several casual eateries near the Gatineau Park Visitors Centre.

Microbrewery **Les Brasseurs du Temps** (170 rue Montcalm, 819/205-4999, ext. 1, www.brasseursdutemps.com, 11:30am-midnight Mon.-Wed., 11:30am-2am Thurs.-Fri., 1pm-2am Sat., 1pm-midnight Sun., $12-22) brews a variety of beers that you can order along with the international pub fare, from sandwiches to fish-and-chips to poutine. They even try to make beer drinking educational with an exhibit on the history of brewing in the Outaouais.

Tiny **Chez Edgar** (60 rue Bégin, 819/205-1110, www.chezedgar.ca, 10am-5pm Tues.-Sat., 9:30am-5pm Sun.) is a popular purveyor of contemporary comfort food for lunch and weekend brunch: pastries, soups, creative sandwiches, and salads.

If you can't drag yourself away from the blackjack tables, or if you just want a comfortable place to stay in Gatineau, you can crash at the **Hôtel Hilton Lac-Leamy** (3 Blvd. du Casino, 819/790-6444 or 866/488-7888, www.hilton.com, $249-439 d), where original works by glass artist Dale Chihuly decorate the lobby. Besides the 349 modern rooms, the hotel has indoor and outdoor pools, a fitness center, tennis courts, a large spa, several restaurants, and three bars. Parking is free in the outdoor lot.

PRACTICALITIES

Ottawa and Gatineau have separate bus systems. Some Ottawa (OC Transpo) buses go to Gatineau, but Gatineau's own bus system, **Société de Transport de l'Outaouais** (STO, 819/778-8327, www.sto.ca), operates within Gatineau and between Gatineau and downtown Ottawa; the STO website has route maps and a trip planner. The regular STO adult cash fare is $4. You can purchase

lunch at the Chelsea Pub near Gatineau Park

an STO day pass, called *La Passe-temps,* for $8.50, good for unlimited travel for one day. Regular OC Transpo bus tickets are not accepted on the STO system. However, you *can* use an OC Transpo DayPass on STO buses. Taxi companies serving Gatineau include **Crown Taxi** (819/777-1645) and **Regal Taxi** (819/777-5231).

For information about Gatineau, contact **Outaouais Tourism** (103 Laurier St., 819/778-2222 or 800/265-7822, www.tourismeoutaouais.com). For more food-centric stops in Gatineau and vicinity, check out the **Outaouais Gourmet Way** (www.outaouaisgourmetway.com), an interactive directory of regional food experiences.

Cottage Country, Algonquin, and the Northeast

Look for ★ to find recommended sights, activities, dining, and lodging.

Highlights

★ **Muskoka Wharf:** Learn how steamships helped develop tourism around the Muskoka Lakes at this Gravenhurst development that includes a boat museum and runs lake cruises aboard a traditional steamship (page 318).

★ **Canoeing in Algonquin Provincial Park:** Ontario's largest provincial park is one of the province's best destinations for canoeing, whether you're paddling on the numerous lakes and rivers or taking a multiday trip across the backcountry (page 333).

★ **Science North:** Sudbury's cool, contemporary science museum is filled with "please touch" exhibits that are particularly eco-friendly (page 344).

★ **Temagami:** This lake region is one of the most accessible places in the north for canoe trips, whether you're a novice or experienced paddler (page 348).

★ *Polar Bear Express* **Train:** Go where no roads go on this rail trip north to James Bay, where you can explore the Cree First Nations communities of Moosonee and Moose Factory Island (page 352).

GRAVENHURST

F or a getaway to the outdoors, head north to Ontario's Cottage Country and to the woodland region that extends northeast all the way to James Bay.

The Muskoka Lakes region north of Toronto has long been a popular weekend getaway for families to escape to their summer cottages or stay at lakeside resorts. Muskoka Cottage Country begins just 100 kilometers (60 miles) north of Toronto, centered on the towns of Gravenhurst, Bracebridge, and Huntsville. Dotted with inland lakes, ski hills, and waterfront towns along Lake Muskoka and numerous smaller lakes, this region offers plentiful opportunities for outdoor adventure and relaxation. The area's top attraction is Algonquin Provincial Park, one of Ontario's largest protected green spaces; visit for a day or a week and take a hike, paddle across an inland lake, or set out on a multiday wilderness adventure.

Beyond Algonquin, smaller provincial parks like Arrowhead, Restoule, or Samuel de Champlain are great for families looking to camp, hike, or swim, while farther north, the lakes and forests surrounding Temagami make it a prime destination for canoe trips.

While the northeast is a natural choice for outdoor adventures, it's ripe for cultural explorations, too. Aboriginal people have lived in Northern Ontario for thousands of years, and many First Nations welcome visitors who want to learn about their culture and traditions. If you venture north to the remote communities of Moosonee and Moose Factory Island on the shores of James Bay, you can explore the culture of the Cree First Nation, one of Canada's largest aboriginal groups.

Northeastern Ontario also has a large francophone population, so don't be surprised to see bilingual signs or hear *"Bonjour"* and *"Merci."* The city of Sudbury is particularly bilingual; it's Canada's third-largest French-speaking community outside Quebec. In some northern towns, you'll find French Canadian influences in the food, with *tourtière* (meat pie) and *poutine* (french fries topped with cheese curds and gravy) almost as common as burgers and fries.

Looking for outdoor adventure? Cultural adventure? Just plain adventure? Then head north.

Previous: canoeing on Ontario's northern lakes; on the lake in Restoule Provincial Park. **Above:** Muskoka Wharf in Gravenhurst.

Cottage Country, Algonquin, and the Northeast

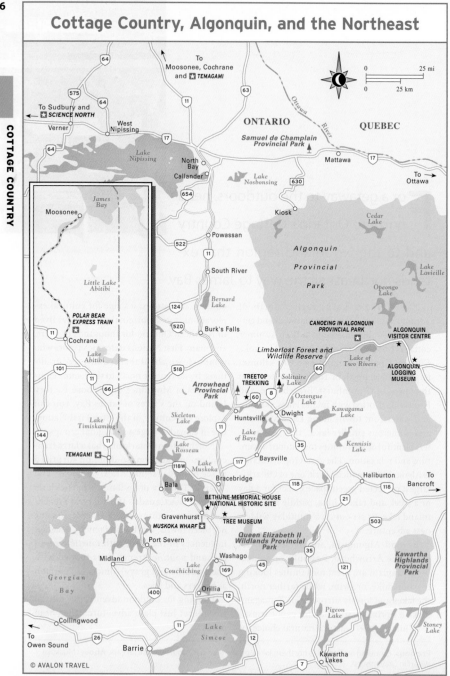

ONTARIO

QUEBEC

Ottawa River

To Moosonee, Cochrane and ✚ TEMAGAMI

To Sudbury and
← ✚ SCIENCE NORTH

Verner

West Nipissing

64

575

64

64

64

11

63

17

Lake Nipissing

North Bay

Callander

654

Samuel de Champlain Provincial Park

Mattawa

17

To Ottawa →

Lake Nosbonsing

630

Kiosk

Cedar Lake

Algonquin Provincial Park

Lake Lavieille

Opeongo Lake

CANOEING IN ALGONQUIN PROVINCIAL PARK ✚

ALGONQUIN VISITOR CENTRE ★

ALGONQUIN LOGGING MUSEUM ★

Limberlost Forest and Wildlife Reserve

Lake of Two Rivers

TREETOP TREKKING ★

Solitaire Lake

60

8

Oxtongue Lake

Kawagama Lake

Arrowhead Provincial Park

Huntsville

Dwight

Skeleton Lake

Lake Rosseau

Lake of Bays

35

Kennisis Lake

Baysville

Haliburton

To Bancroft

118W

Lake Muskoka

117

118

21

118

Bracebridge

Bala

169

BETHUNE MEMORIAL HOUSE NATIONAL HISTORIC SITE ★

503

Gravenhurst

✚ MUSKOKA WHARF

TREE MUSEUM ★

Queen Elizabeth II Wildlands Provincial Park

Port Severn

Midland

Washago

169

45

35

121

Lake Couchiching

Georgian Bay

400

Orillia

12

48

Pigeon Lake

Kawartha Highlands Provincial Park

Collingwood

To Owen Sound ←

26

Barrie

11

Lake Simcoe

12

7

Kawartha Lakes

Stoney Lake

Powassan

522

11

South River

124

Bernard Lake

520

Burk's Falls

518

60

Powassan

Inset map

James Bay

Moosonee

Little Lake Abitibi

POLAR BEAR EXPRESS TRAIN ✚

11

Cochrane

101

Lake Abitibi

11

66

144

Lake Timiskaming

11

✚ TEMAGAMI

© AVALON TRAVEL

0   25 mi

0   25 km

PLANNING YOUR TIME

This region is packed with outdoor activities, but many Cottage Country and northeastern attractions don't begin operation until mid- or late May and close in mid-October, after the Canadian Thanksgiving weekend. July and August are the busiest travel months; fall is the best time to visit, when the foliage is most dramatic. For autumn travel, try to come mid-week to avoid weekend leaf-peeping crowds.

A weekend trip could take you to the Muskokas and **Algonquin** for a relaxing outdoor getaway. You'd want at least a long weekend to take a canoe trip in **Temagami** or to explore the cities of North Bay or Sudbury. With several days to spare, you could travel to Cochrane, then take the **Polar Bear Express Train** onward to the Cree communities of **Moosonee** and **Moose Factory Island.**

Muskoka Cottage Country

TOP EXPERIENCE

With more lakes than you can count, the Muskoka region is one of Ontario's vacationlands. For many Ontarians, Muskoka is Cottage Country, a place to escape from the city, where your obligations are nothing more than to sit on the porch of your cottage and relax. Even people who don't have cottages of their own (or friends with cottages who invite them for weekends) head to Cottage Country to stay in B&Bs, hotels, or the many cottage resorts that dot the lakes.

The Muskoka region, north of Toronto, encompasses the towns of Gravenhurst, Bracebridge, and Huntsville, among others, extending northwest to Georgian Bay and northeast to Algonquin Provincial Park. Tourism to Muskoka began in earnest in the 1800s when steamboats transported visitors across the lakes. These days, nearly all the steamboats are gone (except for a couple used for sightseeing cruises), but the visitors continue to come. And if you're looking for a place to get outdoors, whether to hike, canoe, or just sit on the porch, you should, too.

BARRIE AND ORILLIA

Barrie isn't really part of the Muskoka region, but you'll likely pass through on your way north. Even though it's 105 kilometers (65 miles) north of Toronto, this small city on Lake Simcoe feels like an extension of the metropolitan area (and people do commute daily from Barrie to Toronto). It's a handy spot to break up your drive and have a bite to eat. Continuing north, another interesting stop is in the town of Orillia, 40 kilometers (25 miles) northeast of Barrie via Highway 11, where you can tour the former home of notable Canadian humor writer Stephen Leacock.

Sights

Barrie's small but worthwhile art museum, the **Maclaren Art Centre** (37 Mulcaster St., 705/721-9696, www.maclarenart.com, 10am-5pm Mon.-Fri., 10am-4pm Sat.-Sun., adults $5), exhibits work by established Canadian and emerging regional artists. Half of the building was Barrie's original public library, built in 1917; the other half is an airy contemporary addition. If you're looking for a gift for an arty friend, browse the jewelry and works by local artists in the gallery shop.

Though his day job was as a political science professor at Montreal's McGill University, Stephen Leacock (1869-1944) became famous as a writer and humorist. He published 35 humorous books, including *Sunshine Sketches of a Little Town* (1912) and *Arcadian Adventures of the Idle Rich* (1914). In 1928, Leacock built a summer house near Orillia's Old Brewery Bay. The home, which was his permanent residence following his retirement from McGill in 1936 until his death 12 years later, is now the **Stephen Leacock Museum** (50 Museum Dr., 705/329-1908, www.leacockmuseum.com, 10am-4pm daily June-Sept., 10am-4pm Mon.-Fri. Oct.-May, donation $5). Some parts of the house are nearly as Leacock left them, including the sunroom with his worktable and his living room facing the lake. On the main floor are signed portraits of Leacock that noted photographer Yousuf Karsh took in 1941.

Food

One of Ontario's largest and longest-running farmers markets, the year-round **Barrie Farmers Market** (Collier St. at Mulcaster St., www.barriefarmermarket.ca, 8am-noon Sat.) has been operating since 1846. Selling seasonal produce, prepared foods, yummy baked goods, and crafts, the market is outside city hall from May to October; it moves inside city hall from November to April.

Some of Barrie's most interesting food isn't downtown—it's in the strip malls and industrial parks off Highway 400. A good example is **Cravings Fine Food** (131 Commerce Park Dr., 705/734-2272, www.cravingsfinefood.ca, 9am-6pm Mon.-Tues., 9am-7pm Wed.-Fri., 9am-5pm Sat.), a café and gourmet shop that sells beautifully crafted (and scrumptious) pastries, sandwiches, salads, and other prepared foods, perfect for a quick meal on the road or to take north to the cottage.

If you love butter tarts, find your way to the shopping mall that houses **The Sweet Oven** (90 Park Place Blvd., Unit 2, 705/733-9494, www.thesweetoven.com, 10am-8pm Mon.-Sat.), which makes these tasty tarts ($3, or $15 for six) in numerous varieties. Flavors like peanut butter, mint, or chai are novelties, but the classics—plain, pecan, or raisin—are the best.

Practicalities

The provincially run **Ontario Travel Information Centre** (21 Mapleview Dr. E., 705/725-7280 or 800/567-1140, www.ontariotravel.net, 8am-8pm daily June-Aug., 9am-5pm daily Sept.-May), off Highway 400, can help with travel questions about Barrie and points north.

Pick up information about Barrie and the surrounding region at the helpful **Tourism Barrie Visitor Information Centre** (205 Lakeshore Dr., 705/739-9444 or 800/668-9100, www.tourismbarrie.com, 9am-5pm Mon.-Fri., 10am-4pm Sat. Sept.-June, 9am-5pm Mon.-Fri., 10am-4pm Sat.-Sun. July-Aug.), on the south side of Lake Simcoe. Tourism Barrie also staffs a seasonal **Downtown Information Kiosk** (Bayfield St. at Simcoe St., 9am-7pm daily May-mid-Oct.).

GRAVENHURST

You know you've arrived in Cottage Country when you pass by the **world's largest Muskoka chair** (397 Muskoka Rd. N.), in the parking lot of a craft brewery near the center of town. What's a Muskoka chair, you ask? It's the laid-back wooden porch chair that most Americans call an Adirondack chair. This symbol of relaxation gives you a clue of what Gravenhurst is all about.

Gravenhurst's main attractions are at **Muskoka Wharf** (www.discovergravenhurst.com), the lakefront development where you can tour a boat museum or cruise the lake in a traditional steamship. The town is also the birthplace of Norman Bethune, a Canadian doctor who became wildly famous in China, where he's still considered a hero long after his death.

Gravenhurst Opera House (295 Muskoka Rd. S., 705/687-5550 or 888/495-8888, www.gravenhurstoperahouse.com), built in 1901, hosts concerts, plays, and films. **Music on the Barge** (Gull Lake Rotary Park, Brock St. at Bethune Dr., 7:30pm Sun. mid-June-mid-Aug.) has brought toe-tapping summer concerts, from big band to Dixieland to folk, to the waterfront since 1959.

★ Muskoka Wharf

The Muskoka Lakes Navigation Company opened in 1866, and during its heyday operated the largest fleet of inland lake steamships in North America. The ships carried passengers and freight across the Muskoka Lakes, providing service where the railroads didn't reach and roads either didn't go or were difficult to navigate. More than 100 lakeside hotels once operated in the Muskokas, and guests all arrived by steamship.

One of these ships, the **RMS** *Segwun,* built in 1887 and used as an official Royal Mail Ship, remains North America's oldest operating steamship. **Muskoka Steamships** (185 Cherokee Lane, 705/687-6667 or 866/687-6667, www.realmuskoka.com, mid-June-mid-Oct., adults $21-50, kids $12.50-36) offers 1- to 4-hour sightseeing cruises on the *Segwun,* departing from their Muskoka Wharf docks.

Back on land, explore the region's steamship traditions at the creatively designed **Muskoka Discovery Centre** (275 Steamship Bay Rd., 705/687-2115, www.realmuskoka. com, 10am-6pm Mon.-Fri., 10am-4pm Sat.-Sun. mid-June-mid-Oct., 10am-4pm Tues.-Sat., noon-4pm Sun. mid-Oct.-mid-June, adults $12, seniors $9.50, kids $7, families $30), filled with multimedia exhibits. You can board a re-created steamship, and in a replica lakeside hotel, you can pretend that you're holidaying in the 19th century. Visit the Grace and Speed Boathouse, North America's only in-water exhibit of working antique boats, with up to 20 spiffy craft on view. Admission to the museum is free with a ticket from a Muskoka Steamships cruise.

Bethune Memorial House National Historic Site

Gravenhurst-born surgeon Henry Norman Bethune (1890-1939) became a legendary physician and a hero in China, known largely for a brief tour of service on the other side of the world.

In 1938, after China and Japan went to war, Bethune traveled to China to tend to the injured, and after he arrived at the front, the legend of the foreign doctor's commitment to the Chinese began to spread. Bethune implemented a medical education program and established mobile medical facilities, including an operating theater that two mules could carry. After less than two years in the country, however, Bethune accidentally cut his finger while performing an operation, developed an aggressive form of blood poisoning, and died within the month. Chinese leader Mao Zedong wrote an essay, "In Memory of Norman Bethune," which became required reading for Chinese students and helped solidify Bethune's status as an icon in China.

The **Bethune Memorial House National Historic Site** (297 John St. N.,

Muskoka Discovery Centre in Gravenhurst

705/687-4261, www.pc.gc.ca, 10am-4pm daily July-mid.-Oct., 10am-4pm Wed.-Sun. mid-May-June, 10am-4pm Thurs.-Sun. mid-late Oct., adults $3.90, seniors $3.40) comprises two buildings: a modern museum that recounts Bethune's history, and the 1880 home where Bethune was born. Visit on a weekday if you can, when the house's diminutive rooms are less crowded and staff have more time to explain Bethune's legacy.

Tree Museum

Among Cottage Country's most offbeat attractions is this outdoor art gallery outside Gravenhurst. No, the **Tree Museum** (1634 Doe Lake Rd., 705/684-8185, www.thetreemuseum.ca, dawn-dusk daily May-Oct., free) isn't a museum of trees—it's a gallery outside in an 80-hectare (200-acre) woodland with imaginative sculptures and other eclectic works among the trees. Be prepared for lots of walking along the sometimes-muddy paths. It's one kilometer (0.6 miles) from the parking area to the first sculpture, and another 1.2 kilometers (0.75 miles) to the center of the site; return the way you came. The museum has no restrooms or other facilities, so bring water and a snack.

To get to the Tree Museum, follow Highway 11 north past Gravenhurst, then exit at Doe Lake Road (Muskoka Rd. 6). Go east about eight kilometers (five miles) till you see museum signs on your right.

Food

Though it looks a bit twee, with floral café curtains and blue-and-white china, the **Blue Willow Tea Shop** (900 Bay St., Muskoka Wharf, 705/687-2597, www.bluewillowteashop.ca, 11am-4pm Tues.-Thurs., 11am-8pm Fri.-Sat., 11am-3pm Sun. spring-fall, 11am-3pm Wed.-Sun. winter, $7-17) makes a good lakeside rest stop at Muskoka Wharf. It serves soups, salads, and sandwiches at lunch, along with a large selection of black, green, and fruit teas. Midafternoon, take a tea break with a scone or slice of cake, or settle

in for traditional high tea ($24.50 pp), served June through September.

You'll be fed well at the **Well Fed Deli** (150 Hotchkiss St., 705/684-9355, www.wellfedinc.com, 8am-3pm Mon., 8am-5pm Tues.-Fri., 10am-3pm Sat.), a diminutive downtown shop serving sandwiches (they roast their own turkey, beef, and peameal bacon), seasonal salads, and fresh-baked pastries. Most business is take-out, since there are only two sidewalk tables out front.

The dozen taps at **Sawdust City Brewing Company** (397 Muskoka Rd. N., 705/681-1100, www.sawdustcitybrewing.com, 11am-11pm daily) dispense beer from this local craft brewer and other small local producers. The saloon has pizza to eat, live music most Saturdays (8pm-11pm), as well as weekly trivia nights.

Accommodations

Some of the 106 modern suites with kitchen facilities at **Residence Inn by Marriott** (285 Steamship Bay Rd., 705/687-6600 or 866/580-6238, www.marriott.com, $165-419 d), overlooking Lake Muskoka at Muskoka Wharf, are studios with sleeper sofas, while larger units have one or two bedrooms. Rates include buffet breakfast, parking, and Wi-Fi.

You won't be bored at **Taboo Resort** (1209 Muskoka Beach Rd., 705/687-2233 or 800/461-0236, www.tabooresort.com, May-Oct., $299-639 d), set in the woods on Lake Muskoka north of town. There's a private beach, four outdoor heated pools, golf, tennis, canoes, kayaks, and stand-up paddleboards, plus a lakeside restaurant and bar. The prime picks of the 101 guest rooms, done in sleek satiny woods, are right above the lake. Thirty individually decorated condos, with two to four bedrooms, are scattered around the property, although most don't have lake views.

Information and Services

Muskoka Tourism (1342 Hwy. 11 N., Kilworthy, 800/267-9700, www.discovermuskoka.ca) provides information about Gravenhurst and the Muskoka Lakes region online, by phone, and from its travel information center on Highway 11 south of Gravenhurst. Both the **Gravenhurst Chamber of Commerce** (www. gravenhurstchamber.com) and the **Town of Gravenhurst** (www.discovergravenhurst. com) provide visitor information online.

Getting There and Around
Gravenhurst is 180 kilometers (112 miles) north of Toronto and 75 kilometers (47 miles) north of Barrie. From Toronto, take Highway 400 north to Barrie, then continue north on Highway 11 into Gravenhurst.

From Toronto's Bay Street Station, **Ontario Northland** runs several daily buses to Gravenhurst (290 Brock St., 705/350-0358 or 800/461-8558, www.ontarionorthland. ca, 2.5-2.75 hours, one-way adults $40.20, seniors and students $35, ages 2-11 $20.10). Exploring Gravenhurst is easiest if you have a car, although you can walk between Muskoka Wharf and the town center. The nearest car rental offices are in Bracebridge.

BRACEBRIDGE
Like many Muskoka towns, Bracebridge's tourism industry dates to the late 1800s, when visitors from Toronto arrived by train and boat. Most of the old-time resorts are gone, but the town's main street, Manitoba Street, has an old-timey feel that makes for a pleasant stroll. Bracebridge is a good base for exploring the region—it's an easy drive to Gravenhurst or Huntsville and to other towns along the surrounding lakes.

Since the lakes are an important part of the Muskoka experience, get out on the water with **Lady Muskoka Cruises** (300 Ecclestone Dr., 705/646-2628 or 800/263-5239, www. ladymuskoka.com, noon Sat.-Sun. late May, noon Sat.-Sun. and Wed. June, noon daily July-Aug., noon Sat.-Sun. and Wed. Sept.-mid-Oct., adults $38, ages 13-18 $24.25, ages 4-12 $17), which operates sightseeing boats on Lake Muskoka.

Bracebridge's own microbrewery, **Muskoka Brewery** (1964 Muskoka Beach Rd., 705/646-1266, www.muskokabrewery. com, 9am-6pm Mon.-Fri., 10am-6pm Sat., 10am-5pm Sun. May-Oct., 9am-5pm Mon.-Thurs., 9am-6pm Fri., 10am-6pm Sat., 10am-4pm Sun. Nov.-Apr.), welcomes visitors to its shop. You can also tour the brewery (12:30pm, 1:30pm, and 2:30pm Fri.-Sun., free).

A Bracebridge summer tradition is the free **Bandshell Concert Series** (Memorial Park, Manitoba St., www.bracebridge.ca) on Thursday evenings from late June until late August or early September.

Food
A friendly joint for hanging out and sipping a microbrew, **The Griffin Gastropub** (9 Chancery Lane, 705/646-0438, www. thegriffinpub.ca, noon-late Tues.-Sat. late May-mid-Oct., 4pm-late Wed., noon-late Thurs.-Sat. mid-Oct.-late May, $12-18) serves inventive pub grub, including addictive risotto balls, bison burgers, and sticky toffee pudding. Live folk, rock, blues, or jazz usually starts around 9pm Thursday through Saturday. The pub is at the top of a narrow alleyway, off Manitoba Street.

Don't be put off by the strip mall setting; there's serious sushi savvy at the chic **Wabora Fusion Japanese Restaurant** (295 Wellington St. N., 705/646-9500, www. waborasushi.com, 11am-11pm daily, $8-20). The cavernous room has both an artfully arranged cocktail bar and a well-lit sushi bar where the chefs craft wildly imaginative *maki* rolls, like the Bracebridge (salmon, crab, asparagus, and gobo wrapped in cucumber with lemon-*ponzu*-caramel sauce) or the Spicy Cottage (shrimp tempura, crab, spicy tuna, greens, mango, and avocado in a rice paper roll). The straight-up *nigiri* are first-rate, too.

The owners of **El Pueblito** (155 Manitoba St., 705/645-1935, noon-8:30pm Tues., 8am-8:30pm Wed.-Thurs., 8am-9pm Fri.-Sat., 8am-1pm Sun., $13-20) ran a fine-dining restaurant at this same location, and they've incorporated their kitchen savvy and hospitality into this colorful Mexican eatery. Order a "cerveza local" from an area craft brewery,

Ontario's Cranberry Capital

cranberry wine made in Bala, Ontario's cranberry capital

Of all the foods that you associate with Canada, cranberries might not be high on the list. But the Cottage Country town of **Bala** is Ontario's cranberry capital.

Cranberries once grew wild here, providing food and natural medicine for the indigenous people who lived on the land. Today, family-owned **Johnston's Cranberry Marsh & Muskoka Lakes Winery** (1074 Cranberry Rd., Bala, 705/762-3203, www.cranberry.ca, 10am-6pm daily July-mid-Sept., 9am-6pm daily mid-Sept.-Oct., 10am-5pm daily Nov.-June.) cultivates 11 hectares (27 acres) of cranberries, in a half-dozen varieties. Fruit begins growing on these perennial vines in the spring, and they become heavy with berries by the time the autumn harvest season starts. In winter, though the fruit is gone, the vines turn ruby red.

The Johnstons and their staff sell about a third of their annual crop locally to markets, hotels, and other businesses, and a third becomes jam, preserves, or other cranberry products that they sell in their on-site shop. They use the remainder to produce several types of cranberry wine.

Take the **Bog to Bottle Discovery Tour** (11am, 1pm, and 3pm daily year-round, $15 pp) to learn more about these rosy berries. As you walk through the marsh, your guide will share stories about the Johnston family and how they launched their business, and you'll get the scoop on how cranberries grow and how they're harvested. At the tasting bar, you'll watch a video about the cranberry production process as you sample raw berries and try several types of cranberry wine, including an almost grape-like cranberry-blueberry blend and a cranberry-maple dessert wine.

In summer, the Johnstons grow blueberries, also native to the region, and on the **Blueberry Hill Tour** (noon and 2pm mid-July-early Sept., $20 pp), you'll learn how they grow and sample both fruit and berry products. There are hiking trails around the property; in winter, they build a trail for ice-skating around the marsh, and you can snowshoe, too (rentals are available).

An entertaining time to visit is during the busy harvest season when you can see the harvest process in action. In late September and early October (see the website for exact dates), you can take the **Cranberry Plunge** (10am and 2pm Mon.-Fri. by reservation only, 10am-4pm Sat.-Sun., adults $10, ages 12 and under $8), in which you don waders for a photo op in the berry-filled bogs. The town hosts the annual **Bala Cranberry Festival** (www.balacranberryfestival.on.ca, mid-Oct.), the weekend following Canadian Thanksgiving, an autumn fair with wagon rides, music, and a variety of cranberry-related activities on the farm and around the community.

or a *refresco* like *jamaica* or *tamarindo* to pair with your *carnitas* burrito (stuffed with rich confit-like braised pork), *mole poblano* (chicken in a savory chocolate sauce), or *flautas* (pulled chicken rolled into a fried corn tortilla). Several mornings a week, you can stop in for *molletes* (bean- and cheese-filled breads), *chilaquiles* (crispy tortilla chips topped with eggs and *queso fresco*), and other breakfast dishes.

Accommodations

Sandy Yudin has run **Century House B&B** (155 Dill St., 705/645-9903, www.bbmuskoka. com/centuryhouse, $70-100 s, $110-125 d), the 1855 brick farmhouse she shares with her husband, Norman Yan, for more than two decades, and knows how to make guests feel at home. The three traditional B&B rooms are furnished with quilts and wicker chairs and have all the essentials—comfortable beds, reading lamps, bathrobes—but no extraneous frills; they share two baths. Sandy's a great cook, serving multicourse breakfasts with fresh fruit, eggs, smoked trout, and toast with homemade marmalade. The B&B is a 15-minute walk to Manitoba Street's shops and restaurants.

Although it's near the town center, **Bay House Bed-and-Breakfast** (2 Dominion St., 705/645-7508, www.bbmuskoka.com/ bayhouse, $138-178 d) feels like a cottage in the woods. The three lower-level guest rooms

are done in cheery pastels. The largest has an electric fireplace and four-poster bed, while the Garden Room opens onto the patio. Jan and Peter Rickard are experienced innkeepers who are full of tips for things to do, although after their hearty breakfasts (which might include lemon ricotta pancakes or eggs hollandaise), you may be tempted just to soak in the outdoor hot tub.

Information and Services

Tourism Bracebridge (1 Manitoba St., 705/645-8121 or 866/645-8121, www. tourismbracebridge.com) provides information about the area. Find more trip-planning details online at **Muskoka Tourism** (www. discovermuskoka.ca).

Getting There and Around

Bracebridge is 195 kilometers (121 miles) north of Toronto and 18 kilometers (11 miles) north of Gravenhurst. From Toronto, take Highway 400 north to Barrie, then continue north on Highway 11 to Bracebridge.

Ontario Northland (705/646-2239 or 800/461-8558, www.ontarionorthland.ca, 3 hours, one-way adults $44, seniors and students $37, ages 2-11 $22) buses from Toronto's Bay Street Station stop at the Quality Inn (300 Ecclestone Dr.). Buses continue to Huntsville and North Bay. Bracebridge is fairly compact and walkable, but to explore the Muskoka region further, you need your own vehicle.

Huntsville and Vicinity

West of Algonquin Provincial Park, and close enough for an Algonquin day trip, the attractive town of Huntsville is a favorite destination in its own right, with lots of outdoor activities, good places to eat, and a cute downtown.

SIGHTS AND RECREATION

Start your Huntsville visit walking around downtown, looking for the **Group**

of Seven Outdoor Gallery (www. thegroupofsevenoutdoorgallery.com), a series of colorful murals that decorate town buildings. You'll find additional murals in the nearby communities of Baysville and Dwight and at the Portage Store on Canoe Lake in Algonquin Park. More than 90 in total, the murals are replicas of works by the Group of Seven artists who worked in Canada in the early 1900s.

Huntsville

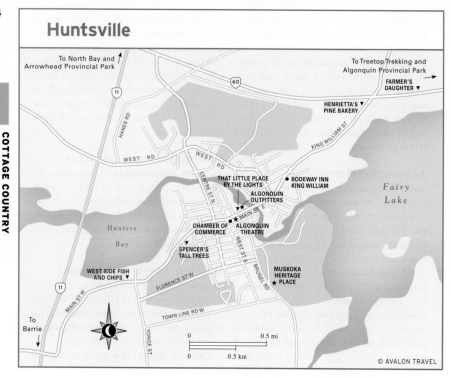

To North Bay and Arrowhead Provincial Park

To Treetop Trekking and Algonquin Provincial Park

FARMER'S DAUGHTER ▼

HENRIETTA'S ▼ PINE BAKERY

HANES RD

KING WILLIAM ST

WEST RD

WEST RD

CENTRE ST N

THAT LITTLE PLACE BY THE LIGHTS

● RODEWAY INN KING WILLIAM

ALGONQUIN OUTFITTERS

Fairy Lake

MAIN ST N

Hunters Bay

CHAMBER OF COMMERCE

ALGONQUIN THEATRE

WEST ST S

SPENCER'S TALL TREES

BRUNEL RD

WEST SIDE FISH AND CHIPS ▼

MUSKOKA HERITAGE PLACE

FLORENCE ST W

MAIN ST W

To Barrie

TOWN LINE RD W

YONGE ST

0   0.5 mi

0   0.5 km

© AVALON TRAVEL

Muskoka Heritage Place

If you're interested in the history of the Muskoka region, there's a lot to see at **Muskoka Heritage Place** (88 Brunel Rd., 705/789-7576, www.muskokaheritageplace. org, adults $17.55, seniors $15.80, ages 3-12 $11.90). Your first stop should be the **museum** (10am-4pm daily mid-May-mid-Oct., 10am-4pm Mon.-Fri. mid-Oct.-mid-May, museum only adults and seniors $2.55, ages 3-12 $1.60), which traces the region's roots from the early First Nations people through the first European contact, the fur trading and lumber eras, and the evolution of the Muskokas as a tourist destination. More fun for kids is the **pioneer village** (10am-4pm daily mid-May-mid-Oct., last admission 3pm), where wandering around the 20 restored buildings takes you back to the period between 1880 and 1910. Costumed interpreters demonstrate blacksmithing,

woodworking, and other trades. Explore a trapper's cabin, a one-room schoolhouse, and a First Nations encampment.

Catch a ride on the **Portage Flyer** steam train (100 Forbes Hill Dr., departs at noon, 1pm, 2pm, and 3pm Tues.-Sat. July-Aug., 1pm Tues.-Fri., noon, 1pm, 2pm, and 3pm Sat. mid-May-June and Sept.-mid-Oct., adults $5.95, seniors $5.40, ages 3-12 $3.70), which ran from 1904 to 1959 in nearby Dwight along the world's smallest commercial railroad. It operated on a 1.8-kilometer-long (1.125-mile) narrow-gauge track as a portage, ferrying supplies and travelers across a sliver of land between Peninsula Lake and Portage Bay. The train trip runs about 30 minutes and includes a stop at the **Rail Museum,** a re-creation of a 1920s train station, where you can learn more about the role of railroads and steamboats in the Muskokas' development. If you're a train enthusiast, note that the steam engine pulls the train only in July and August; in spring and fall, a diesel locomotive does the work in order to preserve the steam engine's life.

Muskoka Heritage Place is a few minutes' drive from downtown Huntsville. From Main Street, go south on Brunel Road. The train depot is a short distance from the main entrance; watch for the signs.

Arrowhead Provincial Park

Through far smaller and less well known than nearby Algonquin, the four-season **Arrowhead Provincial Park** (451 Arrowhead Park Rd., 705/789-5105, www.ontarioparks.com/park/arrowhead, mid-May-mid-Oct. and early Dec.-Mar., $14.50 per vehicle), on Arrowhead Lake 10 kilometers (six miles) north of Huntsville, is a family-friendly outdoor destination with lots to do year-round. If you purchase a day-use pass at either Arrowhead or Algonquin, you can use that pass in both parks.

For day **hiking,** Arrowhead has 15 kilometers (nine miles) of easy-to-moderate trails, including the 5.3-kilometer (3.3-mile) Arrowhead Lake Trail that circles the lakeshore. A short walk from the parking lot on Roe Campground Road leads to **Big Bend Lookout,** which overlooks the winding Big East River. Arrowhead Lake has several **swimming** beaches, and the waters here and on smaller Mayflower Lake are calm spots for **paddling.** You can rent canoes, kayaks, stand-up paddleboards, and bicycles (including fat-tire trail bikes) at the Beach Information Building in July-August and from the main park office in the spring and fall. In winter, Arrowhead's hiking paths become cross-country ski trails; ski rentals are available. The park also floods a road to create a groomed 1.3-kilometer (0.8-mile) **ice-skating trail** through the woods.

Limberlost Forest and Wildlife Reserve

An excellent, less-visited hiking destination is the privately owned **Limberlost Forest and Wildlife Reserve** (S. Limberlost Rd., 705/635-1584, https://limberlostforest.com, 9am-5pm daily, free), where more than 70 kilometers (44 miles) of trails circle many of the property's 20 lakes as they crisscross the forested 4,045-hectare (10,000-acre) reserve. Check the website or ask at the reserve office for the detailed *Master Trail Guide,* which tells you about each trail and its notable features; it also includes trail maps.

From Huntsville, follow Highway 60 east for about 10 kilometers (six miles), then turn

paddling at Arrowhead Provincial Park

The Screaming Heads

One of Ontario's most unusual art attractions extends across a field, along a remote rural road, north of Huntsville. It's known as **The Screaming Heads** (981 Midlothian Rd., Burk's Falls). As soon as you see it, you'll know why.

Planted among the property's pines, grasses, and vegetable plots, these eerie concrete sculptures resemble a field of nightmares. Cartoonish open-mouthed faces contort as if in pain and giant hands rise out of the ground. Artist Peter Camani, a retired teacher, began crafting the unusual works that now loom around his land more than 20 years ago. He lives on-site in the equally surreal Midlothian Castle, with its gargoyles and a turret topped with another screaming head. Visitors are welcome to wander the fields and view the sculptures, but remember that this is a private home, so be respectful of the site and the artist's privacy. Don't try to drive onto the property if the gate is closed.

To reach the Screaming Heads from Huntsville, it's about a 35-minute drive. Go north on Highway 11 to Burk's Falls, then wind through town, following signs for Highway 520 west. Take Highway 520 to Midlothian Road; from there, it's about four kilometres (2.5 miles) to the sculptures. There's no sign, but if you look through the trees, you should see the artworks from the road.

left (north) onto Limberlost Road (Muskoka Rd. 8). Continue another nine kilometers (5.6 miles) and turn right onto South Limberlost Road and follow it for three kilometres (1.8 miles) to the reserve entrance. The gates of the reserve look imposing, but pull up and they'll slide open.

Treetop Trekking

In a wooded park east of Huntsville, this adventure company (1180 Hwy. 60, 705/788-9000 or 855/788-9009, www.treetoptrekking. com, early May-mid-Oct., adults $60, ages 12-15 $50, ages 9-11 $44) offers three-hour outdoor experiences that include up to seven **zip lines** and multiple **aerial ropes courses** ranging 3 to 21 meters (10 to 70 feet) high. A highlight (or terror-inducer) is the Tarzan jump, a controlled leap from a platform high in the trees. Make reservations, which are required, online. Kids under age 16 must be accompanied by an adult, and the website details age, height, and weight requirements. Ask about family discounts.

ENTERTAINMENT AND SHOPPING

The **Algonquin Theatre** (37 Main St. E., 705/789-4975 or 877/989-4975, www. algonquintheatre.ca) stages concerts, plays,

and lectures, featuring performers from near and far. The **Huntsville Festival of the Arts** (705/789-4975, www.huntsvillefestival. on.ca) brings concerts, art workshops, and other events to venues around town; many are outdoors and free. For ticketed events, buy tickets online, by phone, or in person at the Algonquin Theatre.

Shops along Huntsville's Main Street sell outdoor gear, artwork, and souvenirs. **Algonquin Outfitters Huntsville** (86 Main St. E., 705/787-0262 or 800/469-4948, www.algonquinoutfitters.com, 9:30am-8pm Mon. and Thurs.-Fri., 9:30am-6pm Tues.-Wed., 9am-8pm Sat., 10am-5pm Sun. July-early Sept., 10am-6pm Mon.-Fri., 9am-5pm Sat., 11am-4pm Sun. early Sept.-June) stocks outdoor clothing and camping supplies and rents canoes, kayaks, and bikes.

Near Algonquin Park, **Algonquin Outfitters Oxtongue Lake** (1035 Algonquin Outfitters Rd., Dwight, 705/635-2243 or 800/469-4948, www.algonquinoutfitters. com, 8am-6pm Mon.-Thurs., 8am-7pm Fri.-Sun. July-early Sept., 9am-5pm Mon.-Thurs., 8am-6pm Fri.-Sat., 9am-6pm Sun. May-June and early Sept.-mid-Oct., 9am-5pm daily mid-Oct.-Apr.) has canoe, kayak, and bike rentals and offers guided canoe and kayak trips in and around the park.

FOOD
Huntsville

One of the best spots for picnic supplies or a meal to go is located on Highway 60, just east of town. **Farmer's Daughter** (118 Hwy. 60, 705/789-5700, www.fresheverything.ca, 8:30am-6pm Mon.-Fri., 8am-6pm Sat., 8am-5pm Sun.) is a combination prepared-foods counter, bakery, and gourmet market. It sells fresh produce, sandwiches made to order, and fancy fixings like smoked fish pâté and homemade jams. The baked goods, including the addictive trail mix bars, are excellent.

For many Ontarians, a trip to Cottage Country isn't complete without a stop at old-style, family-friendly **West Side Fish and Chips** (126 Main St. W., 705/789-7200, www.westsidefishandchips.com, 8am-8pm daily, $5-17) for a hearty plate of halibut and chips and a gooey slice of coconut cream pie. It's always busy, but you can amuse yourself with trivia game cards while you wait.

You know **That Little Place by the Lights** (76 Main St. E., 705/789-2536, www.thatlittleplacebythelights.ca, 9am-9pm Mon.-Sat., 11am-4pm Sun., lunch $9-12, dinner $13-18)? It's a cozy Italian trattoria masquerading as a touristy ice cream parlor and coffee shop. The sauces for the pastas and pizzas are homemade (try the spicy linguini puttanesca with olives, capers, anchovies, and peppers), and the salads are simple but fresh. It's family friendly, too, especially if you promise the kids gelato for dessert.

Long-established **Spencer's Tall Trees** (87 Main St. W., 705/789-9769, www.spencerstalltrees.com, 5pm-close Mon., 11:30am-2pm and 5pm-close Tues.-Fri., 5pm-close Sat., call for seasonal hours, lunch $11-21, dinner $18-49) is set in a heritage house amid, yes, tall trees. In the several dining nooks, you can sup on classics like venison pie, veal Oscar (topped with crab), or pickerel in a maple-thyme-butter sauce. Lunch options range from salads and sandwiches to pastas. To finish with something sweet, try the chocolate pâté or a seasonal fruit crumble.

Dwight and Oxtongue Lake

The perpetual lines attest to the popularity of **Henrietta's Pine Bakery** (2868 Hwy. 60, Dwight, 705/635-2214, www.henriettaspinebakery.net, 9am-5pm Mon.-Sat., 10am-4pm Sun. May-mid-Oct.), where specialties include sticky buns and a highly recommended scone-like cranberry pastry called the Muskoka Cloud. Come early in the day, since they close when the goodies sell

Algonquin Outfitters Huntsville supplies gear for Cottage Country adventures.

out. There's a second location in Huntsville (92 King William St., 705/787-1084).

ACCOMMODATIONS

Huntsville-area lodgings range from basic in-town motels to B&Bs hidden in the woods, cottage colonies, and upscale resorts. Many accommodations are off Highway 60 east of town. Closer to Algonquin's West Gate, in the tiny town of Dwight, more lodgings cluster around Oxtongue Lake.

Huntsville

The 32-unit **Rodeway Inn King William** (23 King William St., 705/789-9661 or 888/995-9169, www.kingwilliaminn.com, $129-189 d) is the nicest of the in-town motels, upgraded with crisp white linens, newer furnishings, and mini fridges. The standard rooms, with either two doubles or one double and one queen, are slightly smaller but otherwise similar to the queen rooms, which have one queen and a sleep sofa. The largest rooms are kings with a whirlpool tub. Wi-Fi is included.

East of Huntsville

A stay at **The Morgan House** (83 Morgans Rd., 705/380-2566 or 866/311-1727, www.morganhousewoolworks.ca, $100-110 d), a bed-and-breakfast in a comfortable stone country home, is like a holiday with good friends on their mostly organic farm. Co-owner Pam Carnochan, a wool artist, welcomes guests on the screened-in porch or in the parlor with its overstuffed furniture. Upstairs, two simple guest rooms, with traditional quilts on the beds, share one large bath. Breakfast includes homemade baked goods and eggs from the farm's hens. Families are welcome.

A suburban home set amid gardens, and, yes, tranquil woods, the **Tranquil Woods Victorian Inn** (50 North Portage Rd., 705/788-7235, www.tranquilwoods.ca, $130-145 d) is Victorian in style, but it's in a newly built house with high ceilings and an airy feel. Personable owners Judy and Dan offer touring tips while serving a hearty breakfast. The largest of the three guest rooms is on the main floor, with a private patio. Upstairs, the Red Oak room has a sleigh bed and Victorian furnishings, while the red-walled Scarlet Maple room is more country cottage.

Busy with families and outdoor adventurers, **Hidden Valley Resort** (1755 Valley Rd., 705/789-2301 or 800/465-4171, www.hvmuskoka.com, $119-189), on Peninsula Lake, offers plenty to do year-round. In the summer guests can swim in the indoor or outdoor pools, play tennis, or go paddleboarding, canoeing, or kayaking; in the colder months, you can snowshoe, skate on the lake, or walk to the slopes at the small Hidden Valley Highlands Ski Area. The restaurant and bar have an outdoor terrace. The 100 rooms at this ski lodge-style hotel are fairly basic; most have two queen beds (or one king and a sleep sofa), wingback chairs, a mini fridge, and coffeemaker. Three larger family rooms sleep up to six.

You might be able to keep everyone off their screens at classy **Deerhurst Resort** (1235 Deerhurst Dr., 705/789-6411 or 800/461-4393, www.deerhurstresort.com, $239-719 d, resort fee $25 per room), with activities such as golf, tennis, trail rides, and zip-lining. The lake has waterslides, trampolines, and all kinds of water sports. In winter, there's cross-country skiing and ice-skating. Accommodations include standard hotel rooms and 1- to 3-bedroom condos with full kitchens. The main dining room serves contemporary fare with local ingredients; several more casual eateries are set around the property. A high-energy musical show, performed several nights a week in summer and fall, is great fun.

Dwight and Oxtongue Lake

The cheapest beds near Algonquin are at laid-back **Wolf Den Hostel and Nature Retreat** (4568 Hwy. 60, Oxtongue Lake, 705/635-9336 or 866/271-9336, www.wolfdenbunkhouse.com, year-round, $27 dorm, $45-85 s, $68-85 d, $90-125 cabin). Located between Dwight and the West Gate, the property's main lodge has a shared kitchen, large lounge, and guest rooms. Two log bunkhouses have an eight-bed dorm upstairs and rooms for four to five on the main level. Baths are central and shared. There's no meal service, so bring your own provisions.

A small group of lodgings sits along Oxtongue Lake, off Highway 60, about a 10-minute drive from Algonquin's West Gate. It's a pretty setting, although the proximity of Highway 60 and its traffic noise can be bothersome. Under the same ownership as the Bartlett Lodge in Algonquin Park, **The Pines Cottage Resort** (1032 Oxtongue Lake Rd., Dwight, 705/635-2379, www.algonquinparkaccommodations.com, mid-May-mid-Oct., $170-250) has family-friendly one- and two-bedroom cottages with fully equipped kitchens in the woods above Oxtongue Lake, where there's a sandy beach. Rates include the use of canoes and kayaks.

More modern, but a little closer to Highway 60, the year-round **Blue Spruce Resort** (4308 Hwy. 60, Dwight, 705/635-2330, www. bluespruce.ca, $142-339) has both hotel-style suites and stand-alone 1- to 3-bedroom cottages, all with kitchens. There are tennis courts, a swimming beach, coin-operated laundry, and Wi-Fi.

Camping
Arrowhead Provincial Park (451 Arrowhead Park Rd., 705/789-5105, www. ontarioparks.com, mid-May-mid-Oct., tent sites $42-45, electrical sites $47-52) has three campgrounds with a total of 378 campsites, 185 with electrical service. Roe Campground is the most secluded, and forested Lumbly Campground—with no electrical sites—is closest to the lakes and feels the most rustic. The large East River Campground accommodates RVs and also has five heated camping cabins ($142) sleeping up to five. The campgrounds all have central flush toilets and showers.

INFORMATION AND SERVICES
The **Huntsville/Lake of Bays Chamber of Commerce** (37 Main St. E., 705/789-4771, www.huntsvilleadventures.com) can provide more information about events and things to do in the Huntsville-Algonquin region.

GETTING THERE
Car
Huntsville is 215 kilometers (133 miles) north of Toronto and 35 kilometers (22 miles) north of Bracebridge. From Toronto, take Highway

on the waterfront at the Deerhurst Resort

400 north to Barrie, then continue north on Highway 11 to Huntsville.

Bus

Ontario Northland (800/461-8558, www.ontarionorthland.ca, 3.75-4 hours, one-way adults $54, seniors and students $46, ages 2-11 $27) operates buses from the Toronto Central Bus Station to **Huntsville**. In 2018, the Huntsville stop relocated temporarily to the Super 8 Motel (225 Main St. W., 705/789-5504); check the Ontario Northland website to confirm the current stop location. Buses continue from Huntsville to North Bay, where you can change for Temagami, Cochrane, and other northern destinations.

To get to Huntsville directly from Toronto's Pearson Airport, you can take the **Northern Airport Shuttle** (705/474-7942 or 800/461-4219, www.northernairport.com, 2.75 hours, one-way adults $94), which runs two daily trips in each direction.

GETTING AROUND

While it's easy to get to downtown Huntsville without a car, exploring the region around town, including Algonquin Park, is difficult without your own wheels. If you don't have your own car, you can take the bus to Huntsville, then rent a car to explore Algonquin. **Enterprise Rent-A-Car** (174 Main St. W., 705/789-1834 or 800/736-8222, www.enterpriserentacar.ca) and **Discount Car Rentals** (8 Ott Dr., 705/788-3737, www.discountcar.com) have Huntsville locations.

Algonquin Provincial Park

If you visit only one of Ontario's many outdoor destinations, the province's first provincial park is an excellent choice. Measuring 763,000 hectares (1.9 million acres), immense **Algonquin Provincial Park** (705/633-5572, www.ontarioparks.com or www.algonquinpark.on.ca) stretches across a wide swath of Northeastern Ontario. Covered with hardwood and coniferous forests, the region was a major logging area in the 1800s, and many visitors are surprised to learn that limited logging is still allowed in the park. When the park was created in 1893, it wasn't to bring a halt to logging, but rather to protect the region's wildlife. The park's earliest tourists arrived by train, disembarking at a rail depot near Cache Lake and staying in a nearby hotel. In the 1930s, Highway 60 was built across Algonquin's southern sections, and as more tourists came by road, rail service was discontinued. The prevailing wisdom was that eliminating train service would keep the park more "natural."

Highway 60 is still the main access route for visitors entering the West Gate from Huntsville (or Toronto) or the East Gate from Ottawa. If your time is limited, pick a few stops—perhaps a paddle at Canoe Lake, hiking one or two of the shorter trails—and spend an hour at the exhibits in the park Visitors Centre. Despite the park's popularity, you can find quiet trails and canoe routes to explore even if you stay near Highway 60. But Algonquin offers ample opportunities to get out into the wilderness, too; most of the park's vast backcountry is reachable only by canoe. Algonquin Park is open year-round, although many park services and sights operate only from May until mid-October.

SIGHTS

The park's main sights are listed from west to east along Highway 60, the direction you'll reach them coming from Toronto or elsewhere in the Muskokas. Distances are from the park's West Gate, so a sight at "Km. 20" is 20 kilometers east of the West Gate. From Ottawa, Peterborough, and the Kawarthas, or from elsewhere in Eastern Ontario, enter the park from the East Gate (at Km. 56) and follow these locations in reverse.

West Gate (Hwy. 60, Km. 0)

At Algonquin's western entrance, staff can help you get oriented and provide information about things to do. All visitors must purchase a park permit ($20 per vehicle) and display it on the dashboard. Permits are available at the East and West Gates and at the Algonquin Park Visitors Centre. If you're driving across the park on Highway 60 without stopping, you don't need a permit; but if you stop anywhere in the park, even to use a restroom, you must have a permit or else you risk being fined.

If you're spending several days in the park or visiting multiple parks, consider purchasing an **Ontario Parks seasonal pass,** which allows unlimited day visits to any of the Ontario provincial parks. You can buy a summer-only pass (valid Apr.-Nov., $125), a winter-only pass (Dec.-Mar., $85), or a full-year pass (Apr.-Mar., $175).

Canoe Lake (Hwy. 60, Km. 14.1)

The history of Canoe Lake is inextricably linked to the mysterious disappearance of the painter Tom Thomson (1877-1917), who was affiliated with the Group of Seven artists who lived and worked in Ontario in the early 1900s. Beginning in 1912, Thomson spent several years painting in Algonquin Park, mostly on and around Canoe Lake. Thomson was last seen on July 8, 1917, in the vicinity of Canoe Lake—and then he vanished. His overturned canoe was found behind the lake's Wapomeo Island, and several days later, his body was pulled from the lake. The exact circumstances of his death remain a puzzle that has never been solved. In his memory, the **Tom Thomson memorial cairn** was erected in 1930 on one of Thomson's favorite Canoe Lake campsites. The cairn is accessible only by canoe.

The **Portage Store** (Hwy. 60, Km. 14.1,

705/633-5622, www.portagestore.com, late Apr.-mid-Oct.) on Canoe Lake rents canoes and can give you tips on where to go, including how to get to the Thomson cairn. It also offers half-day and full-day guided paddles.

Algonquin Art Centre (Hwy. 60, Km. 20)

The **Algonquin Art Centre** (705/633-5555, www.algonquinartcentre.com, 10am-5pm daily June-mid-Oct.) has a small gallery (donation) that shows changing exhibits of works by artists who have an Algonquin connection. The center also offers drop-in art activities and classes (10:30am-4:30pm daily July-Aug., $10-30) for both children and adults.

Cache Lake (Hwy. 60, Km. 23.5)

Cache Lake was once the center of activity in Algonquin Park. From the 1890s, when the park was first established, until the 1950s, this lake area had a rail depot—Algonquin Park Station—as well as a large hotel. All that remains today, aside from the lovely lake itself, is a short historical walking trail, where several signs with historical photos along a wooded path tell you about the area's interesting past.

Lake of Two Rivers (Hwy. 60, Km. 31)

Lake of Two Rivers is a busy place. In addition to the large **Two Rivers Campground** (705/633-5572), there's a snack bar, grocery store, and mountain bike rentals. East of the campground, **Killarney Lodge** (Lake of Two Rivers, Hwy. 60, Km. 33.2, 705/633-5551 or 877/767-5935, www.killarneylodge.com) is set on the Lake of Two Rivers. Just east of the lodge is a public swimming beach.

Algonquin Visitors Centre (Hwy. 60, Km. 43)

Even if you've entered the park from the west, it's worth stopping into the **Algonquin Visitors Centre** (9am-7pm daily mid-June-mid-Oct., 9am-5pm daily late Apr.-mid-June

Algonquin Provincial Park

© AVALON TRAVEL

and mid-Oct.-late Oct., 9am-4pm Mon.-Fri., 9am-5pm Sat.-Sun. Nov.-late Apr.) to learn more about the park. Start by watching a 12-minute film about the park's history and natural features, and then visit the exhibit area, which covers these topics in more detail. In summer, many interpretive programs are based at the Visitors Centre. A shop sells detailed park maps and guides as well as books about wildlife, camping, and the outdoors. There's a basic cafeteria (spring-fall), and free Wi-Fi.

What's the best feature of the Visitors Centre? It's the deck out back, which overlooks a wide swath of park territory and helps you appreciate Algonquin's expanse. There's another overlook from the short **Fire Tower Trail,** a boardwalk that leads to a reconstructed cupola, the lookout at the top of a fire tower.

Algonquin Logging Museum (Hwy. 60, Km. 54.5)

Logging was an important part of Algonquin's heritage. Learn more about that history and about the delicate balance between industry and preservation at the **Algonquin Logging Museum** (9am-5pm daily late June-mid-Oct., free). You can watch a short video about Algonquin's logging history, but the most interesting parts of this museum are outdoors.

As you follow a walking trail through a re-created logging camp, you can see how loggers cut and squared the trees, hauled them across the lakes, and drove them through water chutes to transport them to the cities. You can climb aboard an "alligator," a steam-powered tugboat used to haul logs. The trail also takes you past a working log dam and chute, a restored blacksmith shop, a locomotive, and a classic 1950s truck. There are enough things to touch and climb on that kids may enjoy it, even if they don't appreciate the historical angle.

East Gate (Hwy. 60, Km. 55.8)

Like the West Gate, Algonquin's eastern entrance has an information office that sells the required park permits ($20 per vehicle), provides park maps, and offers suggestions about things to see and do. If you're driving east toward Ottawa, you can use the restrooms here before hitting the road.

SPORTS AND RECREATION

TOP EXPERIENCE

★ Canoeing

Algonquin Park is one of Ontario's most popular destinations for canoeing. Not only can you paddle on the park's numerous lakes and rivers, but Algonquin also has more than 2,000 kilometers (1,240 miles) of canoe routes across the backcountry, ideal for overnight or multiday canoe trips. A useful planning resource is the *Canoe Routes of Algonquin Provincial Park Map* (www.algongquinpark. on.ca, $5), which you can order online or purchase at any of the park stores or information centers. It details all the lakes, access points, portages, and campsites across Algonquin.

Within the park, you can rent canoes at the **Portage Store** (Canoe Lake, Hwy. 60, Km. 14.1, www.portagestore.com) and the Opeongo Store (6.2 km/3.9 miles north of Km. 46.3), the latter run by **Algonquin Outfitters** (613/637-2075 or 888/280-8886, www.algonquinoutfitters.com). Both outfitters offer shuttle services to take you and your

Howling with the Wolves

One of the many animals that live in the Algonquin Provincial Park wilderness is the wolf. And one of the most popular (and eeriest) activities at Algonquin Park is the Wolf Howl. These events typically attract more than 1,500 visitors, who assemble at the park's Outdoor Theatre (Hwy. 60, Km. 35.4) for a presentation about wolves and their habitat. Then everyone gets in their cars and drives caravan-style to a designated spot where park naturalists have heard a wolf pack on the previous night. Once everyone is in place, the naturalists begin a sequence of howls—hoping that the wolves will respond with howls of their own. Sometimes they do, and sometimes they don't, but if you're lucky enough to hear the wolf pack howling, it's a unique experience.

The Wolf Howls are typically held during August, occasionally the first week of September, the only time of year when wolves are likely to remain in one place for days at a time. The howls are held once a week, at 8pm Thursday, and last about three hours. Check event bulletin boards throughout the park, or phone the **Visitors Centre** (613/637-2828) to confirm if the week's Wolf Howl will be held. Howls are canceled if no wolves are in an area along Highway 60 or if the weather is inclement, so you generally won't know till the day of the event whether it will take place. Updates on the Wolf Howls are also posted on the **Friends of Algonquin Park website** (www.algonquinpark.on.ca), where you can sign up to receive an email update on the week's Wolf Howl.

canoe to various launch points. Many outfitters outside the park will rent canoes with cartop carriers.

Both the Portage Store and Algonquin Outfitters offer guided canoe day trips. The Portage Store runs a full-day trip (9:30am-4:30pm daily July-early Sept., 9:30am-4:30pm Tues., Thurs., and Sat.-Sun. mid-May-June and early Sept.-early Oct., adults $63, under age 14 $31.50) on Canoe Lake, which includes an orientation about the park, basic canoe instruction, and a daylong paddle with a stop for a picnic lunch. In July and August they also offer a half-day trip (1pm-5pm, adults $43, under age 14 $21.50). Reservations are advised for both trips.

From its Opeongo Store, Algonquin Outfitters offers a guided half-day Costello Creek trip (Mon.-Fri. mid-May-Oct., $70 pp for 2 people, $47 pp for 3, $35 pp for 4). They also run a half-day guided canoe trip, exploring the wildlife in the park's Hailstorm Creek Nature Reserve (Mon.-Fri. mid-May-Oct., $160 pp for 2, $140 pp for 3, $130 pp for 4), departing from their Oxtongue Lake store. Reservations are required for all trips. Ask about discounts for kids and teens.

Hiking

All along the Highway 60 corridor are trails for day hikes, ranging from an easy boardwalk path to strenuous all-day excursions. More experienced hikers can tromp along more than 140 kilometers (87 miles) of backpacking trails through the park's interior.

The most accessible park trails are:

- **Whiskey Rapids** (Km. 7.2, 2.1 km/1.3 miles, moderate)
- **Hardwood Lookout** (Km. 13.8, 1 km/0.6 miles, moderate)
- **Mizzy Lake** (Km. 15.4, 10.8 km/6.7 miles, strenuous)
- **Peck Lake** (Km. 19.2, 2.3 km/1.4 miles, moderate)
- **Track and Tower** (Km. 25, 7.5 km/4.7 miles, strenuous)
- **Hemlock Bluff** (Km. 27.2, 3.5 km/2.2 miles, moderate)
- **Bat Lake** (Km. 30, 5.8 km/3.6 miles, moderate)
- **Two Rivers** (Km. 31, 2.3 km/1.4 miles, moderate)

- **Centennial Ridges** (Km. 37.6, 10.4 km/6.5 miles, strenuous)

- **Lookout** (Km. 39.7, 2.1 km/1.3 miles, strenuous)

- **Big Pines** (Km. 40.3, 2.9 km/1.8 miles, moderate)

- **Booth's Rock** (Km. 40.3, 5.1 km/3.2 miles, strenuous)

- **Spruce Bog Boardwalk** (Km. 42.5, 1.5 km/0.9 miles, easy)

- **Beaver Pond** (Km. 45.2, 2 km/1.2 miles, moderate)

Trail guides, with more details about each of these hikes, are available at the trail-heads (spring to fall) and online (www.algonquinpark.on.ca).

Bicycling

Algonquin Park has two cycling trails that are easy to reach from Highway 60. The relatively flat, family-friendly 16-kilometer (10-mile) **Old Railway Bike Trail** follows the route of a former rail line between Cache Lake and the Rock Lake Campground. The trail passes the campgrounds at Mew Lake, Lake of Two Rivers, Kearney Lake, Pog Lake, Whitefish Lake, and Coon Lake. The more challenging **Minnesing Mountain Bike Trail** (Hwy. 60, Km. 23, late-June-mid-Oct.) includes four hilly loops ranging from 4.7 to 23.4 kilometers (2.9 to 14.5 miles). The trail is often quite muddy in June and July.

You can rent bikes at the **Lake of Two Rivers Store** (Hwy. 60, Km. 31.4, 800/469-4948) and the **Opeongo Store** (Lake Opeongo, 6.2 km/3.9 miles north of Km. 46.3, 613/637-2075 or 888/280-8886, www.algonquinoutfitters.com).

Winter Sports

If you want to try dogsledding, a couple of outfitters can get you out on the Algonquin trails. **Voyageur Quest** (416/486-3605 or 800/794-9660, www.voyageurquest.com, Dec.-Mar.) offers one-day ($272-288 pp), weekend-long ($545 pp) and multiday

(from $788 pp) dogsledding trips. **Snow Forest Adventures** (705/783-0461, www.snowforestadventures.ca, late Dec.-Mar.) runs two-, three-, and four-day dogsledding trips (from $550 pp) that depart from the Sunday Lake dogsledding trails (Hwy. 60, Km. 35).

Algonquin Park has several areas that offer trails for cross-country skiing. At the West Gate, the groomed **Fen Lake Ski Trail** has four loops, from 1-18 kilometers (0.6-11 miles). One kilometer (0.6 miles) west of the East Gate, the groomed **Leaf Lake Trail** has routes measuring 5-45 kilometers (3-28 miles) in length. The 16-kilometer (10-mile) linear **Old Railway Bike Trail** becomes a multiuse trail in winter, groomed for cross-country skiing. For more challenging wilderness skiing, head to the **Minnesing Trail** (Hwy. 60, Km. 23), where four ungroomed loops extend from 6 to 32 kilometers (3.7-20 miles). For snowshoeing, you can explore nearly anywhere in the park, including any of the hiking trails along Highway 60. Snowshoes are not allowed on the cross-country trails.

In winter, you still need to purchase a park permit ($20 per vehicle). Also make sure you have ample time to get off the trails before dark, and wear warm clothes, particularly hats, gloves, boots, and multiple layers appropriate for your outdoor activity.

Outfitters

A number of outfitters, both within and outside Algonquin Park, can help organize canoeing, camping, and hiking trips; rent you the gear you need; or take you on a guided journey. Some even organize dogsledding excursions. **Algonquin Outfitters** (800/469-4948, www.algonquinoutfitters.com) has locations throughout the Muskoka region, including the Opeongo Store on Lake Opeongo within the park, Oxtongue Lake outside the West Gate, and Huntsville. They offer a variety of guided or self-guided trips, including half-day, full-day, and multiday canoe and kayak excursions. On Canoe Lake, the **Portage Store** (Hwy. 60, Km. 14.1, 705/633-5622, www.portagestore.com, late Apr.-mid-Oct.)

organizes canoe trips and offers half-, full-, and multiday guided paddles. Outside the East Gate, **Opeongo Outfitters** (29902 Hwy. 60, Whitney, 613/637-5470 or 800/790-1864, www.opeongooutfitters.com, mid-Apr.-mid-Oct.) can rent gear for a multiday canoe trip, including a canoe, tent, pack, sleeping bag, food, cooking utensils, and other supplies. You can also rent a kayak or canoe for the day.

Voyageur Quest (416/486-3605 or 800/794-9660, www.voyageurquest.com) organizes several different Algonquin excursions, such as 3- to 7-day canoe trips (including trips designed for families), a moose photography safari, and winter dogsledding trips. **Northern Edge Algonquin** (888/383-8320, www.northernedgealgonquin.com) runs adventures throughout the year, including a stand-up paddling safari and yoga retreat and a weekend of hiking, canoeing, and wildlife spotting. Run by the Algonquin First Nation of Wolf Lake, **Algonquin Canoe Company** (705/981-0572 or 866/889-9788, www.algonquincanoe.com) offers guided daylong and multiday canoe trips as well as cultural tours. **Snow Forest Adventures** (705/783-0461, www.snowforestadventures. ca) offers multiday dogsledding trips, from late December through March, weather permitting.

FOOD AND ACCOMMODATIONS

If you want to stay within the park, you can choose from three upscale lodges (which also operate restaurants), rustic former ranger cabins, yurts, or camping. The lodges, cabins, and most of the campgrounds are open spring to fall. In winter, you can camp at Mew Lake, off Highway 60, or out in the backcountry. The park cafeterias and snack bars also operate seasonally.

Food

If you're not a lodge guest, you can still come for a meal in the dining room at **Arowhon Pines** (Arowhon Rd., 705/633-5661 or 866/633-5661, www.arowhonpines.ca, late

May-mid-Oct.), where meals are fixed-price: breakfast (8am-10am, $25 pp), weekday lunch (12:30pm-2pm, $35 pp), weekend lunch buffet (12:30pm-2pm, $50 pp), and an abundant multicourse dinner (6:30pm only, $75 pp). The dining room doesn't have a license to serve alcohol, but you can bring your own.

Bartlett Lodge Dining Room (Cache Lake, 705/633-5543 or 866/614-5355, www. bartlettlodge.com, mid-May-late Oct.) is open to nonguests in the evening, when an elaborate four-course prix fixe dinner (adults $67.50, ages 12 and under $30) is served. The dining room isn't licensed to serve alcohol, but you can bring your own.

The main lodge building at **Killarney Lodge** (Lake of Two Rivers, Hwy. 60, Km. 33.2, 705/633-5551 or 866/473-5551, www. killarneylodge.com, mid-May-mid-Oct.) dates to 1935 and now houses the dining room, open to nonguests and serving hearty, fixed-price, three-course menus at lunch (noon-2pm daily, $30) and dinner (5:45pm daily, $70). If you're not a lodge guest, reservations are advised for dinner. Also, the dining room keeps slightly shorter hours in May-June, so phone to confirm.

You can get casual meals at the **Portage Store** (Canoe Lake, Hwy. 60, Km. 14.1, 705/633-5622, www.portagestore.com), which serves breakfast, lunch, and dinner daily late April-mid-October, and at the **Sunday Creek Café** (Hwy. 60, Km. 63, 613/637-1133), the basic cafeteria in the Algonquin Visitors Centre. A seasonal snack bar sells sandwiches and ice cream at the **Lake of Two Rivers Store** (Hwy. 60, Km. 31.4).

Park Lodges

With hiking, swimming, and canoeing, there's plenty to do at **Arowhon Pines** (Arowhon Rd., 705/633-5661 or 866/633-5661, www.arowhonpines.ca, June-mid-Oct., $245-575 pp). The private cabins have a queen bed, lounge area, and private deck. The less-expensive shared cabins have a private room and bath but share the lounge space with other guests. Lodging rates include breakfast, lunch, and dinner as well as use of all the recreational facilities. To reach Arowhon Pines, follow Highway 60 to Km. 16, then turn north onto Arowhon Rd., which winds through the woods to the lodge.

Getting to **Bartlett Lodge** (Cache Lake, 705/633-5543 or 866/614-5355, www.bartlettlodge.com, mid-May-late Oct.) is half the fun; the lodge is accessible only by boat. When you turn off Highway 60 at Km. 23.5, call the lodge, which will send its water taxi. Some of the lakeside one-to-three-bedroom cabins ($225-325 pp) date to the early 1900s. Studio units ($185-242 pp) are in a historic log cabin. Rates include buffet breakfast and a multicourse dinner. The lodge also offers a "glamorous camping" option in a furnished **platform tent** ($115-160 pp, including breakfast); a washroom with showers is in an adjacent building.

Killarney Lodge (Lake of Two Rivers, Hwy. 60, Km. 33.2, 705/633-5551 or 866/473-5551, www.killarneylodge.com, mid-May-mid-Oct., $234-369 pp) is the easiest park lodge to reach, just off Highway 60. With no TVs, radios, or phones, the 25 log cottages are set in the woods, with neat knotty-pine or rough-hewn log interiors. The "one-bedroom" cabins are one room with a king or queen bed; the "two-bedroom" cabins have two rooms, one with a king bed, a second with twin beds. Many cottages are right on the lake, and each comes with its own canoe. Rates include three meals a day.

Ranger Cabins

Algonquin has 14 **Ranger Cabins** (mid-Apr.-mid-Oct., $63-135) that offer indoor camping. They're rustic log structures without running water or electricity where rangers patrolling the park would overnight. You can reach five by car, at Rain Lake, Bissett Creek Road, Kiosk, and two cabins at Brent; others are in the backcountry. Equipped with a table and chairs, a wood stove, and an outdoor toilet, most cabins have bunks but not mattresses, so bring a sleeping pad and a sleeping bag, along with any cooking supplies you

want. The Friends of Algonquin Park website (www.algonquinpark.on.ca) has detailed descriptions of each cabin.

Camping

Algonquin is a popular destination for campers, with the largest number of campsites—more than 1,300—of any Ontario provincial park. **Reserve your campsite** (519/826-5290 or 888/668-7275, www.ontarioparks.com/reservations, tent sites $42-45, electrical sites $52, reservation fee online $11, by phone $13) in advance, particularly for summer and fall weekends. Eight of the front-country campgrounds are accessible by car near Highway 60. Most are seasonal, opening in late April or mid-May and closing between early September and mid-October. Only Mew Lake campground is open year-round.

The front-country campgrounds:

- **Tea Lake** (Km. 11.4, 42 sites) has showers and flush toilets.

- **Canisbay Lake** (Km. 23.1, 242 sites) has secluded campsites, swimming beaches, showers, flush toilets, and laundry facilities.

- **Mew Lake** (Km. 30.6, 131 sites), which has central flush toilets, showers, and laundry, also has seven yurts ($98), available year-round. The yurts, which sleep six, are furnished with two sets of bunk beds (a double below and a single above), a table and chairs, a propane barbecue, cooking utensils, and dishes. They have electric lights and heating. You still need to bring sleeping bags or other bedding, as well as food and other personal items.

- **Two Rivers** (Km. 31.8, 241 sites) is the most centrally located, and frequently the most crowded. It has a beach, a laundry, flush toilets, and showers.

- **Kearney Lake** (Km. 36.5, 103 sites) has two beaches, showers, and flush toilets.

- **Pog Lake** (Km. 36.9, 286 sites) has secluded campsites and central showers, laundry, and flush toilets.

- **Coon Lake** (6 kilometers south of Km. 40.3, 48 sites) has a beach and pit toilets.
- **Rock Lake** (8 kilometers south of Km. 40.3, 121 sites) has two beaches, showers, flush toilets, and laundry.

Algonquin has three more drive-in campgrounds (late Apr.-mid-Oct.) farther north. **Achray** (45 sites), **Brent** (30 sites), and **Kiosk** (22 sites) campgrounds are all accessible from Highway 17 but are far more secluded than the Highway 60 camping areas. Achray and Kiosk have flush toilets, and Achray also has a yurt ($98), but none of these three campgrounds has showers.

Algonquin Park also has numerous **backcountry campgrounds** (adults $12, ages 6-17 $5); most are accessible only by canoe. The Friends of Algonquin Park (www. algonquinpark.on.ca) has detailed information to help plan a trip into the backcountry. Several outfitters also organize backcountry trips.

East of the Park

A short drive outside the park's East Gate, **Couples Resort** (139 Galeairy Lake Rd., Whitney, 866/202-1179, www.couplesresort. ca, $257-1,041 d), on the waterfront, is unabashedly romantic. Some of the large rooms have four-poster beds, hot tubs or whirlpool baths, and wood-burning fireplaces. Enjoy the seasonal outdoor heated saltwater pool, play billiards or table tennis, take a sauna, or use the fitness room and spa. Midweek specials can reduce the rates significantly. Rates include breakfast and a semiformal five-course dinner; for the evening meal, jeans, shorts, and sandals are forbidden, and men must wear a dress shirt with a collar.

INFORMATION AND SERVICES

For questions about Algonquin Park, phone the **Algonquin Park Information Office** (705/633-5572, 8am-4pm daily). You can also get visitor information at the park's West Gate, East Gate, and Visitors Centre. Online, the best source of information is the **Friends** of **Algonquin Park** (www.algonquinpark. on.ca). **Ontario Parks** (www.ontarioparks. com) will give you an overview of the park facilities but doesn't provide as much detail.

Mobile phones do work in Algonquin Park, if you're within about three kilometers (two miles) of Highway 60. There are dead spots, though, and outside this zone, don't count on picking up a phone signal. Within the park, three stores sell camping supplies (including mosquito repellent, rain ponchos, and basic first aid supplies) and a small selection of groceries. The **Portage Store** (Km. 14.1) is on the west end of Highway 60 at Canoe Lake, the **Lake of Two Rivers Store** (Km. 31.4) at the Lake of Two Rivers Campground is at roughly the midway point on Highway 60, and the **Opeongo Store** is to the east, a short drive north of Kilometer 46.3.

GETTING THERE
Car

Algonquin's West Gate is 45 kilometers (28 miles) east of Huntsville via Highway 60. The East Gate is five kilometers (three miles) west of the town of Whitney. From Toronto (270 kilometers, or 168 miles), the most direct, if most heavily trafficked, route is to take Highway 400 north to Highway 11 north, which will take you to Huntsville, where you can take Highway 60 to the West Gate.

An alternate route from Toronto takes you to the East Gate. Go east on Highway 401, then pick up Highway 115 to Peterborough; from there, take Highway 28 north to Bancroft, Highway 62 north to Maynooth, and then Highway 127 north to Highway 60, which will bring you to the park's East Gate. While this route sounds more complicated, it's clearly marked; it's about 310 kilometers (190 miles) from Toronto. From Ottawa, it's 240 kilometers (150 miles) to the East Gate; take Highway 417/17 west to Highway 60.

You can buy gas at the Portage Store (Km. 14.1, early May-mid-Oct.). Otherwise, the nearest gas stations are in Oxtongue Lake and Dwight west of the park, and in Whitney to the east.

Bus

The **Parkbus** (800/928-7101, www.parkbus. ca) provides direct bus service from Toronto to Algonquin (one-way/round-trip adults $64/$89, seniors and students $58/$80, ages 2-12 $32/$45). It's an excellent nonprofit initiative designed to get people out of the city—and out of their cars—by offering transportation to a growing number of national parks and Ontario provincial parks. The bus runs on select weekends throughout the summer season. The bus departs from several points in Toronto, including 30 Carlton Street (between Yonge St. and Church St., 1 block from the College subway station) and Dufferin Street at Bloor Street West, which is at the Dufferin subway station.

You can get off the bus at several points, including the Wolf Den Hostel near Oxtongue Lake, the West Gate, the Portage Store at Canoe Lake, Lake of Two Rivers Store, Pog Lake, and the Algonquin Outfitters store on Lake Opeongo. These locations either have accommodations (you can camp at Lake of Two Rivers or Pog Lake, or bunk at the Wolf Den), or they're departure points for outfitters who organize guided trips.

GETTING AROUND

There is no public transportation within Algonquin Park. If you arrive on the **Parkbus** (800/928-7101, www.parkbus.ca), you can camp at Lake of Two Rivers or Pog Lake, which are both centrally located and have hiking, cycling, and canoeing options nearby, so it's feasible to do without a car. You can also arrive by bus and do a canoeing or hiking trip that you've booked through an outfitter; the bus will drop you at one of several outfitters' locations.

Otherwise, unless you're comfortable bicycling or hiking long distances, you need a car to explore the park. The most convenient place to rent a car in the vicinity of the park is in Huntsville.

North Bay to James Bay

Traveling north from Algonquin Provincial Park or northeast from the Ottawa Valley, the towns get farther apart and the forests get denser. Mining and logging have historically formed the backbone of local economies here, but tourism, particularly outdoor adventure and ecotourism, is a growing business. From the city of North Bay, on the shore of Lake Nipissing, it's a short trip to Mattawa, with a lovely provincial park, or to the lake town of Temagami, which has excellent canoe-trip options. Farther north, you can board the train for a unique journey to First Nations communities along James Bay. Heading west, the city of Sudbury has a growing arts scene, and it's a gateway to outdoor destinations on Georgian Bay and beyond.

For more regional travel details, contact **Northeastern Ontario Tourism** (2009 Long Lake Rd., Unit 401, Sudbury, 705/522-0104 or 800/465-6655, www. northeasternontario.com).

NORTH BAY
Sights

On May 28, 1934, quintuplets were born to Oliva and Elzire Dionne, a French Canadian couple living in Corbeil, outside North Bay. These five identical girls—the now-famous Dionne Quintuplets—became an immediate media sensation. By an act of Parliament, they were removed from their parents, who already had five other children under age seven, and designated wards of the Ontario government, which built an "observation playground" dubbed "Quintland" where Annette, Cécile, Émilie, Marie, and Yvonne lived—in view of more than three million visitors—until 1943. Although they were returned to their family, the transition to normal life was difficult, and their treatment eventually drew public indignation. The house where the quints were born, which was moved to its current location in downtown North Bay, is slated to reopen as the **Dionne Quints Museum**, filled with memorabilia about their lives and information about their complicated history. Contact Northeastern Ontario Tourism (705/522-0104 or 800/465-6655, www.northeasternontario. com) for an update.

The physician who delivered the Dionne quintuplets, Dr. Allan Roy Dafoe, supervised their life at Quintland. In his brick former home, south of North Bay, the **Callander Bay Heritage Museum** (107 Lansdowne St., Callander, 705/752-2282, www.mycallander. ca/museum, 10am-5pm Tues.-Sat., call for off-season hours, adults $5.50, seniors $5, ages 6-12 $4.50, families $15) displays photographs and artifacts about the famous multiples, including a basket where they were kept warm as infants and a 1936 newsreel of crowds flocking to Quintland. The museum's Alex Dufresne Gallery exhibits work by regional artists. A retirement home currently occupies the former Quintland site, which is on Highway 94 in Corbeil, four kilometers (2.5 miles) east of the museum.

The **Heritage Railway and Carousel** (Memorial Dr., 4pm-dusk Fri., 10am-dusk Sat.-Sun. mid-May-late June, 10am-dusk daily late June-early Sept., 10am-dusk Sat.-Sun. early Sept.-mid-Oct., $2) is an old-time miniature train and merry-go-round that will appeal to kids. In the former train station, the **Discovery North Bay Museum** (100 Ferguson St., 705/476-2323, www. discoverynorthbay.com, 10am-5pm Tues.-Fri., 8:30am-3pm Sat., adults $7, seniors and students $6, ages 5-12 $5) has model trains and other changing exhibits, most about local history. Lake Nipissing is a short walk from downtown, and you can explore the lake on a sightseeing cruise aboard the *Chief Commanda II* (200 Memorial Dr., 705/494-8167 or 866/660-6686, www. georgianbaycruise.com, mid-May-early Oct., adults $27-34, seniors $25-32, ages 13-18 $20-22, ages 6-12 $14-18).

Food

Downtown, vegetarian-friendly **Cedar Tree Lebanese Restaurant** (183 Main St. E., 705/472-2405, www. cedartreelebaneserestaurant.com, 11am-8pm Mon.-Sat., $5-18) serves tasty falafel, tabbouleh, *shawarma,* and other Middle Eastern classics.

North Bay's Heritage Carousel

Quirkily named **gd2go** (375 Foran St., 705/472-1111, www.gd2go.ca, 7am-7pm Mon.-Fri., 8am-7pm Sat., 9am-5pm Sun., $5-14) delivers on its slogan, "Fresh Food Fast," with smoothies, wraps, bowls, and salads that include plenty of vegetarian and vegan options.

Inside a homey cottage, brightly painted in primary colors, **The White Owl Bistro** (39 Lakeshore Dr., 705/472-2662, www.thewhiteowlbistro.ca, 11am-9pm Mon.-Sat., 10am-3pm and 5pm-9pm Sun., lunch $12-16, dinner $22-34) sources local ingredients for dishes like potato-crusted pickerel, elk burgers, and a lamb mixed grill. On a warm day, the best seats are on the patio overlooking Lake Nipissing.

Accommodations

Despite its drab exterior, a well-managed option among the chain motels lining Lakeshore Drive south of the city center is the **Best Western North Bay** (700 Lakeshore Dr., 705/474-5800 or 800/780-7234, www.bestwestern.com, $110-175 d), with a good-sized indoor pool and a guest laundry. The 130 rooms have been updated with cherry-toned furnishings, fridges, microwaves, and one-cup coffeemakers. Rates include Wi-Fi, local calls, and parking. At the hotel's **Farina Ristorante** (7am-1pm and 5pm-10pm daily), pastas, including savory mushroom ravioli, are among the Italian specialties.

Off Highway 11, there's **Hampton Inn North Bay** (950 McKeown Ave., 705/474-8400, www.hamptoninn.hilton.com, $118-159 d) and **Holiday Inn Express & Suites North Bay** (1325 Seymour St., 705/476-7700, www.ihg.com/holidayinnexpress, $121-159 d).

Practicalities

At the junction of Highways 11 and 17, North Bay is roughly equidistant to Toronto and Ottawa (355 kilometers, or 220 miles), and 130 kilometers (80 miles) east of Sudbury. **Ontario Northland** (www.ontarionorthland.ca) has bus service to Toronto (via Huntsville) and to Sudbury, while **Greyhound** (www.greyhound.ca) runs buses to Sudbury and Ottawa. The **bus station** (100 Station Rd., 705/495-4200) is east of downtown, near Highway 17.

You really need a car to explore North Bay. Local rental agencies include **Avis** (705/476-9730, www.avis.com), **Enterprise** (705/840-7777, www.enterprise.com), and **National** (705/474-3030, www.nationalcar.com). **Tourism North Bay** (205 Main St. E., 705/472-8480, www.tourismnorthbay.com, 9am-4pm Mon.-Fri.) provides local information.

MATTAWA

Taking its name from an Anishinaabek word meaning "where two rivers meet," the small town of Mattawa does indeed sit at the intersection of two rivers: the Ottawa, which divides Ontario from the neighboring province of Quebec, and the Mattawa, which flows west toward Lake Nipissing, near the present-day city of North Bay. Long a main trading route for local indigenous people, the Mattawa River also became important to the 16th- and 17th-century fur traders and voyageurs who journeyed between Montreal and Thunder Bay.

One of these explorers, French-born Samuel de Champlain (1567-1635), who founded Quebec City in 1608, sent his envoy and interpreter, Etienne Brulé, to the Mattawa region in 1610 to live with its native inhabitants, learn their language, and develop maps of potential routes west. Champlain himself first visited the area in 1615; a provincial park just west of Mattawa now bears his name.

Sights and Recreation

In the visitors center at **Samuel de Champlain Provincial Park** (6905 Hwy. 17, 705/744-2276, www.ontarioparks.com, mid-May-mid-Oct., $14.50 per vehicle), explore exhibits about Samuel de Champlain, the region's fur traders and voyageurs, and the history of its indigenous people. From July through early September, park staff run several different paddling excursions in traditional **voyageur canoes**, each accommodating 6-10 people; get details at the visitors

Side Trip: Nipping into Nipissing

The big woods of Algonquin give way to farm country as you drive north on Highway 11 and then turn west toward the small village of Nipissing (pronounced "NIH-pih-sing"). Nipissing is attracting modern-day pioneers who are simultaneously getting back to the land and welcoming visitors into their lives. It's a funky, little-touristed getaway destination.

Pop in for a quick look through the quirky **Nipissing Museum** (Hwy. 654 at Hwy. 534, 705/724-2938, 10am-4pm Tues.-Sun. mid-June-early Oct., donation), and you may find you're there for an hour or more. The museum was a labor of love for the local resident nicknamed "Museum Joe," who assembled several buildings packed with artifacts reflecting life in Nipissing since the early 1900s. There's the dress of a local woman who met with British royalty, the cash register from the general store, a wide variety of household items, and scads of photos.

Family-run **Board's Honey Farm** (6866 Hwy. 534, 705/729-2939 or 888/363-2827, www. boardshoneyfarm.com, 10am-5pm daily May-Oct.), between Nipissing and Restoule, houses more than 300 colonies of bees and sells a variety of homemade honeys and honey products. On Tuesday (10:30am) and Thursday (1:30pm) in July and August, you can take a guided tour of the beekeeping operations ($7.50 pp); otherwise, explore the gardens, walking trails, and hives on your own.

Continue west on Highway 534 to quiet **Restoule Provincial Park** (8818 Hwy. 534, 705/729-2010, www.ontarioparks.com, mid-Apr.-late Nov., $14.50 per vehicle), where you can swim in one of the lakes and perhaps spot deer or other wildlife nearby. Follow the one-kilometer (0.6-mile) **Rangers Point Trail**, an easy loop through the forest, for views of serene Stormy Lake. Or climb up the more challenging **Fire Tower Trail**; this seven-kilometer (4.3-mile) round-trip hike will take to you the top of the 100-meter (330-foot) Stormy Lake bluffs. The park office rents canoes and kayaks (four hours $25, full day $50), as well as bicycles ($5/hour, full day $20) that you can use to explore the park. Some of the 278 **campsites** (mid-May-mid-Oct., tent sites $42-45, electrical sites $47-52) are right on Restoule Lake.

WHERE TO STAY AND EAT

Staying at the **Piebird Vegan Farmstay** (113 Chapman's Landing Rd., 705/724-1144, www. piebird.org, $195 d) is like escaping to a laid-back farm run by your cool, socially conscious friends. Upstairs in the 100-year-old farmhouse is a country bedroom with a queen bed and en suite bath; the house has two additional bedrooms that can be rented along with the main room for families or groups of friends. Rates include a vegan breakfast. A separate two-bedroom family-friendly cottage on the property ($165) has a full kitchen and bath.

center. Elsewhere in the park, you can go **swimming** in clear Moore Lake, or **hiking** along the Etienne System trails, four forested loops ranging from 2.5 to 9 kilometers (1.5 to 5.5 miles) that take you to overlooks above the Mattawa River. The park entrance, on Highway 17, is 50 kilometers (31 miles) east of North Bay and 13 kilometers (eight miles) west of the town of Mattawa.

Take a short hike through the pretty, wooded **Eau Claire Gorge Conservation Area** (Graham Rd., Calvin, 705/474-5420, www.nbmca.on.ca) for views of a waterfall along the Amable du Fond River. A short trail from the parking area leads directly to the falls; it's about a 10-minute walk. A 1.9-kilometer (1.2-mile) loop trail takes you through the pine and maple forest to the river, follows the river to the waterfalls, and circles back through the woods. To reach the conservation area from Highway 17, turn south on Highway 630 (10 kilometers, or six miles, west of Mattawa), and follow the signs.

In town, the **Mattawa Museum** (285 First St., 705/744-5495, www.mattawamuseum. com, 10am-4pm Thurs.-Mon. mid-July-Aug., 10am-4pm Fri.-Mon. late June-mid-July and Sept.-mid-Oct., adults $7, seniors

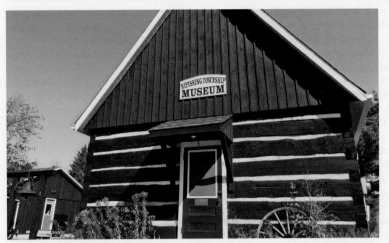

The Nipissing Museum is packed with artifacts about local life.

Piebird owners Sherry and Yan, who grow their own vegetables and operate a farm animal sanctuary on their property, share their love of animals and of organic farming with guests. They'll prepare vegan lunches and dinners by reservation. They also organize workshops about vegetarian food, canning, and other topics related to organic and local food, and they host the annual **Piebird Picnic and Garden Concert,** a day of summer music and outdoor eating; check their website for details.

GETTING THERE

Nipissing is 340 kilometers (210 miles) north of Toronto and 110 kilometers (68 miles) beyond Huntsville. Turn off Highway 11 at Highway 534 and continue west for about 13 kilometers (eight miles). For Nipissing Village, go north on Highway 654; Highway 534 continues west toward Restoule.

$4, students and kids $2, families $12) has three floors of exhibits about the region and its history. Displays in the riverside log building tell the stories of local residents like Firmin Monestime, a Haitian-born doctor who in 1964 became Canada's first Black mayor; Anahareo (1906-1986, aka Gertrude Bernard), an indigenous conservationist and author; and Anahareo's husband, born Archibald Belaney in Britain, who adopted the native identity "Grey Owl" and wrote about the Canadian wilderness. The museum has an original fringed leather jacket that Anahareo wore. As you wander around town, note the nearly two dozen larger-than-life-size carved **wooden statues** that portray voyageurs and First Nations people, explorers, adventurers, and others, including both Anahareo and Grey Owl.

Food and Accommodations

Hearty breakfasts, burgers, and poutine are among the specialties at **Myrt's Family Restaurant** (610 McConnell St., 705/744-2274, www.myrtsfamilyrestaurant.com, 6am-8pm daily, $6-17), a homey spot for a fresh, filling meal. The chicken club sandwich is made with roast chicken, bacon, and cheddar cheese, while other options range from burgers to wings to pizza. And this close to Quebec, of course there's poutine.

Inside Samuel de Champlain Provincial Park but independently run, the ★ **Canadian Ecology Centre** (6905 Hwy. 17, 705/744-1715 or 888/747-7577, www. canadianecology.ca, Aug.-June, $150), a non-profit environmental education facility, rents 32 pine-walled cabins. Most have a double bed with a single bunk above, plus a second double bed, a trundle that pulls out from under the other. The cabins come with linens and towels, electricity (and lots of outlets), heat, bathrooms with hot and cold water, and mini fridges. You can prepare meals in a shared dining cabin, which has a stove, refrigerator, kettle, coffeemaker, and a TV, with tables inside and out. Cabins don't have Wi-Fi, but the main building does. Bring a flashlight; the woods are very dark after sunset. Check the website for special events and for packages including activities and meals.

The two **campgrounds** (6905 Hwy. 17, 705/744-2276, www.ontarioparks.com, mid-May-mid-Oct., tent sites $42, electrical sites $47) in Samuel de Champlain Provincial Park border Moore Lake. Both the 74-site Babawasse Campground and the 137-site Jingwakoki Campground have small sandy beaches, playgrounds for the kids, flush toilets, showers, and laundry facilities.

In an 1881 building on Mattawa's main street, **Le Voyageur Inn** (351 Main St., 705/744-2370, www.levoyageurinn.com, $83-150) has 17 simple updated guest rooms with fridges, flat-screen TVs, and complimentary Wi-Fi. The big surprise? The dining room serves respectable Thai food, including a tasty green curry and pad Thai; a Thai-Pakistani couple owns and runs the property.

Practicalities

Mattawa is off Highway 17, the Trans-Canada Highway, 63 kilometers (39 miles) east of North Bay and 300 kilometers (186 miles) northwest of Ottawa. From Highway 17 near Mattawa, you can also access the northern

sections of Algonquin Provincial Park. The turnoff for Algonquin's Kiosk area is 18 kilometers (11 miles) west of Mattawa. For Brent, continue east from Mattawa on Highway 17; in 32 kilometers (20 miles), at Deux-Rivières, turn south onto Brent Road.

The **Mattawa Information Centre** (705/744-0222 or 800/267-4222, www. visitmattawa.travel) and **Northeastern Ontario Tourism** (705/522-0104 or 800/465-6655, www.northeasternontario.com) can provide more details about travel in the area.

SUDBURY

Sudbury reveals its charms slowly. Belching smokestacks and the rocky pits of many active mines surround this industrial city of 160,000. Yet if you find yourself here while en route to Sault Ste. Marie, Manitoulin Island, Killarney Provincial Park, or wilderness spots farther north or west, it's worth exploring.

Like many smaller Ontario cities, Sudbury has a growing arts scene, with a well-regarded autumn film festival that frequently features movies about northern communities and regional issues. The city's science museum is a don't-miss sight if you have children in tow, and the compact downtown has a handful of interesting restaurants and galleries, including **Artists on Elgin** (168 Elgin St., 705/674-0415, www.artistsonelgin.ca, 10am-5pm Mon.-Sat.) and **One Sky** (125 Durham St., 705/222-1759, 10am-6pm Mon.-Wed., 10am-8pm Thurs.-Fri., 11am-4pm Sat.-Sun.), which both feature local artists' work. Brightly painted murals on downtown buildings also showcase regional artists.

★ Science North

Kids (and their parents) could easily spend a day or more at Sudbury's cool, contemporary science museum, **Science North** (100 Ramsey Lake Rd., 705/523-4629 or 800/461-4898, www.sciencenorth.ca, 9am-6pm daily late June-early Sept., 10am-4pm daily early Sept.-Dec., call or check the website for hours winter-spring; adults $22, seniors and ages 13-17 $20, ages 3-12 $18).

Built into a massive rock on the edge of Ramsey Lake (you enter the exhibit halls through a tunnel blasted from the bedrock), this year-round hands-on museum is packed with "please touch" exhibits focusing on the environment, animals, the human body, and more. In the Nature Exchange, kids can bring in something they've found—a plant, a rock, a bug—learn something about it, and exchange it for something in the museum's collection. Many exhibitions highlight the wildlife, plants, geology, and ecology of Northern Ontario.

Admission packages including Science North and the on-site IMAX theater, planetarium, and science-themed escape room game are available, as are combination tickets to Science North and Dynamic Earth.

Dynamic Earth

In a region where mining, primarily for nickel and copper, is such a big part of the local economy, it's no surprise that a major attraction is the high-tech mining museum **Dynamic Earth** (122 Big Nickel Rd., 705/523-4629 or 800/461-4898, www.dynamicearth.ca, Mar.-Oct., adults $22, seniors and ages 13-17 $20, ages 3-12 $18).

A highlight is the 45-minute Underground Tour through a simulated mine, where you walk through 100 years of mining technology, from the dark, narrow tunnels of the early 1900s to the more high-tech mines of today. Bring a sweater or jacket; the temperature underground is cool, and the floor and walls are damp. Outside, the **Big Nickel**, a really big 13-ton replica of a 1951 Canadian five-cent piece, symbolizes the importance of nickel production to Sudbury's, and Canada's, economy.

Dynamic Earth operates in conjunction with Science North, and you can buy a combination ticket to both; the two attractions are about five kilometers (three miles) apart.

Entertainment and Events

Sudbury hosts a variety of arts festivals, including **Northern Lights Festival Boreal** (www.nlfbsudbury.com, July), a long-running music fest on Ramsey Lake; the **Cinéfest Sudbury International Film Festival** (www.cinefest.com, Sept.); and the **Sudbury Jazz Festival** (www.jazzsudbury.ca, Sept.).

Food

A seasonal **farmers market** (233 Elgin St., 705/674-4455, www.greatersudbury.ca/market, 8am-2pm Sat. June-Oct.) operates

Science North on Ramsey Lake

outside the downtown rail station. The market runs a second summertime location near Science North (York St. at Paris St., 3pm-7pm Thurs. July-Aug.).

Fromagerie Elgin (5 Cedar St., at Elgin, 705/675-1000, www.fromagerieelgin.ca, 4pm-11pm Tues.-Fri., 10am-11pm Sat., $6-12) is part cheese shop and part café, where patrons settle into the long wooden tables for cheese plates, sandwiches, and daily-changing soups. It hosts art exhibits and regular live music nights, too; call for schedules.

At **Leinala's** (272 Caswell Dr., 705/522-1977, 8am-5pm Mon.-Fri., 8am-4pm Sat.), a traditional Finnish bakery, it's difficult to choose among the delicious sweet breads and fresh-cooked doughnuts, including the house specialty, jelly pigs (glazed and filled with jam). It's in a strip mall off Regent Street, south of downtown.

A chill downtown spot for vegetarians and their nonveg companions is the **Laughing Buddha** (194 Elgin St., 705/673-2112, www.laughingbuddhasudbury.com, 11am-2am daily "patio season," 11am-11pm Sun.-Tues., 11am-midnight Wed., 11am-2am Thurs.-Sat. rest of the year, $10-17), a café-bar that hums till the wee hours. Whether you want herbal tea or booze, a classic chicken club sandwich,

a tofu banh mi, or an eclectically topped pizza, the laid-back staff will oblige. You can while away a mild evening in the courtyard garden.

You might not find tacos piled with maple-tamari tempeh or refried black beans with seitan at many classic Mexican cantinas, but then again, you might not expect to find **Tucos Taco Lounge** (582 Kathleen St., 705/222-8459, www.tucostacolounge.com, 11am-10pm Tues.-Thurs., 11am-11pm Fri.-Sat., 11am-9pm Sun., $9-13), a cool spot for drinks and Latin-inspired vegan fare, in Northern Ontario either. Sit on the lively outdoor patio and try the "phish" taco, filled with beer-battered avocado. The same owners run two equally hip eateries across the street: **Beards Coffee Bar & Bakery** (587 Kathleen St., 705/222-6866, 8am-8pm Mon.-Fri., 10am-8pm Sat., 10am-4pm Sun.) serving vegan pastries, pour-over coffee, and espresso drinks, and **Flurple's** (593 Kathleen St., noon-9pm Tues.-Sun., check their Facebook page for off-season hours), a vividly painted take-out shop scooping vegan ice cream.

The staff at family-owned **Verdicchio Ristorante** (1351-D Kelly Lake Rd., 705/523-2794, www.verdicchio.ca, 5pm-10pm Mon.-Sat.) cure their own meats, make their own pasta, and incorporate local

Tucos Taco Lounge

Sudbury's Signature Sandwiches

Ask Sudbury locals about what they have eaten since they were kids, and you'll quickly learn about two Sudbury sandwiches.

Though **Deluxe Hamburgers** looks like your typical fast-food chain, and it does serve an eponymous burger, this Sudbury icon is better known for its **chicken on a bun.** Order the bird in the popular dinner version, and you'll get roasted shredded chicken piled onto a simple burger-style bun that you douse with salty golden gravy and pair with a heap of french fries. Launched by a local family in 1959, the Deluxe mini chain currently has three locations: 1737 Regent Street, 1137 Kingsway, and 1313 Lorne Street. And in contrast to the double-arched logo of a better-known international burger company, the eatery's single golden arch is locally famous, too. As Sudbury residents will tell you, their community is a "one-arch town."

Sudbury's other beloved sandwich is the **porchetta**, particularly the one sold at **Regency Bakery & Deli** (1355 Regent St., 705/522-8861, www.regencybakery.com), an Italian-style grocery and meat store. At lunchtime, grab a bun from the shop's bakery bin, take it to the deli counter, say "Porchetta, please," and you'll get a sandwich overflowing with seasoned roast pork.

This signature Sudbury pork even figures in a legendary weekly game day at a local pub. Every Saturday afternoon from October to May, **Beef 'n' Bird Tavern** (923 Lorne St., 705/675-7833, www.beefnbird.net) hosts **"porketta bingo"** (with their own unique spelling). In this quirky only-in-Sudbury card game, each winner—who must call out "Porketta!"—earns as their prize a pound of roast pork.

ingredients—including trout caught off Manitoulin Island or Ontario quail—into their modern Italian dishes. Choose a wine from their all-Italian list or opt for a classic cocktail like a Negroni. A long-popular destination for a special night out, the restaurant is a little hard to find, located in a business park southwest of the city center.

Accommodations

The "artisan" at the **Artisan Upstairs Guesthouse** (318 Jeanne D'Arc Ave., 705/674-4387, www.artisanupstairs.com, $100 s, $130 d), on a residential street east of downtown, is co-owner Pete Lautenschlager, who carved much of the furniture and woodwork in these two second-floor guest rooms. Popular with couples and business travelers, the bedrooms have sponge-painted walls and private baths. Guests can use the fully equipped kitchenette and relax on the deck overlooking the nearby woods. Rates include full breakfast.

At the two-story brick **Travelway Inn** (1200 Paris St., 705/522-1122 or 800/461-4883, www.travelwayinnsudbury.com,

$129-148 d), across the street from Science North, the handy amenities and 83 well-maintained rooms make up for the stodgy exterior. You can read or play games in the snug den, prep meals in the guest kitchenette (equipped with a microwave and toaster), and buy snacks from the small lobby store. There's a guest laundry, too. Rooms have comfortable beds, plenty of outlets, and mini fridges. Rates include Wi-Fi, parking, and a light breakfast.

Among the nicest of Sudbury's many chain motels along Regent Street south of downtown is the 121-room **Hampton Inn-Sudbury** (2280 Regent St., 705/523-5200, www.sudburyontario.hamptoninn.com, $113-153 d), which makes both business travelers and vacationing families feel at home. The beds are topped with crisp white duvets, and kids will appreciate the indoor pool.

Information and Services

Sudbury Tourism (200 Brady St., 705/674-4455, ext. 7718, or 866/451-8252, www.sudburytourism.ca) has details about the city on its website.

Getting There

Sudbury is well served with air, train, and bus connections, but all its transportation terminals are located outside the city center.

AIR

The **Greater Sudbury Airport** (YSB, 5000 Air Terminal Dr., Garson, 705/693-2514 or 855/359-2972, www.flysudbury.ca) is 25 kilometers (15 miles) northeast of downtown. **Air Canada** (www.aircanada.com) and **WestJet** (www.westjet.com) fly from Toronto's Pearson Airport; **Porter Airlines** (www.flyporter. com) flies from Billy Bishop Toronto City Airport. **Bearskin Airlines** (705/693-9199 or 800/465-2327, www.bearskinairlines.com) serves Ottawa, Sault Ste. Marie, and Thunder Bay.

From the airport to in-town hotels, **Sudbury Cab** (705/626-7968, www.sudburycab.com) runs shared-van shuttles ($36-65) and taxis ($46-80). Both take advance bookings.

TRAIN

VIA Rail's transcontinental Toronto-Vancouver train stops two or three days a week at **Sudbury Junction** (2750 LaSalle Blvd., 705/524-1591), 10 kilometers (six miles) northeast of the city center. The Sudbury-Toronto leg (one-way adults $65-176) takes 7-8 hours. Note that the only trains using the **Sudbury Downtown Station** (233 Elgin St.) travel to the town of White River, between Sault Ste. Marie and Thunder Bay.

BUS

From Sudbury's Ontario Northland Bus Depot (1663 Kingsway), five kilometers (3 miles) northeast of downtown, **Ontario Northland** (705/222-6682, www.ontarionorthland.ca) runs buses to Toronto (5.5-6 hours, one-way adults $80, seniors and students $53, ages 2-11 $40) and north to Cochrane (6 hours, one-way adults $82, seniors and students $70, children $41). **Greyhound** (705/524-9900, www.greyhound.ca) connects Sudbury with Sault Ste. Marie (4.5 hours, one-way adults $35-86)

and Toronto (5 hours, one-way adults $41-97). A taxi from the bus station to downtown will cost about $20-25.

CAR

Sudbury is at the intersection of Highway 69 to Toronto and Highway 17, which goes west to Sault Ste. Marie and east to North Bay and Ottawa. The city is 390 kilometers (242 miles) north of Toronto, a 5-to 6-hour drive. Sudbury is 90 minutes north of Killarney Provincial Park and about the same distance to Manitoulin Island's swing bridge.

Getting Around

Although the city center is compact and walkable, Sudbury's attractions are all outside downtown. You can get around by bus or taxi, but having your own wheels is more convenient. **Greater Sudbury Transit** (705/675-3333, www.greatersudbury.ca) runs the city's bus network. Local cab companies include **Lockerby Taxi** (705/522-2222, www.lockerbytransportation.com) and **Aaron Taxi** (705/670-0000, www.aarontaxi. ca). **Avis** (www.avis.ca), **Enterprise** (www. enterpriserentacar.ca), **Budget** (www.budget. ca), and **Discount** (www.discountcar.com) are among Sudbury's car rental options.

TOP EXPERIENCE

★ TEMAGAMI

If you love to canoe or hike, Temagami, a wilderness region dotted with lakes large and small, makes a great getaway. Outdoor adventurers flock here in summer, increasing the population from 1,000 to over 10,000. Paddlers will find scores of opportunities for multiday canoe trips. Local outfitters help organize active trips.

The town's name, pronounced "Teh-MAW-gah-mee," is an Ojibwa word, roughly translated as "deep water by the shore," a fitting moniker for this lake country.

Sights

For an expansive aerial view of the surrounding

Side Trip: Chutes Provincial Park

If you're traveling between Sudbury and Sault Ste. Marie or the Lake Superior region, or if you'd simply like to make an outdoor detour, consider a side trip to **Chutes Provincial Park** (660 Imperial St. N., Massey, 705/865-2021, www.ontarioparks.com, mid-May-mid-Oct., $14.50 per vehicle), just off Highway 17.

This compact park's highlight are its **waterfalls**—the "chutes" that give the area its name—which cascade down the rocks in the Aux Sables River. There's a parking area near the falls. For a longer hike, follow the moderate **Twin Bridges Trail,** six kilometers (3.7 miles) round-trip, along the river to several lookouts above the falls.

The wooded 130-site **campground** (tent sites $42, electrical sites $47) is divided into four areas, each with restrooms and water taps; a centrally located comfort station has showers. If you want to fall asleep to the sound of the waterfalls, book sites 90-96, in Area C. The small swimming beach on the river below the falls, near Area D, is open to both campers and day-use visitors.

To reach the park from Highway 17, turn north onto Highway 553 (Imperial Street) at the town of Massey and follow the signs. Chutes is 100 kilometers (60 miles) west of Sudbury and 215 kilometers (135 miles) east of Sault Ste. Marie.

lakes and forests, climb the 30-meter (100-foot) **Temagami Fire Tower** (dawn to dusk, $3). At 396 meters (1,300 feet) above sea level, it's the highest point on Yonge Street (Hwy. 11), which runs more or less all the way to Toronto (and at one time was named the longest street in the world).

In the early-1900s stone building that once housed Temagami's train station, the **Living Temagami Heritage & Culture Centre** (6715 Hwy. 11 N., 705/569-3344, www.livingtemagami.ca, free) runs a gallery showing works by artists from local indigenous communities.

Two kilometers (1.2 miles) south of town, **Finlayson Point Provincial Park** (24 Finlayson Park Rd., off Hwy. 11, 705/569-3205, www.ontarioparks.com, late May-late Sept., $14.50 per vehicle) has two small sandy swimming beaches on Lake Temagami. You can rent canoes or explore the park's hiking trails. A museum has exhibits about the park's natural environment.

A vast protected wilderness surrounds Temagami with a network of backcountry parks. The largest is **Lady Evelyn Smoothwater Provincial Park** (www.ontarioparks.com) to the northwest. Exploring this rugged region isn't for outdoor novices; you need backcountry camping, white-water canoeing, and other wilderness skills. Contact local outfitters for information about backcountry trips.

Sports and Recreation

Smoothwater Outfitters & Lodge (705/868-6464, www.smoothwater.com) can organize canoe, kayak, or hiking adventures. The **Temagami Outfitting Company** (6 Lakeshore Dr., 705/569-2595, www.temagamioutfitting.ca) runs an outdoor gear store and plans canoe, kayak, and hiking trips. **Lakeland Airways** (705/569-3455, www.lakelandairways.ca) can take you into the wilderness surrounding Temagami by floatplane. They'll even strap your canoe to the plane and drop you off on a remote lake.

Another way to explore is by houseboat, which you can pilot along the interconnected lakes that wind through the region. Contact **Leisure Island Houseboat Rentals** (705/569-3261, www.leisureislandhouseboats.com) or **Three Buoys Houseboat Rentals** (705/569-3455, www.threebuoyshouseboats.ca) for rentals.

Food and Accommodations

Although the sign at this roadside stand says **B&D Burgers** (6731 Hwy. 11, 11am-7pm daily summer, hours vary in other seasons, weather permitting, $2.50-12), everyone calls it "the Chip Shop," because that's what you should order: chips (french fries), specifically the French Canadian specialty known as poutine. You can get a hamburger, hot dog, or fried fish, but it's the mounds of fries topped with gooey cheese and brown gravy that keep the picnic tables packed. When they ask if you want "shredded or curds" on your poutine, they're inquiring about the cheese; to be authentic, you want curds.

Temagami's best place to stay is **Smoothwater Outfitters & Lodge** (34 Smoothwater Rd., off Hwy. 11, 705/868-6464, www.smoothwater.com, $35 dorm, $108-128 d without meals, $248 d w/breakfast and dinner). The rustic petite doubles and bunkhouse are comfortable, staff are friendly and knowledgeable, and family-style breakfasts and dinners feature local ingredients. Adventures include paddling on the property's lake and multiday canoeing and camping excursions. In winter, you can snowshoe or cross-country ski on 50 kilometers (31 miles) of trails. Lounge lakeside or in the Gathering Hall with comfy sofas, books, and games. Smoothwater is 14 kilometers (8.7 miles) north of Temagami.

Stephanie and Mark Wagner owned the **Temagami Shores Inn & Restaurant** (6612 Hwy. 11N, 705/569-3200 or 866/866-7733, www.temagamishores.com, $109-185 d, $199-215 cabins), on forested grounds above Lake Temagami, for a number of years before they sold it. They've since bought it back. As this book went to press, they were upgrading the property and renovating the motel units (all with fridges and microwaves), the two hillside cabins, and the homestyle restaurant, which serves particularly tasty breakfasts.

CAMPING

Finlayson Point Park (24 Finlayson Park Rd., off Hwy. 11, 705/569-3205, www.ontarioparks.com, late May-late Sept., tent sites $42, electrical sites $47) has 117 campsites, many right on Lake Temagami. The campground has showers, flush toilets, and laundry facilities. The park also rents a two-bedroom **cabin** ($170) with log furniture and an electric fireplace; it has no plumbing, but it's a short walk to the washrooms.

Campers are welcome to pitch a tent on the lawn at **Smoothwater Outfitters & Lodge** (705/868-6464, www.smoothwater.com, $12); you can use the restrooms and showers in the bunkhouse.

Practicalities

The **Temagami Chamber of Commerce Information Centre** (7 Lakeshore Dr., 705/569-3344 or 800/661-7609, www.temagamiinformation.com) can give you information about the area. Temagami is 455 kilometers (285 miles) north of Toronto and 100 kilometers (60 miles) north of North Bay. **Ontario Northland** (www.ontarionorthland.ca) operates a daily bus between Toronto and **Temagami station** (Hwy. 11, 705/569-3310, 6.5 hours, one-way adults $102, seniors and students $87, ages 2-11 $51) and from Temagami on to Cochrane (5.25 hours, one-way adults $72, seniors and students $61, ages 2-11 $36).

COCHRANE

The main reason to come to Cochrane is to leave again. This windswept town with a remote, almost Wild West feel is the starting point for the Polar Bear Express train that runs north toward James Bay, at the edge of the arctic.

While Cochrane isn't far enough north to support arctic wildlife, the town capitalizes on its polar bear connection as the home of the small **Polar Bear Habitat and Heritage Village** (1 Drury Park Rd., 705/272-2327 or 800/354-9948, www.polarbearhabitat.ca, 9am-5pm daily May-Oct., 10am-4pm daily Nov.-Apr., adults $16, seniors $14, students $12, ages 5-11 $10, families $45), a polar bear sanctuary and research facility. Try to visit in the morning, or on a cool day, when the bears are most active, and time your visit so you can hear one of the free twice-a-day **keeper talks** (call or see the website for schedule), when

Cochrane is home to the Polar Bear Habitat and Heritage Village.

3rd Ave./Hwy. 11, 705/272-4926, www.town.cochrane.on.ca).

Food and Accommodations

To rustle up some grub, your best bet is the **J. R. Bar-B-Q Ranch** (63 3rd Ave., 705/272-4999, 11am-9pm Mon.-Sat., 3pm-8pm Sun.), where the family-friendly room, decorated with saddles and trophy fish, feels like the love child of a cowboy and a north-woods fisherman. The hearty barbecued ribs (half rack $18, full rack $24) are worth hooting over, and the menu includes ample portions of barbecue chicken, burgers, steaks, and pizza.

Cochrane's accommodations cluster near the train station, with additional chain motels on Highway 11 south of town. Behind a grim stone facade is Cochrane's most upscale lodging, the **Best Western Swan Castle Inn** (189 Railway St., 705/272-5200 or 800/265-3668, www.bestwesternontario.com, $130-150 d), which has 39 middle-of-the-road rooms and a helpful staff. Rates include continental breakfast.

You can roll out of bed and onto your train from the **Station Inn** (200 Railway St., 705/272-3500 or 800/265-2356, www.ontarionorthland.ca, $109-125 d), with 23 smallish rooms above the depot, as well as a coffee shop. The low-rise **Commando Motel** (80 7th Ave. S., 705/272-2700, www.commandomotel.com, $65 s, $70 d) is another option, with free Wi-Fi, one block from the station.

Getting There and Around

Cochrane is off Highway 11, 725 kilometers (450 miles) north of Toronto and 375 kilometers (235 miles) beyond North Bay. Polar Bear Express passengers who've arrived in Cochrane by car can leave their vehicles in the station parking lot during their journey north.

Cochrane Station (200 Railway St., 705/272-4228) is both the train station and the depot for **Ontario Northland** buses from Toronto (www.ontarionorthland.ca, 13-14 hours, one-way adults $163-174), a long haul with two transfers en route. Cochrane has no

staff tell you about the bears and answer your questions. If you're lucky, you can watch them swim from the other side of a clear enclosure. Because the bear population at the sanctuary fluctuates, check the status before making a special trip; in 2018, three bears were in residence. Also on the grounds is a modest one-street heritage village and a snowmobile museum.

If you still have time to kill, visit the **Tim Horton Museum** (7 Tim Horton Dr., off 4th St. E., 705/272-5084, call for hours, $2), inside the Tim Horton Event Centre, 2.5 kilometers (1.6 miles) east of the station. Born in Cochrane in 1930, Horton played 22 seasons in the National Hockey League, but he's equally well known as the founder of the ubiquitous Canadian doughnut shop chain that bears his name.

For visitor information, look for the giant polar bear. Chimo, an 11-meter (35-foot) bear statue (its name is an Inuit word meaning "welcome"), greets visitors outside the **Town of Cochrane Information Centre** (3 public transit, but you can easily walk around the small town.

★ POLAR BEAR EXPRESS TRAIN

You won't see polar bears en route (it's too far south), nor is the Ontario Northland train particularly "express," yet this 299-kilometer (186-mile) **rail journey** (800/265-2356, www.ontarionorthland.ca, 5 hours, Sun.-Fri. July-Aug., Mon.-Fri. Sept.-June, one-way adults $53, seniors and students $45, ages 2-11 $27) gives you a fascinating glimpse of life in the north. From Cochrane, the train chugs through stands of birch and poplar toward swampier lowlands dotted with skinny, green-tufted black spruce before pulling into the predominantly Cree community of Moosonee, where you can also visit nearby Moose Factory Island, another Cree settlement.

It's not a luxury train, but there's a dome car with broader views of the surrounding terrain, a dining car, an entertainment car (where local bands often perform), and a family car, offering activities and movies to help kids pass the time. You can rent a worthwhile audio tour ($15) that provides background about the region, points out highlights of Moosonee and Moose Factory Island, and introduces you to Cree culture.

Many people take the Polar Bear Express from Cochrane, make a quick tour of Moosonee and Moose Factory Island, and return the same night. If you have time, though, stay at least one or two nights in the north to better experience Cree culture.

In July and August, day-trippers have almost four hours to walk around Moosonee and Moose Factory before the southbound train departs. The rest of the year, the train's tourism amenities are discontinued, and the southbound train leaves three hours after the northbound train arrives, making a day trip less feasible.

Practicalities

The **Polar Bear Express** train departs Cochrane at 9am and reaches **Moosonee**

Station (705/336-2210) about five hours later. The return train leaves Moosonee at 6pm in July-August and at 5pm September-June. Advance reservations are recommended.

MOOSONEE AND MOOSE FACTORY ISLAND

If you look at a map of Northeastern Ontario, you'll notice one important thing is missing: roads. The only way to reach the remote area around James Bay, which has a predominantly First Nations population, is by rail or air.

The Polar Bear Express train travels to Moosonee, a town of about 3,500 near James Bay. The Moosonee area has two main settlements: the dusty frontier town of Moosonee on the mainland, and the island of Moose Factory in the Moose River just offshore, which is the region's primary draw. Home to 2,500 people, Moose Factory is 4.8 kilometers (three miles) long and 3.2 kilometers (two miles) wide; the Moose Cree First Nation Reserve occupies much of the island. Local websites with information about the region include the **Moose Cree First Nation** (www.moosecree.com) and the town of **Moosonee** (www.moosonee.ca).

Sights and Activities

Moosonee's main street is 1st Avenue, which runs from the train station to the river, where you can catch a water taxi to Moose Factory Island. Stop first at the **Railway Car Museum** (1st St., July-Aug., free), opposite the station, to check out the exhibits about the area's culture and history.

Moose Factory Island's main attraction is the **Cree Cultural Interpretive Centre** (Pehdabun Rd., 705/658-4619, ext. 265, www.moosecree.com, 9am-5pm Sun.-Fri. July-Aug., off-season by appointment, adults $12, under age 12 $6), which has well-designed exhibits about Cree culture, language, traditional medicine, and food. Outside the building, you can peek into several tepees. Located on the island's east side, the center is about a 30-minute walk from the Cree Village Ecolodge or from the town docks. The waterfront views along Pehdabun Road are lovely.

In summer, the Cree Village Ecolodge can arrange **boat trips** from Moose Factory to nearby Fossil Island and up to James Bay, 15 kilometers (nine miles) to the north, weather and tides permitting.

Moose Factory Island gets its unusual name from its history as Ontario's oldest fur-trading community. When the Hudson's Bay Company established Ontario's first English-speaking settlement on the island in 1673, the chief agent at a fur-trading post was called a "factor," and the place where a factor worked was called a "factory." Add "Moose," which referred to the island's location in the Moose River, and you have "Moose Factory Island." Today, little remains of this fur-trading era. On Front Street, near the Northern Quickstop store, is the **Hudson's Bay Staff House**, once part of the Hudson's Bay post. A more permanent legacy, perhaps, is the island **cemetery** (Pehdabun Rd.) where some of these early settlers were laid to rest.

Food and Accommodations

The best place to stay in the region is on Moose Factory Island, where the Moose Cree First Nation run ★ **Cree Village Ecolodge** (Hospital Dr., 705/658-6400 or 888/273-3929, www.creevillage.com, $178-258 d) on the banks of the Moose River. The 20 rustically comfortable rooms have organic cotton bedding, birch blinds, and Wi-Fi, and the staff help arrange tours. The lodge's showpiece is the dining room—the best place to eat in the area—with a soaring ceiling and a multistory wall of windows facing the water. The kitchen uses traditional First Nations ingredients in its bison chili, baked pickerel, venison, and other dishes ($17-33).

The whole island seems to gather at the **Moose Cree Complex** (Mookijuneibeg Dr.), part shopping mall and part community center. The **Northern Store** (705/658-4552, 9am-6pm Mon.-Wed. and Sat., 9am-8pm Thurs.-Fri., noon-5pm Sun.) is a well-stocked grocery, although prices—as in many northern towns—are significantly higher than they are down south. The building also houses the **Moose Cree Tourism Office** (705/658-4619, ext. 265), as well as a pharmacy, coffee shop, bank, and post office, and residents often sell homemade baked goods or crafts inside.

You can also pick up provisions at **G. G.'s Corner** (Center Rd., 705/685-4591) or **Northern Quickstop** (Front St., 705/658-4086).

native script on the Railway Car Museum

Getting Around

From Moosonee's train station, it's a 15- to 20-minute walk to the docks; a taxi will cost about $6. In summer, **water taxis** ($15 pp) cross the river between Moosonee and Moose Factory Island in 10-15 minutes. Boats typically wait at the docks on both the Moosonee and Moose Factory sides. The Cree Village Ecolodge has its own dock, on the opposite side of the island from the main public dock, so be sure to tell the boat operator if you're heading to the lodge.

In midwinter, the river freezes solid enough to support an **ice road** between Moose Factory and the mainland; taxis and other vehicles can drive across ($10-15 one-way). During the fall "freeze-up" and spring "break-up" periods, when the river is too icy for boats to cross but not solid enough for cars, the only way on and off Moose Factory Island is by helicopter.

Taxis typically meet trains arriving in Moosonee. For a cab on Moose Factory Island, call **Creeway** (705/658-5256) or **Northway** (705/658-4131).

Georgian Bay

Look for ★ to find recommended
sights, activities, dining, and lodging.

Highlights

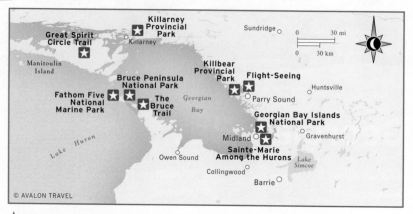

★ **Bruce Peninsula National Park:** This national park is among Ontario's most beautiful settings. Its intricate rock formations, turquoise waters, and more than 40 species of orchids draw hikers, kayakers, and other nature lovers (page 365).

★ **The Bruce Trail:** This iconic Canadian hiking route stretches 845 kilometers (525 miles) from the Niagara region to the end of the Bruce Peninsula (page 366).

★ **Fathom Five National Marine Park:** Best known for its distinctive "flowerpot" rock formations and for the shipwrecks where you can snorkel or explore by boat or even helicopter, this national marine conservation area also has some of North America's finest scuba diving (page 367).

★ **Sainte-Marie Among the Hurons:** This historic village "reimagines" the first European settlement in Ontario, where French Jesuits lived and worked with the indigenous Wendat people in the 1600s (page 393).

★ **Georgian Bay Islands National Park:** Of the thousands of islands that dot Georgian

Bay, 63 are protected in this national park. Visit for a day of hiking and swimming or stay in a quiet cabin by the shore (page 398).

★ **Flight-Seeing:** The most thrilling way to take in Georgian Bay's 30,000 Islands is on a floatplane tour. Soar above the bay by day or take a romantic sunset flight—complete with champagne (page 402).

★ **Killbear Provincial Park:** This waterfront area near Parry Sound offers granite cliffs, sandy beaches, and a lovely destination for hiking, canoeing, swimming, and camping (page 404).

★ **Killarney Provincial Park:** Escape to the wilderness of this vast and dramatic park, with its rugged white dolomite ridges, pink granite cliffs, pine forests, and crystal-clear lakes (page 407).

★ **Great Spirit Circle Trail:** Explore aboriginal culture on Manitoulin Island, the world's largest freshwater island. Take a guided "Mother Earth" nature hike or a workshop on traditional dance, drumming, or food, and stay on a First Nations reserve (page 413).

With Caribbean-blue water, dramatic rock formations, and a network of red-and-white lighthouses standing guard along the shore, Georgian Bay boasts some of Ontario's most spectacular scenery. If you're looking for a

getaway to the outdoors, whether for exhilarating adventure or relaxing by the water, head to this eastern finger of Lake Huron.

Measuring 320 kilometers (200 miles) long and 80 kilometers (50 miles) wide, Georgian Bay is dotted with more than 30,000 islands and offers some of the finest scuba diving in the north. The region has three national parks, several large provincial parks, ski slopes, and canoe routes, as well as the world's longest freshwater beach. It's a hugely popular destination for hikers, too, encompassing the northern portions of the Bruce Trail, one of Canada's longest hiking routes.

You won't want to miss the stunning Bruce Peninsula, with its unusual rock formations, offshore islands, and network of hiking trails. Georgian Bay Islands National Park is the gateway to the 30,000 Islands region, and splurging on a floatplane tour over the area's waters is a new level of thrill. Winter

sports enthusiasts should head to the Blue Mountains, Ontario's top ski and snowboarding region; the surrounding area draws foodies, too, with numerous top-notch restaurants and an "apple pie trail" to explore. If you prefer history and culture with your outdoor adventures, the towns of Midland, Parry Sound, and Owen Sound will oblige.

Another superlative outdoor destination, Killarney Provincial Park lures paddlers and hikers to its shores studded with pink granite and its trails lined with pines. Hike the challenging trail to the Crack for views across the hills, or spend a morning canoeing on a peaceful inland lake.

On Manitoulin Island, the Great Spirit Circle Trail is a leader in aboriginal tourism, offering experiences in music, dance, traditional medicine, hiking, and more that introduce visitors to First Nations culture and heritage. The world's largest freshwater island, Manitoulin has long sandy beaches,

---

Previous: pink rocks on the Chikanishing Trail in Killarney Provincial Park; the powwow grounds on Manitoulin Island. **Above:** overlooking the cliffs from the Cup and Saucer Trail.

Georgian Bay

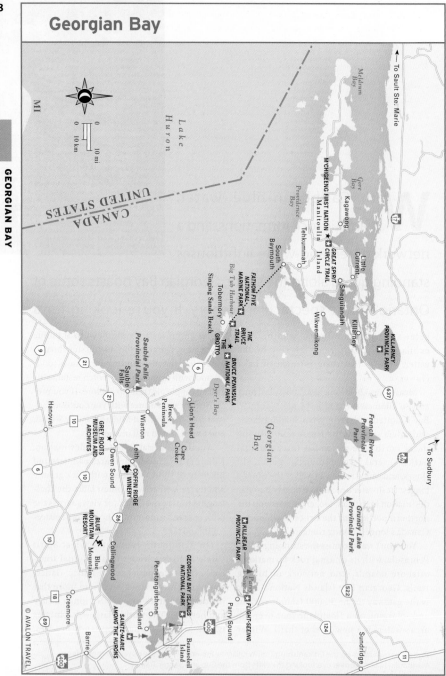

© AVALON TRAVEL

quiet roads for cycling, and—like much of this waterside region—plenty of spots to sit and simply enjoy the bay.

PLANNING YOUR TIME

Many attractions and services around Georgian Bay don't begin operation until mid- or late May and close in mid-October, after the Canadian Thanksgiving weekend. One exception is the Blue Mountains, which draw winter visitors for skiing and snowboarding.

For a long weekend, do a quick tour of the **Bruce Peninsula**, hike or mountain bike at **Blue Mountain Resort**, pair a visit to **Midland**'s historic sites with a day trip to **Georgian Bay Islands National Park**, or base yourself in **Parry Sound** and explore the nearby provincial parks. You can easily spend 3-4 days on the Bruce Peninsula, particularly if you want to hike sections of the Bruce Trail and snorkel or scuba dive in the **Fathom Five National Marine Park.**

An excellent way to explore the region is by following the **Georgian Bay Coastal Route**, a complete loop around the bay. From May to October you can take a ferry between the Bruce Peninsula and **Manitoulin Island**, then continue to **Killarney Provincial Park**, the Georgian Bay Islands, Midland, **Wasaga Beach**, and the Blue Mountains. Although you could cover most of this route in a week, you'll have more time for outdoor activities if you can spend at least 10 days.

The Bruce Peninsula

With limestone cliffs, crystal-blue waters, forested hiking trails, and even a wide variety of orchids, the Bruce Peninsula's striking natural scenery is the main reason to visit this finger of land that juts out between Lake Huron and Georgian Bay. The must-see attractions are its two national parks—Bruce Peninsula National Park and Fathom Five National Marine Park—at the peninsula's north end, around the town of Tobermory. Yet beyond these natural attractions, the friendly, small-town atmosphere draws vacationers, too.

For pre-trip research, check out the detailed **County of Bruce Tourism website** (www.explorethebruce.com), with extensive information about the Bruce Peninsula and its surrounding communities. A fun way to "Explore the Bruce" is with their annual **Adventure Passport** (http://passport.explorethebruce.com), a scavenger hunt that leads you through the region.

TOBERMORY

The most convenient base for exploring Bruce Peninsula National Park and Fathom Five National Marine Park is Tobermory, a pretty waterfront town at the peninsula's northern tip. Highway 6, the peninsula's main north-south road, ends in Tobermory.

National Park Visitors Centre

Start your visit at the **National Park Visitors Centre** (120 Chi Sin Tib Dek Rd., 519/596-2233, www.pc.gc.ca, 9am-5pm daily May-late June and early Sept.-Oct., 8am-8pm daily late June-early Sept., national park admission adults $5.80, seniors $4.90, $11.70 per vehicle) for information about both Bruce Peninsula National Park and Fathom Five National Marine Park. Watch a short film about the area's highlights and explore exhibits about local ecology. Then climb the 112 steps of the 20-meter (65-foot) **Lookout Tower** for views across the peninsula and surrounding islands.

In summer, park staff offer a variety of interpretive programs, including guided hikes and children's activities. If you plan to camp on Flowerpot Island in Fathom Five National Marine Park, or to scuba dive in any park territory, you must register at the Visitors Centre before heading out. Two short hikes start at

Two Days on the Bruce Peninsula

You could spend far more than two days exploring the trails, beaches, and waters along the Bruce Peninsula, but if time is short, follow this guide to the region's highlights.

DAY 1

Take an early-morning walk along Tobermory's **Little Tub Harbour**, then get oriented at the **Bruce Peninsula National Park Visitors Centre.** Check out the exhibits about local ecology and climb the 112 steps of the **Lookout Tower** for a bird's-eye view over the peninsula and nearby islands.

Next, pick up a picnic at **Little Tub Bakery** (and choose a butter tart or other treat for dessert) and head off for a hike, either at the exceedingly popular **Grotto** and **Indian Head Cove** (reserve your parking slot in advance) or along the shorter trail out to the cliff views at **Halfway Log Dump.**

Your next adventure? Take a **snorkeling tour** to see several of the eerie shipwrecks resting on the lake bottom. Don't worry about getting too cold; you'll suit up in an extra-thick wetsuit, hood, booties, and gloves.

After your snorkeling adventure, warm up with a late-afternoon swim or stroll on the sand at **Singing Sands Beach** on Lake Huron, where you can linger till the sun starts to set. Pop back to your lodging for a quick shower, then have a casual dinner in Tobermory at **The Fish and Chip Place** or the town's microbrewery, **Tobermory Brewing Co & Grill.**

DAY 2

After breakfast the next morning, venture out on the water again, this time into **Fathom Five National Marine Park** to explore **Flowerpot Island.** Walk to the unusual rock formations that give the island its name and continue hiking out to the island's lighthouse.

Back on the mainland, drive south to **Lion's Head.** Eat lunch at homey **Marydale's Restaurant,** walk on the beach past the picturesque lighthouse, or go for a hike in **Lion's Head Provincial Park.**

For dinner, either return to Tobermory, or if you have to leave the peninsula, head south and wrap up your Bruce region adventure in Owen Sound with the creative Mexican food at lively **Casero Kitchen Table.**

---

the Visitors Centre, which is the northernmost point on the Bruce Trail. It's an easy 800-meter (0.5-mile) walk to the **Little Dunks Bay Lookout.** The 4.8-kilometer (three-mile) **Burnt Point Loop Trail** meanders through the forest (with some rough, rocky patches) to Georgian Bay, where you can look out over the Fathom Five islands.

The Visitors Centre is a 10-minute walk from Tobermory's Little Tub Harbour along a flat, partly paved section of the Bruce Trail. By car, look for the park sign on Highway 6, just south of town.

Little Tub Harbour

Most of Tobermory's shops and services surround Little Tub Harbour. Boats to the Fathom Five islands leave from Little Tub, as do sightseeing cruises around Tobermory and the islands.

Blue Heron Tours (519/596-2999 or 855/596-2999, www.blueheronco.com, mid-June-early Sept., adults $38, seniors $36, ages 6-16 $29) runs a two-hour tour on a 125-passenger glass-bottom ferry. It sails to Big Tub Harbour, where you see two 19th-century shipwrecks close to the surface, and continues around Cove Island, the Otter Islands, and Flowerpot Island. Another option, for the same price, is a two-hour sunset cruise (May-mid-Oct.). **Bruce Anchor Cruises** (519/596-2555 or 800/591-4254, www.bruceanchorcruises.com, adults $33, seniors $31, ages 6-16 $24) offers two-hour tours that

The Bruce Peninsula

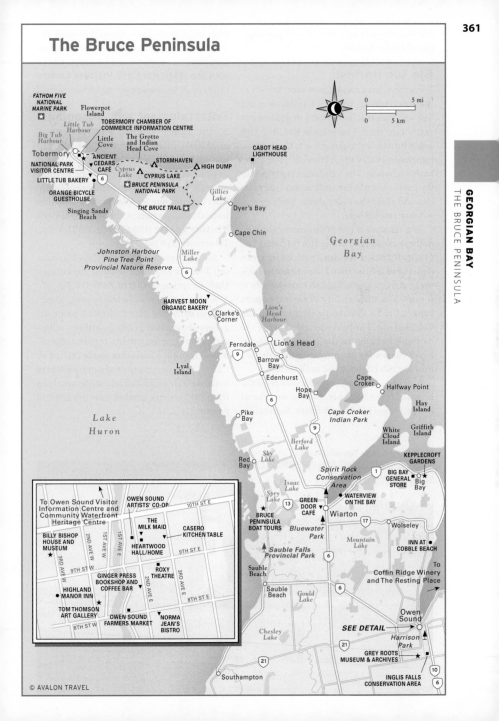

FATHOM FIVE
NATIONAL
MARINE PARK

Flowerpot
Island

Little Tub
Harbour

TOBERMORY CHAMBER OF
COMMERCE INFORMATION CENTRE

Big Tub
Harbour

Little
Cove

The Grotto
and Indian
Head Cove

CABOT HEAD
LIGHTHOUSE

Tobermory

ANCIENT
CEDARS
CAFÉ

STORMHAVEN

HIGH DUMP

NATIONAL PARK
VISITOR CENTRE

Cyprus
Lake

CYPRUS LAKE

LITTLE TUB BAKERY

BRUCE PENINSULA NATIONAL PARK

ORANGE BICYCLE
GUESTHOUSE

Gillies
Lake

THE BRUCE TRAIL

Singing Sands
Beach

Dyer's Bay

Cape Chin

Johnston Harbour
Pine Tree Point
Provincial Nature Reserve

Miller
Lake

*Georgian
Bay*

HARVEST MOON
ORGANIC BAKERY

Clarke's
Corner

Lion's
Head
Harbour

Ferndale

Lion's Head

Lyal
Island

Barrow
Bay

Edenhurst

Cape
Croker

Halfway Point

Hope
Bay

Cape Croker
Indian Park

Hay
Island

*Lake
Huron*

Pike
Bay

Berford
Lake

White
Cloud
Island

Griffith
Island

Red
Bay

Sky
Lake

Spirit Rock
Conservation
Area

KEPPLECROFT
GARDENS

BIG BAY
GENERAL
STORE

Big
Bay

Isaac
Lake

Spry
Lake

GREEN
DOOR
CAFÉ

WATERVIEW
ON THE BAY

To Owen Sound Visitor
Information Centre and
Community Waterfront
Heritage Centre

OWEN SOUND
ARTISTS' CO-OP

10TH ST E

BRUCE
PENINSULA
BOAT TOURS

Wiarton

Wolseley

THE
MILK MAID

CASERO
KITCHEN TABLE

*Bluewater
Park*

INN AT
COBBLE BEACH

BILLY BISHOP
HOUSE AND
MUSEUM

HEARTWOOD
HALL/HOME

9TH ST E

*Mountain
Lake*

Sauble Falls
Provincial Park

To
Coffin Ridge Winery
and The Resting Place

9TH ST W

GINGER PRESS
BOOKSHOP AND
COFFEE BAR

ROXY
THEATRE

Sauble
Beach

HIGHLAND
MANOR INN

8TH ST E

Sauble
Beach

Gould
Lake

Owen
Sound

TOM THOMSON
ART GALLERY

OWEN SOUND
FARMERS MARKET

NORMA
JEAN'S
BISTRO

SEE DETAIL

*Harrison
Park*

8TH ST W

*Chesley
Lake*

GREY ROOTS
MUSEUM & ARCHIVES

INGLIS FALLS
CONSERVATION AREA

Southampton

© AVALON TRAVEL

0   5 mi
0   5 km

follow a similar route aboard a 47-passenger glass-bottom Zodiac.

Big Tub Harbour

Tobermory has a second port area, known as Big Tub Harbour. The first lighthouse at Big Tub was constructed in 1885 to guide ships safely into port. The present-day **Big Tub Lighthouse,** a hexagonal tower that was automated in 1952, still performs that role at the harbor's mouth. The lighthouse isn't open to the public, but you can walk around the exterior and along the rocky shore. You can also swim or snorkel here.

The remains of two 19th-century ships lie in the shallow water of Big Tub Harbour. The *Sweepstakes,* a two-masted schooner, ran aground near Cove Island Lighthouse in 1885; the boat was towed to Big Tub Harbour, where it sank. The steamer *City of Grand Rapids* caught fire in 1907 while docked in Little Tub Harbour. The boat was towed out of the harbor to prevent the fire from spreading to nearby ships; the burning ship then drifted into Big Tub Harbour and sank there.

You can see the shipwrecks on one of the boat tours out of Tobermory or on several of the Flowerpot Island boats. Snorkeling and scuba diving are allowed around the wrecks, but only at designated times, because boat traffic in the area can be heavy. Check with the **National Park Visitors Centre** (519/596-2233, www.pc.gc.ca) for details.

Entertainment and Shopping

At the annual **Orchid Festival** (www.orchidfest.ca, late May or early June), you can join guided orchid-viewing walks, take flower drawing or photography workshops, or learn more about the peninsula's orchid population. Check the website for a schedule or stop into festival headquarters at the **National Park Visitors Centre** (120 Chi Sin Tib Dek Rd., Tobermory, 519/596-2233).

Most shops around Little Tub Harbour sell T-shirts and other ordinary souvenirs. One exception is **Circle Arts** (14 Bay St., 519/596-2541, www.circlearts.com, 10am-5:30pm daily mid-May-mid-Oct.), a fine-art gallery showcasing prints, paintings, sculpture, photographs, jewelry, textiles, one-of-a-kind furniture, and other works crafted by Canadian artists, many of whom have ties to the Bruce Peninsula. You might find anything from a $15 ceramic candleholder to a $20,000 painting.

Big Tub Lighthouse, Tobermory

On the Lookout for Lighthouses

What is it about lighthouses that draw people like a beacon? If you're a lighthouse lover, the Lake Huron and Georgian Bay coasts are prime territory for lighthouse touring. Many of the region's lighthouses were built in the mid- to late 1800s or early 1900s during the heyday of Great Lakes shipping. Today, the lonely job of lighthouse keeper has generally gone the way of the dodo: Most lighthouse operations are automated, although their beacons still guide boats along the shores.

On Lake Huron, visit the **Chantry Island Light** (www.chantryisland.com) near Southampton and **Kincardine Lighthouse** (www.kyc.ca), a lighthouse-turned-museum near Kincardine's downtown. The Bruce Peninsula has several lighthouses, including **Big Tub Lighthouse** in Tobermory, **Cabot Head Lighthouse and Museum** (www.cabothead.ca), **Lion's Head Lighthouse** on Lion's Head Beach, and **Cape Croker Lighthouse** at the tip of Cape Croker, a First Nations reserve. On Flowerpot Island in the Fathom Five National Marine Park, you can visit the **Flowerpot Island Light Station.** One of the most picturesque light stations is the **Killarney East Lighthouse,** on the bay near Killarney Provincial Park.

Food

Most of Tobermory's dining options are near Little Tub Harbour or along Highway 6. In a little house south of town, **Little Tub Bakery** (4 Warner Bay Rd., at Hwy. 6, 519/596-8399, 9am-6pm daily summer, call for off-season hours) is justifiably famous for its gooey butter tarts. The cinnamon rolls and freshly baked pies are also delicious. You can pick up a sandwich or homemade pizza for a picnic.

Surprised to find a vegetarian-friendly eatery on a golf course? **Ancient Cedars Café** (Cornerstone Golf Club, 7178 Hwy. 6, 519/596-8626, 11am-9pm daily summer, call for off-season hours, $11-20) does dish out burgers made from locally raised beef, but the menu also features tofu banh mi, a barbecue seitan sandwich, and a tasty sweet potato-and-black bean burrito.

You can't miss the bright blue and yellow facade of **The Fish and Chip Place** (24 Bay St. S., 519/596-8380, www.thefishandchipplace. com, lunch and dinner daily late May-mid-Oct., call for seasonal hours, $7-13), on Little Tub Harbour. The small menu includes the eponymous whitefish and french fries; the fish taco won't put any Baja joints out of business, but this far north of the border, it will do. On a sunny afternoon, particularly if you've been hiking, a beer on the deck is a perfect reward.

Tobermory has its own microbrewery,

Tobermory Brewing Co & Grill (28 Bay St. S., 519/596-8181, www.tobermorybrewingco. ca, noon-11pm daily spring-fall, noon-11pm Wed.-Sun. winter, lunch $10-25, dinner $17-44) in a pine-walled cottage on Little Tub Harbour. The bar is up front, the dining room and brew tanks are in the rear. At either spot, sip their Bruce Trail blonde ale or Fathom Five porter to accompany plates of beer-braised baby back ribs or trout from Manitoulin Island.

Accommodations

You'll find motels and B&Bs around, or within walking distance of, Little Tub Harbour and along Highway 6 south of town; if you don't want to take your car everywhere, stay near the harbor. In July and August and on holiday weekends, even basic motel rooms go for over $150; book in advance, or at least arrive early in the day. The **Tobermory Chamber of Commerce** website (www.tobermory.com) lists local accommodations with last-minute availability.

Friendly **Blue Bay Motel** (32 Bay St., 519/596-2392, www.bluebay-motel.com, May-mid-Oct., $110-238 d), right above Little Tub Harbour, has 16 basic but comfortable rooms with fridges, coffeemakers, and updated linens; the best are the second-floor units with water views (first-floor rooms face the parking lot). There's also a large three-bedroom suite with a full kitchen. You can borrow one of the motel bicycles to tool around the area.

Inside a nondescript vinyl-sided house about a 15-minute walk from Little Tub Harbour is the surprisingly stylish **Forest House B&B** (68 Harpur Dr., 877/596-1228, www.theforesthouse.ca, May-mid-Oct., $159-349 d), with three modern guest units outfitted with microwaves, fridges, and small flat-screen TVs. On the top floor, the two-bedroom Harbour View Suite can accommodate two couples; one bedroom has glimpses of the bay, while the other looks over the forest. Owners Spencer and Chris serve breakfast around a communal table in the sleek industrial kitchen; there's no other common space, although you can gather around the fire pit or lounge in the hammock between the trees.

As vibrant as the name suggests, the three contemporary guest rooms in the **Orange Bicycle Guesthouse and Gardens** (5 Warner Bay Rd., at Hwy. 6, 519/596-2353, www.orangebicyclebnb.com, $155-200 d) pop with color. The largest unit has a king bed and a sitting area with a double futon couch; the others have queen beds. Rates include a full breakfast and Wi-Fi. The inn is just off the highway south of town; look for the orange bicycle in the yard.

Information and Services

The **Tobermory Chamber of Commerce Information Centre** (7420 Hwy. 6, just south of Little Tub Harbour, 519/596-2452, www.tobermory.com) provides maps and information about attractions, lodging, and services. **County of Bruce Tourism** (www.explorethebruce.com) has extensive information about Tobermory and the rest of the Bruce Peninsula.

Foodland Market (9 Bay St., 519/596-2380, 7am-9pm daily summer, 8am-6pm Mon.-Sat. off-season) at Little Tub Harbour stocks basic supplies for picnics or camping and also has a coin laundry.

Getting There

CAR

Tobermory is approximately 300 kilometers (186 miles) northwest of Toronto, about a four-hour drive, weather and traffic permitting. Parking around Little Tub Harbour is restricted to two hours ($3/hour mid-May-mid-Oct.). Boat tour operators provide parking for their customers; ask for details when you book your tickets. Otherwise, if you're planning a longer stay in town, leave your car in one of the long-term parking lots ($15/day mid-May-mid-Oct.).

BUS

Without a car, the most convenient way to travel from Toronto to Tobermory, Bruce Peninsula National Park, or other peninsula destinations is on the **Parkbus** (800/928-7101, www.parkbus.ca, one-way/round-trip adults $64/$89, seniors and students $58/$80, ages 2-12 $32/$45), which operates on select weekends. The bus departs from several points in Toronto, including 30 Carlton Street (between Yonge St. and Church St., subway: College), and Dufferin Street at Bloor Street West (subway: Dufferin). On the Bruce Peninsula, the Parkbus drops off and picks up at stops in Wiarton, Lion's Head, the national park's Cyprus Lake campground, and Tobermory; check the website for details.

If you can't arrange your schedule to ride the Parkbus, the other bus option is to connect through Owen Sound. **Greyhound** (800/661-8747, www.greyhound.ca) can get you to Owen Sound from Toronto and points farther afield. From Owen Sound to Tobermory, **First Student Canada bus service** (2180 20th St. E., Owen Sound, 519/376-5712, www.tobermory.com, one-way adults $34, seniors and ages 4-12 $32) runs one bus a day in each direction Friday-Sunday and holiday Mondays July through early September. The schedule is timed to connect with the Manitoulin Island ferry.

FERRY

The **MS *Chi-Cheemaun* Ferry** (information 519/376-6601, reservations 800/265-3163, www.ontarioferries.com, mid-May-mid-Oct.), nicknamed "the Big Canoe," runs between Tobermory and South Baymouth on Manitoulin Island. The crossing takes about two hours, and the ship accommodates 638 passengers and 143 cars. The ferry cuts several hours of driving time compared to the road route between Southern Ontario and Manitoulin. Reservations are advised, particularly if you're taking a car. The **Tobermory ferry terminal** is at 8 Eliza Street (519/596-2510).

Getting Around

Without a car, you can easily walk around Tobermory or to the National Park Visitors Centre, catch a boat to Flowerpot Island, and take other short hikes in the area. Some hotel or B&B owners will drop you at the trailhead for a day hike, so inquire when making lodging reservations. **Thorncrest Outfitters** (7441 Hwy. 6, 519/596-8908, www.thorncrestoutfitters.com) runs a shuttle service for hikers or paddlers (they'll also transport your canoe or kayak) between Tobermory and Cyprus Lake, Dyer's Bay, or Lion's Head.

★ BRUCE PENINSULA NATIONAL PARK

Intricate rock formations. Caribbean-blue water. Centuries-old trees. Inland lakes. More than three dozen types of orchids. **Bruce Peninsula National Park** (www.pc.gc.ca, open year-round, $11.70 per vehicle), which encompasses 156 square kilometers (60 square miles) spread over several parcels of land, protects these natural features that are unique in Ontario. The park is at the northern tip of the Bruce Peninsula near the town of Tobermory.

The Grotto and Indian Head Cove

The park's most visited sights are the Grotto, a waterside cave, and the adjacent Indian Head Cove. They're popular for good reason. Through centuries of erosion, the waters of Georgian Bay have sculpted the area's soft limestone cliffs, leaving dramatic overhangs, carved rocks, and underwater caves, such as the Grotto. At Indian Head Cove, the rocks are shaped into pillars, narrower at the bottom and wider at the top, resembling smaller versions of the "flowerpots" in the Fathom Five National Marine Park. Particularly on bright sunny days, the contrast between the brilliant blue-green bay, the polished white rocks along the shoreline, and the layered rock cliffs is striking.

You can climb down to sea level to explore the cave-like Grotto, but even if scrambling down steep rocks isn't your thing, you can still view the Grotto from above. At Indian Head Cove, the rock formations are on the pebbly beach, so no climbing is required. You can swim in Georgian Bay, although the water is cold year-round.

To manage the crowds at this wildly popular spot, Parks Canada has implemented a timed parking program daily from mid-May through the end of October. If you're visiting during this period, you must reserve a Grotto parking pass for one of several four-hour time slots; you cannot stay beyond your allotted time. Reserve your pass online or by phone beginning in May through the **Parks Canada Reservation Service** (877/737-3783, www.reservation.pc.gc.ca, $11.70 per car plus reservation fee $6 online/$8.50 phone); the reservations website also shows parking availability. From November through mid-May, advance parking passes are not currently required. Check the Bruce Peninsula National Park website for updates.

It's a moderate hike to the Grotto from the Cyprus Lake Park Office, where several trails lead to Georgian Bay. Once at the water, head north along the rocky shore to Indian Head Cove and then to the Grotto. Allow about 30-45 minutes to walk each way from the parking area. There are restrooms at the Cyprus Lake office and near the Grotto, but no other services, so bring whatever food and water you need.

Cyprus Lake

From the Cyprus Lake day-use parking area (469 Cyprus Lake Rd., off Hwy. 6), you can walk down to the lake in just a few minutes. There's a sandy beach with water that's somewhat warmer than that in chilly Georgian Bay, as well as picnic tables. The **Cyprus Lake Trail,** a mostly flat, 5.2-kilometer (3.2-mile) loop, follows the lakeshore and is popular for bird-watching. In winter, you can snowshoe along Cyprus Lake and on to the Grotto; park at the Cyprus Lake main gate, then follow Cyprus Lake Trail to the Georgian Bay Trail.

Cyprus Lake is a calm destination for canoeing or kayaking. There are no boat rentals at the lake, but in Tobermory, **Thorncrest Outfitters** (7441 Hwy. 6, 519/596-8908, www.thorncrestoutfitters.com) rents canoes and kayaks and can transport them to the lake. They also offer full- and half-day guided paddling trips at locations across the northern Bruce Peninsula.

TOP EXPERIENCE

★ The Bruce Trail

One of Canada's iconic outdoor experiences is a hike along Ontario's **Bruce Trail** (www.brucetrail.org), an 845-kilometer (525-mile) route that extends from the Niagara region to the tip of the Bruce Peninsula. How long does it take to complete the whole trail? If you hiked eight hours a day, covering about 30 kilometers (19 miles), it would take you roughly a month to hike end to end. However, unless you're an experienced hiker, this pace will likely be much too fast. And while some hikers do the entire trail straight through, you don't have to be an indomitable trekker to enjoy the experience. Far more end-to-end hikers complete the trail in a series of shorter excursions in two-day, three-day, or weeklong increments over several months or years.

PLANNING YOUR HIKE

Some sections of the trail are flat and easy, while others are quite rugged—get information about your route before you start. A good source of trail information is the **Bruce Trail Conservatory** (905/529-6821 or 800/665-4453, www.brucetrail.org), a nonprofit committed to protecting and promoting the trail. They have a free online overview map, and you can download detailed maps of individual trail sections ($3 per map). If you're serious about hiking the entire trail, consider purchasing the **Bruce Trail Reference** ($40), available on the conservatory website or through Canadian bookseller Chapters/Indigo (www.chapters.indigo.ca). Many Canadian libraries stock the guide, too. It's updated regularly—and there are changes and additions to the trail—so check for the most recent edition.

To find hiking companions or join in group hikes, check out one of the nine Bruce Trail clubs, which help maintain the trail and arrange group activities in different regions. The **Peninsula Bruce Trail Club** (www.pbtc.ca) organizes hikes throughout the year on the Bruce Peninsula and publishes guides to peninsula day hikes. The Bruce Trail Conservatory website lists all the trail clubs, campgrounds that are accessible to the trail, as well as B&Bs and inns that welcome trail hikers. Many innkeepers whose lodgings are close to the trail will pick up or drop off hikers at nearby trailheads.

HIKING THE TRAIL

From the Grotto, the Bruce Trail extends along Georgian Bay in both directions. If you continue to the west, you can hike all the way to Tobermory (18 kilometers, 11 miles). Between the Grotto and Little Cove (12.6 kilometers, 7.8 miles) the trail is quite difficult, with very rocky terrain, but you're rewarded with sweeping views of Georgian Bay. From Little Cove to Tobermory (5.4 kilometers, 3.4 miles) the trail flattens out and wends through the cedar forest.

Heading east from the Grotto along the bay, the Bruce Trail hugs the shore to Stormhaven

(2.4 kilometers, 1.5 miles), where there's a primitive camping area and restroom. The trail then gets more difficult for the next 9.5 kilometers (six miles) to the High Dump camping area.

For an easier alternative, park at the **Halfway Log Dump** parking area south of Cyprus Lake and follow the one-kilometer (0.6-mile) trail to the beach. Or park near **Little Cove** north of Cyprus Lake, where it's a short walk down to the pretty shoreline.

Staff at the Cyprus Lake Park Office or National Park Visitors Centre can help match a hike to your ability level.

Singing Sands Beach

On the west side of the peninsula, Singing Sands Beach (Dorcas Bay Rd.) looks like it's part of a completely different natural environment from the rocky eastern shores—and it is. The flat, sandy beach spreads out around Dorcas Bay with vistas across Lake Huron; it's a popular swimming spot. A short boardwalk trail loops around an adjacent marsh, and the three-kilometer (1.9-mile) **Forest Beach Loop Trail** is another easy walk that's good for bird-watching.

Camping

Within Bruce Peninsula National Park, **Cyprus Lake Campground** (469 Cyprus Lake Rd., mid-Apr.-mid-Oct. $23.50, mid-Oct.-Apr. $15.70) has 232 drive-in campsites in three camping areas. All border Cyprus Lake and have restroom facilities with flush toilets and cold-water taps, but no showers; several private businesses outside the park offer showers for campers. No electrical or sewer hookups are available.

The campground has ten furnished **yurts** (May-Oct., $120), with outdoor propane barbecues. A heated washroom with flush toilets and showers, for yurt residents only, is located a short walk from the yurts.

For stays between May and October, reserve campsites and yurts through the **Parks Canada Campground Reservation Service** (877/737-3783, www.reservation.

pc.gc.ca). Reservations typically open in January and are highly recommended for campsites, particularly from July through early September. Reservations are required for yurts. From November to April, campsites are first come, first served.

Also in the park are two primitive backcountry campgrounds ($9.80 pp): **Stormhaven** and **High Dump**. Stormhaven is 2.4 kilometers (1.5 miles) east of the Grotto along Georgian Bay. High Dump is 9.5 kilometers (six miles) east of Stormhaven, or eight kilometers (five miles) from the parking area at Crane Lake (from Hwy. 6, take Dyer's Bay Rd. east to Crane Lake Rd.). To reach either area, you need to backpack in along the Bruce Trail. You must register at the Cyprus Lake Park Office (Cyprus Lake Rd., off Hwy. 6) before heading out. Between May and October, register by phone (519/596-2263) or in person at the office; the rest of the year, register at the self-service kiosk outside the office.

Stormhaven and High Dump each have nine sites with tent platforms and a composting toilet. No water is available, so bring your own or purify the water from the bay.

Outside the park, the closest accommodations are in Tobermory.

Information and Services

For general information about Bruce Peninsula National Park, phone or visit the **National Park Visitors Centre** (120 Chi Sin Tib Dek Rd., Tobermory, 519/596-2233, www.pc.gc.ca). Between May and October, you can also contact the **Cyprus Lake Park Office** (Cyprus Lake Rd., off Hwy. 6, 519/596-2263).

★ FATHOM FIVE NATIONAL MARINE PARK

One of three national marine conservation areas in Canada, **Fathom Five National Marine Park** (519/596-2233, www.pc.gc.ca) encompasses 22 islands in Georgian Bay off the northern end of the Bruce Peninsula. Formed over 400 million years ago, these rocky islands are composed primarily of dolomite, a type of limestone. The main attractions for visitors are the distinctive rock formations known as "flowerpots." Narrow at the bottom and wider at the top, these rock stacks resemble massive stone pots. While the waves have slowly worn away the softer limestone on the pillars' lower ends, the harder dolomite tops have survived, creating the unusual shape. Access to the park is by boat from the town of Tobermory.

More than 20 shipwrecks lie within the park's territory, making it a popular destination for scuba divers. In fact, the park gets its name from William Shakespeare's play *The Tempest*, in which the following lines describe the father of Ferdinand, who is feared dead in a shipwreck:

> Full fathom five thy father lies;
> Of his bones are coral made;
> Those are pearls that were his eyes:
> Nothing of him that doth fade
> But doth suffer a sea-change
> Into something rich and strange.
> Sea-nymphs hourly ring his knell
> Hark! now I hear them, ding-dong, bell.

A fathom is a unit of measure roughly equal to 1.8 meters (six feet), so "fathom five"

is nine meters, or about 30 feet—a long way down!

Flowerpot Island

Unless you have your own boat, only one of the park's 22 islands is accessible to visitors: Flowerpot Island, named for the two towering rock pillars known as the "flowerpots." These rock stacks sit waterside on the island's eastern shore.

Tour boats from Tobermory dock at Beachy Cove on Flowerpot Island's east side. The island isn't large, at about two square kilometers (0.77 square miles), so it's only about a 15-minute walk from Beachy Cove to the first **small flowerpot,** which is seven meters (23 feet) high, and a few minutes farther to the **large flowerpot,** which stands 12 meters (40 feet) high. From the flowerpots, you can follow the **Loop Trail,** passing a small cave. The path up to the cave is easy to miss; it's on the left just beyond the flowerpots. You can't go inside the cave, but you can peer into the entrance.

Beyond the cave, the Loop Trail continues to **Flowerpot Island Light Station** on the island's northeast tip. The first lighthouse on the island went into service in 1897; in the 1960s, the original light was replaced with a

cruising to Flowerpot Island

steel lighthouse tower that's still flashing its beacon today. You can walk out to the tower and to an adjacent observation deck with a view across Georgian Bay. Near the light station is the lightkeeper's house, which contains a small museum (July-Aug.).

To return to Beachy Cove from the lighthouse, either backtrack along the trail past the flowerpots or continue on the Loop Trail up and over the bluffs in the middle of the island. This latter section of the Loop Trail is more rugged; park staff advise allowing at least an extra hour to return via this route.

If you can tolerate cold water (or wear a wetsuit), you can swim or snorkel off Flowerpot Island. The beaches are rocky, so wear protective footwear. The best swimming spots are near Beachy Cove or around the flowerpots. In either location, be alert for boat traffic.

TOP EXPERIENCE

Scuba Diving and Snorkeling

While you might not think of such a northern location as a prime scuba destination, Fathom Five has some of the world's best freshwater diving. Not only is the water generally clear, but the combination of underwater cliffs, caves, and other geological formations, along with the area's more than 20 shipwrecks, give divers plenty to explore.

All divers must register in person in Tobermory at the **National Park Visitors Centre** (120 Chi Sin Tib Dek Rd., 519/596-2233, www.pc.gc.ca, national park admission fee adults $5.80, seniors $4.90). The park charges divers a daily fee of $4.90 per person in addition to the park admission fee and the cost of boat transportation. If you're planning to dive at least four days, buy an annual divers' pass ($19.60).

Several companies in Tobermory, including **Divers Den** (3 Bay St., 519/596-2363, www.diversden.ca) and **G+S Watersports** (8 Bay St. S., 519/596-2200, www.gswatersports.net), run single-day and multiday dive trips to the Fathom Five islands and surrounding areas. They also offer scuba lessons and gear rentals.

While not all the shipwrecks are visible to snorkelers, some are, and you'll see them much more clearly than you would from a glass-bottom boat. Divers Den offers two-hour (adults $60, kids $40) and four-hour (adults $80, kids $50) **snorkeling tours**; they provide guidance, snorkeling gear, and the thick, warm wetsuits you'll need to swim in the chilly water. G+S Watersports runs similar snorkeling excursions.

Helicopter Tours

Another way to see Fathom Five National Marine Park is by air, soaring over the islands by helicopter. **Blue Heron Tours** (7433 Hwy. 6, 519/596-2035, www.blueherontours.ca, May-mid-Oct.) runs several helicopter excursions, departing from the Tobermory Municipal Airport (73 Warner Bay Rd.). The 12-minute **Fathom Five Marine Park Tour** ($109) is a quick flight over the area's lighthouses, shipwreck sites, and islands. The 20-minute **Fathom Five & Flowerpot Island Tour** ($169) adds views of Flowerpot Island, while the **Fathom Five, Flowerpot Island & Grotto Tour** ($249) is a 30-minute flight over the cliffs and coves of the Grotto along with the Fathom Five and Flowerpot Island sites.

Camping

Camping is your only option if you want to spend the night on Flowerpot Island. The park accepts **camping reservations** (519/596-2233, ext. 221) each year beginning in early May. The **Flowerpot Island Campground** ($9.80 pp) has six basic tent sites, all a stone's throw from the shore and a 5-10-minute walk from the Beachy Cove boat dock. There's a composting toilet nearby but no showers or running water. Bring your own water or purify the bay water for drinking. No supplies are available on the island. Parks Canada cautions that campers should bring enough food, water, and warm clothing to last extra days, since boat service back to the mainland can be canceled if the weather turns bad.

Information and Services

Park staff are frequently on duty at Flowerpot Island's Beachy Cove during the summer. Otherwise, get information at the **National Park Visitors Centre** (120 Chi Sin Tib Dek Rd., 519/596-2233, www.pc.gc.ca, 9am-5pm daily May-late June and early Sept.-Oct., 8am-8pm daily late June-early Sept.) before you leave Tobermory.

A small, volunteer-run snack bar near the lighthouse is open in the summer, but hours are erratic. There are restrooms at Beachy Cove between the ferry dock and the campground, and near the lighthouse. It's almost worth hiking to the light station just to use the **Loo with a View**, with its vistas across the bay.

Getting There

The national park does not run its own boats; instead, it works with two private companies that offer boat trips to Flowerpot Island from mid-May to mid-October. Sailing schedules vary seasonally, so check their websites or phone for details. Also confirm when the last boats leave Flowerpot Island to return to the mainland, and get yourself back to the Beachy Cove dock in plenty of time. You don't want an unexpected overnight stay!

Both **Blue Heron Tours** (519/596-2999 or 855/596-2999, www.blueheronco.com) and **Bruce Anchor Cruises** (519/596-2555 or 800/591-4254, www.bruceanchorcruises. com) run boats from Little Tub Harbour to Beachy Cove. Blue Heron operates both speedy jet boats and slightly slower glass-bottom boats (round-trip adults $39-44, seniors $38-42, ages 6-16 $31-35). Bruce Anchor Cruises takes passengers to Flowerpot Island in several different glass-bottom vessels (adults $38-42, seniors $36-40, ages 6-16 $29-33). Both companies operate different boats with varying schedules, so check to see what's most convenient for you. You must pay the national park admission fee (adults $5.80, seniors $4.90) in addition to the boat trip price.

DYER'S BAY

Unlike many of the Bruce Peninsula's lighthouses, which you can see only from the exterior, at **Cabot Head Lighthouse** (806 Cabot Head Rd., Miller Lake, 519/795-7780, www.cabothead.ca), you can normally venture inside. The lower levels of the red-and-white wooden structure are a museum with exhibits about local marine history. Climb up to the observation tower for a lightkeeper's view out across the bay. The original Cabot Head Lighthouse began operation in 1896. It remained in use until 1968, when it was torn down and replaced with the current light, which is an automated beacon. The lighthouse is about 40 kilometers (25 miles) southeast of Tobermory, about a 45-minute drive. From Highway 6, go east on Dyer's Bay Road. (The lighthouse closed temporarily in 2017 to address environmental issues on the site. Check ahead for updates before visiting.)

LION'S HEAD

Lion's Head is a friendly little village on Georgian Bay at the approximate north-south midpoint of the Bruce Peninsula. You can stroll or swim at the beach, browse the village shops, or have a beer in the local pub. With its central location, Lion's Head is another convenient base for traveling around the peninsula, particularly if you want to visit sights beyond the Tobermory area.

On the bay at the mouth of Lion's Head harbor, **Lion's Head Lighthouse** is a re-creation of the original light station built here in 1903. Students at the local high school constructed the current lighthouse in 1983, using the plans for the original structure. The lighthouse is particularly photogenic, with the bay and the cliffs of the Niagara Escarpment as a backdrop.

On the south side of town, **Lion's Head Provincial Park** (519/389-9056, www. ontarioparks.com, free) is known for its "potholes," deep, cylindrical holes carved by erosion into the limestone rocks. It's about a 20-minute walk along a flat section of the Bruce Trail to two of the large potholes. The trail continues toward Georgian Bay, where it becomes more difficult as it hugs the cliffs. The reward for the climb up and along the tops of the rocks is a spectacular view of the cliffs and the bay. This section of the trail isn't recommended for younger children, as the trail veers quite close to the cliffs. Access to the potholes trail is from Moore Street; the trail starts opposite 128 Moore Street. The park has no restrooms or other services.

Lion's Head is about 250 kilometers (160 miles) north of Toronto. There's no public transportation to or around the area. **Visit Lion's Head** (www.visitlionshead.ca) provides local information online.

Food and Accommodations

If you're not a regular at **The Lion's Head Inn & Restaurant** (8 Helen St., 519/793-4601, www.lionsheadinn.ca, 11am-11pm daily May-Oct., 4pm-9pm Wed.-Sat. Nov.-Apr., $10-20), you may feel like one after you've stopped for a beer in this convivial pub. The food, a notch above basic bar grub, includes burgers, pasta, fish-and-chips, and steaks. Built as a boardinghouse in 1879, the inn has three simple guest rooms upstairs ($80-120 d), two with a shared bath and one with private bath.

In the center of Lion's Head village, **Marydale's Restaurant** (76 Main St., 519/793-4224, 8am-8pm daily summer, 8am-7pm daily fall-spring, $5-15) serves substantial breakfasts and simple home-style fare year-round. Known for their baked goods, **Rachel's Bakery and 50's Diner** (79 Main St., 519/793-3982, 7am-9pm Mon.-Sat., 8am-9pm Sun., $5-20) has a sweet-shop vibe, with Formica tables and a checkerboard floor. Sandwiches, pizza, and comfort food classics like potpie or meat loaf round out the menu. Thursday night is a live music jam, and musicians sometimes perform on other evenings, too.

It's worth visiting small **Lion's Head Farmers Market** (1 Forbes St., 9am-noon Sat. late May-mid-Oct.) just for its open-air setting right on Lion's Head Beach. Vendors sell produce, muffins, other baked goods, and crafts.

Pull off Highway 6 at **Harvest Moon Organic Bakery** (3927 Hwy. 6, 519/592-5742, www.harvestmoonbakery.ca, 10am-4:30pm Wed.-Sun. July-Aug., 10am-4:30pm Thurs.-Sun. May-June and Sept.-Oct.) for butter tarts, hearty potato-filled pasties, or homemade multigrain bread. Besides sampling the

Lion's Head Lighthouse

treats that come out of this riotously colorful little house, you can wander around the quirky sculpture garden (free). The bakery is about 10 minutes north of Ferndale, on the west side of the highway.

Hosts Diana Licskai and Doug Kennedy are full of advice about local hikes and other adventures that they share with guests at their comfortable **Taylor-Made B&B** (31 Byron St., 519/793-4853 or 877/434-9464, www.taylormade.bb-bruce.com, $99-139 d), on a quiet residential street. The main floor has a common area for guests with a fridge and coffeemaker, along with two guest rooms (Room 5 is the larger one) with en suite baths. Upstairs are three more rooms; the two bigger units (which each sleep three) have small bathrooms with a sink and toilet, though the hall bath with shower is shared. A hearty breakfast, perhaps scrambled eggs with cheddar cheese and chives or waffles with fresh fruit, will energize you for the trail.

Big rooms, a beachside location, and reasonable rates are the reasons to stay at **Lion's Head Beach Motel and Cottages** (1 McNeil St., 519/793-3155, www.lionsheadbeachmotelandcottages.ca, $148 d). Although the family-friendly motel rooms won't win any design prizes, they're well maintained, larger than average, and include kitchenettes. The newer two- and three-bedroom cottages would be even more comfortable if you've brought Grandma or the kids (call ahead for prices).

WIARTON AND VICINITY

Wiarton sits on Colpoys Bay, an inlet off Georgian Bay, with the cliffs of the Niagara Escarpment towering above the water. Highway 6, the peninsula's main north-south route, runs straight through town, where it's called Berford Street, and many of the limestone or brick buildings date to the mid-1800s.

The community's most famous resident may be **Wiarton Willie,** a weather-forecasting groundhog. Similar to the American Punxsutawney Phil, Wiarton Willie comes out of his burrow annually on Groundhog Day

(Feb. 2). If he sees his shadow, Canada's winter will last another six weeks; if he doesn't, spring is supposedly on the way. Wiarton celebrates its woodchuck during the annual **Wiarton Willie Festival** (519/534-5492, www.wiartonwillie.com, early Feb.), a winter carnival with a parade, fireworks, concerts, pancake breakfasts, sleigh rides, and, of course, Willie's prediction for winter's end. Local sculptor Dave Robinson crafted a 4.5-ton limestone statue of the town's groundhog, *Willie Emerging*, which sits near the beach in **Bluewater Park** (William St.) year-round.

Two fingers of land jutting into Georgian Bay on either side of Wiarton are worth exploring. To the north, Cape Croker is a First Nations reserve. To the east, head toward the village of Big Bay to visit caves, gardens, and a popular ice cream shop.

For visitor information, contact the **Town of South Bruce Peninsula** (315 George St., 519/534-1400 or 877/534-1400, www.southbrucepeninsula.com, 8:30am-4:30pm Mon.-Fri.), or **County of Bruce Tourism** (268 Berford St., 519/534-5344 or 800/268-3838, www.explorethebruce.com).

Wiarton is about 220 kilometers (137 miles) northwest of Toronto. You'll want a car to explore, although **Bruce Peninsula Transit** (www.brucepeninsulatransit.com) has begun piloting limited bus service between Owen Sound and Wiarton. Check their website for updates.

Cape Croker

Part of the Saugeen Ojibway First Nations territory, the 6,000-hectare (14,825-acre) Cape Croker Peninsula juts out into Georgian Bay north of Wiarton. The peninsula's Ojibwa name, Neyaashiinigmiing, means "a point of land nearly surrounded by water," and the name is apt—except for a sliver of land connecting the peninsula to the mainland, it's ringed by the waters of the bay. Cape Croker is a pretty spot for a drive or hike, particularly on the north side of the peninsula with views across the water to the limestone bluffs of the Niagara Escarpment.

Near the mainland end of the peninsula, **Cape Croker Park** (112 Park Rd., Neyaashiinigmiing, 519/534-0571, www.capecrokerpark.com, $10 per vehicle) has a lovely beach and hiking trails as well as a campground. The park is also the site of the annual **Cape Croker Powwow** (www.nawash.ca, late Aug., $5), where you can experience the music, dance, and other traditions of the local First Nations community. Visitors are welcome at the powwow as long as they are respectful of local customs. Ask permission before taking photos or videos, and leave the beer at home—the powwow is an alcohol-free event.

Big Bay

East of Wiarton, stroll among the irises, lilacs, poppies, and lavender in the peaceful, privately owned **Keppel Croft Gardens** (504156 Grey Rd. 1, Big Bay, 519/534-1090, www.keppelcroft.com, 10am-5pm Wed.-Sun. May-mid-Oct., donation $3). With a Zen garden, a woodland garden, and rock sculptures, Keppel Croft Gardens are part of a regional network of private gardens, known as the **Rural Gardens of Grey and Bruce Counties** (www.ruralgardens.ca), that are open to visitors. The website lists gardens hours and locations, with a downloadable map.

Stop nearby at the tiny **Big Bay General Store** (250854 Big Bay Sideroad at Grey Rd. 1, 519/534-3730, daily late May-early Sept., Sat.-Sun. spring and fall, call for hours), which doesn't stock many groceries, but does serve delicious homemade ice cream. They make more than 80 different flavors, with 10-12 available at a time.

Boat Tours

While several cruises leave from Tobermory to explore the national parks, family-run **Bruce Peninsula Boat Tours** (18 Shoreline Ave., South Bruce Peninsula, 519/372-6309, www.brucepeninsulaboattours.com, 9:30am, 11:30pm, and 1:30pm daily May-Oct., adult $43.50, seniors $41.50, ages 6-15 $33.50, ages 1-5 $9.50) take travelers through a different aquatic environment: the marshes, islands, and wide-open vistas of the peninsula's Lake Huron side. Operating in comfortable pontoon boats seating 6-12, these 90-minute guided tours instruct you in the area's ecology, geography, and history.

Tours leave from the Oliphant docks, 13 kilometers (8 miles) west of Wiarton and 15 kilometers (9.5 miles) north of Sauble Beach. Advance reservations are required.

Food and Accommodations

Wiarton's best restaurant, the **Green Door Café** (563 Berford St., 510/534-3278, www.thegreendoorcafe.com, 11am-3pm Sun.-Tues., 11am-8pm Wed.-Sat. late June-Aug., 11am-3pm Sun.-Wed., 11am-8pm Thurs.-Sat. Sept.-late June, $5-14) looks like a small-town coffee shop, where local retirees stop in for cups of joe and grilled cheese sandwiches. At this unassuming eatery, though, the straightforward sandwiches and hearty main dishes are well prepared from fresh ingredients.

Overlooking Colpoys Bay, the three-story, 21-unit **Waterview on the Bay** (501205 Grey Rd. 1, 519/534-0921 or 877/534-0921, www.waterview.ca, $95-170 d) includes simple rooms with two double beds and a fridge and "luxury suites," with whirlpool tubs, sleigh beds, and expansive bay views. Also on the family-friendly property are five two- or three-bedroom cottages ($225-300), plus a swimming pool and a sandy beach.

CAMPING

Owned by the Chippewas of Nawash First Nation, **Cape Croker Park** (519/534-0571, www.capecrokerpark.com, early May-mid-Oct., $36-48) has an enviable waterfront location on Sydney Bay. On the 210-hectare (520-acre) property are 315 campsites with showers, flush toilets, laundry facilities, a swimming beach, and canoe rentals. Prime waterfront sites look across to the cliffs of the Niagara Escarpment, while other sites are tucked into the woods. A small camping cabin with two bunks ($65) is also available.

Definitely reserve in advance for the August powwow, and you may want to book ahead for the popular waterfront sites, for the cabin, or for holiday weekend stays.

SAUBLE BEACH

On Lake Huron at the south end of the Bruce Peninsula, Sauble Beach is a full-fledged beach-holiday town. This sun-and-fun community has burger stands and soft-serve ice cream shops, T-shirt sellers and bikini boutiques, and, yes, a sandy lakeshore beach that seems to go on and on. The world's second-longest freshwater beach, Sauble Beach (Lakeshore Dr.) is a flat paradise of sand that extends for 11 kilometers (nearly seven miles); only Wasaga Beach, east of Collingwood, is longer. The early French explorers who traversed this area named it La Rivière au Sable ("River to the Sand") for the nearby Sauble River, but by the end of the 19th century the town was known as Sauble Beach for its major geographical asset.

Because the water is fairly shallow, Sauble Beach is a good choice for families with younger kids. The atmosphere in July and August can be rather honky-tonk, but the farther you go from the heart of town, the easier it is to find a peaceful spot to lay your towel.

And despite the crowds, the beach is undeniably beautiful, and sunsets over the lake can be spectacular. Outside summer high season, you'll sometimes have the fine golden sand almost to yourself. Beach parking is available in lots right on the sand and along Lakeshore Road. Prepare for epic summer traffic jams. The annual **Sauble Beach Sandfest** (Lakeshore Blvd., www.saublebeach.com, early Aug.) turns the beach into a giant outdoor sand sculpture gallery, drawing both professional and amateur sand sculptors.

Sauble Beach has a large assortment of standard beach motels and cottages. The **Sauble Beach Information Centre** (672 Main St., 519/422-1262, www.saublebeach.com, 9am-5pm Mon.-Fri., 10am-3pm Sat.) has information about cottage rentals and lists of area accommodations. If you prefer a more peaceful atmosphere, you could stay in Wiarton, about 20 kilometers (12.5 miles) from Sauble Beach, or Southampton (18 kilometers/11 miles to the south), and come to the beach during the day. Restaurants, primarily along Main Street and on 2nd Avenue North (one block east of the beach), tend to serve burgers, pizza, and other eat-and-run fare.

Sauble Beach is about 220 kilometers (137 miles) northwest of Toronto via Highways

Sauble Falls Provincial Park

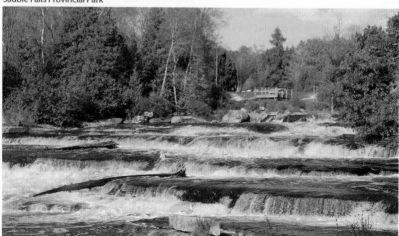

6/10. After you pass through Owen Sound, continue on Highway 6 to Bruce Road 8, which heads west into Sauble Beach.

Sauble Falls Provincial Park

About one kilometer (0.6 miles) north of Sauble Beach, the small **Sauble Falls Provincial Park** (Sauble Falls Pkwy./County Rd. 13, 519/422-1952, www.ontarioparks.com, late Apr.-Oct., $14.50 per vehicle) couldn't feel more different from the frenzied tourist crush of the nearby town. Although it does get busy in summer, it still feels like an escape into the woods.

The petite waterfalls along the Sauble River that give the park its name descend in tiers, almost like an aquatic wedding cake, over a staircase of dolomite limestone. You can watch the falls from a small viewing platform or along either side of the river; it's a scenic spot for a picnic. In spring and fall, you may see salmon and rainbow trout attempting to swim upstream over each ledge of the falls. You can also canoe or kayak on a stretch of the Sauble River that winds through the park. Canoe and kayak rentals (daily mid-June-early Sept., Sat.-Sun. early Sept.-mid-Oct., call for fall hours) are available off Sauble Falls Parkway just north of the river.

Sauble Falls Provincial Park has 152 **campsites** (tent sites $42, electrical sites $47). In both the East Campground and the larger, radio-free West Campground, the nicest sites front the river. Both areas have flush toilets and showers; West Campground has laundry facilities. Reserve campsites up to five months in advance though the **Ontario Parks Reservations Service** (888/668-7275, www.ontarioparks.com, reservation fee online $11, by phone $13).

OWEN SOUND AND VICINITY

It's hard to imagine today that this community of 22,000 was once known as "Chicago of the North." From 1885 through 1912, when the Canadian Pacific Railway (CPR) made Owen Sound the terminus of its steamship line, the town's port was the busiest in the upper Great Lakes. Alas, in 1912, the Canadian Pacific Railway moved its shipping operations farther east to Port McNicoll, Ontario, which had better rail connections, ending Owen Sound's glory years.

For a small city, Owen Sound has a large number of museums and historical attractions. To stroll through the town's history, pick up the *Historic Walking Tour* brochure at the **Owen Sound Visitor Information Centre** (1155 1st Ave. W., 519/371-9833, www. owensoundtourism.ca). Many grand homes, built in the late 1800s, are along 1st Avenue West, while Victorian-era commercial buildings still stand along 2nd Avenue East. Owen Sound was also a destination for formerly enslaved people who came north along the Underground Railroad, and several locations let you explore this heritage.

Beyond its historical attractions, Owen Sound offers outdoor adventures, from hiking to caving and rock climbing, along the steep cliffs of the Niagara Escarpment.

Sights
GREY ROOTS MUSEUM AND ARCHIVES

If you think that a museum about a region's roots is a musty trove of papers and old tools, think again. The contemporary **Grey Roots Museum and Archives** (102599 Grey Rd. 18, 519/376-3690 or 877/473-9766, www. greyroots.com, 10am-5pm daily late May-mid-Oct., 10am-5pm Tues.-Sun. mid-Oct.-Dec. and mid-Mar.-late May, 10am-5pm Tues.-Sat. Jan.-mid-Mar., adults $8, seniors $6, ages 5-12 $4, families $20) showcases the history and culture of Owen Sound and the surrounding region with films, radio stories, and other entertaining multimedia features.

Start in the Grey County gallery, where the permanent *Grey Roots* exhibit introduces you to the people who settled the region— from local First Nations to early pioneers to notable citizens such as Agnes Macphail, a Grey County native who became Canada's first woman elected to Parliament. Other galleries host temporary and traveling exhibitions; recent exhibits have focused on *Saints and Sinners* (how alcohol influenced Grey County's development), *Black in Grey* (about the region's Black heritage and Underground Railroad connections), and Victorian-era death and mourning customs.

If you have kids in tow, visit **Moreston Heritage Village** (11am-4:30pm daily June-early Sept.), the on-site pioneer village staffed by costumed volunteers. Watch the blacksmith at work, visit the 1850s log cabin, or check out the schoolhouse. The museum and village are located about seven kilometers (4.4 miles) south of downtown.

TOM THOMSON ART GALLERY

Known for his affiliation with the Group of Seven—notable early 20th-century Canadian landscape artists—Tom Thomson (1877-1917) grew up outside Owen Sound in the town of Leith. Thomson is celebrated for the paintings he created in Algonquin Park between 1912 and 1917, until his death, reportedly by drowning, in Algonquin's Canoe Lake. The small, modern **Tom Thomson Art Gallery** (840 1st Ave. W., 519/376-1932, www.tomthomson.org, 10am-6pm Mon.-Fri., 10am-5pm Sat., noon-5pm Sun. July-Aug.,

11am-5pm Tues.-Fri., noon-5pm Sat.-Sun. Sept.-June, donation) mounts changing exhibits of work by Thomson and other Ontario artists.

BILLY BISHOP HOME AND MUSEUM

Owen Sound native William Avery Bishop (1894-1956), a fighter pilot with the British Royal Flying Corps, became one of the most decorated Canadians serving in World War I. Bishop's childhood home, a restored Victorian mansion, is now the **Billy Bishop Home and Museum** (948 3rd Ave. W., 519/371-0031, www.billybishop.org, 10am-5pm Mon.-Sat., noon-5pm Sun. late May-early Sept., noon-4pm Tues.-Sun. early Sept.-late May, adults $5). It includes artifacts from Bishop's life and from World Wars I and II, with an emphasis on aviation history.

COMMUNITY WATERFRONT HERITAGE CENTRE

Inside Owen Sound's former Canadian National Railway station (the station's waiting room houses the Owen Sound Visitor Information Centre), the **Community Waterfront Heritage Centre** (1155 1st Ave. W., 519/371-3333, www.marineandrail. ca, 10am-4pm daily late May-early-Oct.,

fall colors in Harrison Park

donation) commemorates the region's glory days as a ship and rail hub in the late 1800s. There are ship models and railroad exhibits; outside, you can climb aboard a restored caboose.

HARRISON PARK AND THE BLACK HISTORY CAIRN

Owen Sound was one of the northernmost stops on the Underground Railroad, the network of safe houses that protected slaves fleeing from the United States in the 1800s.

The **Black History Cairn** (www. owensoundtourism.ca), in **Harrison Park** (2nd Ave. E.), memorializes the journey of enslaved people into the north. This outdoor sculpture comprises eight tiles inlaid in the ground, incorporating quilt patterns that represented coded messages to escaping slaves—according to legend, the patterns were originally sewn into quilts. One pattern symbolizes the North Star, which guided slaves to freedom; a log cabin symbol indicates a safe house; another is a sailboat, signifying a water crossing. Around the tiles is a stone structure representing the ruins of a church, with windows looking toward the Sydenham River. According to Bonita Johnson de Matteis, the artist who designed the cairn, newly freed

people might have looked out similar church windows in Owen Sound as they gave thanks for their freedom. Johnson de Matteis herself is a descendent of a slave who escaped from the United States and settled in Owen Sound.

Harrison Park is located off 2nd Avenue East, south of downtown. To find the Black History Cairn, walk north from the parking area near the Harrison Park Inn; the cairn is past the playground. Trails for hiking, running, and cycling crisscross the park, which is a lovely spot to picnic. The park also has three playgrounds, canoe rentals, a public swimming pool, and a restaurant.

Wineries, Cideries, and Breweries

In the rolling hills east of town, with views to Georgian Bay, small-batch **Coffin Ridge Boutique Winery** (599448 2nd Concession N., Annan, 519/371-9565, www.coffinridge.ca, 11am-6pm Mon.-Sat., 11am-5pm Sun. spring-fall, noon-5pm Wed.-Sun. winter) cultivates 10 hectares (25 acres) of cold-climate grapes that they make into drinkable one-of-a-kind wines. They also produce several small-batch ciders; try the smooth, almost chardonnay-like Honey & Oak made from honeycrisp apples. Sample what's on offer at the tasting

overlooking the vineyards at Coffin Ridge Boutique Winery

bar, or have a glass with a cheese and charcuterie plate overlooking the vineyard. In the restroom, videos of *The Munsters,* the quirky 1960s TV monster show, play up the coffin theme.

Owen Sound and the region along south Georgian Bay was a center of bootlegging activity during the Prohibition era in the early 1900s. Today, winemakers, cider makers, and craft brewers have revived the area's spirit-making tradition. A number of these producers, including Coffin Ridge, have banded together as the **Saints and Sinners Trail** (www.saintsandsinnerstrail.com), a self-guided sipping tour from Owen Sound to Collingwood and into the Blue Mountains. Their website lists participating members and touring tips.

Entertainment and Shopping

The historic downtown **Roxy Theatre** (251 9th St. E., 519/371-2833 or 888/446-7699, www.roxytheatre.ca), built in 1912, hosts live theater and musical performances throughout the year.

On the second floor of a heritage building that once belonged to Eaton's Department Store, **Heartwood Hall** (939 2nd Ave. E., 519/470-2501, www.heartwoodhall.ca) programs concerts, open mike evenings, poetry nights, and other events featuring performers from the local area and around Ontario. The bar, made from repurposed tin panels, stocks local beer, wine, and cider. Beneath the club on the street level is **Heartwood Home** (519/470-2500, www.heartwoodhome.ca, 10am-5:30pm Mon.-Sat.), a shop purveying an eclectic mix of crafts, textiles, and home furnishings. The shop sells tickets for Heartwood Hall events and serves java and locally made biscotti at its coffee bar.

From photography to metalwork to jewelry, **Owen Sound Artists' Co-op** (942 2nd Ave. E., 519/371-0479, www.artistscoop.ca, 9:30am-5:30pm Mon.-Sat.) displays and sells the work of its roughly 45 member artists, all from the area. A small café at the back of the space offers pastries and sandwiches.

Inglis Falls, Owen Sound

The first weekend in August, Owen Sound's annual **Emancipation Celebration Festival** (Harrison Park, 2nd Ave. E., www.emancipation.ca) recalls the struggles of the formerly enslaved people who traveled the Underground Railroad to freedom in Canada. First held in 1862, it's the longest continuously running emancipation festival in North America. Events include a speaker's forum, music, and a picnic.

Sports and Recreation

Around Owen Sound, you can go hiking, caving, and rock climbing along the steep cliffs and cascading waterfalls of the Niagara Escarpment that traverses the region.

At **Inglis Falls Conservation Area** (237785 Inglis Falls Rd., 519/376-3076, www.greysauble.on.ca, parking $3), south of Harrison Park, an 18-meter (60-foot) waterfall rushes over the escarpment. Take a short walk from the parking area to the falls or hike the more than seven kilometers (4.5 miles) of wooded trails.

Outfitter **At Last Adventures** (519/373-6951, www.atlastadventures.com) runs guided half- and full-day excursions to get you onto the rocks and trails. They offer **rock climbing** for beginners and guided adventures for more experienced climbers, as well as cave tours, waterfall hikes, and snowshoe tours, among other programs.

Food

If you'd like to wander and check out food options, go downtown to 2nd Avenue East, between 10th and 7th Streets.

The year-round **Owen Sound Farmers Market** (114 8th St. E., 519/371-3433, www.owensoundfarmersmarket.ca, 8am-12:30pm Sat.) sells baked goods, crafts, and seasonal produce.

Ginger Press Bookshop and Café (848 2nd Ave. E., 519/376-4233, www.gingerpress.com, bookshop 9:30am-6pm Mon.-Fri., 9am-2pm Sat., café 9:30am-2pm Mon.-Fri., 9am-noon Sat., $5-12) is part bookstore and part casual café, serving soup, sandwiches, and other light meals. Fresh-pressed apple-ginger juice is a specialty. Wi-Fi is free.

Known for their scones (they post the daily varieties on their Facebook page), **The Milk Maid Fine Cheese and Gourmet Food** (947 2nd Ave. E., 519/372-1130, www.themilkmaidcheese.ca, 10am-6pm Tues.-Thurs., 10am-10pm Fri., 9am-9pm Sat.) is a café and artisanal cheese shop that carries a variety of Ontario food products.

Why eat Mexican food in Owen Sound? Because the fresh Mexican fare at ★ **Casero Kitchen Table** (946 3rd Ave. E., 519/416-8226, www.caserofood.ca, 11:30am-3pm and 5pm-close Tues.-Fri., noon-close Sat., $6-24), in a garage-like building in a downtown parking lot, is delicious. Look for tacos piled with grilled beets and tomatillo salsa, beer-battered Georgian Bay whitefish, or hickory-smoked brisket with pickled onions. Burritos, quesadillas, and nachos all feature local ingredients, too. Ontario craft beer, beachy cocktails, and a selection of tequilas and mezcals amp up the festive feel. Co-owners Emily Leonard and Beth Milne (Leonard is the chef, while Milne runs the front of the house) started their business as a seasonal taco bus in a 1949 double-decker vehicle; **Casero Taco Bus** (316 Main St., Sauble Beach, 226/909-7694, call or check the website for seasonal hours) still dishes out tacos and burritos at the beach in summer.

Named in homage to Norma Jeane Mortenson, better known as the actress Marilyn Monroe, **Norma Jean's Bistro**

taco plate at Casero Kitchen Table

(243 8th St. E., 519/376-2232, 11:30am-10pm Mon.-Sat., $12-27) has been a downtown fixture since 1984. Though the menu looks fairly standard—pastas, sandwiches, chicken, steak—the creative kitchen livens things up with seasonal ingredients and as many surprising twists as a Hollywood flick.

Accommodations

The most romantic inn in town is the ★ **Highland Manor** (867 4th Ave. "A" W., 519/372-2699 or 877/372-2699, www. highlandmanor.ca, no children under 14, $170-190 d), a grand brick mansion on a shady residential street. Guests can browse books about the area in the library and take their elaborate breakfasts in the formal dining room. Upstairs, the guest rooms have working fireplaces and antique furnishings. Owners Linda Bradford and Paul Neville are passionate about local history, and they're a wealth of information about things to do nearby.

Even if you don't play golf, consider a stay at the **Inn at Cobble Beach** (221 McLeese Dr., Kemble, 519/370-2173 or 888/278-8112, www. cobblebeach.com, $179-459 d), a discreetly posh 10-room lodging overlooking an 18-hole golf course and the waters of Georgian Bay.

The classically furnished rooms are bright and airy; several have water views. Also on the property are five two-bedroom, two-bath cottages ($349-499/night), which would be comfortable for two couples. With bay vistas, the inn's genteel Sweetwater Restaurant serves breakfast, lunch, and dinner; save room for dessert if the apple butter tart with salted caramel sauce is on the menu. The inn is in a residential development 13.5 kilometers (8.5 miles) north of downtown Owen Sound and 26.5 kilometers (16.5 miles) southeast of Wiarton.

Originally built as a private residence for the owners of Coffin Ridge Winery, **The Resting Place at Coffin Ridge** (599450 2nd Concession N., Annan, 226/909-1174, www. coffinridge.ca, $160-220 d) is now a three-unit B&B in a spacious manor overlooking the vineyards on the winery grounds. Guests can swim in the outdoor pool, soak in the hot tub, or watch films in the upstairs theater. The Relic's Room, on the main floor, has a king bed and large bathroom with a whirlpool tub. Upstairs, the black-and-white Widow's Walk has a queen bed and looks out to the gardens. The Writer's Haunt, a separate suite over the garage, has a full kitchen. Fresh fruit, blueberry coffee cake, and baked

Inn at Cobble Beach

eggs with smoked salmon are among the dishes that turn up in the ample breakfast spreads.

Information and Services

The **Owen Sound Visitor Information Centre** (1155 1st Ave. W., 519/371-9833 or 888/675-5555, www.owensoundtourism.ca) provides details about attractions and lodgings around town. The regional tourism association, **Grey County Tourism** (102599 Grey Rd. 18, 519/376-3265 or 877/733-4739, www.visitgrey.ca), has a helpful information desk in the lobby of the Grey Roots Museum.

Getting There and Around

Owen Sound is 190 kilometers (120 miles) northwest of Toronto, about a 2.5-hour drive via Highways 6 and 10. **Greyhound** (City Transit Centre, 1020 3rd Ave. E., 519/371-5111 or 800/661-8747, www.greyhound.ca) runs one direct bus daily in each direction between Toronto and Owen Sound (4 hours, $23-56). **Grey Bruce Airbus** (800/361-0393, www.greybruceairbus.com, adults $79 one-way, $150 round-trip) operates four trips daily in each direction between Toronto's Pearson Airport and the Owen Sound Days Inn (950 6th St. E.).

The majority of Owen Sound's roadways are numbered streets and avenues (streets run east-west, avenues run north-south). The Sydenham River divides the east and west sides, so a "west" address, such as the Tom Thomson Gallery on 1st Avenue West, is west of the river, while an "east" address is east of the river.

Owen Sound's attractions are either around the walkable downtown or south of the center. The main downtown shopping street is 2nd Avenue East, south of 10th Street and east of the river. From downtown, continue south on 2nd Avenue East to Harrison Park and the Grey Roots Museum. During the day, you can get around on **Owen Sound Transit** buses (Downtown Transit Terminal, 1020 3rd Ave. E., 519/376-3299, www.owensound.ca, 6:30am-6pm Mon.-Fri., 9am-4pm Sat., adults $3, students $2.50, under age 6 free). The useful Crosstown loop bus circles between downtown and Harrison Park.

In 2017, **Bruce Peninsula Transit** (www.brucepeninsulatransit.com) began piloting limited bus service between Owen Sound and Wiarton. Check their website for details. Otherwise, to explore the surrounding towns or farther up the Bruce Peninsula, it's much easier to have your own wheels. It's about a 45-minute drive to Wiarton and 75-90 minutes to Tobermory. **Enterprise Rent-A-Car** (www.enterpriserentacar.ca), **Thrifty Car Rental** (www.thrifty.com), and **Discount Car Rentals** (www.discountcar.com) have Owen Sound offices.

Collingwood and the Blue Mountains

The Blue Mountain Resort, just west of the town of Collingwood, is Ontario's top ski destination. If you're expecting the Alps or the Rockies, you may chuckle when you see the size of the "mountains" here, but these rolling hills have enough terrain to keep many skiers and snowboarders occupied. Besides the winter snow-sports season, the busiest times are midsummer (for mountain biking, hiking, golfing, and other outdoor activities) and fall weekends, when the trees blaze with color.

Collingwood (population 21,000) serves skiers and other outdoor adventurers with grocery stores, movie theaters, and excellent restaurants; it's a good base for exploring the region. If your goal is skiing, snowboarding, or other active pursuits, it's most convenient to stay in the Village at Blue Mountain, the resort area at the mountain base. You'll find more café and restaurant options to the west of Blue Mountain Resort in the town of Thornbury.

BLUE MOUNTAIN RESORT

Blue Mountain Resort (108 Jozo Weider Blvd., 705/445-0231 or 877/445-0231, www. bluemountain.ca) is a car-free village, where casually upscale restaurants, bars, and outdoor clothing shops line the pedestrian streets. You can easily walk from village lodgings to the lifts; if you stay in one of the village condo developments, a free shuttle will pick you up.

Blue Mountain Activity Central (705/445-0231, ext. 8273) acts as an activity concierge for guests. Staff keep a schedule of regular events, including free guided hikes or snowshoe tours, sleigh rides, scavenger hunts, toboggan tours, and more, plus activities for kids and teens. They also book activities both on and off the mountain. Prices for many mountain activities are discounted for guests staying in Blue Mountain Village lodgings.

Special events take place at Blue Mountain nearly every weekend from July through early October and on select weekends during the rest of the year. Highlights include the **May Long Weekend Music and Fireworks** (late May), **Salsa at Blue Festival** (late June), and **Apple Harvest Festival** (early Oct.).

Skiing and Snowboarding

Blue Mountain Resort began life as a winter sports mecca and now has 11 lifts serving 43 trails. At 720 vertical feet, it's not a tall mountain, nor does it get buried in snow like western resorts, but an extensive snow-making operation supplements the average annual snowfall of 280 centimeters (110 inches). The winter season typically starts in December and runs through March. Come midweek to avoid the crowds.

Full-day lift tickets (adults $80, seniors and ages 6-17 $63) are valid from 9am to 9pm. You can opt for an **eight-hour day ticket** (adults $70, seniors and ages 6-17 $53) or a **night ticket** (adults $47, seniors and ages 6-17 $41) valid from 3:30pm to 9pm. Ski and snowboard rentals, lessons, and kids camps are all available. For snowboarders, a **terrain park** (9am-9pm daily) has its own chairlift. To access the park, you must purchase a one-time $10 park pass in addition to your lift ticket.

Ice-Skating

Ice skaters of all levels can take spin along the **Woodview Mountaintop Skating Trail** (noon-5pm Mon.-Thurs., 10am-8pm Fri.-Sat., 10am-5pm Sun. late Dec.-Mar., adults $16, ages 3-12 $13), a 1.1-kilometer (.7-mile) groomed loop through the woods along the Niagara Escarpment. Skate rentals ($6) are available.

Swimming and Water Sports

The year-round **Plunge Aquatic Centre** (200 Gord Canning Dr., 705/444-8705, www. plungebluemountain.ca, adults $16, ages 3-12 $13), adjacent to the Westin Trillium House, entertains water-lovers with indoor and outdoor swimming pools, several waterslides, rope swings, hot tubs, and a water playground for toddlers. Schedules vary seasonally, but in general, Plunge is open daily in summer and winter, weekends only in spring and fall. Regular admission tickets are good for a three-hour period or you can buy a full-day pass (adults $29, ages 3-12 $23).

Blue Mountain Resort maintains a **beach** (Blue Mountain Activity Central, 705/445-0231, ext. 8273) on Georgian Bay, open to resort guests daily from late June through early September. A complimentary 10-minute shuttle will take you from the village to the beach.

Mountain Biking

From spring through fall, mountain bikers take over the Blue Mountain Resort trails. The lifts are open to bikers 10am-6pm Sunday through Thursday and 10am-8pm Friday and Saturday late May-late June, 10am-8pm daily late June-early September, 10am-6pm daily early September-mid-October. Daily trail passes are $8 (no lift access), $16 (one lift access), or $45 (unlimited lift access). You can rent bikes and safety gear. There are also

Collingwood and the Blue Mountains

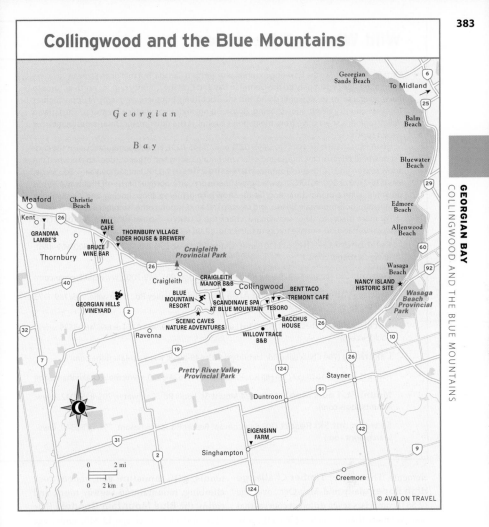

guided mountain biking options for youth, teens, adults, and families, both novice and experienced riders.

Mountain Coaster

Thrill-seekers should fly over to the **Ridge Runner Mountain Coaster** (daily mid-May-Oct. and mid-Dec.-Mar., adults $16 per ride, ages 3-12 $13 per ride), which twists and turns from the top of the Glades area through the trees and down to the village. One or two people can ride together in each car, and riders control the car's speed. For specific operating hours, which vary seasonally, check with Blue Mountain Activity Central (705/445-0231, ext. 8273, www.bluemountain.ca).

More Summer Activities

Two different ropes courses test your agility and balance. On the family-friendly **Woodlot Low Ropes** (daily mid-May-Oct., over age 12 $29, ages 6-12 $23), navigate three routes at different heights, crossing beams, ropes, suspended logs, and other swaying aerial

Wild Winter Adventures

Ontario may not have the towering mountains of western Canada, but that doesn't mean you can't take to the slopes. Not only do the Georgian Bay and Cottage Country regions north of Toronto have several spots for downhill skiing and snowboarding, but there are plenty of opportunities for cross-country skiing, snowshoeing, dogsledding, and other winter adventures. The Ottawa Valley region, a short drive from the nation's capital, is the other major Ontario destination for winter sports.

Blue Mountain Resort (705/445-0231 or 877/445-0231, www.bluemountain.ca) is the largest downhill ski resort in Ontario and offers mountain biking and other outdoor sports when the snow season ends. Closer to Toronto, **Horseshoe Resort** (1101 Horseshoe Valley Rd., Barrie, 705/835-2790 or 800/461-5627, www.horseshoeresort.com), north of Barrie off Highway 400, has downhill skiing and snowboarding, fat-tire snow biking, tubing, snowshoeing, and ice-skating in winter, plus golf, mountain biking, and treetop trekking, among other summer activities.

For more places to ski or snowboard, check the **Ontario Snow Resorts Association** (www.skiontario.ca) or make tracks to these mountain resorts:

- **Calabogie Peaks Resort** (30 Barrett Chute Rd., Calabogie, 613/752-2720 or 800/669-4861, www.calabogie.com)

- **Dagmar Ski Resort** (1220 Lake Ridge Rd., Uxbridge, 905/649-2002, www.skidagmar.com)

- **Hidden Valley Highlands Ski Area** (1655 Hidden Valley Rd., Huntsville, 705/789-1773 or 800/398-9555, www.skihiddenvalley.on.ca)

- **Hockley Valley Resort** (793522 3rd Line EHS, Mono, 519/942-0754 or 866/462-5539, www.hockley.com)

- **Lakeridge** (790 Chalk Lake Rd., Uxbridge, 905/649-2058, www.ski-lakeridge.com)

- **Mount Pakenham** (577 Ski Hill Rd., Pakenham, 613/624-5290, www.mountpakenham.com)

- **Mount St. Louis Moonstone** (24 Mount St. Louis Rd., Coldwater, 705/835-2112, www.mountstlouis.com)

- **Searchmont Ski Resort** (103 Searchmont Resort Rd., Searchmont, 705/781-2340, www.searchmont.com)

---

elements. The tougher **Timber Challenge High Ropes** (daily mid-May-Oct., over age 12 $63) comprises seven different courses that take you more than 15 meters (50 feet) above the forest floor.

Another activity for the adventurous, the **Wind Rider Triple Zips** (daily mid-May-Oct., over age 12 $16, ages 10-12 $13) includes two 122-meter (400-foot) zip lines. Three lines run in parallel, letting you zip with friends or family members. On the **Apex Bagjump** (daily mid-May-Oct., over age 12 $16, ages 8-12 $13), you free-fall from four increasingly higher platforms into a puffy airbag on the ground.

Still want more things to do? Hiking, tennis, golf, miniature golf, indoor rock climbing, mountaintop Segway tours, and riding the **Blue Mountain Gondola** (late May-mid-Oct., over age 12 $16, under age 12 $13) are among the many other mountain activities.

Yoga and Spa Services

When you're ready for some relaxation, head for **IWA Spa** (234 Gord Canning Dr., 705/293-2492, www.iwaspa.com), which not only indulges guests in the normal array of massages, facials, and other spa services, but also offers restorative **yoga classes** ($35) taught on a *ganban*, a gently heated volcanic rock platform. The *ganban* keeps your muscles warm without the extreme sweating of a hot yoga class; it's exceptionally relaxing. Call or check the website for schedules.

Food

Food in the village tends toward either fare to fuel up fast and get back on the slopes or simple but hearty pub-style eats. Start your day with coffee and a pastry at **Royal Majesty Espresso Bar Bakery** (190 Jozo Weider Blvd., 705/812-3476, www.royalmajesty.ca, generally 7am-9pm daily), or stop in later for soup or a sandwich. Wi-Fi is free. The local outpost of a Toronto-based restaurant group, **Oliver and Bonacini Café Grill** (Westin Trillium House, 220 Gord Canning Dr., 705/444-8680, www.obcafegrill.com, 7am-10pm daily, lunch $13-33, dinner $18-45) is one of the best places to eat in the village. The contemporary dishes—Caesar salad updated with broccoli and Brussels sprouts, miso-glazed trout, and balsamic short ribs with mustard greens—are both crowd-pleasing and creative.

If you're hungry for fine dining, detour west to **Thornbury,** on Georgian Bay between Owen Sound and Blue Mountain Village. The town has several good cafés and restaurants. It's worth a drive to ★ **Bruce Wine Bar and Kitchen** (8 Bruce St., 519/599-1112, www.brucewinebar.ca, 11:30am-3:30pm and 5:30pm-close Tues.-Sat., $14-32), which emphasizes local ingredients in its imaginative sharing plates, wood-fired pizzas, and entrées. There's always a daily "chef's creation" pizza, and the mains, from potato gnocchi with kale and pickled squash to short ribs with spiced gourd purée, change regularly as well. The wine list highlights Canadian labels and by-the-glass options; the vibe at the rustic wood tables or along the bar is welcoming and informal. In a restored stone mill building on the Beaver River,

In a restored stone mill building on the Beaver River, **The Mill Café** (12 Bridge St., 519/599-7866, www.themillcafe.com, 11am-9pm Sun.-Mon. and Wed.-Thurs., 11am-10pm Fri.-Sat., lunch $13-17, dinner $24-34) cooks up inventive casual cuisine. Midday menus might feature a pulled pork grilled cheese sandwich, steak and feta salad, or panko-crusted portobello burger, while evening fare could range from seared pickerel with Brussels sprouts to venison with roasted sunchokes. Ontario beers and ciders are continually on tap.

For more dining options, head east to Collingwood.

Georgian Bay views from the Blue Mountain Gondola

The Apple Pie Trail

The Blue Mountain region produces nearly a quarter of Ontario's apples. Crisp ambrosias, honeycrisps, and fujis are local snacking favorites, apples turn up in muffins, pies, and other pastries, and the craft cider business is booming.

The Apple Pie Trail (www.applepietrail.com) makes it easy to find—and sample—this local fruit. This network of apple growers and producers stretches from Collingwood through Thornbury and Meaford along Georgian Bay toward Owen Sound, south to Creemore and other nearby rural communities. Download an Apple Pie Trail brochure and map from the trail website, or pick one up at most locations along the trail.

Start at **Thornbury Village Cider House and Brewery** (90 King St. E./Hwy. 26, Thornbury, 519/599-2616, www.thornburycraft.com, 11am-5pm Sun.-Thurs., 11am-8pm Fri.-Sat.), where you can try a tasting flight or glass at the bar or outdoor patio. The original Thornbury Premium Cider is tart and crisp; they also make a cinnamon-spiced cider and an unusual herbal elderflower blend. Other cider makers include **Coffin Ridge Boutique Winery** (599448 2nd Concession N., Annan, 519/371-9565, www.coffinridge.ca, 11am-6pm Mon.-Sat., 11am-5pm Sun. spring-fall, noon-5pm Wed.-Sun. winter), closer to Owen Sound, and **Georgian Hills Vineyard** (496350 Grey Rd. 2, Blue Mountains, 519/599-2255, http://www.georgianhillsvineyards.ca, 11am-5pm daily), west of Blue Mountain Village.

Pop into **Thornbury Bakery Café** (12 Bruce St. S., 519/599-3311, www.thornburybakerycafe.com, 8am-4pm Mon.-Sat., 9am-4pm Sun.) for a slice of pie, a "sticky knot," or a cinnamon bun. **Thornbury Cheese Gallery** (11 Bruce St. S., 519/599-6699, www.thornburycheesegallery.com, 8am-6pm daily) carries an apple-smoked cheddar, along with other cheeses and gourmet items; sit at the bar for a gourmet grilled cheese. About 10 kilometers (six miles) west of Thornbury, old-timey **Grandma Lambe's** (206570 Hwy. 26, Meaford, 519/538-2757, www.grandmalambes.com, 8am-6pm daily) might not be as old as your own grandmother, but it's been selling pies and jams since 1992.

To combine eating with exercise, take the trail's self-guided **Pedal and Paddle tour** (877/445-0231, www.applepietrail.com/pedal-paddle, mid-May-mid-Oct., $60 pp, plus bike rental). Start in Blue Mountain Village where you can rent a bike and take a shortcut up the Blue

Accommodations

Blue Mountain Village has several hotel and condominium properties, and just outside the village are additional condo and town house complexes. Reserve lodgings through **Blue Mountain Central Reservations** (877/445-0231, www.bluemountain.ca). When booking, ask whether the lodging is ski-in, ski-out or within walking distance of the lifts. Winter room rates typically start at about $180 d, and a variety of lodging and lift ticket packages are available. Although free Wi-Fi is available in the lobbies, Blue Mountain properties charge $9.95/day for in-room access.

Blue Mountain Inn was the village's original lodging, and while it's starting to show its age, it offers moderately priced accommodations. You can walk to the Century Express chairlift. For more style, boutique **Mosaïc** has 163 contemporary suites, from studios to three-bedroom units. The smaller units have kitchenettes, and larger suites, some of which are multilevel town houses, have full kitchens. There's a fitness center as well as a year-round outdoor pool and hot tub. It's not as close to the lifts as **Weider Lodge** or the **Grand Georgian**—both slightly older, well-appointed condo hotels—but the rooms are more stylish and you can walk to the gondola in a few minutes.

The village's most upscale lodging, a short walk from the gondola, is **Westin Trillium House** (220 Gord Canning Dr., 705/443-8080

cider sampling on the Apple Pie Trail

Mountain Gondola, before cycling west through the hills, stopping at apple trail spots as you'd like. After lunch at **Blackbird Pie Company** (108 Main St, Heathcote, 519/599-6573, www.blackbirdpie.ca), where, yes, there's pie, local outfitter **Free Spirit Tours** (www.freespirit-tours.com) will set you up for a one-hour canoe or kayak excursion along the Beaver River. After your paddle, you'll pedal the Georgian Trail, a local rail trail, back to Blue Mountain Village. The round-trip ride totals 40 kilometers (25 miles).

The peak season for touring the Apple Pie Trail is August through October, when the greatest varieties of apples are on the trees, cider making is in full swing, and trees begin to take on their autumn colors.

or 800/937-8461, www.westinbluemountain.com, $235-745 d, parking $15-20/day), designed like a grand Georgian Bay lodge. The 222 spacious units, including standard guest rooms and one-, two-, and three-bedroom suites, have modern furnishings in ski-lodge beiges and browns, as well as TV/DVDs and kitchenettes. There's a 24-hour gym, year-round outdoor pool, sauna, and hot tubs, plus a restaurant and lounge, with room service.

Information and Services

For resort information or reservations, contact **Blue Mountain Resorts** (108 Jozo Weider Blvd., 705/445-0231 or 877/445-0231, www.bluemountain.ca). You can get additional information from the **Blue Mountain Village Association** (705/444-7398, www.bluemountainvillage.ca).

Getting There and Around

Blue Mountain Resort is 170 kilometers (105 miles) northwest of Toronto and 11 kilometers (7 miles) west of Collingwood, off Highway 26. Depending on traffic and weather conditions, it's about a two-hour drive from metropolitan Toronto. From mid-December through late March, **AU Coach Tours** (416/741-5200, www.auctours.ca, one-way $30) runs a daily shuttle between Toronto and Blue Mountain. In Toronto, pickup and drop-off locations include City Hall and the Kipling subway station. Reserve online.

If you're staying in the Village at Blue

Mountain, you don't need a car. The village is car-free and ringed with parking lots where you can leave yours. A free **resort shuttle** (705/443-5519, www.bluemountain.ca) loops through the village Friday through Sunday every 5-10 minutes between 8am and 10pm. Outside of these hours, call for a pickup.

COLLINGWOOD

While many people come to Collingwood to ski or snowboard at nearby Blue Mountain, it's also a pleasant spot for a weekend getaway, even if you're not mountain-bound. The Collingwood area draws gourmets to its many first-rate restaurants. The **Georgian Trail** (www.georgiantrail.ca) is a flat, 34-kilometer (21-mile) rail-trail for hiking and cycling that runs west from Collingwood to the towns of Thornbury and Meaford, passing several beaches en route. In winter, it's a cross-country ski and snowshoeing trail.

To soothe those post-adventure sore muscles, sink into the outdoor baths at **Scandinave Spa at Blue Mountain** (152 Grey Road 21, Blue Mountains, 705/443-8484 or 877/988-8484, www.scandinave.com, 10am-9pm daily, $60, Wed. $50), which offers a Scandinavian-style "bath experience." First, warm up in one of the Finnish saunas, steam baths, or outdoor hot tubs. Then immerse yourself in a chilling plunge pool. After recovering in a relaxation area, repeat the process until you feel totally tranquil; the average stay is 2-4 hours. The experience is even more magical when snow falls on the hot pools. Bathing suits are required, and you must be at least 19 years old.

For several days in July, Collingwood is overrun with Elvis Presley lookalikes. The annual **Collingwood Elvis Festival** (866/444-1162, www.collingwoodelvisfestival.com) features a parade and more than 100 tribute concerts; it ranks among the world's largest Elvis festivals.

Scenic Caves Nature Adventures

In the hills outside Collingwood, **Scenic Caves Nature Adventures** (260-280 Scenic Caves Rd., 705/446-0256, www.sceniccaves.com, 9am-8pm daily late-June-early Sept., call or check the website for spring and fall hours, adults $25, seniors and ages 3-17 $22) is a sprawling outdoor playground. Walking trails wind through the woods, and you can explore a network of underground **caves** (try to squeeze through "Fat Man's Misery," a narrow rock channel). A highlight is a stroll across the 126-meter (413-foot) **suspension bridge,** one of Ontario's longest suspension footbridges, with panoramic views across Georgian Bay. Admission covers access to the caves, suspension bridge, and walking trails.

At 777 meters (2,550 feet) long, the **Thunderbird Twin Zip Line** (adults $47, seniors and ages 10-17 $45) is among Canada's longest twin zip lines, with two zip lines side by side and vistas across the Blue Mountains and Georgian Bay. Twin Zip tickets include access to the caves, suspension bridge, and trails.

Another option is a three-hour guided **ecotour** (adults $85, seniors and ages 10-17 $75), which starts with a short hike to the suspension bridge, followed by a treetop canopy tour on a network of narrow wooden bridges. You'll also tour the caves and whiz along two zip lines, including a 305-meter (1,000-foot) plunge from the top of the Niagara Escarpment.

In winter, the park is open for cross-country skiing and snowshoeing (9am-5pm daily Dec.-Mar., full-day pass: adults $20 weekend, $15 weekday, seniors and ages 6-17 $16 weekend, $13 weekday). You can even snowshoe across the suspension bridge. Ski and snowshoe rentals are available.

Allow a minimum of two hours to explore the site, but you can easily spend most of the day. Wear running or hiking shoes. There's a small snack bar, but for more variety, pack your own picnic lunch.

Food

Restaurants in and around Collingwood range from the foodie to the ardently epicurean.

Most are located on or near Hurontario Street in the town center.

For a fun, casual meal, head for the little white house with rustic wood floors that's home to **Bent Taco** (48 Pine St., 705/445-0202, www.benttaco.com, noon-3pm and 5pm-10pm Wed.-Mon., $7-17), a hipster joint dishing up an eclectic, Mexican-flavored menu. Try the excellent buffalo-fried cauliflower taco or an unusual salad of pickled black plums, peanuts, arugula, cotija cheese, and guacamole. The bar pours lots of tequilas and local microbrews.

Hidden in a lane downtown, **Tesoro** (18 School House Lane, 705/444-9230, www.tesororestaurant.ca, 11am-11pm Mon.-Sat. spring-summer, 11am-9:30pm Mon.-Thurs., 11am-10pm Fri.-Sat. fall-winter, lunch $10-20, dinner $19-35), with its sturdy pine tables and vibrant red chairs, is the sort of welcoming, casual Italian eatery everyone would like to have in their neighborhood. There's a long list of creative pizzas (try the Tre Funghi, with black olives and three types of mushrooms), as well as updated versions of Italian classics like penne *arrabbiata* (pasta with spicy sausage and hot peppers), chicken parmigiano, or lasagna.

In an 1889 former hotel, the classy **Tremont Café** (80 Simcoe St., 705/293-6000, www.thetremontcafe.com, 11am-3pm and 5pm-9pm Sun.-Mon. and Wed.-Thurs., 11am-3pm and 5pm-10pm Fri.-Sat., lunch $14-20, dinner $20-36), with a curved bar, white-painted woodwork, and floor-to-ceiling windows, invites lingering, from weekend brunch to lunch to dinner to evening cocktails. On the plate, expect well-crafted dishes with lots of seasonal ingredients: veggie bowls, hearty salads, or creative flatbreads midday, and mains from braised lamb shank to sesame-crusted rainbow trout for supper.

One of Ontario's most distinctive dining destinations is ★ **Eigensinn Farm** (449357 Concession Rd. 10, Singhampton, 519/922-3128, www.stadtlanderseigensinnfarm.com), which draws well-heeled gourmets from far and wide. Chef-owner Michael Stadtlander, with his wife and business partner, Nobuyo, accommodate no more than a dozen diners nightly, creating extravagant eight-course tasting menus ($300-350). And that's not including wine; the restaurant has no liquor license, so guests bring their own. The restaurant's schedule can be as wildly personal as the dining experience, so make reservations well in advance. It's about 13 kilometers

crossing the suspension bridge at Scenic Caves Nature Adventures

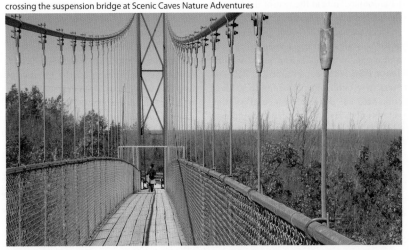

(eight miles) south of Collingwood via County Road 124.

The owners of Eigensinn Farm run a more casual nearby alternative, **Haisai Restaurant** (794079 County Rd. 124, Singhampton, 705/445-2748, www.haisai.ca, 11am-2:30pm Thurs., 11am-2:30pm and 5pm-9pm Fri.-Sat., 10am-3pm Sun., $24-30, no credit cards), serving imaginative pizzas on Thursdays, and other creative dishes with locally sourced ingredients on the weekends.

Accommodations

Some of Collingwood's restored Victorian homes are now inns or B&Bs, and in the hills around town, you'll find more small accommodations. Most motels are west of town along Highway 26.

The four guest rooms at romantic **Bacchus House** (142 Hume St., 705/446-4700, www.bacchushouse.ca, $145-195 d) are decorated with a wine theme: the purple Pinot Noir Suite has an ornate four-poster bed, and the Cabernet Sauvignon Suite has a claw-foot tub. Common spaces in this 1880 yellow-brick Victorian include the living room (with a fireplace), a deck with a hot tub, and the dining room where a full breakfast is served. Only the location on a busy street mars the elegance of this upscale lodging; the golden-hued Chardonnay Suite at the rear of the house is the quietest.

On a six-hectare (15-acre) property with gardens, walking trails, a swimming pool, and a gaggle of ducks and hens, **Willow Trace B&B** (7833 Poplar Side Rd., 705/445-9003, www.collingwoodbedandbreakfast.com, $165-185 d) feels like a rural getaway, yet it's only a five-minute drive from downtown. The four rooms are bright and modern, including one on the lower level facing the gardens. Among the breakfast options that co-owner and chef Philip Tarlo, who runs the B&B with his wife, Leanne Calvert, prepares are cinnamon French toast, customized omelets, or a full English breakfast.

Craigleith Manor B&B (9 Craigleith Ct., 705/293-1170 or 844/412-1170, www.craigleithmanor.com, $190-260 d) caters to active adults. It's in a spacious contemporary home on a residential cul-de-sac, about a 10-minute drive to Blue Mountain Village or Collingwood. The Georgian Trail abuts the one-acre property, and there's space for cyclists to park their bikes. The three guest rooms upstairs have balconies overlooking the woods and bathrooms with heated floors. Like to control your morning schedule? You can select a hot entrée from a changing breakfast menu and choose the time you prefer to eat.

Information and Services

Georgian Triangle Tourist Association (45 St. Paul St., 705/445-7722 or 888/227-8667, www.visitsouthgeorgianbay.ca, 9am-5pm daily) runs a visitor information center that provides information about the Collingwood-Blue Mountain region.

Getting There and Around

Greyhound (800/661-8747, www.greyhound.ca) operates one daily bus in each direction between Toronto and Collingwood (22 2nd St., 705/445-7095, 3 hours); the same buses go on to Blue Mountain, stopping at the **Blue Mountain Inn** (108 Jozo Weider Blvd.) about 15 minutes later.

Simcoe County Airport Service (705/728-1148 or 800/461-7529, www.simcoecountyairportservice.ca) runs regular vans from Toronto's Pearson Airport to Collingwood and Blue Mountain Resort. Prices vary depending on the number of people in your party. From Pearson Airport to Collingwood, the one-way price is $126 for one person, $169 for two; to Blue Mountain, it's $141 for one, $183 for two. **Summer Bound** (705/445-5267 or 888/286-4528, www.summerbound.ca) also operates shuttles between Pearson and Collingwood ($165 for two) or Blue Mountain ($175 for two).

Colltrans (705/446-1196, www.collingwood.ca, 6:30am-9pm Mon.-Fri., 7am-6pm Sat., 9am-5pm Sun., $2) is the town's public transportation service, with several routes around the community and between Collingwood and Blue Mountain.

VICINITY OF COLLINGWOOD
Creemore

This village of 1,200 people makes a great day trip if you're looking for that elusive "small-town charm." The main downtown street—Mill Street—is lined with art galleries, cafés, and shops, ready-made for wandering and browsing. Creemore's main attraction is **Creemore Springs Brewery** (139 Mill St., 705/466-2240 or 844/887-3022, www.creemoresprings.com, 10am-6pm Mon.-Sat., 11am-5pm Sun.), started in 1987 by three beer-loving guys who retired to the area and decided they needed a hobby. The brewery produces several varieties of beer, including its signature Creemore Springs Premium Lager. Free 30-minute tours (noon-4pm Mon.-Sat., noon-3pm Sun.), offered on the hour year-round, wrap up with a beer tasting.

The **Mad and Noisy Gallery** (154 Mill St., 705/466-5555, 11am-5pm Mon.-Fri., 10am-5pm Sat., noon-4pm Sun. summer, call for off-season hours) is neither—it's named for the two rivers that meet near Creemore. It showcases high-quality work of painters, sculptors, photographers, and other artists, most of whom hail from the Southern Georgian Bay area.

Mill Street has several cafés, bakeries, and restaurants, as well as the **100 Mile Store** (176 Mill St., 705/466-3514, www.100milestore.ca), a local grocery that sources its products—from produce and meats to snacks, cheeses, and ice cream—from within 100 miles of town.

Venture east of Mill Street to find the **Creemore Jail** (Library St., between Elizabeth St. and Caroline St.). This diminutive stone structure, built in 1892, claims to be the smallest jail in North America.

Creemore is about 30 kilometers (19 miles) southeast of Collingwood. Take Highway 26 east from Collingwood to Highway 42 south; then go west on Highway 9 into Creemore and turn left onto Mill Street.

Wasaga Beach

The world's longest freshwater beach, with a historical attraction to boot, is an easy day trip from Collingwood.

The Wasaga area had a part in the War of 1812, through a trading ship called the *Nancy*. Built in 1789, the *Nancy* was pressed into service as a British supply vessel. In 1814, American troops attacked the *Nancy* on the Nottawasaga River. The ship sank, and over the next century, the silt and sand flowing through the river collected around the ship's hull, preserving the remains and forming an island around the boat.

The *Nancy* was excavated in the 1920s, and today, at the **Nancy Island Historic Site** (119 Mosley St., 705/429-2728, www.wasagabeachpark.com, 10am-5pm daily mid-June-early Sept., 10am-5pm Sat.-Sun. late May-mid-June and early Sept.-mid-Oct.), you can see the *Nancy*'s hull, watch a video about her story, and join in as park staff reenact elements of the *Nancy*'s history. Also on the site is the **Wasaga Beach Welcome Centre**, which has information about the *Nancy* and the surrounding area, a small museum, and a replica of an 1884 lighthouse that once stood near Collingwood's harbor.

Wasaga Beach Provincial Park (11 22nd St. N., 705/429-2516, www.ontarioparks.com, daily Apr.-mid-Oct., per vehicle $20 weekends, $16 weekdays) is the world's longest freshwater beach. The sand extends along Georgian Bay for 14 kilometers (nearly nine miles) and is divided into eight sections, each with a different personality. Beaches 1 to 4 are closer into town and have more restaurants, shops, and other services; they're also more crowded and honky-tonk. As you move farther from the town center—to beaches 5 and 6 to the south and New Wasaga and Allenwood Beaches to the north—the sand becomes less populated and more peaceful. Because the beach is flat and the bay is shallow, Wasaga is a popular destination for families.

Although most people come for the beach, Wasaga also has 50 kilometers (31 miles) of hiking trails. In winter, there are 30 kilometers (19 miles) of trails for cross-country skiing. Access the trail network from the **Wasaga Nordic Centre** (101 Blueberry Trail, 705/429-0943, 9am-5pm daily mid-Dec.-mid-Mar., adults $15, seniors $10, ages 6-17 $7).

Wasaga Beach Transit (705/429-7873, www.wasagabeach.com/transit, $2) runs a shuttle between the beach and Collingwood Bus Terminal (100 Pine St., Collingwood). Check their website for schedules.

The **Town of Wasaga Beach** (705/429-3844, www.wasagabeach.com) and the **Wasaga Beach Chamber of Commerce** (705/429-2247 or 866/292-7242, www.wasagachamber.com) are good sources of information about accommodations and services in the Wasaga area, which include the usual assortment of modest beach motels, plus privately run campgrounds (the provincial park has no camping facilities). Wasaga Beach is 20 kilometers (12.5 miles) east of Collingwood; take Highway 26 to Highway 92.

Midland and Parry Sound

The peninsula on Georgian Bay's southwestern side that houses the towns of Midland and Penetanguishene played an important role in Ontario's early history. Long populated by First Nations people, in the 1600s a site near present-day Midland became the region's first European settlement, when a group of French Jesuits established a village. Several interesting historic sites, particularly the well-designed Sainte-Marie Among the Hurons, illuminate the region's past. The area retains a strong French and First Nations heritage.

Like other areas around Georgian Bay, the Midland region has its share of beautiful outdoor destinations, particularly Wye Marsh in Midland and the large Awenda Provincial Park in Penetanguishene. It's also a gateway to the 30,000 Islands region of Georgian Bay, some of which are protected in Georgian Bay Islands National Park. You can visit this park in a day trip from Midland or Penetanguishene; it's less than an hour's drive to Honey Harbour, where the boat to the park islands departs.

North along Georgian Bay is Parry Sound, a pleasant community that's both a cultural destination and a base for outdoor activities; ruggedly beautiful Killbear Provincial Park nearby draws travelers to its shores and waterfront campgrounds.

MIDLAND AND PENETANGUISHENE

The largest community along this part of Georgian Bay, Midland (population 17,000) retains a low-key small-town feel along King Street, the main downtown street. The town has begun to sprawl from the center, with malls and other developments, and its sights are spread around the area, but it's a convenient base for exploring the region's historical and outdoor attractions.

As you walk around downtown Midland, look for the 34 wall **murals** (www.downtownmidland.ca). One mural, painted on silos along Midland Harbor, depicts a Jesuit priest and an indigenous Wendat person at Sainte-Marie; it is reportedly the largest outdoor historical mural in North America. Pick up a mural map at the harborfront **Midland Visitor Information Centre** (165 King St., Midland, 705/527-4050 or 855/527-4050, www.midland.ca, 9am-6pm daily May-Sept.).

Nearby Penetanguishene (population 9,000) has a strong French heritage; roughly 16 percent of the residents speak French as their first language. Penetanguishene's main attractions are the restored naval base at Discovery Harbour and the expansive Awenda Provincial Park, which has the region's best beaches.

Midland and Penetanguishene

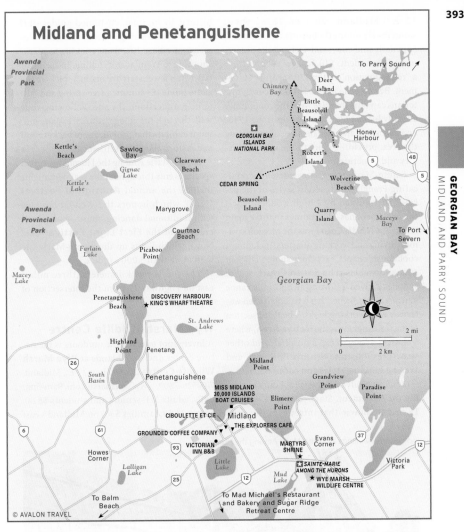

© AVALON TRAVEL

★ Sainte-Marie Among the Hurons

In 1639, a group of French Jesuit missionaries began constructing a community near present-day Midland, establishing the first European settlement in Ontario. Their goal was to bring Christianity to the indigenous Wendat people, whom they called the "Hurons." The Jesuits worked with the Wendat for 10 years, until hostilities worsened between the Wendat and the nearby Iroquois people. After two priests were killed in skirmishes with the Iroquois, the Jesuits abandoned the settlement and burned it to the ground to protect it from desecration. Centuries later, in 1930, Pope Pius XI canonized the murdered priests, Jean de Brébeuf and Gabriel Lalemant.

What you see today at the fascinating historical village **Sainte-Marie Among the Hurons** (16164 Hwy.

12 E., Midland, 705/526-7838, www.saintemarieamongthehurons.on.ca, 10am-5pm daily mid-May-mid-Oct., adults $12, seniors $10, students $10.50, ages 6-12 $9.25) is a "reimagination" of the 17th-century settlement. Because the Jesuits left no records, historians can only theorize what the community actually looked like. It wasn't until the 1940s and 1950s that archeologists began excavating the area, providing clues to the village's history and structure.

Sainte-Marie was reconstructed by replicating French construction styles of the period. Surrounded by a high wooden fence, the settlement has 25 buildings in three main areas. The **North Court** was the mission's primary living and working quarters, including a cookhouse, chapel, carpentry shop, a chicken run, and stables. The **South Court,** where supplies arrived following an 800-mile canoe journey from Quebec, has a reconstructed waterway with working locks. The third section of the settlement was the **Native Area,** where a church, a longhouse, a hospital, and other structures illustrate the mix of French and Wendat building styles and cultures.

You can easily spend several hours exploring the settlement. Start your visit with the 15-minute movie that introduces the site's history. In summer, costumed guides staff the village buildings, demonstrating elements of village life, from cooking to blacksmithing to Wendat storytelling. In spring or fall, when fewer staff are on duty, pick up the audio guide ($3 summer, free spring and fall) to help understand the site. Following your walk through the village, you can explore museum exhibits that provide more background and history about the settlement.

Sainte-Marie Among the Hurons organizes special events throughout the year. Highlights include the annual **Aboriginal Festival** (June), which honors the Wendat heritage with traditional dancing, music, games, and crafts, and the **First Light Festival** (late Nov.), which lights up the Sainte-Marie site with more than 3,000 candles.

The site is five kilometers (three miles) east on Highway 12 from the intersection of Highway 93.

Wye Marsh Wildlife Centre

A lovely spot to enjoy the outdoors is the nature center and marshlands at **Wye Marsh Wildlife Centre** (16160 Hwy. 12 E., Midland, 705/526-7809, www.wyemarsh.com, 9am-5pm daily, adults $11, seniors and students $8.50, ages 4-12 $8, families $30) on Midland's east

indigenous dwellings at Sainte-Marie Among the Hurons

side, next to Sainte-Marie Among the Hurons. The visitors center has exhibits about local ecology, and kids enjoy the live animal presentations, but the real action is outdoors on the network of walking trails. Rent an audio guide about the plants and wildlife, or simply follow the interpretive signs; climb the observation tower for views over the marsh.

The marsh is a nesting habitat for **trumpeter swans,** and one highlight of a visit here is the chance to observe these majestic birds. You can canoe or kayak on the channels that wind through the marsh, and guided canoe excursions ($8 pp) are offered. In winter, there are 22 kilometers (14 miles) of groomed trails for cross-country skiing and 10 kilometers (six miles) of snowshoeing trails (rental skis $15, snowshoes $5-10). Other nature programs are offered throughout the year.

Martyrs' Shrine

Across the highway from Sainte-Marie Among the Hurons, the 1926 **Martyrs' Shrine** (16163 Hwy. 12 W., Midland, 705/526-3788, www.martyrs-shrine.com, 8am-9pm daily mid-May-mid-Oct., ages 12 and over $5), with its two soaring spires, honors the memory of the two Jesuits who worked at

Sainte-Marie but died in a 1649 Iroquois raid. Roman Catholic mass is held several times a day, and you can stroll the gardens and walkways. The site draws religious pilgrims from all over the world.

30,000 Islands Cruises

The two-hour **Miss Midland 30,000 Islands Boat Cruises** (705/549-3388, www. midlandtours.com, mid-May-mid-Oct., adults $32, seniors $30, students $22, ages 5-12 $16) take you around Georgian Bay Islands National Park and other islands in the 30,000 Islands region. Cruises depart from the Midland Town Dock at the foot of King Street.

Discovery Harbour

Ahoy, matey! Climb aboard the replicas of two majestic 18th-century British sailing vessels, the HMS *Bee,* a supply schooner, and the HMS *Tecumseth,* a warship, at **Discovery Harbour** (93 Jury Dr., Penetanguishene, 705/549-8064, www.discoveryharbour.on.ca, 10am-5pm daily late May-early Sept., adults $7, seniors and students $6.25, ages 6-12 $5.25), a restored naval base that the British built following the War of 1812 to protect the Upper Great Lakes region from future American attacks. While only one original building remains (the 1845

tall ships at Discovery Harbour

officers' quarters), the reconstructed site reflects naval and military life here in the 1800s. Guides in period costume conduct tours of the 19 historic buildings and demonstrate various aspects of sailors' lives, including cooking, ropework, and games. Also on-site is the HMS *Tecumseth* Centre, which houses the original hull of this 1815 warship, as well as exhibits about and artifacts from Penetanguishene during the War of 1812.

Awenda Provincial Park

Fronting Georgian Bay 11 kilometers (seven miles) northwest of Penetanguishene, the 2,915-hectare (7,200-acre) **Awenda Provincial Park** (Awenda Park Rd., off Concession Rd. 16 E./Lafontaine Rd. E., 705/549-2231, www.ontarioparks.com, $14.50 per vehicle) is a beautiful destination for hiking and swimming. One of central Ontario's largest parks, Awenda is in a transition zone between north and south, making it home to a diverse array of plants and trees, as well as roughly 200 bird species and many reptiles and amphibians. In summer, park staff offer nature programs, theatrical productions, and other special events; call the park office or check online with **Friends of Awenda** (www.awendapark.ca) for schedules.

The park has approximately 30 kilometers (19 miles) of multiuse trails. The most popular is the easy **Beach Trail,** which connects the park's four beaches. Off the Beach Trail, you can follow the easy, one-kilometer (0.6-mile) **Beaver Pond Trail,** most of which is along a boardwalk, to an area that had extensive beaver activity. Longer park trails include the **Robitaille Homestead Trail,** a three-kilometer (1.9-mile) round-trip trail past ancient sand dunes that begins in the day parking lot near Bear Campground; the five-kilometer (three-mile) **Wendat Trail,** which starts near Kettle's Lake; and the 13-kilometer (eight-mile) **Bluff Trail,** which circles the campgrounds and connects the camping areas to the beach.

Some of the area's nicest swimming spots are within the provincial park, which has four beaches along Georgian Bay. **First Beach,** closest to the parking area, is a sheltered, family-friendly sand beach that also has rocks for the kids to climb. You can continue along the beach trail to **Second Beach; Third Beach,** which has particularly soft sand; and eventually to the more secluded **Fourth Beach.** It's about two kilometers (1.25 miles) from First to Fourth Beach.

You can also swim at **Kettle's Lake,** an inland lake with an easy boardwalk trail to the water. The lake is a calm spot for canoeing, particularly for beginning paddlers; in summer, canoe rentals are available. Around the lake, you might see otters, beavers, loons, or great blue herons. Awenda is open year-round, and you can cross-country ski here in winter.

ACCOMMODATIONS AND CAMPING

The park's **Stone Cottage** (www.ontarioparks.com, May-Oct., reservation fee online $11, by phone $13, late June-early Sept. $1,040 per week, May-June and Sept.-Oct. $150 per night) has a spacious terrace above the water and a huge living room with a stone fireplace and windows facing the bay. One bedroom has a double bed and two bunks, the other twin beds. It has no running water; drinking water is provided, and there's an outhouse but no shower. Bring sleeping bags or linens, food, and cooking gear. While the cottage itself is rustic, the setting is beautiful; reserve well in advance.

Awenda's six **campgrounds** (888/668-7275, www.ontarioparks.com, mid-May-mid-Oct., reservation fee online $11, by phone $13, tent sites $42, electrical sites $47) are set amid maple and oak forests, so the 333 shaded sites feel comparatively private. All the camping areas have flush toilets and showers, and three have laundry, though none are on the waterfront. The Snake, Wolf, and Deer Campgrounds are closest to the bay, but it's still a long walk. Bring bicycles if you can.

Entertainment

Located at Discovery Harbour, **King's Wharf Theatre** (97 Jury Dr., Penetanguishene,

705/549-5555, www.draytonentertainment.com) is a professional summer theater that produces several plays every year from June to early September.

Food

For places to eat in Midland, wander along King Street downtown. Get your caffeine near the waterfront off King Street at **Grounded Coffee Company** (538 Bay St., Midland, 705/527-5997, www.groundedcoffee.ca, 7am-5pm Mon.-Sat., 9am-3pm Sun.).

At **Ciboulette et Cie** (290 King St., Midland, 705/245-0410, www.cibouletteetcie. ca, 8am-5pm Mon.-Sat., 10am-4pm Sun.), a cheerful café and takeout shop (the name is French for "Chives and Co."), the day starts with freshly baked scones and other pastries. Creative sandwiches and delicious ready-to-eat salads, perhaps Brussels sprout slaw or roasted sweet potatoes with cranberries, make a quick lunch.

Decorated with Russian dolls, African drums, and maps of faraway lands, **The Explorers Cafe** (345 King St., Midland, 705/527-9199, www.theexplorerscafe.com, 5pm-9pm Tues.-Sat., $21-32) resembles a Victorian-era adventurer's residence. The menu wanders the world, too, from Indian curry and Singapore noodles to duck confit and Georgian Bay whitefish. Although the restaurant is right downtown, you may need a compass to find it, since it's set back from the main road; look for its signboard on King Street.

Craving Texas-style barbecue pork ribs? Jerk chicken? Barbecue brisket? Head for the little yellow bungalow, about 10 minutes south of Midland, that houses **MAD Michael's Restaurant and Bakery** (8215 Hwy. 93, Wyebridge, 705/527-1666, www.madmichaels. com, noon-8pm Thurs.-Sun. mid-May-mid-Oct., lunch $9-20, dinner $20-28). This isn't any ordinary barbecue shack; chef "Mad" Michael White smokes ribs in his outdoor kitchen, bakes bread, and in his spare time, crafts rustic wood furniture. Save room for a slice of homemade pie.

Accommodations

Midland has the usual selection of chain motels. They cluster along King Street near Highway 12 or on Yonge Street off Highway 93. Try the **Quality Inn** (924 King St., Midland, 705/526-9307 or 800/461-4265, http://www.qualityinnmidland.ca) or **Midland Comfort Inn** (980 King St., Midland, 705/526-2090 or 888/274-3020, www.choicehotels.ca).

breakfast at The Victorian Inn Bed & Breakfast

You feel like part of the family when you stay at **The Victorian Inn Bed & Breakfast** (670 Hugel Ave., Midland, 705/526-4441 or 877/450-7660, www.victorianinn.ca, $119-159), a bright yellow house with a wraparound porch. Two of the three homey guest rooms, with quilt-topped beds, have en suite baths; the larger Royal Suite has a separate sitting area and a private bath across the hall. Well-traveled owners Peter and Kim Hakkenberg have filled the dining room, where they serve a full breakfast, with mementos of their journeys. Children under age 12 are not permitted.

Set amid marshlands south of Midland, the peaceful ★ **Sugar Ridge Retreat Centre** (5720 Forgets Rd., Wyebridge, 705/528-1793 or 866/609-1793, www.sugarridge.ca, $149 s or d, includes breakfast) offers yoga retreats and other workshops. Owners Liz and Kurt Frost have 10 sturdy, simply furnished cabins, which sleep up to four, in the fields around the main lodge, a contemporary Zen-style retreat center with an airy yoga studio and large dining room. Cabins have no plumbing, phones, or Internet; restrooms, showers, and Wi-Fi are available in the lodge, where breakfast is served.

Practicalities

The seasonal **Midland Visitor Information Centre** (165 King St., Midland, 705/527-4050 or 855/527-4050, www.midland.ca, 9am-6pm daily May-Sept.), near the waterfront downtown, has lots of information about the region; Midland Tourism also staffs a year-round Visitor Information Centre in the North Simcoe Sports and Recreation Centre (527 Len Self Blvd., Midland, 8am-8pm daily), off King Street. The **Penetanguishene Tourist Information Centre** (2 Main St., Penetanguishene, 705/549-2232, www.penetanguishene.ca, 9am-6pm daily May-Aug., 10am-6pm daily Sept.-Oct.) is at the town docks.

The Midland-Penetanguishene area is about 160 kilometers (100 miles) from Toronto. From Highway 93, take Highway 12 east, then turn left onto King Street for downtown Midland or continue east on Highway 12 to Sainte-Marie Among the Hurons, the Martyrs' Shrine, and Wye Marsh. For Penetanguishene, stay on Highway 93, which becomes Main Street.

★ GEORGIAN BAY ISLANDS NATIONAL PARK

Georgian Bay is dotted with at least 30,000 islands. Some are not much more than a big rock jutting out of the water, while others are substantial enough to house entire communities. A visit to **Georgian Bay Islands National Park** (705/527-7200, www.pc.gc.ca), established in 1929 and encompassing 63 islands across Georgian Bay, is the easiest way to sample the island experience.

With hiking trails, beaches, and campgrounds as well as a visitors center, Beausoleil Island, the largest of the park's islands, is the most accessible. Parks Canada runs a seasonal boat service from Honey Harbour to Beausoleil to take day-trippers to the island (in fact, the boat is named *DayTripper*). To reach islands other than Beausoleil, you need to have your own boat, make arrangements with a local outfitter, or hire a water taxi.

While experienced kayakers and canoeists can explore the park islands on their own, the park service advises extreme caution due to the frequently heavy boat traffic and the many rocks just under the surface that can surprise the unwary. The park has partnered with **White Squall Paddling Centre** (19 James St., Parry Sound, 705/746-4936, www.whitesquall.com) to offer guided kayak trips to some of the park's northern islands.

Honey Harbour is the jumping-off point to visit the park. It's about 168 kilometers (104 miles) northwest of Toronto and 35 kilometers (22 miles) northwest of Midland, the nearest major town. If you don't have a car, you can ride the convenient **Parkbus** (800/928-7101, www.parkbus.ca, one-way/round-trip adults $61/$85, seniors and students $55/$77, ages 2-12 $31/$44) from Toronto to Honey Harbour on select summer

That's a Lot of Islands

Many people outside Ontario know about the **Thousand Islands,** the chain of islands along the St. Lawrence River in the eastern part of the province. After all, there's even a salad dressing with the Thousand Islands name. Yet the Georgian Bay region has far more than just a thousand isles. Depending on who's counting, Georgian Bay—one of the world's largest freshwater archipelagoes—encompasses at least 30,000 islands. Some of these islands are hardly more than specks of bare rock, while others are quite substantial. Manitoulin Island, which measures 2,765 square kilometers (1,067 square miles) on the bay's northern side, is the largest freshwater island in the world.

What created these many different islands? During the ice age, more than 10,000 years ago, glaciers covered what is now Canada. According to one theory, the movement of these glaciers compressed and reshaped the land, fashioning the distinctive landscape of islands and coves that today surrounds Georgian Bay.

UNESCO has recognized the unique geography of the Georgian Bay region and its islands, designating 347,000 hectares (857,455 acres) of the shoreline between the Severn and French Rivers as the **Georgian Bay Biosphere Reserve** (705/774-0978, www.gbbr.ca). One of 15 such reserves in Canada, it's home to more than 100 species of at-risk animals and plants, including the eastern wolf, the lake sturgeon, and the massasauga rattlesnake. The biosphere's mission is to assist in the conservation of these species and to support education and sustainable development in the region.

The 30,000 islands are a mix of public and private lands. Some, like the 63 islands of **Georgian Bay Islands National Park** (705/526-9804, www.pc.gc.ca) or those of **Fathom Five National Marine Park** (519/596-2233, www.pc.gc.ca), are government-protected natural areas. Many others are privately owned, with a cottage or two offering their owners a waterfront getaway. Visitors to this island region can cruise around the bays and harbors, explore the island parks, and even soar above the islands by floatplane. So come back again; to tour even a fraction of these 30,000 islands will take years of exploring.

weekends. The bus departs from several points in Toronto, including 30 Carlton Street (between Yonge St. and Church St., subway: College) and Dufferin Street at Bloor Street West (subway: Dufferin).

Georgian Bay Islands National Park is technically open year-round, but park services, including boat transportation between Honey Harbour and Beausoleil Island, operate only between mid-May and mid-October.

Beausoleil Island

The main destination for visitors exploring Georgian Bay Islands National Park is this 11-square-kilometer (4.2-square-mile) island, 15 minutes by boat from the Parks Canada marina in Honey Harbour. A unique feature of Beausoleil Island is that it encompasses two different natural environments. The northern part of the island is typical of the Canadian Shield, which extends into Northern Ontario, with its rocky shoreline and its windblown juniper and pine forests. On Beausoleil's southern half, you'll see more hardwood trees, especially maple, beech, oak, and birch, and land that's grassy or marshy rather than rocky. The best sandy beaches are on the southern end, but you can swim almost anywhere that looks inviting. Bring your own food, water, and anything else you need (hiking shoes, swimsuit, towel, and insect repellent). While park rangers are on duty on Beausoleil Island from spring to fall, there are no snack bars or other services.

Beausoleil Island has about a dozen marked hiking trails, including the 6.9-kilometer (4.3-mile) Huron path that runs between the island's north and south and the 2.5-kilometer (1.5-mile) loop around pretty Fairy Lake. Most are for hikers only, but mountain bikes are allowed on two of the routes. For trail details, pick up the free park *Visitor Guide* at any of the park offices or at the Beausoleil welcome center.

Parks Canada runs the *DayTripper* boat (2611 Honey Harbour Rd., 705/526-8907, adults $15.70, seniors $13.45, ages 6-16 $8.55) to transport visitors from Honey Harbour to Beausoleil Island. The *DayTripper* makes the 15-minute trip several times a day from mid-June through early September and Friday through Tuesday mid-May through mid-June and early September through mid-October. The *DayTripper* can take you either to the Cedar Spring dock at the island's south end or to the island's north side at Chimney Bay; the boats to and from these different points depart at different times, so check the schedule carefully before you phone for *DayTripper* reservations, which are required. *DayTripper* rates include park admission.

Two privately owned water taxis also shuttle visitors from Honey Harbour to the park's islands: **Georgian Bay Water Services** (705/627-3062, www.gbws.ca) and **Honey Harbour Boat Club** (705/756-2411, www.hhbc.ca). If you take a water taxi to Beausoleil,

park admission is adults $5.80 and seniors $4.90.

Food and Accommodations

Within the national park, you can camp or stay in one of the camping cabins or oTENTiks (platform tents). Otherwise, you'll need to sleep on the mainland.

CAMPING

Beausoleil Island has nine campgrounds. The largest is **Cedar Spring Campground** (705/526-8907, $25.50, reservation fee $9.80 per campsite), near the boat dock, with 45 tent sites and six family-friendly two-bedroom camping cabins (sleeps up to 5, $175), as well as flush toilets and showers. Five **oTENTiks** ($140), furnished platform tents accommodating up to four people, are available at Cedar Spring as well. Reserve campsites, cabins, and oTENTiks through the **Parks Canada reservation service** (877/737-3783, www.reservation.pc.gc.ca).

In addition to the cabins at Cedar Spring, four lovely secluded **cabins** ($150) overlook the shore at **Christian Beach**, 1.8 kilometers (1.2 miles) from the Cedar Spring boat dock. Sleeping two adults, the cabins come with a queen bed, a table and chairs, barbecues, and

Christian Beach cabins in the Georgian Bay Islands National Park solar-powered electricity. Park staff transport your gear from the *DayTripper* dock and provide water; the cabins have no plumbing, but there's a composting toilet nearby. Consider bringing or renting a mountain bike, which will give you more flexibility in exploring the island or cycling to the showers at Cedar Spring.

You can reserve five of the primitive camping sites at Honeymoon Bay, on the island's northernmost end, and the four sites at Tonch North. The island's remaining primitive campgrounds ($15.70) are first come, first served. All have either pit or composting toilets. Campers must bring their own water:

- **Honeymoon Bay** (11 sites)
- **Chimney Bay** (6 sites)
- **The Oaks** (7 sites)
- **Sandpiper** (8 sites)
- **Tonch North** (4 sites)
- **Tonch East** (7 sites)
- **Tonch South** (7 sites)
- **Thumb Point** (8 sites)

OUTSIDE THE PARK

The village of Honey Harbour, where the park boat dock is located, has a handful of seasonal businesses. Port Severn, a blink-and-you'll-miss-it town off Highway 400's exit 153, just south of the Honey Harbour turnoff, has the nicest lodging in the vicinity of the national park. To stay somewhere with more food and entertainment options, sleep in Midland and spend the day in the national park; it's about an hour's drive.

In partnership with Midland's Ciboulette et Cie, **The Hive** (18 Franks Ln., Honey Harbour, 289/828-4774, www.thehivehoneyharbour. com, May-mid-Oct., call or check the website for seasonal hours) serves coffee, pastries, and light meals. It's also a small spa, yoga studio, and cottage supply shop—a hive of activity in this small village.

The **Rawley Resort and Spa** (2900 Kellys Rd., Port Severn, 705/538-2272 or 800/263-7538, www.rawleyresort.com, $188-415 d)

feels like a waterfront estate, particularly if you sit in the dining room, looking across the manicured lawns to the water. The restaurant (breakfast $8-14, lunch $12-18, dinner $18-36) is rather formal, serving classic dishes such as veal osso bucco, rack of lamb, or seafood paella, with live jazz several nights a week. Accommodations are spread over several buildings and range from upscale guest rooms to large one- or two-bedroom suites to two-story loft units overlooking the water. There's an outdoor pool and a small beach.

Information and Services

The administrative office of **Georgian Bay Islands National Park** (705/527-7200, info. gbi@pc.gc.ca, 8am-4pm Mon.-Fri.) is located in Midland. You can phone or email for information year-round. The park service runs a **Welcome Centre** (9:30am-5pm Sun.-Thurs., 9am-7pm Fri., 9am-6pm Sat. mid-June-early Sept., 9:30am-5pm Fri.-Tues mid-May-mid-June, 9am-4pm Sun.-Tues. and 9am-5pm Fri.-Sat. early Sept.-mid-Oct.) on Beausoleil Island, near the Cedar Spring Campground.

At the **Lock 45 Port Severn Welcome Centre** (175 Port Severn Rd. N., Port Severn, 705/538-2586, mid-May-mid-Oct.), off Highway 400's exit 153 between Midland and Honey Harbour, Parks Canada staff provides information about park and area activities. The Welcome Centre is located on the 386-kilometer (240-mile) **Trent-Severn Waterway,** which connects Lake Ontario with Georgian Bay; the lock station has a small exhibit area about the waterway and the lock system, and you can watch boats transiting the lock.

PARRY SOUND

Fronting Georgian Bay, Parry Sound is a jumping-off point for exploring the 30,000 Islands region. It's a popular destination for kayaking, whether you're just getting started or you're an experienced paddler. For a relatively small community (the year-round population is about 6,400), Parry Sound has a surprisingly robust cultural life, drawing music lovers in particular to the beautifully designed performing arts center.

Parry Sound's most famous native son may be hockey player Bobby Orr, whose legacy lives on in the **Bobby Orr Hall of Fame** (Charles W. Stockey Centre for the Performing Arts, 2 Bay St., 705/746-4466 or 877/746-4466, www.bobbyorrhalloffame.com, 10am-6pm daily late May-mid-Oct., 10am-4pm Mon.-Sat. mid-Oct.-late May, adults $9, seniors and children $6, families $25). The first-floor exhibits document Orr's legendary National Hockey League career, beginning in 1962, when the Boston Bruins recruited him for their junior team at age 14. If you have kids in tow, they'll likely head directly upstairs to play the hockey skills games.

30,000 Islands Cruises

One of the best ways to explore the thousands of islands off Parry Sound's coast is on a boat. The 550-passenger *Island Queen* (9 Bay St., 705/746-2311 or 800/506-2628, www.islandqueencruise.com), which bills itself as Canada's largest sightseeing boat, runs a three-hour cruise (1pm daily June-mid-Oct., adults $42, ages 6-12 $21) that passes Killbear Provincial Park and circles a number of the islands. In July and August, there's also a two-hour morning cruise (10am daily July-Aug., adults $32, ages 6-12 $16) that sticks closer to shore and the inner islands, where you can catch glimpses of cottages and vacation homes.

After years of service as Niagara Falls' *Maid of the Mist,* the **MV *Chippewa III*** (Spirit of the Sound Schooner Co., Seguin River Parkette, off Bay St., 705/746-6064 or 888/283-5870, www.spiritofthesound.ca, July-Aug.) now tours the waters off Parry Sound. It offers a variety of island cruises, including a 90-minute afternoon trip highlighting the Group of Seven artists' connection to the region (adults $22, under age 17 $11), and a sunset dinner cruise (adults $60, under age 16 $4 per year). The company also runs trips to **Henry's Fish Restaurant** (705/746-9040) on Frying Pan Island (adults $38, under age 17 $19), combining a cruise with a stop for a fish-and-chips lunch.

★ Flight-Seeing

Touring the 30,000 Islands by boat is a delightful way to spend an afternoon, but seeing the islands by air is an entirely different thrill. Run by husband-and-wife pilots Keith and Nicole Saulnier, **Georgian Bay Airways** (11A Bay St., 705/774-9884 or 800/786-1704,

The M.V. *Chippewa III* cruises the waters near Parry Sound.

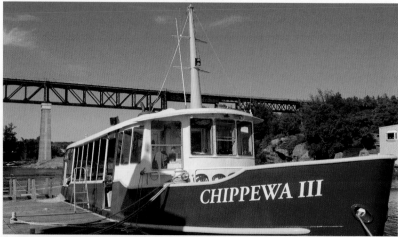

www.georgianbayairways.com, May-Oct.) flies Cessna floatplanes that take off from Parry Sound Harbor and soar over the nearby islands. Seeing the islands from above gives you a much clearer picture of their number and diversity; some are barely more than a boulder in the bay, while others support entire towns. Keith and Nicole know the region well and can tell you all about the islands below.

The basic tour runs 25-35 minutes (adults $115-152), or you can opt for one of several special flights, from a sunset champagne flight ($346 per couple) to a fish-and-chips meal at **Dockside Fish 'n' Chips** (adults $235, meal not included) at Paynes Marine in Pointe au Baril. They've hosted in-flight marriage proposals, and even a wedding, so if you have something special in mind, let them know.

Canoeing and Kayaking

The Parry Sound area is an excellent starting point for canoe or kayak tours, and one well-established local outfitter has two locations to help you get out on the water. **White Squall Paddling Centre** (53 Carling Bay Rd., Nobel, 705/342-5324, www.whitesquall. com, 9am-5:30pm Sat.-Thurs., 9am-8pm Fri. June-Aug., 9am-5:30pm daily Apr.-May and Sept.-mid-Oct.), on Cole Lake, rents canoes and kayaks, offers lessons that include stand-up paddleboarding, and organizes a variety of day trips as well as multiday kayak tours. It's located off Highway 559 en route to Killbear Provincial Park.

In downtown Parry Sound, the **White Squall Town Shop** (19 James St., 705/746-4936, www.whitesquall.com, 9:30am-5:30pm Mon.-Thurs. and Sat., 9:30am-7pm Fri., 11am-4pm Sun.) is primarily a gear shop, but you can get information about rentals and trips here, too.

Entertainment and Shopping

The hub of cultural life in Parry Sound—indeed, in this entire region of Ontario—is the **Charles W. Stockey Centre for the Performing Arts** (2 Bay St., 705/746-4466 or 877/746-4466, www.stockeycentre.com). This striking contemporary building, right on the bay and built of local timber and stone, hosts concerts, lectures, and other events year-round. Parry Sound's major cultural event, held at the Stockey Centre, is the annual **Festival of the Sound** (42 James St., 705/746-2410 or 866/364-0061, www.festivalofthesound.ca). Since 1979, this classical music festival has been drawing Canadian and international musicians and music lovers for three weeks of concerts in July and August.

Food and Accommodations

Families and couples, visitors and locals, even the occasional visiting hockey team all turn up at **Wellington's Pub and Grill** (105 James St., 705/746-1333, www.wellingtonspubandgrill.com, $10-25), a friendly pub-restaurant downtown decorated with black-and-white photos from Parry Sound's past. From salads to steaks to succulent schnitzel, the food is straightforward but tasty, and the bar stocks plenty of local brews.

Though rustic on the outside, the six units (in three cabins) overlooking the river at the **Log Cabin Inn** (9 Little Beaver Blvd., at Oastler Park Dr., 705/746-7122, www.logcabininn.net, $160 d) are country-contemporary inside, with a king or two queen beds, fireplaces, and modern baths. Rates include continental breakfast. You can also book a package with dinner in the upscale **restaurant** (lunch $8-15, dinner $23-40), where both guests and nonguests can dine on applewood-smoked pork chops, pan-seared pickerel, or filet mignon in, yes, a log cabin. Don't expect pioneer hardship, though; the solid log structure with a soaring ceiling overlooks the river, with a fireplace, twinkling candles, and a lengthy wine list setting the mood. The property is three kilometers (1.9 miles) south of town.

The nicest spots to relax at the homey and well-located **40 Bay Street Bed & Breakfast** (40 Bay St., 705/746-9247 or 866/371-2638, www.40baystreet.com, $150-200 d) are the two sunporches overlooking the harbor. The

Bay Room, the smallest of the three cozy guest quarters (all with private baths), has expansive harbor views, too. The Retreat Room's special feature is the oversize bath, and the Garden Room lives up to its name with a private deck facing the flower-filled yard. No kids under age 11.

Built in 1882 (with a 1950s addition), the rambling 11-room **Bayside Inn** (10 Gibson St., 705/746-7720 or 866/833-8864, www. psbaysideinn.com, $138-158 d) is conveniently located near downtown. The well-turned-out rooms, done in a modern country style, all have air-conditioning, flat-screen TVs, Wi-Fi, and refrigerators. Families can book a room with two sleeping areas separated by a divider. Free coffee and tea are available every morning, and guests can have breakfast for a small additional charge (continental $4, full breakfast $8).

Practicalities

Parry Sound is 222 kilometers (138 miles) northwest of Toronto along Highway 400/69. It's 163 kilometers (101 miles) south of Sudbury via Highway 69, and 170 kilometers (105 miles) from Killarney. **Ontario Northland** (800/461-8558, www. ontarionorthland.ca) runs three buses daily in each direction between Toronto and Parry Sound (3-4 hours, adults $58) and between Parry Sound and Sudbury (2-2.5 hours, adults $40). Buses stop at **Richard's Coffee** (119 Bowes St., 705/746-9611), about 1.8 kilometers (1.1 miles) east of downtown.

Most Parry Sound attractions are along the harbor, a short walk from downtown. For taxi service, try **Parry Sound Taxi** (705/746-1221). **Parry Sound Tourism** (www. parrysoundtourism.com) provides information about the region.

★ KILLBEAR PROVINCIAL PARK

With pink granite cliffs, windblown pines, and several long sandy beaches along Georgian Bay, **Killbear Provincial Park** (35 Killbear Park Rd., Nobel, 705/342-5492, www.ontarioparks.com, $14.50 per vehicle) is a spectacular location for hiking, canoeing, and swimming. Somewhat lesser known than Ontario's "destination" provincial parks like Algonquin or Killarney, Killbear is less than an hour's drive from Parry Sound, which makes it an easy day trip. If you'd like to stay longer, Killbear's campgrounds are the third largest in the Ontario provincial park system; only Algonquin and The Pinery have more campsites.

The park **Visitors Centre** (705/342-5492, 10am-5pm daily mid-May-mid-Oct.) has exhibits that illustrate the geology, natural history, and cultural history of the Killbear area. Particularly popular with the kids (well, with most of them) are the snake exhibits; in summer, naturalists give "snake talks" where you can learn about and touch local reptiles. In July and August, you can join in guided hikes, slide shows, kids' activities, and other interpretive programs. Be sure to walk around to the back of the Visitors Centre for great views of Georgian Bay.

Killbear is home to the endangered massasauga rattlesnake. While it's not likely you'll see one, if you do come upon a rattlesnake near the campgrounds or along the road, notify a park staff member, who will relocate the snake to a less-traveled area. Don't try to pick up or move the snake yourself.

The park is officially open mid-May through mid-October, but in the off-season, you can walk in for winter hiking, cross-country skiing, or snowshoeing.

Sports and Recreation

Several easy hiking trails run through the park, making Killbear a pleasant place for novice hikers. Heading along the shoreline out to the far end of the park, the **Lighthouse Point Trail** is an easy one-kilometer (0.6-mile) route that passes a 1904 lighthouse. The 3.5-kilometer (2.2-mile) **Lookout Point Trail** goes through the forest to a lookout above Georgian Bay. For bayside views of the park's pink granite rocks, follow the **Twin Points Trail,** a 1.6-kilometer (1-mile) loop from the day-use parking area. The **Recreational Trail**, a six-kilometer (3.7-mile) walking and cycling path, runs from the park entrance past several of the campgrounds to Lighthouse Point.

Killbear's three kilometers (1.9 miles) of sandy beaches include a swimming beach at the day-use area. You can swim near most of the campgrounds as well. **Harold Point**, with both a sand beach and rocky cliffs, is a pretty spot to watch the sunset.

Surrounded by water on three sides, Killbear is popular for canoeing and kayaking. The most sheltered waters are near the park's day-use area. Canoe and kayak rentals are not available inside the park, but you can rent boats by the day from nearby outfitters from mid-May to mid-October, including **Killbear Park Mall** (495 Hwy. 559, Nobel, 705/342-5747, www.killbearparkmall. com, canoes $35, single kayaks $35, double kayaks $50, stand-up paddleboards $35) and **The Detour Store** (401 Hwy. 559, Nobel, 705/342-1611, www.thedetourstore.ca, canoes $25-33, single kayaks $27-35, double kayaks $39-40). **White Squall Paddling Centre** (53 Carling Bay Rd., Nobel, 705/342-5324, www. whitesquall.com), off Highway 559 en route to Killbear, rents canoes ($35-55 per day), kayaks (single $28-53 per day, double $35-74 per day), and stand-up paddleboards ($28-38 per day) and runs a shuttle service to deliver boats to locations in and around the park.

Camping

Killbear Provincial Park (35 Killbear Park Rd., Nobel, 705/342-5492, www.ontarioparks. com, tent sites $42-47, electrical sites $47-52) has seven different campgrounds, with a total of 880 campsites, most within a five-minute walk of the shore. All the campgrounds, except for the more remote 55-site Granite Saddle area, have restrooms, showers, and laundry facilities. About one-quarter of the sites have electrical hookups. Among the prime sites are the waterfront campsites fronting the beach at **Kilcoursie Bay.** Other campgrounds with waterfront sites include **Beaver Dams, Harold Point,** and **Lighthouse Point.**

Killbear's campgrounds book up early, so reserve well in advance through **Ontario Parks Reservation Service** (888/668-7275, www.ontarioparks.com, reservation fee online $11, by phone $13). You can make reservations up to five months before your stay.

Practicalities

Contact the **Killbear Provincial Park office** (35 Killbear Park Rd., Nobel, 705/342-5492, www.ontarioparks.com) or check online with **Friends of Killbear** (www.friendsofkillbear. com) for more information. Several small stores along Highway 559 stock food and other provisions. For a better selection, shop in Parry Sound.

Killbear Provincial Park is 35 kilometers (22 miles) northwest of Parry Sound, about a 45-minute drive. From Parry Sound, take Highway 69 north to Nobel, where you pick up Highway 559 west to the park. There's no public transportation to or around the park.

HIGHWAY 69 NORTH

Traveling along Highway 69 north of Parry Sound, you'll find two more provincial parks that are worth a stop for an afternoon, a weekend, or more: Grundy Lake and French River.

Grundy Lake Provincial Park

Family-friendly **Grundy Lake Provincial Park** (20400 Hwy. 522, Britt, 705/383-2286, www.ontarioparks.com, mid-May-mid-Oct., $14.50 per vehicle) is filled with lakes, and not just the one that gives the park its name. The forests, wetlands, rocky shores, and sandy beaches feel less wild, at least in the front country, than in the parks fronting Georgian Bay, but Grundy Lake has a gentle beauty and plenty to do.

The park's **Interpretive Centre** at Smokey Point offers summer nature programs, guided hikes, and other activities for kids. You can swim from sandy Main Beach on Grundy Lake and from seven other **beaches** around the park. The calm waters make for peaceful canoeing and kayaking. Though the park doesn't rent boats, nearby outfitters do; the park office can refer you to current suppliers.

For **hiking**, the park has several moderate trails. The 2.5-kilometer (1.5-mile) Gut Lake Trail follows the rock-lined shore that's part of the Canadian Shield, while the 1.5-kilometer (0.9-mile) Swan Lake Trail wanders through the marshlands around Swan Lake. On the 3.6-kilometer (2.25-mile) Beaver Dams Trail, you'll see the dams that give the path its name; park staff report that hikers have spotted deer, grouse, and even moose on this trail.

Campers can choose from 586 sites across nine **campgrounds** (tent sites $42-47, electrical sites $47-52). Most have sites on or near a lakeshore, with showers, flush toilets, and laundry facilities nearby. A camping cabin ($125) overlooking Grundy Lake sleeps up to five; it's equipped with a small fridge, kettle, microwave, and propane barbecue, though you'll need to walk to the water taps, restrooms, and showers.

Grundy Lake offers Ontario Parks's **Learn to Camp** program on several summer weekends. The park provides tents, air mattresses, a camp stove, cooking equipment, and firewood, and staff teach you the basics for getting started outdoors, from pitching a tent to building a campfire. Grundy also runs two-hour **Learn to Fish** programs, where you learn fundamental fishing skills and then go out to catch your own.

Grundy Lake is 85 kilometers (53 miles) north of Parry South and about 20-minutes' drive south of the Highway 637 turnoff for Killarney Provincial Park. If you don't have a car, or if you don't want the hassle of driving, check the schedule for the **Parkbus** (800/928-7101, www.parkbus.ca, one-way/round-trip adults $64/$89, seniors and students $58/$80, ages 2-12 $32/$45), which can take you from Toronto directly to Grundy Lake on selected weekends.

French River Provincial Park

The French River, which runs 110 kilometers (68 miles) from Lake Nipissing to Georgian Bay, was an aboriginal trading route for thousands of years before the first French explorers and missionaries arrived in the early 1600s. The river became an important passage for the fur trade in the 1700s and early 1800s. **French River Provincial Park** (705/857-1630, www.ontarioparks.com) incorporates part of this territory, and it's a good place to take a break along Highway 69.

Grundy Lake Provincial Park

The park **Visitors Centre** (9am-5pm daily July-Aug., 9am-4pm Thurs.-Mon. late-May-June and Sept.-mid-Oct.), in an interesting modern building, has a small **museum** (adults $2, seniors $1.75, ages 6-17 $1), where the *Voices of the River* exhibit illuminates the area's history, particularly the mix of First Nations, French, and English cultures.

A short walk from the Visitors Centre, a suspension bridge soars over the French River. It's the **world's largest snowmobile bridge**, measuring 156 meters (512 feet) long, built in 2005 by the French River Snow Voyageurs Snowmobile Club. The bridge has great views up and down the river. The four-kilometer (2.5-mile) **Recollet Falls Trail,** which starts at the Visitors Centre, follows the French River Gorge to the waterfall, a route that First Nations people, fur traders, and other explorers would have traveled centuries ago. If you want to stay awhile, the park has 230 backcountry campsites. There's no road access to any of the sites, so you need to backpack or paddle in.

French River Provincial Park is about 15 minutes' drive from Grundy Lake. It's 90 kilometers (56 miles) north of Parry Sound and 65 kilometers (40 miles) south of Sudbury.

Killarney

On Georgian Bay south of Sudbury, Killarney ranks among Ontario's most beautiful natural destinations. This wilderness park juts out into the bay with white dolomite ridges and pink granite cliffs providing a striking backdrop for hiking, canoeing, and kayaking.

★ KILLARNEY PROVINCIAL PARK

One of Ontario's premier outdoor destinations, **Killarney Provincial Park** (Hwy. 637, Killarney, 705/287-2900, www.ontarioparks. com, $14.50 per vehicle) is known for its striking scenery, particularly the white quartzite and pink granite cliffs that dominate the ridges throughout the park. Dense pine forests surround more than 40 crystal-blue lakes, and the park is home to approximately 100 bird species. Killarney's rolling hills are what remains of the La Cloche Mountains. Worn down over millions of years, the La Cloche range once had peaks taller than the present-day Rockies. Today, white rocks peek out through the woods near the peaks, and the granite cliffs that surround many of the lakes and the shores of Georgian Bay glow with a pinkish cast, particularly in the early-morning and late-afternoon sun.

At 645 square kilometers (250 square miles), Killarney is tiny compared to mammoth Algonquin Provincial Park. Yet it feels more remote, with secluded wilderness a short hike or paddle away. This wilderness naturally takes some effort to reach. The park is located off Highway 69 between Parry Sound and Sudbury. Within the park, services are limited and camping is the only accommodations option, although lodgings, restaurants, and services are nearby in the village of Killarney.

For most Killarney visitors, the first stop is **George Lake** (off Hwy. 637), where the main park office and campground are located. You can swim or canoe here, and it's the starting point for two of the park's hiking trails. At the **Killarney Park Observatory** (George Lake), evening astronomy programs are held regularly in summer. The park hosts other summer events, from nature presentations to concerts, at the George Lake Amphitheatre. Get schedules from the park office or the **Friends of Killarney Park** (www.friendsofkillarneypark.ca).

Killarney Provincial Park is open year-round, but many businesses in the village close from mid-October to May. And at any time of year, be prepared for sudden storms and rapid weather changes. Even if it's sunny when you head out in the morning, a storm can blow in by afternoon.

Beaches

Killarney's most accessible swimming beaches are two sandy stretches along George Lake. The main beach at **George Lake** is in the day-use area; it's a launching point for canoes and kayaks, so watch for paddling traffic. **Second Beach** is in the George Lake Campground. You can also swim in the park's numerous interior lakes and rivers.

Canoeing, Kayaking, and Paddleboarding

George Lake is the park's most popular spot for short canoe, kayak, or stand-up paddleboard excursions. You can easily paddle for an hour or two, appreciating the striking scenery, with pink granite cliffs surrounding sections of the lake. **Bell Lake**, on the park's east side, is another good canoeing or kayaking spot. From the Bell Lake Road turnoff from Highway 637—21 kilometers (13 miles) east of George Lake or 38 kilometers (24 miles) west of Highway 69—it's about nine kilometers (5.5 miles) farther to the lake. Other paddling destinations include **Chikanishing Creek** (Chikanishing Rd., off Hwy. 637) and areas along Georgian Bay.

Killarney Outfitters (1076 Hwy. 637, 705/287-2828 or 888/222-3410, www.killarneyoutfitters.com) and **Killarney Kanoes** (1611 Bell Lake Rd., 705/287-2197 or 888/461-4446, www.killarneykanoes.com) rent canoes and kayaks at both George and Bell Lakes. Killarney Outfitters also rents canoes and kayaks to paddle Chikanishing Creek and stand-up paddleboards at George Lake.

With more than 40 lakes throughout the park, Killarney is a launching point for multiday canoe trips. Killarney Outfitters offers a trip-planning service ($95) that includes suggesting a route, arranging for permits, and preparing a detailed trip plan. They provide gear packages ($99-109 pp per day) for multiday canoe or kayak trips, including canoe or kayak rental, camping gear, and cooking equipment. Another service is a shuttle for canoeists whose excursions start at one point and end at another. Killarney Kanoes can also outfit you for a multiday canoe, kayak, or backpacking adventure.

Based in Parry Sound, **White Squall Paddling Centre** (705/746-4936 or 705/342-5324, www.whitesquall.com) is another outfitter that organizes multiday kayak trips in the Killarney area.

Hiking

Killarney Provincial Park isn't really a beginner's hiking destination, but the park rates several trails "moderate," suitable for people who can manage some steep sections and rocky terrain. Hiking times are estimates only; it's a good idea to talk with park staff before you head out.

Across the highway from the George Lake park office, you can pick up the **Granite Ridge Trail,** which winds through the forest and climbs up to two lookout points, one overlooking Georgian Bay and the other onto the rocky cliffs of La Cloche Range. Allow 1 to 1.25 hours for this moderate two-kilometer (one-mile) loop trail. The longer **Cranberry Bog Trail** (four kilometers, 2.5 miles) starts in the George Lake Campground; the trailhead is near site no. 101. As the name suggests, it passes through bogs and marshes, and then goes along A. Y. Jackson Lake, named for one of the Group of Seven artists. Allow about two hours round-trip.

A short hike that gives you beautiful views of Georgian Bay's rocky shores is the **Chikanishing Trail.** Allow 1 to 1.5 hours for this three-kilometer (1.9-mile) loop that involves some gentle scrambles across massive granite boulders (best save this hike for a dry day, as the rocks can be slippery when wet). The trailhead is at the end of Chikanishing Road, off Highway 637 about two kilometers (1.2 miles) west of George Lake.

For great vistas across the La Cloche Mountains, climb up through the boulders of **The Crack,** a challenging but rewarding trail. This six-kilometer (3.7-mile) route has difficult, rocky sections, and the trail is not a loop, so you must return the same way you came in. Pick up the trail off Highway 637, seven kilometers (4.3 miles) east of the George Lake park office. Save this hike for a clear day to appreciate the awesome views. The trail to The Crack is part of the 100-kilometer (62-mile) **La Cloche Silhouette Trail,** a difficult backpacking route that will take many hikers at least seven days.

On the east side of the park, the **Lake of the Woods Trail** is a 3.5-kilometer (2.2-mile) loop around Lake of the Woods; part of the route crosses a beaver dam. The trail starts from Bell Lake Road, which is off Highway 637, about 21 kilometers (13 miles) east of George Lake or 38 kilometers (24 miles) west of Highway 69.

Skiing and Snowshoeing

The park has more than 30 kilometers (19 miles) of trails for cross-country skiing and snowshoeing. The trails all start at the George Lake Park Office, which also offers snowshoe rentals. You can usually expect plenty of snow December through March.

Art Programs

If Killarney's natural setting inspires you to make art, look for details about the **Artist-in-Residence Program.** Created by the Friends of Killarney Park, this summer program brings an established artist to the park to work and offer classes to visitors. Check with the park office or the Friends of Killarney Park website (www.friendsofkillarneypark.ca) for details about these art experiences.

Camping

Killarney's car-camping area is the **George Lake Campground** (July-mid-Oct. $45, mid-Oct.-June $36), which has 128 campsites, with flush toilets, showers (July-mid-Oct.), and laundry facilities, but no electricity. The most secluded spots are near Second Beach, along Blue Heron Circle, although those sites are also the farthest from the showers.

To reserve a campsite, contact **Ontario Parks Reservations** (888/668-7275, www.ontarioparks.com, reservation fee online $11, by phone $13) up to five months in advance; early reservations are recommended, particularly for summer weekends. Campsites can be reserved from May to October; the rest of the year, sites are first come, first served.

on the Chikanishing Trail, Killarney Provincial Park

The George Lake Campground also has six **yurts** (year-round, $98) and two rustic **cabins** (year-round, $141); all require reservations. Aluminum-framed yurts, sleeping up to six, have two bunk beds with a double lower and single upper bunk, a table and chairs, and heat. The adjacent deck has a propane-fueled barbecue and a bear-proof box for storing your food. It's a few minutes' walk from the yurt parking area (spring-fall); each yurt has a cart for hauling your gear. With a queen bed plus a bunk with a double bed below and single above, the cabins, which have heat for chilly nights, can sleep five; they have a table and chairs and an outdoor grill, too. In winter, you must ski or snowshoe 500 meters (0.3 miles) to the yurts or cabins from the front gate. Toilets and water taps are located a short walk away.

For a true wilderness experience, head for one of Killarney's year-round **backcountry campsites** (705/287-2900, www.ontarioparks.com, adults $12.45, ages 6-17 $5.65). You can hike in to 33 of these sites; another 140 backcountry campsites are accessible only by canoe.

Killarney Outfitters (1076 Hwy. 637, 705/287-2828 or 888/222-3410, www.killarneyoutfitters.com) and **Killarney Kanoes** (1611 Bell Lake, 705/287-2197 or 888/461-4446, www.killarneykanoes.com) rent tents, sleeping bags, and other camping gear.

Village of Killarney

Fewer than 500 people live in the village of Killarney, which is on the harbor 10 kilometers (six miles) west of the provincial park. Until 1962, when Highway 637 was built between Killarney and Highway 69, the only way to get to the village was by water (or in winter, across the ice to Manitoulin Island). Killarney was originally known by its Ojibwa name, Shebahonaning, and many present-day residents have aboriginal roots.

Most of the town's lodgings and services are on or near Channel Street, named for the Killarney Channel, which the street follows.

The nicest time to stroll along the waterfront is in the early evening, as the sun begins to set. The land you see directly across the channel is George Island. Formerly a logging area, the island is now primarily wilderness. You can hike around the island on the 7.5-kilometer (4.7-mile) **George Island Trail,** which is rated moderate to difficult; make sure you have sturdy hiking boots and enough food and water for the day. Both the **Killarney Mountain Lodge** (705/287-2242, www.killarney.com) and the **Sportsman's Inn** (705/287-9990, www.sportsmansinn.ca) arrange boat transportation to and from George Island.

Originally built in 1868 and rebuilt in 1909, the **Killarney East Lighthouse** (Ontario St.) is at the mouth of the channel on the east side of the village. You can hike or swim nearby, and it's especially pretty just before sunset.

FOOD AND ACCOMMODATIONS

Lines are legendary at **Herbert Fisheries** (21 Channel St., 705/287-2214, www.herbertfisheries.ca, 11am-7pm daily May-June and Sept.-Nov., 11am-9pm daily July-Aug., 11am-7pm Sat.-Sun. Feb.-Apr.), which serves first-rate fish-and-chips ($12-19) on the waterfront.

Opposite the harbor, **The Pines Inn** (36 Channel St., 705/287-1068, www.bbcanada.com, $110 d) is a comfortable, old-time lodge open year-round with a busy pub and restaurant. Upstairs, the six simple guest rooms with quilt-covered beds share two baths; washbasins in the rooms help minimize the wait. Owners Paul and Adele Malcew offer a warm welcome, with Paul pouring cold beer behind the bar and Adele cooking bacon-and-eggs breakfasts, burgers, grilled fish, and other home-style fare. Even if you're not staying here, stop in for a drink and a chat; the pub is a local hangout.

At the **Sportsman's Inn** (37 Channel St., 705/287-9990 or 877/333-7510, www.sportsmansinn.ca) on the harbor, there are several different room types, from plain rooms in a separate motel building ($129 d) to more upscale units overlooking the waterfront ($179-199 d) to large two-bedroom suites ($400). The main dining room, the Anchorage, serves straightforward traditional fare, while the pub, Sporto's Grill, which has live music on weekends, sticks with nachos, burgers, and other basics. The inn is now open year-round, under the same ownership as Killarney Mountain Lodge.

A holiday at the waterfront ★ **Killarney Mountain Lodge** (3 Commissioner St., 705/287-2242 or 800/461-1117, www.killarney. com, mid-May-mid-Oct., $75-329 d) feels like summer camp, with activities from canoeing to cycling to paddleboarding. Guests gather in the main lodge on leather couches in front of the massive stone fireplace, out on the garden patio, in lounge chairs at the pool, or on the pink granite rocks by the lake. The most modern guest rooms are the 32 units in the two-story Portage building; the older cabin-style guest units with rustic pine walls are quite small. The 18 budget shared-bath rooms in the Lacloche Building have either a queen bed or bunks for four. The dining room serves three meals daily (various meal plans are available), and there's live music (from 9pm Tues.-Sun.) in the octagonal window-lined **Carousel Bar.**

There's Wi-Fi in the main lodge, but rooms have no phones, TVs, or Internet access.

Information and Services

When you arrive in the Killarney area, stop at the **Killarney Provincial Park** main office (Hwy. 637, 705/287-2900) at George Lake to pick up the free park information guide and ask questions of the park staff. The **Friends of Killarney Park Store** (George Lake Campground, 705/287-2800, www. friendsofkillarneypark.ca, year-round) sells park guides, maps, books, and other souvenirs; they have a second location at Bell Lake. You can order canoeing and hiking guides online—a boon for trip planning—and their useful website has information about park events, hiking trails, and other activities

The **Killarney Outfitters Store** (1076 Hwy. 637, 705/287-2828 or 888/222-3410, www.killarneyoutfitters.com, 8am-8pm daily July-Aug., 8am-5pm daily spring and fall) is located between the village and the main park entrance at George Lake. They sell outdoor clothing and camping supplies; rent canoes, kayaks, and other gear; and arrange a variety of outdoor excursions. **Pitfield's General Store** (7 Channel St., 705/287-2872) sells basic

Killarney Mountain Lodge

groceries and snacks year-round. They also have a coin laundry.

Getting There and Around

CAR

Killarney is 425 kilometers (265 miles) north-west of Toronto, about a 5- to 6-hour drive. Sudbury is the closest city, a 90-minute drive to the north; Parry Sound is two hours' drive to the south. The only road into Killarney is Highway 637, which is off Highway 69 be-tween Parry Sound and Sudbury. From the Highway 69/637 interchange, it's 67 kilo-meters (42 miles) to the village of Killarney, about an hour by car.

While the village of Killarney is only about 20 nautical miles from the eastern tip of Manitoulin Island, there's currently no public boat service between the two. By car, it's a three-hour drive from Killarney to Little Current (220 kilometers, 137 miles). From Killarney, return to Highway 69 and travel north toward Sudbury; then take Highway 17 west to Espanola, where you pick up Highway 6 south, which crosses the bridge to Manitoulin.

BUS

Without a car, the simplest way to travel from Toronto to Killarney is on the **Parkbus** (800/928-7101, www.parkbus.ca, one-way adults $64, seniors and students $58, ages 2-12 $32, round-trip adults $92, seniors and students $83, ages 2-12 $46), which operates on selected weekends in summer and fall. The bus departs from several points in Toronto, including 30 Carlton Street (between Yonge St. and Church St., subway: College) and Dufferin Street at Bloor Street West (subway: Dufferin). The Parkbus picks up and drops off at three points in the Killarney area: Bell Lake, George Lake (at the park headquarters and main campground), and in the village of Killarney.

Manitoulin Island

Bordered by Lake Huron to the west and Georgian Bay to the east, Manitoulin isn't Canada's largest island (that distinction be-longs to Baffin Island). Yet Manitoulin is still tops for its size: It's the largest freshwater is-land in the world.

Don't expect to make a quick loop around Manitoulin in a couple of hours. Measuring 2,765 square kilometers (1,067 square miles), with good but meandering roads, Manitoulin is a place for leisurely exploration. One of the most significant things to explore is the is-land's indigenous culture. Manitoulin and the surrounding mainland region are home to eight First Nations, collectively known as the Anishinaabe people. An innovative aboriginal tourism association, the **Great Spirit Circle Trail,** offers a variety of cultural programs to introduce visitors to local First Nations tradi-tions. The First Nations communities hold tra-ditional **powwows** that welcome visitors, too.

Because the island is so large, consider your interests in deciding where to stay. If you're interested in aboriginal culture, base yourself on the island's eastern half, where you'll be close to more First Nations attractions. For the best beaches, head south; the nicest sandy spot is Providence Bay on the south shore. And if you're looking for a remote getaway, go west, where villages like Gore Bay and Meldrum Bay have comfortable inns.

Scientists believe that millions of years ago, Manitoulin was connected by land to the Bruce Peninsula. Today, the only land ac-cess is from the north, via Highway 6, where a "**swing bridge**"—similar to a drawbridge, except that it swings sideways instead of lift-ing—links the island to the mainland.

Just across the swing bridge onto the is-land is the town of **Little Current.** The small downtown runs along Water Street, with a handful of shops for browsing. You can also

Manitoulin Island

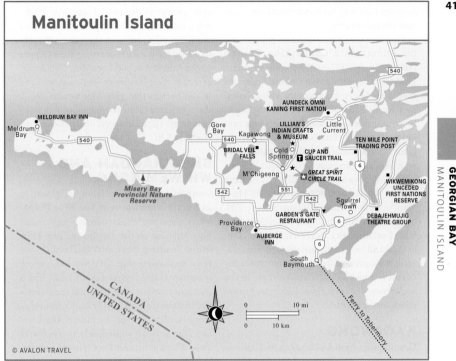

© AVALON TRAVEL

wander along the harbor, which fronts Lake Huron's North Channel, watching the sailboats and the occasional cruise ship.

If you're coming from Toronto and Southern Ontario, the most direct route to Manitoulin is by boat. From mid-May to mid-October, a ferry runs between Tobermory, on the Bruce Peninsula, and South Baymouth, on the southeast corner of Manitoulin Island. The island's high season mirrors the ferry schedule, so when the ferry docks for the winter, many Manitoulin lodgings close and restaurants shut down or reduce their hours.

TOP EXPERIENCE

★ GREAT SPIRIT CIRCLE TRAIL

Based in M'Chigeeng, the **Great Spirit Circle Trail** (5905 Hwy. 540, 705/377-4404 or 877/710-3211, www.circletrail.com), an aboriginal tourism association, offers a number of activities to introduce visitors to First Nations traditions, and several nearby attractions focus on aboriginal culture. The M'Chigeeng First Nation (the *m* is silent) is 34 kilometers (21 miles) southwest of Little Current and 78 kilometers (48 miles) northwest of South Baymouth.

The Great Spirit Circle Trail offers programs that include one- to two-hour introductions to indigenous herbal medicines, First Nations crafts, storytelling, and traditional drumming, as well as longer guided hiking, horseback riding, or canoe experiences. Programs are typically available between late May and early October; call or check the website for details and to make arrangements.

At the **Ojibwe Cultural Foundation and Museum** (15 Hwy. 551, 705/377-4902, www.ojibweculture.ca, 8:30am-4pm Mon.-Fri., 10am-4pm Sat. mid-June-Sept., 8:30am-4pm Mon.-Fri. Oct.-mid-June, donation), exhibits focus on First Nations history and contemporary aboriginal arts.

Opposite the Ojibwe Cultural Foundation, the **Immaculate Conception Church** (Hwy. 551, 705/377-4985, donation) mixes First Nations and Roman Catholic religious traditions. The round structure with a conical roof recalls a traditional tepee; on the bright blue front door, a yellow sun with four rays in the shape of a cross is an indigenous religious symbol. Inside, look for other aboriginal paintings and carvings.

Part shop and part gallery, **Lillian's Indian Crafts and Museum** (5950 Hwy. 540, 705/377-4987, www.lilliansindiancrafts.com, 10am-6pm Mon.-Fri., 10am-5pm Sat.-Sun., free) displays a local First Nations craft: baskets and boxes intricately woven from colorful porcupine quills. Make sure you see the exhibits done by master craftspeople in the back room. The front room sells more typical aboriginal souvenirs.

KAGAWONG

Heading west from M'Chigeeng on Highway 540, you reach Kagawong, a cute village whose Ojibwa name means "where mists rise from the falling waters." It's a fitting moniker, since the town's main attraction is **Bridal Veil Falls,** where you can splash under the waterfall. Stairs lead from a parking area down to the falls, and a walking path follows the riverbank from the falls into the village.

If you need a break after playing in the falls, don't worry—there's chocolate. **Manitoulin Chocolate Works** (160 Main St., 705/282-0961, www.manitoulinchocolate.ca, 10am-5:30pm Mon.-Sat., 11am-5pm Sun. July-Aug., 10am-5pm Tues.-Sat., 11am-4pm Sun. May-June and Sept.-Dec.) crafts chocolates and other confections in a former village blacksmith shop. They sell coffee, tea, and hot chocolate, too.

GORE BAY

Longtime friends Eleanor Charlton and Andrea Smith launched **Split Rail Brewing Company** (31 Water St., 705/370-8284, www.

splitrailmanitoulin.com, 11am-5pm Wed.-Sat.), one of Canada's few women-owned craft breweries, opposite the harbor in Gore Bay. Visit the tasting room to try their Copper Lager, Amber Ale, and LoonSong Oats Stout, as well as their Hawberry Ale, made with the island berries that give Manitoulin locals the nickname "Haweaters." Gore Bay is 19 kilometers (12 miles) west of Kagawong, off Highway 540.

SHEGUIANDAH AND WIKWEMIKONG

South of Little Current along Highway 6, stop at the **Viewpoint at Ten Mile Point,** where vistas stretch east across Sheguiandah Bay. Adjacent to the viewpoint, **Ten Mile Point Trading Post and Gallery** (12164 Hwy. 6, Sheguiandah, 705/368-2377, www.tenmilepointtradingpost.com) looks like a standard souvenir shop, but amid the T-shirts and trinkets are high-quality works, from jewelry to leather to prints, by First Nations artists. They also carry a large selection of books about Manitoulin and First Nations culture, including books for kids.

On the peninsula jutting out from Manitoulin's eastern shore is the **Wikwemikong Unceded First Nations Reserve**—"unceded" because the group never agreed to any treaty that would give title of its land to the government. It's Canada's only officially recognized unceded aboriginal reserve. The Wikwemikong offer a variety of tours and cultural experiences, including walking tours and canoe excursions. Contact the **Wikwemikong Tourism Information Center** (888/801-9422, www.wikwemikong.ca) for details.

If you visit during July or August, don't miss a production by the **Debajehmujig Theatre Group** (office: 8 Debajehmujig Lane, 705/859-2317, www.debaj.ca). They perform works with aboriginal themes in the ruins of Wikwemikong's Holy Cross Mission and host other theater, music, and art events at their **Debajehmujig Creation Centre** (43 Queen St., Manitowaning, 705/859-1820).

Planning to Powwow

One of the most interesting ways to experience aboriginal culture is to attend a traditional pow-wow, a festival that encompasses dance, music, and food. And one of Ontario's best places to find powwows is on Manitoulin Island.

WHERE TO POWWOW

Manitoulin's largest and longest-running powwow is the **Wikwemikong Cultural Festival and Powwow** (www.wikwemikongheritage.org), held annually in early August on the Wikwemikong Reserve on the island's east side. Most of Manitoulin's other First Nations communities hold annual traditional powwows as well, including the **Aundeck Omni Kaning** (June), **Sheguiandah** (July), and **M'Chigeeng** (late Aug. or early Sept.). Get a powwow schedule and details about any of these events from the **Great Spirit Circle Trail office** (705/377-4404 or 877/710-3211, www.circletrail.com).

POWWOW ETIQUETTE

Traditional powwows are generally open to the public, and most are free, although donations are accepted. Competition powwows often charge admission of $10-15. A master of ceremonies leads the powwow and explains the dances and ceremonies. You can purchase food and traditional crafts on-site. Powwows are alcohol-free events.

During certain ceremonial songs or dances, photography and video recording are prohibited; the master of ceremonies will usually explain when these ceremonies are taking place. At other times, you may take photos or videos, but it's polite to ask for permission first, particularly when you're photographing a dancer in traditional regalia. Because many believe that the regalia (which should never be called "costumes") have their own spirit, and frequently are handmade or passed down from an ancestor, you should never touch the regalia either.

To learn more about powwow customs and etiquette, request a copy of the Great Spirit Circle Trail's *Powwow Guide* (705/377-4404 or 877/710-3211, www.circletrail.com).

Miigwetch (Thank you)!

SPORTS AND RECREATION
Hiking

One of Manitoulin's most popular hikes is the **Cup and Saucer Trail** (Hwy. 540 at Bidwell Rd., dawn-dusk daily mid-May-mid-Oct.), which climbs the Niagara Escarpment to spectacular lookouts from the 70-meter (230-foot) cliffs. This 12-kilometer (7.5-mile) route is divided into several shorter trails, including the optional two-kilometer (1.2-mile) adventure trail, which takes hikers up and down ladders and along narrow ledges to a viewpoint overlooking the North Channel. The trailhead is 18 kilometers (11 miles) west of Little Current, just north of M'Chigeeng.

A fascinating way to explore the Cup and Saucer Trail is on a **Mother Earth Nature Hike,** (2.5-3 hours, $49.50 pp), led by an indigenous guide who will help you identify local plants and understand how they're used in aboriginal medicine and cooking. Contact the **Great Spirit Circle Trail** (705/377-4404 or 877/710-3211, www.circletrail.com) to book.

Legend has it that, back in the 1880s, a farmer was cutting grass in southwest Manitoulin when two men approached and asked the place's name. "Misery," the hot, tired farmer called it, and the name stuck. Today, it's the antithesis of misery for hikers who stroll the 15 kilometers (nine miles) of trails in the **Misery Bay Provincial Nature Reserve** (400 Misery Bay Park Rd., 705/966-2315, www.ontarioparks.com and www.miserybay.ca, 10am-5pm daily July-early Sept., 10am-5pm Sat.-Sun. mid-May-June, adults $2, ages 6-17 $1). The park visitors center has exhibits about the area's geological and natural features, which include its wetlands and its alvar ecosystem, a rare type of flat rock landscape found primarily in the Great Lakes region. You can follow a 1.3-kilometer (0.8-mile) trail to a **swimming beach.** The Misery Bay turnoff is 35 kilometers (22 miles) west of Gore Bay along Highway 540.

Beaches

Although Manitoulin is ringed with beaches, the best sandy spots are on the south shore, west of South Baymouth. And the best of the best? **Providence Bay Beach,** a long strip of soft sand along Lake Huron, backed by swaying grasses and a boardwalk trail. The beach's Harbour Centre building (spring-fall) has restrooms, a small exhibit area about the local history and environment, and **Huron Island Time,** an ice cream and snack shop.

In eastern Manitoulin, off Highway 6 between Sheguiandah and Manitowaning, is the largest of the island's 108 freshwater lakes, Lake Manitou.

FOOD AND ACCOMMODATIONS

Manitoulin lodgings include cottages, B&Bs, small inns, and summer camp-style resorts. No chains or megaresorts have set up shop yet. It's a good idea to book ahead, especially in July and August. Manitoulin isn't a fine-dining destination—it's much easier to find burgers and fish-and-chips than a gourmet meal—but most towns have someplace to get a bite.

Little Current

The take-out counter at **Island Jar** (15 Water St., 705/368-1881, www.theislandjar.ca, 9am-7pm Mon.-Fri., 9am-5pm Sat. May-Sept., 10am-3pm Sun., 10am-6pm Mon., 10am-5pm Tues.-Fri., 10am-4pm Sun. Oct.-Apr.), a small organic grocery, whips up smoothies, salads, and sandwiches from chicken to hummus.

Have coffee and check your email at **Loco Beanz** (7 Water St., 705/368-2261, 7am-5pm Mon.-Fri., 8am-4pm Sat., 8am-3pm Sun.), a cheery café with free Wi-Fi. They have other island locations in Gore Bay (50 Meredith St., 705/282-0007, 7am-4:30pm Mon.-Sat., 7am-2pm Sun.) and in Manitowaning (109 Arthur St., 705/859-3722, 7:30am-5:30pm Mon.-Thurs., 7:30am-7pm Fri., 8am-5pm Sat.).

The Great Spirit Circle Trail runs the 57-room **Manitoulin Hotel and Conference Centre** (66 Meredith St. E., 705/368-9966 or 855/368-9966, www.manitoulinhotel.com or www.circletrail.com, $225-235 d), near

summer fun on Providence Bay Beach

Stay in a teepee on Manitoulin Island.

the swing bridge. The expansive lobby overlooking the channel is modeled after a First Nations gathering place, and the guest rooms are decorated with light wood furnishings and First Nations motifs. Amenities include Keurig coffeemakers, flat-screen TVs, and free Wi-Fi.

Both sailors and landlubbers wash into the **Anchor Inn** (1 Water St., 705/368-2023, www. anchorgrill.com, 7am-11pm daily July-Aug., call for off-season hours, lunch $7-27, dinner $8-28) for a beer or for chow that ranges from burgers and sandwiches to steaks and fish plates. Upstairs, the inn has several simple rooms ($50-70 d) and apartments ($80-90 d), although light sleepers should note that rooms over the bar can be noisy, particularly on weekends when bands are playing.

Aundeck Omni Kaning

On this First Nations reserve off Highway 540, five kilometers (three miles) west of Little Current, **Endaa-aang "Our Place"** (705/368-0548, www.aokfn.com) rents four well-kept cabins in parklike grounds near the North Channel waterfront. The wood-paneled cabins sleep six, with a double bedroom, a twin-bed room, and a living room with a sofa bed; they have full kitchens as well as decks with barbecues. Also on the property are **tepee rentals.** Tepees sleep eight but are unfurnished. Bring sleeping bags and other camping gear; restrooms are nearby. Guests can use the reserve's beach along the North Channel, but it's otherwise not open to the public.

M'Chigeeng

A convenient place to eat before or after you visit the Circle Trail or the Ojibwe Cultural Foundation, **Seasons Family Restaurant** (72 Hwy. 551, 705/377-4344, 8am-7:30pm Mon.-Sat., 9am-7:30pm Sun., $5-15) serves bacon and eggs, sandwiches, and other family-style dishes.

Spirit Island Adventures (5905 Hwy. 540, 705/377-4404 or 877/710-3211, www. circletrail.com) rents several furnished **tepees** (May-Oct., $155 d) on the Great Spirit Circle Trail's M'Chigeeng property where visitors can stay. Tepees have propane fire pits to provide heat, and washrooms are a short walk away.

Tehkummah

One of the island's best restaurants is in the countryside 26 kilometers (16 miles) north of South Baymouth. In a house at the end of a garden path, ★ **Garden's Gate Restaurant** (312 Hwy. 542, Tehkummah, 705/859-2088 or 888/959-2088, www.gardensgate.ca, from 5pm Tues.-Sun. May-June and Sept.-Oct., from 5pm daily July-Aug., $16-28), with its floral tablecloths and cozy screened porch, looks grandmotherly, but the food—updated country fare made with fresh local ingredients—is first-rate. Fish is a specialty, and the menu always includes vegetarian options. Save room for the homemade pie.

Providence Bay

What's a day at the beach without fish-and-chips? **Lake Huron Fish and Chips** (20

McNevin St., 705/377-4500, late May-Sept.) is just inland from Providence Bay.

A five-minute walk from Providence Bay Beach, the **Auberge Inn** (71 McNevin St., 705/377-4392 or 877/977-4392, www.aubergeinn.ca, year-round, $40 dorm, $98-142 d), the island's only hostel, is a friendly place with three bunk beds, each with a keyed locker, in a dorm. There are also two private rooms, one with a double bed and one with a queen bed and two bunks. Guests share a large bath upstairs and can use the common kitchen. Rates include self-serve continental breakfast and Wi-Fi.

Gore Bay

Buoys Eatery (1 Purvis Dr., off Water St., 705/282-2869, www.buoyseatery.com, lunch and dinner daily May-Oct., $10-32) looks like an ordinary fish shack (albeit with a lovely deck), but the two specialties make it worth the stop: fish and wedges (local whitefish paired with thick slices of roasted potato) and pizzas with either traditional or out-of-the-ordinary toppings; the Greek Obsession sports *tzatziki* sauce, gyro meat, feta cheese, and olives.

One of Manitoulin's most elegant accommodations is **The Queen's Inn Bed-and-Breakfast** (19 Water St., 705/282-0665, www.thequeensinn.ca, May-Dec., $120-140 s, $155-180 d), overlooking the harbor in Gore Bay. Built in the late 1800s, this Victorian manor has a formal antiques-filled parlor and a saloon-turned-breakfast-room where a hot morning meal is served. On the second and third floors are eight Victorian-style guest rooms, five with private baths. Sit on either of the two verandas to enjoy the harbor views.

Meldrum Bay

To get way, way away from it all, book a stay at the family-run **Meldrum Bay Inn** (25959 Hwy. 540, 705/283-3190 or 877/577-1645, www.meldrumbayinn.com, year-round, $140-180 d), in an 1878 wood-frame building with a wide front porch, overlooking the water on Manitoulin's far west end. Seven simple rooms share two baths; rates include continental breakfast. The home-style dining room (5pm-8pm late May-mid-Sept., dinner $18-27) specializes in local whitefish and barbecue ribs. Meldrum Bay is 167 circuitous kilometers (104 miles) from South Baymouth and 134 kilometers (83 miles) from Little Current; allow at least two hours from the island's east side.

INFORMATION AND SERVICES

Just over the swing bridge, stop into the **Manitoulin Tourism Association Welcome Centre** (70 Meredith St. E./Hwy. 6, Little Current, 705/368-3021, www.manitoulintourism.com), where obliging staff provide maps and brochures, book ferry reservations, and offer advice about things to do and places to stay. Their website is an excellent resource for planning your island visit. If you arrive on the ferry, pick up maps and brochures at the **ferry terminal information center** (41 Water St., South Baymouth, 705/859-3161).

For information about aboriginal tourism on Manitoulin, contact the **Great Spirit Circle Trail** (5905 Hwy. 540, M'Chigeeng, 705/377-4404 or 877/710-3211, www.circletrail.com). The **Wikwemikong Tourism Information Center** (888/801-9422, www.wikwemikong.ca) can tell you about activities on the Wikwemikong Reserve.

Getting There
FERRY

From Toronto or other Southern Ontario destinations, the quickest way to Manitoulin is by ferry from the Bruce Peninsula. The **MS Chi-Cheemaun Ferry** (800/265-3163, www.ontarioferries.com, mid-May-mid-Oct., one-way adults $16.50, seniors $14.25, ages 5-11 $8.25, cars $27.75-45)—its Ojibwa name means "The Big Canoe"—makes the two-hour run between Tobermory and South Baymouth several times daily. Discounts are available for families and for same-day returns. Make a reservation if you're taking a car; a $15 reservation fee applies to many sailings.

CAR

By road, it's a long slog—about 510 kilometers (320 miles) from Toronto to Manitoulin. After taking Highway 400/69 north toward Sudbury, it's still 90 minutes farther on Highway 17 west and Highway 6 south to Manitoulin's **swing bridge.** In summer, every hour on the hour (dawn-dusk), the bridge swings sideways to allow boats to pass, halting road traffic for 15 minutes. The bridge is only one lane, so even when it's open, traffic alternates in each direction. Don't be in a rush to make the crossing.

GETTING AROUND

Highway 6 runs along the island's east side between Little Current and South Baymouth, passing Sheguiandah and Wikwemikong en route. From Little Current, Highway 540 goes west to M'Chigeeng, Kagawong, Gore Bay, and Meldrum Bay. From South Baymouth to M'Chigeeng, take Highway 6 north to Highway 542 west, then, at Mindemoya, pick up Highway 551 north to M'Chigeeng. To Providence Bay, turn south onto Highway 551. For Gore Bay, continue west on Highway 542.

Manitoulin has no public transportation. If you're an avid cyclist able to ride fairly long distances, **bicycling** is a reasonable way to tour the island. From South Baymouth, it's 30 kilometers (19 miles) to Providence Bay and 62 kilometers (39 miles) to Little Current. For cycling tips, check with the **Manitoulin Tourism Association** (705/368-3021, www.manitoulintourism.com).

Lake Superior

Biggest, deepest, longest—Northern Ontario is a place of geographical superlatives, and the region encompassing Lake Superior is no exception. Not only is Superior the deepest of the five Great Lakes, it is the largest body of fresh water in the world. No wonder it's frequently called an inland sea. Unless you taste the salt-free water as you listen to the waves crashing on the shores of this immense lake, which stretches 560 kilometers (350 miles) from end to end and 260 kilometers (160 miles) across, you'd swear you were looking out across the ocean.

Lake Superior's land borders include not just Ontario, but the U.S. states of Minnesota, Wisconsin, and Michigan, and a popular driving route circles the lake on both sides of the international boundary. On the Ontario shores, connected by the Trans-Canada Highway, two cities bookend the Lake Superior region: Sault Ste. Marie to the east and Thunder Bay in the west. While each has several worthwhile attractions and a diverse cultural heritage stretching from the aboriginal peoples to more recent immigrant Italians, Scandinavians, and Asians, it's the landscape and outdoor activities outside the metropolitan areas—on land and on the water—that make Lake Superior special.

From Sault Ste. Marie, you can take a one-day rail journey into the wilderness of Agawa Canyon. North and west of the Sault, the shores of Lake Superior are lined with spectacular beaches, canoe or kayak routes, and rocky cliffs crisscrossed with hiking trails, many in beautiful provincial parks and in Ontario's largest national park. From Thunder Bay, you can make day trips into nearby parks to wander amid waterfalls, canyons, and dramatic foliage, especially when the autumn leaves turn red and gold.

Lake Superior figures prominently in art and literature, from paintings by Canada's Group of Seven to the 19th-century epic poem, *The Song of Hiawatha,* that Henry Wadsworth Longfellow set "By the shores of Gitche Gumee" (from the lake's Ojibwa name, *Gichigami*). Whether on foot, with a paddle, or behind the wheel, or with your own camera,

---

Previous: rocky shores in Pukaskwa National Park; road-tripping through Lake Superior Provincial Park.
Above: Fort St. Joseph National Historic Site.

Look for ★ to find recommended
sights, activities, dining, and lodging.

Highlights

★ **Agawa Canyon Tour Train:** A car-free day trip into the northern wilderness, this rail journey is particularly spectacular during the fall foliage season (page 426).

★ **Lake Superior Provincial Park:** One of Ontario's most beautiful outdoor destinations, this provincial park extends along the eastern shore of the world's largest body of fresh water. You'll find sandy beaches, rocky coves, rugged hiking trails, and even ancient rock paintings (page 431).

★ **Pukaskwa National Park:** Explore First Nations culture at Ontario's largest national park, where you can also hike and paddle amid stunning Lake Superior terrain (page 436).

★ **Fort William Historical Park:** Journey back to the time of the voyageurs and their indigenous trading partners at this re-created early-1800s fur-trading post near Thunder Bay (page 446).

★ **Sleeping Giant Provincial Park:** Jutting into the lake across the harbor from Thunder Bay, this craggy, forested park has more than 100 kilometers (60 miles) of hiking trails, including the challenging "Top of the Giant," which rewards hikers with expansive cliff-top vistas (page 453).

★ **Ouimet Canyon Provincial Park:** Carved by natural forces over millions of years, Ouimet Canyon spans a 150-meter (495-foot) gorge with jagged cliffs on either side and lookout points high above the canyon floor (page 455).

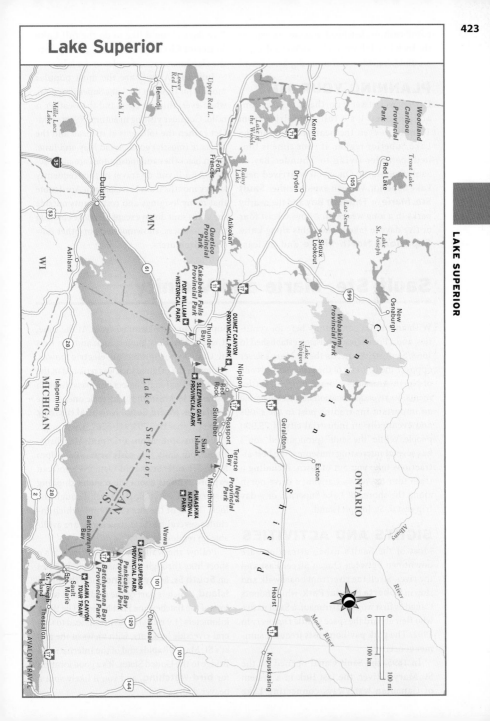

Lake Superior

© AVALON TRAVEL

paintbrush, or sketchpad, you too can explore the rock-lined shores and wooded landscapes around Longfellow's "shining Big-Sea-Water."

PLANNING YOUR TIME

Distances between northern destinations are long, and it's a full day's drive from Toronto to even the nearest points in the Lake Superior region. If your time is limited, consider flying to Thunder Bay or Sault Ste. Marie. Once you've arrived near Lake Superior, you can explore either **Sault Ste. Marie** or **Thunder Bay** and the nearby parks in a long weekend. Allow at least four or five days to take in the sights along **Lake Superior's North Shore** and at least

7-10 days if you'd like to do the full **Lake Superior Circle Route,** encompassing both the Canadian and U.S. sides of the lake.

July and August are the most popular months for travel in the Lake Superior region, when everything is open and the weather is mild. Consider visiting in autumn (Sept.-mid-Oct.) when the foliage is at its peak and the bugs are (mostly) gone. Avoid May and June, when blackflies and mosquitoes are most active. And if you do travel in the frequently snowy months from November to April, note that many lodgings and restaurants outside the cities shut down except for those catering to snowshoers, snowmobilers, or other outdoor adventurers.

Sault Ste. Marie and Vicinity

With an Ojibwa community here for centuries, and a French Jesuit mission established in 1668, Sault Ste. Marie, on the St. Mary's River opposite the U.S. city of the same name, is one of North America's oldest European settlements. Its riverside location helped it become an important fur-trading post in the 1700s and eventually an industrial city of 75,000 people. While "the Sault" (pronounced "soo") has several interesting museums, the best attractions take you out of town, including a train tour to Agawa Canyon, a drive north along the shores of Lake Superior, or a day trip east to St. Joseph Island.

SIGHTS AND ACTIVITIES

Most of the Sault's urban attractions are downtown between Queen Street East and the river. Stroll the riverfront boardwalk and stop in **Roberta Bondar Park,** which honors Canada's first woman astronaut, a Sault native who flew aboard the space shuttle *Discovery* in 1992. The park pavilion hosts frequent summer concerts.

In 1895, the Sault Canal opened on the St. Mary's River, the last link in a system of Canadian waterways connecting Lake

Superior to the Atlantic Ocean. At the time, it was the world's longest lock and the first in Canada to operate on electric power. Although the original lock was replaced in the 1990s, recreational boaters now pass through a smaller lock within the historic one. At the **Sault Ste. Marie Canal National Historic Site** (1 Canal Dr., 705/941-6262, www.pc.gc. ca, 10am-5pm Mon.-Fri. mid-May-June, 10am-5pm daily July-early Sept., 10am-4pm Mon.-Fri. early Sept.-mid-Oct., free), you can explore exhibits about the region's shipping history and watch boats travel through the lock. Tours of the site ($5.80 pp), which includes several historic structures, are available on request.

Follow the walkway over the lock for a short hike through the grasses and marshes on **South St. Mary's Island** and **Whitefish Island**, which is part of the traditional territory of the Batchewana First Nation. The three kilometers (1.9 miles) of easy trails lead to several riverside lookouts, with views of the river's St. Mary's Rapids and of the International Bridge to the United States. It's a good location for **bird-watching,** and you'll likely spot a beaver dam or two.

Sault Ste. Marie

Two unusual historic buildings and a modern heritage center constitute the **Ermatinger-Clergue National Historic Site** (800 Bay St., 705/759-5443, www.ecnhs. com, 9:30am-4:30pm daily late May-mid-Oct., 9:30am-4:30pm Tues.-Sat. mid-Oct-late May, adults $12, seniors and ages 6 and older, $10). In the Heritage Discovery Centre, a worthwhile 20-minute film illustrates the Sault's history, first as a fur-trading outpost and later as an industrial community, bringing to life the stories of the two businessmen whose residences now sit on the site. The stately, Georgian-style Old Stone House, built in 1814, was home to wealthy fur trader Charles Oakes Ermatinger, his Ojibwa wife, Mananowe (Charlotte), and their 13 children. Next door is the Clergue Blockhouse, a replica of a frontier fort cantilevered above a former gunpowder

magazine. Francis Hector Clergue, an industrialist and (ultimately failed) entrepreneur, had this odd structure built in 1895 as his home and office. Costumed interpreters guide you through both buildings and detail 19th-century local life.

Small, rugged aircraft known as bush planes traditionally provided a vital transportation link throughout Northern Ontario, offering access to regions with few roads. At the **Canadian Bushplane Heritage Centre** (50 Pim St., 705/945-6242 or 877/287-4752, www.bushplane.com, 9am-6pm daily mid-May-mid-Oct., 10am-4pm daily mid-Oct.-mid-May; adults $12, seniors $11, students $7, children $3), in a cavernous former air service hangar, you can learn about the importance of these planes past and present and have some fun, too. Climb aboard several of the 25 historic airplanes, check out exhibits on fighting forest fires, or take a video flight tour of Agawa Canyon.

The waterfront **Art Gallery of Algoma** (10 East St., 705/949-9067, www. artgalleryofalgoma.ca, 9am-5pm Tues.-Sat., adults $7, students $5) has three galleries with rotating contemporary art exhibits that showcase established and emerging regional artists. Among the permanent collection are works by Group of Seven artists and aboriginal artists such as Norval Morrisseau. The gallery shop sells jewelry, cards, and other pieces, many by Northern Ontario artists.

★ Agawa Canyon Tour Train

In 1918, artists Lawren Harris, J. E. H. MacDonald, and Frank Johnston rented a boxcar in which to travel and paint along the Algoma Central Railway, which runs north from Sault Ste. Marie into Agawa Canyon and beyond. These painters, along with several colleagues who later joined them, became known as the Group of Seven, creating and exhibiting the works that these wilderness sojourns inspired.

You don't have to travel by boxcar to explore the same scenery that motivated these artists. Book a seat on the **Agawa Canyon Train** (Algoma Central Railway, 129 Bay St., 705/946-7300 or 800/242-9287, www. agawatrain.com, daily late June-mid-Oct., summer prices adults $92, seniors $82, ages 2-18 $46, fall prices adults and senior $110, ages 2-18 $76), a one-day trip into the wilderness.

Agawa Canyon is tiny compared to Arizona's Grand Canyon or Mexico's Copper Canyon, but with a river winding amid the trees and below the rock walls, it's an attractive—and car-free—destination. The most popular times for the trip are the last two weeks of September and the first week of October, when fall colors typically peak.

After the train pulls out of Sault station at 8am, beginning the four-hour, 184-kilometer (114-mile) ride north, the city's mills and factories give way to forests, hills, and lake after lake. At Mile 92, the train crosses a curved trestle bridge over the Montreal River; near Mile 102, look left and you can see all the way to Lake Superior. You can take in the "engineer's view," too; cameras mounted on the engine periodically project onto monitors inside the coaches. Recorded commentary tells you about other scenic spots en route.

Passengers disembark at the canyon, where they have about 90 minutes to explore before

the Clergue Blockhouse at the Ermatinger-Clergue National Historic Site

Three Days in Sault Ste. Marie

DAY 1

Sault Ste. Marie is an excellent base for outdoor adventures, offering a diverse set of activities within day-tripping distance of downtown. Even if you spend your first day in the city, there's plenty to do outside. Tour the **Sault Ste. Marie Canal National Historic Site,** watch a ship travel through the historic locks, and go for a walk on nearby **Whitefish Island,** a traditional First Nations territory. After your stroll, have brunch at **The Breakfast Pig** and then spend the afternoon on a guided **fishing adventure** along the St. Mary's River. Even if you've never held a rod, local guides can show you what to do. Share your fish stories over a dinner of the locally famous broasted chicken at **Muio's.**

DAY 2

Get to the train station early this morning, ready for your 8am departure on the **Agawa Canyon Tour Train,** a full-day trip through the wilderness terrain that inspired Ontario's early-20th-century landscape artists, the Group of Seven. When the train pulls into the canyon, hike up to the lookout or walk to the waterfalls. You'll be back in the city by 6pm. In the evening, choose among the city's many pizza spots—**Mrs. B's** and **Fratelli's** are both popular—or if you'd rather a more upscale Italian dinner, try **Solo Trattoria** or **Quattro Vinotecca.**

DAY 3

Today, you're exploring **Lake Superior Provincial Park,** northwest of the city. Along the way, take a break in Batchawana Bay for an abundant breakfast at **Voyageurs' Lodge and Cookhouse;** if you're not ready for a full meal, grab one of their giant apple fritters to go.

When you get to the provincial park, your first stop should be the **Agawa Bay Visitors Centre** to see the well-designed exhibit center. Continue north of the Visitors Centre, and if the lake is calm enough, follow the short but steep trail to the **Agawa Rock Pictographs,** red ocher graphics that Ojibwa people painted several hundred years ago; it remains a sacred site for local First Nations people. Other park highlights are scenic **Katherine Cove** and **Old Woman Bay,** both along the Lake Superior shore.

If you're continuing north and west along Lake Superior, stop for dinner in **Wawa** at **Kinniwabi Pines International Restaurant,** where the kitchen prepares dishes from the owners' native Trinidad, and then stay the night nearby. Otherwise, return to Sault Ste. Marie with ample memories and plenty of photos of your three days adventuring outdoors.

the return train leaves. The prettiest hike climbs 320 steps up the **Lookout Trail** (30-40 minutes round-trip), the best vantage point for photos over the canyon. The flatter **Bridal Veil Falls Trail** (30 minutes round-trip) goes to the 68.5-meter (225-foot) waterfall of the same name. As you walk back from the falls, take the path across the train tracks (carefully) to follow the **Black Beaver Falls Trail** to a second, smaller waterfall. If you don't dawdle, you should have time to see both the lookout and the falls.

The train's dining car begins serving breakfast shortly after the morning departure and is open for lunch until late afternoon. You're also welcome to bring your own food to eat en route or picnic at the canyon. However, you may prefer to eat on the train and use the relatively brief canyon stopover to explore. The train returns to Sault Ste. Marie around 6pm.

SPORTS AND RECREATION
Hiking

Take a short hike through the forests of maples, white pines, and other trees at **Hiawatha Highlands Conservation Area** (1100 5th Line E., 705-946-8530, www.ssmrca.ca, 9am-9pm daily, free). In the Kinsman Park section of the conservation

Side Trip: St. Joseph Island

The second-largest freshwater island in the world after Manitoulin, rural St. Joseph is dotted with farms, beaches, and two tiny villages, Richards Landing and Hilton Beach, where you can stop for a bite to eat. The St. Joseph turnoff from Highway 17 is just 45 kilometers (28 miles) east of downtown, making it a leisurely day trip from the Sault.

The island's main attraction is **Fort St. Joseph National Historic Site** (Fort Rd., 705/246-2664, www.pc.gc.ca, 10am-5pm Wed.-Sun. June and early-Sept.-mid-Sept., 10am-5pm daily July-early Sept., adults $3.90, seniors $3.40). The British built the fort in the 1790s; the Americans burned it to the ground during the War of 1812. What remains are the excavated ruins of the fort buildings, from the powder magazine to the kitchen to a surprisingly intact chimney.

The Visitors Centre exhibits detail life in this remote outpost and the alliances between the British and the First Nations; guided tours are available ($4). You can also hike the trails around the property. Note that the fort overlooks the lakeshore on St. Joseph's southwestern tip, a meandering 37-kilometer (23-mile) drive from the island bridge.

North of the fort, another scenic strolling spot is the lovely **Adcocks' Woodland Gardens** (4757 5th Side Rd., 705/246-2579, www.adcockswoodlandgardens.com, dawn-dusk daily, donation), part cultivated grounds and part wild woods.

area, a pretty walk takes you along a boardwalk and up a staircase to Crystal Falls. Hiawatha Highlands is 12 kilometers (7.5 miles) northeast of downtown.

Northwest of the city, **Lake Superior Provincial Park** (Hwy. 17, 705/856-2284, www.ontarioparks.com or www.lakesuperiorpark.ca, mid-May-mid-Oct., $14.50 per vehicle) has an extensive network of hiking trails.

Fishing

Have you always wanted to learn to fish? Try your hand at hooking a big one without even leaving the city by booking a guided **fishing** excursion on the St. Mary's River. Several local operators offer half- or full-day fishing packages, both on the river and on the lakes throughout the Algoma region.

Adam Valee is a competitive tournament bass fisher and fishing guide. Through his company **Angling Algoma** (705/943-5286, www.anglingalgoma.com), he'll take you out on the river, show you how to cast, and point out where the largemouth bass are hiding. And while he's a pro, he's patient with beginners. He can arrange half-day (1-2 people $300, each additional person $75) or full-day

(1-2 people $475, each additional person $75) river trips.

Other local fishing guides include **Tyler Dunn Guiding** (705/206-0984, www.tylerdunnguiding.ca) and **John Giuliani's Fishing Adventures** (906/203-9112, www.stmarysrapidsguiding.com). For guidance in booking a fishing adventure, contact **Sault Ste. Marie Tourism** (705/759-5442 or 800/461-6020, www.saulttourism.com), which works with several of these local companies and periodically offers discounted fishing packages.

FOOD

Dining options are plentiful around Queen Street East downtown and amid Great Northern Road's strip malls. The city has a large Italian population, which makes Italian eating a good choice; finding the best pizza is a competitive sport.

The cheery vibe at **Vibe Eatery & Juice Co** (112 March St., 705/949-8423, vibeeatery.ca, 8am-6pm Mon.-Wed., 8am-8pm Thurs.-Fri., 9am-6pm Sat., 10am-4pm Sun., $6-15) draws diners to this vegetarian café on a downtown side street for light breakfasts and lunches, from fresh juices, smoothies, and muffins to salads, beet burgers, and falafel wraps.

Calling itself a "badass eatery," **The Breakfast Pig** (265 Bruce St., 705/450-6911, www.thebreakfastpig.com, 8am-4pm daily, $10-15) dishes out substantial morning meals featuring local ingredients; all their pork products come from a nearby farm. Among the specialties: "The Angela" (named for the owner), a veggie-filled, balsamic-glazed potato hash with poached eggs on top; waffle poutine, a serving of deep-fried waffles piled with mozzarella, gravy, and pulled pork; and eggs Benedict with locally caught smoked trout.

Popular with everyone from young folks on dates to old folks on pensions, ★ **Muio's** (685 Queen St. E., 705/254-7105, www.muios.com, 7am-close daily, lunch $5-12, dinner $11-24) is so retro, it's hip. The must-have dish is the "broasted" chicken (the Sault's version of southern fried chicken), which comes as chicken on a bun or as a heaping platter with potatoes and salad or coleslaw. The ravioli is another favorite, and other options include pizza, burgers, and steaks. Breakfast is served as well.

Looking for classic Italian downtown? **Solo Trattoria** (250 Queen St. E., 705/254-7656, www.solotrattoria.ca, 11am-10pm Mon.-Sat., lunch $9-15, dinner $14-30) serves up grilled panini and salads midday, pastas, seafood, and steaks in the evenings, and pizza all the time.

Among pizza partisans, popular picks include **Mrs. B's** (76 East St., 705/942-9999, www.mrsbspizza.ca, 11am-10pm Mon.-Thurs., 11am-11:30pm Fri.-Sat., noon-7pm Sun., $7-27) in a bright red building downtown, with a second location (97 Great Northern Rd., 705/575-7522) open the same hours, and **Fratelli's** (522 Great Northern Rd., 705/256-1313, www.fratellisrestaurant.ca, 11:30am-11pm Mon.-Sat., 11:30am-10pm Sun., $9-29), which also makes tasty *panzarotti,* Ontario's version of a calzone.

For a classy evening out, meat lovers head for **The Mill Steakhouse + Wine Bar** (83 Huron St., 705/942-3051, www.machineshopinc.ca, 11am-10pm Sun.-Thurs., 11am-midnight Fri.-Sat., lunch $10-15, dinner $22-40) near the Sault Canal. It's set in a former machine shop built in the late 1890s and retains its exposed brick walls, ceiling pipes, and other industrial features. The evening menu leans heavily toward classic steaks paired with potatoes and vegetables. At lunch, choose from burgers, steak sandwiches, and salads.

Finding the best pizza is a competitive sport in Sault Ste. Marie.

ACCOMMODATIONS

The city's most upscale lodging is the riverfront **Delta Sault Ste. Marie Waterfront Hotel** (208 St. Mary's River Dr., 705/949-0611 or 888/236-2427, www.marriott.com, $128-260 d), where many of the 195 contemporary rooms, with mini fridges, flat-screen TVs, and free Wi-Fi, have water views. The fitness center, indoor pool, and restaurant overlook the river.

If you have a car, an excellent-value lodging for both families and business travelers is **The Water Tower Inn** (360 Great Northern Rd., 705/949-8111 or 888/461-7077, www.watertowerinn.com, $115-155 d). Although the surroundings are typically suburban, once you're inside, it feels like a mini resort, particularly in the Aqua Spa, with its indoor pool and indoor-outdoor hot tubs.

Another good choice if you have your own transportation is the **Quattro Hotel and Conference Centre** (229 Great Northern Rd., 705/942-2500, www.quattrossm.com, $119-169 d). Decorated with dark woods, white linens, and purple accents, the 157 rooms are all suites, with sitting areas, fridges, and microwaves. For exercise, head for the indoor pool or large fitness room. Rates include a buffet breakfast in **Quattro Vinotecca** (11:30am-2pm and 5pm-11pm Mon.-Fri., 5pm-11pm Sat., 5pm-10pm Sun., lunch $10-22, dinner $23-48), which is also a good option for Italian-influenced meals of spinach and mushroom ravioli, grilled branzino, or filet mignon.

Among the midrange chain hotels downtown, the renovated 115-room **Holiday Inn Express Sault Ste. Marie** (320 Bay St., 705/759-8200, www.ihg.com/holidayinnexpress, $121-214 d) is a short walk from the Agawa Canyon train station and the waterfront.

INFORMATION

The helpful crew at **Tourism Sault Ste. Marie** (99 Foster Dr., 705/759-5442 or 800/461-6020, www.saulttourism.com), and their equally informative website, can clue you into things to do in the Sault. For more information about the region surrounding Sault Ste. Marie, contact the **Algoma Kinniwabi Travel Association** (334 Bay St., 705/254-4293 or 800/263-2546, www.algomacountry.com).

GETTING THERE AND AROUND

The Ontario Sault is across the river from its Michigan namesake. Michigan's I-75 crosses the International Bridge into the Canadian Sault's downtown. Remember that passports are required for travel between the United States and Canada. Within Ontario, it's an easy 3.5-hour drive between Sault Ste. Marie and Sudbury, 300 kilometers (186 miles) to the east. The Sault is roughly equidistant (700 kilometers, or 435 miles) to Toronto and Thunder Bay.

From **Sault Ste. Marie Airport** (YAM, 475 Airport Rd., 705/779-3031, www.saultairport.com), 20 kilometers (12 miles) west of downtown, **Air Canada** (www.aircanada.com) and **Porter Airlines** (www.flyporter.com) fly to Toronto. **Bearskin Airlines** (www.bearskinairlines.com) has flights to Thunder Bay.

The **Greyhound Bus Station** (Howard Johnson's, 503 Trunk Rd., 705/541-9305 or 800/661-8747, www.greyhound.ca), northeast of downtown, has buses to Sudbury (4.5 hours, $35-86), Toronto (10.5 hours, $72-138), and Thunder Bay (9.75 hours, $72-181), among other destinations. At the same location, **Ontario Northland** (800/461-8558, www.ontarionorthland.ca) buses arrive from North Bay (6.5 hours, $94) and Sudbury (4.5 hours, $68), daily except Saturday.

The city's attractions cluster in the walkable downtown. The 25-kilometer (15-mile) **John Rowswell Hub Trail,** for pedestrians and cyclists, loops through the city center connecting all the main sights. However, to explore Lake Superior Provincial Park or other day-trip sights, you'll need your own wheels. All the major car rental companies have offices in Sault Ste. Marie.

Planning a Lake Superior Circle Tour

Circumnavigating Lake Superior is a 2,000-kilometer-plus (1,300-mile) road trip that not only runs through some of Ontario's most dramatic scenery, it also crosses through the U.S. states of Minnesota, Wisconsin, and Michigan. Whether by car, on a motorcycle, or even by bike, it's an epic but manageable journey.

On the Ontario side, Thunder Bay is just an hour's drive from the U.S. border, while the city of Sault Ste. Marie is across the International Bridge from its U.S. namesake. In between you'll find small towns but far more forests, wooded parks, and beaches. The U.S. shores are more developed, including the cities of Duluth (Minnesota) and Marquette (Michigan), though you'll still find plenty of open spaces.

For more information about planning a Lake Superior Circle Tour, contact the **North of Superior Tourism Association** (https://superiorcountry.ca). Duluth-based *Lake Superior Magazine* (www.lakesuperior.com) features lots of regional destinations online and in its print publications. Several Moon guides (www.moon.com) to the Midwestern United States cover Lake Superior territory, including *Moon Michigan* by Paul Vachon, *Moon Wisconsin* by Thomas Huhti, and *Moon Minnesota* by Tricia Cornell.

BATCHAWANA BAY

Batchawana Bay Provincial Park (Hwy. 17, 705/882-2209, www.ontarioparks.com, mid-May-mid-Oct., $11.25 per vehicle), on Lake Superior 70 kilometers (44 miles) north of the Sault, has a long sandy beach that's a pleasant place to swim or lounge by the lake. Fun fact: Batchawana Bay is the approximate east-west midpoint of the Trans-Canada Highway, the world's longest national highway.

Even lovelier is the smooth stretch of sand backed by dunes and trees at **Pancake Bay Provincial Park** (Hwy. 17, 705/882-2209, www.ontarioparks.com, early May-mid-Oct., $14.50 per vehicle), 10 kilometers (6.2 miles) farther north. Hikers may want to follow the **Edmund Fitzgerald Lookout Trail** (Lookout Trail Rd.) to a viewing platform above the section of the lake where the SS *Edmund Fitzgerald* sank in 1975; allow two to three hours to hike the seven-kilometer (4.4-mile) trail. The trailhead is across the highway from the rest of the park, two kilometers (1.2 miles) to the north.

A popular place for **camping** (tent sites $42-45, electrical sites $47-52), Pancake Bay has 328 campsites along the water; try to book a lakefront site or one up in the Hilltop Campground, as others are quite close to the highway. The campground has showers, flush toilets, and laundry facilities, as well as five **yurts** ($98) that each sleep six. Reserve campsites and yurts through the **Ontario Parks Reservations Service** (888/668-7275, www.ontarioparks.com, reservation fee online $11, by phone $13).

For a big bite to eat in Batchawana Bay, try the hearty fare at **Voyageurs' Lodge and Cookhouse** (Hwy. 17, 705/882-2504, www.voyageurslodge.com), including burgers, *tourtière* (Quebec meat pie), and traditional baked beans with bannock. They're especially busy Friday evenings for their weekly fish fry. If you can't bear to get back on the road after stuffing yourself on the blueberry crisp, check into one of the motel rooms. The Voyageurs' store sells essentials, booze, and delicious, supersized apple fritters.

★ LAKE SUPERIOR PROVINCIAL PARK

One of Ontario's most beautiful outdoor destinations, **Lake Superior Provincial Park** (Hwy. 17, 705/856-2284, www.ontarioparks.com or www.lakesuperiorpark.

ca, mid-May-mid-Oct., $14.50 per vehicle) stretches 115 kilometers (72 miles) along Lake Superior's eastern shore. As you sit on a sandy beach or scramble up the rocky cliffs, you could be forgiven for thinking you were actually at the ocean, as surf crashes onto the rocks and the steely blue-gray water disappears into the horizon, with no land in sight.

For park information, contact the main park office, located in the northern half of the park near Red Rock Lake, or the **Agawa Bay Visitors Centre** (705/882-2026, 9am-8pm daily mid-June-early Sept., 9am-5pm daily mid-May-mid-June and early Sept.-mid-Oct.). If you're coming from the north, pick up a park brochure and map at the Wawa Tourist Information Centre (Hwy. 17 at Hwy. 101, Wawa).

The Lake Superior region famously inspired the Group of Seven landscape painters in the early 1900s. Find your own inspiration with the **Art in the Park** programs, which might include painting or printmaking workshops. Throughout the summer, park staff offer guided hikes, kids' programs, evening presentations, and other activities. Get program details from the Visitors Centre or the website of the Friends of Lake Superior Park (www.lakesuperiorpark.ca).

Sights

At the park's south end, stop at the well-designed and modern **Agawa Bay Visitors Centre** (705/882-2026, 9am-8pm daily mid-June-early Sept., 9am-5pm daily mid-May-mid-June and early Sept.-mid-Oct.) to learn more about Lake Superior, which is not just the largest, deepest, and coldest of the Great Lakes—it's the largest body of freshwater in the world. Other exhibits illustrate the lake's legendary storms, including the one that sank the freighter SS *Edmund Fitzgerald* in 1975, immortalized in Ontario-born singer Gordon Lightfoot's ballad "Wreck of the Edmund Fitzgerald." The knowledgeable staff here can help you plan your time in the park. Wi-Fi is available by donation.

A few kilometers north of Agawa Bay, a short (0.5-kilometer, 0.3-mile) but steep and rocky trail leads to the **Agawa Rock Pictographs** (late-May-mid-Sept.), red ocher graphics that Ojibwa people painted on a lakefront rock face several hundred years ago. It's still an active sacred site; park staff are usually on hand in July and August to help interpret its significance to the indigenous people. The rocky shore here is especially beautiful. Because you have to venture out onto slippery rocks to see the pictographs, you can visit only

Batchawana Bay Provincial Park

when the lake is calm; otherwise, the surf can crash dangerously onto the rocks.

Continuing north is **Katherine Cove,** with a sheltered beach of fine white sand that is a pretty picnic spot. If the surrounding trees were palms instead of evergreens, you could imagine that you were in the Caribbean. The terrain changes again at **Old Woman Bay,** approaching the park's northern boundary. Evergreen hills rise and fall around the bay, and waves often pound the broad, sandy beach.

Recreation

Hikers will find a wide variety of terrain on the park's 11 trails, ranging from easy paths like the two-kilometer (1.2-mile) **Crescent Lake Trail,** the longer six-kilometer (3.7-mile) but still fairly flat **Pinguisibi-Sand River Trail,** or the rugged 65-kilometer (40-mile) **Coastal Trail** that extends from Agawa Bay north beyond Gargantua Harbour; allow five to seven days to hike the entire coastal route, though you can do sections as day hikes. Pick up hiking information and maps at the park office or the Agawa Bay Visitors Centre.

You can swim in Lake Superior if you're hardy; the surf is often strong, and even in August the average surface temperature is a chilly 14.5°C (58°F). Head for one of the more sheltered bays to find warmer water. The park has several interior lakes, which are warmer, calmer places to swim or boat. You can rent **canoes** (mid-June-early Sept., $10 per hour, $30 per day) at Agawa Bay and Rabbit Blanket Lake, and from the Red Rock Park Office near Mijinemungshing Lake.

Camping

The park has 206 campsites in three different areas. To camp beside Lake Superior, book a site at the park's largest and most popular camping area, **Agawa Bay Campground** (mid-May-mid.-Oct., tent sites $42-45, electrical sites $47-52), where the premium sites are right on the beach. Agawa has showers, flush toilets, laundry facilities, and an outdoor amphitheater offering summer nature programs. In the park's northern half, on a smaller interior lake, **Rabbit Blanket Lake Campground** (mid-May-mid-Oct., tent sites $42, electrical sites $47) has flush toilets, showers, and a laundry. To reserve campsites at Agawa Bay and Rabbit Blanket Lake, contact the **Ontario Parks Reservations Service** (888/668-7275, www.ontarioparks. com, reservation fee online $11, by phone $13).

The park's 200 **backcountry campsites**

on the beach in Lake Superior Provincial Park

(mid-May-Oct., adults $11, ages 6-17 $5) are accessible on foot or by canoe.

If you don't want to camp, the closest accommodations are south of the park in Batchawana Bay or Montreal River Harbour with more options to the north in Wawa. You can also stay in Sault Ste. Marie and spend the day in the park.

Outfitters

Naturally Superior Adventures (705/856-2939 or 800/203-9092, www.naturallysuperior.com) is based at the Rock Island Lodge, near Wawa. Rent kayaks, take kayaking lessons, or sign up for day hikes or canoe or kayak excursions. In July and August, they arrange **stand-up paddleboarding** sessions at Rabbit Blanket Lake. They can also organize multiday adventure trips in the park and around the Lake Superior region.

Headquartered south of the park in Goulais River, **Caribou Expeditions** (705/649-3540 or 800/970-6662, www.caribou-expeditions.com) focuses on water-based adventures, including kayak or canoe rentals and guided tours, lodge-to-lodge kayaking trips, and wilderness excursions.

Getting There

Highway 17 from Sault Ste. Marie to Wawa bisects Lake Superior Provincial Park; you can tour the park on a day trip from either town. From the Sault, it's 140 kilometers (87 miles)—less than two hours by car—to the Agawa Bay Visitors Centre, and another 64 kilometers (40 miles) from Agawa Bay to Old Woman Bay.

There's **no food, gas, or other services within the park,** so check your fuel in Sault Ste. Marie or Wawa and bring whatever supplies you need.

WAWA

Wawa is derived from an Ojibwa word meaning "wild goose," so it's fitting that the chief landmark in this community is the 8.5-meter-tall (28-foot-tall) *Wawa Goose.* The current goose perches south of town outside the **Wawa Tourist Information Centre** (Hwy.

17 at Hwy. 101, www.experiencewawa.ca, 8am-8pm daily July-Aug., 9am-5pm daily mid-May-June and Sept.-mid-Oct.). Installed in 2017 to replace its decaying predecessor, it's an exact replica of the goose statue that sculptor Dick Vandercliff crafted in the 1960s. After taking your obligatory goose photo, head inside to pick up information about the Lake Superior region or check your email (there's free Wi-Fi).

While most travelers use Wawa as a base for exploring Lake Superior Provincial Park or as a stopover between Sault Ste. Marie and Thunder Bay, you can stretch your legs at a couple of other outdoor stops. With an interpretive display about the local First Nations, the large **Sandy Beach** fronts Lake Superior south of town; take Michipicoten River Village Road west off Highway 17 and follow the beach signs. In town, there's an attractive beach on **Wawa Lake.**

At the intersection of Highways 17 and 101, Wawa is 230 kilometers (145 miles) north of Sault Ste. Marie and 475 kilometers (295 miles) east of Thunder Bay.

Food and Accommodations

The best place to stay near Wawa is ★ **Rock Island Lodge** (10 Government Dock Rd., 705/856-2939 or 800/203-9092, www.rockislandlodge.ca, mid-May-mid-Oct., $118-138 d). The four rooms don't have phones or TVs, but they do have private baths, Wi-Fi, and awe-inspiring views of Lake Superior. Out on the deck, the lake is so close that you're practically in the water. Rates include breakfast; staff will prepare lunch and dinner on request, or you can use the lodge kitchen to cook your own meals. You can also "glamp" in their "Geo Dome" ($60 d without breakfast, $75 d with breakfast), a yurt-like tent with a wood floor, queen bed (linens are provided), and a nearby composting toilet. The on-site outfitter, **Naturally Superior Adventures** (705/856-2939 or 800/203-9092, www.naturallysuperior.com), rents kayaks, leads day hikes, and offers canoe and kayak excursions.

Winnie the Pooh: Born in Ontario?

The wilderness outside the tiny Ontario town of White River may have been the original home of a beloved children's literary icon: Winnie the Pooh. Legend has it that, during World War I, a Canadian army veterinarian named Harry Colebourn purchased an orphaned bear cub from an Ontario trapper when the train on which his regiment was traveling made a stopover in White River. Colebourn named the bear for his hometown, Winnipeg. Colebourn brought "Winnie" to England as his regiment's mascot and eventually gave her to the London Zoo. It was there that writer A. A. Milne and his son Christopher first met the bear that was to inspire Milne's famous stories.

Located 95 kilometers (60 miles) west of Wawa, White River has commemorated its honey-loving bear connection by building a public **park** (Hwy. 17) with a children's playground and a statue of Winnie. The **White River Heritage Museum** (200 Elgin St., 807/822-2657, www. whiteriver.ca, 10am-6pm Tues.-Sat. May-Sept.) has a collection of Pooh memorabilia.

Five kilometers (three miles) south of the Wawa visitors center, **Best Northern Motel** (150 Hwy. 17, 705/856-7302 or 800/434-8240, www.bestnorthern.ca, mid-Apr.-mid-Dec., $99-105 d, $135 cottages) is an updated road-side lodging with 11 guest rooms, all with microwaves, refrigerators, coffeemakers, and flat-screen TVs, as well as three two-bedroom cottages. The main lodge has a sauna, a rec room with a pool table, and a **restaurant** (7:30am-10am and 5pm-9pm daily, dinner $12-30) that's worth a visit for its Polish specialties, including excellent pierogi and cabbage rolls. For dessert, if there's no homemade pie, consider the cheese-filled crepes with berry sauce.

Surprise—you can travel to the Caribbean at friendly ★ **Kinniwabi Pines International Restaurant** (106 Hwy. 17, 705/856-7226, 8am-9pm daily, lunch $8-13, dinner $16-25), with tables overlooking the river. The owners hail from Trinidad, so don't miss the top-notch chicken, potato, and chickpea curry, served with roti. The spicy baked pork chop is another popular choice from the world-roaming menu that also spans Chinese and Canadian dishes. For breakfast, try Trinidadian-style scrambled eggs with tomatoes or salt cod with fry bread.

Next to a car dealership, in an unassuming motel block eight kilometers (five miles) west of town, longtime owners Maureen Hutchinson-Parker and John Parker have outfitted their homey guest rooms at the **Northern Lights Motel** (1014 Hwy. 17, no phone, http://nlmotel.com, mid-May-mid-Oct., $99-119 d) with plenty of personality, from trivia quizzes taped to the bathroom door to humorous illustrated notes outlining everything you need to know about the property. Four rooms have two queen beds with blue and white quilts; another room has two doubles; and there's a two-bedroom cottage ($144-174) and a three-bedroom chalet ($225-255). While you have to head into town to dine out, rooms come with microwaves, fridges, coffeemakers, and a book of local restaurant menus.

You'll find more basic motels and eateries in town, along Mission Road and Broadway Avenue, Wawa's main streets. The 21 cozy rooms at the two-story **Beaver Motel** (148 Mission Rd., 705/856-2294 or 866-819-4286, www.beavermotel.com) are more modern than the exterior suggests, with updated furnishings, contemporary baths, and in-room fridges. You can grab a free cup of morning coffee in the lobby. The **Wawa Motor Inn** (118 Mission Rd., 705/856-2278 or 800/561-2278, www.wawamotorinn.ca, $91-169 d) has adequate rooms in its main motel block and in a rustic "log village" set back from the road, plus several two-bedroom cottages ($225-325).

Lake Superior's North Shore

The Trans-Canada Highway runs along Lake Superior's northern shore, lined with boreal forests and rocky evidence of the Canadian Shield. The road dips and rises, gently curving toward or away from the lake, with wow-inducing landscapes and water vistas surprising you as you round a bend or crest a hill. One of Ontario's most beautiful driving routes, this section of the Trans-Canada connects Wawa to the city of Thunder Bay and beyond, with stopover towns and both national and provincial parks along the way.

A 10,000-square-kilometer (3,900-square-mile) section of Lake Superior forms the **Lake Superior National Marine Conservation Area** (807/887-5467, www.pc.gc.ca), the marine equivalent of a Canadian national park. Beginning east of Terrace Bay, the conservation area encompasses a third of the lake's Canadian waters and approximately 600 islands west to the Sibley Peninsula (home of Sleeping Giant Provincial Park) and south to the U.S. border. When its establishment is finalized, it will become the largest protected freshwater area in the world.

While the conservation area doesn't have a visitors center or official facilities, Parks Canada staff work with local communities and First Nations to develop programs for visitors, host special events, and promote the region's numerous land- and water-based recreational activities, such as hiking, wildlife viewing, cross-country skiing, canoeing, kayaking, sailing, fishing, scuba diving, and even surfing on the lake. Outfitters in Wawa, Terrace Bay, Rossport, Nipigon, and Red Rock organize all manner of outdoor trips, and the Parks Canada website has details about local hiking trails and other recreational opportunities.

You can make the 485-kilometer (300-mile) drive from Wawa to Thunder Bay in a leisurely day, but plan to make stops along the way. You could spend weeks here before you'd run out of outdoor adventures. Except in the cities of Sault Ste. Marie and Thunder Bay, the Lake Superior region has little in the way of public transportation. While **Greyhound** (www.greyhound.ca) does provide bus service to towns along Lake Superior's North Shore, it's not practical to explore without a car unless you've arranged with an outfitter for local transportation.

TOP EXPERIENCE

★ PUKASKWA NATIONAL PARK

The largest national park in Ontario spreads across Lake Superior's northeastern reaches, encompassing 1,878 square kilometers (725 square miles) of northern forest and Great Lake coastline that are home to moose, woodland caribou, wolves, and bears. Pronounced "PUCK-a-saw," **Pukaskwa National Park** (off Hwy. 627, Heron Bay, 807/229-0801, www.pc.gc.ca, late May-mid-Oct., adults $5.80, seniors $4.90) draws both novice outdoorspeople and experienced adventurers who come to hike or kayak amid Lake Superior's dramatic terrain. The park also offers interesting programs to introduce visitors to the region's First Nations culture.

In summer, the waterside **Hattie Cove Visitors Centre** (9am-4pm Sun.-Thurs., 9am-8pm Fri.-Sat. July-Aug.) is a hub of activity, with daily interpretive programs ranging from art workshops to guided hikes to presentations about the park's prescribed fire program for maintaining the health of its forests. Check out the colorful wall mural full of First Nations symbols. The center has free Wi-Fi.

Park cultural interpreters run unique programs at the **Anishinaabe Camp,** which has several traditional First Nations wigwams and other structures near the Visitors Centre. Staff demonstrate and interpret aspects of Ojibwa culture, including traditional medicines, drumming, and ceremonies, sharing not just aboriginal heritage but present-day life and teachings of the First Nations communities who make their home in this region. Get a program schedule from the Visitors Centre.

Hiking

Pukaskwa has lots of choices for day hikes of varying levels of difficulty:

- **Beach Trail** (1.5 km, easy): Follows the boardwalk along the Lake Superior shore.

- **Manitou Miikana** (2 km, moderate): Known as the "Spirit Trail," this route wends through the woods to two lookouts high above the lake.

- **Southern Headland Trail** (2.2 km, moderate): Top-notch lake views can be had as you wander through the pine forests and along the rocky shores.

- **Bimose Kinoomagewnan** (2.6 km, moderate): An interpretive trail around Halfway Lake, highlighting the Ojibwa people's Seven Grandfather Teachings. Park cultural interpreters lead periodic guided hikes on this trail; check with the park office for schedules.

- **White River Suspension Bridge** (18 km

round-trip, moderate): This demanding but popular full-day hike leads to a suspension bridge 23 meters (75 feet) above Chigaminqinigum Falls.

For experienced backcountry hikers who want a multiday adventure, the park's **Coastal Hiking Trail** runs 60 kilometers (37 miles) one-way through rugged wilderness terrain. Refer to the Coastal Hiking Trail Trip Planner, available on the park website (www.pc.gc.ca), for more details about backcountry hiking.

Kayaking

Pukaskwa's offshore waters aren't a beginner kayaking or canoeing destination, as Lake Superior's weather and water conditions can be changeable and challenging. Unless you're an experienced kayak tripper, consider working with a local outfitter to plan your paddling adventure. **Naturally Superior Adventures** (705/856-2939 or 800/203-9092, www.naturallysuperior.com) offers guided sea kayaking trips along the Pukaskwa coast. The park publishes a detailed Coastal Paddling Route Trip Planner, available online, to help you prepare for a paddling journey.

Camping

Hattie Cove Campground (late May-early

hiking along the rocks in Pukaskwa National Park

Once a POW Camp, Now a Park

If you were looking for a remote encampment to sequester prisoners of war, you'd want a place where your charges would be unlikely to escape, right? Maybe you'd choose a region with sandy soil too soft to tunnel out, bounded by a huge frigid lake that's too rough to flee in a makeshift boat. Perhaps you'd consider the wilds of Northern Ontario, on the shores of Lake Superior. In fact, the Lake Superior region did house German POWs during World War II. The site of one POW camp, known as Camp 100, is now **Neys Provincial Park** (807/229-1624, www.ontarioparks. com, mid-May-mid-Sept., $11.25 per vehicle).

German prisoners were sent to Canada when European POW camps began to run out of capacity. Chosen for its remote location and for the difficulty it would pose for an attempted escape, Neys Camp 100 housed high-ranking German officers. It was an active POW camp from 1941 to 1946, accommodating 650 prisoners at its peak. Many were allowed to work at nearby logging camps, which were short-staffed because of the war. In 1948, after all the prisoners had been repatriated to Germany, Neys began receiving new residents—Japanese Canadians who had been interned during the war. Neys became a temporary relocation facility, housing these displaced Japanese Canadians until they were reunited with their families or found more permanent homes.

Neys has a place in art history, as well. Lawren Harris, A. Y. Jackson, and other members of the Group of Seven painted along the Lake Superior shore in and around the present-day provincial park. Harris painted views looking out to Pic Island, a vista that you can still see today. You can learn more about Neys's heritage in the park's Visitors Centre. This lakeside park has a long, sandy swimming beach and several easy-to-moderate hiking trails, including the one-kilometer (0.6-mile) Under the Volcano Trail along the rocky shoreline, and the two-kilometer (1.2-mile) Lookout Trail that climbs up to viewpoints over the park.

For campers, Neys has 144 wooded, well-spaced **campsites** (tent sites $36, electrical sites $42). Areas 1, 2, and 3 all have sites near the Lake Superior shore, while Area 4 is close to the Little Pic River. Only Area 2 has a full-service comfort station with flush toilets, showers, and laundry facilities. A rustic one-room **cabin** ($141.25) overlooking the beach in Area 2 can sleep up to four. Neys Provincial Park is off Highway 17, 30 kilometers (19 miles) west of Marathon and 55 kilometers (35 miles) east of Terrace Bay.

Sept. tent sites $25.50, electrical sites $29.40, May and Sept.-mid-Oct. tent sites $15.70, electrical sites $19.60) has 67 well-spaced wooded sites. The 29 electrical sites are all in the larger south loop area; tent campers may prefer the quieter north loop. Both areas have comfort stations with hot showers and flush toilets. The park does not accept advance reservations for Hattie Cove sites. In spring and fall, some campground facilities, including restrooms, are closed; campsite fees are reduced accordingly.

If you don't have your own tent, book one of the park's five **oTENTiks** ($100-120), platform tents sleeping up to six, near the Hattie Cove Visitor Centre. The cabin-like shelters come with one queen and two double sleeping platforms, a table and chairs, grill, and a food locker; bring your own bedding, food, and cooking equipment. Reserve oTENTiks in advance (877/737-3783, http://reservation. pc.gc.ca).

Backpackers traveling the Coastal Hiking Trail can set up camp at primitive backcountry sites along the route, which are equipped with a tent pad, privy, fire pit, and bear box. You must book backcountry sites in advance; reserve online or by phone (807/229-0801 or 877/737-3783, http://reservation.pc.gc.ca).

Practicalities

Pukaskwa National Park is approximately 410 kilometers (255 miles) northwest of Sault Ste. Marie and 310 kilometers (195 miles) east of Thunder Bay. It's located off Highway 17, the Trans-Canada Highway, 180 kilometers (115

the Terrace Bay Lighthouse

has enough services to make it a handy stop as you're traveling across the lake's North Shore.

A collection of rocky islands in Lake Superior, 13 kilometers (eight miles) off the coast of Terrace Bay, the Slate Islands are home to the largest known herd of predator-free woodland caribou. In the early 1900s, during particularly cold winters when Lake Superior froze all the way to the islands, caribou crossed from the mainland, where they have remained and thrived. Beavers, red foxes, snowshoe hares, and other small mammals also live on the islands, which offer lots of adventures for kayakers and hikers.

Sights and Recreation

The **Terrace Bay Lighthouse** (Simcoe Plaza, off Hwy. 17, Terrace Bay, 8am-10pm Mon.-Fri., 9:30am-9pm Sat.-Sun., free) never guided any ships ashore. The town built this 15-meter (50-foot) tower as a replica of the lighthouse on the nearby Slate Islands; sitting at 68 meters (224 feet) above sea level, the Slate Island Light is considered the tallest lighthouse on the Great Lakes. The replica lighthouse is a lookout tower, with views over the town to the lake.

About one kilometer (0.6 miles) west of town, a short walkway leads to a viewing platform above pretty **Aguasabon Falls** (Hwy. 17, Terrace Bay, www.terracebay.ca). Pronounced "AUG-was-saw-bin," the falls cascade 30 meters (100 feet) into a deep gorge.

On Lake Superior, wide, sandy **Terrace Bay Beach** (Beach Ave.) is a five-minute drive south of Highway 17. In the small town of Schreiber, 15 kilometers (nine miles) west of Terrace Bay, **Schreiber Beach** is a little harder to find, but its secluded shores, lined with pink-tinged stones, are worth seeking out. The beach is three kilometers (1.9 miles) from Schreiber's town center. From Scotia Street, take the underpass on Subway Street beneath the railroad tracks, then turn right to follow steep Isbester Drive until it ends just above the beach.

Hikers can explore sections of the challenging, 52-kilometer (32-mile) **Casque Isles**

miles) west of Wawa, about a two-hour drive. Take the Heron Bay exit onto Highway 627 and follow it 15 kilometers (nine miles) to the park entrance.

You can pick up basics at convenience stores in Biigtigong Nishnaabeg, the indigenous community formerly known as the Pic River First Nation (www.picriver.com), bordering the park on Highway 627. The nearest town with lodging, restaurants, and other services is **Marathon** (www.marathon.ca), eight kilometers (five miles) west of the Highway 627 turnoff. Terrace Bay, 98 kilometers (60 miles) west of the park, has additional lodging options.

TERRACE BAY AND THE SLATE ISLANDS

Overlooking Lake Superior, the town of Terrace Bay (population 1,800) grew from the surrounding woods; for decades, its main employer has been a pulp mill. It's now a jumping-off point for exploring the Lake Superior National Marine Conservation Area, and it

Trail (www.voyageurtrail.ca) that connects Terrace Bay, Schreiber, and Rossport. You can pick up the trail near Terrace Bay Beach or Schreiber Beach.

The two largest Slate Islands, Patterson and Mortimer, along with several smaller islands and their surrounding waters, make up **Slate Islands Provincial Park** (www.ontarioparks.com), which currently has no visitor facilities. Several outfitters run day trips or overnight trips to the Slates. Departing from Terrace Bay or Rossport, the **Bluebird Charter Boat** (807/824-3353, www.bluebirdcharterboat.com, $124 per hour for 1-4 people) runs sightseeing tours to the Slates and other Superior islands. Wawa-based **Naturally Superior Adventures** (705/856-2939 or 800/203-9092, www.naturallysuperior.com) offers guided kayak trips in the Slate Islands.

Food and Accommodations

You can buy snacks and groceries at **Costa's Foods** (Simcoe Plaza, Terrace Bay, 807/825-4501, www.costasfoods.ca, 9am-6pm Mon.-Fri., 8:30am-5:30pm Sat.). Also in the plaza are a liquor store, bank, post office, bakery, and Chinese restaurant.

Terrace Bay has several basic roadside motels. The 16-room **Norwood Motel** (Hwy. 17, Terrace Bay, 807/825-3282, $75 d) looks straight from the 1950s, pink bath tile and all, but the rooms have microwaves, mini fridges, free Wi-Fi, and (surprise!) Keurig coffeemakers.

Although they face a gas station, many rooms at **Drifters Imperial Motel** (Hwy. 17, Terrace Bay, 807/825-3226 or 877/825-1625, $89-109 d) have been updated with woodsy log furnishings and free Wi-Fi. Adjacent to the motel, friendly **Drifters Restaurant** (807/825-3226, 6am-10pm daily, lunch $5-13, dinner $12-35) specializes in Italian dishes, like the ample "roadhouse pasta" with chicken, bacon, mushroom, and peppers. It also serves burgers, steaks, and salads, including a meal-size spinach salad with feta cheese and figs or a romaine, cranberry, and chicken plate.

Practicalities

Terrace Bay is on Highway 17, 260 kilometers (160 miles) west of Wawa and 225 kilometers (140 miles) east of Thunder Bay. The **Terrace Bay Tourist Information Centre** (1008 Hwy. 17, 807/825-3315, ext. 235, or 800/968-8616, www.terracebay.ca, 9am-6pm daily late May-Sept.) provides information about the Lake Superior North Shore and has free Wi-Fi. The town of Terrace Bay offers free Wi-Fi that you can pick up around Simcoe Plaza.

ROSSPORT

The waterside hamlet of Rossport is another worthwhile stopover along Lake Superior's North Shore. Watch carefully for the exit, or you'll easily blow right past the tiny town, which is home to fewer than 100 souls. You can hike, swim, canoe, or kayak in a nearby provincial park, or use the village as a launching point for Slate Islands trips. Unlike many North Shore communities, which have only simple roadside motels, Rossport has several bed-and-breakfasts.

Sights and Recreation

Tiny **Rossport Museum** (Main St., July-Aug.), housed in a Canadian Pacific Railroad caboose, has exhibits on the area's rail and marine history.

For a short hike along the Lake Superior shore, follow the 1.5-kilometer (0.9-mile) **Rossport Coastal Trail.** Some sections are close enough to Highway 17 that you can hear the cars whiz by, but the lake views make up for it. It's a linear trail, so you need to return the way you came. The trailhead is at the east end of Rossport village.

Eleven kilometers (seven miles) east of Rossport, **Rainbow Falls Provincial Park** (Hwy. 17, spring-summer 807/824-2298, fall-winter 807/825-3403, www.ontarioparks.com, mid-May-mid-Oct., $11.25 per vehicle) has several popular hiking trails, including the three-kilometer (1.9-mile) Rainbow Falls trail, which follows a boardwalk down 180 steps to a bridge, with views of the falls along the way; across the bridge, the trail turns more rugged as it climbs to a viewpoint with vistas to Lake Superior. The 52-kilometer (32-mile) **Casque Isles Trail** (www.voyageurtrail.ca), linking Terrace Bay and Rossport, passes through the park. You can swim, or rent canoes and kayaks, in a sheltered cove at Whitesand Lake's East Beach; West Beach has a small swimming area as well.

Experienced scuba divers head out from Rossport to explore the **wreck of the Gunilda,** a steam yacht that hit a shoal off the coast and sank in 1911. Lying 81 meters (265 feet) beneath Lake Superior's surface, the ship is considered one of the most intact freshwater wrecks in the world. **Discovery Charters** (807/824-3323, www.discoverycharters.ca) organizes dive trips to the *Gunilda* and other nearby shipwrecks.

Food and Accommodations

Rossport's most distinctive place to stay is the **Serendipity Gardens Guest House** (807/824-2890, www.serendipitygardens.ca, $125 d), with four guest rooms in a unique dome-like building. Choose one of the upstairs units with Gothic-inspired arched windows; all the wood-paneled rooms have queen beds and kitchenettes. Rates include "breakfast in a box" (yogurt, a muffin, and

juice). The same owners run **Serendipity Gardens Café** (222 Main St., 807/824-2890, 11am-9pm daily, call for off-season hours, $12-30), which serves salads, sandwiches, and home-style dinners; baked lake trout is a specialty. Check-in for the Guest House is at the café.

In a renovated 1940s log cabin five kilometers (three miles) east of town, **B&B on the Beach** (237 Lakeshore Rd., 807/824-2155, www.bbcanada.com, $129 d) occupies an enviable site directly on Lake Superior. Upstairs, guests have their own living room facing the lake, plus two homey guest rooms, each with a queen bed. There's a shared half bath opposite the bedrooms and a larger bathroom with a shower and whirlpool tub on the main floor. Gregarious owner Billie Jo Keating, who runs the B&B with her husband, Bill, is a wealth of local information. She grows berries for homemade jam and regularly bakes pies for guests, in addition to serving a full breakfast.

Other B&Bs in town include the four-room **Willows Inn B&B** (116 Main St., 807/824-3389 or 877/825-1275, www.bbcanada.com, $90-110 d) and the three-room **Island Shores Bed & Breakfast** (440 Main St., 807/824-1182, www. bbcanada.com, $110-130 d).

Rainbow Falls Provincial Park

CAMPING

Rainbow Falls Provincial Park (Hwy. 17, spring-summer 807/824-2298, fall-winter 807/825-3403, www.ontarioparks.com, tent sites $36, electrical sites $42) has two camping areas, both with showers and flush toilets. Eight kilometers (five miles) east of Rossport, the **Rossport campground** (mid-May-mid-Oct.) has 36 sites on a lakeside point; although they're not very shaded, several are right on Lake Superior. The larger **Whitesand Lake campground** (mid-May-mid-Sept.), along with the rest of the park's facilities, is 11 kilometers (seven miles) east of Rossport, where most of the 97 sites are set among the pines. For views of Whitesand Lake, book a site in the Lakeside camping area.

Practicalities

Rossport is just off Highway 17, 37 kilometers (23 miles) west of Terrace Bay and 190 kilometers (118 miles) east of Thunder Bay.

Based in Rossport, **Superior Outfitters** (807/824-3314, www.kayakrossport.ca) rents kayaks and canoes, offers kayak day trips (July-Aug., $95 pp), and organizes multiday kayak excursions to the Slate Islands and other Lake Superior destinations. In addition to offering shipwreck scuba diving trips,

Discovery Charters (807/824-3323, www.discoverycharters.ca) runs 1.5- to 2-hour boat tours of the islands around Rossport ($55 pp) and 4-hour trips out to the Slate Islands ($140 per hour).

NIPIGON

In 1941, American author Holling C. Holling penned a tale of an aboriginal boy living in the Ontario highlands near Nipigon, who carves a figure in a small canoe and sends him off to try to reach the ocean. Calling him *Paddle to the Sea,* the boy sets the canoe in the snow, and when spring comes, the little boat begins its journey down a stream into Lake Superior. The intrepid wooden canoe survives encounters with beavers and boys, freighters and frozen winters, even a tumble over Niagara Falls, before finally reaching the Atlantic. You can watch a 28-minute film, adapted from the book in 1966, online through the National Film Board of Canada (www.nfb.ca).

The town of Nipigon, 72 kilometers (45 miles) west of Rossport, has brought Paddle's journey back to life in its **Paddle to the Sea Park,** a children's playground with interpretive panels recounting parts of the Paddle story. The main section of the park is downtown behind the public library, and like

B&B on the Beach is on Lake Superior near Rossport.

Paddle, the park itself continues toward the water, with sections near the town marina.

Sports and Recreation

Nipigon-based **Epic Adventures** (807/887-1008, www.epicadventures.ca) offers guided hiking, mountain biking, and snowshoeing tours, ranging from two hours to a full day ($25-185 pp), and leads multiday multisport outdoor trips along the Lake Superior North Shore. It also provides a hiker shuttle service, which can take one-way hikers back to their starting point; book in advance.

Several day hikes that enable you to explore the mainland sections of the Lake Superior Marine Conservation Area and the surrounding region. The 8.2-kilometer (five-mile) linear **Nipigon River Recreation Trail** follows the wetlands along the Nipigon River and climbs up to viewpoints over Lake Superior as you hike between the Nipigon Marina (25 2nd St.) and the town of Red Rock. Parks Canada staff recommend hiking this rugged 3- to 4-hour one-way route from Red Rock to Nipigon; remember to arrange transportation back to your starting point if you don't have a full day to hike both ways. For great views over Lake Superior, hike the **Kama Cliffs Trail.** Rated moderate with one steeper, more difficult section, this trail is a five-kilometer (three-mile) out-and-back hike to its first lookout and an eight-kilometer (five-mile) round-trip to a second lookout. The trailhead is 24 kilometers (15 miles) east of Nipigon's Highway 11-17 junction, on the north side of Highway 17. Even if you're not planning to hike, watch for the viewpoint markers as you're driving between Rossport and Nipigon, and pull over at the **Kama Bay Lookout** for spectacular lake vistas.

Recommended for experienced hikers, the **Mazukama Falls Trail** is a challenging 3.1-kilometer (two-mile) loop that climbs uphill through an old-growth cedar forest to the 25-meter-tall (82-foot) waterfalls. The route continues past huge boulders and through more forests before returning to its starting point. To find the trailhead, follow Highway 17 twenty kilometers (12.5 miles) east of Nipigon and turn north (left) onto the gravel Camp 81 Road.

Food

Casual **La Luna Café** (46 Front St., 807/889-1537, www.lalunacafe.net, 8:30am-5:30pm Tues.-Fri., 9am-6pm Sat., $5-10), opposite Paddle to the Sea Park, serves breakfast, soups, salads, sandwiches, and pastries. The

lake views from Lloyd's Lookout

gingersnap cookies go well with coffee or a latte.

RED ROCK

The village of Red Rock is another base for outdoor activities. Start exploring the area at the Nipigon Bay shore and the **Red Rock Marina and Interpretive Centre** (7 Park Rd., www.redrocktownship.com, 8am-6pm Mon.-Fri., 8am-8:30pm Sat.-Sun. mid-May-Sept., adults $5, seniors and ages 4-17 $3), which has high-tech interactive exhibits about the region, as well as a small café.

From the Red Rock end of the 8.2-kilometer (five-mile) linear **Nipigon River Recreation Trail,** it's a gentle 20-minute hike through the forest up to **Lloyd's Lookout,** where the panoramas from the viewing platform extend across the water, down to the marina and to several lake islands. A second viewpoint, the **Nipigon Bay Lookout,** is a few minutes farther. To continue all the way to Nipigon Marina, allow at least 3-4 hours; the trail has some more rugged sections. The Red Rock trailhead is off Highway 628, 6.4 kilometers (4 miles) from Highway 11/17; turn left onto 3rd Street, just before the railroad tracks, and you'll see a small parking area. If you're coming from Red Rock Marina, follow Highway 628 1.2 kilometers (.75 miles) west.

Every summer, the town hosts **Live from the Rock** (www.livefromtherockfolkfestival.com, Aug.), a weekend-long folk festival, and the Red Rock Indian Band, an Ojibwa First Nation, welcomes visitors to its annual pow-wow, the **Opwaaganasining Traditional Gathering** (www.rrib.ca, July).

Nipigon River Adventures (807/621-6342, www.nipigonriveradventures.com) can organize fishing, kayaking, hiking, sailing, and other trips in the Lake Superior National Marine Conservation Area. They accommodate guests at their Red Rock-area **Lodge** ($90 s, $135 d, with meals $120 s, 200 d).

To reach Red Rock, exit Highway 17 south of Nipigon onto Highway 628 and follow it into the village.

Thunder Bay and Vicinity

The largest city on Lake Superior's Canadian shores, Thunder Bay is a natural starting point for exploring this lake region, whether you're spending a weekend, circling the lake, or stopping off on a cross-Canada road trip. Once a key fur-trading post, Thunder Bay is still an important trade location. Its port, one of the world's largest grain-handling facilities, draws major ships transporting cargo along the Great Lakes and the St. Lawrence. The forest industry, with its pulp and paper mills, dominated the economy for many years, supplemented more recently with jobs in tourism, health care, education, and other service industries.

The present-day city of Thunder Bay, with a population of 120,000, grew out of two nearby towns: Fort William to the south and Port Arthur to the north. The city's main downtown is now the northern one, around Water Street, Red River Road, and Marina Park. A smaller downtown district in former Fort William centers on Arthur and May Streets. Strip malls and big-box stores occupy much of the area between these two districts, creating a suburban strip inside the city rather than around the outskirts.

From Thunder Bay, you can set out on all manner of outdoor adventures. Three provincial parks—Sleeping Giant, Ouimet Canyon, and Kakabeka Falls—are within an hour's drive of the city, and opportunities for hiking, kayaking, sailing, and other sports abound.

SIGHTS AND ACTIVITIES

An interesting historic neighborhood to explore is the **Bay & Algoma Historic District.**

Thunder Bay

Once a center of the region's Scandinavian community, Bay Street still houses the Finnish Labour Temple and its well-loved Hoito Restaurant, a Scandinavian deli, and gift shops selling Scandinavian products and souvenirs. Around the corner, Algoma Street is morphing into a funkier strip, with a juice bar, tea purveyor, yoga studio, and other eclectic shops.

Prince Arthur's Landing

A public park extending along the lakeside marina, **Prince Arthur's Landing** (Marina Park, Water St., www.thunderbay.ca) is filled with outdoor sculptures and ways to enjoy the outdoors. The park has become a major step toward reclaiming the city's formerly industrial lakeshore.

Explore the park for its most distinctive feature: a diverse collection of **public art.** On the patio of the Water Garden Pavilion (which houses Bight Restaurant) are the graceful

giant water droplets of *Traveller's Return* by Andy Davies. In the aboriginal culture-inspired Spirit Garden, a series of panels on the *Celebration Circle,* by Randy Thomas and Roy Thomas, incorporates images from the artists' Ojibwa culture. Throughout the park, literary quotes are etched into stones, on walls, and other unexpected locations; one example is *Round Dance,* by Sarain Stump, set into the ground on Pier 2: "Don't break this circle / Before the song is over / Because all of our people / Even the ones long gone / Are holding hands."

Three kilometers (1.9 miles) of trails for **walking** and **cycling** wind along Lake Superior's lakeshore. Daredevils demonstrate their skills in the **skateboard park,** and in the Water Garden, kids play on the **splash pad** (it's a **skating rink** in winter). One section of the park is designated as the **International Tai Chi Park** (www.pengyou-taiji.ca), where morning tai chi practitioners

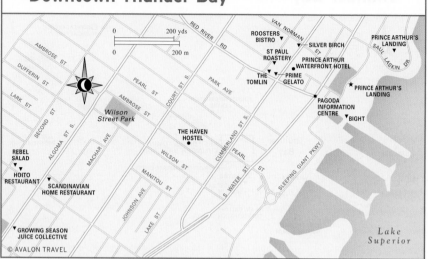

Downtown Thunder Bay

VAN NORMAN
RED RIVER RD
ROOSTERS BISTRO
ST PAUL ROASTERY
SILVER BIRCH ST
PRINCE ARTHUR'S LANDING
SAUL LASKIN DR
AMBROSE ST
DUFFERIN ST
PRINCE ARTHUR WATERFRONT HOTEL
THE TOMLIN
PRIME GELATO
PEARL ST
PARK AVE
COURT ST S
LARK ST
SECOND ST S
AMBROSE ST
MACHAR AVE
PRINCE ARTHUR'S LANDING
Wilson Street Park
PAGODA INFORMATION CENTRE
BIGHT
REBEL SALAD
ALGOMA ST S
THE HAVEN HOSTEL
WILSON ST
CUMBERLAND ST S
PEARL ST
HOITO RESTAURANT
SCANDINAVIAN HOME RESTAURANT
MANITOU ST
JOHNSON AVE
S. WATER ST
SLEEPING GIANT PKWY
GROWING SEASON JUICE COLLECTIVE
LAKE ST
Lake Superior
© AVALON TRAVEL

0   200 yds
0   200 m

perform their graceful moves on the yin-yang practice pad.

In the **Baggage Building Arts Centre** (807/684-2063, 11am-5pm Tues.-Fri., noon-4pm Sat.-Sun.), in a former freight shed, there's a small gallery and gift shop as well as periodic art workshops. Prince Arthur's Landing has a regular schedule of movies, concerts, and other special events, including the weekly summer **Live on the Waterfront concerts** (6pm-9pm Wed. early July-Aug.). Find out what's happening by checking the website of **Tourism Thunder Bay** (www. thunderbay.ca).

★ Fort William Historical Park

How many beaver pelts does it take to buy a wool blanket or a musket? You can travel back to the fur-trading days of the early 1800s at **Fort William Historical Park** (1350 King Rd., 807/473-2344, www.fwhp.ca, 10am-5pm daily June-mid-Aug., 10am-5pm Sat.-Sun. May and mid-Aug.-mid-Sept., mid-June-mid-Aug. adults $14, seniors and students $12, ages 6-12 $10, May-mid-June and mid-Aug.-mid-Sept. adults $12, seniors and students $11, ages 6-12 $9), a family-friendly living-history site on the banks of the Kaministiquia River.

Fort William served as the inland head-quarters of the North West Company, a fur-trading operation based in Montreal that was established in 1783 as a rival to the Hudson's Bay Company. Not a military outpost, Fort William was set up in 1803 as a trading post. It served as a rendezvous point between voya-geurs—French Canadian traders who traveled several weeks by canoe from Quebec, bringing goods from eastern Canada and Europe—and the traders and their First Nations allies from the west who arrived bringing beaver pelts and other valuable furs. The fort was a vital link in Canada's fur trade for over a decade. However, in 1821, the North West Company, facing stiff competition from the Hudson's Bay Company, merged with its rival. Trade routes shifted, and the fort's importance began to decline, until it closed permanently in the 1880s.

At the fort **Visitors Centre,** a short film introduces the history of the North West Company and its relationship with the re-gion's First Nations. Visitors then proceed to the fort itself, which has been reconstructed

Finland on the Lake

pickled herring plate at Hoito Restaurant

Beginning in the 1870s and continuing until World War I, immigrants from Finland settled in the Thunder Bay area. Some came to Canada seeking land to farm, and more found work in Northern Ontario's burgeoning lumber and railroad industries. Subsequent waves of immigration—after World War I and later in the 1950s—continued to increase the number of Finnish settlers until the Thunder Bay region housed the largest community of Finns outside of Finland. Today, roughly 12,000 local residents claim Finnish ancestry.

For visitors, the region's Finnish culture remains most accessible in two places: the restaurant and the sauna. Both locals and travelers have long flocked to eateries like **Hoito Restaurant** (314 Bay St., 807/345-6323, www.thehoito.ca) and the **Scandinavian Home Restaurant** (147 Algoma St. S., 807/345-7442, www.scandihs.com) for Finnish pancakes—plate-size hotcakes that are slightly thicker than a French crepe. Another locally popular treat is *pulla,* a cardamom-scented coffee bread, which you can find at Finnish bakeries and shops like the **Scandinavian Delicatessen** (307 Bay St., 807/344-3632), across the street from the Hoito, which sells other traditional food products from Finland, Sweden, Norway, and Denmark. The Scandinavian custom of smoking fish continues at the family-run **Fish Shop** (960 Lakeshore Dr., 807/983-2214, www.thefishshop.ca, Apr.-Dec.), where you can purchase ready-to-eat smoked trout, whitefish, and salmon—worth a detour on your way to or from Sleeping Giant Provincial Park.

In Finland, saunas are an important element of the culture, providing both health benefits and social relaxation. In Thunder Bay, you can enjoy an in-town steam—solo, with friends, or with family members—at **Kangas Sauna** (379 Oliver Rd., 807/344-6761, www.kangassauna.ca). While it may not have the same cachet as a log sauna out in the woods, it has been providing locals with private sauna sessions for decades, and you'll still sweat plenty. Saunas at Kangas rent for 90 minutes and include use of the communal hot tub. Prices vary depending on the number of people and the size of the sauna: small ($22 for 1 person, $30 for 2, $45 for 3, $60 for 4), medium ($30 for 1, $40 for 2, up to $100 for 5), and large ($30 for 1, $40 for 2, up to $120 for 6). Saunas include a changing room and shower. You can rent towels ($4). Bathing suits aren't required (just lock your sauna door), although you have to wear suits in the hot tub. And if you haven't had your fill of Finnish pancakes, the on-site restaurant serves 'em by the plateful.

to represent life in 1815-1816. **Tours** of the fort, its 40-plus buildings, and its working farm run 60-90 minutes. You might start at the wigwams in the aboriginal encampment outside the fort, where costumed interpreters expand on First Nations life. Within the fort, you can visit the canoe shed, where the vessels that carried traders and their goods were built, or the fort doctor's office, where your guide might demonstrate instruments used for pulling teeth or administering enemas. Another stop is the trading post, piled high with furs, where you learn the trade value of various pelts.

In summer, you can talk with interpreters representing Scottish fur traders, French voyageurs, Ojibwa and Métis people, farmers, and others who "live" at the fort. You might also ride down the river in a **voyageur canoe.** Fewer hands-on activities are available between mid-September and April, when the fort is open by appointment only (10am-5pm Mon.-Fri., ages 6 and up $7.50); phone to reserve a tour time. The fort hosts special events throughout the year, including **Anishnawbe Keeshigun** (June), a festival of indigenous culture, and the **Voyageur Winter Carnival** (Feb.).

An on-site **canteen** (lunch $8-12) serves rib-sticking voyageur beef stew and French Canadian pea soup as well as more modern sandwiches and pizzas. To reach Fort William, which is south of Thunder Bay Airport, follow Highway 61 south, then turn west onto Broadway to the park.

Museums

The **Thunder Bay Museum** (425 Donald St. E., 807/623-0801, www.thunderbaymuseum. com, 11am-5pm daily mid-June-early Sept., 1pm-5pm Tues.-Sun. early Sept.-June, adults $3, ages 6-17 $1.50, free admission Tues.) recounts the region's history through a series of small rooms, each reflecting a particular business or social organization: a school, a post office, a medical office, a shoemaker, a real estate office. Rotating exhibits showcase area architecture, military history, and music.

Focusing on regional artists, including aboriginal artists, the **Thunder Bay Art Gallery** (Confederation College Campus, 1080 Keewatin St., www.theag.ca, noon-8pm Tues.-Thurs., noon-5pm Fri.-Sun., donation $5, free admission Wed.) changes the displays in its three small exhibit rooms several times a year.

Animal pelts were a valuable trade commodity at Fort William.

Two Days Outdoors in Thunder Bay

If you love the outdoors, base yourself in Thunder Bay, on the shores of Lake Superior, with several provincial parks right outside the city. Here's a two-day plan for adventuring outdoors from this Northwestern Ontario urban center.

DAY 1

Get ready for adventure with a plentiful plate of Finnish pancakes at **Hoito Restaurant**, the classic Scandinavian eatery. After breakfast, try rock climbing—**Outdoor Skills and Thrills** offers lessons and guided climbs, even for beginners, on cliffs around Thunder Bay—or if you prefer a gentler activity, walk along the lakeshore at **Prince Arthur's Landing** for a self-guided tour of the park's public artworks.

Lunch on a build-your-own salad bowl at **Rebel Salad** or get a sandwich and fresh juice at vegetarian-friendly **Growing Season Juice Collective**, then head for **Kakabeka Falls Provincial Park,** west of the city. Snap photos of these double cascades, which are often called the "Niagara of the North," and take a hike along the river. If it's a hot day, you can go for a swim.

Return to the city in time for a sunset sailing tour with **Sail Superior.** For dinner, stroll along the docks and take a seat overlooking the waterfront at lively **Bight,** before calling it a night.

DAY 2

Start your day bright and early with coffee at **St. Paul Roastery** or with something more substantial, like eggs Benedict or pan-fried walleye at **Roosters Bistro** downtown. Get a sandwich to go or stop at the grocery store for a picnic lunch, and then drive east toward **Ouimet Canyon Provincial Park,** a deep and dramatic gorge with jagged cliffs on either side. It's an easy walk to two lookout points above the canyon floor. On your way to the canyon, pull off at the **Terry Fox Tourist Information Centre** to see the larger-than-life-size bronze **statue of Terry Fox,** who embarked on a cross-Canada run in 1980 to raise money for cancer research after he had lost his own leg to the disease.

Spend the rest of the day in vast **Sleeping Giant Provincial Park,** where you can choose among numerous hiking trails. The park's signature hike is the 22-kilometer (14-mile) round-trip Top of the Giant, which rewards hikers with great views across Lake Superior, but there are plenty of shorter options, including the mostly flat Sea Lion Trail, leading to an unusual and vaguely animal-shaped geological formation that gives the route its name. Have a picnic on the beach at **Marie Louise Lake,** where you can also go for a paddle; the Visitor Centre nearby rents canoes, kayaks, and stand-up paddleboards. Before leaving the park, drive the winding road to the **Thunder Bay Lookout,** a spot atop some of Ontario's highest cliffs that allows views across the lake all the way back to the city.

Return to Thunder Bay for a shower and brief rest before dinner at one of the downtown bistros, such as **The Tomlin** or **Silver Birch.** After your two days of outdoor adventures, you've earned your dessert. Fortunately, **Prime Gelato** is right nearby.

Flight-Seeing

For a unique perspective on the islands of Lake Superior and the topography of the Sleeping Giant, take a 20- to 30-minute flight-seeing tour with **Wilderness North** (807/983-2047 or 888/465-3474, www.wildernessnorth.com, from $150 pp). You fly in a classic bush plane, a De Havilland Beaver, built in 1953. They can also fly you east of the Sleeping Giant to

Porphyry Point Lighthouse (from $240 pp), where you can take a tour.

SPORTS AND RECREATION
Sailing

To experience Lake Superior from the water, book a cruise with **Sail Superior** (807/628-3333, www.sailsuperior.com), which takes passengers on 90-minute sailing tours of Thunder Bay harbor (daily mid-May-mid-Oct., adults $59, ages 11-18 $39, ages 3-10 $25), departing from Marina Park. They also run half-day excursions to the Welcome Islands ($465 for up to 8 people) and organize other day or overnight sailing trips. Another option is a full-day or overnight trip to the **Porphyry Point Lighthouse** (from $1,195 for up to 6 people) east of the Sleeping Giant, where you can stay in the refurbished lightkeeper's residence.

Rock Climbing

The numerous cliffs around Thunder Bay and along Lake Superior's North Shore are magnets for rock climbers. Climbing guide Aric Fishman launched **Outdoor Skills and Thrills** (807/472-4742, www.outdoorskillsandthrills.com) to offer **rock climbing** lessons for beginners (half-day $79, full-day $149) and intermediates (full-day $149), as well as a variety of private or small-group guided climbing adventures for climbers of all abilities. Rock climbing season is normally May through October; in winter (December to March), the company leads ice climbing programs.

FOOD

Plan to attend the annual **Savour Superior Food and Drink Festival** (www.savoursuperior.com, Sept.) to sample what's new and local from around the region. The rest of the year, visit the **Thunder Bay Country Market** (Dorothy Dove Bldg., Canadian Lakehead Exhibition grounds, off Memorial Ave., 807/622-1406, www.thunderbaycountrymarket.com, 8am-1pm Sat. year-round, 4pm-7pm Wed. late May-early Sept.) for local products, such as elk jerky, homemade pickles, and baked goodies; look for **Boreal Birch Syrup** (www.birchsyrup.ca)—an alternative to maple—and for several varieties of gouda from **Thunder Oak Cheese Farm** (807/628-0175 or 866/273-3329, www.cheesefarm.ca).

Finnish

Originally opened to offer reasonably priced meals to Finnish bush workers when they came to the city (an average dinner in the 1930s cost 25 cents), ★ **Hoito Restaurant** (314 Bay St., 807/345-6323, www.thehoito.ca, 8am-7pm daily, breakfast $5-15, lunch and dinner $6-17) has become a Thunder Bay breakfast tradition, especially for its crepe-like Finnish pancakes, served plain or piled high with eggs, bacon, or ham. Expect weekend brunch lineups, but don't expect high style; the restaurant is on the lower level of the 1910 Finnish Labour Temple, with all the atmosphere of a church basement. Later in the day, try the pickled herring or smoked salmon plates.

Like the Hoito around the corner, **Scandinavian Home Restaurant** (147 Algoma St. S., 807/345-7442, www.scandihs.com, 7am-8pm daily, $5-20) was established as part of a support network for Scandinavian immigrants. These days, families, visitors, and old-timers all pack this cheery Viking-themed diner for substantial all-day breakfasts and a mix of home-style and Scandinavian specialties, like the salted salmon sandwich and *mojakka* (Finnish beef stew). Of course, they've got Finnish pancakes, too.

Contemporary

A boisterous downtown bistro, **The Tomlin** (202 1/2 Red River Rd., 807/346-4447, www.tomlinrestaurant.com, 5pm-10pm Tues.-Thurs., 5pm-11pm Fri.-Sat., sharing plates $12-29) reels in a diverse crowd with creative cocktails like the Green Lily (a sparkling blend of cucumber, elderflower, and pisco) or the Tomlin Collins (made with olive oil-infused gin, fennel, and coriander tincture), and with a long list of Ontario microbrews. Bring your sense of adventure for the eclectic menu, too, with sharing plates like sweet-and-crispy chicken karaage, roasted cauliflower with charred corn and manchego, or grilled herring with salsa verde.

Its wallpaper adorned with

photos of silvery trees, **Silver Birch** (28 N. Cumberland St., 807/345-0597, www. thesilverbirchrestaurant.com, 5pm-10pm Tues.-Sat., dinner $18-38) hums with quiet conversation and emphasizes northern ingredients in dishes like bacon-wrapped pickerel glazed with birch syrup or garlicky Caesar salad topped with bannock croutons and elk sausage chips. It often features wild game in dishes like elk shepherd's pie. You can drink a "Birch Bark Canoe"—Crown Royal whisky with birch beer.

Choose a seat overlooking the waterfront or on the patio at lively **Bight** (2201 Sleeping Giant Pkwy, Unit 100, 807/622-4448, www. bightrestaurant.ca, 11:30am-10pm Sun.-Thurs., 11:30am-11pm Fri.-Sat., lunch $14-20, dinner $18-44) in Marina Park. The small plates range from poutine topped with braised beef short ribs and Thunder Oak cheese curds to inventive pizzas, while the more substantial entrees, with plenty of regional ingredients, might pair local whitefish with roasted root vegetables or duck breast with a sweet potato latke and fried Brussels sprouts.

Excellent pizza from the wood-burning oven, seasonal specialties like fresh corn salad, and internationally inspired entrées—perhaps duck with Korean-style barbecue sauce, *piri piri* chicken, or pasta with braised rabbit—make contemporary **Caribou Restaurant & Wine Bar** (727 Hewitson St., 807/628-8588, www.caribourestaurant.com, 5pm-10pm Mon.-Wed., 11:30am-2pm and 5pm-10pm Thurs., 11:30am-2pm and 4:30pm-11pm Fri., 4:30pm-11pm Sat., 5pm-9pm Sun. $16-33) a long-running favorite for dinner with family or friends.

Diner

It's worth getting up when the cock crows for a hearty breakfast at **Roosters Bistro** (32 St. Paul St., 807/344-7660, www.roostersbistro. com, 8am-3pm daily, $6-16), a downtown diner serving morning classics with a Northern Ontario twist. Top your eggs Benedict with pan-fried walleye (a local fish) or pair your scramble with Finnish pancakes.

At lunch, burgers and sandwiches rule the roost.

Cafés and Light Meals

The aroma of freshly roasted coffee envelops you as you enter **St. Paul Roastery** (11 St. Paul St., 807/344-3900, 7:30am-5pm Mon.-Fri., 9am-5pm Sat.). Take a break at this hip brick-walled coffeehouse downtown with a pour-over or an espresso.

Squeezed into a tiny storefront, vegetarian-friendly **Growing Season Juice Collective** (201 Algoma St. S., 807/344-6869, www. growingseason.ca, 11am-8pm Mon.-Sat., $8-13) serves fresh-pressed juices and smoothies, sandwiches with locally made Thunder Oak gouda, and rice bowls. Try the sesame-ginger dressed Living Salad with greens, baked tofu, avocado, and sprouted lentils. The same team operates **Rebel Salad** (320 Bay St., 11am-8pm Mon.-Fri., $13-15), where you can customize your salad bowls with a mind-boggling array of ingredients, from roasted sweet potatoes to shredded beets to a chia-flax-sesame seed mix.

Dessert

The ice cream masters at **Prime Gelato** (200 Red River Rd., 807/344-1185, www. primegelato.ca, noon-10pm daily summer, call or check the website for off-season hours) concoct inventive flavors, like miso caramel or apple pie, made with local ingredients or with products imported from Italy. Also on the menu are nondairy *sorbettos*, including lemon or red wine and pear.

ACCOMMODATIONS

To stay downtown, consider the **Prince Arthur Waterfront Hotel** (17 Cumberland St. N., 807/345-5411 or 800/267-2675, www. princearthurwaterfront.com, $137-185), a redbrick landmark built in 1911, a short stroll from the harbor. The aging property could use some TLC, but many of the 120 rooms are large, with fridges, microwaves, and one-cup coffeemakers; the best have lake views. The restaurant serves a basic continental breakfast. Rates include Wi-Fi, parking, and a complimentary shuttle to or from the airport.

New in 2018, **The Haven Hostel** (226 Ambrose St., 807/629-2225, www.thehavenhostel.ca, $45-50 dorm, $95-100 d), on a downtown side street, is targeting budget-minded travelers with simple private rooms with en suite baths, standard four-bed mixed dorms, and six-bed male or female "pod" dorms, where each pod, behind a curtain for privacy, has a locker, shelves, electrical outlet, and lighting. There's a communal kitchen, lounge, and book exchange. Rates include Wi-Fi, continental breakfast, and all-day coffee and tea.

Also downtown, the upscale **Marriott-Delta Hotel at Prince Arthur's Landing** (www.marriott.com), slated for completion in 2018, will overlook the city's waterfront. The location opposite the lake is fantastic; get updates on opening dates and prices online.

There's nothing picturesque about the surroundings of the **Marriott Towneplace Suites** (550 Harbour Expressway, 807/346-9000, www.marriott.com, $144-269 d), overlooking the parking lot of a big-box store. Still, as one of Thunder Bay's newer chain motels, this family-friendly five-story property covers the essentials: colorful modern studio, one-, and two-bedroom suites with full kitchens, granite countertops, flat-screen TVs, and free Wi-Fi; a modest complimentary breakfast; a compact pool and fitness facility; and a central location.

Convenient if you're traveling by air or exploring attractions surrounding Thunder Bay, **Valhalla Inn** (1 Valhalla Inn Rd., 807/577-1121 or 800/964-1121, www.valhallainn.com, $134-219 d) is adjacent to the city's airport. Recent renovations have upgraded this older 264-room property with white duvets, electrically equipped desks, and free Wi-Fi.

INFORMATION AND SERVICES

Tourism Thunder Bay (www.thunderbay.ca) runs two local visitor information centers that are both attractions as well. On a hill east of the city, the **Terry Fox Tourist Information Centre** (off Highway 11/17, 1 km/0.6 miles east of Hodder Ave., 807/983-2041 or 800/667-8386, 8:30am-7pm daily mid-June-early Sept., 9am-5pm daily Sept.-mid.-June) looks out across Lake Superior to the Sleeping Giant, but it's worth stopping to see the 2.7-meter (nine-foot) bronze **statue of Terry Fox.** A young British Columbia man, Fox embarked on a cross-Canada run in 1980 to raise money for cancer research after losing his own leg to the disease. He unfortunately had to stop his "Marathon of Hope" as he neared Thunder Bay, after running 5,342 kilometers (3,339 miles). Though Fox succeeded in raising more than $24 million, his own cancer had returned and would end his life at age 22 on June 28, 1981.

Downtown near Marina Park, the distinctively shaped **Pagoda Information Centre** (Water St. at Red River Rd., 807/684-3670, 10am-6pm Tues.-Sat. June-early Sept.) claims to be Canada's oldest continuously operating tourism office, dating back to 1909.

For the scoop on the city's arts and entertainment scene, check out *The Walleye* (www.thewalleye.ca), the local alternative arts and culture publication.

GETTING THERE
Air
Thunder Bay International Airport (YQT, 100 Princess St., off Hwy. 61, 807/473-2600, www.tbairport.on.ca) is southwest of the city center. **Air Canada** (www.aircanada.com) and **Westjet** (www.westjet.com) fly to Thunder Bay from Toronto's Pearson Airport and from Winnipeg; **Porter Airlines** (www.flyporter.com) has flights from Billy Bishop Toronto City Airport. **Bearskin Airlines** (www.bearskinairlines.com) flies between Thunder Bay and Sault Ste. Marie and to several towns in Northwestern Ontario. **Wasaya Airways** (www.wasaya.com) flies to several northern communities.

Bus
Buses run to the Thunder Bay **Greyhound**

Bus Station (815 Fort William Rd., 807/345-2194 or 800/661-8747, www.greyhound.ca) from Sault Ste. Marie (9.75 hours, $72-181), Toronto (20.75 hours, $137-295), and Winnipeg (9.5 hours, $62-142).

Car

Thunder Bay is approximately 700 kilometers (435 miles) northwest of Sault Ste. Marie and the same distance east of Winnipeg. It's 80 kilometers (50 miles), along Highway 61, from the U.S. border near Grand Portage, Minnesota. Toronto to Thunder Bay is 1,375 kilometers (860 miles)—a two-day drive. If you're interested in exploring Lake Superior and other points in Northwestern Ontario, consider flying to Thunder Bay and either renting a car or arranging with a local outfitter for onward transportation. All the major car rental companies have Thunder Bay offices.

GETTING AROUND

Highway 11/17, the Trans-Canada Highway, skirts the western side of Thunder Bay. From the east, Hodder Avenue will take you toward downtown and the marina. The Harbour Expressway runs east-west from the Trans-Canada to Fort William Road, close to the lakeshore.

Thunder Bay's attractions are scattered throughout the surrounding region, making it challenging to explore without a car. Within the city, you can get to many destinations on buses run by **Thunder Bay Transit** (807/684-3744, www.thunderbay.ca/transit, $2.75).

TOP EXPERIENCE

★ SLEEPING GIANT PROVINCIAL PARK

From Thunder Bay's waterfront, you can see a hulking forested peninsula looming just offshore. If you look closely, and use your imagination, you can glimpse in the peninsula's terrain the reclining profile of a gigantic humanlike figure, its arms crossed over its chest. The Ojibwa have many legends surrounding the creation of this Sleeping Giant, which they call Nanabijou, the Spirit of the Deep Sea Water. In one tale, Nanabijou was turned to stone after the location of the peninsula's rich silver deposits was disclosed to outsiders. Regardless of its origin, this craggy neck of land with cliffs rising 240 meters (780 feet) above the lake has become one of Lake Superior's most iconic outdoor destinations.

An hour's drive east of Thunder Bay on the Sibley Peninsula, vast **Sleeping Giant Provincial Park** (Pass Lake, 807/977-2526, www.ontarioparks.com, $14.50 per vehicle) offers lots of opportunities for visitors to enjoy the outdoors. The park's boreal forest is home to moose, wolves, deer, foxes, and lynx. You can fish for yellow perch and northern pike in several inland lakes; in the park's largest lakes, you might catch walleye or smallmouth bass. Birders, take note: more than 200 avian species have been spotted in the region.

Near the park's northern entrance, **Thunder Bay Lookout**—atop some of Ontario's highest cliffs—has views across the lake to the city of Thunder Bay. If you're not afraid of heights, peer through the slatted lookout platform to the cliffs and rocky shores below. The nine-kilometer (5.5-mile) gravel and dirt road to the lookout can be steep and potholed in sections, but once you arrive in the parking lot, the lookout is only a minute's walk away.

The **Visitors Centre** and park information office are at Marie Louise Lake, near the park's south end, where the main campground is also located. The Visitors Centre rents watercraft (two hours $15, four hours $25), including **canoes, kayaks,** and **stand-up paddleboards,** as well as **mountain bikes** (four hours $20). In summer, park staff run numerous interpretive programs, including nature walks, campfires, and children's activities.

Hiking

Sleeping Giant has more than 100 kilometers (60 miles) of hiking trails that range from easy lakeside strolls to challenging daylong or multiday adventures. Because weather along Lake Superior can change rapidly, always carry rain gear and warm clothing, even if the sun is shining when you set out.

The park's signature hike is the **Top of the Giant**, a 22-kilometer (14-mile) round-trip climb across the peninsula's southern sections to scenic lookouts across Lake Superior. Starting from the Kabeyun South trailhead, this route follows several different trails. The Kabeyun Trail leads past Tee Harbour, where it meets the Talus Lake Trail; from there, you continue toward the Top of the Giant, where an additional two-kilometer (1.25-mile) steady climb leads to one of Ontario's highest lookout points. Park staff caution that you shouldn't attempt this tough hike unless you're in good physical condition, but dramatic views are the hiker's reward.

A far easier path is the **Sea Lion Trail,** a mostly flat, 2.5-kilometer (1.5-mile) walk to the lakeshore, where an unusual rust-tinged, vaguely animal-shaped geological formation jutting into the water gives the route its name. The Sea Lion Trail branches off from the Kabeyun Trail toward the park's southern end. Other day hikes include the family-friendly **Sibley Creek Trail** (2.3 km, 1.4 miles, round-trip) that starts from the Marie Louise Lake campground; the **Wildlife Habitat Trail** (2.1 km, 1.3 miles, round-trip), where you might spot deer or even moose; and the **Middlebrun Bay Trail** (10 km, 6 miles, round-trip), which traverses wetlands en route to a sandy beach.

Seasoned backpackers can explore the dramatic 37-kilometer (23-mile) linear **Kabeyun Trail,** which begins at the Thunder Bay Lookout and follows the coast around the Sleeping Giant.

Mountain Biking

Experienced cyclists can tackle several park trails and roads by mountain bike. The Sawyer Bay, Sawbill Lake, Burma, and Pickerel Lake Trails are open to mountain bikers, as is a section of the South Kabeyun Trail to the junction with Talus Lake Trail. Cyclists can pedal the steep rutted road to the Thunder Bay Lookout and the easier route along Marie Louise Drive, which starts from the campground.

Winter Sports

When the snow falls, the park grooms 50 kilometers (31 miles) of trails for cross-country

In Sleeping Giant Provincial Park, this "sea lion" rock formation gives the Sea Lion Trail its name.

skiing and snowshoeing. The Visitors Centre remains open as a warming station and restroom stop for winter adventurers.

Camping

Marie Louise Lake Campground (www. ontarioparks.com, mid-May-mid-Oct., tent sites $42-45, electrical sites $47-52) has 200 campsites, including 85 with electrical service. The campground's comfort stations have hot showers and laundry facilities. It's a short walk to a swimming beach and playground. Also in the campground are five **cabins** (year-round, $169.50). Sleeping six, each cabin has three bedrooms (one with a double bed and two with bunk beds), a kitchen, bath, and sunporch. Linens, dishes, and cooking equipment are provided. The park rents three **camping trailers** (May-Oct., $98-142), which also sleep six. Although the trailers have showers, air-conditioning, and TV, you need to bring your own bedding and walk to the nearby campground for toilets.

Book campsites, cabins, or trailers up to five months in advance through the **Ontario Parks Reservation Service** (888/668-7275, www.ontarioparks.com, reservation fee online $11, by phone $13).

Getting There

Because Sleeping Giant's territory spreads across 244 square kilometers (60,300 acres), it's not a quick drive-in, drive-out destination. Plan to spend at least a full day to explore the park. The park turnoff from Highway 17 is Highway 587 south at Pass Lake, 50 kilometers (32 miles) east of Thunder Bay. From there, it's another 30 kilometers (19 miles) south to the Visitors Centre and main campground at Marie Louise Lake.

★ OUIMET CANYON PROVINCIAL PARK

Northern Ontario has plenty of places where the forested landscape gives way to more extreme topography. Ouimet Canyon, in the small **Ouimet Canyon Provincial Park** (Ouimet Canyon Rd., Dorion, 807/977-2526, www.ontarioparks.com, mid-May to mid-Oct., $2), is one of those places. Carved by natural forces over millions of years, Ouimet Canyon is a 150-meter (495-foot)-wide **gorge** with jagged cliffs on either side. An easy one-kilometer (0.6-mile) loop trail leads to two lookout points, 100 meters (330 feet) directly above the canyon floor.

The canyon is especially striking in the fall when clusters of trees and plants turn gold

jagged cliffs at Ouimet Canyon Provincial Park

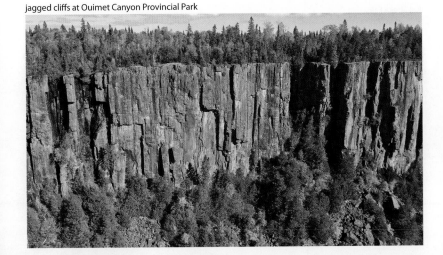

and red; autumn colors are typically the most vibrant from the second half of September through early October. While it's difficult to tell from above, several varieties of arctic plants, normally found in much more northern regions, thrive on the canyon floor. In part to protect this fragile vegetation, visitors are not allowed into the canyon.

Ouimet Canyon is a day-use park, with no camping facilities. Most visitors come from Thunder Bay or stop off as they're driving along Lake Superior's North Shore. You can combine a stop at Ouimet Canyon with a day at Sleeping Giant Provincial Park. The Ouimet Canyon turnoff from Highway 11/17 is 75 kilometers (47 miles) east of Thunder Bay and 35 kilometers (22 miles) west of Nipigon.

Nearby Sights

The Ouimet Canyon area has two other points of interest.

Off Ouimet Canyon Road, **Eagle Canyon Adventures** (275 Valley Rd., Dorion, 807/355-3064, www.eaglecanyonadventures.ca, 10am-6pm daily May-mid-Oct., adults $20, ages 4 and over $10) boasts **Canada's longest suspension bridge,** a 183-meter (600-foot) span high above a canyon. If that's not enough adventure, there's a second

92-meter (300-foot) suspension bridge to cross, as well as a **zip line** ($60) that whizzes you through the air for more than 800 meters (0.5 miles).

Some of the rocks and boulders around the Lake Superior region are rich with amethysts, and **Amethyst Mine Panorama** (500 Bass Lake Rd., Shuniah, 807/622-6908, www.amethystmine.com, 10am-5pm daily mid-May-June and Sept.-mid-Oct., 10am-6pm daily July-Aug., ages 6 and over $8), part working mine and part tourist attraction, is Canada's largest amethyst deposit. The stones were discovered here in 1955, and the mine has been operating since 1960.

Your admission price includes a 5- to 10-minute tour that covers the mine's history and facts about amethyst. What's more entertaining, particularly for the kids, is to dig for your own amethysts in the rock-studded field. If you'd like to keep what you dig up, it's $3 per pound. A gift shop sells amethyst jewelry, decorative stones, and other products.

The turnoff for the mine from Highway 11/17 is at East Loon Road, 55 kilometers (35 miles) east of Thunder Bay. From there, it's about 8 kilometers (5 miles) along a well-marked, mostly dirt road to the mine.

Kakabeka Falls

Northern Adventures Farther Afield

Vast—really vast—tracts of wilderness stretch north from Lake Superior to Hudson Bay and west to the Manitoba border. Adventurous travelers could explore for years in this immense region. Thunder Bay is a starting point for many more travels throughout Northwestern Ontario. Here are a few ideas to assist in planning additional adventures:

CANOEING IN QUETICO PROVINCIAL PARK

Known for its world-class wilderness paddling, **Quetico Provincial Park** (108 Saturn Ave., Atikokan, 807/597-2735, www.ontarioparks.com) has more than 2,000 lakes. Much of the immense forested territory in this 4,600-square-kilometer (1,775-square-mile) provincial park is accessible only by canoe.

You can sample Quetico's pine forests, cliffs, waterfalls, and lakes with a stay in the park's Dawson Trail campground, which has 106 car-camping sites as well as three rustic **cabins;** two of the cabins are available year-round, while one is a winter retreat only (Oct.-Apr.). The park's main entrance is off Highway 11, 165 kilometers (103 miles) west of Thunder Bay. To really experience Quetico's terrain, though, you need to get out into the backcountry. Outfitters like **Canoe Canada Outfitters** (807/597-6418 or 877/597-6418, www.canoecanada.com) and **QuetiQuest** (807/929-2266, www.quetiquest.com) can help plan Quetico trips.

NORTHERN WILDERNESS WITH WILDERNESS NORTH

Based in Thunder Bay, outfitter **Wilderness North** (807/983-2047 or 888/465-3474, www.wildernessnorth.com) organizes multiday trips throughout Northwestern Ontario. They own several lodges, accessible only by floatplane, that they use as bases for many trips, and they work with aboriginal guides in the surrounding First Nations communities.

One such adventure, the "Iconic Canadian," starts in Toronto, where you'll travel on Via Rail's long-distance Canadian train and disembark (with your guide) in the wilderness near **Wabakimi Provincial Park** (www.ontarioparks.com)—Ontario's second-largest provincial park. You'll spend several nights canoeing and camping in this remote region, before you paddle into one of the outfitter's wilderness lodges for two more days of adventures. You'll return to civilization by floatplane. They can tailor this trip to your paddling background; no prior canoe-tripping experience is required. Check Wilderness North's website or give them a call to discuss these and other wilderness trip ideas with a cultural slant.

WEST TO LAKE OF THE WOODS

With more than 105,000 kilometers (65,000 miles) of shoreline, Lake of the Woods wraps around more than 14,000 islands as it extends from Northwestern Ontario into Manitoba and across the U.S. border into Minnesota. The city of **Kenora** (www.kenora.ca), 500 kilometers (310 miles) west of Thunder Bay via the Trans-Canada Highway, is one starting point for exploring this expansive lake region. You could also base yourself in another Lake of the Woods destination, **Sioux Narrows Provincial Park** (www.ontarioparks.com), for fishing, swimming, sailing, and canoeing.

The **Northwest Ontario Sunset Country Travel Association** (807/468-5853 or 800/665-7567, www.ontariossunsetcountry.ca) has information to help plan a Lake of the Woods adventure. Another source of online information about travel in the province's north is **Explore Northwest Ontario** (http://visitnorthwestontario.com).

KAKABEKA FALLS PROVINCIAL PARK

Northern Ontario's largest waterfall is located in **Kakabeka Falls Provincial Park** (Hwy. 11/17, Kakabeka Falls, 807/453-9231, www.ontarioparks.com, year-round, $14.50 per vehicle), a 30-minute drive west of Thunder Bay. Viewing platforms and boardwalk paths on both sides of the Kaministiquia River give you excellent vantage points for admiring the 40-meter (130-foot)-high falls. Sometimes called the "Niagara of the North," Kakabeka is a more modest than its famous southern neighbor yet still an impressive cascade of water.

In addition to the boardwalk trail overlooking the falls, Kakabeka has several longer **hiking** routes. The easy Mountain Portage Walking Trail, a 1.25-kilometer (0.75-mile) loop, follows the portage route that early explorers took to bypass the falls. The 2.5-kilometer (1.5-mile) Little Falls Walking Trail is another loop with views along the river and a climb up the Mountain Portage. Upriver from the falls, there's a small beach and riverside **swimming** area.

Camping

The park has 169 **campsites** (www.ontarioparks.com, mid-May-mid-Oct., tent sites $36-42, electrical sites $42-47) in three campgrounds. Whispering Hills Campground is in the woods up a steep road from the falls; it has central showers and laundry facilities. Bordering the Kaministiquia River, the Riverside Campground and the adjacent Fern's Edge Campground have vault toilets as well as central flush toilets but no showers.

Practicalities

Kakabeka Falls Provincial Park is 35 kilometers (22 miles) west of Thunder Bay, off Highway 11/17. Unless you plan to camp, most visitors day-trip from Thunder Bay. If you're taking a quick look at the falls and moving on, pay for parking by the hour instead of buying a full-day pass. The park **Visitors Centre** (late May-mid-Oct.) on the river's west bank provides information and runs summer interpretive programs.

You'll find basic services, including a couple of places to eat, just east of the park in the village of Kakabeka Falls. For coffee, fresh baked goodies, and light meals, stop into the cabin that houses **Metropolitan Moose Beanery & Café** (4770 Hwy. 11/17, Kakabeka Falls, 807/473-5453).

Background

The Landscape

Covering 1.1 million square kilometers (425,000 square miles), Ontario is nearly as large as France, Italy, and Germany combined. It's not Canada's largest province (Quebec has that distinction), but it's twice as big as Texas, the second-largest U.S. state, and just slightly smaller than Alaska. Ontario's northernmost regions share the same latitude as southern Alaska, while Point Pelee, the southernmost point on the Ontario mainland, is at the same latitude as Northern California's wine country. No wonder, then, that Southern Ontario is a major wine-producing region.

Ontario sits between Manitoba to the west and Quebec to the east, but if you think it's landlocked in the middle of the country, think again. The province borders four of the five Great Lakes—Ontario, Erie, Huron, and Superior—along more than 3,000 kilometers (2,300 miles) of shoreline. Ontario even has over 1,000 kilometers (680 miles) of saltwater shores on its northern boundary with Hudson Bay.

Beyond these major bodies of water, Ontario has nearly 250,000 lakes holding one-third of the world's freshwater, as well as numerous rivers and streams. Of course, the province's most impressive water feature may be Niagara Falls, which thunder down the Niagara River separating Canada from the United States.

GEOGRAPHY

With its granite rock formations and pine forests, the Canadian Shield covers two-thirds of Ontario, extending from Manitoba across the province nearly to Ottawa and to the Thousand Islands farther south. In the far north, in the Hudson Bay lowlands along Hudson and James Bays from Moosonee to Fort Severn, the rocks and pines give way to swamps and meadows.

In the south, in the ecological zone known as the Mixedwood Plain, more lowlands along the Great Lakes are flat farm country, while the woodlands include a mix of deciduous trees and evergreens. Bisecting a 725-kilometer (450-mile) section of Southern Ontario, extending roughly between the Niagara and Bruce Peninsulas, is the Niagara Escarpment, a forested ridge of sedimentary rock that juts above the region's otherwise flat terrain. The highest point on the escarpment is 510 meters (1,625 feet) above sea level.

CLIMATE

Although Toronto is northwest of Buffalo, Torontonians are quick to point out that the lake effect that dumps piles of snow on their New York State neighbors has a different result in their city. Toronto's position on Lake Ontario's northern shore moderates the winter weather, and the city averages 115 centimeters (45 inches) of snow per year, less than Buffalo can get on a single day. Winter is still cold and frequently snowy—January's average temperatures range from -10°C (14°F) to -2°C (28°F)—but at least you might not always be battling major blizzards if you visit midwinter.

Toronto's spring is fairly short, beginning in late April or May, and summers can turn hot and humid. In July, the average temperatures range from a low of 15°C (59°F) to a high of 27°C (81°F). Fall is a lovely time of year, and the best season to travel across much of the province, particularly in late September and early October when the trees put on their annual autumn color show.

South of Toronto, on the Niagara Peninsula, the Niagara wineries claim that the

Ontario's Average Temperatures

These are the average annual temperatures in several of Ontario's cities. Keep in mind that temperatures can fluctuate on a given day. On a typical July day in Toronto, for example, the temperature might be as low as 18°C (64°F) at night and as high as 26°C (79°F) during the day.

City	January	April	July	October
Toronto	-4°C, 25°F	7.5°C, 46°F	22°C, 72°F	10.5°C, 51°F
Niagara Falls	-4.5°C, 24°F	7.5°C, 46°F	22°C, 72°F	10.5°C, 51°F
Ottawa	-10.5°C, 13°F	6°C, 43°F	21°C, 70°F	8°C, 46°C
Windsor	-4.5°C, 24°F	8°C, 46°C	23°C, 74°F	11°C, 52°F
Sudbury	-13.5°C, 8°F	3°C, 38°F	19°C, 66°F	6°C, 43°C

Source: Environment Canada

region's climate is similar to that of France's Burgundy region and Loire Valley, with Lake Ontario again moderating the more extreme winter weather found in nearby New York State. Temperatures are slightly more moderate than in Toronto, too: slightly hotter in summer, not quite as frigid in winter. Niagara's warm summers and temperate autumns are the busiest times here, when tourism is in full swing.

As you travel north of Toronto, into the Muskoka Cottage Country and along Georgian Bay, the slightly cooler summers have made these regions popular with Torontonians escaping the city's heat and humidity. It's still hot midsummer, but at least you can cool off with a swim in the lake. In winter, a snow belt starts north of Toronto around the city of Barrie. It can be snowing in Barrie (and on the ski hills between Barrie and Collingwood) when it's raining or dry in Toronto.

Ottawa residents will maintain, with a certain perverse pride, that their city is the coldest capital in the world. Moscow may also claim that distinction, but there's no disputing that winter in Ottawa—320 kilometers (200 miles) north of Syracuse, New York—can be frigid. While Ottawa may not get the heavy snows that towns like Syracuse do, it's definitely in the snow belt, averaging 235 centimeters (nearly eight feet) of snow per year. Still, the city celebrates its winter weather with the popular Winterlude Festival in February and with lots of outdoor activities. Spring comes late to Ottawa (it might begin to warm in April, but it's not consistently springlike till May), and summers, as in Toronto, are hot and sticky. Fall, as it is throughout Ontario, is one of Ottawa's best seasons.

Across Northern Ontario, winter temperatures, as you'd expect, dip well below freezing, and snowfall is heavy. Summers, though, can be surprisingly hot and humid, with daytime highs above 30°C (86°F). Even along Hudson and James Bays, expect warm temperatures if you're traveling in July and August.

Plants and Animals

PLANTS

Although you might not know it from a down-town Toronto street corner, forests dominate Ontario's landscape, covering more than 60 percent of the province's land. The types of trees you'll find vary from the southern to northern regions.

In the south, along Lake Erie and Lake Ontario and extending to Lake Huron's south-eastern shore, **deciduous forest** is domi-nant. Trees common to this region include maple, oak, and walnut. You'll find the white trillium, Ontario's official provincial flower, blooming in deciduous forests in late April and early May.

Moving north, the forests become a mix of deciduous and **coniferous trees,** the for-mer including red maples, sugar maples (ac-counting for most of the province's maple syrup production), yellow birch, and red oak, and the latter including eastern white pine (Ontario's official provincial tree), east-ern hemlock, red pine, and white cedar. This forest region, known as the Great Lakes-St. Lawrence Forest, extends across the central part of the province, along the St. Lawrence River, on the Lake Huron shores, and in the area west of Lake Superior.

If you think of **orchids** as tropical plants, you may be surprised to learn that more than 40 species of orchids grow on the Bruce Peninsula, which juts into Lake Huron. The best time to see the orchids in bloom is mid-May through early June.

Boreal forest spreads across most of Northwestern Ontario, covering 49 million hectares (121 million acres). The predominant species here are jack pine and black spruce, as well as white birch, poplar, and balsam fir.

In the far north's Hudson Bay Lowlands, constituting the remaining 25 percent of Ontario's land and bordering the subarc-tic tundra, trees include black spruce, white spruce, white birch, balsam fir, and balsam poplar. This area is also one of the world's largest expanses of wetlands.

Ontario's provincial government owns more than 90 percent of the province's forests. About one-third is classified as "production forest," meaning that it's available for logging. Although some provincial parks and reserves, like Algonquin Provincial Park, are protected from further development, logging has histor-ically been part of their economy, and limited logging is still allowed.

Even in its urban areas, Ontario is begin-ning to realize that its trees are an important asset. In Toronto, which currently has an estimated 10 million trees, the city is work-ing toward a goal of increasing its tree can-opy from 28 percent to 40 percent by 2057. The city hosts annual tree-planting days and plants free trees on residential streets.

ANIMALS

Southern Ontario is home to the white-tailed deer as well as other small animals, including raccoons, skunks, beavers, red foxes, and gray squirrels. In fall, thousands of monarch but-terflies typically pass through the province's southwest, crossing Lake Erie as they migrate south to Mexico. Although butterfly numbers have been fluctuating in recent years, Point Pelee National Park remains one of the best spots to witness the monarch migration. The Point Pelee region is also prime bird-watch-ing territory. More than 370 species of birds have been recorded in the vicinity, and in the spring, thousands of birders come to witness the migration of songbirds returning to the north.

In the Canadian Shield region that cov-ers much of central Ontario, the animals get bigger. While you'll still see foxes, squirrels, and beavers, this region is also home the east-ern timber wolf, the gray wolf, white-tailed deer, caribou, Canadian lynx, and black bear. One of the most popular events in Ontario's

Algonquin Provincial Park is the summer Wolf Howl, when park naturalists imitate wolf calls and wild wolves may howl in response. Many of the fish that you see on Ontario tables, including pike, lake trout, and walleye, come from this region.

In the far north, caribou, moose, and black bears become more prevalent, and in the extreme northern reaches, including the vast protected territory of Polar Bear Provincial Park (accessible only by air), there's a small population of polar bears. Seals, walruses, and beluga whales can sometimes be spotted off the northern coasts.

History

INDIGENOUS PEOPLES AND THE FIRST EUROPEANS

Archaeologists have found evidence of human settlement in Ontario dating back more than 10,000 years. In the north, early aboriginal people hunted and fished, while farther south, they were the region's first farmers. The province's name, Ontario, comes from an Iroquoian word that's loosely translated as "sparkling water."

The first Europeans to explore Ontario arrived in the early 1600s. French explorer Étienne Brulé sailed along the St. Lawrence River and into Lake Ontario in 1610, while his countryman Samuel de Champlain followed in 1615, after overseeing the construction of a fort at what is now Quebec City. British explorer Henry Hudson claimed the Northern Ontario region that now bears his name—Hudson Bay—for Britain in 1611.

A group of French Jesuit missionaries began constructing a community near present-day Midland in 1639, establishing the first European settlement in Ontario. Their mission was to bring Christianity to the indigenous Wendat people, whom they called the "Huron." You can visit a re-created version of this settlement, where the Jesuits worked with the Huron for 10 years. It's now known as Sainte-Marie Among the Hurons.

In 1670 the Hudson's Bay Company was established, and the British monarch granted the company exclusive trading rights to the land around Hudson Bay. Over the next 100 years, the fur trade flourished across Northern Ontario and the rest of Canada's far north. Aboriginal hunters sold furs to the Hudson's Bay Company in exchange for knives, kettles, and what became the company's signature wool blankets.

FRANCE VS. BRITAIN

Both France and Britain staked claims to territory in present-day North America during the 1600s and 1700s, and battles broke out as the two countries fought over these territorial claims.

During the Seven Years' War (1756-1763), while many conflicts took place in what is now Quebec and Eastern Canada, others were waged in what is now Ontario, along Lake Ontario and in the Niagara region. In 1759 the British defeated the French in Quebec City, during the Battle of the Plains of Abraham, which turned the tide of the war. The Canadian territories became part of the British Empire.

Over the subsequent decades, the British found that their vast colony was difficult to govern. In 1791, the British Parliament passed the Constitutional Act, which divided the territory in two. The region encompassing present-day Ontario became Upper Canada, and what is now Quebec became Lower Canada.

Upper Canada's first capital was the town of Newark, now called Niagara-on-the-Lake. In 1793, the capital was moved farther north, away from the volatile American border, to the settlement of York, which eventually grew to become the city of Toronto.

THE UNITED EMPIRE LOYALISTS

In the late 1700s, a wave of immigration to Upper Canada came from south of the border. The 13 British colonies south of Canada declared their independence from Britain, launching the American Revolutionary War, which resulted in the creation of the United States. After the war, many Loyalists—Americans who remained loyal to the British Crown—found that they were no longer welcome in the new United States.

The Loyalists came north to the still-British colony of Upper Canada, where many received land grants from the British government. Many of the early settlers to Eastern Ontario, along the Thousand Islands, in Kingston, in Prince Edward County, and in what is now the Rideau Canal region, were Loyalists, who kept British traditions alive in their new colony.

THE WAR OF 1812

Tensions between Britain and France flared up again in the early 1800s. The British navy eventually set up a blockade, preventing French ships from reaching the Americas and stopping American ships heading for Europe. In North America, where Britain and the United States still had an uneasy relationship in the aftermath of the American Revolution, the shipping blockade became one more significant source of conflict. In 1812, the United States attacked the closest outpost of the British Empire: Canada.

Many battles during the War of 1812, which lasted until 1815, were fought on Ontario soil, in the regions bordering the United States: the Niagara Peninsula, Toronto, the Windsor-Detroit area, and along the St. Lawrence River in Eastern Ontario. The Americans burned the legislative buildings in Toronto; the British in turn attacked Washington DC and set the White House aflame.

The British and American governments eventually negotiated a settlement, and the war officially ended with the Treaty of Ghent,

signed on December 24, 1814, and ratified February 16, 1815.

BUILDING CANALS AND WATERWAYS

After the War of 1812, Canadians were concerned that the St. Lawrence River—a vital shipping channel between Montreal and the Great Lakes—could be vulnerable to another U.S. attack, since the Americans controlled the river's southern banks. In 1826, British lieutenant colonel John By arrived on the site of what is now Ottawa and made plans for a new town—christened Bytown—and for a canal that would run south to Lake Ontario through a series of connected lakes, rivers, and waterways. The canal, which opened in 1832, became the Rideau Canal.

During the same period, entrepreneur William Hamilton Merritt proposed the idea of a canal across the Niagara Peninsula to provide a passage for ships traveling between Lake Ontario and Lake Erie. The Niagara River connected the two lakes, but a significant natural feature prevented the river from becoming a shipping route: the unnavigable Niagara Falls. Construction began on the Welland Canal, which included a series of locks to help ships "climb the mountain"—the Niagara Escarpment—between the two lakes. The canal opened in 1829.

Settlers in Ontario were also looking to improve shipping routes across the central sections of the province. In 1833, the first lock was built on what would eventually become the Trent-Severn Waterway, connecting Lake Ontario with Georgian Bay.

FIRST STEPS TO A UNITED CANADA

Upper and Lower Canada, which had been split in 1791, were joined again in 1840 as the Province of Canada. Toronto had been the capital of predominantly British Upper Canada, while Quebec City was the capital of francophone Lower Canada. However, when the two provinces were united, neither would accept the other's capital as the seat of government. As a compromise, the city of Kingston became the first capital of the Province of Canada. But the political wrangling continued, and two years later, the capital was moved to Montreal. In the meantime, the frontier outpost of Bytown that Lieutenant Colonel John By had settled in the 1830s had become the city of Ottawa. By 1857, when the legislature still hadn't been able to agree on a permanent home for the Canadian capital, they referred the problem to the British monarch, Queen Victoria. The queen and her advisers unexpectedly chose the comparatively remote outpost of Ottawa.

Situated between English Upper Canada and French Lower Canada, Ottawa had a relatively central location. But another important factor was that other potential capitals—Toronto, Kingston, and Montreal—were extremely close to Canada's boundary with the United States. Ottawa, in contrast, was at a safer distance from the American border. Since 1857, Ottawa has been the nation's capital.

THE UNDERGROUND RAILROAD

In the mid-1800s, thousands of enslaved African Americans fled from the United States to freedom in Canada. Following what was known as the Underground Railroad, a network of safe houses and churches that gave shelter to the refugees, the vast majority of those slaves crossed into Canada into what is now Southwestern Ontario. Many remained in the region, with significant settlements in Windsor, Sandwich, Amherstburg, Chatham, Dresden, and Buxton, and many of their descendants live here today.

CONFEDERATION

The Province of Canada was split once again in the 1860s, creating the new provinces of Quebec and Ontario. But this time, these provinces joined with Nova Scotia and New Brunswick to establish a new nation: the Dominion of Canada. The British Parliament passed the British North America Act in 1867, which officially created this fledgling country, joining these four original provinces in confederation on July 1, 1867. Kingston lawyer and politician John A. Macdonald became the first prime minister of the new nation of Canada. Today, Canadians celebrate Confederation on July 1, Canada Day. The country marked its 150th birthday in 2017.

ONTARIO'S DEVELOPING INDUSTRIES

In the late 1800s and early 1900s, Ontario began the transition from a primarily agricultural province to a more industrial one. In 1903, a huge silver vein was discovered in Northern Ontario, near the town of Cobalt, launching the mining industry in this region. In Southwestern Ontario, the industry was automobiles; the year after Henry Ford founded the Ford Motor Company, the company set up a manufacturing plant across the river from Detroit, in the Ontario city of Windsor.

During this same era, tourism became important to the Ontario economy. Railroads and steamships ferried visitors to lakeside resorts in the Muskoka region, the Kawarthas, the Thousand Islands, and Niagara Falls. The falls also became a source of hydroelectric power, beginning in 1906.

The province's industrial development continued throughout the 20th century, during and after both World Wars, and into the 1950s and 1960s. The Toronto subway—Canada's first—opened in 1954, and the Macdonald-Cartier Freeway (Hwy. 401), which crosses the province from Windsor to the Quebec border, opened in 1968.

More recently, an Ontario company helped usher in the smartphone era when the Waterloo-based outfit formerly known as Research in Motion introduced the BlackBerry. The province now claims to be the second-largest information technology region in North America (after California); Toronto, Ottawa, and Kitchener-Waterloo are all major high-tech industry hubs.

Government and Economy

GOVERNMENT

Canada has a three-tiered governmental structure, with federal, provincial (or territorial), and municipal governments. The federal government, headquartered in Ottawa, is responsible for foreign policy, national defense, immigration, and other national issues. The provincial governments handle health care, education, policing, and the highways, among other things. Local issues, such as zoning, city policing and firefighting, snow removal, garbage, and recycling, are the municipal governments' purview.

Retaining its roots as a British Commonwealth country, Canada is a constitutional monarchy. The country's head of state is officially the monarch of the United Kingdom. That means that the Queen of England is also the Queen of Canada. Although Canada has preserved many of its British influences and traditions, including the summer Changing the Guard ceremony in Ottawa, the monarch's role in Canada is largely symbolic, and it's Canada's **prime minister** who is the country's chief executive.

The queen's official representative in Canada as head of state is the **governor general.** This, too, is largely a ceremonial role. The governor general functions something like a governmental ambassador, officiating at ceremonies, bestowing awards, and opening and closing Parliament sessions. With the prime minister's advice, the queen appoints the governor general for a five-year term.

Parliament is the national legislature, which has two bodies: the elected 338-member House of Commons and the appointed 105-member Senate. The governmental structure at the provincial level parallels that of the federal government. The head of each provincial government is the premier, a position analogous to a U.S. state governor. Each province and territory has its own legislature.

Toronto is Ontario's provincial capital; the Legislative Assembly building is in Toronto's Queen's Park.

ECONOMY

In Ontario's early days, the region's economy was based on its natural resources, including timber, fur, and minerals. Logging, trapping, and mining are still important components of Northern Ontario's economy. In cities like Sudbury and Timmins, mines dominate the skyline, and across the north, you'll share the highways with massive logging trucks.

Southern Ontario was formerly agricultural, and while you'll see plenty of farms, orchards, and vineyards, the province's southern sector is now heavily industrial. Manufacturing, particularly in the automotive, pharmaceutical, and aerospace sectors, has been a foundation of Ontario's economy for many years. The province produces more than half of all manufactured goods that are exported from Canada.

As in many other countries, the service industries have become more and more important in Ontario, now accounting for more than 75 percent of the province's economy. Toronto is Canada's financial capital; not only is Canada's major equities market, the Toronto Stock Exchange, based here, but so are the headquarters of scores of banks and financial services companies.

High technology has become a major Ontario business, too. Greater Toronto, the Kitchener-Waterloo region, and Ottawa are major centers for software and hardware development, telecommunications, and biotechnology. Toronto is a hub for Canada's communications industries as well, including TV and film production, broadcasting, publishing, performing arts, design, and advertising.

With more than 30 colleges and universities, education is a significant component of Ontario's economy. Canada's largest university—the University of Toronto—is in Ontario. Other major Ontario universities include York University, Ryerson University, and the Ontario College of Art and Design, all based in Toronto; McMaster University in Hamilton; the University of Waterloo and Wilfred Laurier University in Waterloo; the University of Western Ontario in London; the University of Windsor; Carleton University and the University of Ottawa in the nation's capital; and Queen's University in Kingston.

ENVIRONMENTAL ISSUES

Like many heavily industrialized regions, Ontario has its environmental challenges. Along the lakeshores, particularly sections of Lake Erie, Lake Ontario, and Lake Huron, you'll still see power plants and other reminders of the province's industrial heritage—some still active, some long abandoned. In northern towns like Sudbury and Timmins, where mining remains an important part of the local economy, barren rocky pits mar parts of the landscape, and smoke can darken the skies. Similarly, the logging industry has cut wide swaths across Ontario's north.

Another industrial legacy, unfortunately, is water pollution. The Great Lakes can be plagued with poor water quality, although significant efforts have been made in recent years to clean up the lakes and make them again fit for recreation. Many beaches now have a Blue Flag program in place, where a blue flag identifies areas that are clean and safe for swimming.

As Ontario's cities continue to grow, urban sprawl, increasing traffic, and worsening air quality are challenges to address. These issues are most acute in Toronto, the province's largest metropolitan area, and in the Golden Horseshoe, the suburban ring around metropolitan Toronto. But Ontario is continuing to promote alternatives to car travel, with increasing options for train, bus, and ferry travel across the province.

People and Culture

Ontario is Canada's most populous province, home to more than 14 million people, or roughly 40 percent of Canadians. Most of Ontario's population lives in the cities, with over six million concentrated in the Greater Toronto region.

DEMOGRAPHY

Canada's government actively encourages immigration as a way to counterbalance the country's declining birthrate and provide workers for the nation's growing economy. Due to these immigration policies, which began in earnest in the 1970s, Canada's largest cities have become among the most multicultural on the planet. Half of all immigrants to Canada settle in Ontario.

Toronto, in particular, is a city of immigrants. Roughly half of the metropolitan area's residents were born outside Canada, and tens of thousands of new immigrants move to the city every year. While the majority of Toronto's early settlers were of British origin, Torontonians now come from all over the globe. In the 2016 census, 51.5 percent of Toronto residents identified as a member of a visible minority community, and in some suburban cities in Greater Toronto, that percentage is even higher, from 60 percent in Richmond Hill to more than 75 percent in Markham. South Asian, Chinese, Black, and Filipino people are Toronto's largest visible minority groups.

After English and French, Chinese is the most widely spoken language in Ontario. Ontario also has significant Punjabi-, Urdu-, Italian-, Persian-, and German-speaking populations.

RELIGION

Christianity is the major religion in Canada. More than 40 percent of Canadians are Roman Catholic, and about one-quarter are Protestant; in Ontario, Protestants are the predominant religious group, with Roman Catholics a close second. Recent census figures indicate that more than 15 percent of Canadians claim no religious affiliation at all.

Although only about 1 percent of Canada's population, or roughly 350,000 people, is Jewish, Canada has the fourth-largest Jewish population in the world, after Israel, the United States, and France. More than half of Canada's Jews live in Toronto.

Canada's largest non-Christian religious group is Muslim, representing about 2 percent of the population nationwide. In Ontario, Muslim communities are concentrated in the large urban areas of Toronto and Ottawa.

FRENCH LANGUAGE AND CULTURE

Ever since European explorers first landed on Canada's shores, the country was settled by both English- and French-speaking colonists. While many people assume that Quebec is Canada's only French-speaking region, Ontario, in particular, had a large francophone population during colonial times. Even as late as the mid-1800s, more than half of Ontario's population were native French speakers.

Today, English is the first language throughout most of the province of Ontario, and there's no need to brush up on your *bonjour* and *merci* to travel here. However, because the province shares a long border with francophone Quebec, French is widely spoken throughout the region, and Ontario's francophone community is the largest in Canada outside Quebec. Roughly 500,000 Ontario residents, or just under 5 percent of the population, speak French as their first language. More than 60 percent of Ontario's francophones live in the province's eastern and northeastern regions.

Ottawa has a particularly large francophone and bilingual community. In fact, as the capital of bilingual Canada, Ottawa is itself a bilingual city, closer in linguistic mindset—and physical proximity—to Montreal than to Toronto. The Ottawa metropolitan area spans two provinces, Ontario and Quebec. The city of Ottawa is on the Ontario side of the Ottawa River, but on the opposite riverbank is the community of Gatineau in French-speaking Quebec. Residents easily go back and forth across the bridges between the two provinces, many living on one side and working on the other. Reflecting this linguistic diversity, nearly half the population of the Ottawa region is fully bilingual. The government operates in both languages, as do many businesses.

Across the province, Ontario's francophone community continues to grow through immigration, as French-speaking immigrants from Africa, the Caribbean, and Europe have settled here. Today, about 10 percent of Ontario's francophones are members of a visible racial minority.

ABORIGINAL CULTURE

Canada has three officially recognized aboriginal groups: the First Nations, the Inuit, and the Métis. *First Nations* is the modern term for indigenous people who are neither Inuit nor Métis. The Inuit people live primarily in Canada's far north, while the Métis—descendants of French settlers and their First Nations spouses—have historically settled in the prairies and the west.

Canada's aboriginal peoples—totaling just over one million people—make up about 4 percent of the nation's population. Roughly one-quarter of Canada's aboriginal people, most of whom fall under the "First Nations" designation, live in Ontario.

Ontario's aboriginal people are divided primarily into two groups, based on their linguistic heritage. The Cree, Oji-Cree, Algonquin, Ojibwa, Odawa, Potawatomi, and Delaware, whose historical territory has spread across central and Northern Ontario, speak languages that derive from Algonquian, while the Six Nations people, who are concentrated in the southern part of the province and include the Mohawk, Oneida, Onondaga, Cayuga, Seneca, and Tuscarora, are Iroquoian-speaking.

Some of Ontario's aboriginal peoples—including the Anishinaabe on Manitoulin Island, the Cree along James Bay, the Ojibwa near Peterborough in Eastern Ontario, and the Six Nations near Brantford and Hamilton—are beginning to open their communities to tourism, offering opportunities for visitors to learn about their cultures while bringing in new revenue.

The Arts

As you travel around Ontario, you can't help but see works by the Group of Seven, Canadian landscape painters who worked primarily in the 1920s and whose works have become associated with Ontario. The original members, Franklin Carmichael, Lawren Harris, A. Y. Jackson, Frank Johnston, Arthur Lismer, J. E. H. MacDonald, and Frederick Varley, were all based in Ontario. Although artist Tom Thomson died (under mysterious circumstances in Algonquin Provincial Park) before the group was officially formed, he worked with most of its members and is normally considered part of the group.

The National Gallery of Canada in Ottawa has an extensive collection of Group of Seven works, as do Toronto's Art Gallery of Ontario and McMichael Canadian Art Collection. In Owen Sound, there's a small museum, the Tom Thomson Art Gallery, devoted to Thomson's work.

In the Lake Superior region, look for the "Moments of Algoma" interpretive panels (www.momentsofalgoma.ca) that highlight either an actual location where Group of Seven members painted or spots that have some connection to the artists' experiences around northern Ontario. You'll find these panels at the CN Railway Station in Sault Ste. Marie, Agawa Canyon, Lake Superior Provincial Park, Pukaskwa National Park, Terrace Bay, and a number of other places.

LITERATURE

Many of Canada's notable contemporary authors live and work in Ontario or have made the province their home. **Margaret Atwood,** born in Ottawa in 1939, is one of Canada's best-known novelists. She writes on themes including feminism (*The Edible Woman,* 1969), science fiction (*The Handmaid's Tale,* 1985), life in Toronto (*The Robber Bride,* 1993), and ancient Greece (*The Penelopiad,* 2005).

Another of Canada's most notable writers, **Carol Shields** (1935-2003), was born in the United States but moved to Canada at age 22. She lived in Ottawa, Winnipeg, and Victoria, authoring 10 novels, three collections of short fiction, three volumes of poetry, and four published plays. She won the Pulitzer Prize for *The Stone Diaries* (1993). Her other books include *A Fairly Conventional Woman* (1982), *Larry's Party* (1997), and *Unless* (2002).

Short-story writer and novelist **Alice Munro,** who was born and continues to live in Ontario, writes frequently about growing up female in the province's rural communities in the 1940s and 1950s. Among her works are *Lives of Girls and Women* (1971), *Who Do You Think You Are: Stories* (1978), *The View from Castle Rock* (2006), and *Dear Life* (2012). Her stories also appear periodically in *The New Yorker* and *The Atlantic.* Munro won the Nobel Prize in Literature in 2013. Her daughter Sheila Munro wrote a memoir about her mother, *Lives of Mothers and Daughters: Growing Up With Alice Munro* (2001).

Timothy Findley was born in Toronto and began his professional career as an actor, performing with the Stratford Festival in 1953. He later became the first playwright-in-residence at Ottawa's National Arts Centre and author of more than a dozen novels, including *The Wars* (1977). Sri Lankan-born novelist **Michael Ondaatje** has lived and worked in Ontario for many years, teaching at the University of Western Ontario, York University, and the University of Toronto. His best-known works, including *The English Patient* (1992), *Anil's Ghost* (2000), and *The Cat's Table* (2011), don't draw on Ontario life, but one of his earlier novels, *In the Skin of a Lion* (1987), is set in 1930s Toronto.

With so many Ontarians hailing from abroad, it's no surprise that many of the province's modern writers deal with immigrant themes. **Rohinton Mistry,** born in India and now living in Toronto, writes about the Indian and Indian Canadian communities in novels such as *A Fine Balance* (1995) and *Family Matters* (2002). Toronto novelist **M. G. Vassanji** also tackles immigrant themes, particularly about Indians and Africans. His books include *No New Land* (1991), *The In-Between Life of Vikram Lall* (2003), and *The Assassin's Song* (2007). Another Toronto writer, **Dionne Brand,** born in Trinidad in 1953, considers immigrant issues in her works as well, including the 2005 novel *What We All Long For.*

Born in Ontario in 1959, **Nino Ricci** drew on his experiences as an Italian Canadian in his first novel, *Lives of the Saints* (1990). His subsequent books include *In a Glass House* (1993), *Where She Has Gone* (1997), *Testament* (2003), and *The Origin of Species* (2008). One of Ontario's earliest "immigrant" writers was **Susanne Moodie,** who came with her husband from England in 1832 and settled in Upper Canada, in what is now Ontario. She described their experiences in her autobiographical works, *Roughing It in the Bush; or, Life in Canada* (1852) and the sequel, *Life in the Clearings Versus the Bush* (1853).

Humorist **Stephen Leacock** offered up a different take on small-town Ontario life in *Sunshine Sketches of a Little Town* (1912), which was among his 35 books of humor. His former home in Orillia, north of Barrie in central Ontario, is now a museum. Ontario-born playwright and novelist **Robertson Davies** set many of his novels, such as *Fifth Business* (1970) and *What's Bred in the Bone* (1985), in his home province. Novelist **Jane Urquhart,** who was born in the small Northern Ontario town of Little Long Lac and now lives in the southern part of the province, considers regional themes in works such as *The Stone Carvers* (2001).

More recently, Ireland-born writer **Emma Donoghue,** who resides with her partner in London, Ontario, rocketed to fame with the novel *Room* (2010), which she adapted into a 2015 film starring Brie Larson, who won an Academy Award for her role. Born in Toronto in 1966, **Joseph Boyden** authored a controversial novel, *The Orenda* (2013), set in the often-violent 17th-century world of the French missionaries and indigenous Wendat people in central Ontario. Ontario-born Ojibway author **Richard Wagamese** (1955-2017) explored the legacy of trauma that Canada's residential schools inflicted on generations of indigenous people, in novels like *Indian Horse* (2012), set in northern Ontario. A 2017 movie based on Wagamese's novel was filmed in Sudbury and elsewhere in Ontario's north.

MUSIC

Ontario has contributed many performers to the music and dance worlds. Rock-and-roll legend **Neil Young** hails from Toronto, as does classical pianist and composer **Glenn Gould** (1932-1982), where a concert hall in the Canadian Broadcasting Company building bears his name. Singer-songwriter **Gordon Lightfoot,** born in Orillia, is perhaps best known for "The Wreck of the Edmund Fitzgerald," his ballad about a Lake Superior shipwreck. Stratford's hometown heartthrob is former teen pop sensation **Justin Bieber;** country singer **Shania Twain** was born in Windsor and raised in Timmins. The bands **Barenaked Ladies** and **Tragically Hip** both have Ontario roots, as do singer-songwriters **Alanis Morissette,** who was born in Ottawa, and **Avril Lavigne,** born in Belleville.

THEATER AND FILM

Toronto is a major center for English-language theater, with more than 90 theater venues around the metropolitan region. A number of the city's professional repertory companies focus on Canadian plays. Toronto is also home to a theater landmark. The **Elgin and Winter Garden Theatres** compose Canada's only "double-decker" theater—one auditorium is stacked atop the other—and one of fewer than a dozen ever built worldwide. In Ottawa, the **National Arts Centre** (NAC) is the theater hub. The NAC has resident English- and French-language companies and often hosts national and international theater troupes and special events.

North America's two largest theater festivals take place in Ontario: the **Stratford Festival** and the **Shaw Festival** in Niagara-on-the-Lake. The Stratford productions, which run annually from late April through October, include works by Shakespeare and by many other classical and more contemporary playwrights. Similarly, the Shaw Festival was launched in 1962 to produce works by Irish playwright George Bernard Shaw but now mounts plays by Shaw, his contemporaries, and more modern authors during its annual April-to-October season.

Toronto is often called "Hollywood North" for the number of movies made here. Among the films shot on location in Toronto are *Chicago, Hairspray, The Time Traveler's Wife, Mean Girls, Harold and Kumar Go to White Castle,* and *Cinderella Man.* To see what's currently filming in the city so you can be on the lookout for the stars, check the lists that the Toronto Film and Television Office publishes on its website (www.toronto.ca/tfto).

Every September, Ontario hosts one of the industry's major film fests: the **Toronto International Film Festival.** Headquartered in the distinctive glass TIFF Bell Lightbox theater building, the festival screens more than 300 movies from around the world and draws celebrities from across the globe. Though much smaller, the well-regarded **Cinéfest Sudbury International Film Festival,** in late September, highlights regional films, particularly those with connections to Canada's northern communities.

Ontario has contributed many actors to Hollywood. Among the many film-industry notables who were born in Ontario are **Dan Aykroyd** (Ottawa), **John Candy** (Toronto), **Jim Carrey** (Newmarket), **Ryan Gosling** (London), **Rachel McAdams** (London), **Sandra Oh** (Ottawa), **Catherine O'Hara** (Toronto), **Christopher Plummer** (Toronto), and **Martin Short** (Hamilton). Even early film star **Mary Pickford,** who became known as "America's Sweetheart," was actually born in Toronto.

Essentials

Transportation

GETTING THERE
Air

If you're flying to Ontario from abroad, Toronto will likely be your gateway city. The province's largest metropolitan area is also its transportation hub. Ottawa, Canada's national capital, has an international airport as well, with flights from across Canada, several U.S. cities, and some European destinations.

ONTARIO AIRPORTS

Toronto's **Pearson International Airport** (YYZ, 6301 Silver Dart Dr., Mississauga, 416/247-7678 or 866/207-1690, www. torontopearson.com) is Ontario's major airport, with flights from across Canada, the United States, and European and Asian countries. Canadian carriers **Air Canada** (888/247-2262, www.aircanada.ca) and **WestJet** (800/538-5696, www.westjet.com), along with a number of U.S., European, and Asian airlines, fly into Pearson. **Flair Airlines** (204/888-4357, www.flairairlines. com), a Canadian discount operator, flies between Toronto Pearson and Vancouver, Kelowna (BC), and Edmonton. **Sunwing** (877/786-9464, www.sunwing.ca), which flies primarily to the Caribbean and other sunny destinations, also has summer service between Toronto and Vancouver.

Toronto has a second, smaller airport, the **Toronto City Airport** (YTZ, www. billybishopairport.com), located on the Toronto Islands a short walk or even shorter ferry ride from downtown. You can fly here from New York City (Newark), Boston, Washington DC (Dulles), and Chicago, and from a number of Canadian cities. **Porter Airways** (888/619-8622, www.flyporter. com) is the main carrier serving this airport, although Air Canada also flies here from Montreal.

Ottawa International Airport (YOW, 1000 Airport Pkwy., 613/248-2000, www. ottawa-airport.ca) has flights from most major Canadian cities, U.S. destinations that include Boston, New York, Washington DC, Detroit, Tampa, Fort Lauderdale, and Orlando, as well as London. **Air Canada** (888/247-2262, www. aircanada.ca) and **WestJet** (800/538-5696, www.westjet.com), along with a number of U.S. airlines, fly to Ottawa.

Most of Ontario's other large cities, including two that are within 90 minutes' drive of Toronto, have airports with flights from other parts of Canada and the United States. You can fly nonstop to **Hamilton International Airport** (YHM, 9300 Airport Rd., 905/679-1999, www.flyhamilton.ca), southwest of Toronto, from Calgary and Montreal year-round, and seasonally from Vancouver, Edmonton, Halifax, Winnipeg, Orlando, and Las Vegas. In the Kitchener-Waterloo area, the **Region of Waterloo International Airport** (YFK, 4881 Fountain St., Breslau, 519/648-2256 or 866/648-2256, www. waterlooairport.ca) has nonstop flights from Calgary.

Other regional Ontario airports include:

- **London International Airport** (YXU, 519/452-4015, www.londonairport.on.ca)
- **Windsor International Airport** (YQG, 519/969-2430, www.yqg.ca)
- **Greater Sudbury Airport** (YSB, 705/693-2514, www.flysudbury.ca)
- **Sault Ste. Marie Airport** (YAM, 705/779-3031, www.saultairport.com)
- **Thunder Bay International Airport** (YQT, 807/473-2600, www.tbairport.on.ca)

Previous: a historic locomotive in Kingston; cliffs along Highway 17, on Lake Superior's north shore.

U.S. AIRPORTS

If you're flying to Ontario from the United States, it's worth checking airfares to nearby airports just across the U.S. border. Airline taxes are lower in the United States than in Canada, so airfares may be cheaper, too.

For Toronto and the Niagara region, check the **Buffalo-Niagara International Airport** (BUF, 716/630-6000 or 877/359-2642, www.buffaloairport.com). For Windsor and points in Southwestern Ontario, look at flying into **Detroit Metro Airport** (DTW, 734/247-7678, www.metroairport.com).

Train

VIA RAIL

Canada's national rail carrier, **VIA Rail** (888/842-7245, www.viarail.ca), can take you to Ontario from across the country. VIA's flagship route, **The Canadian,** crosses Canada from Vancouver to Toronto via Jasper, Edmonton, Saskatoon, and Winnipeg. If you do the trip nonstop, it takes 3.5 days. There are departures three times a week in each direction May through mid-October and twice a week the rest of the year.

From Atlantic Canada, **The Ocean** travels overnight from Halifax to Montreal, where you can make connections for Ottawa, Toronto, or other Ontario destinations. The train runs three days a week in each direction. Between Montreal and Toronto, VIA Rail runs several trains a day; the trip takes 5-6 hours. Between Montreal and Ottawa, a quick two-hour ride, there are also several daily trains.

You can purchase train tickets online, by phone, or in person at most stations. VIA Rail fares are cheaper when you buy your tickets in advance. You'll get the lowest fare if you're willing to buy a nonrefundable ticket at least four days before you plan to travel. Fares are typically lowest from mid-October through May. Fares also depend on the class of service. On shorter routes, such as Montreal-Toronto, you can choose between economy and business class. A business-class ticket includes a multicourse meal with cocktails and wine on board the train; you also get to wait in the more comfortable Panorama lounge, with complimentary drinks and newspapers, in the station. On the Canadian, options range from a basic economy seat to several types of sleeping berths and cabins; sleeper tickets include meals as well as access to a shower room and an observation car.

VIA Rail periodically runs last-minute specials on its website, offering significantly discounted rates for travel within the upcoming weeks. If you're planning a lot of train travel, it's worth checking the VIA Rail website, signing up for their newsletter, or following them on Twitter to learn about additional sales and discount offers.

AMTRAK

From the United States, American rail carrier **Amtrak** (800/872-7245, www.amtrak.com) has limited service into Ontario, and most routes involve a lengthy layover. The one exception is the train between New York City and Niagara Falls or Toronto, the **Maple Leaf,** which makes the 12.5-hour trip between New York City and Toronto daily, stopping in Niagara Falls along the way.

From Chicago and U.S. points farther west, or from Boston and other northeastern U.S. cities, there's no direct rail service to Toronto or anywhere else in Ontario. Coming from the west, you could take the Amtrak **Wolverine** train from Chicago to Detroit, where you can cross the border to Windsor to continue your travels or transfer to the Toronto-bound VIA Rail train. Alternatively, you can take the Amtrak **Lake Shore Limited** from Chicago to Buffalo, where you can change to the Maple Leaf or catch a bus to Toronto.

If you're starting your trip in Boston, you can catch the **Lake Shore Limited** westbound to Buffalo and transfer there, or go first to New York City and change to the Maple Leaf. Unless you're a real rail buff (or you're coming from New York City), flying or even taking the bus is more efficient.

Bus

MEGABUS

Megabus (705/748-6411 or 866/488-4452, www.megabus.com) has some of the best fares and service to Toronto from Montreal and from the eastern United States, including New York City, Syracuse, Washington DC, Baltimore, and Philadelphia. Megabus can also take you to Kingston (from Montreal) and Niagara Falls (from New York City). On some routes, Megabus periodically offers one-way sale fares as low as $1, so check the website, particularly if you're flexible with your travel dates.

Note that Megabus allows passengers to travel with only one piece of luggage weighing less than 23 kilograms (50 pounds), plus one small hand-baggage item. To bring an additional bag, you must buy an extra ticket.

GREYHOUND

Greyhound (800/661-8747, www.greyhound. ca) can take you to Toronto from many Canadian and U.S. cities, although you'll frequently have to change buses along the way. They run frequent buses between Montreal and Ottawa; change in Ottawa if you're going on to Toronto. Greyhound's long-haul western routes travel to Ontario from Calgary and Winnipeg, stopping in Thunder Bay, Sault Ste. Marie, Sudbury, and Toronto. From Vancouver, you have to change buses in Calgary. From Edmonton, transfer in either Calgary or Winnipeg.

From the United States, Greyhound runs direct buses to Toronto from New York City (with stops in Syracuse and Buffalo, and on some buses, Niagara Falls), Detroit (stopping in Windsor and London), and Chicago. To reach Toronto from Boston, you need to transfer in Buffalo or Syracuse. From Philadelphia, transfer in New York City.

DETROIT-WINDSOR TUNNEL BUS

If you're crossing the border between Michigan and Southwestern Ontario, you can take the **Detroit-Windsor Tunnel Bus** (www.citywindsor.ca). Assuming no traffic

or border delays, the trip takes only 20-25 minutes. The buses begin running at 5:30am Monday-Saturday, 8am Sunday, and continue until 12:30am Monday-Saturday, midnight on Sunday.

Car

REQUIRED DOCUMENTS FOR DRIVERS

If you have a valid driver's license from your home country, that license will be valid in Canada for three months. If you're driving over the border from the United States, bring the car's registration forms and proof of insurance. Either carry the insurance policy itself or get a free Canadian Non-Resident Insurance Card from your insurance agent. You must have a minimum of $200,000 combined liability insurance in Ontario.

If you're planning to rent a car in the United States and drive it across the border, confirm with your car rental company in advance that you're allowed to drive out of the country. Make sure you have a copy of the rental contract handy at the border crossing.

If you're driving a borrowed car across the border, bring a letter of permission signed by the owner, even if the owner is a family member. The border agents may not ask for the letter, but you can save some hassles if you have it on hand.

ONTARIO LAND BORDER CROSSINGS

You can cross the border between the United States and Canada at a number of Ontario points. In the Niagara Falls area, four bridges cross the Niagara River, which separates Ontario from New York State: the **Peace Bridge** (www.peacebridge.com), linking Fort Erie, Ontario, with I-190 from the Buffalo area; the **Rainbow Bridge** (www.niagarafallsbridges.com), which directly links Niagara Falls, Ontario, with Niagara Falls, New York; the **Whirlpool Bridge** (www.niagarafallsbridges.com), north of the Rainbow Bridge, available to NEXUS cardholders only; and the **Queenston-Lewiston Bridge** (www.niagarafallsbridges.com) between Queenston, Ontario, and Lewiston, New York.

Between Michigan and Southwestern Ontario, you can cross from Detroit to Windsor via the **Ambassador Bridge** or the **Detroit-Windsor Tunnel.** The **Blue Water Bridge** (www.bwba.org) connects Port Huron, Michigan, and Sarnia, Ontario. The **International Bridge** connects the cities of Sault Ste. Marie, Michigan, and Sault Ste. Marie, Ontario.

Three international bridges cross the St. Lawrence River between New York State and Eastern Ontario. The **Thousand Islands Bridge** (www.tibridge.com) is a major crossing linking I-81 with Highway 401; the **Ogdensburg-Prescott International Bridge** (www.ogdensport.com) runs between Ogdensburg, New York, and Prescott, Ontario; and the **Seaway International Bridge** (www.sibc.ca) links Massena, New York, and Cornwall, Ontario.

GETTING AROUND
Air

Ontario covers a lot of ground, and when you're traveling from one end to the other, or if your time is limited, consider flights within the province. On shorter, well-traveled routes, like Toronto to Ottawa or Montreal, airfares are often priced competitively with the train or bus. On longer routes or in more remote areas, airfares tend to be high.

Toronto is the hub for flights within Ontario, although Ottawa has convenient air connections as well. **Air Canada Jazz** (888/247-2262, www.flyjazz.ca), Air Canada's regional affiliate, flies between Toronto and Ottawa, Windsor, North Bay, Sudbury, Timmins, Sault Ste. Marie, and Thunder Bay. Ontario routes on **WestJet** (888/937-8538, www.westjet.com) include Toronto-Ottawa, Toronto-Sudbury, and Toronto-Thunder Bay. Within Ontario, **Porter Airways** (888/619-8622, www.flyporter.com), based at Toronto City Airport on the Toronto Islands, flies

between Toronto and Ottawa, Windsor, Sudbury, Sault Ste. Marie, and Thunder Bay.

Bearskin Airlines (800/465-2327, www.bearskinairlines.com) flies across Northern Ontario, including service to Sudbury, Sault Ste. Marie, and Thunder Bay. **Air Creebec** (819/825-8375 or 800/567-6567, www.aircreebec.ca) can take you between Timmins, Moosonee, and points farther north. **Wasaya Airways** (877/492-7292, www.wasaya.com) connects Thunder Bay to several northern communities.

Train

VIA Rail (888/842-7245, www.viarail.ca) runs trains across Southern Ontario. You can travel between Toronto and Niagara Falls, Stratford, London, Windsor, and Sarnia. In the eastern part of the province, VIA Rail trains connect Ottawa, Brockville, Kingston, Belleville, Cobourg, and Toronto. **Ontario Northland** (800/461-8558, www.ontarionorthland.ca) operates the **Polar Bear Express** train from Cochrane north to Moosonee.

GO Transit (416/869-3200 or 888/438-6646, www.gotransit.com) operates a network of commuter trains from Toronto to the surrounding communities, including Oakville, Burlington, Hamilton, Brampton, Barrie, Richmond Hill, and Markham. GO provides seasonal service to Niagara Falls, running weekends and holidays from June through early September (and on holiday weekends in May and October), also operating as the Niagara **bike train,** which has a bike rack-equipped baggage car.

Bus

Buses connect most Ontario cities and smaller communities. **Megabus** (www.megabus.com) has direct buses and great prices between Toronto and Niagara Falls and between Toronto and Kingston, with one-way sale fares sometimes going as low as $1.

Greyhound (www.greyhound.ca) has the most extensive bus service across Ontario. It operates regular buses between Toronto and Kitchener, Waterloo, London, Windsor,

Owen Sound, Collingwood, Blue Mountain, Sudbury, and Sault Ste. Marie. Greyhound also runs most of the bus routes in and out of Ottawa, including service to Toronto, Kingston, North Bay, and Sudbury. Heading northwest, you can take Greyhound buses between Sudbury, Sault Ste. Marie, and Thunder Bay. Greyhound transports passengers between Toronto's Pearson Airport (Terminal 1) and a number of Ontario cities, including Niagara Falls, Hamilton, Kitchener, London, Windsor, Peterborough, and Ottawa as well.

To travel between Toronto and the Muskoka Lakes or to Ontario towns farther north, **Ontario Northland** (www.ontarionorthland.ca) has regular bus service. Check its schedules if you're going to Gravenhurst, Bracebridge, Huntsville, Parry Sound, Sudbury, North Bay, Temagami, or Cochrane. **GO Transit buses** (www.gotransit.com) connect Toronto with Hamilton and other surrounding suburbs and towns.

Car

If most of your time in Ontario will be in Toronto, Ottawa, or Niagara Falls, you can get around without a car. It's possible to travel to other destinations car-free, and we've detailed car-free options throughout the book. However, for the greatest flexibility in exploring the province, either drive your own vehicle or rent one along the way.

To get information about highway conditions, including winter weather and summer construction status, phone the **Ontario Ministry of Transportation**'s toll-free 24-hour road conditions line (800/268-4686). On Twitter, **@511Ontario** reports on road closures and other highway issues.

CAR RENTALS

The major North American car rental companies have outlets at Toronto's Pearson Airport, at Ottawa International Airport, and at regional airports around the province. A number of smaller car rental agencies also have offices near Pearson Airport; it's worth comparing their rates to other major companies.

Ontario's cities and most small towns also have at least one or two car rental offices. **Enterprise** (800/261-7331, www.enterpriserentacar.ca) has an extensive network of rental offices around Ontario; both **National** (877/222-9058, www.nationalcar.ca) and **Discount Car Rentals** (800/263-2355, www.discountcar.com) have offices in many towns as well.

One strategy that can sometimes save money on car rentals is to take the bus or train from Toronto to your next destination and rent a car from there. Toronto rates are sometimes higher than those in nearby cities such as Kitchener or Hamilton, although at times you'll find better deals in Toronto. Most agencies provide discounts for weekly rentals and additional discounts for rentals of a month or more. Some also offer discounts for members of the Canadian Automobile Association (CAA) or American Automobile Association (AAA).

DRIVING

Ontario law requires adults and children weighing over 18 kilograms (40 pounds) to wear seat belts with both lap and shoulder belts. Toddlers who weigh 9-18 kilograms (20-40 pounds) must ride in a forward-facing child safety seat, and infants weighing up to 9 kilograms (20 pounds) must travel in a rear-facing infant safety seat.

Most Ontario highways have a speed limit of 100 km/h (62 mph). On the Trans-Canada Highway, the speed limit is typically 90 km/h (56 mph), and country roads have a speed limit of 80 km/h (50 mph).

You can make a right turn at a red light in Ontario (as long as you stop and make sure it's clear), unless it's otherwise posted. Hitchhiking is not allowed on major (controlled-access) highways, such as Highway 401. Radar detectors are illegal in Ontario. If the police stop you, officers can confiscate a radar device—and fine you—even if the device is turned off.

EMERGENCY SERVICES

Dial 911 to reach the police, ambulance, or other emergency service if you have an automobile accident, or phone the **Ontario Provincial Police emergency line** (888/310-1122). If you're involved in a car accident where someone is injured or where the estimated property damage is more than $1,000, Ontario law requires you to contact the police and stay at the scene of the accident until the police officers give you the OK to move on.

Boat
GREAT LAKES FERRIES

The **Owen Sound Transportation Company** (www.ontarioferries.com) operates two ferry services on Ontario's Great Lakes. Between April and mid-December, ferries run to Pelee Island, Ontario's southernmost point, from Leamington or Kingsville in Southwestern Ontario.

To travel from Toronto or other points in Southern Ontario to Manitoulin Island, the quickest route is to take the MS *Chi-Cheemaun* ferry from Tobermory at the tip of the Bruce Peninsula. The ferry runs mid-May to mid-October.

NATIONAL PARK FERRIES

Ontario's Georgian Bay Islands National Park is composed entirely of islands, so you can reach the park only by water. Parks Canada (www.pc.gc.ca) runs the *DayTripper* boat service from the town of Honey Harbour to the park's Beausoleil Island from late spring through early fall.

One of only three national marine conservation areas in Canada, **Fathom Five National Marine Park** (www.pc.gc.ca) includes 22 islands in Georgian Bay off the northern end of the Bruce Peninsula. Access to the park is by boat from the town of Tobermory. Parks Canada has partnered with two private companies, **Blue Heron Tours** (www.blueheronco.com) and **Bruce Anchor Cruises** (www.bruceanchorcruises. com), which offer several types of boat trips to the park's Flowerpot Island from mid-May through mid-October.

Visas and Officialdom

ENTERING CANADA

For the most up-to-date requirements for visitors coming to Canada, visit **Citizenship and Immigration Canada** (CIC, www.cic. gc.ca).

Important note: If you have a criminal record, including misdemeanors or driving while impaired (DWI or DUI), no matter how long ago, you can be prohibited from entering Canada, unless you obtain a special waiver well in advance of your trip. Refer to the Application Forms and Guides section of the CIC website for additional information.

U.S. Citizens

The simple answer to the question of what documents U.S. citizens need to visit Canada is "a valid **passport.**" It's always a good idea to travel with your passport, if you have one.

If you are driving over the border, you can use a **NEXUS** card, issued as part of the U.S. government's Trusted Travel Program, as your entry document. See the U.S. Customs and Border Protection website (www.cbp.gov) for NEXUS details. Drivers can also use a valid **U.S. Passport Card** instead of a passport. Get more information about U.S. Passport Cards, which cannot be used for air travel, from the U.S. State Department (www.travel. state.gov).

Several U.S. states and Canadian provinces issue **Enhanced Drivers Licenses** that can be used as an alternative to a passport or passport card when you're crossing a land border; they're not valid for air travel. The

U.S. Customs and Border Protection website (www.cbp.gov) has details about Enhanced Drivers Licenses.

Citizens of the United States do not need a visa to visit Canada for stays of less than six months.

Citizens of Other Countries

All other foreign visitors to Canada must have a valid passport, and depending on your nationality, you may also need either a visitor visa or an Electronic Travel Authorization (eTA). Check with Citizenship and Immigration Canada (www.cic.gc.ca) to confirm what documents you require.

British, Australian, and New Zealand citizens don't require a visa, nor do citizens of many European nations. However, in 2016, Canada introduced the **Electronic Travel Authorization (eTA)**, which is required for visa-exempt visitors who are traveling to Canada **by air.** For example, a British citizen who is driving into Canada from the U.S. would not require a visa or an eTA but would need the eTA to fly into Canada. If you need an eTA, apply for this document online on the **Citizenship and Immigration Canada** website (www.cic.gc.ca).

CUSTOMS

Visitors to Canada can bring a reasonable amount of personal baggage, including clothing, camping and sports equipment, cameras, and computers for personal use.

As long as you're at least 19 years old, you can bring in a limited amount of alcoholic beverages duty- and tax-free. You're allowed *one* of the following: two bottles of wine (up to 53 fluid ounces or 1.5 liters), one standard bottle of other alcohol (40 ounces or 1.14 liters), or 24 cans or bottles of beer or ale (up to a total of 287 ounces or 8.5 liters). Visitors are also allowed to bring in up to 200 cigarettes or 50 cigars. You can bring gifts for friends or family into Canada duty- and tax-free as long as each gift is valued at $60 or less; if it's worth more, you'll have to pay duty and taxes on the excess amount. Alcohol and tobacco don't count as gifts. They're subject to the limits above, even if you're bringing them to give as gifts.

Travelers must declare all food, plants, or animals they bring into Canada. In general, you're allowed to bring food for personal use, although there are some restrictions on fresh fruits, vegetables, meats, and dairy products. Get the latest information from the **Canadian Food Inspection Agency** (www.inspection.gc.ca).

In general, visitors cannot bring weapons into Canada. You're specifically prohibited from bringing automatic weapons, sawed-off rifles or shotguns, most handguns, and semi-automatic weapons into Canada. There are some exceptions for hunters, and all visitors must declare any firearms in writing. Check the detailed requirements with the **Canada Border Services Agency** (www.cbsa.gc.ca).

Recreation

NATIONAL PARKS

Ontario is home to five of Canada's national parks: Bruce Peninsula National Park, known for its spectacular rock formations, beaches, and wide range of hiking trails; Georgian Bay Islands National Park, comprising 63 islands large and small; Point Pelee National Park, marking the southernmost point on the Canadian mainland; Thousand Islands National Park, in Eastern Ontario; and Pukaskwa National Park on Lake Superior's North Shore. The province also has two national marine conservation areas: Fathom Five National Marine Park and the Lake Superior National Marine Conservation Area. Just outside Toronto, Rouge National Park will be the country's first urban national park.

Parks Canada (888/773-8888, www.

pc.gc.ca) is the agency responsible for the country's national parks. You can purchase an annual **Parks Canada Discovery Pass** (adults $67.70, seniors $57.90, family or group $136.40), valid at more than 100 national parks, national marine conservation areas, and national historic sites across the country. The family or group pass is good for up to seven people arriving together at a particular site. If you're going to visit several parks and historic sites during your travels, a Discovery Pass can be a good value. As of January 2018, admission to Parks Canada parks and historic sites is free if you're under 18 years old.

If you purchase your Discovery Pass at the beginning of a month, your pass will be valid for 13 months, rather than 12, because the pass expires on the last day of the month in which you bought it. That is, if you purchase your pass on March 1, 2019, it will be valid until March 31, 2020. You can buy a Discovery Pass online or by phone from Parks Canada or in person at any national park or historic site. If you've already bought a day pass to a park or historic site within the past 30 days, you can credit the price of that ticket toward a Discovery Pass.

When you're spending several days in just one park, you're better off purchasing a **seasonal pass** for that particular park. For example, at Bruce Peninsula National Park, a day pass is $11.70 per vehicle, and a seasonal pass is $49 per vehicle, so the season pass would save you money if you were staying five days or more.

PROVINCIAL PARKS

Ontario has more than 300 provincially managed outdoor spaces, run by **Ontario Parks** (www.ontarioparks.com). Among the province's most popular parks are Algonquin Provincial Park in Cottage Country near Huntsville, Killarney on Georgian Bay, Lake Superior north of Sault Ste. Marie, Wasaga Beach near Collingwood, and The Pinery on Lake Huron, outside Grand Bend. It's hard to narrow down more favorite parks, but others worth exploring include Sandbanks on Lake Ontario, in Prince Edward County; Awenda, near Midland on Georgian Bay; Killbear and Grundy Lake, also on Georgian Bay, north of Parry Sound; Sauble Falls, on the Bruce Peninsula; and Sleeping Giant, near Thunder Bay.

Daily park entrance fees range $11.25 to $20 per vehicle. If you're going to visit several provincial parks, or if you're going to return to the same park over multiple days, consider purchasing a **provincial park pass** (800/668-9938, www.ontarioparks.com). You can buy a seasonal pass good for unlimited park visits during either the summer (Apr.-Nov., $125) or the winter (Dec.-Mar., $85), or an annual pass ($175) valid for the entire year. Buy park passes online, by phone, or at most provincial parks.

HIKING

Ontario has plenty of opportunities to hit the trail, whether you're looking to tromp around in the woods or along the lake for an afternoon or set off on a multiday hiking adventure. The **Ontario Trails Council** (www.ontariotrails.on.ca) provides information about trails province-wide.

One of Canada's iconic outdoor experiences is a hike along Ontario's **Bruce Trail** (www.brucetrail.org), an 845-kilometer (525-mile) route that extends from the Niagara region to the tip of the Bruce Peninsula. While some hikers do the entire trail straight through, far more end-to-end hikers complete the trail in a series of shorter excursions over several months or years. And many more hikers use the trail only for day hiking.

The world's longest network of trails, the **Trans-Canada Trail**, also known as "the Great Trail" (www.tctrail.ca, or www.thegreattrail.ca), extends—as its name suggests—across the country. Some sections of the trail are urban walks, like parts of Ottawa's **Capital Pathway** (www.ncc-ccn.gc.ca) or Toronto's **Waterfront Trail** (www.waterfronttrail.org). Others, like the

Voyageur Trail (www.voyageurtrail.ca) in Northern Ontario, are wilderness routes. Check the Trans-Canada Trail website for more hike ideas.

CYCLING AND MOUNTAIN BIKING

Ontario has an extensive network of trails for both road cycling and mountain biking. Some regions of the province, particularly along the lakeshores, are fairly flat. Inland, it's not the Rockies, but you'll find enough rolling hills to get your heart pumping. **Ontario By Bike** (www.ontariobybike.ca) can give you more ideas about where to cycle around the province.

The Niagara region is an excellent spot for cyclists, even if you're a not a hard-core long-distance rider. The **Greater Niagara Circle Route** (www.niagararegion.ca), with more than 140 kilometers (87 miles) of mostly paved cycling trails, loops around the Niagara Peninsula. You can bring your bike from Toronto on the seasonal **bike train,** run by GO Transit (www.gotransit.com).

Running nearly 2,100 kilometers (1,300 miles), the **Great Lakes Waterfront Trail** (www.waterfronttrail.org) follows the Lake Huron, Lake Erie, Lake Ontario, and St. Lawrence River banks, between Grand Bend and the Quebec border; a second section in Northern Ontario connects Sudbury and Sault Ste. Marie. Another long-distance route, the 450-kilometer (280-mile) mixed-use **Central Ontario Loop Trail,** circles from Port Hope on Lake Ontario, through Peterborough and the Kawarthas region, north to Haliburton and Bancroft. Many sections of the **Trans-Canada Trail** (www.tctrail.ca or www.thegreattrail.ca) are also open to cyclists.

Hardwood Ski and Bike (www.hardwoodskiandbike.ca), in the hills northeast of Barrie, has 80 kilometers (50 miles) of mountain bike trails. Some of Ontario's downhill ski resorts become mountain bike meccas in summer, including **Blue Mountain** (www.bluemountain.ca), near Collingwood.

WATER SPORTS

Surrounded by four of the five Great Lakes, with over 200,000 inland lakes large and small, Ontario is a popular destination for all types of water sports. You can go **swimming** in most of these lakes, although the water, particularly in the Great Lakes, can be quite chilly. Pollution or increased bacteria levels can also close beaches temporarily. The **Blue Flag** (www.blueflag.global) program assesses the environmental safety of participating beaches, so swim when the blue flag is flying; their website also lists Ontario's approved Blue Flag beaches.

Ontario is a hugely popular destination for **canoeing** and **kayaking,** whether you want to paddle around a lake for an hour or two or embark on a multiday expedition. The most popular destinations include Algonquin Provincial Park, Killarney Provincial Park, and Temagami. **Stand-up paddleboarding** has grown in popularity throughout Ontario. Look for paddleboard rentals and lessons at many lake destinations.

For **white-water rafting,** head for the Ottawa River region, west of Ottawa; you can even do a gentle raft trip within the Ottawa city limits. For **scuba diving,** the Fathom Five National Marine Conservation Area, off the Bruce Peninsula, has some of the finest diving in the north; you can **snorkel** here, too.

Ontario may not have oceans or palm trees, but yes, you can go **surfing.** Lake Superior routinely sees waves of 3 to 4.5 meters (10 to 15 feet) that bring out hardy surfers and their boards. Even in midsummer, it's critical to prepare for the cold, though, with thick wetsuits, gloves, hoods, and booties. Thunder Bay is a good place to start your surfing adventure, and many surfers head for Terrace Bay on the lake's north shore.

WINTER SPORTS

Oh, yes, Ontario has plenty of winter weather, so if you like to get outdoors, you'll have copious opportunities for winter sports. In winter, you can **ice-skate** almost anywhere in

Ontario. Practically every city or town has a rink or a frozen pond where you can strap on your skates. But the best place to skate is on Ottawa's Rideau Canal, which becomes the world's largest rink.

Compared to the snow resorts in the mountains of Western Canada, Ontario's **ski and snowboard** spots are smaller and more modest. But there are plenty of places where you can schuss down the mountain within a short distance of either Toronto or Ottawa. The province's largest ski area is the Blue Mountain Resort, near Collingwood. Other downhill destinations include Horseshoe Resort near Barrie, or Calabogie Peaks and Mount Pakenham near Ottawa.

While Ontario's rolling hills may seem small for downhill skiing or snowboarding, they offer excellent terrain for **cross-country skiing** or **snowshoeing.** A number of the provincial parks remain open in winter for skiers and snowshoers, including Algonquin, Arrowhead (near Huntsville), Awenda (outside of Midland), Killarney (between Parry Sound and Sudbury), The Pinery (on Lake Huron), and Wasaga Beach (near Collingwood). Gatineau Park, near Ottawa, is also a popular cross-country ski destination.

If you ever wanted to learn about **dogsledding** and lead your own team of dogs, you can give it a try in Ontario. Several outfitters offer dogsledding excursions in and around Algonquin Provincial Park.

Accommodations

Room rates are listed for high season—generally May or June through September or October, except at the ski resorts or other winter destinations, when high season typically runs from late December through February or March. Even within that time period, rates can fluctuate significantly, depending on the lodging's occupancy, nearby special events, and even the weather, so check current rates before making your plans. You'll need to add the 13 percent HST (harmonized sales tax) to the listed rates.

In Ontario's cities, especially Toronto and Ottawa, accommodations rates tend to be highest midweek when vacationers are competing for lodging space with business travelers. Hotels catering to road warriors will often discount their rates Friday through Sunday. Conversely, in areas that are primarily tourist destinations, including Niagara Falls, the Bruce Peninsula, Georgian Bay, Prince Edward County, and any of the national or provincial parks, weekends are busiest, and you might find lower lodging prices and more availability between Sunday and Thursday.

In most of the province, you'll save money on lodging by visiting in winter. A room for a midwinter weekend in Toronto may cost as much as 50 percent less than that same accommodation in July. However, outside the urban areas, since many attractions close from mid-October through mid-May, accommodations may shut down as well.

COTTAGE RENTALS AND RESORTS

Throughout Ontario, going to "the cottage" is a long-established summer ritual. Even if you're not fortunate enough to own a country getaway or have friends or family willing to invite you to their cottage, you can still join the throngs of summer cottagers. Many cottages are available for summer rentals, and cottage resorts—essentially a hotel where you sleep in a cottage but have hotel services like a dining room, water sports, and organized activities for the kids—are also popular. Cottages frequently rent for a minimum of a week, at least in summer, while you can usually book shorter stays at cottage resorts. Weekly rentals most often run Saturday to Saturday.

The Muskoka region north of Toronto is often known simply as Cottage Country, where Huntsville, Bracebridge, Gravenhurst, and the surrounding communities are all magnets for cottagers. You'll find cottages and cottage resorts around Georgian Bay, along Lake Huron, in the Kawarthas region around Peterborough, and pretty much anywhere that there are lakes and woods.

If you're renting a cottage, ask what's included and what's nearby: Do you need to supply your own linens and towels? What appliances—stove, oven, dishwasher, washing machine, clothes dryer—does the cottage have? What types of beds are in each bedroom? Is there a patio or deck? A barbecue? Wi-Fi? A TV? DVD player? Is the cottage on a main road, or at the end of a quiet lane? How far is the nearest beach? Where's the closest grocery store?

The Ontario Tourism website (www. ontariotravel.net) has information about and listings for cottage rentals, and tourism offices and visitors bureaus in most regions can provide details about cottage rentals in their vicinity. **AirBnB** (www.airbnb.ca) lists cottages for rent across Ontario.

BED-AND-BREAKFASTS

Ontario has bed-and-breakfast accommodations in major cities, smaller towns, and out in the country. Some are upscale and modern, with private baths and high-tech amenities like flat-screen TVs, iPod docks, and espresso machines. Others are homey but more modest—like staying with your aunt and uncle, where the bath is down the hall and you get a bed and a morning meal but not much else.

If a room has an en suite bath, it's in your suite, that is, it's inside your room, for your own use. A private bath can sometimes be en suite, but the term often refers to a bath that's outside of your room but reserved for you only; you might have to walk down the hall, but you won't have to share. A shared bath is just that: a bath used by guests of more than one room. Ask how many guest rooms share each bath; when there are two baths for three

guest rooms, you're less likely to have to wait than when six rooms take turns for a single bath.

Wireless Internet access is widely available at Ontario B&Bs, and it's generally included in the rates, but always ask if Wi-Fi is important to you. Some B&Bs will have a computer for guest use; again, if that's something you need, ask. Outside major cities, most B&Bs have parking available. In the cities, they may not, or there may be a parking fee.

Remember that in a bed-and-breakfast, you're usually a guest in the owner's home. Many people enjoy staying at B&Bs, where they can chat with the owner and meet other guests over a cup of coffee or breakfast. Most owners will respect your privacy, but they're also your hosts, who can make recommendations about things to see and do nearby.

HOSTELS

If your vision of a hostel includes crowded, run-down dormitories filled with unwashed backpackers, it may be time to update your perception. Hostels do still tend to draw younger people, but older travelers and families have discovered the benefits of hostel travel, too.

Some hostels, like Toronto's Planet Traveler, are very modern and very wired—with free Wi-Fi, phone booths where you can make calls via Skype, and lockers with electrical outlets to plug in your laptop or phone charger. While others may not be as well outfitted, Wi-Fi is standard, as are shared kitchens, laundry facilities, and common areas for lounging and meeting other guests. Hostels often organize local activities, from pub crawls to city tours, to acquaint you with the area and with other travelers.

While the standard hostel accommodations are a shared dorm with bunk beds and shared baths, accommodating anywhere from 4 to 10 travelers, there are lots of variations. Dorms can be female-only, male-only, or mixed, so ask if you have a preference. Many hostels now offer options for rooms that you share with only two or three other

Cool Sleeps

Is a bed too boring? If you're looking for an unusual place to lay your head, check out these unique Ontario accommodations.

- You can bed down in a tepee on a First Nations reserve, when you stay at **Endaa-aang "Our Place"** or with **Spirit Island Adventures** on Manitoulin Island.

- At the **HI-Ottawa Jail Hostel,** in the nation's capital, some of the beds are in cells of the 19th-century former Carleton County Gaol.

- Combine a sailing excursion on Lake Superior with an overnight at the **Porphyry Point Lighthouse**, where you can sleep in the refurbished lightkeeper's residence.

- Want to know what it was like to be a soldier in the 1800s? You won't be issued a musket or army rations, but you can spend the night in Kingston's **Fort Henry.**

- The **Sugar Ridge Retreat Centre,** with 10 cabins surrounding a contemporary Zen-style lodge near Midland, may be one of the quietest places you'll ever stay, whether you come for a yoga retreat or simply a peaceful escape.

- Fancy a "glamping" adventure? Consider the upscale camping options at **Whispering Springs Wilderness Retreat** near Grafton or **Fronterra Farm** in Prince Edward County, both in Eastern Ontario.

people; you're still not getting hotel amenities, but you are getting a little more space. Many have private rooms, with a double bed or two twins, or family rooms, where you share with your family members but no one else. For two or more travelers sharing a room, hostel prices can sometimes approach those of bed-and-breakfasts or lower-end hotels, so shop around. Hostels generally supply sheets, a blanket, and a towel. To prevent bedbug infestation, most prohibit travelers from bringing their own linens.

Many Canadian hostels are affiliated with **Hostelling International** (HI, www. hihostels.com) and offer discounts to HI members. Not only do you get discounts on hostel stays, but you're also eligible for up to 15 percent off VIA Rail tickets and 25 percent off Greyhound bus travel within Canada. In Ontario, HI members also get discounts on some tours or museum admissions.

You typically buy a membership from your home country's HI association, which you can do online. For Canadian citizens and residents, **Hostelling International-Canada** (613/237-7884 or 800/663-5777, www.

hihostels.ca) sells adult memberships, valid for two years, for $35; junior memberships, for kids under 18, are free. At **Hostelling International-USA** (240/650-2100, www. hiusa.org), memberships are valid for one year for adults (US$18) and youths under 18 (free). Other international hostel organizations include **YHA England and Wales** (www.yha.org.uk), **Fédération Unie des Auberges de Jeunesse** (France, www.fuaj. org), **YHA Australia** (www.yha.com.au), and **Youth Hostels Association of New Zealand** (www.yha.co.nz). Get a complete list of international chapters from Hostelling International (www.hihostels.com).

For more information about privately run hostels and other budget accommodations in Ontario and across Canada, see **Backpackers Hostels Canada** (www.backpackers.ca).

UNIVERSITY RESIDENCES

You don't have to be a student or professor to stay in a university residence. Many Ontario universities open their residence halls to visitors during the summer months (generally mid-May through August). Accommodations range from basic dormitory rooms with shared baths down the hall to suites with kitchen facilities that would be comfortable for families. Some residence halls provide breakfast, some give you an option to eat at campus dining facilities, while at others, you're on your own for meals.

Staying in residence is best for independent travelers, since you don't have a hotel staff to help you out, and you won't get room service or other hotel-style frills. The advantage? The cost can be lower than for nearby hotel accommodations, and the locations are often quite central.

- Hamilton: **McMaster Summer Residences** (905/525-9140, http://conference.mcmaster.ca, $66-74 s, $95-105 d, 4-bed apartment $200)

- Kingston: **Queen's University Residence Halls** (613/533-2223, http://eventservices.queensu.ca, $50 s, $60 d, 2-bedroom suite $109-119)

- London: **Western Summer Accommodations** (University of Western Ontario, 519/661-3476, www.stayatwestern.com, $72-77, suite $144)

- Niagara-on-the-Lake: **Niagara College Residence** (137 Taylor Rd., 905/641-4435 or 877/225-8664, www.stayrcc.com, 2-bedroom suite $100-140)

- Ottawa: **University of Ottawa Residences** (613/562-5885 or 888/564-4545, www.accommodation.uottawa.ca, $159 d)

- Toronto: **Massey College Residences** (4 Devonshire Pl., at Hoskin Ave., 416/978-2895, www.masseycollege.ca, $87-120, suite $130-180)

- Waterloo: **University of Waterloo Residences** (519/884-5400, www.uwaterloo.ca/summer-accommodations, $60 s or d); **Hotel Laurier** (Wilfred Laurier University, 200 King St. N., 519/884-0710, ext. 2771, www.wlu.ca/hotel, $55-75 s, $93 d)

CAMPING

In Ontario, you can camp in many of the national and provincial parks, and in private campgrounds. In addition to sites where you can pitch a tent or park your RV, many national and provincial parks have cabins or yurts to rent (the latter are tent-like structures modeled after the dwellings of nomads in Mongolia, China, and other regions). You usually have to bring your own sleeping bags and linens, as well as cooking supplies, but you don't have to bring or set up a tent. In the national parks, you can also stay in an "oTENTik," a furnished platform tent.

You can camp at four of the five Ontario national parks; there are no individual campgrounds at Point Pelee National Park, although the park does have oTENTiks available year-round. At Pukaskwa National Park, campsites are available on a first-come, first-served basis, but reservations for oTENTiks are required. You can (and should) make campsite reservations if you're planning to camp at the Bruce Peninsula, Georgian Bay Islands, and Thousand Islands National Parks. Book through the **Parks Canada reservation service** (877/737-3783, www.reservation.pc.gc.ca).

To find a campsite at one of the many campgrounds run by the provincial **Ontario Parks** (888/668-7275, www.ontarioparks.com) agency, search the park reservation website, which not only lists park campgrounds, but also lets you search online for campground availability. For campgrounds that accept reservations, you can book a site up to five months in advance.

For information about Ontario's more than 400 private campgrounds, contact the **Ontario Private Campground Association** (www.campinginontario.ca).

Learn to Camp, Ontario Style

What if you've never been camping, but you've always wanted to give it a try? Or you camped a couple of times as a kid, but don't have the gear you need now?

Ontario Parks (www.ontarioparks.com) offers a **Learn to Camp** program to help get you started on your outdoor adventure. Park staff teach you the basics, from how to pitch a tent to how to build a campfire. The park provides tents, air mattresses, a camp stove and cooking equipment, firewood, even flashlights; you bring your food, clothes, and other personal items, as well as a sleeping bag or bedding. The program is offered at certain provincial parks on select dates. Some parks even run two-hour **Learn to Fish** programs, where you learn basic fishing skills, before trying to catch your own fish.

"Roofed accommodations," including cabins, camping trailers, and yurts, are available in a growing number of provincial parks. You may still need to bring sleeping bags and other gear, but you don't need to pitch your own tent.

Parks Canada (www.pc.gc.ca) also offers periodic Learn to Camp programs in some national parks, and many parks now offer roofed accommodations, too. In the national parks, these include cabins, yurts, and "oTENTiks," platform tents that are essentially a cabin floor with tent walls. Another alternative, in the Thousand Islands National Park, is an "equipped camping service," in which park staff set up a large tent for you (or arrange a stay in an oTENTik) and provide various gear.

Food and Drink

The "eating local" movement—choosing foods that are grown or produced locally—has swept Ontario in a big way. From the biggest cities to many a small town, Ontario chefs are sourcing and promoting local products. The **Ontario Culinary Tourism Alliance** (www.ontarioculinary.com) is a good resource for learning more about the province's locally raised foods. **Farmers Markets Ontario** (www.farmersmarketsontario.com) lists farmers markets around the province.

While local food is booming, Ontario's long history of immigration has influenced its cuisine, too. Many formerly unknown foods are now routine parts of Ontario meals, sometimes adapted to use locally grown ingredients. You'll find the legacy of Italian immigration in many communities, especially in the Niagara region, in Sault Ste. Marie, and in Thunder Bay; German and Eastern European fare from Kitchener-Waterloo and St. Jacobs west to Lake Huron and south toward Windsor; Scandinavian heritage in the Thunder Bay area; and French Canadian influences in Eastern and Northeastern Ontario and in the Ottawa region. Multiethnic Toronto has historically Italian, Portuguese, Greek, Indian, and Korean neighborhoods, as well as several Chinatowns, and across the city you'll find foods from around the globe.

REGIONAL SPECIALTIES

Outside Canada, it's known as Canadian bacon, but in Canada, the thickly sliced cured pork commonly served for breakfast or in sandwiches is called back bacon or **peameal bacon.**

Ontario's numerous lakes yield several varieties of fresh fish, including pickerel and perch. It's baked, grilled, or fried up for fish-and-chips.

Artisanal cheese making is a growing business in Ontario, particularly in Prince Edward County, the Ottawa region, and the region between Kitchener and Lake Huron, where you can even do a self-guided cheese tour on the **Oxford County Cheese Trail** (www.oxfordcountycheesetrail.ca). Look for Ontario cheeses at farmers markets and specialty cheese shops around the province. One distinctive use of cheese that you'll now find across the country is **poutine,** french fries topped with brown gravy and melted cheese curds. Originally from Quebec, poutine is gooey, salty, savory, and surprisingly addicting.

Central and Eastern Ontario is maple country, so you'll find lots of maple products, including syrup, maple butter, and taffy. In late winter (usually Mar.-Apr.), you can visit **sugar shacks** that tap the sap from maple trees and produce syrup, although most are now large commercial operations rather than little shacks in the woods. Many operate seasonal pancake houses to showcase their maple products. A particular treat is **maple taffy on snow;** hot syrup is poured onto snow, which firms it into taffy that's rolled on a stick. While late winter is the production season, you can purchase Ontario-made maple syrup at farmers markets and groceries year-round.

In late spring and early summer, you'll find strawberries and rhubarb. As the summer goes on, the markets fill with raspberries, blueberries, and peaches, then grapes, apples, and pears. Look for farms where you can pick your own fruit for the absolute freshest produce (and are fun for the kids).

Panzarotti are Ontario's version of calzone. It's baked dough stuffed with tomato sauce and cheese, often including sausage, peppers, or other toppings typically found on pizza. You'll see *panzarotti* in Sault Ste. Marie (which also has excellent pizza) and anywhere there's a large Italian community.

Summer in Ontario is **fruit pie** time, with strawberry, raspberry, blueberry, peach, apple, and other varieties appearing on bakery and farm-stand shelves as each fruit comes into season. Year-round, in francophone communities, you might see *tourtière,* a savory meat pie. Found in many of Canada's First Nations communities, **bannock** is a biscuit-like bread, baked, fried, or grilled over an open fire.

BeaverTails aren't actually the tails of beavers; they're just shaped like them. They're fried slabs of whole-wheat dough topped with cinnamon sugar and a squeeze of lemon (or with all sorts of other sweet toppings). They're an Ottawa tradition, but you can find them in many parts of Canada and abroad.

If you have only one dessert in Ontario, it should be a **butter tart.** No, it's not a pie shell filled with butter; it's a single-serving pastry filled with a gooey mix of brown sugar, butter, and eggs. The dark-sugar custard filling resembles American pecan pie without the nuts, although butter tarts sometimes have pecans or raisins added. You can find butter tarts at bakeries across the province.

ONTARIO WINES

Ontario is Canada's main wine-producing region, with vineyards and wineries concentrated in several areas. The largest is the Niagara region, with more than 100 wineries in and around the town of Niagara-on-the-Lake and in the Twenty Valley, incorporating the towns of Beamsville, Vineland, and Jordan. In Eastern Ontario, Prince Edward County is a growing wine district, and in the southwestern corner of the province is the small wine-producing area known as the **Essex Pelee Island Coast (EPIC) Wine Country** along Lake Erie's North Shore. More recently, wineries have opened farther north, along Lake Huron and Georgian Bay. Most wineries welcome visitors, and you can buy their wines at the winery shops; larger wineries also sell to restaurants and wine stores around the province.

Ontario may be best known for its **ice wine,** a sweet, intense dessert wine that's made from grapes that are allowed to freeze on the vine. The production process is labor-intensive (the frozen grapes must be hand-picked) and very sensitive to temperature variations, which makes ice wine an expensive, if delicious, treat.

The **Wine Council of Ontario** (www.

winecountryontario.ca) is a good source of information about Ontario wines and wineries.

CRAFT BEER AND CIDER

These days, you can hardly raise a glass in Ontario without bumping into a new craft brewery. By 2018, the province had more than 200 small artisanal beer makers, with reports of at least 100 more in development. Both Toronto and Ottawa have active, growing craft beer scenes, and you'll find local brews to sample all across the province. Most craft brewers have tasting rooms where you can taste their products, and many offer tours. Ontario even has an annual province-wide festival to celebrate its local suds: **Ontario Craft Beer Week** (www.ocbweek.ca, June). On its website, **Ontario Craft Brewers** (www.ontariocraftbrewers.com) lists the province's craft brewers by region, while the **Ontario Beverage Network** (www.momandhops.ca) publishes maps of "Brewery Discovery Routes"—self-guided tasting tours (www.brewerydiscoveryroutes.ca).

Despite Ontario's long history as an apple-growing region, it's only recently that artisanal cider making has enjoyed a renaissance. As recently as 2008, the province had only one craft cider maker, but by 2018, that number had grown to more than 50. Many cider makers have set up shop in the Blue Mountains, along the south shore of Georgian Bay, where you can sample your way along the **Apple Pie Trail** (www.applepietrail.com), a network of orchards, bakeries, restaurants, and cider makers—basically anyone who has apple deliciousness to share. The **Ontario Craft Cider Association** (www.ontariocraftcider.com) and the **Ontario Beverage Network** (www.momandhops.ca) can direct you to more of the province's cider makers.

Travel Tips

OPPORTUNITIES FOR STUDY AND EMPLOYMENT

To go to school or work in Canada, you must apply for and receive a study or work permit before you enter the country. The government agency responsible for study and work permits is **Citizenship and Immigration Canada** (www.cic.gc.ca). For specific information about studying and working in Ontario, also see the **Ontario Ministry of Citizenship and Immigration** (www.citizenship.gov.on.ca).

ACCESS FOR TRAVELERS WITH DISABILITIES

Many, but not all, of Ontario's attractions, hotels, restaurants, entertainment venues, and transportation options are accessible to travelers with disabilities. A useful general resource that provides information about accessible travel to and around Canada is the Canadian government's **Access to Travel** website (www.accesstotravel.gc.ca). It includes helpful details about transportation between and around Ontario cities and towns, as well as general tips and travel resources.

Many Canadian national parks and Ontario provincial parks offer accessible facilities. Many picnic areas, campsites, and park restrooms, as well as some trails, can accommodate wheelchairs and other mobility aids. Get details on facilities in specific parks from **Parks Canada** (www.pc.gc.ca) and **Ontario Parks** (www.ontarioparks.com).

TRAVELING WITH CHILDREN

Ontario is an extremely family-friendly destination. Not only are there tons of fun things for families to do, there are lots of resources to help support traveling families or make travel more affordable. Many museums and attractions offer free admission for kids under a certain age (often 5 or 6, but sometimes 11 or 12). Many offer discounted family admission rates, which generally include two adults and at least two children.

During the summer (late June-Aug.) and during school holiday periods, including Christmas-New Year's (late Dec.-early Jan.) and March break (mid-Mar.), many attractions offer kids' camps or other activities for children. Just note that these periods will also be the most crowded times at family-friendly places.

Kids stay free at many major hotels. Other good lodging options for traveling families, besides the typical chain motels, include suite hotels (in cities) and cottages (in more rural areas), which often provide more space for the money, as well as kitchen facilities where you can prepare your own food. Cottage resorts, which offer cottage accommodations as well as the services of a hotel (a dining room, water sports, or other kids' activities), are great fun for families; many specifically target multiple generations traveling together.

Some bed-and-breakfasts don't accept kids, so always ask. One type of B&B that's typically great for kids is a bed-and-breakfast on a farm. There's usually space for kids to run around, as well as animals to look at; children may even be able to help with farm chores.

Many Ontario restaurants have children's menus with burgers, chicken, sandwiches, or other nonthreatening foods. Some will also make smaller portions of regular menu items or prepare a simple pasta dish. Encourage your kids to eat what you're eating, though, since they may surprise you (and themselves) with a new food that they like.

WOMEN TRAVELING ALONE

Overall, Ontario is a relatively safe destination compared to many spots around the world, and women shouldn't hesitate to travel alone. However, exercise caution wherever you go, and particularly in urban areas, avoid venturing out alone late at night or in the wee hours

of the morning. If you are out late on your own, don't walk—take a cab. Take your cues from local women, too; if you don't see other women walking or waiting for the bus, that's a clue that maybe you shouldn't either.

Carry a cell phone with you, so you can phone for assistance if you need it. However, be aware that some parks and remote regions have limited or no cell phone coverage.

When hiking, many women suggest finding other groups of travelers that you might join, or hiking on busier trails where you won't be alone for long periods of time.

An excellent resource for women travelers is **Journeywoman** (www.journeywoman.com), a Toronto-based worldwide website where women travelers can share tips and ask for advice from local women. Another great site for women's travel tips, particularly for solo travelers, is **Wanderlust and Lipstick** (www.wanderlustandlipstick.com).

SENIOR TRAVELERS

The good thing about getting older is that you can often get discounts. Many Ontario attractions, lodgings, and transportation providers offer discounts for seniors. Normally, you need to be 65 to qualify for a senior discount, although occasionally these discounts are extended to travelers at age 60 or 62.

For seniors who love the outdoors, **Ontario Parks** offers discounts at the provincial parks, with reduced rates for day-use admission and camping fees. **Parks Canada** offers similar senior discounts at the country's national parks and national historic sites.

LGBTQ TRAVELERS

Canada is far more welcoming to LGBTQ travelers than many other destinations. Marriage equality is the law in Canada, and Ontario was among the first provinces to make same-sex marriage permissible, in 2003. Ontario's largest LGBTQ community is in Toronto, and the city's annual Pride Week is one of the biggest gay and lesbian pride celebrations in the world. Though the hub of the community was once the Church and Wellesley neighborhood, known as the Gay Village, queer culture now extends around the city. Accommodations, restaurants, and other facilities throughout Toronto (and indeed across the province) welcome LGBTQ travelers.

Resources for LGBTQ travel to Ontario include:

- **Travel Gay Canada** (www.travelgay canada.com): The country's LGBTQ tourism association

- **TAG Approved** (www.tagapproved.com): Gay-friendly hotels and attractions

- **Ontario Tourism** (www.ontariotravel. net): Search for "LGBTQ Travel" for information about accommodations, festivals and events, and other travel tips

- **Tourism Toronto** (www.seetorontonow. com/toronto-diversity): Toronto travel tips and resources, including information about same-sex weddings in the city

- **Ottawa Tourism** (www.ottawatourism. ca): Lists resources and events for LGBTQ travel in the nation's capital.

CONDUCT AND CUSTOMS
Smoking

Smoking is not allowed in any enclosed public space in Ontario. That means you can't smoke in restaurants, bars, offices, stores, sports arenas, casinos, theaters, or other entertainment venues. In hotels, you can smoke in your room only if it's a designated smoking room (which are becoming less and less common); smoking is prohibited everywhere else in the hotel.

So where can you smoke? Smoking is permitted on outdoor patios, but only if there's no roof. You can smoke in your car, unless you're traveling with a child who's under 16. And you're still allowed to smoke outdoors on the sidewalk. You must be at least 19 to purchase cigarettes or other tobacco products in Ontario.

Alcohol

The legal drinking age in Ontario is 19. Liquor, wine, and beer are sold in government-run

---

Ontario Holidays

Ontario observes all of Canada's national holidays, as well as additional provincial holidays. Banks, post offices, and government offices are typically closed on major holidays; stores may or may not be open. For example, most stores are closed on Christmas Day but reopen for major sales on Boxing Day.

National Holidays

- New Year's Day (Jan. 1)

- Good Friday

- Easter Monday

- Victoria Day (3rd Mon. in May)

- Canada Day (July 1)

- Labour Day (1st Mon. in Sept.)

- Thanksgiving (2nd Mon. in Oct.)

- Christmas Day (Dec. 25)

- Boxing Day (Dec. 26)

Ontario Provincial Holidays

- Family Day (3rd Mon. in Feb.)

- Civic Holiday (1st Mon. in Aug.)

---

liquor stores. Because the Liquor Control Board of Ontario operates these stores, they're known by the acronym LCBO. There are separate stores that sell beer called the Beer Store. Driving under the influence of alcohol or drugs is a criminal offense. The law applies not only to cars, but also to boats, snowmobiles, and all-terrain vehicles. You can immediately lose your driver's license for 90 days if you're found to have a blood-alcohol level of more than 0.8 or if you refuse to take a Breathalyzer test.

Tipping

In restaurants, the expected tip is 15 percent, with 18-20 percent for particularly good service. You should also tip around 15 percent in bars and taxis. Give hotel baggage handlers at least a dollar or two for each bag they carry, and tip concierges in proportion to the services they provide; if they've gotten you seats for a sold-out play or reservations at the booked-for-months restaurant, compensate them for their service. Many people also leave tips of at least $5 per night for hotel housekeeping staff.

Etiquette

Canadians have a reputation for being polite, and for the most part, that reputation is well deserved. People generally wait patiently in line to board buses and streetcars and give up their seats on public transit to seniors, pregnant women, and anyone with a disability.

The Canadian Human Rights Act prohibits discrimination on the basis of "race, national or ethnic origin, colour, religion, age, sex, sexual orientation, marital status, family status, disability and conviction for which a pardon has been granted." Discrimination still exists, of course, but most Canadians pride themselves on getting along, and they try to respect other cultures and customs. When you enter a Canadian home, you may be expected to remove your shoes. Many bed-and-breakfasts want you to leave your shoes by the front door, as well.

Health and Safety

Travelers should always carry a basic first-aid kit, including bandages, aspirin or another pain reliever, sunscreen, insect repellent, and an antiseptic or antibiotic ointment. You might want to include an ointment or other product to relieve the itching of mosquito bites; if you're prone to allergic reactions, consider packing an antihistamine as well. If you wear glasses, bring an extra pair. If you take prescription medication, carry a copy of your prescription.

EMERGENCIES

In an emergency, call **911** to reach police, fire, ambulance, or other emergency services. In some remote areas of the province without 911 service, dial 0 and say "This is an emergency" to be transferred to the police. You can also reach the **Ontario Provincial Police emergency line** (888/310-1122).

HEALTH CARE AND INSURANCE

If you become ill or injured while in Ontario, you can go to the nearest hospital emergency room or walk-in health clinic. If you're a resident of another Canadian province, your provincial health plan may not provide health coverage while you're in Ontario. If the plan does provide coverage, it may pay only the amount it would pay for the service in your home province, not what you might be billed in Ontario. Either way, before your trip, it's a good idea to purchase supplemental travel health insurance to cover any unexpected medical costs while you're in Ontario.

If you live outside of Canada, make sure that you have health insurance that will cover you and your family in Canada. You will normally have to pay for the service provided in Ontario and then file a claim with your health insurance provider after you return home.

MOSQUITOES AND BLACKFLIES

Mosquitoes in Ontario may not be a "hazard," but they're surely a major nuisance, particularly from May through August. Try to avoid being outside at dusk or in the early evening when mosquitoes are most active. Outdoors, cover up with long pants and a long-sleeved shirt, and don't forget socks. Using an insect repellent is also a good idea; you can get recommendations from a good outdoors store, like Mountain Equipment Co-op.

Blackflies are buzzing, biting insects that

live in forested areas, particularly in the late spring, and they're a hugely annoying pest. Across much of Ontario, blackflies are worst in May and at least the first half of June; the farther north you go, the later the blackfly season. The flies can't bite through clothing, but they can certainly find their way *under* your clothing, especially around your ankles or wrists. Tucking your pants into your socks, while perhaps not the most fashionable solution, will help prevent bites, as will a good insect repellent. Blackflies are attracted to darker colors, so wearing lighter hues may help keep them away.

If you're camping, make sure your tent has a screen panel that's not ripped, and always keep the screen closed. The kids may whine when you tell them, for the 100th time, to zip the tent fly, but they'll thank you if it keeps the bugs out of the tent. And even if you're staying indoors, make sure the windows have screens. Ceiling fans or window fans that circulate the air around you make it more difficult for bugs to alight.

Information and Services

MONEY

Canada's currency is the Canadian dollar, and like its U.S. counterpart, it's divided into 100 cents. Canadian bills include $5, $10, $20, $50, and $100 denominations. Coins include 5, 10, and 25 cents, and one and two dollars. The gold-colored one-dollar coin is called the loonie, for the picture of the loon on its back. The two-dollar coin is nicknamed the "toonie," because it's equal to two loonies. Canada has been phasing out its penny, or one-cent piece; if you purchase something with cash, the price will be rounded up or down to the nearest five-cent increment. Throughout this book, prices are listed in Canadian dollars unless otherwise specified.

Major credit cards, including Visa, MasterCard, and American Express, are accepted throughout the province, as are debit cards, although some smaller establishments may take payment in cash only. You'll find Automated Teller Machines (ATMs)—which Canadian banks call Automated Banking Machines, or ABMs—in almost every town.

The Bank of Canada (www.bankofcanada.ca), Canada's central bank, publishes the official exchange rate between Canadian dollars and other currencies. You can exchange U.S. dollars, euros, British pounds, Australian dollars, and other major currencies for Canadian dollars at banks across Ontario or at currency exchange dealers in Toronto, Ottawa, and towns near the U.S. border. Most of the Ontario travel information centers around the province can exchange currency. In tourist areas close to the border, like Niagara Falls or the Thousand Islands, some businesses will accept U.S. dollars, although the exchange rate is usually worse than the official rate, and you'll get change back in Canadian funds. You're nearly always better off paying in Canadian currency or using a credit card.

Ontario has a 13 percent sales tax, the **HST,** or harmonized sales tax. Not every purchase a traveler might make is subject to HST, but many are. You don't pay sales tax in Ontario on basic groceries.

COMMUNICATIONS AND MEDIA
Telephone

Across most of Ontario, you must dial the full 10-digit number (the area code plus the seven-digit local number) in order to place a call, even if you're within the same area code. If you're calling from outside Ontario or from a different area code, you must also dial "1" (which is the country code for Canada, the same as for the United States), followed by the 10-digit number.

Toll-free numbers, which you can call for free from a landline and some mobile phones, depending on your plan, begin with the area codes 800, 855, 866, or 877. You must dial "1" before the toll-free number.

Cellular phone service is widely available across Ontario, although you may find dead zones in more remotes areas.

Internet

Internet access is widely available across Ontario. Ontario's major airports have free Wi-Fi service. VIA Rail offers complimentary Wi-Fi in major Ontario train stations and on board most of their trains in the Windsor-Quebec City corridor, which includes trains to Windsor, London, Toronto, Kingston, Ottawa, and Montreal.

Most hotels, motels, bed-and-breakfasts, and hostels provide Internet access for guests, and many also have a computer you can use. Larger hotels sometimes charge a daily fee for Wi-Fi access; it's always a good idea to ask. Many coffee shops and cafés have free Wi-Fi, but they expect that you'll purchase at least a cup of coffee or tea before tapping into the network. Some require you to ask for a password. Some libraries have public Internet access, available free or for a small fee. Visitor information centers may offer free Wi-Fi, or staff can tell you where you can get online.

Even in fairly remote areas, most accommodations have Internet access for guests. In rural areas, the signal may be less reliable; sometimes you might be able to get online in the lobby or other public space, but not in your room or cottage.

MAPS AND VISITOR INFORMATION

The best source of information about travel in Ontario (in addition to this book, of course) is **Ontario Travel** (www.ontariotravel.net). Created by Destination Ontario, an agency of the provincial government, this site provides details about things to see and do all across Ontario, including a calendar of upcoming events. The **Canadian Tourism Commission** (www.canada.travel) is the government of Canada's official guide to travel across the country and includes information about travel in Ontario.

If you're a member of either the **American Automobile Association** (AAA, www.aaa.com) or the **Canadian Automobile Association** (CAA, www.caa.ca), you can request free maps of Ontario and its major cities. If you belong to AAA, you can get maps from the CAA, and vice versa.

Ontario Travel Information Centers

The province operates a number of travel information centers that offer travel and visitor information, either by phone or in person. Some are open year-round, while others operate seasonally. The major locations are listed here; you can get a complete list at www.ontariotravel.net.

In Toronto and Central Ontario:

- **Toronto** (Union Station, 65 Front St. W., 416/314-5899, ontariotravel.toronto@ontario.ca)
- **Barrie** (21 Mapleview Dr. E., at Hwy. 400, 705/725-7280, ontariotravel.barrie@ontario.ca)

In the Niagara Region:

- **Niagara Falls** (Rainbow Bridge, 5355 Stanley Ave., 905/358-3221, ontariotravel.niagarafalls@ontario.ca)
- **Niagara-on-the-Lake** (251 York Rd., St. Catharines, 905/684-6354, ontariotravel.stcatharines@ontario.ca)

In Southwestern Ontario:

- **Sarnia** (Blue Water Bridge, 1455 Venetian Blvd., 519/344-7403, ontariotravel.sarnia@ontario.ca)
- **Tilbury** (62 Hwy. 401 E., 519/682-9501, ontariotravel.tilbury@ontario.ca)
- **Windsor** (Detroit-Windsor Tunnel, 110 Park St. E., 519/973-1338, ontariotravel.windsorp@ontario.ca)

In Eastern Ontario:

- **Bainsville** (22064 N. Service Rd., Hwy.

401, at the Ontario-Quebec border, 613/347-3498, ontariotravel.bainsville@ontario.ca)

In Northwestern Ontario:

- **Sault Ste. Marie** (Sault Ste. Marie International Bridge, 261 Queen St. W., 705/945-6941, ontariotravel.ssm@ontario.ca)
- **Pigeon River** (7671 Hwy. 61, Neebing, south of Thunder Bay, 807/964-2094, ontariotravel.pigeonriver@ontario.ca, mid-May-Oct.)

Regional Tourism Organizations

Tourism agencies in the regions and major cities around Ontario provide detailed information about their districts.

In Toronto and Central Ontario:

- **Tourism Toronto** (416/203-2500 or 800/499-2514, www.seetorontonow.com)
- **Tourism Hamilton** (905/546-2666 or 800/263-8590, www.tourismhamilton.com)

In the Niagara Region:

- **Niagara Falls Tourism** (905/356-6061 or 800/563-2557, www.niagarafallstourism.com)
- **Niagara-on-the-Lake Chamber of Commerce** (905/468-1950, www.niagaraonthelake.com)

In Southwestern Ontario:

- **Ontario's Southwest** (519/290-8687, www.ontariossouthwest.com)
- **Waterloo Regional Tourism Marketing Corporation** (519/585-7517 or 877/585-7517, www.explorewaterlooregion.com), including Kitchener-Waterloo, Cambridge, St. Jacobs, and surrounding communities
- **Stratford Tourism Alliance** (519/271-5140 or 800/561-7926, www.visitstratford.ca)
- **Tourism London** (519/661-5000 or 800/265-2602, www.londontourism.ca)
- **Tourism Windsor, Essex, and Pelee Island** (519/255-6530 or 800/265-3633, www.visitwindsoressex.com)

Around Georgian Bay:

- **Bruce Peninsula-County of Bruce Tourism** (519/534-5344 or 800/268-3838, www.explorethebruce.com)
- **Grey County Tourism** (519/376-3265 or 877/733-4739, www.visitgrey.ca), providing information about Owen Sound, Collingwood, and the Blue Mountains

In Cottage Country and the Northeast:

- **Muskoka Tourism** (705/689-0660 or 800/267-9700, www.discovermuskoka.ca) covering Gravenhurst, Bracebridge, Huntsville, the Muskoka Lakes, and the region surrounding Algonquin Provincial Park
- **Northeastern Ontario Tourism** (705/522-0104 or 800/465-6655, www.northeasternontario.com), covering Sudbury, North Bay, and other Northeastern Ontario communities
- **Sudbury Tourism** (705/674-4455, ext. 7718, or 866/451-8252, www.sudburytourism.ca)

In Eastern Ontario:

- **Ottawa Tourism** (613/237-5150 or 800/363-4465, www.ottawatourism.ca)
- **Peterborough and the Kawarthas Tourism** (705/742-2201 or 800/461-6424, www.thekawarthas.ca)
- **Prince Edward County Tourism** (613/476-2421 or 800/640-4717, www.thecounty.ca or http://prince-edward-county.com)
- **Tourism Kingston** (613/544-2725 or 866/665-3326, www.visitkingston.ca/)
- **Tourism 1000 Islands** (613/381-8427, www.1000islandstourism.com)

In Northwestern Ontario:

- **Algoma Kinniwabi Travel Association** (705/254-4293 or 800/263-2546, www.algomacountry.com), including Sault Ste.

Marie, Wawa, and Lake Superior's North Shore

- **Tourism Sault Ste. Marie** (705/759-5442 or 800/461-6020, www.saulttourism.com)
- **Tourism Thunder Bay** (807/983-2041 or 800/667-8386, www.thunderbay.ca)
- **Explore Northwest Ontario** (www. visitnorthwestontario.com), covering Thunder Bay, Lake Superior's North Shore, and the province's northwestern destinations.

WEIGHTS AND MEASURES

Canada officially uses the metric system. Distances and speed limits are marked in kilometers, gasoline and bottled beverages are sold by the liter, and weights are given in grams or kilograms. Because the country didn't adopt metric units until the 1970s, however, you'll still occasionally see grocery items measured with pounds or ounces, and older folks, who didn't grow up with the metric system, will sometimes use imperial units.

Electricity in Canada is 120 volts, 60 hertz, the same as in the United States, with the same types of plugs.

Ontario has two time zones. Most of the province, including cities as far west as Thunder Bay, is in the eastern time zone. The westernmost part of the province, on the Manitoba border, is in the central time zone. Ontario observes daylight saving time. Clocks move forward one hour on the second Sunday in March and turn back one hour on the first Sunday in November.

Resources

Suggested Reading

FICTION

Atwood, Margaret. *Cat's Eye*. Toronto: Mc-Clelland & Stewart, 1988. One of Ontario's most eminent writers, Atwood (www.margaretatwood.ca) has written more than a dozen novels, including this one about a painter who returns to her native Toronto.

Brand, Dionne. *What We All Long For*. Toronto: A. A. Knopf Canada, 2005. A novel about a young Toronto artist from a Vietnamese immigrant family and several of her friends.

Boyden, Joseph. *The Orenda*. Toronto: Penguin Canada/Hamish Hamilton, 2013. A controversial novel set in the often-violent 17th-century world of the French missionaries and indigenous Wendat people in central Ontario.

Lansens, Laurie. *Rush Home Road*. Toronto: A. A. Knopf Canada, 2002. Set in the fictional town of Rusholme, an all-black community in Southwestern Ontario settled by fugitive slaves, which the author modeled after the village of Buxton, this novel follows their descendants in their rural surroundings.

Munro, Alice. *Lives of Girls and Women*. New York: McGraw-Hill, 1973. A collection of linked stories chronicling a young woman's coming-of-age in small-town Ontario, by the 2013 winner of the Nobel Prize in Literature. For more Ontario stories, check out Munro's *Dear Life* (Toronto: McClelland and Stewart, 2012).

Shields, Carol. *Unless*. Toronto: Random House Canada, 2002. The eldest daughter of an Ontario novelist becomes a mute panhandler in downtown Toronto. Shields (1935-2003, www.carol-shields.com) wrote several other novels set in Ontario or elsewhere in Canada.

Wagamese, Richard. *Indian Horse*. Vancouver: Douglas & McIntyre, 2012. A novel about a young indigenous Canadian boy sent to a residential school in Northern Ontario, who attempts to overcome his challenging life circumstances through hockey.

FOOD AND WINE

Norton, James, and Becca Dilley. *Lake Superior Flavors: A Field Guide to Food and Drink along the Circle Tour*. Minneapolis: University of Minnesota Press, 2014. A guide to local food along the Lake Superior Circle Route, on both the Canadian and U.S. sides of the lake.

Ogryzlo, Lynn. *Niagara Cooks: From Farm to Table*. Toronto: Epulum Books, 2008. Part cookbook and part local food guide, this book (www.niagaracooks.ca) features the foods and wines of the Niagara region.

Ogryzlo, Lynn. *Ontario Table: Featuring the Best Food from Across the Province*. Toronto: Epulum Books, 2011. A cookbook and agricultural guide (www.ontariotable.com) that highlights local growers, foods, and wines from around Ontario.

Rosen, Amy. *Toronto Cooks: 100 Signature Recipes from the City's Best Restaurants*. Vancouver: Figure 1 Publishing, 2014. A cookbook featuring dishes from many of Toronto's top chefs.

Rosen, Amy. *Toronto Eats: 100 Signature Recipes from the City's Best Restaurants*. Vancouver: Figure 1 Publishing, 2017. A follow-up to Rosen's *Toronto Cooks* title, this cookbook features recipes from more top Toronto chefs.

Sanders, Moira, and Lori Elstone. *The Harrow Fair Cookbook*. Toronto: Whitecap Books, 2011. Recipes, featuring regional produce and products, from Southwestern Ontario's Harrow Fair, one of Canada's oldest country fairs.

NONFICTION

Christmas, Jane. *The Pelee Project: One Woman's Escape from Urban Madness*. Toronto: ECW Press, 2002. A Toronto journalist takes a sabbatical on Pelee Island to reevaluate her life and values, learning something about Canadian island life along the way.

Wilkens, Charles. *Walk to New York: A Journey Out of the Wilds of Canada*. Toronto: Viking Canada, 2004. A 50-something author decides to shake up his life by walking 2,200 kilometers (1,300 miles) across Ontario from Thunder Bay to New York City.

TRAVEL

Bogue, Margaret Beattie. *Around the Shores of Lake Superior: A Guide to Historic Sites*. Waterloo: Wilfred Laurier Press, 2007. As the title suggests, this book provides background about historic sites along Lake Superior.

Brown, Ron. *Top 150 Unusual Things to See in Ontario*. Toronto: Firefly Books, 2016. Author Ron Brown (www.ronbrown.ca) has written more than 20 books about Ontario, including this one about the province's quirkiest attractions. His other recent books include *Rails across Ontario: Exploring Ontario's Railway Heritage* (Toronto: Dundurn Press, 2013) and *Backroads of Ontario* (Toronto: Firefly Books, 2016).

Esrock, Robin, *The Great Central Canada Bucket List: One-of-a-Kind Travel Experiences* (Toronto: Dundurn Press, 2015). Travel writer and adventurer Esrock (www.robinesrock.com) highlights the best travel experiences in Ontario and Quebec.

McGuffin, Gary, and Joanie McGuffin. *Great Lakes Journey: Exploring the Heritage Coast* (Toronto: McClelland & Stewart, 2003) and *Superior: Journeys on an Inland Sea* (Toronto: Boston Mills Press/Firefly Books, 1995). These photo-filled books by husband-and-wife adventurers (www.themcguffins.ca) document their travels through the Northern Ontario wilderness.

Runtz, Michael. *The Explorer's Guide to Algonquin Park*. Erin, ON: Boston Mills Press, 2008. A detailed guide to Algonquin Provincial Park, one of Ontario's largest protected green spaces.

Internet Resources

GOVERNMENT
Citizenship and Immigration Canada
www.cic.gc.ca
The federal government agency responsible for overseeing visitors and immigrants to Canada, including information about visitor visas, work permits, study permits, and applications for permanent residence.

Government of Ontario
www.ontario.ca
The provincial government's website with information for visitors and residents about travel, recreation, money, documents, and more.

PARKS
Ontario Parks
www.ontarioparks.com
Information about, and reservations booking service for, Ontario's more than 330 provincial parks.

Parks Canada
www.pc.gc.ca
The federal government agency that manages the country's national parks and national historic sites.

Parks Canada
Campground Reservation Service
https://reservation.pc.gc.ca
Reservations booking service for Canada's national park campgrounds, including those in Ontario.

TRANSPORTATION
Major Airlines
Air Canada
www.aircanada.com

Porter Airlines
www.flyporter.com

Westjet
www.westjet.com

Trains and Buses
Amtrak
www.amtrak.com
U.S. rail carrier that provides train service to Toronto and Niagara Falls from American cities.

Greyhound Bus Lines
www.greyhound.ca
Provides the most extensive network of bus services across Ontario, as well as buses from the eastern United States to Ontario.

Megabus
www.megabus.com
Operates buses between Toronto and Niagara Falls, Kingston, and Montreal, as well as buses between Toronto and the eastern United States, including New York City, Syracuse, Washington DC, Baltimore, and Philadelphia.

OC Transpo (Ottawa)
www.octranspo.com
Ottawa's public transit system, including a Trip Planner routing feature.

Ontario Northland
www.ontarionorthland.ca
Runs buses between Toronto and various points in Northern Ontario, including service to the Muskoka region and the northeast. Also operates the Polar Bear Express train from Cochrane to Moosonee.

Toronto Transit Commission
www.ttc.ca
Toronto's public transit system, including subways, streetcars, and buses. The website includes a Trip Planner to help you plan the best route to your destination.

VIA Rail
www.viarail.ca
Canada's national rail system, which operates trains across the country.

TRAVEL

Canadian Tourism Commission
www.canada.travel
The government of Canada's official guide to travel across the country.

Environment Canada
www.weather.gc.ca
Provides weather forecasts and historical weather data for more than 150 locations across Ontario and many more destinations across Canada.

Ethan Meleg Outdoor Photography
www.ethanmeleg.com
For more photographs to inspire your Ontario travels, check out the work by Ontario-based photographer Ethan Meleg.

Festival and Events Ontario
www.festivalsandeventsontario.ca
A guide to festivals and special events around the province, including an annual Top 100 Ontario Festivals list.

Ontario Culinary Tourism Alliance
www.ontarioculinary.com
An organization that promotes Ontario's food producers and culinary travel destinations.

Ontario Travel
www.ontariotravel.net
Created by Destination Ontario, an agency of the provincial government, this website provides details about things to see and do all across Ontario.

Ottawa Tourism
www.ottawatourism.ca
Guide to travel in Ottawa, the nation's capital.

Tourism Toronto
www.seetorontonow.com
A guide to festivals and events, things to see and do, and other travel details in and around the city of Toronto.

Visit Niagara Canada
www.visitniagaracanada.com
Travel information for the Niagara Peninsula, including Niagara Falls, Niagara-on-the-Lake, and the Niagara wine country.

Wine Country Ontario
www.winecountryontario.ca
A guide to Ontario's wineries in the province's main wine-producing regions: the Niagara Peninsula, Prince Edward County, and the North Shore of Lake Erie.

Index

List of Maps

In Memory of

Ruth Wehage

Schroer

Provinces & Regions

MOON

ATLANTIC CANADA
Nova Scotia, New Brunswick, Prince Edward Island, Newfoundland & Labrador
ANDREW HEMPSTEAD

MOON

BANFF
NATIONAL PARK
ANDREW HEMPSTEAD

MOON

BRITISH COLUMBIA
Including the Alaska Highway
ANDREW HEMPSTEAD

MOON

CANADIAN ROCKIES
Including Banff & Jasper National Parks
ANDREW HEMPSTEAD

MOON

NEWFOUNDLAND & LABRADOR
ANDREW HEMPSTEAD

MOON

NOVA SCOTIA
NEW BRUNSWICK & PRINCE EDWARD ISLAND
ANDREW HEMPSTEAD

MOON

TORONTO & ONTARIO
With Niagara Falls, Ottawa & Georgian Bay
CAROLYN B. HELLER

MOON

VICTORIA & VANCOUVER ISLAND
ANDREW HEMPSTEAD

Road Trips

MOON

PACIFIC NORTHWEST
Road Trip
SEATTLE, VANCOUVER, VICTORIA, THE OLYMPIC PENINSULA, PORTLAND, THE OREGON COAST & MOUNT RAINIER
ALLISON WILLIAMS

MOON

VANCOUVER & CANADIAN ROCKIES
Road Trip
VICTORIA, BANFF, JASPER, CALGARY, THE OKANAGAN, WHISTLER & THE SEA-TO-SKY HIGHWAY
CAROLYN B. HELLER

Cities

Across the Border

MONTRÉAL
ANDREA BENNETT

QUÉBEC CITY
ANDREA BENNETT

VANCOUVER
Including Victoria, Vancouver Island, and Whistler
CAROLYN B. HELLER

MAINE, VERMONT & NEW HAMPSHIRE
JEN ROSE SMITH

NEW ENGLAND
JEN ROSE SMITH

NEW YORK STATE
JULIE SCHWIETERT COLLAZO

NIAGARA FALLS
Including the Canadian & U.S. Sides
JOEL A. DOMBROWSKI

SEATTLE
ALLISON WILLIAMS

PACIFIC NORTHWEST
ALLISON WILLIAMS

Pack up the pemmican, grab a guide, and find your next adventure with Moon!

MAP SYMBOLS

══════ Expressway	○ City/Town	✈ Airport	⛳ Golf Course		
═══ Primary Road	◉ State Capital	✈ Airfield	🅿 Parking Area		
─── Secondary Road	⊛ National Capital	▲ Mountain	⛟ Archaeological Site		
- - - - Unpaved Road	★ Point of Interest	✛ Unique Natural Feature	⛪ Church		
─── Feature Trail	• Accommodation	𖣯 Waterfall	⛽ Gas Station		
- - - Other Trail	▾ Restaurant/Bar	⛢ Park	Glacier		
········ Ferry	■ Other Location	🛈 Trailhead	Mangrove		
═══ Pedestrian Walkway	Λ Campground	✗ Skiing Area	Reef		
▥▥▥ Stairs			Swamp		

CONVERSION TABLES

°C = (°F - 32) / 1.8
°F = (°C x 1.8) + 32
1 inch = 2.54 centimeters (cm)
1 foot = 0.304 meters (m)
1 yard = 0.914 meters
1 mile = 1.6093 kilometers (km)
1 km = 0.6214 miles
1 fathom = 1.8288 m
1 chain = 20.1168 m
1 furlong = 201.168 m
1 acre = 0.4047 hectares
1 sq km = 100 hectares
1 sq mile = 2.59 square km
1 ounce = 28.35 grams
1 pound = 0.4536 kilograms
1 short ton = 0.90718 metric ton
1 short ton = 2,000 pounds
1 long ton = 1.016 metric tons
1 long ton = 2,240 pounds
1 metric ton = 1,000 kilograms
1 quart = 0.94635 liters
1 US gallon = 3.7854 liters
1 Imperial gallon = 4.5459 liters
1 nautical mile = 1.852 km

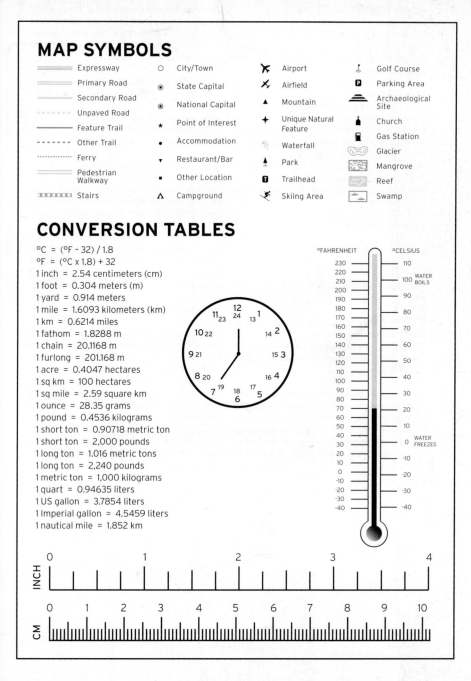

MOON TORONTO & ONTARIO
Avalon Travel
Hachette Book Group
1700 Fourth Street
Berkeley, CA 94710, USA
www.moon.com

Editor: Kevin McLain
Series Manager: Kathryn Ettinger
Copy Editor: Brett Keener
Graphics and Production Coordinator: Darren Alessi
Cover Design: Faceout Studios, Charles Brock
Interior Design: Domini Dragoone
Moon Logo: Tim McGrath
Map Editor: Kat Bennett
Cartographers: Brian Shotwell, Stephanie Poulain, Chris Henrick
Proofreader: Gillian Perry
Indexer: Rachel Kuhn

ISBN-13: 978-1-64049-238-7

Printing History
1st Edition — January 2019
5 4 3 2 1

Front cover photo: Toronto, Marina Quay West, Skyline with CN Tower © Alan Copson / Getty Images
Back cover photo: Bruce Peninsula National Park © Filtv | Dreamstime.com
All interior photos: © Carolyn B. Heller

Printed in China by RR Donnelley.